Dictionary of the Middle Ages

AMERICAN COUNCIL OF LEARNED SOCIETIES

The American Council of Learned Societies, organized in 1919 for the purpose of advancing the study of the humanities and of the humanistic aspects of the social sciences, is a nonprofit federation comprising forty-three national scholarly groups. The Council represents the humanities in the United States in the International Union of Academies, provides fellowships and grants-in-aid, supports research-and-planning conferences and symposia, and sponsors special projects and scholarly publications.

MEMBER ORGANIZATIONS

AMERICAN PHILOSOPHICAL SOCIETY, 1743
AMERICAN ACADEMY OF ARTS AND SCIENCES, 1780
AMERICAN ANTIQUARIAN SOCIETY, 1812
AMERICAN ORIENTAL SOCIETY, 1842
AMERICAN NUMISMATIC SOCIETY, 1858
AMERICAN PHILOLOGICAL ASSOCIATION, 1869
ARCHAEOLOGICAL INSTITUTE OF AMERICA, 1879
SOCIETY OF BIBLICAL LITERATURE, 1880
MODERN LANGUAGE ASSOCIATION OF AMERICA, 1883
AMERICAN HISTORICAL ASSOCIATION, 1884
AMERICAN ECONOMIC ASSOCIATION, 1885
AMERICAN FOLKLORE SOCIETY, 1888
AMERICAN DIALECT SOCIETY, 1889
AMERICAN PSYCHOLOGICAL ASSOCIATION, 1892
ASSOCIATION OF AMERICAN LAW SCHOOLS, 1900
AMERICAN PHILOSOPHICAL ASSOCIATION, 1901
AMERICAN ANTHROPOLOGICAL ASSOCIATION, 1902
AMERICAN POLITICAL SCIENCE ASSOCIATION, 1903
BIBLIOGRAPHICAL SOCIETY OF AMERICA, 1904
ASSOCIATION OF AMERICAN GEOGRAPHERS, 1904
HISPANIC SOCIETY OF AMERICA, 1904
AMERICAN SOCIOLOGICAL ASSOCIATION, 1905
AMERICAN SOCIETY OF INTERNATIONAL LAW, 1906
ORGANIZATION OF AMERICAN HISTORIANS, 1907
AMERICAN ACADEMY OF RELIGION, 1909
COLLEGE ART ASSOCIATION OF AMERICA, 1912
HISTORY OF SCIENCE SOCIETY, 1924
LINGUISTIC SOCIETY OF AMERICA, 1924
MEDIAEVAL ACADEMY OF AMERICA, 1925
AMERICAN MUSICOLOGICAL SOCIETY, 1934
SOCIETY OF ARCHITECTURAL HISTORIANS, 1940
ECONOMIC HISTORY ASSOCIATION, 1940
ASSOCIATION FOR ASIAN STUDIES, 1941
AMERICAN SOCIETY FOR AESTHETICS, 1942
METAPHYSICAL SOCIETY OF AMERICA, 1950
AMERICAN STUDIES ASSOCIATION, 1950
RENAISSANCE SOCIETY OF AMERICA, 1954
SOCIETY FOR ETHNOMUSICOLOGY, 1955
AMERICAN SOCIETY FOR LEGAL HISTORY, 1956
AMERICAN SOCIETY FOR THEATRE RESEARCH, 1956
SOCIETY FOR THE HISTORY OF TECHNOLOGY, 1958
AMERICAN COMPARATIVE LITERATURE ASSOCIATION, 1960
AMERICAN SOCIETY FOR EIGHTEENTH-CENTURY STUDIES, 1969

Dictionary of the Middle Ages

JOSEPH R. STRAYER, *EDITOR IN CHIEF*

Interim Index

CHARLES SCRIBNER'S SONS • NEW YORK

Library of Congress Cataloging in Publication Data
Main entry under title:

Dictionary of the Middle Ages.

Includes bibliographies and index.
1. Middle Ages—Dictionaries. I. Strayer,
Joseph Reese, 1904–
D114.D5 1982 909.07 82-5904
ISBN 0-684-16760-3 (v. 1)
ISBN 0-684-17022-1 (v. 2)
ISBN 0-684-17023-X (v. 3)
ISBN 0-684-17024-8 (v. 4)
ISBN 0-684-18161-4 (v. 5)
ISBN 0-684-18467-2 (Interim Index)

1 3 5 7 9 11 13 15 17 19 Q/C 20 18 16 14 12 10 8 6 4 2

PRINTED IN THE UNITED STATES OF AMERICA.

The *Dictionary of the Middle Ages* has been produced with
support from the National Endowment for the Humanities.

The paper in this book meets the guidelines for
permanence and durability of the Committee on
Production Guidelines for Book Longevity of the
Council on Library Resources.

Editorial Board

Advisory Committee

Editorial Staff

Preface

The *Dictionary of the Middle Ages* is a reference source for the events from roughly A.D. 500 to 1500 in the Latin West, the Slavic lands, the territories of the Byzantine Empire, and the Islamic world as far east as Iran. Its approach is interdisciplinary, treating subjects that range from politics to philosophy, from technology to art. In a work as broad in scope and conception as the *Dictionary,* it is impossible to cover every person, place, work of art, and event in separate articles. Variations in the spelling of names are legion throughout the medieval period, and it can be very difficult to discover where to look for information. Great stores of information are contained in articles on general subjects, and many topics insufficiently important to be treated by themselves are explained in wider contexts.

In a reference work published serially it is necessary to make information from the early volumes accessible before the work is complete. To meet these needs and problems, the Editors decided to publish this interim index. It covers the material contained in Volumes 1 through 4 and also includes the entries in Volume 5. After completion of the entire twelve-volume *Dictionary,* a final, cumulative index will be published in hardcover.

Dictionary of the Middle Ages

A

AACHEN 1–1a
adoptionism dispute 1–57b
Carolingians 3–110a
coronations 4–426b
German capture (1248) 4–59b
palace school 1–142b-143a; 3–100a; 4–412a
translatio studii 1–142a,b
Aachen, Council of (816-817) 4–117b
church organization 3–375a
Divine Office 4–230a
monasteries 3–347b
Aachen, Diet of (818)
blasphemy 2–272a
AACHEN, PALACE CHAPEL 1–2b; 1–1b
architecture 1–641a; 4–347a
Aälof
Romance of Horn 1–266b
Abacus
Exchequer 4–531b, 533b
Abar 2–12a
Abas (ruler) 1–482a
Abasgia
See Georgia
Abba Giyorgis of Gasečča 1–155b
ʿAbbāsah 2–110b
ʿABBĀS IBN ʿABD AL-MUṬṬALIB IBN HĀSHIM, AL- 1–3b
Abbasids 1–6b
Alids 1–30a
Muḥammad 1–15a
See Also Shīʿa
ʿAbbās ibn Aḥmad ibn Ṭūlūn
Tripoli 3–209a
ʿAbbās ibn al-Aḥnaf, al- 1–401a
ABBASID ART AND ARCHITECTURE 1–5a
ABBASIDS 1–6b
ʿAbbās, al- 1–4a
Abode of Islam--Abode of War 1–21b
administrative complexes 2–45a
Afghanistan 1–64b
Aghlabids 1–70a
Aleppo 1–145a
Alids 1–174b-175a
alms tax 1–202a
Ankara occupation 1–302a
Antioch domination 1–326a
Arcrunis 1–451a
Armenia 1–479a-480a
ʿAskar, al- 3–13b-14a
Baghdad 2–44b
Barmakids 2–109b
Basra 2–127b
Buyids 2–435b-436a,b
caliphate 3–41b, 42a-b
Christian church 3–312b
commander of the faithful 3–488b
concubinage 3–528b
cookery 3–584a
Córdoba 3–599b
costume 3–616b, 618a
Damascus 4–81b-82a, 83a,b, 84b
diplomacy 4–200a-b
Egypt 4–405b-406a
emirs 4–437a
exilarch 4–552a
poetry 1–400b
princes 1–449a
Syria 4–27b
See Also Arabia, Islamic
ʿAbbāsiyya, al- 1–70a-b, 71b
Abbatibus, De (Ethelwulf) 1–254b
Abbess 3–443a
ABBO OF FLEURY (FLORIACENSIS) **1–12b**; 3–103b
Aimoin de Fleury 1–109b, 110a
literature 1–261a
Saint Dunstan 4–311b
Abbo of Saint Germain-des-Prés
See Adbo of Saint Germain-des-Prés
Abbot
See Clergy
Abbreviatio de gestis Francorum 3–331b
ABBREVIATOR 1–13b
Alberti 1–126a
chancery 3–253a
ʿAbda ibn al-Ṭabīb 1–399b
ʿAbd al-Ḥakam, Ibn 1–154b; 4–407b
ʿAbd Allāh I 1–70a
ʿAbd Allāh II 1–72a
ʿAbd Allāh ibn al-ʿAbbās 4–442b
ʿAbdallah ibn al-Fadl 3–617a,b
ʿAbd Allāh ibn ʿAlī 1–7b; 3–46a
ʿABD ALLĀH IBN AL-ZUBAYR 1–15a; 1–115a
anticaliphate 3–38b, 39b
Abdallah ibn Mawhub 1–386a
ʿAbd Allāh ibn Saʿd ibn Abī Sarḥ 1–15b, 237a
ʿAbd Allāh ibn Yāsīn al-Jazūlī 1–198a-b
ʿAbd al-Malik ibn Nūḥ
Alptigin 1–220a
ʿAbd al-Muʾmin 1–200b
Almohads 1–193b-194b
ʿABD AL-MUṬṬALIB 1–14a
ʿAbbās, al- 1–4a,b
See Also Kaaba
ʿAbd al-Qāhir ibn ṭāhir al-Baghdādī 1–585a
ʿAbd-al-Raḥmān I
Córdoba 3–598a
slaves 2–268a
ʿAbd al-Raḥmān III
commander of the faithful 3–488b
Spain 1–627a-b
ʿAbd al-Raḥmān Ghāfiqī
Bordeaux 2–327b
ʿAbd al-Raḥmān ibn Muljam al-Murādī 1–173b
ʿAbd al-ʿUzzā 1–15a
Abdlmseh, Saint 1–520a
ʿAbd Manāf ibn ʿAbd al-Muṭṭalib ibn Hāshim
See Abū Ṭālib
ʿAbd Rabbih, Ibn 1–380b; 4–445a
ʿAbd Shams
Abū Sufyān 1–28b
Abel (son of Waldemar) 4–154b
ABELARD, PETER 1–16b
adoptionism 1–58a
Anselm of Laon 1–315b, 316a
antifeminism 1–323a, 324a
Aquinas, Saint Thomas 1–365a
Aristotelianism 1–460b
Arnold of Brescia 1–539b
autobiography 2–237a
Christology 3–322a
conceptualism 3–510a
Dialectica 4–169b
exegesis 2–213b; 4–543b
heresy 2–192a
Abenes, King 2–54b
Abengue-fith
See Wāfid, Ibn
Abergele Rhos Monastery 2–71a
Aberlemno 1–26b
Abgar of Edessa, King 4–384a
Abgitir Crabhai
See Fenian poetry
ABIELL, GUILLERMO 1–20a
Abī Laylā, Ibn 1–26b
Abī ʾl-Jawād, Ibn
Koran 1–71a
Abingdon Abbey
chronicles 1–284b
Ethelwold 4–518a
scriptoria 1–276a
Abisolom, Saint 1–518b
Abitur, Ibn
levirate duty 4–607a
Abī Uṣaybiʿa, Ibn 4–408a
Abjad (letters) 3–55a
See Also Arabic Numerals
Abkhazia
See Georgia
Ableiges, Jacques d' 3–279b
Abner of Burgos
cabala 3–3a
converso 3–577b
Abode of Covenant 1–21a
diplomacy 4–197b
ABODE OF ISLAM--ABODE OF WAR 1–20b
calligraphy 3–52a
diplomacy 4–197a
Abode of Truce 1–21a
diplomacy 4–197b
Abortion
contraception 3–573a
Islamic 3–574a,b, 575b
ABRABANEL, ISAAC BEN JUDAH 1–21b
Abraha, King 1–14b, 371b; 2–33a
ABRAHAM BAR ḤIYYA 1–22a
exegesis 4–540a
ABRAHAM BEN DAVID OF POSQUIÈRES 1–22b
cabala 3–1b
Abraham ben Eliezer
cabala 3–3a
ABRAHAM BEN MEÏR IBN EZRA 1–23a
cabala 3–1b
exegesis 2–212a; 3–313b; 4–540a
ABRAHAM IBN DAUD 1–24a
Aristotelianism 1–460a
Abraham of Kashkar
Mount Izlā 3–312b
Abridged Report of the Conference with the Donatists 1–652a
Absalon, Bishop 4–153b
ABSIDIOLE 1–24a
Abtar, al- 2–185b
Abū ʿAbd Allāh
Aghlabids 1–72a
Abū ʿAlī al-Balʿamī
Alptigin 1–220a
Abū ʿAlī al-Ḥasan ibn ʿAlī ibn ʿUmar al-Marrākushī
sundials 3–457b
Abū ʿAlī Chaghānī
Alptigin 1–220a
Abū ʿAlī Lawīk 1–220a
Abū al-Khair 1–106a
Abū al-Qāsim Khalaf al-Zahrāwī (Albucasis)
agriculture 1–106a
cosmetics 2–147b
faience 4–582a
Abū ʿAmr al-Shaybānī 4–442b

Abubacer
  See Tufail, Ibn
ABŪ BAKR (CALIPH) **1–24a**; 3–385b, 387b
  ʿAbd Allāh ibn al-Zubayr 1–15a-b
  ʿĀʾisha 1–112a-b, 113a
  alms tax 1–201b
  caliphate 3–32a, 33a-34a
  Cid, the 3–384b
  commander of the faithful 3–488a
  Muḥammad 1–171b, 172a, 373b
Abū Bakr al-Muṭahhar Jamālī 4–445b
Abū Bakr ibn ʿUmar 1–198b-199a
Abū Dulaf Mosque 1–197a
Abū Firās 1–403a
Abū Ghōsh 4–24b
Abū Ḥafṣ ʿUmar 1–194a,b, 195a
ABŪ ḤANĪFA AL-NUʿMĀN IBN THĀBIT IBN ZŪṬĀ 1–26a
Abū Hāshim ibn Muḥammad ibn al-Ḥanafiyya
  Abbasids 1–7a, 9a
  Kaysanid sect 1–174b
Abū Ḥayyān al-Tawḥīdī
  astrology 1–618a
  prose 1–381a
Abū Ibrāhīm Aḥmad
  Great Mosque of Qayrawān 1–69a,b
Abū ʿImrān al-Fāsī 1–198a
Abū ʿInān
  Baṭṭūṭa, Ibn 2–130b
Abū ʿIqāl 1–70b
Abū Jaʿfar
  See Manṣūr, al-
Abū Jahl 1–28b; 2–42b
Abū Kāmil 1–390b
Abū ʾl-ʿAbbās al-Saffāḥ 1–7b; 3–42b
Abūʾl-ʿAbbās ibn al-Bannāʾ 1–385a
ABULAFIA, ABRAHAM BEN SAMUEL 1–27a
  cabala 3–2b
Abulafia, Todros ben Joseph
  cabala 3–2a
Abū Lahab 1–30a
  Muḥammad 1–15a
Abū ʾl-ʿAlāʾ al-Maʿarrī (poet) 1–401b
Abułamrencʿ family
  Church of Saint Grigor (Ani) 1–292a
Abū ʾl-ʿAtāhiya 1–400b
Abū ʾl-Faraj (hist.)
  See Bar Hebraeus
Abū ʾl-Faraj al-Iṣfahānī (biographer) 1–381a; 2–238b
Abū ʾl Fidāʾ 1–485b; 3–398a
Abū ʾl-Ḥasan ʿAlī ibn Hilāl
  See Bawwāb, Ibn al-
Abul Kasim
  See Abū al-Qāsim Khalaf al-Zahrāwī
Abū ʾl-Maḥāsin ibn Taghrībirdī 2–238b, 272b
Abū ʾl-Salt Umayya
  Arnald of Villanova 1–538a
Abū ʾl-Wafāʾ 1–383a, 384b
Abū Maʿshar 1–385b, 386a, 387b, 606b, 617b, 618b
Abū Muḥammad ʿAbd al-Wāḥid 1–195a
Abū Muḥammad ibn Abī Ḥafṣ 1–200b
Abū Mūsā al-Ashʿari 1–173a,b
Abū Muslim
  Abbasids 1–7a-b
Abū Muslim ibn Khaldūn 1–385b
Abū Naṣr Manṣūr ibn ʿIrāq
  Bīrūnī 2–248b
ABŪ NUWĀS 1–27b
ABŪ NUWĀS 1–400b-403a
Abū Sahl ibn Tamīm 1–387b
Abū Saʿid 1–106b
Abū Salama 1–7b
ABŪ SUFYĀN IBN ḤARB IBN UMAYYA 1–28a
  Badr, battle of 2–42b
ABŪ ṬĀLIB 1–29b; 1–68a,b
Abū Tammām al-Ḥabīb ibn Aws 1–400b
  astrologers 1–617b
Abū Turāb
  See ʿAlī ibn Abī Ṭālib
Abū ʿUbayda 4–443a
  Abū Nuwās 1–27b
Abū ʿUbayda ibn al-Jarrāḥ
  Beirut 2–164a
Abū Yaḥyā 1–627b
Abū Yaʿqūb Yūsuf 1–194b
Abū Yūsuf Yaʿqūb 1–194b-195a
Abū Zayd al-Anṣārī 4–443a
Abydos, Battle of (989) 2–118b
ABYSSINIA 1–30a
  Aksumite art 2–17a
  Alexandrian rite 1–155a-b
  churches 1–157a
  exploration 4–563a
  map 1–31a-b
  trade 4–558b
Acacius of Melitene, Bishop
  Maštocʿ 1–507b
***ACALLAM NA SENÓRACH* 1–33a**
Acarnania
  Epiros despotate 4–499a
Acca of Hexham, Bishop
  Bede 2–154a
Acceptatio of Mainz 3–367a, 526a, 654a
***ACCESSUS AD AUCTORES* 1–34b**
Acciaiuoli, Nerio
  Athens 3–157a
Acciaiuoli, Niccolò
  Boccaccio 2–287a, 288b
Acciaiuoli company of Florence 2–77a
Acciaiuoli family in Greece
  estate yields 1–78a
ACCIDENT 1–35a
  letters 1–218b
ACCLAMATIONS 1–35b
  Asturias-León 1–630a-b
  Byzantium 2–123a
Accomendatio
  See Commenda
ACCOUNTING 1–36a
  bailli 2–52b
  Court of Exchequer 4–533b
  estate management 4–513b-514b
  Exchequer 4–530b
Accounts of the Psalms (Augustine) 1–648b, 651b, 654b, 657a,b
Accursius
  corpus iuris civilis 3–609b
  glossa ordinaria 2–312a
Achaemenid Palace 3–238a
Achaemenids
  Saffarids 1–64b
  Sasanians 1–451b
  south Caucasia 3–195b
ACHARD 1–43a
Acheiropoietos Church 4–552b
***ACKERMANN AUS BÖHMEN, DER* 1–43b**
Ackropolites, George 1–614a
Acolyte 3–441a, 442a,b
Acquasparta, Matteo d' 4–98b
Acre
  Acre Bible 2–219a
  Assizes of Jerusalem 1–599b
  crusader art and architecture 4–25b
  crusades 4–18b, 25a, 26a, 31b, 32b, 40b, 49b
  Guillaume de Beaujeu 3–304b
  Mamluks 4–26a, 54b
  Muslim victory (1291) 3–643b; 4–20b
  Saladin 4–31a
ACRE (LAND MEASURE) 1–45b
ACROSTICS-WORDPLAY 1–45b; 1–207b, 218a
  Eugenius Vulgaris 4–521a
  Hrabanus Maurus 3–103a
  Old English 1–275a
Actes des apostres 4–264b
Actibus apostolorum, De 1–422a
Acts: Against Fortunatus the Manichee (Augustine) 1–648b
Acts of the Apostles, Church of the 1–657b
ACTUALISM 1–46b
Acute arch
  See Lancet arch
Adab 4–444b
  contraception 3–574a
  Ḍiyāʾ al-Dīn 1–635a
  prose 1–379b-380a
Adab al-kabīr
  Arabic adaptation 1–379a
Ad abolendam 3–186b
Ad adolescentes, quomodo possint ex gentilium libris fructum capere (Basil the Great) 2–121a, 122a
Adalard of Corbie
  statutes 4–512a
Adalbero II, Bishop 1–203b
ADALBERO OF LAON 1–46b
Adalbert, Count 2–6a
Adalbert, Margrave 2–6a
ADALBERT, SAINT 1–47b
ADALBERT OF BREMEN 1–47a; 1–50a
  Billungs 2–235a
Adalbert of Mainz 4–427a
Adalbert of Prague
  Bruno of Querfurt 2–391b
  martyrdom 2–64b
Adalbert of Samaria
  dictamen 4–174a
ADALBOLD OF UTRECHT 1–47b
Adalhard 1–143a
  Charlemagne 3–111a
Adalia (Antalya)
  Cilician Kingdom 3–393a
  crusades 4–37b
Adam, Guillaume 1–32b
Adam d'Arras
  See Adam de la Halle
ADAM DE LA BASSÉE 1–48a
ADAM DE LA HALLE 1–48a
  ars antiqua 1–547a
  Bamberg manuscript 2–68b
  congé 3–536b
  fabliau 4–577a
  Jeu de la feuillée 4–264a
  Jeu de Robin et de Marion 4–283b
Adam era 3–25a
Adam le Roi
  See Adenet le Roi
Adam Lock
  See Lock, Adam
Adam Marsh
  See Marsh, Adam de
ADAMNAN, SAINT 1–52b; 3–232a
  Ascension 1–582a
  Columba, Saint 3–485a,b
  dating of Easter 3–228b
Adam of Balsham
  See Adam of the Little Bridge
ADAM OF BREMEN 1–49b
  Denmark 4–152a
Adam of Buckfield 1–461b
Adam of Domerham
  Historia de rebus gestis Glastoniensibus 1–337a

Adam of Fulda 3–658a
Adam of Perseigne 3–405a
ADAM OF SAINT VICTOR 1–51a
ADAM OF THE LITTLE BRIDGE 1–51b; 4–170a
Adana, Council of (1316-1317)
Cilician-Roman church union 3–394b
Ada of Hennegau 2–13b
Adarbadagani
See Azerbaijan
Adarga 1–528a-b
Adarnase II, King 1–481b, 482a
Adarnase IV, King 2–48b
Adarnase, Prince 2–48b
Adarnase of Tao 4–113b
Ada style 1–273a
ADBO OF SAINT GERMAIN-DES-PRÉS 1–53a
Ad Catacumbas 3–154a,b
Adda bar Ahaba 3–27a
Addai, Saint 1–519b
Additiones in codicem (Cino da Pistoia) 3–397b
Address on the Word of Four Letters 1–537b
Adelantado mayor 3–139a
ADELARD OF BATH 1–53b
animal studies 2–244a
ars antiqua 1–544a
astronomy 1–611b
dualism 4–298a
Latin translations 1–378b
Adelard of Ghent
Vita Dunstani 4–311b
Adele, Queen 3–247a
Adelelmus
See Aléaume
ADELMAN OF LIÈGE 1–54b
ADÉMAR OF CHABANNES 1–54b
fables 4–572a
Aden
exploration 4–562b
Aden, Gulf of
Bāb al-Mandab 2–32a
ADENET LE ROI 1–54b
chansons de geste 3–261b
Adeodatus 1–646a, 647a, 648a
Ad Felicem episcopum (Venantius Fortunatus) 3–57b
ADGAR 1–55a
Ādharbādhagān
See Azerbaijan
Ādharbayjān
See Azerbaijan
Adhémar of Le Puy
Council of Clermont 3–449b
death 4–35b
First Crusade 4–30a, 33b, 35a
Adhruḥ 1–237b
Adiabene (Nor Širakan) 1–451a; 2–140a
ʿĀdil, al- 1–195b; 2–23b, 24a
Damascus 4–83b
ʿĀdiliyya, Al- 2–21b
Administrando imperio, De (Constantine VII) 4–446b
ADMIRAL 1–55b
ADMIRALTY, COURT OF 1–56a
See Also Consulate of the Sea
Admiralty, English Black Book of the 3–570a
Admonitio (Saint Basil) 1–62a
Admonitio ad filium spiritualem (Aelfric) 1–61b
"Admonition to a Spiritual Son"
See Admonitio ad filium spiritualem
Admont
Engelbert 4–451b
Adolf of Nassau
Göllheim 2–7b
ADOPTIONISM 1–57b
Alcuin of York 1–143a
Christology 3–321b
Nicene-Constantinopolitan Creed 3–677a
Adoration and Worship in Spirit and Truth (Cyril of Alexandria) 4–75a
Adoration of the magi (Bartolo di Fredi) 2–116b
Ad organum faciendum 3–542a
Ad pauca respicientes (Nicole Oresme) 1–608a
Ad reprimendum (Bartolo da Sassoferrato) 2–115a
Adrevald de Fleury 1–110a, 244a
Adrian I, Pope 1–333b; 2–11a
adoptionism 1–57b
canon law 3–349a
canons and decretals 4–193a
catacombs 3–154b
Christology 3–321b
collectarium 3–479b
Divine Office 4–230a
Donation of Constantine 3–110a
Adrian II, Pope
Anastasius 1–239a
Byzantine church 2–463b
Cyril and Methodios, Saints 4–73b
Fourth Council of Constantinople 3–632a
ADRIAN IV, POPE 1–58a; 4–427b
Arnold of Brescia 1–540a
death 3–637b
lay benefices 2–180a
Adrian V, Pope
papal conclave 3–524a
ADRIANOPLE (**EDIRNE**) **1–59a**; 2–408b, 413a
barbarian victory 1–121a
battle of (378) 1–122a; 2–90b; 3–201a
sack by Bulgarians (813) 2–117a
Adriatic Sea
Dalmatia 4–79b
Dyrrachium 4–329b
trade 2–114a
Ad Sethum (Saint Columbanus) 3–486b
Adso of Montier-en-Der
Antichrist 1–321b; 2–226b
ʿAḍud al-Dawla
Buyids 2–436a
Adulis 1–30b
Adultery
Islamic law 3–527a; 4–598b
ADVENT 1–59a
ember days 4–435b
Adventu antichristi, De (Arnald of Villanova) 1–537b
Adventus
See Entry into Jerusalem
Adversus haereses (Irenaeus) 3–335a
angelology 1–249b
Adversus nationes (Arnobius the Elder) 1–539a
ADVOCATE 1–59b
Advowson
See Presentation
Aedan
See Also Aidan
ÁEDÁN MAC GABRÁIN 1–60a
Dál Riata 4–78a-b
Aedan m Lugar, Bishop 1–107a
AEDDI 1–61a
Áed Find, King 4–78b
AEDICULA 1–61a
Áed mac Ainmuirech, King
Áedán mac Gabráin 1–60a
ÁED SLÁNE 1–60b
Aegean Sea
Anatolia 1–239b
Crete 3–678a
Dardanelles 4–105a
Aegidius (Roman general) 2–94a
Aegidius Romanus
See Egidius Colonna
AELFRIC 1–61b; 1–273b; 4–459a
Bible 2–221a
brewing 2–374b
exegesis 4–546a, 548b-550a
homilies 1–275b, 276b, 281b-285b
textbooks 4–578b
AELFRIC BATA 1–62b
Aelfryth, Queen
Anglo-Norman chronicles 1–265a
Ælle 4–454a
Aelred
See Ethelred
Aelred of Rievaulx, Saint
See Ethelred of Rievaulx, Saint
Aemilia
Ambrose, Saint 1–230b
Ravenna exarchate 4–529b
Aeneas Sylvius Piccolomini
See Pius II
Aeneid (Vergil) 1–180b, 181b
adaptation 4–451a
Douglas translation 4–262b
Aequitas
See Equity
ÆSIR 1–62b
Aesop
beast epic 2–140b-141a
fables 4–572a,b, 573a
Aestiorum gentes (Tacitus) 2–61b
Aethelberht, Archbishop
Alcuin of York 1–142a-b
Aethelbert of Kent, King
laws 1–275a, 286a
Æthelfrith
Bangor Iscoed 2–71a
Alfred the Great 1–163b
Æthelred
See Ethelred the Unready
Aethelwig of Evesham 2–173b
Æthelwold, Bishop 1–273a
Æthelwulf the poet 1–163b, 254b
Aetheria of Gaul
Peregrinatio ad loca sancta Silviae 1–332a
Aethicus Ister 1–217b
Aethiopia credet Deo 1–32a
Aëtius 1–121a
Burgundians 2–422b
Huns 2–92a,b
Aetolia
Despotate of Epiros 4–499a
AEVIA 1–63b
Afḍal ʿAlī, al-
Ḍiyāʾ al-Dīn 1–634b-635a
Afḍal Shānānshāh, al-
Godfrey of Bouillon 4–36a
Afer
See Arnobius the Elder
Afflighem, John of
See John of Afflighem
AFGHANISTAN 1–63b
agricultural products 1–96a
map 1–64
Afonso I Henriques of Portugal, King 1–200a
Order of Aviz 2–16b
Afonso II of Portugal, King
Order of Aviz 2–17a
Afonso III of Portugal, King
deposition of rulers 4–160a

AFONSO III OF PORTUGAL, KING (cont.)
poets 4–189b
Afonso IV of Portugal, King
Poema del Salado 1–163a
Afonso V of Portugal, King 1–21b
Azores 2–29b; 4–559b
Guinea 4–561b
slaves 2–268b
Afonso Sanches
poetry 4–190a,b
Africa
Abyssinia 1–30a-33a
Atlas Mountains 1–639b-641a
Bāb al-Mandab 2–32a
climatology 3–451a
exarchate 4–529b, 530a
exploration 4–561a-562b, 563a
fairs 4–589a-b
map 1–31a-b, 640a-b; 4–404a-b, 553b
slave trade 2–268a-270a
trade 4–556a, 557b
Vandals 2–91b
Afrīqīn 3–619a
Afshīn ibn Abū 'l Sāj
Ašot II Erkatʿ 1–588b
Dwin 4–324a
"Against Christians" (al-Jāḥiẓ) 1–379b
Against Faustus the Manichee (Augustine) 1–651a
Against Gaudentius (Augustine) 1–651b
Against Julian the Pelagian (Augustine) 1–649b
Against Maximus the Arian (Augustine) 1–654a
Against the Letter Called "The Foundation" (Augustine) 1–650b
Against the Letter of Petilianus (Augustine) 1–651b
Against the Skeptics (Augustine) 1–647b
***AGAPE* 1–66a**
Agapetus II, Pope
Cluny 3–470a
AGATʿANGELOS 1–66a; 2–48a
Ardešir legend 1–452a
Armenian literature 1–508a
Armenian saints 1–517b, 518a, 519b
Ējmiacin 4–417a
Agatha, Saint 1–261b
AGATHIAS 1–67b; 2–512a
Agenardus
See Einhard
Agenda dioecesis Aquileiensis 1–353a
Age pyramid
demography 4–145a, 146a
AGHKAND WARE 1–68a
AGHLABID ART 1–69a
AGHLABIDS 1–70a
Tunisia 3–49a
Aghri Dagh
See Ararat, Mount
Aghts
See Ałc
Agila
See Córdoba
Agilofings 2–134a
AGINCOURT, BATTLE OF (1415) **1–72a**; 3–205b
bow and arrow 2–352b
Charles of Orléans 3–273a
AGIUS OF CORVEY 1–72b
AGNELLUS OF PISA 1–72b
AGNELLUS OF RAVENNA, SAINT 1–73a; 4–361b
Agnes, Saint 1–261b
Agnes (Anna) of France, Princess 1–245a; 2–521b
AGNOLO DI VENTURA 1–73b
AGNOLO DI VENTURA 1–76b
AGNUS CHANT 1–73b
AGNUS DEI (MUSIC) **1–74a**
AGNUS DEI (SYMBOL) **1–74a**
AGNUS DEI (SYMBOL) **1–344a**
crucifixion 4–13b
AGOBARD 1–75a; 1–228a
anti-Semitism 3–620b
Carthusian rite 3–118a
Divine Office 4–223a
exegesis 2–213a
reforms 3–112a,b
AGOSTINO, GIOVANNI D' 1–76b; 1–73b
Agrafe 3–624b
Agricola, Rodolphus
dialectic 4–171a
Agricultura, De (Palladius) 3–168b
AGRICULTURE AND NUTRITION 1–76b
Asturias-Len 1–629b
banal monopolies 2–69b
botany 2–347b-348a
bread 2–364b-365a
brewing 2–373b
Burgundy, Duchy of 2–428a
Byzantine 1–76b-79b; 2–475b, 476b-477a, 480a; 4–595a
Castile 3–135a-136a
climatology 3–451a, 456a
corvée labor 3–613a
Cyprus 4–72a
Dauphiné 4–110a
demesne farming 1–39a-40a
draft animals 1–293a
England 2–52a; 4–457b, 482a
estate management 4–511b-514b
fairs 4–584a, 592a
Islamic regions 1–103a-106b
Jewish dietary laws 4–180a-181b
land subdivision 3–415a
Mediterranean 1–79b-88b
northern Europe 1–89a-96a
Slavic regions 1–96b-103a
See Also Class Structure, Western
See Also Climatology
Ağri Daği
See Ararat, Mount
Agri decumates 2–88b, 89b
Alamanni 2–94b
Aguilar Palace 2–104a
ʿAhd 3–39a
Aḥdāth 4–82a, 84a
ʾAḥkām
See Astrology/Astronomy, Islamic
Ahl al-bayt 1–174b
Ahl al-dhimma 3–34a, 43b
Ahl al-kitāb 3–34a
Aḥmad 1–70b
Aḥmad al-Badawī 4–407a
Aḥmad ibn Abī Du'ād 3–44b
Aḥmad ibn Ismāʿīl
Alptigin 1–220a
Aḥmad ibn Muḥammad Abū al-Fazl Maydānī Nīshāpūrī 4–444b
Aḥmad ibn Ṭūlūn
Aleppo 1–145a
Qaṭāʾiʿ, Al- 3–13b
Aḥmadīya 4–407a
AḤMAD MŪSĀ 1–106b
Aḥmad Qadi 3–54a
Aḥmed Dānishmend ibn ʿAlī ibn Mizrāb 4–91b
Ahura Mazda temple (Ani) 1–290a
Aias
See Āyās
Aiazzi
See Āyās
Aichardus
See Achard
Aid (feudal)
See Feudalism
Áidán
See Also Áedán
AIDAN OF LINDISFARNE 1–107a
Celtic church 3–226a
monastery 3–344b
Aigai
See Āyās
Aigues-Mortes 2–129a
city walls 3–151a
Louis IX 4–52b
Aileran the Wise
Brigit, Saint 2–376b
Ailettes 1–525a, 530b
Aillenn 1–34a
AILLY, PIERRE D' 1–108a; 2–41a
astrology 1–608b
Biel, Gabriel 2–234a
calendars 3–23a
conciliar theory 3–365b, 511a-514b, 517a, 518a,b, 521b
councils 3–646a, 647a, 648a, 650a-651a
ecclesiology 4–377b
nominalist theory 3–371a
Ailred of Reievaulx
See Ethelred of Rievaulx
Aimeric of Angoulême 1–422b
Aimerus
ars antiqua 1–545a
AIMOIN DE FLEURY 1–109b
Abbo of Fleury 1–13a
André de Fleury 1–244a
Áine Cliach 4–492b
Ainhardus
See Einhard
Ain Jalut
See ʿAyn Jālūt
AIRBERTACH MAC COISSE 1–110a
***AIRDENA BRÁTHA* 1–111a**
See Also Apocrypha, Irish
Airec Menman Uraird meic Coisse 1–114a
Airgailla
Cinéal Eóghain 3–397a
Airne fingein
See Apocrypha, Irish
Airther Cliach 4–492b
ʿĀʾISHA 1–112a
ʿAbd Allāh 1–15a-b
Abū Bakr 1–24a
ʿAlī ibn Abī Ṭālib 1–172b
First Civil War 3–35b
***AISLINGE MEIC CON-GLINNE* 1–113b**
Aistian
See Baltic countries/Balts
Aithallah of Edessa, Bishop 1–508a
Aix-en-Provence 2–88b
Aix-la-Chapelle
See Aachen
Ajazzo
See Āyās
***AJÍMEZ* 1–114a**
Ajoie 2–424a
Ajuda 3–86b
Ajwad ibn Zāmil 2–51a
***AKATHISTOS* 1–114b**; 2–511a
Aken, Hein van 4–319a
Akhbār al-ṭiwāl, al- (al-Dīnawarī) 4–188a
Akhī associations
Ankara 1–302b
Akhlat
See Xlatʿ
AKHṬAL, AL- 1–115a; 1–400a

Akiba ben Joseph 2–210b
Akilisene, Peace of 3–308a
Akindynos, Gregory 3–632b
Akolouthia
  See Canticle
Akominates, Michael
  estates 1–77b-78a
***AKRITAI* 1–115b**
Akropolites, George 3–642a
Aksum, Kingdom of 2–17a-b
AKSUMITE ART 2–17a
Al-
  See next element of name
'Alā' al-Dīn Beg
  execution 2–136b
'Alā' al-Dīn Kai-Kobadh I
  Anatolia 1–241b
***ÁLA FLEKKS SAGA* 1–116b**
Alain de Lille
  See Alan of Lille
ALAMANNI 1–117a; 2–128b
  Bavaria 2–133b
  Clovis 3–466b-467a
  invasions 2–89a, 94b
  law 1–90b
  Merovingians 3–104a
ALAMUT 1–118a
ALANI 1–120b
  Alamanni 1–117a
  arms and armor 1–522a, 534b
  Burgundians 2–422b
  Byzantine church 2–464a
  northern Caucasia 3–195a
  Romans 3–200b, 201a
  Visigoths 1–122a
ALAN OF LILLE 1–119a; 1–48a
  allegory 1–182a, 183a-b, 188b, 189a
  ars antiqua 1–544a
  ars praedicandi 1–555b, 557b
  prosimetrium genre 1–642b
Alan of Walsingham
  See Walsingham, Alan of
Alans
  See Alani
Alan the Great, King
  Brittany 2–379a
Alanus Anglicus
  conciliar theory 3–516b
Alanus de Insulis
  See Alan of Lille
Alarcos, Battle of (1195) 1–195a, 410a; 3–131a
ALARIC 1–122a; 2–90b
  Byzantine Empire 2–485b
Alarodioi
  See Ayrarat
Álava
  Asturian raids 1–626a
  Basques 2–126a
  Castilian expansion 3–130b
ALAVERDI 1–122b
Alb
  See Vestments
ALBA 1–122b
  aubade 1–642a
  Aucassin et Nicolette 1–643b
Alba Bible 2–215b
Ałbak 1–451a
Alban, Saint 1–261a
Albana
  See Derbent
ALBANIA (CAUCASIAN) **1–123a**
  Azerbaijan 2–26a-27a
  Bagratids 2–47b, 48b
  Bardha'a 2–107a
  Baylakān 2–139b
  Bulgaria 2–406b, 409b, 410a
  Derbent 4–162a
  Epiros, Despotate of 4–500a
  map 1–124a-b; 3–194a-b
Albano, Pietro d' 1–613a
Albarracín 1–415b
Albergamenta 4–110a
Albergati, Nicolas 4–567b
Alberic, Saint
  Cisterican order 3–403b
Alberic de Bisançon
  Alexander romances 1–150a, 151a
Alberich of Trois Fontaines
  chronicle 1–644a
ALBERIC OF MONTE CASSINO 1–125b
  dictamen 4–174a
Albert, Antipope 1–330a
Albert, Bishop
  crusades 2–64b
Albert, Pere 1–413b
Albertano of Brescia 3–169a, 671a
ALBERTI, LEON BATTISTA 1–126a; 1–438a
Albert of Cologne
  See Albertus Magnus
Albert of Lauingen
  See Albertus Magnus
Albert of Mecklenburg, King 4–156a
Albert of Morra
  See Gregory VII, Pope
ALBERT OF SAXONY 1–125b; 1–396b, 435a, 464b
  alchemy 1–137a
  dialectic 4–170b
Albert of Vercelli, Saint
  Carmelites 3–96b
Albert the German
  See Albertus Magnus
Albert IV the Wise, Duke
  Bavarian unity 2–135b
ALBERTUS MAGNUS 1–126b; 2–13a, 35b
  alchemy 1–137a,b
  angelology 1–250a
  Aquinas 1–353b, 354b
  Aristotelianism 1–462a-b
  astrology 1–607b
  Augustinism 1–660b
  Bacon 2–37a, 39a
  baptism 2–84a
  bestiary 2–205a
  biology 2–142b, 242a, 243b-244a, 246a
  Cavalcanti, Guido 3–197a
  Christology 3–323b
  contraception 3–573a,b
  dialectic 4–170a
  doctors of the church 4–234b
  Dominican theology 4–246b
  draft animals 1–296b, 298a
  exegesis 4–544a
  Great Arbitration of 1258 3–481b
  theology 4–245b
  University of Paris 1–543b
Albertus of Brudzewo
  Ptolemy 1–614b
ALBIGENSIANS 1–130b
  beguins 2–162b
  Bible 2–215a
  crusade 1–410b; 3–188a-189b, 255a; 4–15a, 17b, 347b
  Dauphiné 4–109b
  Docetism 4–233b
  Dominic, Saint 4–239b
  Dominicans 4–243b
  dualism 2–296b; 4–297b
  See Also Cathars
Albin, Saint
  Brut, The 2–393a
Albinus
  See Alcuin of York
Albinus of Canterbury 1–645a
  Bede 2–155b
Albinus (Senator)
  Boethius 2–291b
"Albion" 1–613a,b
Albon 4–109a
ALBORNOZ, GIL 1–130b
Albrecht
  See Also Albert
Albrecht I, Emperor 2–7b
Albrecht II, Emperor 2–8b
Albrecht VI, King 2–9a
Albrecht II of Austria, Duke 2–8a
Albrecht III of Austria, Duke 2–8b
Albrecht IV of Austria, Duke 2–8b
Albrecht V of Austria, Duke 2–8b
Albrecht VI of Austria, Duke 2–9a
Albrecht of Brandenburg
  Teutonic Knights 2–262a; 3–306a
Albrecht I of Brunswick, Duke 2–199a
Albrecht of Mecklenburg 2–247a
Albrecht the Bear 2–360b
ALBRECHT VON HALBERSTADT 1–131b
ALBRECHT VON JOHANSDORF 1–132a
ALBRECHT VON SCHARFENBERG 1–133a
Albucasis
  See Abū al-Qāsim Khalaf al-Zahrāwī
Albumasar
  See Abū Ma'shar
Albuquerque, Juan Alfonso de 3–137a
ALBURANUS 1–134a
Albuzale
  See Abū 'l-Salt Umayya
ALC 1–134a
  architecture 1–493a-b
  hypogeum 1–290b
  sculpture 1–495a
Alcalá de Henares
  cortes (1348) 3–135a
  fairs 4–587b
Alcama, Ibn 3–386a
Alcañiz 3–16b
Alcazaba 1–168a,b
Alcázar 1–169a
  Córdoba 3–598a, 600b
ALCHEMY 1–134b
  alcohol 4–219b
  astrology 1–604b
  Canterbury Tales 3–294b
  textbook 4–580a
ALCHEMY, ISLAMIC 1–140b
  West 1–136a-b
Alcibiades
  Aquinas 1–357b
Alcira 1–83b
Alcobaça
  hall church 3–379a
Alcock, Simon
  ars praedicandi 1–557a
Alcohol
  Alderotte, Taddeo 4–219b
  Ankara 1–302b
  distillation 4–219a
ALCUIN OF YORK 1–142a; 1–228a; 2–173b; 4–374a
  adoptionism 1–57b
  All Saints' Day 1–176b
  Angilbert, Saint 1–254a
  Bede 2–154a
  Bible 3–313b
  Carolingians 3–100a-101b, 110a,b, 111a
  Charlemagne 3–109b, 268b

ALCUIN OF YORK (cont.)
confirmation 3–536a
dialectic 4–169a
England 4–455a, 458b
exegesis 4–542b, 548b, 549a
literary studies 3–433a
Nicene-Constantinopolitan Creed 3–676b
poetry 1–254b
seven liberal arts 1–580a
Vulgate 2–211b
Alda 4–283a
Aldeigjuborg 4–555a
ALDERMEN 1–143b
See Also Consuls
Alderotte, Taddeo
alcohol 4–219b
Aldfrid of Northumbria, King
Adamnan, Saint 1–52b
Wilfrid 1–144a,b
Aldfrith
See Aldfrid of Northumbria, King
ALDHELM 1–144a
Celtic church 3–229a, 232a
England 4–458b
poetry 1–254b, 277b, 278a
Aldus Manutius 2–203a
ALÉAUME 1–144b
Alegre, Francesc 3–169a
Alemannic Law 1–90b
See Also Alamanni
Alembic 1–139a-b
Alentejo
agriculture 1–85a
ALEPPO 1–145a
Ayyubids 2–21a,b, 22b, 23b
Bar Hebraeus 2–108b
crusades 4–37b
exilarch 4–552b
Saladin 4–31a
ALEXANDER V, ANTIPOPE 1–147a; 1–330b, 342a
church councils 3–646b, 647a
conciliar movement 3–365b, 366a
election 1–108b
Alexander, Archbishop 1–453b
ALEXANDER II, POPE 1–146a; 1–311a; 3–351b
Benzo of Alba 2–182b
Camaldolese order 3–56a
elections, church 4–421a
excommunication 4–536b
Norman Conquest 4–465b
ALEXANDER III, POPE 1–146b; 4–395b
Adrian IV 1–58b
"antipope" 1–331b
Becket 2–151b, 152a
Bernard of Clairvaux 2–192b
Bucentaur 2–395b
Burgundy 2–429b
canonization 3–68a
Christology 3–323a
church councils 3–637b-638a
clerics 4–133b
coronation 3–604a,b
Danish church 4–153b
decretum 4–129b
Edward the Confessor 4–475a
Ethelred, Saint 4–517a
letters 3–353b
Licet de vitanda 3–94b
military orders 2–17a
reform 3–352b, 353a
University of Bologna 2–312a
vandalism 1–334a
Alexander IV, Pope
Albertus Magnus 1–128b
Bulla Cypria 4–72b
Carthusians, 3–119b
curia 1–128a
Dominicans 4–251b
Franciscans 2–315a
Grand Union 1–659b
Alexander de Villa Dei
Carmen de algorismo 1–396a
grammar 3–434b
Alexander Hegius
Brethren of the Common Life 2–369a
Alexanderlied 2–228a
Alexander of Alexandria 1–633a; 3–627b
Alexander of Aphrodisias 1–457a
dialectic 4–170b
Alexander of Ashby
ars praedicandi 1–556a
Alexander of Byzantium, Emperor
Bulgaria 2–404b
Alexander I of Georgia, King 2–49a; 4–110b
ALEXANDER OF HALES 1–148a; 1–461b
Augustinism 1–660b
Biel, Gabriel 2–234a
Bonaventure, Saint 2–313a
Christology 3–323a
exegesis 4–544a
ALEXANDER OF ROES 1–148b
Alexander I of Scotland, King 4–110b
Alexander III of Scotland, King 4–396a
Alexander of Stavensby
Dominicans 4–245a
ALEXANDER ROMANCES 1–149b
Alexanders Saga 1–152a
Byzantine 2–509b
cuaderna vía 4–63a
Latin epic 4–496a
Libro de Alexandre 1–152b
See Also Anglo-Norman literature
Alexander's Death 1–151a
Alexanders geesten 4–318b
***ALEXANDERS SAGA* 1–152a**; 1–286a
Alexander the Great
astrology 1–604a
Cilician Gates 3–390b
literary studies 3–430a
romances 1–149b, 266a
Alexander the monk
Dicta Anselmi 1–314a
***ALEXANDRE, LIBRO DE* 1–152b**
cuaderna vía 4–63a
Poema de Alfonso XI 1–162b
Alexandre de Paris
Alexander romances 1–151a
Anglo-Norman literature 1–266b
Alexandreis (Gautier de Châtillon) 1–150a; 4–496a
Norse adaptation of 1–152a
ALEXANDRIA 1–153a
alphabetization 1–204a
ʿAmr ibn al-ʿĀṣ 1–237a; 4–403b
Athanasius, Saint 1–632a
Byzantine church 2–459b-460a, 462b
calendars 3–18b
Catechetical School 3–335b, 336a, 593b-594a
Cyril, Saint 4–74b
exploration 4–553b
Peter de Lusignan 4–55a
Saladin 4–31a
theology 3–320a, 336a
ALEXANDRIAN RITE 1–155a
Alexandrine verse
See Cuaderna vía
Alexiad
See Anna Komnena
Alexios III Angelos 1–251b; 2–469a-497a; 3–391a
crusades 4–45a,b-46b
Alexios IV Angelos 1–251b
Boniface of Montferrat 4–43a,b
coemperorship 2–496a; 4–46a-b, 47b
crusades 4–46a-47b, 48b
Alexios Apokavkos
Byzantine Empire 2–501a
Alexios V Doukas 1–251b; 2–496a, 497a
ALEXIOS I KOMNENOS 1–157b; 1–303a; 2–491b-492a, 493b-494a; 4–344a
Angelos family 1–251b
art 2–443b
Bogomils 2–295b, 296a
Bohemond I 2–308b-309b
crusades 4–34a-b, 35a,b
Doukas 4–263a
dux 4–323a
Great Palace 3–553a
histories 2–514b-515a
marriage 4–595b
papacy 4–30a
Venice 4–556a
Alexios II Komnenos
Andronikos I Komnenos 1–245a
ALEXIOS I OF TREBIZOND 1–159a
Byzantine Empire 2–498a
Alexios III of Trebizond, Komnenos 1–159a
Alexios Philanthropenos
Andronikos II Palaiologos 1–245b
Alexios Slav
Bulgaria 2–409a
Alexis, Guillaume
Debat de l'omme et de la femme 1–324b
ALEXIS OF MOSCOW 1–159a
Alexius
See Alexios
Alfaquí 4–85b
Alf layla wa layla (Thousand and one nights) 4–407b
Alfons
See Alfonso
Alfonsi, Petrus 1–264a; 3–167b
ALFONSINE TABLES 1–159b; 1–162a, 612b, 614b-615a
calendars and reckoning of time 3–23a
Alfonso
See Also Afonso
Alfonso, Peter
See Alfonsi, Petrus
Alfonso de Aveiro
Niger 4–562a
Alfonso de la Cerda 1–414b; 3–135a
Alfonso de Paiva 4–562b-563a
***ALFONSO XI, POEMA DE* 1–162b**
Alfonso of Aragon (son of James I) 1–412b
ALFONSO I OF ARAGON 1–160a; 1–406a-407b; 3–178b
marriage 3–129b-130a
reconquest 1–200a
Alfonso II of Aragon (Alfons I of Catalonia) 1–408b-410a,b, 411a; 3–187a
Alfonso III of Aragon (Alfons II of Catalonia) 1–414a
Arnald of Villanova 1–537b
Bible 2–215b; 3–166b
cortes 3–611a,b
slaves 2–268a
Alfonso IV of Aragon (Alfons III of Catalonia) 1–415a,b

Alfonso V of Aragon (Alfons IV of Catalonia) 1–417b-418b, 419a-b
Baçó, Jame 2–34b
Alfonso I of Asturias, King
Galicia 1–626a
Alfonso II of Asturias, King 1–626a-b
Alfonso III of Asturias, King 1–627a
Alfonso IV of Asturias, King 1–627b
Alfonso V of Asturias, King 1–628a-b
Alfonso VI of Castile, King 1–160b, 406a; 3–129a-b, 131b
Almoravids 1–199b
Cantar de mío Cid 3–73a,b, 76a
Alfonso VII of Castile, King 1–628b; 3–138a-b
Crown of Aragon 1–408a,b
reconquest 1–200a
Alfonso VIII of Castile, King 1–409a; 3–76b-77a, 130b
Bordeaux 2–328a
Crown of Aragon 1–410a
death 3–133b
ALFONSO X OF CASTILE, KING 1–161a; 1–413b
Alfonsine tables 1–159b
Bible translations 2–215b
Calila e Digna 3–31b
cantigas de amor 3–87a
cantigas de Santa Maria 3–85a,b
Castile 3–134a-b, 136a, 139a, 142a
chroniclers 3–71a
Córdoba 3–600b
dictamen 4–175b
election 4–428a
Latin translations 1–378b
legal code 1–190b
Libros del saber de astronomía 3–458a
Alfonso XI of Castile, King 3–134b-135a, 136b
Córdoba 3–600b
cortes 3–610b, 611a
Ordenamiento de Alcalá 3–611b
Alfonso IX of León, King 1–629a
Castile 3–133b
marriage 3–77a, 131a
taxes 3–132a
Alfonso of Valladolid
converso 3–577b
Alfonso Raimúndez
See Alfonso VII of Castile
Alfons Pecha 2–247a
Alfred of Sareshel 1–136b
Alfred the Englishman
See Alfred of Sareshel
ALFRED THE GREAT 1–163b
agriculture 1–90b
art 1–272a
biography 2–239b
burhs 4–457b
Chester Treaty 3–300a
Christianity 4–458b-459a
Danelaw 4–91a, 456a-b
exegesis 4–549b
fairs 4–586b
poetry 1–278b
West Saxon supremacy 4–455b
ALFRED THE GREAT AND TRANSLATIONS 1–164b; 1–274b, 276a, 284a-285b
Asser 1–456a, 593a
fables 4–573a
Algarve
agriculture 1–85a
Algazel
See Ghazālī, al-
Algebra
See Mathematics
Algebra (Abū Kāmil) 1–390b
Algeciras
capture (1344) 1–162b; 3–135a
Algeciras, Battle of (1369) 1–170b
Algeria
agriculture 1–80a
Knights of Malta 3–304a
Alger of Liège 1–167b
Alghero 1–416a
Algiers, Great Mosque of 1–196a-b, 197a
Algirdas, Prince 1–159b; 2–67a
Algorismus 1–388a-389a, 395b-396a
Algorismus vulgaris (John of Sacrobosco) 1–396a, 612a
ALHAMBRA 1–168a
Alhazen
See Haytham, Ibn al-
Āl-i Būyih
See Buyids
Alicante 1–414b
Alidade 1–602a,b, 603b, 611a; 3–29a
ALIDS 1–174b
Abbasids 1–7a, 9a, 11a-b
Abū Ṭālib 1–30a
Buyids 2–435b, 436a
caliphate 3–46a
Faḍl ibn Yaḥyā's, al- 2–110b-111a
See Also ʿAlī ibn Abī Ṭālib
Alieniloquium
See Allegory
Āli flekkr 1–116b
ʿAlī ibn Abī Ṭalḥah al-Hāshimī 4–442b
ʿALĪ IBN ABĪ ṬĀLIB 1–171b; 1–15b, 373b, 374a
Abū Bakr 1–25a
ʿĀʾisha 1–112b, 113a-b
Alids 1–174b
caliphate 3–35a,b-36b
ʿAlī ibn Ghāniya 1–194b-195a
ʿAlī ibn Hilāl
See Bawwāb, Ibn al-
ʿAlī ibn ʿĪsā al-Asṭurlābī 1–617b
ʿAlī ibn Muḥammad ibn Jaʿfar al-Himmānī 1–175b
ʿAlī ibn Mūsā al-Riḍā 1–175a
ʿAlī ibn Yūsuf 1–194a, 200a
ʿAlī Mashhadi 3–54a
ALIMPI 1–175b
Aliovat-Arberani 1–423a
Aliscans 3–258b
Alixandre, Libro de
See Alexandre, Libro de
Alix of Champagne (of Cyprus), Queen 3–249a
Conon de Béthune 3–538a
ALJAMIADO LITERATURE 1–176a
Aljarafe
See Sharaf, al-
Aljnikʿ 1–472a, 513a; 2–140b
Alkimia minor (Albertus Magnus) 1–137a
ALLAH 1–177a
ALL'ANTICA 1–177a
Allegoresis 1–180a-186b
Allegoriae (Isidore of Seville) 1–188a
Allegories on Ovid (Giovanni del Virgilio) 1–183b
Allegories on the Metamorphoses (Arnulf) 1–183b
ALLEGORY 1–178b
Alan of Lille 1–119b-120a
alchemy 1–138b, 141a,b, 142a
beast epic 2–140a
bestiaries 2–203b, 243b
courtly love 3–670b
Dante 4–103b
Dutch literature 4–319a
Everyman 4–527b-529a
exegesis 2–212b; 4–544a,b
French literature 1–188a-189b
hermetic 1–141a,b
Islamic alchemy 1–141a,b
Liber officialis 1–228a
Libro de Alexandre 1–153a
Pavo 1–148b
religious dramas 4–286b-287a
Zosimus 1–135b-136a
ALLEGORY, FRENCH 1–188a
Charles of Orléans 3–273a
ALLELENGYON 1–189b
epibolé 4–495b
Allemaine
cookery 3–582b
Allerheiligenthal priory 3–118b
Alliterative patterns
Old English poetry 1–276b-277a
Allocutio super Tetragrammaton (Arnald of Villanova) 1–537b
Allod
See Alod
Allodium
See Alod
ALL SAINTS' DAY 1–176b
ALL SOULS' DAY 1–177a
Almagest (Ptolemy) 1–604b, 610a, 612a, 613b, 614a, 620a,b
Almain, Jacques
conciliar theory 3–519b, 520b
Almanac 1–609a
Almanach perpetuum (Zacuto) 1–613a
Alma Redemptoris mater 1–329a
Almenar 1–405b
Almería 1–408a
capture (1147) 3–130a
trade 4–557b
ALMOGÁVARES 1–190b
Catalan Company 3–156a
ALMOHAD ART 1–191a
Alhambra 1–168a
Almoravid art 1–197a
ALMOHADS 1–193b
Almoravids 1–191a-b, 193b-194a, 200a-201a; 3–130a
Atlas Mountains 1–641a
Calatrava, capture of (1195) 3–16b
Castile 3–130b
Córdoba 3–600a
Crown of Aragon 1–410b
dirham 4–215b
Las Navas de Tolosa 3–131a
Almoin of Fleury
See Aimoin de Fleury
Almojarife mayor 3–139a
ALMORAVID ART 1–196a
Alhambra 1–168a
ALMORAVIDS 1–198a
agriculture 1–105a
Atlas Mountains 1–641a
Barcelona 2–103a
Castile 3–129b, 130a
Catalonia 3–178a,b
ceramics 3–237b
Cid, the 3–384b, 385a-b
commander of the faithful 3–488b
Córdoba 3–600a
Saragossa 1–160b
See Also Almohads
Almos 4–6b-7a
ALMS TAX, ISLAMIC 1–201b
Almucantars 1–602a,b, 603b
ALNAGE 1–202b
ALOD 1–190a-b
Alodia
Nubian Christianity 3–314b
Alodis
See Alod

Alovania
See Albania
ALP ARSLAN 1–203a; 1–484b
Ani in Širak 1–290b
Ankara 1–302a,b
Byzantine Empire 2–493a
Seljuks 4–33b
ALPERT OF METZ 1–203b
Alpetragius
See Biṭrūjī, al-
ALPHA AND OMEGA 1–204a
Apocalypse 1–343b
ALPHABETIZATION, HISTORY OF 1–204a
ALPHABETS 1–207b
Armenian 1–491a-492b
Greek 1–204a
Old English texts 1–275a
Slavic dialect 2–299a
Alphabets of tales 4–551a
Alphabetum narrationum 4–551a
Arnold of Liège 1–206a
ALPHANUS OF SALERNO 1–218b
Constantine the African 3–548b
***ALPHARTS TOD* 1–219a**
Buch von Bern, Das 2–395b
See Also Eckenlied
Alphege, Saint 3–82a
Alphonse
See Also entries under Afonso, Alfonso
Alphonse-Jourain, Count 2–128a
Alphonse of Poitiers 1–412b; 2–270b, 271a
bastides 2–128b
Burgundy 2–429b
French chronicles 3–332a
Alphonsine Tables
See Alfonsine Tables
Alpin, Kenneth mac
See Kenneth I MacAlpin
Alps
agricultural division 1–89a
Álptafjörðr clan 4–568a
ALPTIGIN 1–219b
Alquimia
See Alchemy
Alsace
Alamanni 2–94b
Black Death 2–262b
AŁTʿAMAR 1–220b; 1–451b, 496a
Armenian church 1–503b-504a
ALTAR, PORTABLE 1–225a
ALTAR--ALTAR APPARATUS 1–221a
antependium 1–316b
apse 1–352a
baldachin 2–55a
brandeum 2–362a
chancel 3–251b
ciborium 3–383b
golden, San Abrogio 1–254b
liturgical aspects 1–442a, 443, 444b-445a
Altar cross 4–9a
"Altar of Victory" controversy
Ambrose, Saint 1–231a
ALTARPIECE 1–225b
Baerze, Jacques 2–44b
Bouts, Dirk 2–350a
Broederlam, Melchior 2–383a
Eyck, Jan van 4–566b
Altarpiece of the Baptism (David) 4–115a
Altarpiece of the Deposition (Robert Campin) 3–61a
Altarpiece of the Holy Sacrament 2–350a
Altdeutsche Exodus 2–227a
Altdeutsche Genesis 2–226b
Altdorfer, Albrecht
etching 4–516b
Altercatione ecclesiae et synagogae dialogus, De (Augustine) 4–371a
Alternating supports
See Alternation
ALTERNATION 1–225b
ALTFRID OF MÜNSTER 1–226a
ALTICHIERO 1–226b; 2–11b
Altmark
Brandenburg 2–360b
Altsächsische Genesis 2–225a-b
Altun 4–301b
Altus prosator
Columba, Saint 3–485b
Ałuan
See Albania
Aluank
See Albania
Alum
dyeing 4–327a
Aluminibus et salibus, De 1–136b
Alusianos 2–407b
Álvaro de Luna 3–138a
ALVÍSSMÁL 1–226b; 4–386b-387a, 390a,b, 391a,b
Aʿłwankʿ
See Albania
Alypius 1–647b, 648a
journeys 1–658a
***AMADAS ET YDOINE* 1–227a**; 1–267a
Amadeo VI of Savoy, Count
crusade 4–56a
John V 2–502a
Amadeus VIII of Savoy, Duke
See Felix V, Pope
***AMADÍS DE GAULA* 1–227b**; 1–573a, 576b
Amae 1–223a
Amalar, Bishop 1–75b
Amalaric the Visigoth 2–102b
AMALARIUS OF METZ 1–228a; 3–112a; 4–373a
cantor 3–88a
Divine Office 4–222b-223a, 230a
exegesis 4–542b
liturgical drama 4–274a
Amalbert 1–109a
Amalfi
commerce 4–556a
Amalric, Arnold
Albigensian Crusade 3–187b, 188a, 405b
Amalric I, King
Alexandria 1–153b
Assizes of Jerusalem 1–599a
Byzantine Empire 2–495a
Church of the Nativity (Bethlehem) 4–24b
Latin crusader states 4–38b-39a
AMALRIC OF BÈNE 1–228a
dualism 4–297b
rejection by Lateran council 3–640b
Amalric of Cyprus 4–71a
Amalu/Noravank
See Noravankʿ at Amału
Amanus Mountains 3–391a
Amaous 2–424a
AMARCIUS 1–228b; 1–318b
Amasia 1–241a
AMATUS OF MONTE CASSINO 1–229a
Amaury, Arnold
See Amalric, Arnold
Amaury de Montfort
Albigensian Crusade 3–189a
Amaya 3–128a
Ambassador
Western European diplomacy 4–205a-208a
"Amber routes" 2–61b
AMBO 1–229a; 1–442b, 443, 444a-b; 4–335b
***AMBRASER HELDENBUCH* 1–229b**
Biterolf 2–253a
Ambrogio, Giovanni d'
See Giovanni d'Ambrogio da Firenze
Ambrogio Maitani
See Maitani, Ambrogio
Ambrogio Traversari
See Traversari, Ambrogio
AMBROSE, SAINT 1–230b; 1–454a
antifeminism 1–323a
archaeological excavations 1–336b, 337a
Augustine of Hippo 1–647a-b
bestiary 2–204a
Christmas 3–318a
doctors of the church 4–234a
exegesis 2–224a; 4–547b
exempla 4–551a
pagan practices 1–650b
sarcophagus 4–354b
theology 3–336a-b, 342a
AMBROSIAN CHANT 1–232a; 2–181a
Cistercian chant 3–402b
Ambrosiani 1–231a
Ambrosian number symbolism
eight 2–88a
Ambrosian rite
See Milanese rite
Ambrosius Aurelianus
See Aurelianus, Ambrosius
Ambrosius Autpertus
See Autpertus, Ambrosius
Ambry 1–223b
Ambulate dum lucem habetis (John Gerson) 3–648a
AMBULATORY 1–234a
Aachen Palace Chapel 1–2b, 3a
Aléaume 1–144b
Amiens Cathedral 1–234b
baptistery 2–88a
basilica 2–124b
chapel 3–264a
chevet 3–300b
ʿAmda Ṣeyyon 1–31b
America
exploration 4–560b, 561a
Vikings 4–554a,b-555a
Amice
See Vestments
Āmid
Ayyubids 2–21a,b
Amida
See Diyarbakir
Amiens
commune 3–496a
AMIENS CATHEDRAL 1–234b; 3–276a
cross style 3–379b
engineering 3–567b-568a, 569a
***AMI ET AMILE* 1–234a**; 1–260b, 267a; 3–259a
assonance 1–600b
ʿĀmil (financial official) 3–44b
Amīn, al-
Abū Nuwās 1–27b
reign 2–46b; 3–43a, 48a
Āmina
Muḥammad 1–15a
Amīr
See Emir
Amīr al-muʾminīn
See Commander of the Faithful
Amīr al-Muslimīn 1–199a

Amīr al-umarā' 3–50a
See Also Emir
Amirids
Córdoba 3–600a
AMIRSPASALAR 1–235b; 1–490b
Amis and Amiloun
See Ami et Amile
Amis e Amilun 1–234a, 267a
Amis et Amille 1–234a
AMMIANUS MARCELLINUS 1–235b
Aršak II 1–559b
Ammonius 1–457b
Boethius 2–291a
Amöneburg
Boniface, Saint 2–321b
Amore libri tres, De (Andreas Capellanus) 3–88b, 669b, 672a-b
Amores (Ovid) 1–184a
AMORIANS 1–236a
AMORION 1–236a
Anatolikon, theme of 1–242a
capture (838) 1–241a
Amorium
See Amorion
Amorosa visione (Boccaccio) 2–281a-282a
Amos
Bohemian Brethren 2–307b
Amour courtois
See Courtly love
"Amours dont sui espris" (Gautier de Coincy) 3–576a,b
AMPULLA 1–236b; 1–223a
early Christian art 4–348b
Amra Choluim cille (Dallán Forgaill) 3–233a, 485a
ʿAMR IBN AL-ʿĀṢ 1–236b; 1–153a, 173a,b; 4–403b, 408a
Copts 3–594b
mosque 3–13b
ʿAmr ibn al-Zubayr
ʿAbd Allāh 1–15b
ʿAmr ibn Maʿdīkarib 1–399a
Amthāl 4–442b
Anabaptists
Bohemian Brethren 2–307b
Anacletus II, Antipope 1–330a; 3–636b, 637a
Anagogical allegory 1–180a, 186a,b
Anagogy 1–182a
Anahit 4–508b
Anak 1–66b
Analdi
See Arnoldi, Alberto
Anales toledanos primeros 1–576a
Analogy
Aquinas, Saint Thomas 1–359b-360b
***ANALOI* 1–238a**
Analytica posteriora (Aristotle) 4–510a
Anan ben David
exegesis 2–212a
Anania, Katʿołikos 1–290b
Anania Mokkʿacʿi 1–483b
Anania Narekacʿi 1–510b, 511a
Anania Sanahnecʿi 1–511a
ANANIA ŠIRAKACʿ 1–238a
calendar 3–31a
literature 1–509b
Anaphora
Antiochene rite 1–328a
Armenian 1–516a
Basilian 1–155b; 2–120b-121a
eucharistic 1–155a-157a
Mark 1–155b, 156a-b
Twelve Apostles 1–328a
Anaphoric clocks 3–457b, 458a
Anastasia of Sirmium, Saint
Christmas Mass 3–318b
Anastasis
Seinte Resurreccion 1–270a
Anastasios
See Anastasius
Anastasis (Jerusalem) 4–336b-337a
Christmas 3–318b
crusader art and architecture 4–26a
Anastasis of Christ (Veroia) 2–450a
Anastasius I, Emperor
diplomacy 4–196b
literature 1–508b
reign 2–486a
ANASTASIUS BIBLIOTHECARIUS 1–239a
angelology 1–250a
antipope 1–330a
Anastasius IV, Pope 1–58b
ANATOLIA 1–239b
agriculture and nutrition 1–76b-79b
Alexios I 1–159a
Almogávares 1–191a
Alp Arslan 1–203b, 302a
Aq Qoyunlu 1–352a
Arabs 3–199b
architecture 4–337a-b
Bāyazīd I 2–136a
Bogomils 2–295b, 296a, 297a
Bohemond I 4–35a
Byzantine Empire 2–492a, 493a
Caesarea 3–9a
Cappadocia 3–92a
Cilicia 1–240a; 3–390b
Danishmendids 4–91b
Ephesus 4–494b
Euphrates River 4–521b
Goths 2–89b-90a
Palaiologoi 1–246b, 245b
Seljuks 1–302a,b; 4–27b, 344a
Umayyads 3–38a
water buffalo 1–298a
ANATOLIKON, THEME OF 1–242a
Amorion 1–236a
Anazarba
See Cilician kingdom
Anchialo 2–405a, 410a,b, 411b, 412a,b
Anchiskʿati Icon 2–164b
ANCHORITES 1–242b
Ancrene Riwle 1–243a
Celts 3–231b
Mount Athos 1–636b
Anciens usages d'Artois 4–515b
ANCIENT OF DAYS 1–242b
Emmanuel 4–437a
tympanum 1–496a
Ancona
Pius II, Pope 4–21a
***ANCRENE RIWLE* 1–243a**
Ancrene Wisse
See Ancrene Riwle
Ancyra
See Ankara
ANDACHTSBILD 1–243b
Andalò del Negro 1–613a
Boccaccio 2–278a
Andalus, Al-
Almohads 1–195b, 626a
Almoravids 1–199a-200b, 296a
Andalusia 1–244a
Asturias-León 1–625b-626a, 627a
cavalrymen 3–209a
Mudejars 3–134a
See Also Spain, Muslim Kingdoms of
ANDALUSIA 1–243b
agriculture 1–81a, 82a,b, 84a-b
ceramics 4–64a
commerce 4–558a
Córdoba 3–597b
fairs 4–587a-b
land tenure 3–136a
András II, King
chrysobullon 3–334a
Andrea da Fiesole
See Andrea da Firenze
ANDREA DA FIRENZE 1–244a; 1–343a
Andreas 1–279a
Andreas, Capellanus
See Capellanus, Andreas
Andreas, Era of 3–30b
Andreas de Florentia
ballata 2–61a
ANDRÉ DE FLEURY 1–244a
André le Chapelain
See Capellanus, Andreas
Andrew II, King
crusades 4–49b
Teutonic Knights 3–306a
Andrew, Bishop 2–304a
Andrew, Saint 4–9a
Andreas 1–279a
Andrew cross 4–9a
Andrew of Crete, Saint 2–13a, 511b, 524b
ANDREW OF SAINT VICTOR 1–244b
Christian Hebraists 3–313b
exegesis 2–213b
Andrew the Chaplain
See Capellanus, Andreas
Andrieu, Michel 4–130b
Andronikos Kamateros 1–78a
ANDRONIKOS I KOMNENOS 1–244b; 1–159a; 2–496a; 4–70b
Manuel I 2–495b
ANDRONIKOS II PALAIOLOGOS 1–245b; 1–633b; 2–499b-500b
Almogávares 1–191a
Andronikos III 1–246b
Bulgaria 2–412a
Catalan Company 3–156a
civil war 2–450b
excommunication 3–439a
ANDRONIKOS III PALAIOLOGOS 1–246a; 2–500b
Andronikos II 1–246a
Bulgaria 2–412a
Epiros 4–500a
peasantry 2–481a
Andronikos IV Palaiologos
reign 2–502a-b
Anecdota
See Procopius
Anecdote books 1–380b
ANEGENGE 1–246b
ANEIRIN 1–247a
Arthurian literature 1–565b, 577a
poems 3–234a
Anelida and Arcite (Chaucer) 3–286a
ANGEL 1–247b
crucifixion 4–13b
ANGEL, ISLAMIC 1–248b
ANGELA MERICI, SAINT 1–250b
ANGEL/ANGELOLOGY 1–249a
archangels 1–433a
Angela of Brescia
See Angela Merici, Saint
ANGELA OF FOLIGNO 1–251a
Angelenē
See Angeł-tun
Angelico, Fra
See Giovanni da Fiesole
Angelino, Joseph
cabala 3–2b
Angelino del Tegghia
Canary Islands 4–558b
ANGELO DA ORVIETO 1–251a
ANGELOMUS OF LUXEUIL 1–251b

ANGELOS 1–251b; 2–469a-b, 498a-b
art 2–443b-446a
holdings 2–479b
ANGELRAM OF SAINT RIQUIER 1–252a
Angeł-tun 1–472b
ANGELUS 1–252a
Angelus bell 2–166a
Angelus locutus est Mariae 1–252a
Angelus Urbsveterensis
See Angelo da Orvieto
Angers
fairs 4–586a
ANGEVINS: FRANCE, ENGLAND, SICILY 1–253a; 1–413b; 4–461a
Andronikos II Palaiologos 1–245b
Aquitaine 1–368a-b
Burgundy 2–429b
Byzantine Empire 2–499a-b
Dyrrachium 4–330a
Eleanor of Aquitaine 4–419b, 420a
Guelphs 1–131a
ANGIER 1–254a
saints' Lives 1–261b
ANGILBERT, SAINT 1–254a; 1–3a, 143a
Carolingian poetry 3–100a, 101b
pseudonym 3–100a
ANGILBERT OF MILAN 1–254b
carroccio 3–117a
Angł 1–515a
Angles
arms and armor 1–522a
invasions 2–96b-97a
literature 1–274a
origins and migration 1–289a
Anglicus, Bartholomaeus
See Bartholomaeus Anglicus
ANGLO-LATIN POETRY 1–254b
ANGLO-NORMAN ART 1–255b
Norman-Angevin England 4–472b
Anglo-Norman dialect 1–255b, 259a, 263a
ANGLO-NORMAN LITERATURE 1–259a
Adgar 1–55a
Amadas et Ydoine 1–227a
Ami et Amile 1–234a
Andrew of Saint Victor 1–244b
Anonimalle Chronicle 1–309a
Apocalypse 1–344a
Arundel Psalter 1–480b
Boethius 2–291a
Cambridge Psalter 3–57a
Cato's Ditichs 3–193b
Chardri 3–267b
Chroniques de Londres 3–334a
courtesy books 3–661a
Crusade and Death of Richard I 4–18b
Disciplina clericalis 4–216b
Donnei des amants 4–261b
Espurgatoire St. Patrice 4–509b
Norman-Angevin England 4–471b
See Also Chronicles, French
ANGLO-SAXON ART 1–272a
See Also Celtic art
Anglo-Saxon Chronicle 1–264b; 4–455b, 456a, 461b
Alfred the Great 1–163b
Orosius 1–165b
poetry 1–278b, 279a
prose 1–284a,b
West Saxon dialect 1–276b
Whelock edition 1–287a
Wulfstan homilies 1–281b
ANGLO-SAXON LITERATURE 1–274a
Alfred the Great 1–163b, 164b
Beowulf 2–182b
Bible 2–220b-222b
exegesis 4–548b
Anglo-Saxon: Middle English
chansons de geste 3–258a
courtesy books 3–661a
Anglo-Saxons
Alfred the Great 1–163b
alphabets 1–212b, 215a,b
butler 2–434b
Christian era 3–19b
cosmetics 2–146b, 147b
hair care 2–148a
invasions 2–96a-97a
kingship 1–35b
kinship group 4–599b
sundials 3–28a
ANGLO-SAXONS, ORIGINS AND MIGRATION 1–288b
Chester, Treaty of 3–299b
England 4–452b-455a
Angl-tun
See Angełtun
Angora
See Ankara
Ani 1–474a, 482b, 484a, 485a; 2–48b
Alp Arslan 1–203b
architecture 1–494a
Armenian church 1–503b
Ašot III Ołormac 1–589a
Muslim emirates 1–513b
ANI, MONUMENTS OF 1–291b; 1–68b
Anian, Bishop
Bangor rite 2–72a
Anianos 3–18b
ANICONISM 1–293a
Aniér mac Con-Glinne 1–113b
ANI IN ḌARANAŁIK' 1–290a
ANI IN ŠIRAK 1–290b; 1–450b
Arcrunis 1–451a-b
Byzantine Empire 2–493a
Ani-Kamaχ
See Ani in Daranałik'
Anima, De (Cassiodorus) 3–123b
Anima in arte alchemie, De (Ibn Sīnā) 1–136b, 137b
Animalibus, De (Albertus Magnus) 1–128b
Animal ornament
See Celtic art
Animals
beast epic 2–140b
bone remains 1–300a-301a
breeding 1–301b
charms, old High German 3–274a
study of 2–240b-244b
ANIMALS, DRAFT 1–293a
Byzantine agriculture 1–78b
horses 1–93a-b
Islamic 1–103a,b
ox 1–93a
Slav 1–98b
ANIMALS, FOOD 1–299a
Islamic 1–103b
Jewish dietary laws 4–181b-183b
northern European 1–95a-b
ANIMAL STYLE 1–293b
Bulgarian art and architecture 2–417a
Anime 1–531b
Animosus 2–377a
Anjit
See Angełtun
Anjou
fairs 4–586a
Henry I of England 4–462b
ANKARA 1–302a
Anatolia 1–239b
battle (1402) 1–302b
Danishmendids 4–91b
Tamerlane 2–136a,b
Ankh 4–9a, 11a
Anmchara 3–230b
ANNA KOMNENA 1–303a
Alexiad 2–514b-515a
Annales (Tacitus) 3–334b
Annales Alamannici 4–426a
Annales Cambriae 1–565b, 577a
Annales de gestis Caroli Magni ("Poeta Saxo") 4–496a
Annales Fuldenses 3–202a
Annales Lugdunenses (Agobard) 1–76a
Annales Petaviani 3–201b
Annales sex regum Angliae 1–265b
Annals
See Chronicles
See Historiography
Annals of Inisfallen 1–110a,b
Annals of the Four Masters
Clonard 3–466a
Anna of Savoy, Empress 1–246b; 2–501a
ANNA (PRINCESS) 1–303a
ANNATE 1–304b
Anna (wife of Michael Šišman) 2–411b, 412a-b
Anne of Bohemia 1–319b; 3–289a,b
Anne of Hungary
Andronikos II Palaiologos 1–245b
Annibaldi, Richard 1–659b
ANNO 1–306a
Anno II, Archbishop 3–481a
Anno, Archbishop 1–306a
***ANNOLIED* 1–306a**
Annular vault
See Vault, Types of
ANNULMENT OF MARRIAGE 1–306a
Byzantines 4–594b
ANNUNCIATION 1–307b
engraving 4–489b
fresco 3–198a
Annunciation, Church of the (Nazareth)
Lietard 4–24b
"Annunciation" style calendar 3–20a
Annunziata, Order of 3–307a
ANOINTING 1–308a
basileus 2–123a
Anomoeans 1–453b-454a
***ANONIMALLE CHRONICLE* 1–309a**; 1–265b
ANONYMOUS IV 1–309a; 1–545a
Bamberg manuscript 2–68b
conductus 3–532a,b
discantor 4–216b
duplum 4–312b
Anonymous VII 1–544b
Anonymous of Saint Emmeram
ars antiqua 1–545a
Anonymous of York
See York Tractates
Anonymus Mellicensis 2–239b
Año y vez 1–83a, 84b
Ansāb al-Ashrāf (Balādhurī) 2–54a
Anṣār 1–115a
Ansegis of Fontenelle 2–178b
Anselm of Aosta
See Anselm of Canterbury
Anselm of Bec
See Anselm of Canterbury
ANSELM OF BESATE 1–311b
ANSELM OF CANTERBURY 1–311b; 1–19a; 2–174a
Bradwardine, Thomas 2–358b
Canterbury 3–82b-83a

Christology 3–322a, 323b
Clarendon, Constitutions of 3–409b
De grammatico 4–169b
doctor of the church 4–234b
Eadmer of Canterbury 4–330b
Norman-Angevin England 4–466a-b, 470b
Proslogion 1–649b
translation 4–135b
Anselm of Havelberg
canonical reform 3–356b
ANSELM OF LAON 1–315b
Abelard 1–16b, 17a
exegesis 2–213a; 4–543b
ANSELM OF LIÈGE 1–316b
Anselm of Lucca
See Alexander II, Pope
ANSELM II OF LUCCA 1–311a
crusades 4–16b
Anselm of Milan, Archbishop
Crusade of 1101 4–36a
Anselm of Saint Rémi 3–634a
Anselmus Peripateticus
See Anselm of Besate
Ansgar, Saint
Birka 2–247b, 248a
Denmark 4–151a
ÁNS SAGA BOGSVEIGIS 1–310b
Antakya
See Antioch
Antalya
See Adalia
Antapodosis
See Liutprand of Cremona
ʿAntar 1–382a
Antelami, Benedetto
See Benedetto Antelami
ANTEPENDIUM 1–316b; 1–222a, 224a
Antequera, Battle of (1410) 3–138a
Antes 2–12b
ANTHEMIOS OF TRALLES 1–317a; 4–339a
Archimedes 1–434a
Constantinople 3–555b
***ANTHOLOGIA LATINA* 1–317a**
ANTHOLOGIES 1–317a
commonplace books 3–492b
Anthologies (Vettius Valens) 1–617a
Anthonello of Caserta
ars subtilior 1–558b
ANTHONY OF PADUA, SAINT 1–320b
doctor of the church 4–234b
Anthony the Hermit, Saint 1–518b, 519b; 3–342b
Anthusa
See Constantinople
Anti-Atlas chain 1–639b
ANTICHRIST 1–321a
Albertus Magnus 1–128a
Armilus 1–345a
Bacon, Roger 2–38b
Holy Roman Empire 1–149a
Jewish apocalyptic literature 1–345a
William of Saint Amour 1–128a
Antichrist plays
Chester plays 3–299a
Germany 4–268b-269a
Ludus de adventu et interitu Anti Christi 4–281b-282a
Anticlaudianus (Alan of Lille) 1–48a, 119b, 120a, 182a, 183a, 288b, 544a
ANTIFEMINISM 1–322b
Anglo-Norman poetry 1–269b
Aristoteles und Phyllis 1–455a
Capellanus, Andreas 3–89a
Christine de Pizan 3–315b
courtly love 3–673b
Antiga Casa da Corõa 1–448b
Anti-Lebanon 4–80b, 81a
ANTIOCH 1–325b
architecture 4–332a
Assizes of Jerusalem 1–599b
Bar Hebraeus 2–108a
Baybars al-Bunduqdārī 2–138b
Bohemond I 1–158a-b; 2–308b, 309a-b, 495a; 4–20a, 30b
Byzantine church 2–459b, 460a-461a, 462b
Byzantine Empire 2–493a
Chanson d'Antioche 3–254b
Cilicia 3–391b
crusades 1–158a-b; 2–495a; 4–30a-b, 35a-b, 37a, 38a,b
Nūr al-Dīn 4–38b-39a
Saladin 4–25a
schism 2–120b
tyche of 4–12b
Antioch, Council of (341) 3–607a
Antioch, Song of
See Chanson D'Antioche
Antiochene church
Christmas 3–318a
Christology 3–320a, 336a
ecumenical councils 3–629a,b
ANTIOCHENE RITE 1–326b
apostolic constitutions 1–350a
Antiochos, Gregory
agriculture 1–78a-b
Antipater 1–150b
ANTIPHON 1–328b
Angelus locutus est Mariae 1–252a
breviary 2–370b-373b
Celtic liturgy 3–230a,b
differentia 4–185a
Divine Office 4–221b, 224b-225a, 230a,b
ANTIPHONAL (ANTIPHONER, ANTIPHONARY) **1–329a**
Cistercian chant 3–402b
ANTIPOPE 1–330a
Alexander III 1–146b
Avignon 2–16a
Babylonian Captivity 2–33b-34b
Clement VII 1–147a
Honorius II 1–146a,b
Victor IV 1–146b
ANTIQUARIANISM AND ARCHAEOLOGY 1–331b
Antiquities of the Jews (Josephus) 3–166b
ANTI-SEMITISM 1–338b
Black Death 2–263b
blood libel 2–276a
converts 3–577b
expulsion of Jews 4–564b
Jewish costume 3–620b-621a
Antoine de la Sale
fabliau 4–577a
Antoniana
See Constantinople
Antoni de Genebreda 3–168b
Antonine Hospitalers
See Hospitalers
ANTONINUS, SAINT 1–342a
contraception 3–573a
Dominican theology 4–248a
preaching missions 3–368a
Antoninus Pierozzi
See Antoninus, Saint
Antonio da Noli
Cape Verde Islands 4–561b
ANTONIO DA VINCENZO 1–342b
Antonio di Francesca da Venezia
See Antonio Veneziano
ANTONIO VENEZIANO 1–342b
Antonius of Lérins 4–491b
Anton Pilgrim
See Pilgrim, Anton
ANTRUSTIONES 1–343a
Antsha Gospels 2–164b
Antwerp
arms and armor 1–529a
Bruges 2–387b
fairs 4–586b
Antwerp Songbook 4–321a
Anu Sarga
Coptic architecture 3–586b
Anzitenē
See Angełtun
Apa Apollo Monastery (Bawit) 3–585b
Apahunikʿ
Muslim emirates 1–513a
Apar
See Abar
Aphetis 1–619b
Aphetos
agriculture 1–79a
Aphraates 1–508a
Apocalypse
See Millenialism
APOCALYPSE, ILLUSTRATION OF 1–343b
Beatus manuscripts 2–143b
Emeterius of Tábara 4–436b
Ende 4–450b
Apocalypse of Elijah
angelology 1–249b
Apocalypse of Thomas (Airdena Brátha) 1–111a-112a, 347b
Old English translation 1–285b
Apocalypse Tapestries (Nicholas Bataille) 2–129b
Apocalypsis Mosis 1–347b
APOCALYPTIC LITERATURE AND MOVEMENT, JEWISH 1–344b
Apocalyptic man 1–242b
APOCRYPHA, IRISH 1–346b
Apokatastasis 3–335b
Apollinare Nuovo, S. (Ravenna)
Agnellus of Ravenna, Saint 1–73a
Apollinarianism
azymes 2–31b
See Also Apollinarius
Apollinaris of Laodicea
See Apollinarius
Apollinaris Sidonius
Troyes fair 4–590b
APOLLINARIUS 1–348a; 2–31b; 4–75a
Apollonius of Perga 1–438b, 439a
APOLLONIUS OF TYANA 1–348b
Apollonius of Tyre 1–285a
Apologetics
See Polemics
Apologeticum (Tertullian) 3–334b
Apologeticus (Abbo of Fleury) 1–13a
Apologeticus martyrum (Eulogius of Córdoba) 4–521b
Apologia sacri Pisani concilii moderni (Zacharia Ferreri) 3–520b
Apology (Eunomius) 2–121a
Apology Against Julian (Cyril of Alexandria) 4–75a
Apolonii gesta
See Gesta Apollonii
***APOLONIO, LIBRO DE* 1–348b**
Apophthegmata 1–204b
APOSTASY 1–349b
Apostle of the North
See Ansgar, Saint
Apostles' Creed 3–676a
Apostolic Age
church fathers 3–334b
clergy 3–440a

Apostolic Camera
  annate tax 1–304b
  archives 1–448a
  Urban II 3–352a
"Apostolic Canons" 1–350a
  Byzantine clergy 3–446b
***APOSTOLIC CONSTITUTIONS* 1–349b**; 1–327a
  Ascension feast 1–582a
Apostolic poverty
  John XXII, Pope 3–363b
Apostolic See
  Alexander III 1–146b
  archives 1–448a
  Celtic church 3–232a
  See Also Conciliar theory
APOSTOLIC SUCCESSION 1–350a; 3–338b
  Cathars 3–183b
Apostolic Tradition, The (Hippolytus of Rome) 3–602b, 675b
Apothecaries
  liquors 4–220a
  plague 2–264b
APPANAGES 1–351a
  Armenia 1–481a, 490a
Apparellamentum 3–185b
Apparitio domini in carne 3–318a
Appendix Laterani concilii 4–123b
Appendix Vergiliana 1–320b
Appiliyōn 3–619a
Apprentice/apprenticeships
  See Guilds
Apprise 3–661a
Aprisio 3–174b
APSE 1–352a
  ambulatory 1–234a
  basilica 2–124a,b
  cathedra 3–191a
  Chapels 3–264a
  chevet 3–300b
  choir 3–307b
  Coptic and Ethiopian churches 1–157a
  See Also Church, types of
APSE ECHELON 1–352a
Apsidiole
  See Absidiole
Apuleius Barbarus
  See Pseudo-Apuleius
Apuleius of Madauros 1–646b, 651b
  dialectic 4–168b, 169a
Apulia (Italy)
  Bari 2–108b
  Ipomedon 1–266b
  Ravenna, exarchate of 4–530a
  Swedes 4–555b
Apulia (Kurland) 2–62b
Aqbiya 3–618a
AQ QOYUNLU 1–352a
  Armenia 1–486a, 514a
  Azerbaijan 2–27a
Aqṣā, Al-, Mosque (Jerusalem) 1–196b
Aquae Grani
  See Aachen
Aquae Sextiae
  See Aix-en-Provence
Aquamanile 3–237a, 581b
Aquavit 4–220a
Aquila (Onkelos) 2–210b
Aquileia
  council (381) 1–231a
  double cathedral 3–378b, 381
  Lombard invasion 2–95b
AQUILEIA, RITE OF 1–352b
AQUINAS, SAINT THOMAS 1–353b
  actualism 1–46b
  Albertus Magnus 1–127a-129a
  alchemy 1–137b, 138a
  angelology 1–250a,b
  antifeminism 1–323a,b
  Aristotelianism 1–462a,b-463a, 466a-b; 2–243b
  Ars praedicandi 1–555b
  astrology 1–607b
  Augustinism 1–660b
  Augustinus Triumphus 2–1a
  Bacon, Roger 2–37a
  baptism 2–84a
  Biel, Gabriel 2–234a
  Bradwardine, Thomas 2–358b
  Burley, Walter 2–433a
  Cavalcanti, Guido 3–197a
  confirmation 3–536a
  Corpus Christi 3–608b
  death 4–119b
  Demetrios Kydones 4–135b
  doctor of the church 4–234b
  dualism 4–298a-b
  Easter 4–366a
  ecclesiology 4–375b-376a
  Egidius Colonna 4–400a
  equity 4–501a-b
  exegesis 2–214a, 216b, 222a, 224a-b; 4–544a, 547b
  fables 4–572b
  Greek translations 3–632b
  missionaries 4–252b
  sacraments 2–177b; 4–565a-b
  Scholasticism 4–381b
  theology 2–36a; 3–323a; 4–245b, 246b-247a, 510a
  University of Paris 1–543b
Aquisgranu
  See Aachen
AQUITAINE 1–366b
  Alani 1–121b
  alodial tenure 1–190b
  bastides 2–128b
  Bordeaux 2–327b-328a,b
  canonical reform 3–355a
  champlevé enamel 4–438b
  Chaucer 3–280b
  Merovingians 3–104a
  subkingdom 3–112a
  Visigoths 2–91a
ARABESQUE 1–369b
ARABIA, ISLAMIC 1–373a
  Aksum 2–17a
  Aleppo 1–145a
  Alexandria 1–153a
  Badr, battle of 2–45b
  Barcelona 2–102b-103a
  Bulgaria 2–401a
  caliphate 3–35b, 36b, 49a
  Crete 3–678a
  Croatia 4–2b
  "Green Revolution" 1–80a-b, 81a-83a
  horse breeding 1–295a
ARABIA, PRE-ISLAMIC 1–369b
  Ankara 1–302a
  fairs 4–588b
  water buffalo 1–298a
Arabian architecture
  See Islamic art and architecture
Arabian March 2–140b
ARABIC LANGUAGE 1–376b; 2–54a
  alchemy 1–140b
  alphabet 1–207b-210a
  Castilian 3–141b
  Coptic art 3–591a
  Egypt 4–405a
  Hebrew alphabet 1–208a
  script 3–51b-52a
ARABIC LITERATURE, POETRY 1–398a
  ʿĀʾisha 1–113b
  Akhṭal, al- 1–115b
  Aleppo 1–145a
  Aljamiado literature 1–176a
  Balādhurī 2–54a
  courtly love 3–671b-672a
ARABIC LITERATURE, PROSE 1–379a
  alchemy 1–140b-142a
  Aljamiado literature 1–176a
  Ibn al-Athīr family 1–634a
  biography 2–237b
  Egypt 4–407a-b
  encyclopedias and dictionaries 4–443b, 444b, 446a
ARABIC NUMERALS 1–382b
  astronomy 1–611b, 612a, 619b-620a
ʿAr-abshah, ibn 1–381b
Aragats Mountains 1–470b
ARAGON (800-1137) **1–403b**
  agriculture and nutrition 1–83a-84b
  Alfonso I of Aragon 1–160a
  archives 1–448b
  Catalonia 3–174a, 178b
  excommunication 4–538a
ARAGON, CROWN OF (1137-1479) **1–408a**
ARAGON, CROWN OF (1137-1479) **1–413a-b**
  Almogávares 1–190b
  Barcelona 2–104b
  Canary Islands 4–559a
  castellans 3–125a, 156b
  Castile 3–137a
  Catalan Company 3–156a
  Catalan language 3–157b
  cortes 3–610b, 611b-612a
  Fourth Crusade 3–357a
  hearth lists 4–138a
  Innocent III, Pope 3–353b
  Order of la Jara 3–307a
  political crusades 4–61a-b
  Sicily 1–253b
  slaves 2–268a,b, 269b, 270a
  Union Aragonese 1–414a; 3–611a
  See Also James the Conqueror
Aragon River 1–403b, 404a
ARAKS RIVER 1–421b; 1–125a, 470b, 473b; 2–26a
  Ayrarat 2–19b
Aramaic language
  Syria 1–378a
  See Also Arabic language
Aran
  See Albania (Caucasian)
Aranšahikid dynasty 1–123b
Ararat (province)
  See Ayrarat
ARARAT, MOUNT 1–421b; 1–470b; 3–195a
Aras River
  See Araks River
ARATOR 1–422a-b
Araxenon Pedion
  See Ayrarat
Araxes River
  See Araks River
Arbalest
  See Bow and Arrow/Crossbow
Arbela, Battle of (331 B.C.) 1–150b
ARBEO OF FREISING 1–422a
Arbogast 2–4a
Arbor consanguinitatis 3–539b
Arbre des batailles (Honoré Bonet) 3–169a, 205b, 302a

Arcade, blind
See Arch
Arcadiopolis 2–408a
Arcadius, Emperor 2–485b
architecture 3–586a
Arcae 1–223b
Arcarius 3–444b
Arc'aχ 1–123b, 472b, 473b; 2–48b
ARČĒŠ 1–423a; 1–513a
Erzincan 4–508b
ARCH 1–423b
archivolt 1–449a
Bulgarian art and architecture 2–417a
buttress 2–435a
centering 3–234b
Cluny, Abbey Church 3–468a
See Also Construction: building materials
ARCHAEOLOGY OF MEDIEVAL MONUMENTS 1–425a
Archaionomia (William Lambarde) 1–287a
ARCHANGEL 1–433a; 1–248a,b
Archbishop
See Clergy
Archbishop's Chapel (Ravenna) 4–359a
Archdeacon 3–444b
Archembaud de Saint Amand
Knights Templars 3–304a
Archery 2–352a-b
ARCHES, COURT OF 1–433b
Archicancellarius
See Chancery
Archiepiscopal cross 4–9a
Archil 4–326b
ARCHIMANDRITE 1–433b
ARCHIMEDES IN THE MIDDLE AGES 1–433b
ARCHITECT, STATUS OF 1–440a
castle building 3–150b-151a
See Also Construction: building materials
Architectura, De (Vitruvius) 1–331b
Architecture
Abbasid 1–5a
Absidiole 1–24a
aedicula 1–61a
alternating supports 1–225b
ambulatory 1–234a
Anglo-Norman 1–255b
Ani monuments 1–291b
arch 1–423b
Archaeology of medieval monuments 1–425a
Armenian 1–493a-494a
Ayyubid 2–20b
Cluny 3–469a
collar beam 3–479b
Coptic 3–585b-587a
early Christian and Byzantine 4–331a
pre-Islamic Arabia 1–371a
Roman 3–234b
ARCHITECTURE, LITURGICAL ASPECTS 1–441b
altar apparatus 1–221a
Anglo-Norman 1–255b
baptistery 2–87b
bema 2–167a
Cistercian order 1–404b
early Christian and Byzantine 4–333a, 335b-336a, 343b-344a
Architekton 4–335b
ARCHIVES 1–445b
cartulary 1–120a
Iceland 1–537a
ARCHIVOLT 1–449a
***ARCHON TON ARCHONTON* 1–449a**
Ašot II Erkat' 1–588b
Ašot I Mec 1–588a,b
ARCHPOET 1–449b
Arcila
fairs 4–589a
ARCN 1–450a; 1–513a
ARCOSOLIUM 1–451a; 3–155a
ARCRUNIS 1–451a
Abbasids 1–479b
archon ton archonton 1–449b
Berkri 2–189a
Arculf 1–154b
Adamnan, Saint 1–53a
fairs 4–589a
Holy Land 4–553b
Ardaburius 1–121b
Ardagh chalice 3–220a-222
Ardashir
See Ardešīr I
Ardawān (Artabanus) V 1–451b
Ardebīl 1–125a
ARDEŠĪR I 1–451a-452b; 2–54a
Avesta 2–14b
AREITHIAN PROSE: PROSE RHETORICS 1–452a
ARENA CHAPEL 1–453a
Areopagite
See Pseudo-Dionysios the Areopagite
Arest River 2–189a
Arethas, Archbishop
classical literary studies 3–431a
education 3–556b
Aretissa
See Arčēš
Arezzo 4–99b
Camaldolese Order 3–56a
commune 3–500a
Arfon 2–71a
Argens
agriculture 1–85a
Argentille
Lai d'Haveloc 1–268a
Argina 1–290b
Arguim
slave trade 2–268b, 269a; 4–561a
ARGUN 1–453a
Argyn 3–680a
Arian Baptistery (Ravenna) 2–86b, 88a; 4–359a
ARIANISM 1–453a; 1–231a, 453a-b
Agnellus of Ravenna, Saint 1–73a
Arsacids 1–559a-b
Athanasians 1–632b, 633a
Augustine of Hippo 1–650a, 654a
Basil the Great 2–121a,b-122a
Burgundians 2–423a
Byzantine Empire 2–485a-b
Cathars 3–183b
Christology 3–320b, 336a
Constantine I, the Great 3–545b
Constantinople 3–555b
early church 3–339a
ecumenical councils 3–627b-628a
Eusebius of Caesarea 4–523b
Franks 2–94b
Nicene Creed 3–676a,b
Roman Catholicism 2–93b
Vandals 2–92a
Visigoths 2–91a
Aribert II of Milan 3–557b-558a
Aribo of Mainz 4–427a
Ariminum (Rimini) Council (359) 3–225b
Arinbjarnarkviđa 4–401a, 403a
Arinbjorn hersir Þórisson 4–401a
Ariosto, Ludovico 3–258a
'Arish, Al- 2–58b
Arista, Iñigo 2–126b
ARISTAKĒS LASTIVERTC'I 1–454b; 1–66b, 484a
literature 1–511a
Aristakes Rhetor 1–512a
Aristenos
canon law 2–468a
Aristides of Athens
literature 1–508a
Aristocracy
See Class structure, Western
***ARISTOTELES UND PHYLLIS* 1–455a**
ARISTOTLE IN THE MIDDLE AGES 1–456a
Ackermann aus Böhmen, Der 1–43b-44a
actualism 1–46b
Adelard of Bath 1–53b, 54a
Albertus Magnus 1–127a-129a
alchemy 1–136b, 137a-b, 140a, 141a
Amalric of Bène 1–228b
Anselm of Canterbury 1–314b, 315a
antifeminism 1–323a,b
Aquinas, Saint Thomas 1–355a, 358a-359b, 360b, 361a,b
Aristoteles und Phyllis 1–455a-b
Armenian Hellenizing School 1–505b
astrology 1–604b, 607b
astronomy 1–614b, 615b
Bacon, Roger 2–35b, 36a-b, 37b, 40b
bestiaries 2–203b
biology 2–241b, 242a, 243b
Boethius 2–292a
Bruni, Leonardo 2–391a
Buridan, Jean 2–430a-b
Burley, Walter 2–432b
Crescas, Ḥasdai 3–677b
Dialectic 4–169a,b, 171a
dualism 4–298a
Egidius Colonna 4–400b
equity 4–501a
essence and existence 4–510a
exegesis 4–544a,b
John Duns Scotus 4–309a-b
Latin translations 3–358a
subject indexes 1–205b, 206a
Arithmetic
Islamic science 1–377b
See Also Arabic numerals
Arithmetic (Boethius) 1–396a
Arius
See Arianism
Arjish
See Arčēš
ARK OF THE COVENANT 1–469a
Arlanza River 3–128a
Arlanzón River
agriculture 1–84a
Castile 3–128a
Arles
agriculture 1–85a
Arles, Council of (314) 3–225b
Arles, Kingdom of
See Burgundy, Kingdom of
ARMA CHRISTI 1–469b
ARMAGH 1–469b
See Also Cinéal Eóghain
Armagh, Book of
See Patrick, Saint
Armagnac
Charles of Orléans 3–272b
ARMENIA, GEOGRAPHY 1–470b; 1–474b-475a
Araks River 1–421b
Arčēš 1–423a
Arcn 1–450b
Armenian Geography (Ašχarhac'oyc') 2–20a

ARMENIA, GEOGRAPHY (cont.)
Artašat 1–563a
Ayās 2–19a
Ayrarat 2–19b
Baylakān 2–139a
Byzantine Empire 1–477a-b
Caucasia 3–195a,b
Cilician Gates 3–390b
Dwin 4–323a
Erzincan 4–508b
map 1–471
Mount Ararat 1–421b
ARMENIA, SOCIAL STRUCTURE 1–488a; 1–476b, 485b, 486a
Albania 1–123b-125a
archon ton archonton 1–499a-b
classes 2–25b
Pentarchy 1–515a-b
ARMENIA: HISTORY OF 1–474b
Agat'angełos 1–66a-67a
Andronikos I Komnenos 1–245a
Ani in Daranałik' 1–290a
Ani in Širak 1–290b
Antioch 1–326a
Arcrunis 1–451a
Aristakēs Lastivertc'i 1–454b-455a
Arsacids 1–559a-b
Aršak II 1–559b-560a
Artašat 1–563a
Avarayr 2–12a
Bagratids 2–47b, 48b
Bahrām VI Čōbēn 2–50a
Baylakān 2–139a
Byzantine Empire 2–118b, 492a, 493a
cavalry 3–198b
conversion 1–66a-67a
crusades 4–55b
David of Sasun 4–112a
Dominicans 4–252b
Dwin 4–323a
Seljuks 3–356a
Shaddādid dynasty 2–27a
viceroys 2–140a
ARMENIAKON, THEME OF 1–491b; 1–474a
Armenia Minor
See Cilician Kingdom
ARMENIAN ALPHABET 1–491b; 1–207b, 214a,b, 477a, 506b
Arsacids 1–559b
ARMENIAN ART 1–493a; 1–479a, 482b
Ałc hypogeum 1–134a
Ałt'amar 1–220a
Ani monuments 1–291b
Aštarak 1–601a-b
Constantine the Armenian 3–549a
crusades 4–22a
early Christian and Byzantine architecture 4–337b, 343b
Ereroyk' 4–504b
Armenian Chapel (Jerusalem) 4–359b
Armenian church
Albania 1–123a, 125a
Ałt'amar 1–220a
Arabia 1–478b
Arsacids 1–559b
Ašot I Mec 1–480b
Byzantine Empire 1–478a
Christmas celebration 3–318a
(Georgian) church 1–477b
origin 1–475b-476a
ARMENIAN CHURCH, DOCTRINES AND COUNCILS 1–498a
Ašot I Mec 1–588a
Bible 2–217a
Byzantine church 2–460a
Ējmiacin 4–417a
Eznik of Kołb 4–571a
See Also Cilician-Roman church union
ARMENIAN CHURCH, STRUCTURE 1–502b
Ašot III Ołormac 1–589a-b
bishops' status 2–10a
Armenian Geography
See Ašχarhac'oyc'
ARMENIAN HELLENIZING SCHOOL 1–505a; 1–506b, 509a
David the Invincible 4–114a
ARMENIAN LANGUAGE 1–506a; 1–509a
Agat'angełos 1–66b-67a
ARMENIAN LITERATURE 1–507b; 1–505a-507a
Agat'angełos 1–66a
David of Sasun 4–112a
Ełišē 4–433a
Eznik of Kołb 4–571b
ARMENIAN MUSLIM EMIRATES 1–512b; 1–474a, 478a-480a, 481a,b, 485a
Arčēš 1–423a
Ašot I Mec 1–588a
Ayrarat 2–20a-b
Berkri 2–189a
ARMENIAN PENTARCHY 1–514b
ARMENIAN RITE 1–516a; 1–326b
baptism 4–497a-b
ARMENIAN SAINTS 1–517b
Armenian science
Anania Širakac'i 1–238b
Armenians, Decree for the 3–535b
Armetà rondelle 1–527b, 530a
Armies
See Warfare
Armiger (scutifer) regis 3–282b
ARMILLARY SPHERE 1–521b; 1–603a
astronomy 1–611a
Armilus (Antichrist) 1–345a
ARMS AND ARMOR 1–521b
botany 2–347b
bow and arrow/crossbow 2–352a-b
bronze and brass 2–384b
castles and fortifications 3–143a-b, 150a-b, 152a
cataphracti 3–179a
cavalry 3–200a-b, 202b, 203a, 205b-206a, 209a-b
cost 3–412a
etching 4–516b
infantry 3–204b-205a
missile weapons 3–148a-b
toolmaking 3–145b
ARNALD OF VILLANOVA 1–537b; 1–415b
alchemy 1–138a,b
beguins 2–162a,b, 163a
Catalan language 3–157b
Catalan literature 3–165a
***ÁRNA SAGA BISKUPS* 1–537a**; 2–252a
ARNAUT DANIEL 1–539a
Arnès del cavaller (Pere March) 3–171a
Arneway, Sir John 3–298b
Arnhem
fairs 4–586b
Árni Þorláksson, Bishop 1–537a
Arnkell goði 4–568a
ARNOBIUS THE ELDER 1–539a
ARNOBIUS THE YOUNGER 1–539b
ARNOLDI, ALBERTO 1–540b
ARNOLD OF BRESCIA 1–539b
Adrian IV, Pope 1–58b
ecclesiology 4–374b
Arnold of Guînes 3–145a
Arnold of Liège 1–206a
Arnold of Lübeck
Assassins 1–590b, 592a
ARNOLD OF SAINT EMMERAM 1–540b
Arnold of Saxony 1–137a
Arnolfini Wedding Portrait (Jan van Eyck) 4–567a
ARNOLFO DI CAMBIO 1–541a
Brunelleschi, Filippo 2–388b
Arno of Salzburg, Archbishop
All Saints' Day 1–176b
ARNULF 1–541b
Bohemia 2–299b
Burgundy 2–428b
Carolingians 3–114a-b
election 4–426a
Arnulfingians 3–104b
Arnulf of Metz
Carolingians 3–104a-b
ARNULF OF MILAN 1–541b
Arnulf of Orléans 1–13a, 143a, 183b
Lidia 4–283a
Arnulf of Rohea 4–22b
ARPENT 1–542a
Arqa 4–35b
Arques, Battle of (1053) 3–203b
Arrān
See Albania
Arra de ànima, De (Hugh of Saint Victor) 3–167b
Arras
Adam de la Halle 1–48a
drama 4–264a
Arras, Mathieu d'
See Mathieu D'Arras
Arras, Treaty of (1435) 3–271a
Arrian
See Arrianus Flavius
Arrianus, Flavius
Alani 1–120b-121a; 3–200b
ARRICCIO 1–542b
ARSACIDS/ARŠAKUNI, ARMENIAN 1–559a
Albania 1–123b
Ałc hypogeum 1–134a
Arcrunis 1–451a
Aršak II 1–559b
Artašat 1–563a
Ayrarat 2–20a
Bagratids 2–48a
Bahrām VI Čōbēn 2–50a
cavalry 3–198b
Christianity 1–475b-476a
decline 1–476a-b
Iran 1–66b, 451b
magnates 2–140a
ARŠAK II 1–559b; 1–476a
Aršak III 1–476a
Aršakuni
See Arsacids/Aršakuni, Armenian
Ars alchemie (Michael Scot) 1–136b-137a
Ars amatoria (Ovid) 1–184a; 3–101b, 667b, 671A
***ARS ANTIQUA* 1–542b**; 1–548b
Anonymous IV 1–309a
Aršarunik' 2–20a
Ars cantus mensurabilis (Franco of Cologne) 1–544b
Ars contrapunctus secundum Philippum de Vitriaco 3–657b
Ars dictaminis
See Dictamen
Ars disserendi (Adam of the Little Bridge) 4–170a
Arsenal Bible 2–215a, 447a
Arsendi da Forlì, Raniero 2–115a
Arsenites
Andronikos II Palaiologos 1–245b
Athanasius I 1–33b

ARSENIUS AUTORIANUS 1–560a
Michael VIII Palaiologos 2–499a
patriarchy 2–462a
Arsenius of Orta, Bishop
Jewish costume 3–620b
Ars epistolaris ornatus (Geoffrey of Eversley) 4–175b
Arsessa
See Arčēš
Ars grammatica (Clemens Scotus) 3–438a
Ars grammatica (Donatus of Fiesole) 4–504a
Arsissa
See Arčēš
Arslan, Kılıj
crusades 2–308b-309a
Arslānshāh I 2–43b
Arslānshāh II 2–43b
Ars magna (Ramon Lull) 1–138b
***ARS MORIENDI* 1–547b**
Everyman 4–527b-528a
***ARS NOVA* 1–548a**
motet manuscripts 1–545b
***ARS POETICA* 1–553b**
See Also Areithian prose
***ARS PRAEDICANDI* 1–555b**; 1–120a
Ars praedicandi populo (Francesc Eiximenis) 4–416b
***ARS SUBTILIOR* 1–558a**
ars nova 1–550a,b
ballade 2–59a
See Also Ars antiqua
Arsūf
crusades 4–40b
Arṣuniuni
See Arcrunis
Ars veterum
See Ars antiqua
Ars vetus
See Ars antiqua
Art
Abbasid 1–5a
Aksumite 2–17a
Almohad 1–191a
Almoravid 1–196a
Anglo-Norman 1–255b
Anglo-Saxon 1–272a
aniconic 1–293b
Arabia 1–370b
Asturian 1–624b, 630b-631a
Ayyubid 2–20b
Bulgarian 2–414b
Byzantine 2–437b
Celtic 3–218a
early Christian 4–348a
ART, COMMERCIAL TRADE OF 1–560b
Arta 4–499a-b
Artabanus
See Ardawān (Artabanus) V
Art and Craft to Know how Well to Die, The 3–210b
ARTAŠAT 1–563a; 2–20a
Council 1–498b
Dwin 4–323b
Artašēs V, King 2–49b
Artašēs, King
Artašat 1–563a
Artawazd, King 2–49b
Artawazd II, King 3–198b
Artaxata
See Artašat
Artaxeres
See Ardešīr I
Artaxiad dynasty
Ayrarat 2–20a
Artaxias
See Artašēs, King
Art d'aimer
Anglo-Norman courtoisie 1–268b
Art d'amour (Jacques d'Amiens) 1–189a; 3–672b
Art de chevalerie, L' (Jean de Meun) 3–302a
Art de dictier et de fere chançons, balades, virelais, et rondeaux, L' (E. Deschamps) 4–163b
Arte dei Medici e Speziali 2–99b
Arte de trovar (Enrique de Villena) 3–170b
Arte honeste amandi, De (Andreas Capellanus) 1–189a; 3–88b, 669b
Arte loquendi et tacendi, De (Albertano da Brescia) 3–671a
Arte metrica, De (Bede) 2–154b
Artes dictandi 4–67a,b
Artesonados 1–171a
Arte venandi cum avibus, De (Frederick II) 2–244b
Arthur de Richemont 3–271a
biography 3–333a
Brittany 2–380b
ARTHURIAN LITERATURE 1–564a
Alani 1–121b
Alexander romances 1–151a
archaelogical excavations 1–337a,b
Aurelianus 2–3a
Breton literature 2–370a
Brut, The 2–393a
Chrétien de Troyes 3–308b
courtly love 3–671a-b
Dutch literature 4–318b-319a
Erex Saga 4–504b
Excalibur 4–530a
kingship 4–475a
See Also Chronicles
ARTHURIAN LITERATURE, SPANISH AND PORTUGUESE 1–575b
ARTHURIAN LITERATURE, WELSH 1–576b
Excalibur 4–530a
Arthur of Bardsey, Bishop 2–71b
Arthur of Brittany 4–420a, 468a-b
Artibus ac disciplinis liberalius litterarum, De (Cassiodorus) 1–188b
Articles of the Barons
See Magna Carta
Artillery
cannon 3–64a
Artisans
Barcelona 2–103b-104b
See Also Class structure, Western
See Also Commune
ARTIST, STATUS OF THE 1–578b
See Also Architect, Status of
Artists' manuals
See Modelbooks
Art of Love, The (Chrétien de Troyes) 3–308b
Art of loving honorably, The
See Arte honeste amandi, De
Artophorion
See Darokhranitelnitsa
Artrí mac Cathail, King 4–493a
ARTS, SEVEN LIBERAL 1–580a
Artukids
See Artuqids
Artuqids 1–514a
Armenia 1–485a
Artzn
See Arcn
Arundel
Boeve de Haumtone 1–267b
Arundel, Thomas, Archbishop
angelus 1–252b
anointing of kings 1–308b
Arundel Lyrics 1–319b
ARUNDEL PSALTER 1–580b; 1–262b
Arzan
See Arcn
Arzan ar-Rūm 1–450b
Arzanenē
See Ałjnik
Arzanjān
See Erzincan
Arzinjān
See Erzincan
Arzn
See Arcn
Asadī al-Ṭūsī 4–444b
Asad ibn al-Furāt 1–71a
Aghlabids 1–70b
ʿAsāqir, Ibn 4–84b
Asās al-balāgha (al-Zamakhsharī) 4–443b
Ascalon
crusades 4–36a, 37a, 40b
Ascelin
See Adalbero of Laon
ASCENSION 1–580b
ASCENSION, FEAST OF THE 1–582a
Bucentaur 4–395b
ASCENSION OF THE PROPHET 1–581a
Burāq 2–419b
Ascetica (Basil the Great) 2–120b, 121b, 122a
Asceticism
antifeminism 1–323a
Basil the Great 2–120a, 121b, 122a
Cassian 3–122a
charismatic 2–121b
church-oriented 2–121b
Mount Athos 1–636b
ASHʿARĪ, ABŪ'L-ḤASAN ʿALĪ IBN ISMAʿĪL AL- 1–582b; 4–84b
Ashʿath, Ibn al-
revolt 3–38b
Asher ben David
cabala 3–1b
Ashes
blessing of 2–177b-178a
Ashīr 1–197b
ASHKENAZ 1–585b
alphabet 1–208a
cabala 3–2b
Ashrāf 3–34a, 35a; 4–83a
Alids 1–175b
Muʿāwiya 3–36a,b-37a
Second Civil War 3–38b
Ashraf, al- 4–32a
Ashrafti 4–301b
Ashtarak
See Aštarak
Ash Wednesday 3–99b
Asia
Antiochene rite 1–326b
Black Death 2–258a-259a
Byzantine church 2–460b, 462a
exploration 4–556a-557b
Asia Minor
See Anatolia
ʿAskar, Al- 3–13b-14a
ʿAskar al-Mahdi
See al-Ruṣāfah
Asmā' 1–15a
Asmā' al-ḥusnā 3–52b
Aṣmaʿī, al- 4–443a,b
ASMATIKON 1–586b
ÁSMUNDAR SAGA KAPPABANA 1–586b
Asołik
See Step'anos Asołik Tarōnecʿi
Ašot II Bagratuni 2–48b
Ašot Bagratuni, *Išχan* 1–478b

Ašot Bagratuni, King 1–449a, 500b
AŠOT II ERKAT' 1–588b; 1–449a, 482a
Dwin 4–324a
Ašot IV K'aǰ 1–483a
AŠOT I MEC (THE GREAT) **1–587b**; 1–449a, 479b
achievements 1–480a-481b
Armenian literature 1–510b
Bagratids 2–48a-b
Dwin 4–324a
Ašot Msaker Bagratuni 2–48a
Ani in Širak 1–290b
AŠOT III OŁORMAC (THE MERCIFUL) **1–589a**; 1–290b, 482a,b, 483a
Dwin 4–324a
Aspacures III 3–308a
Aspar 1–121b
Asperukh
See Isperikh
Aspet 3–199a
Ass 1–295b
Aṣ-Ṣāliḥ Ayyūb
death 4–53a
ASSASSINS 1–589b
Alamūt 1–118a
As-Sayyida Arwā 1–375a,b
ASSER 1–593a; 4–456a
Alfred the Great 1–163b, 164b; 2–239b
Assisi, Francesco d'
See Francis of Assisi, Saint
ASSISI, SAN FRANCESCO 1–593b
ASSIZE 1–594a
ASSIZE, ENGLISH 1–596a
Bracton, Henry de 2–356b
Brittany 2–379b
Britton 2–382b
Norman-Angevin England 4–470b
Assize of mort d'ancestor 3–414a
Assizes of Antioch
Cilician court 3–393b
Assizes of Building (1189) 3–560b
ASSIZES OF JERUSALEM 1–598b
consulate of the sea 3–569b
See Also Cilician Kingdom
ASSIZES OF ROMANIA 1–600a
ASSONANCE 1–600a
Spanish epic 3–72a-b
See Also Chansons de geste
ASSUMPTION OF THE VIRGIN 1–601a
Assumption of the Virgin (Bartolo di Fredi) 2–116b
Assumptus homo 3–322b, 323a
Assyrian art
angel 1–248a
AŠTARAK (ASHTARAK) **1–601a**
Asthianenē
See Hašteark'
Asti
banking 2–76a
commune 3–500a
Aštišat 1–498a; 4–417a
Astorga 1–626a,b; 3–132a
Astrakhan khanate 3–679b
Astral religion 1–604a
Astrapas, Michael 4–524b
Astrarium 3–461b, 462a; 4–260b
Giovanni de' Dondi 3–464b
ASTROLABE 1–602a; 3–28b-29a
astronomy 1–611a-b, 622b
Bīrūnī 2–250a
illustration 1–603
planetary clocks 3–465a
ASTROLOGY/ASTRONOMY 1–604a
Alfonsine Tables 1–159a, 162a
armillary sphere 1–521b
astrolabe 1–602a
Bacon, Roger 2–35b, 38a-b
Bīrūnī 2–248b, 250a-b
Buridan, Jean 2–430b-431b
calendars and reckoning of time 3–17a
Catalan literature 3–168b
cross-staff 4–12a
equatorium 4–500b
impact 1–611a-613b, 614a
Islamic 1–616b-624b
judicial 2–38a
See Also Arabic numerals
Astronomical clock 3–29b
Richard of Wallingford 3–461a
Astronomical Tables (al-Khwārizmī) 1–385b, 391a
Astronomicon (Marcus Manilius) 1–605a
Astronomy
See Astrology/Astronomy
Astuacašunč' Girk'
See Bible, Armenian
Astuacatur-Maxož 1–518b
ASTURIAN ART 1–624b
ASTURIAS-LEÓN 1–625a
Castile 3–125b, 128a
Rome 2–126a
Ašχarhac'oyc' 1–238b
Anania Sirakac'i 1–238b
Ašxēn 1–519b
ASYLUM, RIGHT OF 1–631a
ATABEG 1–632a
Atapuerca, Battle of (1054) 3–128b
Ataulf, King 1–121a, 122b; 2–91a, 102a
ATELIER 1–632b
ATENIS SIONI 1–632b
Athanaric 2–90b
Athanasian Creed
Ambrose, Saint 1–231b
Cluniac rite 3–467b
ATHANASIANS 1–632b
ATHANASIUS I, PATRIARCH OF CONSTANTINOPLE 1–633b
Andronikos II Palaiologos 2–499b
ATHANASIUS OF ALEXANDRIA, SAINT 1–633a; 1–31b-32a, 453b
Apollinarius 1–348a
Armenian literature 1–508b
Armenian rite 1–516b
Athanasians 1–632b
Byzantine tools 1–77b
Catechetical School of Alexandria 3–594a
Celtic church 3–225b
Christian dogma 3–336a
doctor of the church 4–234a
early church 3–339a
Life of St. Anthony 2–518a
Nicene Creed 3–627b, 628a
veneration 2–459a,b
Athanasius the Athonite, Saint
Mount Athos 1–636b, 637b-638a
Āthār al-Bāqiya 'an al-Qurūn al-Khāliya, al- (Bīrūnī) 2–248b
Athaulf
See Ataulf
Athelstan, King 1–278b; 4–400b, 456b
bell towers 2–166b
Brittany 2–379a
Athelstan Psalter 1–273a
Athenagoras of Athens 3–335a
Athenogenes, Bishop 1–518a
Athens
Alexander romances 1–150b
Catalan Company 2–500a; 3–156a-b
Constantine I the Great 1–334b
Crown of Aragon 1–415a
traveler accounts 1–333a
Athens-Thebes
See Latin Principalities
ATHIR, IBN AL- 1–634a
Bar Hebraeus 2–108b
***ATHIS UND PROPHILIAS* 1–635b**
ATHOS, MOUNT 1–636b; 4–347b
Byzantine church 2–469b
monasteries 4–333b, 341b
ATHOS, MOUNT, MONUMENTS OF 1–637b; 2–448a-b
Atik Mustafa Pasha Camii (Constantinople) 4–341a
***ATLAKVIÐA* 1–638a**; 4–386b, 390a
***ATLAMÁL* 1–638b**; 4–386b, 390a,b, 391b
Atlakviđa 1–638a
ATLAS MOUNTAINS 1–639b
Almoravids 1–198a
Berbers 2–186a,b
map 1–640a-b
Atli, King 1–638a
See Also Attila the Hun
'Atlīt
Pilgrim's Castle 4–25b
Atom Anjewac'i 1–519b
Atours 3–624a
ATRIUM 1–641a
basilica 2–124a,b
Atrpatakan
See Azerbaijan
Attainder
See Impeachment
Attaleia
Anatolia 1–239b, 241a
ATTALEIATES, MICHAEL 1–641b; 1–303b
akritai 1–116a
Attica
Catalan Company 3–156a-b
Atticism
Byzantine poetry 2–523b
classical literary studies 3–430b
Attila the Hun 2–92b, 93a
Atlakviđa 1–638b
Atlamál 1–638b
Champagne 3–243b
ATTO OF VERCELLI 1–641b
Attribution, False 1–135a
Attuyer 2–427a
Āturpātākān
See Azerbaijan
AUBADE 1–642a
alba 1–123a
Aube
See Aubade
AUBERT, DAVID 1–642b
Aubusson, Pierre d'
Knights of Saint John 3–304a
***AUCASSIN ET NICOLETTE* 1–642b**
Auchinleck Manuscript 1–320a
Auctoritate summi pontificis et generalis concilii, De (Denys the Carthusian) 3–519b
Audelay, John
carols 3–116a
Audgarius
Breviary of Alaric 2–373a
Audience Court (Canterbury) 1–433b
Audiencia 3–139a
Auditing 1–36b, 38a,b
AUDRADUS MODICUS 1–644a
Audrey, Saint 1–261a
Augen, Saint 3–595a
Augrym 1–396a
Augsburg
arms and armor 1–529a
Augsburg Bible 2–215b

***AUGUSTA* 1–644a**; 2–122b
despot 4–165a
Augustine of Ancona
See Augustinus Triumphus
AUGUSTINE OF CANTERBURY 1–644b; 4–454b, 458a
Benedictines 2–170a, 172a
Canterbury Cathedral 3–81b, 84a
celibacy laws 3–216b
Easter dating 3–228b
ember days 4–436a
Kent 3–343a,b, 344b
migration 1–288b, 289a
rechristianization 2–97a
Augustine of Dacia
exegesis 2–224a,b
AUGUSTINE OF HIPPO, SAINT 1–646a; 1–284a
Alfred the Great 1–164b, 167a
allegory 1–181b, 188a
altar apparatus 1–221b
Ambrose, Saint 1–231a
angelology 1–249b
Aristotelianism 1–465b-466a
Arnobius the Younger 1–539b
ars praedicandi 1–556b
Ascension 1–582a
astrology 1–605b
Augustinian canons 1–659a
Augustinian friars 1–659b
Augustinism 1–660a
Bacon, Roger 2–36a-b, 37b
barbarian invasions 2–91a
Boethius 2–292b
Bonaventure, Saint 2–314b
Bradwardine, Thomas 2–358b
Brut, The 2–393a
Cassian 3–122b
casuistry 3–153a
church unity 3–336b
classical literary studies 3–432a
concubinage 3–530a
crusade concept 4–15b, 17b
death and burial 4–118b-119a
Demetrios Kydones 4–135b
deposition of rulers 4–158a
dialectic 4–168b
doctor of the church 4–234a
Donatism 4–260a
dualism 4–297b-298a
early church 3–342a,b
Ecclesia and Synagoga 4–371a
ecclesiology 4–372a,b
encyclopedias 4–447b
exegesis 2–216a, 219a, 224a; 4–544a, 546b, 548a, 550a
exempla 4–551a
Hebrew writing 1–218a
homilies 1–284b
influence 1–148b
monasticism 3–343a
monastic rule 4–222a
Orosius 1–166a-b
virginity 1–323a
works 1–207a
AUGUSTINIAN CANONS 1–659a
Divine Office 4–222a
AUGUSTINIAN FRIARS 1–659b
AUGUSTINIAN FRIARS 1–661a
Aristotelianism 1–465a
Armagh 1–470a
Capgrave, John 3–90a
Augustinianism
See Augustinism
Augustinians
chivalry, orders of 3–303b
Council of Lyons (1274) 3–641b
Latin church 3–368a
AUGUSTINISM 1–660a
Bacon, Roger 2–36a-b
Durand of Saint Pourçain 4–313b
John Duns Scotus 4–309a-b
Louis, Emperor 3–111b
AUGUSTINUS TRIUMPHUS 2–1a
Augustus 2–122b; 3–8b
Augustus, Emperor 2–88b
Aumônière 3–625a
Aunage
See Alnage
Aunes
alnage 1–202b
Aura, Ekkehard of
See Ekkehard of Aura
***AURAICEPT NA NÉCES* 2–1b**
bardic grammars 2–107b
Aurelian, Emperor
barbarian invasions 2–89b, 90b
Dacia 2–90b
AURELIAN OF RÉÔME 2–2b
Cistercian chant 3–402b
AURELIANUS, AMBROSIUS 2–2b
Aurelianus Reomensis
See Aurelian of Réôme
Aurelius Ambrosius
See Ambrose, Saint
Aurelius Augustinus
See Augustine of Hippo, Saint
Aureoli, Peter
Christology 3–324a
Aurès Mountains 1–639b
Auricept na nEces
See Auraicept na nÉces
Auroch 1–301a
Aurora (Petrus Riga) 1–319a
Aurora consurgens 1–138b
***AUSCULTA FILI* 2–3b**
Ausiàs March
See March, Ausiàs
Ausonius 2–102a
AUSPICIUS OF TOUL 2–4a
Austin friars
See Augustinian Friars
Austrasia
aristocracy, revolt of (613) 3–104a-b
Boniface, Saint 2–322a
Charles Martel 3–272a
Merovingian Francia 3–104a-106a
Merovingians 1–117b; 3–104a-106a
AUSTRIA 2–4b
archives 1–448b
Avars 2–12b
Babenberg family 2–33a
Bohemia 2–300a
camels 1–296b
chivalry, orders of 3–306b
Cistercian order 3–404a
courtly lyric 1–132b
Eleonore 4–429a
Lombard settlement 2–95a
map 2–5
Autier, Peter 3–190b
AUTOCEPHALOS 2–9b
AUTOCRATOR 2–10b
basileus 2–122b-123a
***AUTO DE LOS REYES MAGOS* 2–9a**
Autopertus, Ambrosius
See Autpertus, Ambrosius
Autorlegion 3–79a
AUTPERTUS, AMBROSIUS 2–11a
Marian office 2–274a
patristic heritage 4–372b
Autun Cathedral 1–344a
Autunois 2–427a
Auvergne
constable 2–53a
Auvergne, Martial d' 3–332b
Auvezère Valley
agriculture 1–85b
Auxerrois 2–427a
AUXILIUS 2–11b
Eugenius Vulgarius 4–520b
Avalois 2–427a
AVANZO, JACOPO 2–11b
frescoes 1–226b
AVARAYR 2–12a
Battle of (451) 4–433a
AVARS 2–12a
Austria 2–4b
Bosnia 2–334b
Bulgaria 2–399a, 401a
Byzantine Empire 2–486b, 487a
cavalry 3–199b, 202a
Charlemagne 3–107a
Croatia 4–1a,b
Dalmatia 4–79b
water buffalo 1–298a
AVE MARIA 2–13a
Avempace
See Bājja, Ibn
Avendouth
See Abraham ibn Daud
Avengalvón of Molina 3–76a
Cid 3–73b, 74a
Aventiurehaft 4–380a
Avenzoar
See Zuhr Abū Marwān, Ibn
Ave phoenice, De (Lactantius) 1–280b
Averçó, Lluís d' 3–170b
Ave regina caelorum 1–329a
Averroës
See Rushd, Ibn
AVESTA 2–14a; 1–452a
Bundahishn 2–419a
Dēnkard 4–148b
Aveyron
See Villefranche-de-Rouergue
AVIANUS 2–15b
fables 4–572a,b, 573a
Avicebrol
See Solomon ben Judah ibn Gabirol
Avicebron
See Solomon ben Judah ibn Gabirol
Avicenna
See Sīnā, Ibn
AVIGNON 2–15b
Albornoz, Gil 1–130b
art trade 1–562a
Black Death 2–260b
Buridan, Jean 2–430a
church union 2–109b
city walls 3–151a
money markets 2–78b
Avignon papacy 2–34a; 4–376a-377a
ars subtilior 1–558b
Babylonian captivity 2–33b
Catalans 3–156b
church organization 3–377a
Cistercian order 3–405b
See Also Church, Latin: 1305 to 1500
Avignon Pietà (Enguerrand Charonton) 3–274b
Ávila
Asturians 1–626a
Caballeros villanos 3–136b
city walls 3–151b
fueros 3–131b
ÁVILA BIBLE, MASTER OF THE 2–16b
Avinyó, Mossèn 3–171b
Avionnets
See Isopets
Avision-Christine (Christine de Pizan) 3–315b

Avitus of Vienne, Bishop 3–100a
true cross 4–553a-b
AVIZ, ORDER OF 2–16b; 3–306b
Avlona 2–308b
Avoué
See Advocate
Avradaka 2–417a
Avranches
fairs 4–586a
Awāl
See Baḥrayn, Al-
ʿAwāṣim, Al- 1–326a
Awdaghost
Almoravid conquest (1055) 1–198b
Awdlau 4–76b
Casnodyn 3–121b, 122a
ʿAwn al-Dīn 2–43b
Awqāf 1–175b
ʿAwwām, Ibn al- 1–106a
Awzāʿī, al- 4–84b
Beirut 2–164a
Ax 1–522b
Axum
See Aksum, Kingdom of
***¿AY, IHERUSALEM!* 2–18a**
Ayala, Pedro Lopez de
See Lopez de Ayala, Pero
AYAS 2–19a
Aya Sofya
See Hagia Sophia (Constantinople)
Ayasuluk
See Ephesus
Āyāt 1–177b
Āyāt al-kursī 3–55a
Aybak 2–272b
Aybert 2–13b
Aydakīn 2–272b
Aydamir ibn ʿAlī al-Djildakī
alchemy 1–141b
Aydin, emirate of
Andronikos III Palaiologos 1–246b
Ephesus 4–495a
Aymard of Cluny 3–469a
Aymeric III of Norbonne 3–188a
Aymeri de Narbonne 2–201b
ʿAyn al-Dawla
Danishmendids 4–93a
AYNARD OF SAINT ÈVRE 2–19b
ʿAynī, al- 4–407b
ʿAyn Jālūt
battle (1260) 2–138a; 3–391b; 4–406b
AYRARAT 2–19b; 1–472b, 473a,b
Ayvalı Kilise 3–92a
ʿAyyārūn 2–437a
Ayyūb ibn Shadhi 2–23a
AYYUBID ART AND ARCHITECTURE 2–20b; 2–25a
AYYUBIDS 2–22b; 1–123b
agriculture 1–105a
Aleppo 1–145b
Alexandria 1–153b
Arčēš 1–423a
Armenia 1–485a
Baybars al-Bunduqdārī 2–138a
Coptic church 3–594b
crusades 4–31a-32a
Damascus 4–82b, 83b, 84a,b-85a
Egypt 3–14a; 4–406a, 408a
military dress 3–618a-b
***AZAT* 2–25b**; 1–488b, 489b
Albania 1–123b
aznauri 2–28b
cavalry 3–198b
AZERBAIJAN 2–25b; 1–451a, 513b; 2–139a
Albania 1–125a
Baylakān 2–139a
Caucasia 3–195a
Ildeñizids 1–632a
map 2–26a-b
Azerbaijan S.S.R.
See Utikʿ
Azevedo, Diego de, Bishop
heretics 3–187b
AZHAR, AL- (CAIRO) 2–27b; 4–407a
construction 3–14a
ʿAZĪZ BIʾLLĀH NIZĀR ABŪ MANṢŪR, AL- 2–28a
Aznar Galindo 1–403b
Aznar II Galindo 1–404a
***AZNAURI* 2–28b**
azat 2–25b
eristʿaw 4–506a
AZO 2–29a
Bulgarus 2–418a
AZORES 2–29b
exploration 4–560a
Flemings 4–559a-b
Italians 4–559a
map 2–30a-b
ʿAzrāʾīl 1–248b
Azriel of Gerona
cabala 3–1b
AZULEJO 2–30b
ʿAzyāj 1–620a, 621b-622a
AZYMES 2–31b

B

Baalbek
Ayyubids 2–24a; 4–39a
Baʿalei ha-Nefesh (Rabad) 1–22b
Baardson, Ivar 3–455a
Baarlam
See Barlaam
BĀB 2–32a
Almohad art 1–193a
Babai the Great 3–312b
Babak 1–479b
Bāb al-Abwāb
See Derbent
Bāb al-Futūḥ 2–44b
BAB AL-MANDAB 2–32a
map 2–32b
Bāb al-Naṣr 2–44b
Bāb al-Ruwāḥ 1–193a
Bāb al-Ṭāq (Baghdad) 2–46a
Babawīya 4–407a
Babees Book 3–661a
BABENBERG FAMILY 2–33a
Austria 2–6a-7b
Bavarian rule 2–134a,b
Přemysl Ottokar II 2–300a
Babio 4–283a
Babowai, Katholikos
Christian church in Persia 3–312a
Babrius
fables 2–15b; 4–572a
Bāb Ṣaghīr 4–83a
Bāb Tūmā 4–83a
Babuni
See Bogomils
Babylon (Egypt)
ʿAmr ibn al-ʿĀṣ 1–237a; 4–403b
Babylon (Iraq)
Alexander the Great 1–150b
ceramics 3–238a
traveler accounts 1–332a
Babylonia
See Iraq
BABYLONIAN CAPTIVITY 2–33b
Avignon 2–15b
Clement VI, Pope 3–439a
See Also Church, Latin: 1305 to 1500
See Also De captivitate Babylonica ecclesiae praeludium
Babylonian Hebrew alphabet 1–208a, 218a
Bāb Zuwayla 2–44b
Bachkovo monastery 2–417a
Bachya ben Asher
cabala 3–2b
BAÇÓ, JAIME 2–34b
BACON, ROGER 2–35a; 1–435a, 438b, 461b
Albertus Magnus 1–129a
alchemy 1–137a-b
Alexander of Hales 1–148a
Arabic numerals and mathematics 1–396b
Aristotle 1–53b
astrology 1–607b
calendar reform 3–23a
dialectic 4–170b
exegesis 2–214a
experimental science 2–244a
Hebrew grammar 3–314a
languages 1–336b
Badakhshān 1–63b-64a,b
BĀDGĪR 2–42a
Badīʿ Palace (Marrakech) 1–169a
BĀDIYA 2–42b
Badla mawkibiyya 3–618a
BADR, BATTLE OF (624) 2–42b; 1–24b
ʿAbbās, al- 1–4a
Abū Sufyān 1–28b-29a
BADR AL-DĪN LUʾLUʾ 2–43b; 1–634a,b, 635a
BADR AL-JAMĀLĪ 2–44a
Badr al-Mawʿid 1–29a
Bādūrayā 2–45a
Baena 3–140a
BAERZE, JACQUES DE 2–44b
Báetán mac Cairill, King 4–78a-b
Áedán 1–60a
Baetica
agriculture 1–82a
Bagarat
See Bagrat
Bagh
See Rauḍa
BAGHDAD 2–44b
Abbasids 1–8a-b, 10a-b, 11b; 2–127b; 4–81b-82a
architecture 1–5a
bāb 2–32a
Balādhurī 2–54a
Barmakids 2–110b
Buyids 2–435b, 436b, 437a
caliphate 3–42a,b, 43a, 45b, 50a
Mongol conquest 1–12a
Nestorians 4–552a
Seljuks 3–50b
Swedes 4–555b
Talisman Gate 1–6b
Tamerlane 2–113b
writers and poets 1–400b
Bagrat I Bagratuni 1–480a; 2–48a
Bagrat II Bagratuni 1–449a
Bagratid churches
Ani 1–292a
BAGRATIDS, ARMENIAN 2–47b; 1–473b-474a, 499a-b; 3–308a
Ani in Širak 1–290b
Arab conquest 1–478b
Arcn 1–450b

Arcrunis 1–451a
Ašot II Erkatʿ 1–588b
Ašot III Ołormac 1–589a
Ašot I Mec 1–587b-588b
Ayrarat 2–20a,b
Derbent 4–162b
Dwin 4–323b, 324a
history 1–480a-483a
literature 1–510a-511a
Muslim emirates 1–513b
social structure 1–489a
BAGRATIDS, GEORGIAN 2–48b
David II (IV) the Builder 4–112a
David of Tao 4–113b
Bagrat III of Abkhazeti 4–113b
See Bagrat III of Georgia
Bagrat III of Georgia 2–49a; 4–113b
cathedral 2–47b
BAGRAT'S CATHEDRAL 2–47b
Bagratuni
See Bagratids
Bagravand
See Bagrewand
Bagrewand 2–20a, 48a
Bahamas
exploration 4–560a,b
Bahīrā 1–30a
Bahou
See Qbou
BAHR AL-MUHĪT 2–49b
BAHRĀM VI ČŌBĒN 2–50a
Bahrām Čōbēn Nāmag 2–50b
BAHRĀM V GŌR 2–49b
Bahrām Warzāwand
See Bahrām VI Čōbēn
BAHRAYN, AL- 2–50b
Bahrī Mamluk period 4–406b
Bahriyya regiment 2–138a
Bahya ben Asher ben Hlava
exegesis 4–540a
BAHYA BEN JOSEPH IBN PAQUDA 2–51a; 1–23a
exegesis 4–540a
Bailan Pass
See Cilician Gates
Bailey 3–144a
BAILIFF 2–51b; 2–52a
Cyprus 4–71b-72a
échevins 4–379b
estate management 4–514a,b
BAILLI 2–52a
assize 1–594b, 595b
bailiff 2–51b
Burgundy, Duchy of 2–427a-b
Castile 3–132b
Dauphiné 4–109b
Baird
See Bard
Baiuvarii 2–133b
Bājja, Ibn (Avempace)
Aristotelianism 1–459a
Burley, Walter 2–433a
Cavalcanti, Guido 3–197a
Bakers
Byzantine guilds 2–478a
Bakhtīshū family 3–313a
Bakrī, al- 1–83b
Bakr tribe 4–231b
Baku 2–26a, 27a
Bakuriani brothers 2–417a
Balabitenē
See Balahovit
Balade 1–269a
BALĀDHURĪ, ABŪ HASAN AHMĀD IBN YAHYA IBN JĀBIR, AL- 2–54a; 1–478a
Artašat 1–564a
Balaguer 1–413b
Balahovit 1–472b, 515a
Balavar and Būdasaf 2–54b
***BALAVARIANI* 2–54b**; 2–109a
Chardri 3–267b
Balbi, Giovanni
Catholicon 4–248a, 449b, 547a
Balbus, John
See Balbi, Giovanni
Baldacco
See Baldachin
BALDACHIN 2–55a
See Also Ciborium
Balder
See Baldr
Baldo degli Ubaldi da Perugia
See Baldus
BALDR 2–55a; 1–63a
Baldrs Draumar 2–56a
charms 3–273b
***BALDRS DRAUMAR* 2–56a**; 2–55a
eddic poetry 4–385b, 390a, 391a,b
Bald's Leechbook 1–286a
Balduino, Lambertino
tomb 2–324b
BALDUS 2–57a
Bartolo da Sassoferrato 2–116a
Baldwin of Boulogne
See Baldwin I of Jerusalem
BALDWIN I OF FLANDERS 2–58a
Boniface of Montferrat 2–323a
Bruges 2–386a
Baldwin II of Flanders 2–58a
Bruges 2–386a
Baldwin IX of Flanders
See Baldwin I of the Latin Empire
Baldwin of Ford, Archbishop
Cistercian order 3–405b
Baldwin of Hainaut
Mongolia 4–556a-b
BALDWIN I OF JERUSALEM 2–58b; 2–309a; 4–30b
crusades 4–34a, 35a, 36a,b
Edessa 4–30a, 384a
Montreal 4–22b
Baldwin II of Jerusalem
Knights Templars 3–304a
Baldwin III of Jerusalem
Latin States 4–38b
BALDWIN I OF THE LATIN EMPIRE 2–58b; 3–552a; 4–105a
Bulgaria 2–408b
chronicles 3–332a
crusades 4–31b, 42a, 45b
Baldwin II of the Latin Empire
Bulgaria 2–409a
Michael VIII Palaiologos 2–499a
Balearic Islands 1–412a, 413a
Almohads 1–195a, 200b
Almoravids 1–194a, 200a
Catalan language 3–157b, 159a-b
Catalonian conquest 3–178a
Bali 1–31b
Balian of Ibelin 4–39b
Balian of Sidon
Assizes of Jerusalem 1–599a
Balik 2–412b
Balīnās 1–136a
Balkans
agriculture and nutrition 1–76b-79b, 98b-99a
Bāyazīd I 2–136a
food animals 1–299b, 301b
Goths 2–89b-90a
Normans of Sicily 4–27b
Ottomans 4–32b
Balkh 1–65b
Balkhash, Lake
exploration 4–556b
BALLADE 2–59a; 1–558b
ars nova 1–552a-b
ballette 2–61a
chansonnier 3–255a
chant royal 3–263a
Charles of Orléans 3–273a
Chartier, Alain 3–275b
Chaucer, Geoffrey 3–281a, 290b
dance 4–86b
envoi 4–492a
BALLADS, MIDDLE ENGLISH 2–59b
Arthurian literature 1–574a
Ballaghmoone
See Belagh Mugna
BALLATA 2–60b
ars nova 1–553a
carols 3–116a
dance 4–86b
BALLETTE 2–61a
Anglo-Norman lyric poetry 1–269a
See Also Dance
BALL-FLOWER 2–61b
Balli 4–88b, 89a-b
Ballista 3–143a-b, 180a
Ballymote, Book of 3–224b
Balša Balšić 4–330a
Balsamon, Theodore 3–615b
canon law 2–468a
Balsham, Adam of
See Adam of the Little Bridge
Balsora
See Basra
Balthasar of Mecklenburg
Dresdener Heldenbuch 4–292b-293a
BALTIC COUNTRIES/BALTS 2–61b
banking 2–74a
Denmark 4–148b-156b
map 2–63a-b
Teutonic Knights 4–17b
Baltic Sea 2–61b
barbarian invasions 2–88a
Universal History 1–166b
Bambergensis 4–123b
BAMBERG MANUSCRIPT 2–68b
Bamborough Castle 4–316b
BAN, BANALITÉ 2–69a
capitulary 3–91a
Carolingian kings 3–107b
estate management 4–513a
BANA 2–70a
Banastre 1–268b
BANAT 2–70a
banus 2–82b
Bancherius 2–73a
Banchi a minuto 2–75b
Banda 3–199b
***BANDAMANNA SAGA* 2–70b**; 4–613b, 614a
Bandello, Matteo 3–277b
Bandinelli, Rolando
See Alexander III, Pope
Bandini, Domenico 4–449a
Boccaccio 2–287b
Baneli, Kvirike
See Kvirike Baneli, Bishop
BANGOR (WALES) 2–71a
BANGOR, RITE OF 2–72a
Bangor Antiphonary 3–230b, 231a
Bangor Iscoed 2–71a
BANKING, EUROPEAN 2–72b
Bruges 2–386b-387a
Castile 3–139a-b
Cistercians 3–404a
feudalism 4–470a
indexes 1–206b
BANKING, ISLAMIC 2–79a
BANKING, JEWISH, IN EUROPE 2–80b; 2–76a, 80a

Bannatyne Manuscript 1–320a
BANNERET 2–82a
Bannockburn, Battle of (1314) 2–102a; 3–204b; 4–397b
Bannum
See Ban, Banalité
Bannus
See Ban, Banalité
Banovina 4–4a, 6b-7a
Banquet, The (Arius) 1–453b
***BANSENCHAS* 2–82b**
Banū Ghāniya 1–194a, 200b, 201a
Banū Hāshim 1–6b-7a
Alids 1–175b
Banū Hilāl
agriculture 1–105a
Almohads 1–194a
saga 1–382a
Banū Ḥumayd 1–71a
Banū Majīd 2–32b
Banū Marīn
See Marinids
Banū Mūsā (mathematicians) 1–435b
See Also Muḥammad ibn Mūsā ibn Shākir
BANUS 2–82b
banat 2–70a
Banyas 2–24a
Bapheus
Ottomans 1–246a
BAPTISM 2–83a
Alexandrian 1–156b-157a
Armenian 1–516a
Augustine of Hippo 1–648a
baptistery 2–87b
Cathars 3–183b
Celtic church 2–381b; 3–229a, 230b
ceremonies 1–327a
creeds, liturgical use 3–675a-676a
early church 3–338a
Easter 4–367b
Epiphany 4–496b
See Also Confirmation
Baptismal registrations
demography 4–138b
BAPTISMAL VOWS, OLD HIGH GERMAN/OLD SAXON 2–87a; 2–83b-84a
Baptismal water 2–177a,b
BAPTISM OF CHRIST 2–86b
Epiphany 4–496b
BAPTISTERY 2–87b; 2–85b-86a
art and architecture 4–336a, 349b, 350a, 358a
Barcelona 2–102b
Brunelleschi, Filippo 2–388a
Diotisalvi 4–193b
Baptistery of the Arians (Ravenna) 4–352a
Baptistery of the Orthodoxy (Ravenna) 4–359a
Bāqillānī, al- 1–585a
caliphate literature 3–50b
Baradā River 4–81a, 83a
Barānis 2–185b
See Also Berbers
Barbar
See Berbers
BARBARIANS, INVASIONS OF 2–88a; 2–90a,b
Almoravid art 1–197a
Anglo-Saxons 1–288b
animals, food and draft 1–293b, 294b, 299a
bracteates 2–355b
Brittany 2–377b-378a
Buch von Bern, Das 2–396a
Burgundians 2–422b-423b
demography 4–136a
fortifications 3–143b, 144b
heroic poetry 1–638a-639a
See Also Berbers
Barbastro 1–404a, 405a,b, 406b, 407a
Barbato da Sulmona 2–278a
Barberino, Francesco da 3–664a
courtesy books 3–665b
Barbero, Giosophat
travel accounts 1–332b
BARBERS, BARBER-SURGEONS 2–97b
shaving 2–148a
Barbetorte, Alan 2–379a
Barbette 3–623a, 624a
Barbiano, Alberico da
condottieri 3–531a
Barbieri 2–99b
BARBOTINE 2–101a
BARBOUR, JOHN 2–102a
Bar branch
See Bar tracery
Barbute 1–527a, 530a
Barca Peninsula
slaves 2–268b, 269a,b
BARCELONA 2–102a; 3–174b
banking 2–74a,b, 75b, 78b
Borrell, Raymond 3–175b
Borrell II 3–175b
Celestine foundations 3–214b
Charlemagne 3–174a
counts 3–175b, 186b-187a
Crown of Aragon 1–408a, 409b-410a,b, 411b-412a, 414a, 415b, 417a, 418a,b, 419b-420a
shipping 3–178a
slaves 2–268b
Barcino
See Barcelona
BARD 2–105b
bardic grammar 2–107a
eisteddfod 4–415a
Barda
See Bardhaʿ
BARDAS CAESAR 2–106a
assassination 2–117a
classical literary studies 3–431a
Michael III 2–489a
"Philosophical School" 1–392a
BARDAS PHOKAS 2–106b; 1–483b
Bardas Skleros 2–106b
Basil II 2–118b
David of Tao 4–113b
BARDAS SKLEROS 2–106b; 1–483b
Bardas Phokas 2–106b
Basil II 2–118b
David of Tao 4–113b
Bardd
See Bard
Bardd teulu 2–106a; 4–69b
Bardesanes 3–335a
BARDHAʿA 2–107a; 1–123b, 124b-125a; 2–26a
Muslim emirates 1–513b
Bardi banking company 2–77a,b, 277b, 287a
diplomatic loans 4–211a
BARDIC GRAMMARS 2–107a
Auraicept na nÉces 2–2a
bards 2–105b
Bardic poetry
See Irish literature
Bardulia
See Castile
Barford Church
sculpture 1–256a
BARGEBOARD 2–107b
Barghawāṭa 1–198b
Bārghirī
See Berkri
Bargus
See Bargeboard
BAR HEBRAEUS 2–108a
BARI 2–108b
Black Death 2–259a
Bohemond I 2–308b
Byzantine acquisition (875) 2–118a
council (1098) 1–312b
Norman capture (1071) 2–492b
Barid 2–138b; 3–45a
Baris
See Ararat, Mount
BARISANUS OF TRANI 2–109a
Barjr Haykʿ 1–472a
Barking Abbey 1–216b
BARLAAM AND JOSAPHAT 2–109a
Balavariani 2–54b
Chardri 3–267a
Everyman 4–528a
BARLAAM OF CALABRIA 2–109a; 1–614a; 3–632b
Boccaccio 2–278a
Barley
See Grain crops
BARMAKIDS 2–109b; 1–10a
caliphate 3–44a,b, 48a
BARNA DA SIENA 2–111a
BARON 2–111a
Baronet
banneret 2–82a
BARONS' WAR 2–111b
Edward I of England 4
Parliament 4–481a
BARONZIO, GIOVANNI 2–112b
Barozzi, Francesco 1–439a
Barqa
See Pentapolis
BARQŪQ, AL-SULṬĀN AL-MALIK AL-ẒAHIR SAYF AL-DĪN 2–113a
Cairo 3–14b
Barr 2–185b
BARREL (MEASURE) 2–113b
BARRELS 2–114a
Barrel vault
See Vault, Types of
Barrientos brothers 3–306b
Barrili, Giovanni
Boccaccio 2–278a
Barroso, Pero 3–87a
Bar Ṣauma, Bishop 3–312a
Bar-sur-Aube
fairs 4–590b, 591a-592a
Bartholomaeus Anglicus 1–137a; 2–39a; 3–168b
bestiary 2–205a
child care 4–602a
encyclopedias 4–448b-449a
plant study 2–245b
Bartholomeus Brixiensis 4–127b
Bartholomew the Englishman
See Bartholomaeus Anglicus
Bartians
insurrection (1260) 2–67a
BARTOLINO DA NOVARA 2–114b
Bartolino da Padova
ballata 2–61a
Bartolismo 2–116a
Bartolo, Nanni di
See Nanni di Bartolo
BARTOLO DA SASSOFERRATO 2–114b
Baldus 2–57a
BARTOLO DI FREDI 2–116b
Bartolomeo, Michelozzo di
See Michelozzo di Bartolomeo
Bartolomeo da Noli 4–561b

Bartolomeo de Las Cases
West Indies 4–560a
Bartolomeo Marchionni
slaves 2–269a, 270a
Bartolomeus Anglicus
See Bartholomaeus Anglicus
Bartolus
See Bartolo da Sassoferrato
Barton, John 1–270b
Barton-le-Street Church 1–256b
BAR TRACERY (BAR BRANCH) **2–116b**
Baryn 3–680a
Barzillai
cabala 3–1b
BAS-DE-PAGE 2–117a
Basel
antependium 1–316b
anti-Semitism 2–263b
Basel, Council of
See Councils, Western
Bashkale 1–451a
Bashmouric Rebellion (829-830) 3–594b
Bashshār ibn Burd 1–400b
Basileia
See Genesios, Joseph
Basileios
See Basil the Great of Caesarea, Saint
Basiles, Fadrique Alemán de
See Biel, Friedrich
BASILEUS 2–122b
autocrator 2–10b
Basiliada 2–120a
BASILICA 2–123b
Barcelona 2–102b
Bulgaria 2–403b
Coptic and Ethiopian churches 1–157a; 3–585a, 586a
early Christian and Byzantine architecture 4–331b, 332b, 333a, 335a-337a
Ereroyk' 4–504b
See Also Architecture, liturgical aspects
See Also Church, types of
Basilica cistern
See Yerebatan
Basilicarius 3–444b
BASILICS 2–125a
Basilides 3–335a
Basilis, Basilissa
See Augusta
Basilius
Church of the Nativity (Bethlehem) 4–24b
crusader art and architecture 4–23a-b
BASIL THE GREAT OF CAESAREA, SAINT 2–119b; 2–13a
Admonitio 1–62a
Apollinarius 1–348a
Arianism 1–454a
Armenian literature 1–507b
Armenian Rite 1–516a-b
astrology 1–605b
bestiary 2–204a
Catechetical School of Alexandria 3–594a
Christian dogma 3–336a
Christmas 3–318a
classical literary studies 3–430b
Coptic church 3–595a
Divine Office 4–229b
doctors of the church 4–234a
ecumenical councils 3–628b
eucharistic canon 2–468a
salvation theory 3–342a
BASIL II THE "KILLER OF BULGARS," EMPEROR 2–118b; 1–303a, 483b-484a; 2–118b
allelengyon 1–189b
Armenia 2–493a
art patron 2–438b, 442a-443a
Bardas Skleros 2–106b
Bogomilism 2–295b
Bosnia 2–334b
Bulgaria 2–406b-407a
Dalmatia 4–5b-6a
David of Tao 4–113b
dunatoi 4–307a
economy and society 2–477b
Menologion 2–456a
monasticism 2–478b
reign 2–490b, 492a-b
BASIL I THE MACEDONIAN, EMPEROR 2–117a; 1–480b, 483b; 2–489b
Bardas Caesar 2–106b
Croatia 4–2b
eastern frontier 4–523a
Epanagogue 4–493a
gifts 2–453b
Great Palace (Constantinople) 3–553a
Methodios, Saint 4–74a
reign 2–489b
Basil the monk
Bogomils 1–158b; 2–295b
Basil II the Muscovite Grand Prince 1–101b
Basil the Parakoimomenos 2–118b
Basil the *Proedros*
art patron 2–455a, 456b
Basil the Robber
See Goi Vasil
Basinet 1–526a, 527a,b
Basing, Battle (871) 1–163b
Basket capital 3–90b
Bas-Languedoc
agriculture 1–85b
See Also Languedoc
Basmala 3–52b
BASMENOYE DELO 2–125b
Basprakania
See Vaspurakan
BASQUES 2–125b
Castilian language 3–141b
fruit cultivation 1–84a
BASRA 2–127a
Battle of the Camel (656) 1–172b
culture 3–42a
settlements 1–377a
Basrah, Al-
See Basra
BASSA, FERRER 2–128a
Bassadanza 4–88b, 89a-b
Baṣṣāl, Ibn 1–106a
agriculture 1–82a
Bassām, Ibn 3–386a
Bassedanse 4–88b-89a,b
Basse-Navarre
Basques 2–126a,b
See Also Navarre
Basset, Johan 3–171a
Basse-taille enamel
See Enamel, basse-taille
Bassianus, Johannes
Azo 2–29a
Bassora, Bassorah
See Basra
BASTIDE 2–128a
castles and fortifications 3–151a-b
Bastions 3–152a
Baston-course 1–533a
See Also Tournament
Bata
See Aelfric Bata
BATAILLE, NICHOLAS 2–129b
art trade 1–561b
Batailles 3–204a
Bateman of Norwich, Bishop 2–262b
Bath
Black Death 2–261b-262a
Cathedral 3–265a
Bath, Order of the 3–307a
Baths of Diocletian 1–334a
Bāṭin
alms tax 1–202a
Battānī, al-
zij 1–611b
Battering ram 3–146b-148a
Battle Abbey
construction 3–562a
Battle axe
See Arms and Armor
See Ax
Battle Cathedral 1–255b
Battle flags
See Chivalry, orders of
Battle of Brunanburh, The 1–278b, 287a
Battle of Maldon, The 1–277a, 279a
Battle of the Seven Arts (Henri d'Andell) 3–434b
BAṬṬŪṬA, IBN 2–130a; 1–382a; 2–50b
Alexandria 1–154a
Basra 2–127b
Caesarea 3–9b
Nineveh 1–332b
BATU 2–131a
Baturich of Regensburg, Bishop 3–479b
Batyi
See Batu
Baudouin de Lannoy
Jan van Eyck 4–567b
BAUDRI OF BOURGUEIL 2–132a
***BAUERNHOCHZEIT, DIE* 2–132a**
Baugulf of Fulda 4–412a
Einhard 1–143a
Baux, Les 1–408b
BAVARIA 2–132b
administration 2–4b
Babenberg family 2–33b
Boniface, Saint 2–322a
brewing 2–375a
Carolingians 2–6a
Charlemagne 2–4b-6a; 3–107a
invasions 2–94b-95a
Merovingians 3–104a
settlement 2–94b
subkingdom 3–112a
Bawit
Coptic art 3–588a
BAWWĀB, IBN AL- 2–135b
script styles 3–54b
Bay'a
caliphate 3–33a,b
succession 3–39a, 42b
BĀYAZĪD I, YILDIRIM 2–136a
Anatolia 1–242a
Ankara, Battle of (1402) 1–302b
Byzantine Empire 2–502b-a
Constantinople 3–552b
BĀYAZĪD II 2–137a
BAYBARS AL-BUNDUQDĀRĪ 2–138a
Azhar, al- 2–27b
crusades 4–32a,b
Baybars II 3–398b
Bayeux manuscripts 1–256b
BAYEUX TAPESTRY 2–139a; 1–212b, 273b
arms and armor 1–523a
draft animals 1–93b
wooden castles 3–145a

Bāyezīd I
See Bāyazīd I, Yildirim
BAYLAKAN 2–139a; 1–123b, 124b-125a, 472b, 473b
BAY SYSTEM 2–139b
alternating supports 1–225b
basilica 2–125a
***BAYT* 2–140a**
Bayt al-Ḥikma 1–391b; 3–45a, 313a
Bayt al-mal 3–34a
Bayundur
Aq Qoyunlu 1–352a
Bazzazistan
See Also Bedestan
***BDEŠX* 2–140a**; 1–488b
Bear
beast epic 2–141a,b-142a
cookery 3–581b
hunting laws 1–301a
Béarn
Crown of Aragon 1–408b, 410a
Beast canon table 3–66b
BEAST EPIC 2–140b
Dutch literature 4–319a
Ecbasis captivi 4–369a
Latin epic 4–495b
See Also Bestiary
See Also Fables
BEATIFICATION 2–142b
canonization 3–67b
Beatrice
Divine Comedy 4–96a-98a
Beatrice of Nazareth 2–160b
Beatrice of Provence 1–253b
Beatrice of Swabia 1–161a
Beatrijs 4–320a
Beatrijs van Nazareth
mysticism 4–319a
Beatriz of Portugal 3–137b
BEATUS MANUSCRIPTS 2–143b
Dominicus 4–255b
Emeterius of Tábara 4–436b
Ende 4–450b
See Also Beatus of Liébana
Beatus of Liébana 1–630b, 631a; 2–143b
Tractatus de apocalypsis 1–343b, 344a, 630b, 631a
Beaucaire
fairs 4–586a
Beauchamp, Sir William
See Clanvowe, Sir John
Beaujeu, Anne de 3–333b
Beaujeu, Guillaume de 3–304b
Beaujeu, Pierre de 3–333b
BEAUMANOIR, PHILIPPE DE 2–143b
Coutumes de Beauvaisis 3–674b
Beaumont-en-Argonne
rural commune 3–500b
BEAUNEVEU, ANDRÉ 2–145a
Beaunois 2–427a
Beauseant
Knights Templars 3–304b
Beautiful and the Suitable, The (Augustine) 1–646b
BEAUTY AIDS, COSMETICS 2–145b
botany 2–347b
costume 3–624a
dyes 4–326a
Beauvais
commune 3–496a,b
stoneware 3–238a
Beaver 2–243a, 244a
bestiaries 2–204b-205a
cookery 3–581b
BEBO OF BAMBERG 2–150b
Bec, Abbey of 1–311b
Béchada, Grégoire
Chanson d'Antioche 3–255a
Becket, Gilbert 2–60a
BECKET, THOMAS, SAINT 2–151a; 4–471a
anointing of kings 1–308b
Anselm of Canterbury 1–311b
biography 2–236a
Canterbury 3–83a,b, 84a
Clarendon, Constitutions of 3–409b
Henry II of England 1–147a
murder 4–420a
BECKET, THOMAS À
Bangor bishops 2–71b
BEDE 2–153a; 1–262a; 2–174a
acrostics 1–218a
Adamnan, Saint 1–52b
Aidan of Lindisfarne 1–107a
Alfred the Great 1–164b
altars 1–225a
Ambrosius Aurelianus 2–2b
angelology 1–250b
Anglo-Latin poetry 1–254b
Anglo-Saxon England 1–289a; 4–454b, 455a,b, 458a,b
Anglo-Saxon literature 1–274a, 277a, 284a
Antichrist doctrine 1–321b
Arthurian literature 1–564a
Ascension 1–582a
astrology 1–606a-b
astronomy 1–610b
Augustine of Canterbury 1–644b, 645a-b
barbarian invasions 2–96b
Benedict Biscop 2–168a
Bible 2–211b, 212b
Brut, The 2–393a
Cædmon 2–221a; 3–7b
calendar 3–19b, 20b
classical literary studies 3–432b
Dál Riata 4–78a
De die judicii 1–280a
doctor of the church 4–234b
Easter 4–364b
encyclopedias and dictionaries 4–448a
exegesis 4–542b, 546a, 547b-548a, 548b-549a, 550a
Historia ecclesiastica 1–166b, 275b, 277b, 347b
oral literature 1–274b
postpatristic view 4–372b
travel accounts 1–333a
***BEDESTAN* 2–156a**
Bedford, William
Chester plays 3–299a
BEDLAM 2–157a
Bedouins 4–596b
language 1–377a
poetry 1–398a-400a
pre-Islamic Arabia 1–370b-371b
Beef
cookery 3–581b
Hungarian gray cattle 1–301b
Beekeeping 1–100a,b
Byzantium 1–79a
Cistercians 3–404a
Slavs 1–98b
Beer
See Brewing
Beg 3–209b
Beghards
See Beguines and Beghards
Beginnings of an Explanation of the Epistle to the Romans (Augustine) 1–649a
BEGUINES AND BEGHARDS 2–147b; 3–368b
BEGUINS 2–162a
Behetría
See Benefactoría
Beira
agriculture 1–85a
BEIRUT 2–163b
BEK'A OPIZARI 2–164b
Béker, Sir ben Abu 3–76a
Bekynton, Thomas, Bishop
"Bekynton Anthology" 1–319a
Bel 3–30b
Belach Mugna, Battle of (908) 3–602a
Béla I of Hungary, King 4–6a-b
Béla II of Hungary, King
water buffalo 1–298b
Béla III of Hungary, King 2–494a
camels 1–296b
Béla IV of Hungary, King
Bogomils 2–295a
Belchite 1–406a
"Bele Doete" 3–263a
"Bele Oriolanz" 3–263a
Beleth, John 4–223a
"Bele Yolanz" 3–263a
Bel fiore dança 4–88b
Belgium
archives 1–447b
banalité 2–69a
religious communities 3–368b
See Also Flanders
Belgrade
See Beograd
Belibasta 3–190b
BELISARIOS 2–165a
Vandals 2–91b
Bellatores 3–358a
Bella Venus, A (Francesc de la Via) 3–173b
Belle Dame sans merci, La (Alain Chartier) 3–275b
Belleperche, Pierre de
See Pierre de Belleperche
"Bell Harry"
Christ Church Cathedral (Canterbury) 3–83b
Bellifortis (Konrad Kyeser) 1–318a
illustration 3–65b
Bellin, George
Chester plays 3–299a
BELLINI, JACOPO 2–165a
frescoes 1–226b
sketchbook 4–292a
BELLS 2–165b; 3–28b
altar apparatus 1–225a
bronze and brass 2–384b
Bulgarian 2–417a
Bell tower
See Campanile
Bellum civile (Lucan) 3–331b
Bellum intestinum 1–181a
Bellville Breviary 2–117a
Beltraneja, le
See Juana of Castile
Belvoir Castle 4–24b
figural carving 4–25b
BEMA 2–167a; 1–442b
Bemoin, Prince
slave trade 2–269a
Benabila 1–515a
Ben Asher Bible 2–210b
Bendimahi River
See Arest River
Benedetti, Giovanni Battista 1–438a
BENEDETTO ANTELAMI 2–167a
***BENEDICAMUS DOMINO* 2–167b**
conductus 3–532a,b
Benedict X, Antipope 1–330b

Benedict XIII, Antipope 1–108b, 330b; 2–16a
Constance, Council of (1414-1418) 3–649a
Crown of Aragon 1–417b
Eiximenis, Francesc 4–416a
Great Schism 3–365b, 366a, 645b
papal conclave 3–524b
Pisa, Council of (1409) 1–147b
Benedict VIII, Pope
Henry II of Germany 2–150b
Nicene Creed 3–677a
Benedict XI, Pope 3–362a
Arnald of Villanova 1–537b
Florence 4–99a-b
Philip IV of France 3–643b-644a
Benedict XII, Pope 1–14a; 4–109a
Avignonese papacy 3–362a-364a, 377a
breviary 2–372b
church union 2–109b
Curia 3–364a
BENEDICT BISCOP, SAINT 2–168a; 4–421b, 458b
Bede 2–153b, 155a
manuscript authenticity 1–336a
Benedictine Office, The 1–280a, 281a
BENEDICTINE RULE 2–171a
Benedict of Aniane 2–168a
Benedict of Nursia 2–169a-170b
Camaldolese order 3–56a
canonical hours 3–67a
Carthusians 3–118b
Cassian 3–122b
celibacy laws 3–216b
Celtic church 2–382a
church reforms 3–347b, 368a
Cistercian order 3–402a, 403a, 406a
Cluniac order 3–467b, 468b
Divine Office 4–222a, 229b-230a
election of abbots 4–421b
Ethelwold 4–517b
Old English translation 1–286a,b
Order of Aviz 2–17a
West Saxon dialect 1–276b
BENEDICTINES 2–171b
Ancrene Riwle 1–243a
Angelus 1–252b
Anglo-Norman literature 1–261b
Baudri of Bourgueil 2–132a
Bavaria 2–134a
bells 2–165b-166a
benedictions 2–178a
Bernard of Clairvaux 2–191a
calendar 3–19b
Candidus of Fulda 3–63b
chapter house design 3–266b
chapter meeting 3–265a,b
chivalric orders 3–303b
Christian of Stablo 3–311b
Cluniac Order 3–468b
Crown of Aragon 1–410b
Dead, Office of the 4–117b
Divine Office 4–222a, 225b-226a, 229a,b
historical writing 3–326a
Vulgate 2–211a-b
BENEDICTIONAL 2–176b
BENEDICTIONS 2–177a
Celtic church 3–231a
ordination rites 3–442b
BENEDICT OF ANIANE 2–168a
Benedictine Rule 2–170b
benedictions 2–178a
Carolingians 3–111b, 112a
church reforms 3–347b
Cluniac Order 3–368b
Divine Office 4–222a
liturgy 2–172b
Virgin, Office of the 2–325b
Benedict of Arezzo
Angelus 1–252a
BENEDICT OF NURSIA, SAINT 2–168b; 1–165b
Aelfric 1–62a
Benedictine Rule 2–171a
canticles 3–84b
monasticism 3–343a
See Also Church, early
Benedict of Saint Peter's 4–223a
Benedict the Levite
See Benedictus Levita
Benedictus 3–84b
BENEDICTUS LEVITA 2–178b; 4–125a
Benediktbeuern 2–134a
Carmina Burana 3–97b; 4–380a
Benediktbeuern Passion 4–267a
Benefactoría 1–630a; 3–131b
BENEFICE, ECCLESIASTICAL 2–179a; 3–374b
annate 1–304b
Avignonese papacy 3–364a,b
chaplain 3–264b
charistikion 3–268a
Chartier, Alain 3–275a
Clarendon, Constitutions of 3–409b
Clement VI, Pope 3–439a
datary, apostolic 4–107a
BENEFICE, LAY 2–179b
Islamic 1–105b
Benefit of clergy
Henry II of England 2–151b; 3–410a
Beneit 1–262a
Bene of Florence
Candelabrum 4–174b
BENEVENTAN RITE 2–180a
choral manuscripts 2–181a
Benevento, Battle of (1266) 3–196b; 4–60b, 95b
Bengal, Bay of
maps 4–553b
Benin 4–562a
Benjamin I, Patriarch 3–594b
Benjamin ben Moses Nahāwendī
exegesis 4–539a
BENJAMIN OF TUDELA 2–181b; 1–154a; 2–51a
Baṭṭūṭa, Ibn 2–130a
dyeing 4–328a
travel accounts 1–332a; 2–103b
BENNO OF OSNABRÜCK 2–182a
BENOÎT DE SAINTE-MAURE 2–182a; 1–261b; 2–182a, 509b
French chronicles 2–236b; 3–331a
Troy story 2–522b
Ben Sira
See Sira, Simeon ben Jesus ben
Benvenuto da Imola 2–289a
BENZO OF ALBA 2–182a
Beograd
Bulgaria 2–401b, 409b, 410a
Hungarians 2–493a
Beornrad 1–142b
***BEOWULF* 2–182b**
***BEOWULF* 2–221b**; 3–325b
background 1–276b-280b
Brut, The 2–394a
Christian warrior 2–216b
date of composition 1–275b
oral poetry 1–274b
scholarship 1–287a,b
BERBERS 2–185b
Aghlabids 1–71b
Almoravids 1–198a
cavalry 3–208b, 209a
Córdoba 3–598b
Donatism 4–259b
Kutāma 1–72a
language 1–378a; 2–186a,b
Tūmart, Ibn 1–193b
BERCEO, GONZALO DE 2–186b; 1–152b
cuaderna vía 4–63a
Berengaria of Navarre 4–40b, 420a, 468a
***BERENGARII IMPERATORIS GESTA* 2–188b**; 4–496a
Berengar I of Friuli 2–188b; 4–496a
Louis the Blind 2–428b-429a
Berengar of Italy
See Berengar I of Friuli
BERENGAR OF TOURS 2–188a
Adelman of Liège 1–54b
councils 3–634b, 635a
Eusebius Bruno 4–523b
exegesis 2–213a; 4–543a
investiture controversy 1–125b
Bérenger of Rennes 2–379a
Berenguela of León 2–270b; 3–133b
Berenguer I Ramón 3–176a
Berenguer II Ramón 3–177b-178a
Berenguer III, Ramón 3–76a
Berenguer IV, Ramón 3–570a
Berenguer, Joan 3–171a
Berenguer d'Anoya 3–170a
Berenguer de Entenza 1–191a
Berenguer de Palol
See Palol, Berenguer de
Beresford Hope cross 4–437b
Bergamo
fairs 4–587a
Bergen
Black Death 2–261a-b
Bergen op Zoom
fairs 4–586b
Bergfried
See Dungeons
Berghe, Jan van den 4–322b
Berguedà, Guillem de 3–164b
Berit milah
See Circumcision, Jewish
BERKELEY, WILLIAM 2–188b
Berkeri
See Berkri
BERKRI 2–189a; 1–513a
Berlin-Cőlln
Brandenburg 2–360b
BERLINGHIERI, BONAVENTURA 2–189a
Berlin Passion, Master of the 4–488b, 489a
BERMEJO, BARTOLOMÉ 2–189b
Bermudo II of Asturias-León 1–628a
Bermudo III of Asturias-León 1–628b
Bernard de Tremelay 3–304b
BERNARDINO OF SIENA, SAINT 2–195b; 2–13b
contraception 3–572b; 4–144a
preaching missions 3–368a
Bernardo Ciuffagni
See Ciuffagni, Bernardo
BERNARDO DA VENEZIA 2–196b
Bernard VII of Armagnac 3–270b
Bernard III of Besalú 3–178a
Bernard of Bessa 2–315b
Bernard of Bologna
Introductiones prosaici dictaminis 4–175a
BERNARD OF CHARTRES 2–189b
Bernard Silvester 2–194b
classical literary studies 1–331b; 3–434a
BERNARD OF CLAIRVAUX, SAINT 2–190b; 1–607a; 3–244b; 4–101a, 419a
Abelard 1–18a, 19a
Arnold of Brescia 1–539b-540a

BERNARD OF CLAIRVAUX, SAINT (cont.)
baptism 2–84a
Berceo, Gonzalo de 2–187b
biblical poetry 2–230b
Burgundy, Duchy of 2–428a
cardinals 3–94b
Carthusians 3–119a
Christology 3–322b
Cistercian chant 3–402a,b
Cistercians 3–355a, 403b
crusades 2–216a; 4–20b, 37b
Dante 4–94b
decretum 4–129b
doctor of the church 4–234b
exegesis 2–213a,b; 4–543a
heresy 3–186b
Himmerod 1–43a
Knights Templars 3–304b
reform 3–352b
Scholasticism 3–357b
sermons 2–228a
Bernard of Gui 4–247b-248a
Bernard of Italy, King 3–112a
Bernard of Meun
dictamen 4–175a
Bernard of Pavia
decretals 4–123b-124a
BERNARD OF SANTIAGO 2–194b
Bernard of Septimania 3–174b
BERNARD OF SOISSONS 2–194b
Bernard of the Lateran 4–223a
Bernard of Tiron 3–354b
Bernard of Trier
alchemy 1–138a
Bernard of Vézelay 4–37b
BERNARD SILVESTER 2–194b
allegory 1–183a-b
housekeeping manual 4–579a
Bernard Silvestris
See Bernard Silvester
Bernart de Cabrera 1–416a
BERNART DE VENTADORN 2–197a; 4–419b
contrafactum 3–576b
Bernat Metge
See Metge, Bernat
Bernay, Alexandre de
Roman d'Alexandre 1–152b
Bernay Cathedral 1–255b
Berners, Lord (John Bourchier) 3–325a
Bernerton strophe 4–380a
See Also Eckenstrophe
Bernhard of Saxony 2–235a
See Billungs
Bernicia, Kingdom of 4–454b
BERNOLD OF CONSTANCE 2–197b
Council of Piacenza 3–449a
dispensation 4–217a-b
Divine Office 4–223a
Bernold of Sankt Blasien
See Bernold of Constance
Bernold of Strasbourg, Bishop 4–507b
Berno of Cluny 3–469a
Berno of Reichenau 4–223a
BERNORINUS 2–197b
BERNWARD 2–197b
beatification 2–143a
Beroia
See Aleppo
Berolinensis prima (decretals) 4–123a
Berossus 1–604a
Béroul
See Tristan, Roman de
BERRUGUETE, PEDRO 2–198a
BERSERKS 2–198a
Bersuire, Pierre 1–183b; 4–449a
exegesis 4–544b
Berte aus grans piés (Adenet le Roi) 1–55a; 3–261b
BERTHARIUS 2–199a
Berthold, Saint
Carmelites 3–96b
Berthold of Mossburg 1–129b
BERTHOLD VON HOLLE 2–199a
BERTHOLD VON REGENSBURG 2–199b
Albertus Magnus 1–128b
marriage 3–359b
Bertken, Zuster 4–321a
Bertoldus de Holle
See Berthold von Holle
Bertrada
Pepin the Short 3–268a
Bertrada of Anjou
Philip I of France 3–449a
BERTRAM, MEISTER 2–201a
BERTRAND DE BAR-SUR-AUBE 2–201b; 3–258b
Bertrand de Déaulx 3–478b
Bertrand de Got
See Clement V, Pope
Bertrand du Guesclin
Aquitaine 1–368a
Brittany 2–380b
cannon 3–151b
BERTRAN DE BORN 2–201b
Bertrand of Toulouse
crusades 4–37a
BERTUCCIO 2–202a
Bertucius
See Bertuccio
BERWICK, TREATY OF (1357) **2–202b**; 4–111a
Berwick-on-Tweed
Exchequer 4–534a
Berytus
See Beirut
Besagues 1–530b
Besalú, Council of 3–177b
Besançon 1–58b; 2–424a-b, 426a
architecture 2–426b
Diet of (1157) 4–427b
BESANT 2–203a
Besant de Dieu (Guillaume le Clerc de Normandie) 1–264a
Besesten
See Bedestan
BESSARION 2–203a
Bestiaire (Philippe de Thaon) 1–188b, 262a, 271a
***BESTIAIRE D'AMOUR* 2–203b**; 1–188b; 2–205b
Bestiaire divin (Guillaume le Clerc de Normandie) 1–188b; 2–205b
BESTIARY 2–203b; 2–204a, 242b-243b
Anglo-Norman literature 1–262a, 271a
Arabic 1–379b
Catalan 3–168b
French 1–188b; 2–203b, 205b
BETANIA 2–207a
Beth din
See Jewish communal self-government
Béthencourt, Jean de 3–62a-63a
Beth ha-
See Schools, Jewish
Bethlehem
art and architecture 4–21b, 24b, 335a
crusades 4–21b, 32a
Frederick II 4–51b
Bethlehem Royal Hospital
See Bedlam
BETROTHAL 2–207b
Byzantine 4–594b
Jewish 4–606a
Western European 4–599b, 610a
BEVERAGES, ISLAMIC 2–208b
See Also Cookery, Islamic
***BEVERS SAGA* 2–209b**
Beweddung
See Betrothal
Beylerbey 3–678b
Beza, Theodore
Du droit des magistrats 3–521b
Bezaleel
See Einhard
Béziers
Albigensian Crusade 3–188a
Crown of Aragon 1–410a-b
Biar 1–412a
Bibbesworth, Nicholas 3–582b
BIBLE 2–210b
Alcuin 1–143a
alphabetization 1–205a,b
Antichrist doctrine 1–321b
antiphon 1–328b
art, Anglo-Norman 1–258a
art, Celtic 3–221b, 223b
art, early Christian 4–355b-357a
canon table 3–66a
Christian Hebraists 3–313b
illustrated 2–216a, 222b, 223a; 3–276b, 459b
paraphrases, Old English 1–279b-280a
schools, Celtic 2–220a; 3–231b
translations, Anglo-Norman 1–262b
translations, Old English 1–275a, 285a,b
Vulgate 3–336b
See Also Exegesis
BIBLE, ARMENIAN 2–217a
exegesis 2–214b
BIBLE, CISTERCIAN 2–218a
exegesis 2–213a-b
BIBLE, FRENCH 2–218b
vernacular 2–215a
BIBLE, GLOSSES AND COMMENTARIES (IRISH) 2–220a
BIBLE, OLD AND MIDDLE ENGLISH 2–220b
exegesis 1–244a; 4–545a-550b
translations 2–211b
vernacular 2–215a
Bible historiale (Guyart des Moulins) 2–219a-b
***BIBLE MORALISÉE* 2–222b**
water clock illustration 3–459b
Bible of Jumièges 1–258a
Bible of the Poor
See Biblia pauperum
Bible of the Thirteenth Century 2–219b
Biblia parva (Pere Pasqual) 3–167b
***BIBLIA PAUPERUM* 2–223a**; 2–216a
Chartres Cathedral 3–276b
Biblical handbooks
alphabetization 1–204a,b
BIBLICAL INTERPRETATION 2–223b
allegory 1–180a-b
Ibn Ezra 1–23b
Jewish 4–538b
Latin 4–542a
Middle English 4–545a
Old English 4–548b
School of Saint Victor 1–51a
See Also Exegesis
BIBLICAL POETRY, GERMAN 2–224b
Bibliographies
alphabetization 1–204a
Bibliotheca
See Photios

Bicester
  Black Death 2–262a
Bidpai 1–379a
BIDUINO 2–233b
Biel, Friedrich 3–212b
BIEL, GABRIEL 2–233b
  Brethren of the Common Life 2–368b-369a
  Christology 3–324a
  Devotio Moderna 4–167a
  nominalism 3–371a
Bien Advisé et Mal Advisé 4–265a
Biffa
  See Trebuchet
Biga 1–418a, 419a; 2–104b
Bigorre 1–410a
Bijns, Anna 4–322b-323a
Bika Valley 4–81a
Biket, Robert 1–268a
Bilād al-Sūdān 1–198b, 199a
Bilbais 4–39a
Bilbao 2–127a
  trade 4–558a
Bills of exchange 2–78a
  fairs 4–584b
BILLUNGS 2–235a
  Adalbert of Bremen 1–47a
  Bernhard I 2–235a
  Bernhard II 2–235a
  Hermann 2–235a
  Magnus 2–235a-b
  Ordulf 2–235a
  Thietmar 2–235a
Bimaristan
  See Hospitals, Islamic
Binbirdirek 4–334b
Binchois 3–256b; 4–567b
Bingöl Plateau 4–522a
Biograd 4–5b
Biographical Dictionary (Ibn Khallikān) 1–634a
Biography
  chronicles 3–328a
  Icelandic sagas 4–614a
Biography, English
  Arthurian literature 1–574b
  Chaucer, Geoffrey 3–284b-286a
BIOGRAPHY, FRENCH 2–235b
BIOGRAPHY, ISLAMIC 2–237b
Biography, religious
  See Hagiography
BIOGRAPHY, SECULAR 2–239a
  Byzantine 2–517b-518a
  Carolingian 4–412b-413a
BIOLOGY 2–240b
Birch Island (Björkö) 2–247b
Birds
  food animals 1–301a; 3–581b
Birger Jarl, King 4–505b
Birgisson, Jón 4–411b
BIRGITTA, SAINT 2–246b
Biringuccio 2–384b; 3–267a
BIRKA 2–247b
  bracteates 2–355b
Birōs 3–618b
Birr, Synod of (697) 1–52b
Birrus
  See Birōs
Birs Nimrud (Borsippa) 1–332a
BIRUNI, MUHAMMAD IBN AHMAD ABU 'L-RAYHAN AL- 2–248a; 1–618a, 619b, 620b
  calendar 3–25a
  observational astronomy 1–622a
Bisat
  See Rugs and Carpets, Islamic
Biscay, Bay of
  Asturias-León 1–625a
  Basques 2–125b
  Castilians 3–128b
Biscop Baducing
  See Benedict Biscop, Saint
BISHAPUR 2–251b
  barbotine technique 2–101a
Bishavur
  See Bishapur
Bishop 3–440b-442b, 443a-445a
BISHOPS' SAGAS 2–252a; 1–537a; 4–612b
Bishr ibn Abī Khāzim 1–399b
Bīsitūn 1–332b
Biskupa sögur
  See Bishops' Sagas
Bison
  food animal 1–301a
Bisot, Godeffroi 3–304a
***BITEROLF UND DIETLEIB* 2–253a**
  Ambraser Heldenbuch 1–230a
Bithynia
  bridge 4–334a
  Komnenoi 1–245a
  monasteries 1–241a
  Palaiologoi 1–246a,b
  Turks 2–500a, 600b
Biṭrīq al-baṭāriqa
  See Archon ton archonton
Biṭrūjī, al- 1–614b, 621a
BITSHVINTA 2–253b
Bivaly 1–298b
***BJARKAMÁL* 2–254a**; 4–388a, 390a, 391b
***BJARNAR SAGA HÍTDŒLAKAPPA* 2–255a**; 4–612b-613a
Bjarni Herjulfsson 4–555a
BJARNI KOLBEINSSON 2–255b
Bjelo Osero 4–555a
Björkö
  See Birch Island
Bjǫrn á Haugi, King 2–359a
Bjǫrn Arngeirsson 2–255a
Blachernai Palace (Constantinople) 4–45b, 334b
BLACHERNITISSA 2–256b
Black Book of the Admiralty, The 1–56a; 3–570a
BLACK DEATH 2–257a
  Aleppo 1–145b
  Alexandria 1–154b
  Anatolia 1–240a
  Andrea da Firenze 1–244b
  anti Semitism 1–341b; 3–481b
  Aragon, Crown of 1–416a, 419a-b
  Barcelona 2–104a,b
  Bordeaux 2–328b
  Caffa 3–12b
  Cairo 3–14b
  Carmelites 3–96b
  Carthusians 3–119a
  celibacy laws 3–217b
  Champagne 3–250a
  chaplains 3–264b
  Cistercians 3–404a, 405b
  Clement VI, Pope 3–439b
  costume 3–622b
  Denmark 4–149b
  Edward III 4–398a,b
  Egypt, Islamic 4–406b
  England 4–484a,b
  estate management 4–514b
  population 1–94b; 4–142a,b
  See Also Death and Burial, in Europe
Blackfriars 4–393b
Black monks
  See Benedictines
BLACKS 2–268a
Black Sea
  Anatolia 1–239b, 240a-b
  asses 1–295b
  Caucasia 3–193b, 195b
  Crimea 3–678b
  Danes 4–554a
  Huns 2–90a
  trade 4–557b
Black Sheep Turkomen
  See Qara Qoyunlu
Black Stone 1–372a, 375a
Bladín de Cornualha 1–576a
Blanche Anne of France
  Cleomadés 1–55a
***BLANCHEFLOUR ET FLORENCE* 2–271a**; 1–268b
Blanche of Anjou 1–415b
Blanche of Bourbon, Queen 3–137a
BLANCHE OF CASTILE 2–270b; 4–420a
  Bonaventure, Saint 2–317b
  Champagne 3–247b
Blanche of Navarre
  Champagne 3–247b
Blandin de Cornualha 3–173a
Blasco of Alagón 1–412a
Blasme des fames, Le 1–269b
BLASPHEMY 2–271b
Blathmac 1–111a
BLAZON 2–272b
Blemmydes, Nikephoros 1–614a
BLESSED VIRGIN MARY, LITTLE OFFICE OF 2–273b
  canonical hours 2–325a; 3–67b
Blessings
  See Benedictions
Blickling homilies 1–276a, 281b, 284b
BLIGGER VON STEINACH 2–274a
Blind arch 1–423b, 424
BLOCK BOOK 2–275a
  ars moriendi 1–547b
Block capital 3–90b
Blois 3–243b-245a
Blondel, David 4–126a
BLONDEL DE NESLE 2–276a
  contrafactum 3–576a
Blood circulation 1–377b
Bloodletting 2–99a
BLOOD LIBEL 2–276a
Blood money, Germanic
  See Wergild
BLOOD MONEY, ISLAMIC LAW 2–276b
Blood right 4–425b, 427a
Bnabel
  See Benabila
Boar
  cookery 3–581b
Bobbio Missal 3–230a
Bobovac 2–338a, 341b
Boccaccino di Chellino 2–277b
BOCCACCIO, GIOVANNI 2–277b; 1–180a; 2–522b; 4–102b
  biography 2–239b, 240a
  Black Death 2–259a-260a, 261a, 267a
  Chaucer, Geoffrey 2–285b, 286b, 287a
  fabliaux 4–577a
  translations, Catalan 3–169b
Boccanegra family 4–558a
BOCHKA 2–290b
BODEL, JEAN 2–290b
  congé 3–536b
  fabliaux 4–574a
  Jeu de St. Nicolas 4–264a
Bodin, Constantine 2–407b
Boendale, Jan van 4–319b
Boeotia 3–156a-b

BOETHIUS, ANICIUS MANLIUS SEVERINUS 1–34b, 277b, 434b; 2–291a
Alfred the Great 1–164b
allegory 1–188b, 189a
Aquinas, Saint Thomas 1–355a, 357b
Aristotelianism 1–460a, 461b
ars antiqua 1–543b
Asser 1–593a
Bacon, Roger 2–36a-b
Bovo II of Corvei 2–350b
Carolingian renaissance 3–100a
Christology 3–321a
Consolation of Philosophy 1–182b-183a, 280b; 3–283b-284a
counterpoint 3–657a
dialectics 4–169a
dualism 4–298a
Gilbert de la Porrée 1–119a
philosophy 2–241a; 4–510b
Theodoric the Ostrogoth 2–93b
theology 3–342b
translations, Old English 1–284a
Boeve de Haumtone 1–267a; 2–201b
Bevers saga 2–209b
Bogoliubovo Palace 2–293b
BOGOLIUBSKII, ANDREI 2–293b
Bogomil 2–294a
BOGOMILISM 2–294a
Alexios I Komnenos 1–158b
Bulgaria 2–405b
Cathars 3–181a,b
Docetism 4–233a-b
early church 3–340a
theology 2–467a
"Bogomil tombstones" 2–341a
BOHEMIA-MORAVIA 2–297b
Angevins 1–253b
anthologies, Latin 1–319b
arms and armor 1–528a
Bavaria 2–133a
Black Death 2–262b
brewing 2–375a
butler 2–434b
Celestine foundations 3–214b
chamberlain 3–242a
Cisiojanus 3–21b
Cistercians 3–404a
clergy, Roman 3–366a
Cosmas of Prague 3–614a
dictamen 4–176a
German migrants 1–97b-98a
Hussite wars 3–65b
monasteries 2–172a
reform movement 3–649b-650a
serfdom 1–102a
BOHEMIAN BRETHREN 2–305b
Bohemian Forest Mountains 2–132b
BOHEMOND I, PRINCE OF ANTIOCH 2–308a
Alexios I Komnenos 1–158a-b; 2–494a
Anatolia 4–35a
Antioch 1–158a-b; 2–495a; 4–30b
Cilician Kingdom 3–391b
crusades 1–158a-b; 4–34a,b, 35a-b, 36b, 301
Danishmendids 4–91b
propaganda 4–20a
Bohemond III, Prince of Antioch 4–38b
Bohemond IV, Prince of Antioch 3–395a
Boii 2–297b
Boileau, Etienne
Livre des métiers 4–328b
***BOIS PROTAT* 2–309b**
BOISSEAU 2–310a
Bojana 2–416a-b, 417a
Boke of Cupide, The (Sir John Clanvowe) 3–408a
Boke of Curtasye 3–661a
Boke of Kervinge (Wynkyn de Worde) 3–661b
Boke of Nurture (John Russell) 1–135b
Bokšić, Žore 2–341a
BOLL 2–310b
Bollandists
Acta sanctorum 2–519a
BOLNISI SION 2–311a
Bologna
Antonio da Vincenzo 1–342b
Cathars 3–190b
Eugenius IV 3–652b
money markets 2–78b
vineyards 1–87a
BOLOGNA, UNIVERSITY OF 2–311b
Aristotelianism 1–461a
Bartolo da Sassoferrato 2–115a
Boncompagno 2–320a
Bulgarus 2–417b
Cistercians 3–405a
Corpus iuris civilis 3–609b
dictamen 4–173b
surgery 2–98b
Bolognese, Franco 1–579a
Bolos of Mendes
Physika kai mystika 1–135b
Bolts 2–353b-354a
Bolzano 2–132b
fairs 4–586a, 587a
Bombasts 3–625b
Bona, Giovanni 2–171b
Bonaccorso of Milan 3–182a
Bonadies Codex
See Faenza Codex
Bona of Luxembourg 3–269a
Bonatti, Guido 1–607b
BONAVENTURE, SAINT 2–313a; 1–128a, 462a; 3–641b, 642a
angelology 1–250a
ars praedicandi 1–555b
Augustinism 1–660b
Bacon, Roger 2–35b, 36b
baptism interpretation 2–84a
Biel, Gabriel 2–234a
Contemplatio 3–167a
doctor of the church 4–234b
ecclesiology 4–375a,b
exegesis 4–544b
Paris, University of 1–354a, 543b
BONCOMPAGNO (BUONCOMPAGNO) OF SIGNA **2–320a**
dictamen 4–174b, 176b
BONDOL, JEAN 2–320b; 2–129b
Bone carvings
Coptic art 3–587b
Bon enfant 3–661a
Bonet, Honoré 3–169a
L'arbre des batailles 3–302a
Bonfils of Tarascon, Immanuel 1–613a
Bonhomme of Brittany 4–245b
Dominican studies 4–245b
Boniface VII, Antipope 1–330b
papal conclave 3–523b
Boniface I, Pope 1–331b; 3–213b
BONIFACE VIII, POPE 2–323a; 3–642a
advocate 1–59b
Arnald of Villanova 1–537b
Arnolfo di Cambio 1–541a
Augustinus Triumphus 2–1b
Ausculta fili 2–3b
burial practices 4–120b
cameo collections 1–335b
cardinals 3–95b
Celestine V, Pope 3–214a
Cilician-Roman church union 3–394b
Clericis laicos 3–447b
clerics, degradation of 4–133b-134a
Crown of Aragon 1–414b
Curia 3–363b
Dante 4–98a,b-99a
Disputatio inter clericum et militem 4–218a
doctor of the church 4–234a
Dominicans 4–251b
Donation of Constantine 4–259a
ecclesiology 4–376a
Egidius Colonna 4–400a
heresy 4–483b, 484b
John Duns Scotus 4–308b
law 3–352b
Liber sextus 4–133b
papal power 3–354a
Philip IV the Fair 3–438b, 515a, 643b-644a
Ricciardi company 2–77b
Unam Sanctum 2–418b
See Also Church, Latin: 1305 to 1500
Boniface IX, Pope
angelus 1–252b
Great Schism 3–365b, 645b
BONIFACE, SAINT 2–134a
BONIFACE, SAINT 2–321a
anointing 1–308b
Benedictines 2–170a-b, 172a
Carolingians 3–106a
celibacy laws 3–216b
England, Anglo-Saxon 4–458b
horsemeat prohibition 1–300a
Martel, Charles 3–272a
riddles 1–254b
Salzburg 2–4b
BONIFACE OF MONTFERRAT 2–323a; 4–31b
chronicles 3–332a
Crete 3–678b
crusades 4–42b-43a,b, 44b, 46b, 47a
Bonifaci Ferrer
See Ferrer, Boniface
Boni homines 3–658b
BONINO DA CAMPIONE 2–324b
Bonizo of Sutri
altar apparatus 1–221b
ordo laicus 3–358b
BONNANO (BONNANUS) **DA PISA 2–324b**
Bonne of Armagnac 3–272b
Bonnes villes
See Commune
Bonsenyor, Jafuda 3–168a
Bonsignori, Bonifazio 2–76b
Bonsignori, Orlando 2–76b
Bonsignori company 2–76b, 77b
Bonvicino da Riva 3–665a
Bonvicino de Ripa
angelus 1–252b
Book
See Manuscripts and books
Book illumination
Anglo-Norman art 1–258a
Bookkeeping
See Accounting
Book of Adam and Eve 1–347b
Book of Armagh 1–347a
Book of Astronomy (Levi ben Gerson) 1–613a
cross-staff 4–12a-b
Book of Balances (Jābir ibn Ḥayyān) 1–136a
Book of Brome 3–299b
Book of Causes (Proclus) 1–357b
Book of Ceremonies 3–552b
Book of Cerne 4–280b-281a

Book of Creatures (al-Aṣma'ī) 4–443a
Book of Curtesye 3–661a-b
Book of Deeds 1–413a
Book of Deer 3–407a
Book of demonstrations (Eutychios) 4–525b
Book of divine consolation (Meister Eckhart) 4–381a
Book of Durrow 4–64b
Book of Ecclesiasticus (Simeon ben Jesus ben Sira) 3–15b
Book of 83 Different Questions (Augustin) 1–54a
Book of Eloquence and Exposition (al-J?al9hiẓ) 1–379a,b
Book of Enlivenment and Good Company (Abū Ḥayyān al-Tawḥīdī) 1–381a
Book of Excerpts (Richard of Saint Victor) 4–448b
Book of expressions or words (Ibn al-Sikkīt) 4–443a
Book of Faiths and Beliefs, The (Saadiah Gaon) 1–345b
Book of Fortune and Prudence (Bernat Metge) 3–173b
Book of Fortune and Prudence
 See Libre de Fortuna e Prudencia
Book of Friar Bernat (Francesc de la Via) 3–173b
Book of Friar Bernat
 See Libre de Fra Bernat
Book of good advice (Jaume Roig) 3–173b
Book of Great Conjunctions (Abū Ma'-shar) 1–386a
Book of Hearths 4–138a
"Book of Holy Remedies" (Henry, duke of Lancaster) 1–263b
BOOK OF HOURS 2–325a
 botany 2–348b
 Boucicaut Master 2–349b
 canonical hours 3–67b
 Catherine of Cleves, Master of 3–192b
 death and burial 4–121b
 Marian office 2–274a
Book of Jean d'Ibelin 4–71b
Book of Judith 4–26a
Book of Just Rewards, The (Ibn al-Dāya) 1–380b
Book of Long Narratives (al-Dīnawarī) 4–188a
Book of Misers (al-Jāḥiẓ) 1–379b
Book of Plants (al-Dīnawarī) 4–188a
Book of Remedy (Ibn Sīnā) 1–136b
"Book of Rights"(Cormac mac Cuilennáin) 3–602a
"Book of Sins" 1–263a
Book of Songs (Abū 'l-Faraj al-Isfahānī) 1–381a
Book of Songs, Th 2–44a
Book of the Consulate of the Sea (Francis Celelles) 1–413b; 3–570b
Book of the Duchess (Chaucer) 3–281b-282b
Book of the Eparch 3–554b
"Book of the Kings of Brittany and Book of the Kings of England" 1–265a
Book of the Knight of the Tower, The 3–672b
Book of the letter 'ain, Th (al-Khalīl ibn Aḥmad) 4–443b-444a
Book of the letter jim (Abū 'Amr al-Shaybānī) 4–442b
Book of the Ordre of Chyvalry 3–666b
Book of the perfumer (Eleazar Ben Judah of Worms) 4–420b
Book of the Revolutions of the Years of Nativities (Abū Ma'shar) 1–386a
Book of the Sea Consulate 1–413b; 3–165a, 169a
 See Book of the Consulate of the Sea
Book of the Secrets of Creation (Apollonius of Tyana) 1–136a
Book of the Taking of Ireland
 See Leabar Gabálá Érenn
Book of the Three Virtues (Christine de Pizan) 3–672b
Book of the Twelve Gates (George Ripley) 1–139a
Book of the Two Principles (John of Lugio) 3–182a
Book of Travels (Benjamin of Tudela) 2–181b
Book of women (Jaume Roig) 3–173b
Book of Zerubbabel 1–344b-345b
Books, liturgical
 Apostolic Constitutions 1–349b
Books of Enoch 1–249b
Books of Secrets 2–345a
Books of the Dead 4–138b
Book Without a Name 2–34b
Boon works 4–512b
Boot, Order of the 3–307a
Boots
 Western European 3–625b
"Boots the Bishop"
 See Albertus Magnus
Bóraime Laigen 1–34a
Borau Valley 1–404a
Bordars 4–512b
BORDEAUX 2–327b
 Black Death 2–260b
Bordet, Robert 3–178a-b
Bordeus
 See Bordeaux
Borgognoni of Lucca, Theodoric 4–247b-248a
Borgo San Donnino (Fidenza) Cathedral 2–167a
Boril 2–492a
Boril of Bulgaria 2–408b-409a
 Bogomils 2–294a,b, 297a
BORIS I OF BULGARIA 2–329a; 2–402a-404a
 Byzantine church 2–464a
Boris II of Bulgaria 2–406a-b
Borna of Dalmatia 4–2a
BOROUGH (ENGLAND-WALES) **2–329b**
 Anglo-Saxons 4–457b, 458a
 bailiffs 2–52a
 Norman-Angevins 4–465a-b, 469b
Boroughbridge, Battle of (1322) 4–397b
BOROUGH-ENGLISH 2–332a
 burgage tenure 2–420b-421a
BORRASSÁ, LUIS 2–332b
Borrell of Barcelona and Girona, Raymond 3–175b
Borrell II of Barcelona and Urgell 3–175a,b
BORRE STYLE 2–332b
Borsa, Roger 2–308b
Borshevo I
 camels 1–296b
Borsippa
 See Birs Nimrud
Boru, Brian
 See Brian Boru, King
***BÓSA SAGA OK HERRAUÐS* 2–333b**
Boscà, Joan Francesc 3–166b
Bosch, Hieronymous 4–370b
"Böse Frau, Die" 1–230a
Bosna River 2–334a
BOSNIA 2–334a
 banus 2–83a
 Bulgaria 2–406b
 Croatia 4–4a, 8a
 metal trade 4–300a
 serfdom 1–102a
BOSNIAN CHURCH 2–341b
 Bogomils 2–296b
Boso of Provence 2–428b
BOSPORUS 2–343b
 Crown of Aragon 1–416a
 Danes 4–554a
 Dardanelles 4–105a
 Galata 4–45a
Bosra
 Ayyubids 2–24a
 conch church 3–378a
BOSS 2–344a
Bossu, Le
 See Adam de la Halle
Bossuet, Jacques
 conciliar theory 3–521b
Boston
 fairs 4–586b
Bosworth, Battle of (1485) 4–473a, 479a, 485b
Botafumeiro 1–224b
Botaneiates 2–493b
BOTANY 2–344b
 biology 2–241a, 244b-246a
 Dīnawarī, al- 4–188a
Boto da Vigevano 2–320a
BOTTEGA 2–349a
"Bottom of the page"
 See Bas-de-page
Bottrigari, Iacopo 2–115a
BOUCHER, GUILLAUME 2–349b
Boucicaut, Jean 4–56a
 Byzantine Empire 2–503a
 Christine de Pizan 3–316b
BOUCICAUT MASTER 2–349b
 Coene, Jaques 3–478a
Boukeleon (Constantinople) 4–48a
Bourchier, John
 See Berners, Lord
BOURDICHON, JEAN 2–349b
Bourgeoise d'Orléans, La 1–269b
Bourgeoisie, Rights of
 See Rights of the Bourgeoisie
Bourges Cathedral 1–427a; 3–276a
 engineering 3–565a, 568a,b
Bourghtheroulde, Battle of (1124) 3–203b
Boustron, George 2–522b; 4–73a
Boustronios
 See Boustron, George
BOUTS, DIRK 2–350a
Bouvet, Honoré 3–205b
Bouvines, Battle of (1214) 3–204a; 4–469a
BOVO II OF CORVEI 2–350b
BOW AND ARROW/CROSSBOW 2–350b; 1–521b, 522b, 532a; 3–179b, 205a-b
 castle location 3–143a-b
 catapults 3–179b
 crenels 3–146b
BOYAR 2–354b
 Bulgaria 2–401a,b, 402b-403a, 406a, 408a, 409b, 410b-411a
 duma 4–305b, 306a-b
Bozen Passion 4–270a,b
Božidarević, Nikolas 4–300b
Bozon, Nicole 1–263b, 264a
 Anglo-Norman literature 1–261b
 metrical sermons 1–262b
Brabant
 accounting 1–39a
 fairs 4–586b
 hearth lists 4–138a
Brabantsche yeesten, Die 4–319b
Braccio da Montone 3–531b, 651a

Bracciolini, Gian Francesco Poggio
 3–235a, 654b
BRACTEATES 2–355b
BRACTON, HENRY DE 2–356b; 1–144b
 Britton 2–382b
 concubinage 3–530b
 equity 4–501b
BRADWARDINE, THOMAS 2–357b; 1–396b, 435a, 464b
 Albert of Saxony 1–125b
 Canterbury 3–83b
 death 2–262b
 predestination 3–371a
 universe 1–615b
Braga, Council of (561) 1–606a
Bragi 4–414b
BRAGI BODDASON THE OLD 2–359a
 dróttkvætt 4–295a
Brahe, Tycho 1–613b
 armillary sphere 1–521b
 astronomy survey 1–615a
 cross-staff 4–12a
 graduated scales 1–613a
BRAILES, WILLIAM DE 2–360a
Brama dels llauradors, La (Gasull) 3–171b
Branching tracery
 See Bar tracery
BRANDENBURG 2–360a
 map 2–361a
 Waldensians 2–306b
***BRANDEUM* 2–362a**
"Brand New City"
 See Basiliada
Brandy 4–220a
Braničevo 2–401b, 408b, 409a,b, 410a, 411a
Branimir of Croatia 4–2b
Brañosera 3–127b
BRANT, SEBASTIAN 2–363a
Branwen Daughter of Llyr 1–567a
Braquemont, Robert de
 Canary Islands 3–62a
Brass
 See Bronze and Brass
Bratislava, Battle of (907) 2–6a
BRATTISHING 2–364a
BRAULIO OF SARAGOSSA, SAINT 2–364b
Braunschweigische Reimchronik 4–505b
Braye, Cardinal de 1–541a
Brazilwood 4–328a,b
BREAD 2–364b
 cookery 3–580b, 581b
 unleavened 3–349a
Breakspear, Nicholas
 See Adrian III, Pope
Breastplate 1–526b, 528a,b, 534a
Breath deodorizers 2–147b
Brebario sunnī (Içe de Gebir) 1–176a
Breeding, selective 1–293b, 294a
Brega Kingdom 1–60b
Brehon Law
 See Law, Irish
Bremen
 See Hamburg-Bremen
Bremen, Adam of
 See Adam of Bremen
Brémule, Battle of (1119) 3–203b
Brendan, Saint
 Anglo-Norman life of 1–261a
 voyage to Promised Land 1–262a
Brendan of Birr 3–465b
Brendan the Navigator of Clonfort 3–465b
Brenhinedd y Saesson 3–300a
Brescia
 Angela Merici 1–250b
 commune 3–500a
Bressos
 See Erzincan
***BRETA SǪGUR* 2–365b**
Bretèches 3–146b
Bretel, Jehan 1–49a
Brethren, Bohemian
 See Bohemian Brethren
Brethren of Purity 4–445a
BRETHREN OF THE COMMON LIFE 2–366a
 Biel, Gabriel 2–233b, 234a
 Devotio Moderna 4–166a
 Latin church 3–368b-369b
 religious communities 3–368b, 369a
Brethren of the Free Spirit 4–376b
 heresy 3–370a
Brethren of the Sword 3–306b
 Baltic countries 2–64b, 65b, 66b
Brétigny, Treaty of (1360) 1–368a; 3–269b
 Chaucer 3–280b
Břetislav I of Bohemia 2–299b
Breton Lays
 See Lai
BRETON LITERATURE 2–370a; 3–234a
 Arthurian literature 1–567b-568a
Brevary or Some Fewe Collectiones of the Cittie of Chester 3–298b; 4–285a
Breve 1–549a
Breve breviarum 1–137b
Breviari d'amor (Matfre Ermengaud) 3–169a, 672b; 4–506b
Breviarium de dictamine (Alberic of Monte Cassino) 4–174a
Breviarium extravagantium (Bernard of Pavia) 4–123b-124a
BREVIARY 2–370b
 Bellville 2–117a
 books of hours 2–326a
 canonical hours 3–67b
 Divine Office 4–225a-b
BREVIARY OF ALARIC 2–373a
 Codex Theodosianus 3–475b
Breviary of love (Matfre Ermengaud) 3–169a, 672b; 4–506b
Breviloquium (Boncompagno of Signa) 2–320b
Breviloquium (John of Wales) 3–167b
Breviloquium (Saint Bonaventure) 2–314b
Breviloquus (Johann Reuchlin) 4–450a
Brevis introductio ad dictamen (Giovanni di Bonandrea) 4–174b
BREWING 2–373b; 4–219a
 European 1–94b-95a; 3–583b
Brian Boru, King 1–110b; 4–77b
 Cinéal Eóghain 3–397a
Bribir 4–4a
BRICK 2–375a
Bridlington Church 1–256a
Brie
 fairs 4–590b
Brienne
 butler 2–434b
Brigandage
 France 3–269b, 271b
Brigandine 1–526b, 528a, 535a
Brigid, Saint
 See Brigit, Saint
BRIGIT (BRIGID), **SAINT 2–376a**; 4–376a
 brewing 2–374a
 monasteries 3–227b
Brisebarre, Jean 1–151b
Bristol
 Black Death 2–261b, 262a
 countyship 2–331b
Britain
 See England
Britannia (William Camden) 1–337b
Brito, Bonhomme 1–128a; 4–450a
Brittanie de Engleter
 See Livre de Reis
BRITTANY, CELTIC 2–381a
 church 3–226a, 227b
BRITTANY, DUCHY 2–377b; 4–304a
 fairs 4–586a
 map 2–378a
BRITTON 2–382b
Brixiensis, Bartholomeus
 See Bartholomeus Brixiensis
Broad Manner
 engraving 4–489a
Brocades
 Córdoba 3–599b
Brocarda 4–127b
Brocard of Mount Carmel 3–96b
Brocardus
 Assassins 1–591a
Broce, Pierre de la
 chamberlain 3–242b
BROEDERLAM, MELCHIOR 2–383a; 2–44b
Brogne Abbey 3–348a
Bro Gynin 4–76a
Bromflet
 See Carver, William
Bromyard, John 3–59b-60a
 Summa praedicantium 4–250b
Bronze Age
 food animals 1–299a, 300a
BRONZE AND BRASS 2–383a
 art trade 1–562a
 Celtic art 3–219a
Brot af Sigurdharkvidhu
 See Sigurđarkviđa in Forna
Brother of Joy and Sister of Pleasure
 See Frayre de Joy e Sor de Plaser
Brothers of the Law of Christ
 See Bohemian Brethren
Brothers of the Sword
 See Brethren of the Sword
Brouchard of Vienne, Archbishop 4–108b, 109a
BROUN, ROBERT 2–385a
Bruce, Edward, of Scotland 4–299b
Bruce, Robert
 See Robert I of Scotland
Bruce, The (John Barbour) 2–102a
BRUDER HANS 2–385a
BRUGES 2–386a; 3–497b
 art trade 1–562a
 banking 2–74a,b, 75a, 78b
 Caxton, William 3–210a
 échevinages 4–379b
 fairs 4–557b, 585a-b
Brugge, Jacob van 2–29b
Brulé, Gace
 See Gace Brulé
Brun, Garin lo
 See Garin lo Brun
Brunanburh, Battle of (937) 4–402b
BRUNELLESCHI, FILIPPO 2–388a
 dome 4–236a
Brunetto Latini
 See Latini, Brunetto
Brunhild
 See Brynhild
Brunhilde of Austrasia 1–117b; 3–104a-b
BRUNI, LEONARDO 2–390b; 3–654b
Bruno I of Cologne, Archbishop 3–481a

BRUNO OF MAGDEBURG 2–391b
martyrdom 2–64b
BRUNO OF QUERFURT, SAINT 2–391b
BRUNO OF SEGNI, SAINT 2–392a
Bruno of Toul
See Leo IX, Pope
BRUNO OF WÜRZBURG, SAINT 2–392a
exegesis 4–543a
BRUNO THE CARTHUSIAN, SAINT 2–392a
Carthusians 3–118a
Grande Chartreuse 4–109b
monasticism 3–122b
BRUNSBERG, H(E)INRICH VON 2–392b
Brunswick
chronicles 4–505b
BRUSA 2–392b
Ottomans 2–500b
Brussels
arms and armor 1–529a
Brussels Cross
inscription 1–281a
***BRUT, THE* 2–393a**; 1–573a; 3–329b
Anonimalle Chronicle 1–309a
Arthurian literature 1–565a-b
Brute d'Angleterre abrégé 1–265b
Brut y Tywysogion 4–415b
Bruun
See Candidus of Fulda
Bryennios, Nikephoros 1–303a
Brykhulle 1–268b; 2–271a
BRYNHILD 2–394b
Brynjólfr Sveinsson
Codex Regius 4–385a-387a
Brythonic
See Celtic Languages
Bubonic plague
See Black Death
Búcar of Morocco
Cantar de mío Cid 3–73b
See Also Béker, Sir ben Abu
Buccolicum carmen (Boccaccio) 2–280b
***BUCENTAUR* 2–395b**
Buchanan, George 3–522a
Buch der Abenteuer (Ulrich Füetrer) 1–133a
Buch der Göttlichen Tröstung (Meister Eckhart) 4–381a
Buch der Natur (Conrad of Megenberg) 3–539a
"Büchlein, Das" (Hartmann von Aue) 1–229b
***BUCH VON BERN, DAS* 2–395b**
Ermenrîkes Dôt 4–507a
Bucinobantes 1–117a
Bucintoro
See Bucentaur
Buckingham 1–267b
Buckingham, Thomas 2–358b
Buckinghamshire
Black Death 2–262a
Buckler 1–528a; 3–205a
BUDA 2–396b
animal bone remains 1–300b
Buddhism
food prohibitions 1–300a
Budva 4–1b
Bueil, Jean de 3–333a
Buern Bucecarle 1–264b
Bueve d'Hantone
See Boeve de Haumtone
Buevon de Conmarchis (Adenet le Roi) 1–55a; 3–261b
Buffe 1–534a
Bug River 1–96b
Buḥturī, al- 1–400b, 403a
Buik of Alexander 1–151b
Buik of King Alexander (Sir Gilbert Hay) 1–151b
Building
See Construction
Buke of Knychtede (Sir Gilbert Hay) 3–666b
BUKHARA 2–396b
Bukhārī, al- 2–398b
fairs 4–589a
BUKHĀRĪ MUḤAMMAD IBN ISMĀ'IL, AL- 2–397b
Bulbous dome 4–236a
Bulgari
See Cathars
BULGARIA 2–399a
Adrianople 1–59a; 2–117a
agriculture 1–78a
alphabet 1–216b
Avars 2–12b
Baldwin I of the Latin Empire 2–58b
Basil II 2–118b
Bogoliubskii, Andrei 2–293b
Bogomils 2–294a
Boris 2–329a
Boyar 2–354b
Byzantine Empire 1–246b; 2–464a, 465a, 469a, 488a, 489b-490a,b, 492a
camels 1–296b
crusades 4–56a
map 2–400a
water buffalo 1–298a
BULGARIAN ART AND ARCHITECTURE 2–414b; 2–403b, 404b, 413b
ceramics 3–237a
Bulgarian church 2–117b, 403a
Bogomilism 2–294a
prelates 2–10a
See Also Byzantine church
Bulgars
See Bulgaria
BULGARUS 2–417b
Azo 2–29a
Corpus iuris civilis 3–609b
BULL, PAPAL 2–418a
chancery 3–254a
crusade propaganda 4–19b
Bulla Cypria 4–72b
Bullatores 3–254a
"Bull of Union" 3–395b
Bulls of provision 1–305b
***BUNDAHISHN* 2–419a**
Bunyan, John 1–185b
BUON, GIOVANNI AND BARTOLOMEO 2–419a
Buonaccorso, Nicolò di
See Nicolò di Buonaccorso
Buoncompagno of Signa
See Boncompagno of Signa
Buondelmonti, Esau 4–500a
Buraburg 2–322a
BURĀQ 2–419b
Ascension of the Prophet 1–581a
Burchard, Margrave 2–6a
Burchard of Mount Sion
missions 4–253a
theology, Dominican 4–246b
BURCHARD OF WORMS 2–420a; 2–86a
contraception 3–572a
decretals, forged 3–349a
Liber decretorum 4–128b
Burchard of Würzburg, Bishop 3–106b
Burchio
See Bucentaur
Burci, Salvo 3–184a
Burd 3–616b
Burdigala
See Bordeaux
Bureba Plateau
Asturians 1–626a
Castilian settlement 3–128a
BURGAGE TENURE 2–420b; 2–330b, 331b
Burgesses 4–465a-b
Burggraf 3–481a
Burgh
See Borough
BURGH, DE 2–421a
Burgh, Queen Elizabeth de 4–111a
BURGHAUSEN, HANNS VON 2–422a
hall church 3–379a
Burgkmair, Hans 4–516b
Burgonet 1–527b, 531b
Burgos 3–128a, 131b
Caballeros villanos 3–136b
Cantar de mío Cid 3–70b-71b
Castilian language 3–142a
Cid 3–73a
fairs 4–587b
Burgos, Council of (1080) 3–129a
BURGUNDIANS 2–422b; 2–94a
Alamanni 1–117a
Arianism 1–454b
Burgundy, County of 2–424a
Charles of Orléans 3–272b-273a
Charles VII of France 3–270b-271a
Clovis 3–466a
Franks 2–94b
Huns 1–638a-639a
invasions 2–92a-b
Merovingians 3–104a
BURGUNDIO OF PISA 2–423b
BURGUNDY, COUNTY OF 2–424a
charcoal 3–267b
map 2–425
BURGUNDY, DUCHY OF 2–427a
appanages 1–351b
arms and armor 1–529a
Bruges 2–387b
chivalric orders 3–307a
map 2–425a-b
BURGUNDY, KINGDOM OF 2–428b
alodial tenure 1–190b
Dauphiné 4–107b, 108a
establishment 3–104a-106a, 114a
map 2–425
Burhred of Mercia 1–163b
Burhs 4–457b-458a
Burial
See Death and Burial
BURIDAN, JEAN 2–430a
Albert of Saxony 1–125b
Aristotle 1–464b-465a
astrology/astronomy 1–608a, 615b
BURIN 2–432a; 4–488a, 516a
Burjī period 4–406b
BURLEY (BURLEIGH), **WALTER 2–432b**
Burma 4–557a
Burmus
See Barnis
Burriana 1–412a
Bursa
See Brusa
Burton-on-Trent
brewing 2–375a
Bury, Richard de 1–324a
Bury Saint Edmunds
Anonymous IV 1–309b
architecture 1–255b
water clock 3–458b
Busant, Der
See Bussard, Der
Busca 1–418a-b, 419b-420a; 2–104b

Busch, Jan
Devotio Moderna 3–369a; 4–167a
BUSCHETO OF PISA 2–433b
Busfurradjān
See Vaspurakan
BUSHEL 2–433b
Buskenblaser 4–321b
***BUSSARD, DER* 2–433b**
Bustan
See Rauḍa
Bustanai 4–552a
Bustia 1–223b
Bustra
See Bosra
BUTLER 2–434a
Butr 2–185b
BUTTRESS 2–434b
Chartres Cathedral 3–276a
construction 3–565a-b, 567a-b, 568a
Buwayhids
See Buyids
BUYIDS 2–435a
Abbasids 1–11b
Baghdad 2–46b-47a
Bawwāb, Ibn al- 2–136a
caliphate 3–50a,b
BVM, Little Office of
See Blessed Virgin Mary, Little Office of
Byblos
See Jubail (Gibelet)
Byrhtferth of Ramsey 1–284a, 285b; 2–174a
Dunstan, Saint 4–311b
Byrhtnoth of Essex
poetry 1–279a
Byrnie
See Mail
Byskupa sǫgur
See Bishops' Sagas
Byton 1–256a
Byzantine architecture
See Early Christian and Byzantine Architecture
BYZANTINE ART, 843-1453 2–437b
Annunciation 1–308a
Assumption of the Virgin 1–601a
Blachernitissa 2–256b
Bulgaria 2–413b, 414a,b
Deesis 4–131b
Dionysios of Fourna 4–191b
donor portrait 4–261b
drawings 4–292b
Eutychios 4–524b
ex voto images 4–529b
figural arts, Islamic 3–53a
See Also Constantinople
BYZANTINE CHURCH 2–458b
Alexandrian rite 1–155a
Ambrosian chant 1–232b
analoi 1–238a
Anastasis 1–239a
Anthemios of Tralles 1–317a
Armenian church 1–499b-500a
autocephalos 2–10a
Basil the Great 2–119b
Bogomils 2–294b-297b
Bulgaria 2–403a
caesaropapism 3–10a-11a
celibacy 3–215b
charistikion 3–268a
Constantine I the Great 2–484b
costume 3–615b-616a
councils 3–631b
Cyril and Methodios, Saints 4–73a
Demetrios Kydones 4–135b
ecumenical patriarch 4–383a
exegesis 2–214a-b
exonarthex 4–552b
iconoclasm 2–488a
Latin church 3–355b-357a
liturgy 1–326b, 444a-b; 3–675b-677a
marriage 4–594b
schism 2–485b-486a
See Also Clergy, Byzantine
Byzantine Empire
admiral 1–55b
Adrianople 1–59a
Alexandria 1–153a
Anatolia 1–239a
Ani in Širak 1–290b
Ankara 1–302a
Arabic numerals 1–382b, 391b, 392a
astronomy/astrology 1–606a, 613b-614a
Bosporus 2–343b
calendars 3–18b
cosmetics 2–146a,b, 147b, 149a-b
crucifixion 4–13a,b
crusader art and architecture 4–22a
crusades 1–158b; 4–25a, 27b, 31b, 55b-56a
Cyprus, Kingdom of 4–70b, 71b, 72a
Dardanelles 4–105a
diplomacy 4–193b
Dyrrachium 4–329b
fairs 4–588a-b
See Also Constantinople
BYZANTINE EMPIRE: BUREAUCRACY 2–471b; 2–493b
acclamations 1–35b
archives 1–446a
augusta 1–644a; 2–122b
autocrator 2–10b, 122b
basileus 2–122b
Book or the Eparch 4–493b
caesar 3–9a
chancery 3–252a, 253b
chrysobullon 3–334a
costume 3–614a
curopalates 4–66b
despot 4–165a
domestic 4–239a
drungarios 4–295b
dux 4–323a
eparch 4–493b
exarchate 4–529b
themes 2–487b
BYZANTINE EMPIRE: ECONOMIC LIFE AND SOCIAL STRUCTURE 2–475a; 1–490a
agriculture and nutrition 1–76b-79b, 98b-99a
nomisma 2–493b
Slavic merchants 4–587b, 588a
taxes 2–472a
BYZANTINE EMPIRE: HISTORY (330-1025) 2–481b
Abbasids 1–9b
Abū Bakr 1–25b
akritai 1–115b
Amorians 1–236a
ʿAmr ibn al-ʿĀṣ 1–237a
Anatolikon 1–242a
Antioch 1–326a
Arcrunis 1–451a
Armenia 1–476b, 477a-478a,b, 483a-484a
Ašot II Erkatʿ 1–588b
Ašot III Ołormac 1–589b
Ašot I Mec 1–588a-b
Avars 2–12a
Bardas Caesar 2–106a
Bardas Phokas 2–106b
Bardas Skleros 2–106b
Basil I the Macedonian 2–117a
Beirut 2–164a
Belisarios 2–165a
Berkri 2–189a
Boris of Bulgaria 2–329a
Bosnia 2–334b
Bulgaria 2–329a, 399a-407b; 4–4b
Caesarea 3–9a
caliphate 3–38a, 40a
Constans II 3–544a
Constantine IV 3–546a
Constantine V 3–546a
Constantine VII Porphyrogenitos 3–546b
Crete 3–678a
Dalmatia 4–79b
diplomacy, Islamic 4–200a-b, 201a
Diyarbakir 4–231b
Dubrovnik 4–300a
Dwin 4–323b
Eclogue 4–382b
Euphrates River 4–523a
Irene, Empress 3–110a
Moravia 2–299a
Ostrogoths 2–93b-94a
papal coronation 3–603a
Svetoslav 4–5a
Swedes 4–555a-b
Symeon of Bulgaria 4–4b
BYZANTINE EMPIRE: HISTORY (1025-1204) 2–491b
Alexiad 1–303a
Alp Arslan 1–203b
Andronikos I Komnenos 1–244a
Angelos family 1–251b
Arčēš 1–423a
Bohemond I 2–308b
Bosnia 2–334b
Bulgaria 2–407b-408b
Constantine IX Monomachos 3–548a
Doukas 4–263a
Kresimir IV 4–6a
Manazkert 1–203b
Normans 4–6a
Seljuks 4–27b-30a, 33b, 61
BYZANTINE EMPIRE: HISTORY (1204-1453) 2–498a
Almogávares 1–190b-191a
alphabet 1–209b
Bohemond I 1–158b
Brusa 2–392b-393a
Bulgaria 2–408b-414a
Catalan Company 3–157a
Constantine XI Palaiologos 3–548a
Crònica da Sant Joan de La Penya 3–166a
Demetrios Kydones 4–135b
Epiros, Despotate of 4–499a
Ottomans 4–32b
Palaiologoi 1–245b, 246a
BYZANTINE LITERATURE 2–505a
Cosmas Indicopleustes 3–613b
Digenis Akritas 4–185a
encyclopedias and dictionaries 4–446b
BYZANTINE LITERATURE: POPULAR 2–521a
BYZANTINE MINOR ARTS (843-1453) **2–452b**
Anglo-Saxon art 1–273a
cloisonné enamel 4–437b, 441a
Deesis 4–131b
BYZANTINE POETIC FORMS 2–523b
Byzantine rite 1–326b, 444a-b; 3–675b-677a
Byzantium
See Constantinople

C

CABALA 3–1a
Abulafia 1–27a
Eleazar ben Judah of Worms 4–420b
exegesis 2–212a
Jewish apocalyptic literature 1–345b-346a
Rabad 1–23a
Cabalga Diego Laínez 3–389a
Caballeros villanos 1–629b; 3–131b
taxation 3–136a-b
Cabestany, Guillem de
See Guillem de Cabestany
CABOCHIEN RIOTS 3–3b
CACCIA 3–4a
ars nova 1–553a
Caccia di Diana, La (Boccaccio) 2–278a-b
Cáceres
Alfonso IX 3–133b
Cadastres 4–513b
CADE, JACK/CADE'S REBELLION (1450) **3–4b**
CADENCE 3–5b
ars nova 1–551b
contratenor 3–577a
Cadera 2–269b
Cade's Rebellion (1450)
See Cade, Jack/Cade's Rebellion
Cadi
See Qadi
Cádiz
commerce 4–558a
CADOC, SAINT 3–6b
Ca' d'Oro 2–419b
Caecilian of Carthage, Bishop 1–651b
Caelo, De (Aristotle) 1–615b
CÆDMON 3–7b
exegesis 2–221a, 273b; 4–550b
Hymn 1–275b, 277b
Cael 1–34a
Caelestius 1–652b
Caelius Sedulius 1–144b
CAEN 3–8b
Black Death 2–261a
fairs 4–586a
Norman Exchequer 4–532a
Caergybi 2–71a
Caerwys 4–415b
CAESAR 3–8b
caesaropapism 3–11a
Caesar, Julius
biographies 2–236b
chronicles, French 3–331b
Cilician Gates 3–390b
Gaul 2–88b, 89a
Caesar Bardas
See Bardas Caesar
CAESAREA 3–9a; 1–484a
Anatolia 1–239b, 241b
Armenia 1–472b
Basil the Great, Saint 2–119b
Baybars al-Bunduqdārī 2–138b
Byzantine empire 2–493a
Danishmendids 4–91b
Gregory, Saint 1–66b
Louis IX of France 4–25b
Caesaria (sister of Caesarius) 3–9b
CAESARIUS OF ARLES, SAINT 3–9b
contraception 3–573a
Divine Office 4–229b
homilies 1–284b
CAESARIUS OF HEISTERBACH 3–10a
exempla 3–405a; 4–551a
CAESAROPAPISM 3–10a; 3–341a
Cafaggiolo 1–561b
CAFFA 3–12a
Black Death 2–258b-259a
Khanate of Crimea 3–678b
trade 4–557b
Caffarello, Facio
fables 4–572b
CAFTAN 3–12b
Cahors
canvas production 3–88b
pawnbroking 2–76a
wine 2–328b
Cahorsins
See Lombards
Caillau family 2–328a,b
Caílte mac Rónáin 1–33b, 34a
Caimi, Prostaso 2–324b
Cáin Adamnáin 1–52b
Cainnech of Aghaboe 3–465b
CAIRO 3–13a; 4–406a
Amalric I of the Latin Empire 4–39a
Arab settlement 1–377a
art 1–5b
Ayyubids 2–21a, 24a, 25a
Azhar, Al- 2–27b
ʿAziz, al- 2–28b
bāb 2–32a
Badr al-Jamālī 2–44b
crusades 4–32a
Damascus 4–81b, 82a
Egypt 4–405b, 406a, 408a
Genizah 3–15a
history 3–13a-14b
CAIRO GENIZAH 3–15a; 2–80a
costume, Jewish 3–620a-b
Dukus Horant 4–304b
Cairpre Riata 4–78a
Caisel
See Cashel
Cajetan of Thiene 1–465a
Calabria
Barlaam 2–109a
Ipomedon 1–266b
Lombards 2–95b
Ravenna exarchate 4–530a
Caladbolg
See Excalibur
Calamus 1–222b
Calatayud 1–160a, 406a, 407a
CALATRAVA, ORDER OF 3–16b; 2–17a; 3–306b
CALBULUS 3–17a
Calcidius
Timaeus 1–610b
Calculation methods
See Arabic numerals
Calculation with the Hindu Numerals 1–383a
Calculus
Arabic numerals 1–386b
Calderino, John 1–252b
Calendar of Córdoba 1–81b, 82b
Calendar of Deng
See Martyrology, Irish
CALENDARS, ARMENIAN 3–30b
Anania Širakacʿi 1–238a
Armenian church 1–520b-521a
CALENDARS AND RECKONING OF TIME 3–17a; 2–38b
Alfonsine Tables 1–159b
astrolabe 1–602a
astronomy 1–610a,b, 611b, 612b, 614a, 615a
Bede 2–154b-155a
Dionysius Exiguus 4–193a
Easter 3–228a; 4–365a
illustrations 1–95b
printed 1–609a
West Slav 1–96b
See Also Clocks and reckoning of time
Calendrical machine
See Clocks and reckoning of time
Calepino, Ambrogio 4–450a
Calicut 4–563a
***CALILA E DIGNA* 3–31b**
CALIPHATE 3–32a; 2–28b
Abbasids 1–6b
Commander of the Faithful 3–488a
Calix
See Chalice
Calixtines
See Hussite church
Calixtus III, Antipope 1–330a
Calixtus I, Pope 1–330b
Calixtus II, Pope
Burgundy, County of 2–424b
camel use 1–296b
councils 3–636a-b, 637a
reform 3–352a
vandalism 1–334a
Calixtus III, Pope 1–14a
Call 2–103a, 104b
CALLIGRAPHY, ISLAMIC 3–51b
Bawwāb, Ibn al- 2–135b
Callimachus 3–430a
Pinakes 1–204a
Callis, Jaume 3–611b
Calpich 3–407b
CALPURNIUS SICULUS TITUS 3–55b
Caltabelotta 1–414b
treaty (1302) 1–246a; 3–156a
Calvary Chapel 4–22b
Calvary cross 4–9a
Calvin, John 4–538a
Camail 1–526b, 527a,b
CAMALDOLESE, ORDER OF 3–55b; 2–14a
Carthusians 3–118a
Cluny 3–348a
Cambaluc
Marco Polo 4–556b, 557b
Cambellanus
See Chamberlain
Cambitor 2–73a
Cambium 2–78a
Cambrai
commune 3–496a
Cambrensis, Giraldus
See Gerald of Wales
CAMBRIDGE, UNIVERSITY OF 3–58b
Black Death 2–262b
medical training 2–98b
CAMBRIDGE PSALTER 3–57a; 1–262b; 3–56b
Cambridgeshire
Black Death 2–262b
***CAMBRIDGE SONGS* 3–57a**; 1–318b, 319a
Camden, William 1–337b
Camel 1–296a,b
Camel, Battle of (656) 1–15b, 113b, 172b; 2–127b; 3–35b
Camelot
See Arthurian Literature
Cameos
collections 1–335a,b

Camera
cardinals 3–94a
creation 4–66a
papal funds 2–77b
Cameracensis
See Ailly, Pierre d'
Camera obscura 1–377b
Camerarius 1–37a-b
See Chamberlain
Camerlengus
See Chamberlain
Campagna
See Commune
Campaldino, Battle of (1289) 4–96b
Campania Castle 3–151a
Campanian liturgical books 2–180a-b
Campanian Romanesque sculpture
Barisanus of Trani 2–109a
CAMPANILE 3–60a
Palaiologan architecture 4–345b
Campanus of Novara 1–612b; 4–500b
Theorica planetarum 3–461b
Campeador
See Cid, The, History and legend of
CAMPIN, ROBERT 3–60b
Annunciation 1–308a
Daret, Jacques 4–105b
Campionesi 2–324b
Campo Santo (Pisa)
frescoes 1–244a
Campsores 2–74a
Campsores domini papae 2–76b
Canaanites 2–185b
Canals, Antoni 3–167b, 169b
CANARY ISLANDS AND BÉTHEN-COURT 3–61b
Castilians 3–137b
commerce 4–558b, 559a
map 3–62a-b
slaves 4–561a
Canbiac 3–186a
Cancellarius
See Chancery
Cancioneiro geral (Garcia de Resende) 3–63b
Cancioneiros 3–86b
Cancionero de Baena 3–86b
Cancionero de obras de burlas provocantes a risa 3–63b
***CANCIONERO GENERAL* 3–63a**
Cancionero musical de palacio 3–85b
Cancioneros 3–140a
Cançó de Santa Fe 3–164a-b
Cançoner de Masdovelles 3–171a
Cançoner Vega-Aguiló 3–171a
Cancun d'Antioche
See Chanson d'Antioche
Candelabrum (Bene of Florence) 4–174b
Candia
See Crete
CANDIDUS OF FULDA 3–63b
Eigel 4–408b
Candidus Wizo 3–64a
Candle clock 3–458a
Candles
See Lighting devices
Canfranc 1–404b
Can Grande della Scala 4–103a,b
Cannanore 4–563a
CANNON 3–64a
catapults 3–180b
fortifications 3–151a,b-152a
Cano 3–407a
Canon, Cathedral
See Clergy
Canones Hibernenses
See Law, Canon: Before Gratian
Canones Wallici 3–229b
CANONICAL HOURS 3–66b
bells 2–165b; 3–28b
books of hours 2–325a
breviary 2–371a
calendars and reckoning of time 3–24a
collectarium 3–479b
Divine Office 3–230a,b; 4–221b
CANONIZATION 3–67b
Armenian saints 1–520a
beatification 2–142b
bull, papal 2–418a
Latin church 3–353b
Canon of Medicine (Ibn Sīnā) 1–458b; 3–572a
Canons
See Law, Canon
Canons of Edgar (Wulfstan) 1–286a
Canons of Prémontré
Augustinism 1–661a
Canons of Saint Victor
Augustinism 1–661a
Canons of the Apostles 4–125a
CANON TABLE 3–66a
early Christian art 4–356a
Canopy 1–222a
CANOSSA 3–69a; 3–351b
CANSO 3–69b
Cantabrians
Castilian language 3–141b
Roman assimilation 2–126a
Cantacuzeni
See Kantakouzenoi
***CANTAR DE MÍO CID* 3–70a**
assonance 1–600b
Castilian language 3–133a, 142a
Cid legend 3–386b-389a
See Also Cid, the, history and legend of
CANTATORIUM 3–80b; 1–329b
Cant de la Sibilla 3–164a
Cantefable
See Aucassin et Nicolette
CANTERBURY 3–81a
Anglo-Saxon art 1–273b
archbishopric 4–458a,b, 466a
Augustine 1–644b
Bangor 2–71b
Becket, Thomas 2–151a
Bradwardine, Thomas 2–358b
chronicles, Old English 1–284b
convocations 3–578a
courts, ecclesiastical 1–433b
Eadmer 4–330b
elections, church 4–423b
scriptoria, Old English 1–276a
CANTERBURY CATHEDRAL 3–84a; 1–426a
Anglo-Norman features 1–255b
Anselm 1–311b
Becket, Thomas 4–471a
Conrad, Prior 3–539a
construction 3–81b, 90b-91a, 562a
Ernulf 4–508a
Forma compoti 4–513b
monastery church 3–265b
reconstruction 3–83a-b
school 4–472a
Canterbury Tales (Chaucer) 1–568b; 3–83a, 290b-296a
crusades 4–54b-55a, 57a
Dominicans 4–249a
CANTICLE 3–84b
breviary 2–371b
***CANTIGA* 3–84b**; 3–84b, 86b
Cantigas de Santa María 1–162a; 3–85a
Dinis 4–189b
CANTIGAS DE AMOR, AMIGO, AND ESCARNIO 3–86b
chansons de femme 3–257a
Dinis 4–190a-b
Cantigas de Santa María
See Cantiga
Cantilena
See Diaphonia
***CANTILÈNE* 3–87b**
Bible 2–216b
carols, Middle English 3–116a
chansons de geste 3–259b
Séquence de Sainte Eulalie 4–521a
CANTOR 3–87b
ars antiqua 1–546a
Cantor, Peter
See Peter the Chanter
Cantum quem Cisterciensis 3–402b
Cantus
ars nova 1–551a
Cantus fractibilis 3–657b
Cantwaraburh
See Canterbury
Canute
See Cnut the Great
CANVAS 3–88a
Canvis de la Mar 2–74a
Canvis Nous 2–74a
Canvis Vells 2–74a
Canzoniere (Cecco Angiolieri) 3–211b
Cape Bojador 4–561a
Cape Cross 4–562a
Cape Farewell
Eric the Red 4–554b
Capella, Martianus
See Martianus Capella
Capella di Piazza (Siena) 3–572a
Capellani
Carolingian 3–107b-108a
CAPELLANUS, ANDREAS 3–88b; 1–189a
Arthurian literature 1–572b
courtly love 1–269a; 3–669b, 670b-671b, 672a-b, 673a; 4–420a
Cape of Good Hope
discovery 4–560b
exploration 4–562b
Cape of Tempests
See Cape of Good Hope
Cape Padrão
exploration 4–562b
Cape Palmas
exploration 4–561b, 562b
Capet, Hugh 1–46b
appanages 1–351a
Capetian dynasty
Aragon, Crown of 1–409b, 412a,b, 414a
archives 1–447a
Burgundy 2–424b, 427a,b, 429b
Carolingian Empire 3–115a
Occitania 3–189a,b
CAPETIAN FAMILY ORIGINS 3–89a
Cape Verde Islands
Portuguese 4–561b
slaves 2–269a
Cape Volta
See Lüderitz
CAPGRAVE, JOHN 3–90a
***CAPILLA MAYOR* 3–90a**
Capità 3–156b
CAPITAL 3–90a
Anglo-Norman 1–256a
basket 3–90b
Capitalism
double-entry accounting 1–41a, 42a-b
Capitanei 3–557b
Capitols del consolat de mar 3–570a

Capitula 4–127b
Capitula agendorum 3–650a
Capitula Angilramni
False Decretals 4–125a
Capitulare de villis
stewardship accounting 1–36b-37a
Capitulare nauticum 3–570a
CAPITULARY 3–91a
Carolingians 3–108a, 109a
cavalry 3–202a-b
Charlemagne 3–268b
estate management 4–511b
forgeries 2–178b-179a
Louis I 3–111b-112a
Quierzy 3–114b
Capitula (Theodulf of Orléans) 1–286b
Capocci, Peter 4–59b
CAPPADOCIA 3–92a
Anatolikon theme 1–242a
Arianism 1–454a
Armenians 2–492a
Caesarea 3–9a
exploration 4–556b
monasteries 1–241a
Nicene faith 3–628b
paintings 2–439a, 441b-442a
Cappadocian fathers 2–467a
Cappella Palatina (Palermo) 4–346b
Capreolus, John 4–247a
Caprids 1–299a
Caprini, John de Plano
See Plano Caprini, John of
Caprona, Battle of (1289) 4–96b
Capsae 1–223b
Captivitate Babylonica ecclesiae praeludium, De (Martin Luther) 2–34b
Capture of Defur 1–151a
Capuano, Peter 4–44a
Caracalla, Emperor 1–117a
Caradoc of Llancarfan 1–578a
Carantania 2–6a
Caravans
See Han; Trade, Islamic; Travel and Transport, Islamic
Caravansary, Caravanserai
See Han
Carbonell, Pere Miquell 3–171a
Carbon 14 dating
climatology 3–451b, 453b
Carcassonne 2–129a
Albigensian Crusade 3–188b
Aragon, Crown of 1–410a-b
city walls 3–151a
Ramon Berenguer III 3–178a
Cardeña 3–76a-b
Cardiff Castle 4–462b
Cardigan
See Ceredigion, Kingdom of
Cardigan Castle
eisteddfod 4–415b
CARDINALS, COLLEGE OF 3–93b
canonization process 3–68a,b
Church, Latin 3–352a, 364b-365a, 377a
conciliar theory 3–366a-367a, 514b, 516b-517a, 519b-520a
conclave, papal 3–523b, 634b, 638b, 642a
ecclesiology 4–374b
Martin V 3–651b
papal curia 4–65b
Carentan 4–586a
Caribbean 4–561a
Caribert 1–366b
Carileffus 2–16b
Carinthia 2–4b, 7b, 8a,b, 9a, 132b
Bohemia 2–300a
Caritas 3–669a
Carladès 1–410a
Carlisle
Durham treaties 4–316a
Carlisle Cathedral 3–265b
Carloman, King (brother of Charlemagne) 3–268a
Carloman, King (son of Charles the Blad) 3–114b, 115a
Carloman, Prince (son of Charles Martel) 3–272b
Boniface, Saint 2–322a
Carolingians 3–106a-b
Carlos of Viana 1–418b
Carmarthen 4–329a
eisteddfod 4–415b
Carmatiens
See Karamans
Carmel, Mount 3–96b
Carmel, Use of
See Carmelite Rite
CARMELITE RITE 3–96a
CARMELITES 3–96a
Cyprus 4–72b
Lyons, Council of (1274) 3–641b
Carmelite Water 2–147a
Carmen 3–256b
Carmen ad Robertum regem (Adalbero of Laon) 1–46b
Carmen Campidoctoris 2–18b; 3–76b
Carmen de algorismo (Alexander of Villa Dei) 1–396a
Carmen de Bello Lewensi
See Lewes, Song of
***CARMEN DE BELLO SAXONICO* 3–97a**
Carmen paschale (Caelius Sedulius) 1–144b, 422a; 4–371a, 496a
***CARMINA BURANA* 3–97b**; 3–57a; 4–380a
Latin anthologies 1–318a, 319a
Carmina Cantabrigiensia
See Cambridge Songs
Carmina figurata 4–521a
Carmina rhythmica 1–144b
Carniola 2–7b, 8a,b, 9a
Bohemia 2–300a
CARNIVAL 3–99a
Carnival plays
Germany 4–271a-272a
Caroline minuscule 3–110a
Carolingian architecture
See Pre-Romanesque architecture
Carolingian art
See Pre-Romanesque art
CAROLINGIAN LATIN POETRY 3–99b; 3–100a,b
Agius of Corvei 1–72b
Cambridge Songs 3–57b
Ermoldus Nigellus 4–507b
Carolingian renaissance 3–100a
CAROLINGIANS AND THE CAROLINGIAN EMPIRE 3–104a
Aachen 1–1a-2a
Agnus Dei 1–74a
arms and armor 1–522b
astronomy/astrology 1–606b, 611a
Austria 2–6a
Baldwin I of Flanders 2–58a
ban, banalité 2–69a
baptism 2–85b, 86a
Bavarians 2–134a
Bible texts 2–212b-213a
Bordeaux 2–327b
bracteates 2–356a
Brittany 2–378b-379b
Bruges 2–386a
Burgundy, Kingdom of 2–428b
Capetian family origins 3–89a
capitulary 3–91a
cavalry 3–202b
chancery 3–252b
Charlemagne 3–268a
Charles Martel 3–272b
church 3–108b-110a, 373b
classical literary studies 3–433a
Claudius of Turin 3–436b
Clemens Scotus 3–438a
counts 3–658b
duchies 4–303b
ecclesiology 4–372a-374a
Einhard 4–412a
elections, royal 4–425b-426a
estate management 4–511b-512a
exegesis 4–542b
Italy 2–96a
map 3–105, 113
CAROLS, MIDDLE ENGLISH 3–116a
antifeminism 1–324b
ballads 2–60a-b
dance 4–86b-87a
Carpathian Basin
animals 1–296b, 298a, 301b
Carpathian Mountains
banats 2–70a
Visigoths 2–90b
West Slav boundary 1–96b
Carpenter, Alexander 3–459b
CARPET PAGE 3–117a
Celtic art 3–219a, 220a
Carpets
See Rugs and carpets
Carrand diptych 4–352a
Carrer de Montcada (Barcelona) 2–103a
Carrick 3–407a
CARROCCIO 3–117a
Carruca
See Plow
Cartage 3–613b
Cartagena 1–121a
agriculture 1–82a,b, 84b
Carthage
Cyprian, Saint 4–70a
exarch 4–530a
Fifth Council of (401) 3–67b-68a
Pelagius 1–652a, 653a,b
CARTHUSIAN RITE 3–118a
CARTHUSIANS 3–118a
angelus 1–252b
Bruno the Carthusian, Saint 2–354b, 392a-b
Burgundy, Duchy of 2–428a
Chartreuse de Champmol 4–186a
church, Latin 3–368a
Cartoixà (Roís de Corella) 3–167a
CARTULARY 3–120a; 1–446b
chancery 3–252b, 253a
Cistercians 3–405a
demography 4–138b
dictamen 4–173b
English 1–286b
John the Scribe 2–73a
Lembiotissa monastery 1–78b-79a
Cartulary (Heming) 1–286b
Cartusia
See Carthusians
Carucages 4–90b, 469b
CARVER, WILLIAM 3–120b
Carving
Anglo-Saxon 1–273b, 274a
Coptic 3–587a-588b
Casa di San Giorgio 2–75b-76a
CASBAH 3–120b
Casbah Mosque (Marrakech) 1–191b-193a
Casbah of Ūdāya (Rabat) 1–193a

CASHEL 3–121a; 1–470a; 4–492b
stone monuments 3–223a
Casibus virorum illustrium, De (Boccaccio) 2–286a-b, 288b
Caskets
Coptic art 3–587a
Časlav of Serbia 2–334b; 4–5a
CASNODYN 3–121b
Caspian Sea
Albania 1–123b
Araks River 1–421b
Caucasia 3–193b, 195b
Danes 4–554a
exploration 4–556b
Cassal, Battle of (1328) 2–387b
CASSIAN, JOHN 3–122a; 3–343a
Augustine of Hippo 1–653b
Coptic church 3–595a
Divine Office 4–222a, 229b
monasticism 2–170a; 3–344b
Cassianus Bassus 1–106a
Cassiciacum 1–647b-649a
CASSIODORUS SENATOR, FLAVIUS MAGNUS AURELIUS 3–123a; 1–188b, 434b; 3–252b
Arator 1–422a
calendars 3–18b-19b
classical literary studies 3–432b
encyclopedias and dictionaries 4–447b-448a
pattern books 4–291b
philosophy 2–241b
Theodoric the Ostrogoth 2–93b
theology, early church 3–342b
Variae 3–252b
Cassius Dio 1–117a
Casteleyn, Mathys 4–322b
Castella
Hadrian's Wall 3–143b
CASTELLAN 3–124b
castles and fortifications 3–143a
Catalonian 3–176a, 178b
commune 3–494a,b, 496a
Dauphiné 4–109b
militarism 3–176a,b
veguer 3–156b
Castellany 4–379a
Castello di Corte 2–114b
Castello Estense 2–114b
Castellón de la Plana 1–81b, 83b
Castel Nuovo
Giotto 2–278a
Castel Sant'Angelo 1–448a
Castigas y doctrinas que un sabio dava a sus hijas 3–663b
Castiglione, Baldassare 1–580a
CASTILE 3–125b
agriculture and nutrition 1–83a-84b
Albornoz, Cardinal 1–130b
Alfonso I of Aragon 1–160b
Alfonso XI of Castile 1–162b
Alfonso X of Castile 1–161a
Almoravids 1–199b
Aragon, Crown of 1–405a-b, 406a, 407a, 408b, 410a, 413a, 415b, 416b, 417a,b, 418a,b, 419a-b
archives 1–448b
Asturias-León 1–626b-628a,b, 629a
Calatrava, Order of 3–16b
Canary Islands 3–61b; 4–559a
Columbus 4–560b
commerce 2–127a; 4–557b, 558a
cortes 3–610b, 611a
maps 3–125-127
Navarre 2–126b
slaves 2–268b, 269a
Castilian Inquisition 2–105a
CASTILIAN LANGUAGE 3–141a
Cantar de Mío Cid 3–71b-72a, 137a
Catalan language 3–158a, 160a-b
Catalan literature 3–172a
Castilian literature 3–140a
Castillon, Battle of (1453) 2–328b; 3–65b-66a
Casting, metal
cannon 3–65a
Castlans
See Castellans
Castle Acre 1–256a
***CASTLE OF PERSEVERANCE* 3–142b**; 4–286b, 528b
allegory 1–186a
CASTLES AND FORTIFICATIONS 3–143a
animals, draft 1–295b
animals, food 1–299b
cannon 3–65a-66a
castellan 3–124b
castrum 3–152b
crusader art and architecture 4–22a
double-enceinte system 4–333b-334a
dungeon 4–308a
family 3–412b
Parthian 4–313a
Castra Regina 2–133a,b, 134a
Castration of cattle 1–294a
Castro, Guillén de 3–388b
Castrogiovanni 1–70b
Castros (magnate family) 3–130b
CASTRUM 3–152b
crusader art and architecture 4–22b
See Also Castles and fortifications
Casu diaboli, De (Anselm of Canterbury) 1–312a, 314b
CASUISTRY 3–153a
Casus 4–127b
Casus sancti Galli (Ratpert/Ekkehard IV) 4–418b
Catacomb of Priscilla
Annunciation 1–307b
CATACOMBS 3–154a; 1–451a
altar apparatus 1–221b
angel 1–248a
cubiculum 4–64a
death and burial 4–121a
early Christian and Byzantine art and architecture 4–336a, 350a, 351a, 358a
excavation 1–337a
CATALAN COMPANY 3–156a
Almogávares 1–190b
Andronikos II Palaiologos 1–246a
Byzantine Empire 2–500a
CATALAN LANGUAGE 3–157a; 3–157b
Bible translations 2–215b
CATALAN LITERATURE 3–164a
Arnald of Villanova 1–538b
Arthurian literature 1–573a, 575b-576a
CATALAN NARRATIVE IN VERSE 3–173a; 3–169a
Catalaunian Fields, Battle of (451) 2–92b
Catalogus codicum astrologorum graecorum 1–606a
Catalogus scriptorum ecclesiae 1–206b
CATALONIA (800-1137) **3–174a**; 1–406a, 407a
agriculture and nutrition 1–83a-84b
Aragon, Crown of 1–408a
art trade 1–562a
Barcelona 2–104b
Black Death 2–263b
Civil War (1462-1472) 2–104b
cortes 3–610b
Generalitat 2–75b
mandamentum 2–69a
map 3–176, 177
slaves 2–269b
Catania
Black Death 2–259a
***CATAPHRACTI* 3–179a**; 3–199a,b, 200a-b
CATAPULTS 3–179b; 2–354b
castles and fortifications 3–143a, 150b
Catasto 4–138a
Catchword
See Manuscript and Book Production
Catechetical School of Alexandria
Copts and Coptic church 3–593b
Scripture interpretation 3–335b
Catechumen
baptismal liturgy 3–675b
ceremonies of 2–83b, 84a
instruction 2–85b
Categories (Aristotle) 1–356a
Categorized (Ibn Sīda) 4–443a
Catena aurea (Aquinas) 2–222a
Catepan
See Katepano
Catepanagium 4–72a
Cathach of Saint Columba 2–220a; 3–485b
Hiberno-Saxon style 3–219b
incised cross motif 3–218b
shrine 3–223a
Cathal mac Finguine 1–114a; 3–121a; 4–493a
CATHAR LITURGY 3–181a
CATHARS 3–181b; 4–374b
Alan of Lille 1–119a
Albigensians 1–130b
councils 3–353a, 638b, 640a,b
courtly love 3–669a
crusades 3–353a, 357a
dualism 2–296b; 3–340a
Innocent III 3–353a
Cathay
Columbus 4–560b
Marco Polo 4–556b
CATHEDRA 3–191a; 1–442a, 443; 3–191b
CATHEDRAL 3–191b
Bulgaria 2–403b
chapter 3–265b
church organization 3–375a
liturgical aspects 1–444b
Cathedral of Ani 1–291b
Cathedral of Saint Mary the Great (Dubrovnik) 4–300a
Cathedral of Saint Pierre (Poitiers) 3–379a
Cathedral of the Dormition (Moscow) 4–192a
Catherine, Saint 1–261a
Catherine of Alexandria, Saint
miracle plays 4–268b
CATHERINE OF CLEVES, MASTER OF 3–192b
Catherine of Courtenay 1–245b
Catherine of Lancaster 3–138a
Catherine of Siena, Saint 3–168a; 4–476a
contraception 3–572b
doctor of the church 4–234b
Latin church 3–368b
mysticism 4–248b
Cath Finntrága 1–34a
Cathmail
See Cadoc, Saint
Catholic Homilies (Aelfric) 1–61b, 62a
Catholicon (Giovanni Balbi) 4–449b, 450a

Catholicon
  See Katholikon
Catholicus
  See Katholikos
Catihern 2–382a
Catilina (Sallust) 3–331b
Cato, Angelo 3–333b, 487b
CATO'S DISTICHS **(LATIN) 3–193a**
CATO'S DISTICHS **(OLD FRENCH) 3–193b**
Catraeth, Battle of 1–247b
Catterick
  See Catraeth, Battle of
Cattle 1–78b, 293b-294a, 299a
CAUCASIA 3–193b
  Aghkand ware 1–68b
  Albania 1–123a
  Armenia 1–473b, 588a-589b
  Armenian church 1–500b
  Bardha'a 2–107a
  Byzantine church 2–461b
  Georgia 4–113b
  map 3–194
CAUCASUS MOUNTAINS 3–195b; 3–193b
  Albania 1–123a
CAUDA 3–196a
Caupo 2–65a
Causis, De (Aquinas) 4–510b
Cautionary tale
  See Exemplum
Cavalca, Domenico 3–168a
CAVALCANTI, GUIDO 3–196a; 4–96b, 98b
  Cino da Pistoia 3–397b
Cavalcanti, Mainardo 2–286a, 288b
CAVALLERO ZIFAR, LIBRO DEL **3–197b**
CAVALLINI, PIETRO 3–198a; 3–396a
CAVALRY, ARMENIAN 3–198b
CAVALRY, BYZANTINE 3–199b
  arms and armor 1–522a
  cataphracti 3–179a
CAVALRY, EUROPEAN 3–200a
  arms and armor 1–522a, 528a, 531b, 534b
CAVALRY, ISLAMIC 3–208b
  development 1–294b
CAXTON, WILLIAM 3–210a
  ars moriendi 1–547b
  ballads 2–60a
  beast epic 2–142a
  Chronicles of England 3–329b
  courtesy books 3–661a, 662b, 666b
  Diodorus Siculus 3–325a
Cazola, Treaty of (1179) 1–409a; 3–130b
Ceadda
  See Chad, Saint
Cecaumenus
  See Kekaumenos
CECCO ANGIOLIERI 3–211b
Cecco d'Ascoli 1–613a
Cedrenus
  See Kedrenos
Cedrus (Boncompagno of Signa) 2–320b
Cefalù 4–346b
Céle Dé
  See Culdee movement
Celelles, Francis 3–570b
Celestial globes 1–622b
Celestial Hierarchy (Pseudo-Dionysios the Areopagite) 1–248a, 249b
CELESTINA, LA **3–212a**
Celestine II, Antipope 1–330a
CELESTINE I, POPE 3–213b
  elections, church 4–421a
Celestine III, Pope 3–131a
  clerics 4–133b
Celestine IV, Pope
  papal conclave 3–523b
CELESTINES 3–214b
  Celestine V 3–214a,b
CELESTINE V, POPE 3–214a
  Boniface VIII 2–323a-b
  deposition of rulers 4–160a
  papal conclave 3–524a, 642a
  renunciation of papacy 4–483b, 484b
CELIBACY 3–215a
  Anselm II of Lucca 1–311a
  Cathars 3–185a-185b
  clerical reform 3–417b
  law 3–443b
  Leo IX 3–351a
  religious communities 3–369a
  Western Councils 3–634a,b, 635a,b, 636b, 637a
Cellachán of Cashel, King 4–493a
Cellach Ó Sínaigh
  See Ó Sinaich, Cellach
Cellarer 3–444b
Cell-dara
  See Kildare
Cellerier (bp.) 3–183b
Cellini, Benvenuto 4–438b
Celsus 3–334b
CELTIC ART 3–218a
  Brittany 2–382a-b
"Celtic Catechesis, The" 1–111a
CELTIC CHURCH 3–225a
  Adamnan, Saint 1–52b, 53a
  Aidan of Lindisfarne 1–107a
  Armagh 1–469b
  Bangor bishopric 2–70a
  Bible glosses and commentaries 2–220a
  Brittany 2–381b-382a
  Clonard 3–465b
  Columbanus, Saint 3–485b
  Dyfed 4–329a
  Latin Church 3–344a-345a
  monasticism 2–170a, 172a
Celtic cross 4–9a
CELTIC LANGUAGES 3–232b
  Alexander romances 1–150a
  Anglo-Saxon literature 1–274a
  assonance 1–600b
  Breton 2–380b
Celtic literature
  See Irish, Scottish, Welsh literature
Celts
  Aachen 1–1a
  alphabet, Oghamic 1–215a
  Anglo-Saxons 1–288b
  barbarian invasions 2–96b
  Bordeaux 2–327b
  classes 2–105b
  enamel 4–441b
  field systems 1–91a
  horses 1–294b
Cemetery
  See Death and Burial
Cencio Savelli
  See Honorius III, Pope
Cenél Comgaill family 4–78a
Cenél Gabráin family 4–78a,b
Cenél Loairn 4–78b
Cenél nEógain
  Áedán 1–60a
Cennétig mac Lorcáin, King 4–77a-b
Cenn Fáelad mac Colgan
  See Connacht
CENNINI, CENNINO 3–234a
Censiers 4–513a
Censorinus 1–605a
CENTERING 3–234b
Centiloquium 1–606b
CENT NOUVELLES NOUVELLES **3–235a**
Centonarii 3–607a
CENTONIZATION 3–235b
Centurioni firm
  Columbus 4–560b
Ceolfrid 2–153b, 154a
  tonsure 3–229a
Ceolwulf, King 4–456a
  Bede 2–155b
Cephissus, Battle of (1311) 1–191a
CERAMICS, EUROPEAN 3–236a
  art trade 1–561b
  Bulgaria 2–404b, 417a
  Byzantines 2–457a
  cooking 1–95a
  cuerda seca 4–64a
  Della Robbia 4–134b
CERAMICS, ISLAMIC 3–238a
  Abbasids 1–5b
  Aghkand ware 1–68a
  Ayyubids 2–22a-b
  azulejo 2–30b
  barbotine 2–101a
  cuerda seca 4–64a
  faience 4–582a
CERCAMON 3–240a
Cercapou (Francesc Eiximenis) 4–416b
Cerdagne
  See Cerdanya
Cerdanya 1–413a, 416a, 418b-419a; 3–174b
  agriculture 1–84a, 85b
  Ramon Berenguer III 3–178a
Cerddor 2–106a
Cerdic
  Estoire des Engleis (Geffroi Gaimar) 1–264b
Cereal prices
  demography 4–139a
Ceredigion, Kingdom of 4–329a,b
Ceremoniis, De 4–446b
Cérisy-la-Forêt 1–256a
Cerne, Book of 3–231a
Cerne Abbas 1–281b
  Aelfric 1–61b
Cerroni, Petro dei
  See Cavallini, Pietro
Certosa
  See Carthusians
Certosa (Pavia) 2–196b-197a
Cervantes, Miguel de 1–227b; 3–212b
  Don Quixote 3–258a
  Libro del Cavallero Zifar 3–197b
Cervera 1–410b
Cerverí de Girona
  See Guillem de Cervera
Cesare de Barchi
  slaves 2–270a
Cesarini, Giuliano 4–56a
  Basel, Council of 3–652b, 653a
Cesaris 3–256b
Cetina River 4–2a, 4a
Ceuta 1–639b
Ceyhan River 2–19a
Ceylon
  map 4–553b
  traveler accounts 1–332b
Chad, Saint 1–285a
Chaghri-Beg 1–203a
CHAINED BOOKS 3–240b
Chain Tower 4–50a
CHAIRETE 3–240b
Chair of Elijah 3–401b
Chalcedon, Council of (451) 1–32a; 2–10a; 3–628b, 629a-630a; 4–114a, 383b, 524a, 525a
  Antioch 2–460a

CHALCEDON, COUNCIL OF (cont.)
Armenia 1–477b, 482b, 483b
Armenian church 4–114a
autocephalos 2–10a
Byzantine church 2–459b, 460a, 462a-b, 467a; 3–446b, 447a
Christology 3–320a-b, 321a, 336a, 339b
church unity 3–336b
Constantinople 3–555b
Copts 3–594a
corporation 3–607a
decisions 2–485b
early church 3–337b, 338b-339a, 342a
Monophysitism 1–32a
ordination 3–443b
papal power 3–342a
theology, mystical 2–467a
Chaldean alphabet 1–218a
Chaldean rite
See Antiochene rite
Chaldean sages
astrology 1–604a, 605a
CHALDER 3–241a
CHALICE 3–241b
altar apparatus 1–222b
ciborium 3–383b
ordination rites 3–442b
Chalice of San Girolamo 3–239a
Chalke Gate (Constantinople) 3–379a
Chalkoprateia basilicas (Constantinople) 4–337b
Chalon 2–424b, 426a
Châlons-sur-Marne
Catalaunian Fields, Battle of (451) 2–92b
fairs 4–590b, 592a
Chalon-sur-Saône
fairs 4–585b
Chalon-sur-Saône, Council of (603) 3–486a
Châlus
Richard I 4–420a, 468a
Chamber, royal
finances 4–532b
CHAMBERLAIN 3–242a
Chambre des Comptes
butler 2–434b
chamberlain 3–242b
Chamfrain 1–529a, 534b
Chamois
hunting laws 1–301a
CHAMPAGNE, COUNTY 3–243a; 3–658b
Arthurian literature 1–569a
Capellanus, Andreas 3–88b
courtly love 3–672a, 673a
fairs 2–78a; 4–470a, 590b
timber 3–267b
Champain, Cecily 3–286b-287b
Champart, Robert
See Robert of Jumièges
Champion des dames (Martin le Franc) 3–256b
CHAMPION IN JUDICIAL COMBAT 3–250b
Champion of England 3–251a
Champlevé enamel
See Enamel, champlevé
Champmol priory
See Dijon, Chartreuse de Champmol
CHANCEL 3–251b
church types 3–379b
Coptic architecture 3–587a
Chancellor
See Chancery
Chancel screen
See Screen, chancel
CHANCERY 3–251b; 4–502a,b
abbreviator 1–13b
apostolic datary 4–106b
capitulary 3–91a
Catalan language 3–158a
curia, papal 4–66a
cursus 4–67a
equity 4–502b, 503a
Norman-Angevin England 4–469b
Urban II 3–352a
Chandos, Sir John 3–408a
Chandu 4–557a
Chang-Chou
See Zayton
Changer
See Banking, European
CHANSON 3–254b
Chartier, Alain 3–275b
Chanson à carole 3–116a
Chanson avec refrain 3–255b
Chanson d'ami
See Chansons de Femme
***CHANSON D'ANTIOCHE* 3–254b**
crusades 3–331a
Chanson de Guillaume 3–258b, 259a
Chanson de Jérusalem 3–331a
***CHANSON DE LA CROISADE CONTRE LES ALBIGEOIS* 3–255a**
Chanson de malmariée
See Also Chansons de femme
Chanson de nonne 3–263a
Chanson des Saxons (Jean Bodel) 2–290b, 291a
***CHANSONNIER* 3–255b**; 1–269a
Chansons à danser
See Chanson
Chansons d'amour
See Chanson
Chansons de croisade 3–538b
***CHANSONS DE FEMME* 3–257a**
Chansons de malmariée 3–262b
Chansons de toile 3–263a
***CHANSONS DE GESTE* 3–257a**
Anglo-Norman literature 1–266b, 267a
assonance 1–600b
Aucassin et Nicolette 1–642b
Bayeux Tapestry 2–139a
Bertrand de Bar-sur-Aube 2–201b
Bible 2–216b
cantilène 3–87b
chansonnier 3–255b
chronicles, French 3–330b-331a
divisions 3–72a
Elisabeth of Nassau-Saarbrücken 4–432b
Elis Saga ok Rosamundu 4–431b
knights' sagas 4–612b
Romance of Horn 1–266b, 267a
scholarship 3–78b-79b
Spanish epic 3–73a, 75a, 77b
See Also Chanson d'Antioche
***CHANSONS DE MALMARIÉE* 3–262b**
***CHANSONS DE TOILE* 3–263a**
Chansons d'histoire 3–263a
Chant
See individual articles
Chantefable
See Aucassin et Nicolette
CHANT ROYAL 3–263b
envoi 4–492a
Chantry chapel 3–264a
Chapbooks
See Volksbüch
CHAPEL 3–263b
absidiole 1–24a
apse echelon 1–352a
basilica 2–124b
Capilla Mayor 3–90a
chaplain 3–264a
chasovnya 3–277a
chevet 3–300a
lady chapels 1–423b; 3–264a, 379b
liturgical aspects 1–442b, 444b-445a
papal 3–352a
Chapel-de-Fer 1–526a, 527b
Chapel of Dominus Flevit (Jerusalem) 4–359b
Chapel of Saint Bartholomew (Paderborn) 3–379a
Chaperons 3–623b
CHAPLAIN 3–264a
clerical hierarchy 3–444b
Chaplet 3–624a
Chaplet of pearls (Eutychios) 4–525a
Chappes 4–590b
CHAPTER 3–265a
Brethren of the Common Life 2–367b
cathedral 3–191b
CHAPTER HOUSE 3–266a
"Chapter of Mats" 1–320b-321a
CHARCOAL 3–267a
botany 2–347b
Char d'Orgueil (Nicole Bozon) 1–263b, 264a
CHARDRI 3–267b; 1–260b, 261b
moral writings 1–264b
CHARISTIKION 3–268a
Charité-sur-Loire, La, church architecture 2–428a
CHARLEMAGNE 3–106b-111a
CHARLEMAGNE 3–268a
Aachen 1–1a-b
Aachen palace chapel 1–2b
adoptionism dispute 1–57b
agriculture 1–92a, 95b
Alcuin of York 1–100a, 142b, 143a-b; 3–433a
Alexander of Roes 1–149a
altars 1–225a
Amalarius of Metz 1–228a
Angilbert, Saint 1–254a
Anglo-Saxon art 1–273a
Apostles' Creed 3–676a
Aquitaine 1–366b
Asturias-León 1–626b
Avars 4–1b-2a
baptism 2–84a
Barcelona 2–102b-103a
Bavaria 2–4b, 95a
Benedictine Rule 2–170b, 172a
Bible texts 2–211b
building projects 1–333b
Bulgaria 2–401a
Burgundy, County of 2–424a
Byzantine Empire 2–465a, 488b
caesaropapism 3–11b
cancellarius use 3–251b
capitularies 3–91b
Catalonia 3–174a
cavalry 3–202a-b
celibacy, clerical 3–216b
chanson de geste 3–258b-259b
church reforms 3–109a, 347b, 348b-349a, 373b, 374a,b; 4–373a
Collectio Dionysio-Hadriana 4–193a
coronation 3–11b, 110a-111a, 346b
Divine Office 4–230a
dye industry 4–328a
educational reforms 1–100a; 3–433a
Einhard 4–412a
Hārūn al-Rashīd 2–147a
Islamic diplomacy 4–200b
liturgical drama 3–676b-677a; 4–274a
maps 1–333b
Offa 4–455a

poets and poetry 3–100a, 102a
religious wars 4–15b
romances 1–151b; 4–318b
Saxony 2–96b
Spanish campaign (778) 2–126a
successor 4–425b-426a
Tassilo III 2–134a
Charles (son of Lothar) 3–114a
Charles d'Anjou
See Charles of Anjou
Charles de Valois
See Charles of Valois
Charles d'Orléans
See Charles of Orléans
Charles IV, Emperor
Bavaria 2–135b
Bohemia-Moravia 2–300b, 301a-b
Bohemian reform 2–304a,b; 3–368a
Brandenburg 2–361a-b
Burgundy, Kingdom of 2–429b
Dauphiné 4–109a
Golden Bull 1356 2–8a; 3–334a; 4–428b
Petrarch 1–335b
CHARLES MARTEL 3–272a
CHARLES MARTEL 3–345b
Alamanni 1–118a; 2–94b
Boniface, Saint 2–321b, 322a
Carolingians 3–106a
cavalry 3–201a-b
commendation 3–491a
diet 1–95a
ecclesiastical reform 3–108b
Islamic expansion 1–374a
Charles of Anjou, King of Sicily 1–48b, 253a, 437a; 2–270b; 3–641b; 4–499b
Aragon, Crown of 1–412b-413a, 414a
Arnolfo di Cambio 1–541a
Bulgaria 2–410b
Burgundy, Kingdom of 2–429b
Byzantine Empire 2–499a-b
Celestines 3–214b
Conradin of Sicily 4–95b-96a
consulate 3–571b
crusades, political 4–60b-61a
Dyrrachium 4–330a
fiscal agents 2–77b
Louis IX 4–53b-54a
Manfred of Sicily 4–95b-96a
Peter II 3–165b
Charles of Blois 2–380a
Charles IV of France, King
Aquitaine 1–367b
Champagne 3–249b
CHARLES V OF FRANCE, KING 3–269a; 1–447a
art trade 1–561a
astrology 1–608a
Bois Protat 2–310a
Bondol, Jean 2–320b
Brittany 2–380a
cameo collection 1–335b
Carmelite Water 2–147a
Castile 3–137a
Celestines 3–214b
Christine de Pizan 3–316a
Clement VII 1–108a
clock, portable 3–462a
Dauphiné 4–109a
diplomacy 4–210a
Edward the Black Prince 4–399a
Eustache Deschamps 4–163b
Knights of Malta 3–304a
manuscript collections 1–336a
tombs 2–145a
Charles VI of France, King
acclamations 1–36a
Burgundy, Kingdom of 2–429b
Byzantine Empire 2–503a
Cabochien riots 3–3b
cameo collection 1–335b
Châtelet 3–278b
Eustache Deschamps 4–163b
proto-stoneware 3–238a
CHARLES VII OF FRANCE, KING 3–270b
Bordeaux 2–328b
butler 2–434b
Chartier, Alain 3–275a
clock, portable 3–462b
fairs 4–585b
Ferrara-Florence Council 3–653b
military reform 3–206a-b
Pragmatic Sanction of Bourges (1438) 3–367a
siege train 3–65a
Charles VIII of France, King
Bourdichon, Jean 2–349b
Brittany 2–380a,b
chronicles 3–487b
fables 4–572b
Jem Sultan 2–137a
Charles X of France, King
appanages 1–351b
Charles II of Naples 1–414b
Charles III of Naples 2–337a
Charles I of Naples and Sicily
See Charles of Anjou
Charles II the Bad of Navarre, King 3–269a; 4–490b
Charles III of Navarre, King
Fuero general 3–611b
CHARLES OF ORLÉANS 3–272b
ballade 2–59a
chant royal 3–263b
Charles of Salerno 1–414b
Charles of Valois 1–414a
Almogávares 1–191a
Andronikos II Palaiologos 1–246a
Aragon 4–61a,b
Florence 4–98b-99a
Charles Robert of Hungary 2–336b
Charles II the Bald, Emperor 3–112b-114a,b
Baldwin I of Flanders 2–58a
Bible 2–211b
Brittany 2–379a
Burgundy 2–424a, 427a, 428b
Capetians 3–89b
capitulary 3–91b
classical literary studies 3–433a
codex aureus 3–474b
Sunifred 3–174b
Charles II the Bold, Duke 3–333b, 487a
Charles III the Fat, Emperor 3–114a, 115a
Arnulf 1–541b
Burgundy, Kingdom of 2–428b
Charles the Good, Count
Bruges 2–386b
communes 3–497a
Charles the Great
See Charlemagne
Charles the Noble
See Charles III of Navarre, King
Charles the Rash, Duke 2–427a
Charles III the Simple, King 3–114b, 115a
Catalonia monasteries 3–175a
Charlier de Gerson, Joannes 1–608b
Charms
Old English poetry 1–281a
CHARMS, OLD HIGH GERMAN 3–273b
baptismal vows 2–87a
CHARONTON (QUARTON), EN-GUERRAND **3–274b**
Charrino y Meendinno, Payo Gomez 3–87a
Charroi de Nîmes 3–257b
CHARTER 3–274b
aldermen 1–143b
Buda 2–396b
bull, papal 2–418a
cartulary 3–120a
chancery 3–252a, 253a
communes 3–494b
corporation 3–607a-b
Old English manuscripts 1–286b
"Charterhouse"
See Carthusians
CHARTIER, ALAIN 3–275a; 1–189b
CHARTRES CATHEDRAL 3–276a; 1–425b, 428a, 429b, 442b
Annunciation carving 1–308a
Apocalypse illustration 1–344a
Bernard of Chartres 2–189b
cathedral school 1–183a
chevet 3–300b
column figures 3–487a,b
construction 1–226a; 3–568a-569a
crocket capital 3–91a
Latin-cross church 3–379b
rebuilding 3–192a
Chartres Isopet 4–573b
Chartreuse de Champmol (Dijon)
See Dijon, Chartreuse de Champmol
Chartreux, use of
See Carthusian Rite
Charudes 1–117a
***CHASOVNYA* 3–277a**
Chasteau d'amour (Robert Grosseteste) 1–263b
***CHASTELAINE DE VERGI, LA* 3–277a**
Chastoiement des dames (Robert of Blois) 3–664a
Chasuble
See Vestments
Château de Gaillon 3–482b
Château Gaillard 4–111a
Château of Blois 2–344b
Château Porcien
fairs 4–590b
Châtelain 3–625a; 4–379a
***CHÂTELAIN DE COUCY* 3–277b**
CHÂTELET 3–278a
Établissements de Saint Louis 4–515b
Châtellenie 4–379a
Chatton, Walter 2–358a
CHAUCER, GEOFFREY 3–279b
alchemy 4–580a
allegory 1–185a
Anglo-Latin poetry 1–255a
antifeminism 1–322b
Arthurian literature 1–568b
astrolabe 1–603b, 611a; 3–29a
ballade 2–59a
Boccaccio 2–285b, 286b, 287a
Caxton, William 3–211a
Charles of Orléans 3–273a
Clanvowe, Sir John 3–408a-b
contraception 3–572b, 573a
courtly love 3–669b
exempla 4–551b
fables 4–572b
fabliaux 4–577a
knighthood 3–83a
Knight's Tale 3–302b
Chaucer, John 3–280a
Chaucer, Philippa 3–280b-281a
Chaunois 2–427a
Chausses 3–626a

Cheb 2–300b
Cheese 1–95b-96a
rent 1–302a
Cheirothesia 3–442b
Cheirotonia 3–442b
Chelčický, Peter 2–306a-b
Chelles, Jehan de
See Jean de Chelles
Chemistry of Moses 1–135b
Cherbourg
fairs 4–586a
Cherchell
fairs 4–589a
Chernigov 2–131b
Chernomen, Battle of (1371) 4–56a
Cherson 2–118b
Chertsey Abbey 3–237a
CHERUB 3–297b
Chess-book (Jacobus de Cessolis) 3–169a
Chester
Anglo-Saxon migrations 1–290a
CHESTER, TREATY OF (973) **3–299b**
CHESTER PLAYS 3–298a; 4–284b
Corpus Christi, feast of 3–608b
Chestre, Thomas 1–573b, 574b
Chétifs 3–331a
Chetmno
See Culm
Chevalier, Étienne 2–326b
Chevalier, sa dame et un clerc, Le 1–269b
Chevalier à la corbeille, Le 1–269b
Chevalier au cygne et enfances Godefroi 3–331a
Chevalier au Lion, Le (Yvain) (Chrétien de Troyes) 1–643b; 3–308b; 4–520a
Chevalier de la Charrette (Chrétien de Troyes) 3–308b, 671a
Chevalier du Papagau 4–380b
Chevalier qui faisaient parler les cons, Le 1–269b
Chevauchée 3–206a
CHEVET 3–300b; 1–234a
apse 1–352a
Canterbury Cathedral 3–84a
chapel 3–264a
church types 3–379b
development 1–144b
Chichele, Henry 3–83b, 578b
Chicken 1–300a; 3–581b, 584a
Chierheit der gheestelijker brulocht, Die 4–320b
Chieri 2–76a
Chiesa del Loretino (San Miniato al Tedesco) 3–572a
Chilandari Monastery 1–638a; 2–448a
Childbirth
churching of women 3–382a
Childeric I, King 2–94a; 3–466b
Childeric III, King
deposition of rulers 4–158b, 159a,b, 160a
Children
clothing 3–626a
urban environment 4–144a
Children's Crusade
See Crusade, Children's
Chiliasm
See Millenialism
Chilperic I, King 1–212b
CHIN 3–301a
China
alchemy 1–135a
Black Death 2–258a
ceramics 3–240a, 328b, 329b
clocks 3–459b, 460a-b
Marco Polo 4–556b-557a
routes 4–558a-b
traveler accounts 1–332a,b
Chindaswinth, King 4–520b
Chingiz-nama 1–106b
Chinon
fairs 4–586a
Chioggia War 2–502b
Chios 1–246b
CHIP CARVING 3–301a
Celtic art 3–220a
Chippenham, Peace of 1–164a
Chiton 3–614a
CHIVALRY 3–301b
allegory, French 1–188b-189b
Amadís de Gaula 1–227b
Arthurian literature 1–576b
birth 3–203a-204a
Boniface 4–43b
Brittany 2–379b
Burgundy, Duchy of 2–428a
Catalan literature 3–170a
courtesy books 3–665b-666b
courtly love 3–670b
Ovid 1–183b-184b
romances 1–151a; 4–318b
See Also Champion in Judicial Combat
CHIVALRY, ORDERS OF 3–303b
arms and armor 1–524a
Aviz 2–16b
Calatrava 3–16b
crusades 4–32b
See Also Chivalry
Chlamys 3–615a,b
Chlodomer 2–423b
Chludov Psalter 2–440b
Choice Stories (Ibn Qutayba) 1–379b
CHOIR 3–307b
basilica 2–124b
Coptic and Ethiopian churches 1–157a
Cholarzene-Javakheti 3–308a
Chonai 2–493a
Chora, Monastery of Christ in 2–448b
Chorbishop, chorepiskopos
See Clergy, Byzantine
Chosrau I Anōšarwān
See Xusrō I Anōšarwān
Chosrau II Parwez
See Xusrō II Abarwēz
CHOSROIDS (MIHRANIDS) **3–307b**; 2–48b
decline 2–27a
Gardman 1–124a, 125a
Choumnos, Nikephoros 1–246a
CHRÉTIEN DE TROYES 3–308b; 1–184a, 189a; 2–370a; 3–246b
Arthurian literature 1–566b-567a, 568b-569a, 571b, 574b
Aucassin et Nicolette 1–642b
Breta Sǫgur 2–365b
courtly love 3–668a, 669b, 671a, 672a
Eleanor of Aquitaine 4–419b
Erex Saga 4–504b
Eufemiavisor 4–520a
fabliau 4–574b
Guillaume d'Angleterre 1–267b
Chrism
anointing of kings 1–308b
confirmation 3–535b
dedication of churches 4–130b
ordination rites 3–442b
postbaptism ceremonies 2–83b
See Also Baptism
CHRISMON 3–311b
Christ 1–280a
apostolic succession 1–350a
Chairete 3–240a
Seinte Resureccion 1–270a
Christ II (Cynewulf) 1–278a
Christ and Satan 1–280b
Christburg, Treaty of (1249) 2–66b
Christ Carrying the Cross (Barna da Siena) 2–111a
Christ Church Cathedral
See Canterbury Cathedral
Christ Church Monastery 1–256a
Christ Fantokrator
Coptic art 3–592b
Christherre-Chronik 2–229a
Christian I, King
Nordic Union 4–156a
Christian II, King
Nordic Union 4–156a
Christian, Bishop
Prussian conversions 2–66a-b
Christian, Friar
Dominicans 4–244a
Christian architecture
See Early Christian and Byzantine architecture
Christian art
See Early Christian art
Christian calendar 3–18a-24b
CHRISTIAN CHURCH IN PERSIA 3–312a
Armenian saints 1–518b-519a
Christian Gnostic sects
angel/angelology 1–249b
CHRISTIAN HEBRAISTS 3–313b
Christianity
See Church
CHRISTIANITY, NUBIAN 3–314a
CHRISTIAN OF STABLO 3–311b
Latin exegesis 4–542b
Christians in the Islamic World
See Abode of Islam--Abode of War
See Crusades and Crusader States
See Islam, Conquests of
Christian Topography (Cosmas Indicopleustes) 3–613b
Christi Hort 2–230a-b
Christina, Saint 1–261b
Christina of Sweden, Queen
song anthologies 1–319a
CHRISTINE DE PIZAN 3–315b; 1–189b
antifeminism 1–324a
ballade 2–59a
biographical writing 2–240a; 3–333a
Charles V of France 3–269a, 333a
chivalry 3–302a
courtesy books 3–662a, 664b, 665b-666a, 672b
Christ in Glory (Pietro Cavallini) 3–198a
CHRISTMAS 3–317a
Assumption of the Virgin 1–601a
Brigit, Saint 2–376a
Bruno of Würzburg, Saint 2–392a
calendar 3–19b-20a, 21b-22b
canonization 3–68a
carnival 3–99a
cookery 3–580b-582b
Corpus Christi, feast of 3–608a
dance 4–86a
Easter 4–364b
Epiphany 4–496b
liturgical colors 3–484b
plays, German 4–268a-b
tree 3–319a
Christodoulos of Alexandria
Nubian Christianity 3–315a
CHRISTOGRAM 3–319b
Chrismon 3–311b
See Also Cross, Forms of
CHRISTOLOGY 3–319b
Ancient of Days 1–242b

Apollinarius 1–348a
baptism, concept 4–497a-b
Constans II 3–544b
See Also Antichrist
Christopher I, King 4–154b
Christopher II, King 4–154b, 155a
Christopher, Antipope 1–330a
Christopher of Bavaria
Nordic Union 4–156a
Christopher of Mytilene 2–507a, 524a
Christopher of Paris 1–138b
Christophorus of Rivoalto, Bishop
Aquileia, rite 1–353a
Christopolis 2–479b
Christ Order of 3–306b
Christ Pantokrator, Monastery of 2–443b
CHRISTUS, PETRUS 3–324b
***CHRISTUS UND DIE SAMARITERIN* 3–325a**; 2–226a
Chrodegang of Metz, Saint
canon rules 3–108b, 191b, 216b
Capetian family kinship 3–89b
Divine Office 4–222a, 230a,b
Chromatius, Bishop
Aquileia, rite 1–352b
Chronica (Cassiodorus) 3–123a
Chronica actitatorum (Martin de Alpartils) 3–645b
Chronica Boemorum (Cosmas of Prague) 3–614a
Chronica majora (Matthew of Paris) 1–333a; 3–326b
Chronica monasterii Casinensis (Constantine the African) 3–548b
Chronica XXIV generalium 1–252b; 2–35b
Chronicle (Anania Širakac'i) 1–238b
Chronicle (Gaimar) 1–271a
Chronicle (Jocelin of Brakelond) 3–458b
Chronicle (Prosper of Aquitaine) 3–214a
Chronicle (Nicholas Trivet) 1–265b
Chronicle of England (John Capgrave) 3–90a
Chronicle of the Princes, The
See Brut y Tywysogion
Chronicle of the Saxon Kings
See Brenhinedd y Saesson
Chronicle of the Twenty-four Generals
See Chronica XXIV generalium
CHRONICLES 3–325a; 1–296b
Anglo-Norman literature 1–264b-266a
Anglo-Saxon prose 1–284a,b
Arthurian literature 1–564a-565b
Bruno of Magdeburg 2–391b
Byzantine 2–512a-b, 522b
Cantar de Mío Cid 3–71a,b
Catalan literature 3–164a, 165a-166b
Chester, Treaty of 3–299b-300a
Cistercian order 3–405a
Comines 3–487a-488a
crusade 4–20a
Ekkehard of Aura 4–417b
Old English 1–275a
Chronicles (Froissart) 3–325a
CHRONICLES, FRENCH 3–330b
Chronicles of England (Caxton) 3–329b
"Chronicles of Fredegarius" 3–485b
Chronicon (Eusebius) 1–162a
Chronicon de Lanercost 1–309a
Chronique (Jean le Bel) 3–333a
Chronique des ducs de Bourgogne (Georges Chastellain) 3–333a
Chronique des ducs de Normandie (Benoît de Sainte-Maure) 3–331a
Chronique rimée (Philippe Mousket) 3–258a
Chronique rimée des rois de France, La 3–332b
***CHRONIQUES DE LONDRES* 3–334a**; 1–266a; 3–329b
Chronographia (Michael Psellos) 1–641b
Chronography (Bar Hebraeus) 2–108a
Chronology (Bīrūnī) 2–249a
Chrysippus 4–168b
CHRYSOBULLON 3–334a
Chrysocheir 2–118a
Chrysologus, Peter, Saint
church unity 3–336b
Chrysoloras, Manuel 3–435b
Chrysostom, John, Saint
See John Chrysostom, Saint
Church
anti-Semitism 1–339a-342a
apostasy 1–349b
architecture 1–441b
archives 1–445b-446a,b, 448a
astrology 1–605a-606b, 607a-608b
clergy 3–440a
confession 3–533a
ex voto 4–529b
food prohibitions 1–95b, 300a
CHURCH, EARLY 3–337a
angelus 1–252a
Augustine of Hippo 1–646a
caesaropapism 3–10a
clergy 3–440b-441a,b, 442b-443a, 445a
Constantine I, the Great 3–545a-b
Ethiopia 1–31b-32a
excommunication 4–536a
CHURCH, LATIN: TO 1054 3–343b
basileus 2–123b
Córdoba 3–599b, 600a
early Christian and Byzantine architecture 4–337b-338a
ecumenical councils (325-787) 3–627a
excommunication 4–536a-b
Kiev 1–303a
missionaries to Baltic countries 2–64a-b
Western councils 3–632b
CHURCH, LATIN: 1054 TO 1305 3–350b
Aristotelianism 1–461a, 462a,b
Armenian Rite 1–516b
excommunication 4–536b
Henry II of England 2–151a
Jews in Europe 1–586a
CHURCH, LATIN: 1305 TO 1500 3–361a
Andronikos III Palaiologos 1–246b
Bosnian church 2–341b-343b
Western councils 3–642b
CHURCH, LATIN: ORGANIZATION 3–372b
clergy 3–440b-441b
convocations of Canterbury and York 3–578a
dioceses 4–191a
doctors of the church 4–234a
early church 3–341a-b
CHURCH, TYPES OF 3–378a; 3–404b
double-ended basilica 2–124b
Church architecture
apse 1–352a
Armenian 1–493a-494a
ceramics, European 3–237b
chapel 3–264a
chapter house 3–266a
chevet 3–300b
choir 3–307b
Croatia 4–8b
diaconicon 4–167b
early Christian and Byzantine 4–335a-347b
exonarthex 4–552b
wooden construction 3–559a,b
CHURCH FATHERS 3–334b
Augustine of Hippo 1–646a
Christology 3–321a-b
Copts and Coptic church 3–593b-594a
Cyprian, Saint 4–70a
doctors of the church 4–234a
early church 3–338a
Ecclesia and Synagoga 4–371a
mathematics, condemnation 2–38b
CHURCHING OF WOMEN 3–382b
"Church of the East"
See Christian Church in Persia
Ciarain of Clonmacnois 3–465b
Ciarain of Saigir 3–465b
CIBORIUM 3–383b; 1–222a, 223b
Cicero
astrology 1–605a
Augustine 1–646b, 647b-649a; 2–320b
classical literary studies 3–430b
commentary on 1–610b; 2–292a
dialectic 4–169a
equity 4–501a
fables 4–572a
Ciconia 2–61a
Cid, Le (Corneille) 3–388b
CID, THE, HISTORY AND LEGEND OF 3–383b
Almoravid assaults (1099) 1–199b
Berenguer Ramon II vs. 3–177b
Cantar de Mío Cid 3–70b
Castile 3–129b
Cilician Chronicle (Smbat Sparapet) 3–199a
CILICIAN GATES 3–390b
CILICIAN KINGDOM 3–390b; 1–474a; 2–493b
Anatolia 1–240a
Andronikos I Komnenos 1–245a
Antiochene rite 1–326b
Armenian church 1–500b-501a, 504a
Armenian language 1–507a
Armenian literature 1–511b-512a
Armenian painting 1–497a-b
Ayās 2–19a
Byzantine empire 2–492a, 495a
crusades 4–35a
independence 1–241b
map 3–392
CILICIAN-ROMAN CHURCH UNION 3–394a; 1–500b-501a
CIMABUE, CENNI DI PEPI 3–395b
Assisi 1–593b
Duccio di Buoninsegna 4–301b, 302a
status 1–579a
Cimbri 2–88b
Cina da Pistoia 2–278a
Cináed mac Ailpín
See Kenneth I MacAlpin
Cináed of Tara, King 1–60b
Cinca River 1–406a
CINÉAL EÓGHAIN 3–396b
Cinkante balades (John Gower) 1–269a
Cino
See Cino da Pistoia
CINO DA PISTOIA 3–397a; 2–115a,b
Cipangu 4–559b, 560b
Cipolla, Carlo 2–98b
Ciprianus, Saint
See Cyprian, Saint
Ciranawor (Aštarak) 1–601a-b
CIRCASSIANS 3–398a
Barqūq 2–113a
Circumcelliones 1–651b
CIRCUMCISION, ISLAMIC 3–400b
CIRCUMCISION, JEWISH 3–401a
"Circumcision" style calendar 3–20a
Cisiojanus 3–21a-b

Cisjurane Burgundy
See Provence
CISTERCIAN CHANT 3–402a
See Also Cistercian rite
CISTERCIAN ORDER 3–403a; 2–171b; 3–118a, 368a; 4–292b
Achard 1–43a
Alan of Lille 1–119a
Albigensian crusade 3–188a
alchemy 1–137b
Ancrene Riwle 1–243a
Aragon, Crown of 1–410b, 420a
bastides 2–128b
beguines 2–158a
Bernard of Clairvaux 2–190b, 191a, 192b
Bible 2–218a
Birgitta, Saint 2–246b
Boniface VIII 2–323b
Brittany 2–379b, 382a
Burgundy, County of 2–426b
Burgundy, Duchy of 2–428a
Calatrava Order affiliation 3–16b
campaign vs. heretics 3–187b
Castile 3–133a
Celestines 3–215a
chapter house design 3–266b
Christian Hebraists 3–313b
Cluny, order of 3–471a,b
Divine Office 4–222a
Ethelred of Rievaulx, Saint 4–516b
Florentine style calendar 3–20a
Marian office 2–274a
plainsong 4–241a
CISTERCIAN RITE 3–406a
Cistercians of the Strict Observance 3–403a
Cîteaux Bible
See Bible, Cistercian
Cîteaux monastery
Bernard of Clairvaux 2–190b
Robert of Molesme 3–355a
See Also Cistercian Order
Citizens
See Class structure, Western
Citobus
See Civetot
City
See Urbanism
City of God, The (Augustine of Hippo) 1–181b, 218a, 605b, 648a, 649a, 650a, 651a, 654a, 656b, 657a,b; 2–91a; 3–167b, 342b; 4–118b
City of Peace
See Round City
CIUFFAGNI, BERNARDO 3–406b
Ciutadans honrats 2–103b
Civetot 4–34b
Cividale 3–64a-b
Cividale del Friuli, Council of (1408) 3–646a
Cividale del Fruili, Synod of (797) 3–677a
Civitas
Bartolo da Sassoferrato 2–115b-116a
county 3–658a
Civitate, Battle of (1053) 3–203b
Civitate dei, De
See City of God, The
Cizre
See Jazīrat ibn ʿUmar
Clairvaux, Saint Bernard of
See Bernard of Clairvaux, Saint
Clairvaux abbey 3–403b
Clairvaux II (church) 1–43a
Clann Cholmáin 1–60b
CLANS, SCOTTISH 3–407a
CLANVOWE, SIR JOHN 3–408a
Clare 4–77a
CLARENDON, ASSIZE OF 3–408b
CLARENDON, CONSTITUTIONS OF 3–409b; 2–151b-152a; 3–83a
assize 1–596a
church elections 4–422b-423a
clergy, criminous 4–471a
Clari, Robert de 3–332a
Clári Saga
See Klári Saga
CLASSICAL LITERARY STUDIES 3–430a
antiquarianism and archaeology 1–332a, 337b
Chaucer 3–287b, 289b, 294a
Classical Old Irish period
See Celtic languages
Classical sagas 4–612b
See Family sagas, Icelandic
CLASS STRUCTURE, WESTERN (1000-1300) 3–410b
Armenia 1–488a-491b
Asturias-León 1–629b-630a
Barcelona 2–103b-104a
Castile 3–131a-b
Catalonia 3–176b-177a
chivalry 3–301b
clerk 3–448b
costume 3–618b, 621b-622a
demography 4–143b-146b
CLASS STRUCTURE, WESTERN (1300-1500) 3–419a
barbers, barber-surgeons 2–100a
Castile 3–131a-b, 139b
costume 3–621b
Claudian 1–182a-b
Claudius, Emperor 1–212b
Claudius Clemens
See Clemens Scotus
CLAUDIUS OF TURIN 3–436b
Latin exegesis 4–542b
Claudius Ptolemaeus
See Ptolemaic system
CLAUSULA 3–437a
ars antiqua 1–544b, 546a-b
Bamberg manuscript 2–68b
Clauwaerts 2–387a
Clavendier 3–625a
Clavijo
See Gonzalez de Clavijo, Ruy.
Clavis sapientiae (al-Tughraʾi) 1–137b
Clay glazing
See Ceramics, European
CLEF 3–438a
Clef d'amour 1–189a; 3–672b
CLEMENS SCOTUS 3–438a
Clement VII, Antipope 1–108a, 147a, 330b; 2–16a
Charles V 3–270a
election 3–95b
Great Schism 3–365a,b, 645b
Clement, Bishop
Bulgaria 2–403b, 404a
Clement I, Pope 3–341b
apostolic constitutions 1–349b
Clement II, Pope 3–348b
Clement III, Pope 1–312a, 330a; 3–635a
Clement IV, Pope
Bacon 2–35a, 37b
Bonaventure, Saint 2–317a
Dominican rite 4–242a
Durand, Guillaume 4–314a
political crusades 4–60b
CLEMENT V, POPE 3–438b
angelus 1–252b
annate 1–304b
Arnald of Villanova 1–538a
Avignon papacy 4–99b, 362a,b, 363a, 376a
benefices 2–179b
Boniface VIII 2–324a
Bordeaux, archbishop 2–328b
cardinal-priests 3–94b
clerical requirements 3–443a
Corpus Christi, feast 3–608a
Edward II 4–475b
election 2–15b-16a
Henry VII 4–102a
Knights Templar 3–304b
Latin church organization 3–377a
papal conclave 3–524a
Western councils 3–643b-644b, 645a
CLEMENT VI, POPE 3–439a
Avignon papacy 2–15b; 3–362a, 363a
Birgitta, Saint 2–247a
Black Death 2–264a, 265a
Bradwardine 2–358b
Caffa 3–12a
calendar 1–612b; 3–23a
Cola di Rienzo 3–478a-b
crusades 4–20b-21a, 55b
flagellants 2–263a
Jews 2–263b
papal conclave 3–524a
Clement XI, Pope 1–311b
Clement, Saint 1–261b
Bulgaria 2–407a
Clemente Sánchez, Archdeacon
exempla 4–551b
Clementines 3–645a
Clement of Alexandria 2–510a; 3–342a; 4–349a-b
bestiary 2–203b, 204a
catechetical school of Alexandria 3–335b, 593b
Christmas, celebration 3–317b
Docetism 4–233a
Clement of Ireland, Saint
See Clemens Scotus
Clement of Llanthony 4–547b
Clement of Rome 3–334b
apostolic succession 1–350b
Clement of Sosandra 2–296a
Clement Scottus
See Clemens Scotus
Cleomadés (Adenet le Roi) 1–55a
Clepsydra
See Clocks and reckoning of time
CLERESTORY 3–440a; 2–125a; 3–379a
construction 3–565a-b
CLERGY 3–440a
annate payments 1–305a
apostolic succession 1–350a
Armenia 1–488b, 489b, 502b-505a
autocephalos status 2–9b
Bovo II of Corvey 2–350b
Bruno of Magdeburg 2–391b
Cardinals, College of 3–93b
Carolingian reform 3–109b
Cathars 3–186a
cathedral 3–191b
celibacy 3–215a, 349a
Celtic church 3–228b
chaplain 3–264a
chapter 3–265a,b-266a
Chaucer 3–294b, 295a-296a
choir 3–307b
Clarendon, Constitutions of 3–409b
class structure, western 3–416a, 417a-418a, 421b-422a
clerk 3–448b
congé d'élire 3–536b
elections, church 4–421a
False Decretals protection 4–125b-126a
Latin church organization 3–372b

medical practice 2–98a
Norman-Angevin England 4–465b-466b
papal coronation 3–602b
patristic view of church 4–372b
CLERGY, BYZANTINE 3–446a
chorepiscopus 1–75a
clerical hierarchy 3–444b
***CLERICIS LAICOS* 3–447b**
Clerico faciendo, De 3–442a
CLERK 3–448b
Armenia 1–488b
clergy 3–440a
Clermont 2–144a,b
CLERMONT, COUNCIL OF (535) 3–216b
CLERMONT, COUNCIL OF (1095) **3–449a**; 1–93b; 3–635a,b, 636b
Decretum of Ivo of Chartres 4–128b
First Crusade 4–15b, 19a, 20b
Urban II 4–19a, 33b
Clermont-Ferrand Abbey 1–144b
Cletorologion
See Philotheus
"Clever Madmen" (al-Nisābūrī) 1–380b
Clever Men and Women (Ibn al-Jawzī) 1–380b
Clibanarii 3–200b
Clientage 1–8a
Clifford, Sir Lewis 3–408a
Cligés (Chrétien de Troyes) 1–568b-569a; 3–308b
Climacus, John 3–215a
CLIMATOLOGY 3–450a
Byzantium 1–76b-77a
food habits 1–299a,b
Islamic 1–103b-104a
Mediterranean region 1–79b-80a
northern Europe 1–89a, 94b
Western European costume 3–623a
Clipeatus
See Clipeus
CLIPEUS 3–457a
Agnus Dei 1–74a
Clisson, Olivier de 3–270a
Clock of Wisdom (Heinrich Suso) 3–462b
CLOCKS AND RECKONING OF TIME 3–457a
calendars 3–24a-b, 29a-b
Hipparchus 3–457b
mechanical clocks 3–29b
water 3–27b-28a
CLOCKWORK, PLANETARY 3–464b; 3–460b-462a
astrarium 4–260b-261a
Cloisonné enamel
See Enamel, cloisonné
CLOISTER 3–465a
food animals 1–299b-300a
Cloitech, Battle of (789) 3–396b
CLONARD (CLUAIN-IRAIRD) **3–465b**
Clontarf, Battle of (1014) 4–77b, 106a,b
Cloth and clothmaking
alnage 1–202b
altar apparatus 1–224a
fairs 4–585a, 586a-b, 587a, 588a, 592a, 593a
Clothar I 3–243b
Clothing
See Costume
Clotilda (wife of Clovis) 2–423a; 3–466b
Cloud of Unknowing 3–368b
CLOVE 3–466b
Clovesho, Council of (747) 4–230a
CLOVIS 3–466b; 1–454b
Alamanni 2–94b, 117a-b
baptism 2–147a
Bordeaux 2–327b
Burgundians 2–423a
Champagne 3–243b
deposition of rulers 4–158a
Franks 2–94a,b; 3–104a
Cluain-Iraird
See Clonard
CLUNIAC RITE 3–467b
All Souls' Day 1–177a
See Also Cluny, order of
CLUNY, ABBEY CHURCH 3–468a; 1–426b; 3–347b-348a
CLUNY, ORDER OF 3–468b; 2–172b, 173a
Asturias-León 1–628b, 630b
Burgundy 2–426b, 428a
Castile 3–133a
Cluniac rite 3–467b
Dauphiné 4–109b
death and burial practices 4–117b, 119b-120b
Divine Office 4–222a
Latin exegesis 4–543a
reforms 3–347b-348a; 4–33b, 374a,b
Cluny III
See Romanesque architecture
Cnoberesburgh monastery 3–226a
Cnut IV of Denmark, King 4–152b
Cnut VI of Denmark, King 4–153b
Cnut Lavard (Bread Giver) 4–152b, 153a
CNUT THE GREAT 3–471b; 4–151b, 394b, 457a,b
Anglo-Saxon laws 1–286a
Coadjutor 3–444b
COAL, MINING AND USE OF 3–472b
Cistercians 3–404a
Coats of arms
See Heraldry
Coats of Plates 1–525a
Coblas 3–70a
Coblas capfinades 1–269a; 3–70a
Coblas doublas 1–269a
Coblas singulars 1–269a
Coblas unissonans 1–269a
Coblenz
Burgundians 2–422b
Códax, Martín
cantigas de amigo 3–86a, 87a
Code of Huesca 3–611b
CODEX 3–473b
Carmina Burana 3–97b
codicology, Western European 3–476b-477a
Codex Argenteus 1–212b
CODEX AUREUS 3–474b
Codex Barberinus 1–516b
Codex Buranus 1–319a
Codex Calixtinus 3–531b
Codex Florentinus 3–609b
Codex grandior (Cassiodorus) 4–357a
Codex Hermogenianus 3–608b
Codex iuris canonici 3–642a,b
Codex Justianianus
See Corpus Iuris Civilis
Codex Regius 4–385a
Icelandic Eddic poems 1–319b
Codex Salmasianus 1–317a, 318b
***CODEX THEODOSIANUS* 3–475a**; 3–474a
Augustine of Hippo 1–650a, 652a
Corpus iuris civilis 3–608b
Codex Usserianus I 2–220a,b
Codicillus 1–138b
CODICOLOGY, WESTERN EUROPEAN 3–475b
See Also Codex
Codification, age of 3–54b
Codolades 3–173a,b
COENE, JAQUES 3–478a; 2–349b
Coenobium 3–122b
Coffee, 2–209b
Cogitosus
Brigit, Saint 2–376b
Cohen, Yehuda ben Moses 1–159b
Coif 3–623a
Coimbra 1–625a; 3–128b
Coinage
See Mints and Money
Coisi-dobráin
See Airbetach mac Coisse
Col, Gontier and Pierre 3–316b
COLA DI RIENZO 3–478a
archaeology 1–336b
Colas, Antoine 1–426a
Colatorium 1–222b
Colchis
See Georgia: Geography
COLIN MUSET 3–479a
COLLAR BEAM 3–479b
Collationes (John Cassian) 3–122b, 167a
Colle, Francesco da 3–397a
Collectanea 1–111b
***COLLECTARIUM* 3–479b**; 4–223b
breviary 2–370b, 371a
Collectio Britannica 4–128b
Collectio canonum (Abbo of Fleury) 1–13a
Collectio canonum (Deusdedit) 4–165b
Collectio canonum Hibernensis (Saint Adamnan) 1–53a, 347a; 3–229a
Collectio Dionysiana (Dionysius Exiguus) 1–350a; 4–193a
Collectio Dionysio-Hadriana 4–193a
Collection (Ibn Durayd) 4–442a
Collection des anciens alchimistes grecs 1–135b
Collectorium (Gabriel Biel) 2–234a
Collectors and collections, antiquarian 1–335a-336a
Collegantia
See Commenda
Colletin 1–530a-b
Colle Val d'Elsa, Battle of (1269) 4–96b
Colloquy (Aelfric) 1–61b, 62b
"Colloquy of the Old Men, The"
See Acallam na Senórach
COLMAN, BISHOP OF LINDISFARNE 3–480a
Colman mac Telduib 3–465b
Colmán Már 1–60b
Colobion
See Colobium
COLOBIUM (COLOBION) **3–480b**; 4–13a
Colocci-Brancuti 3–86b
COLOGNE 3–480b
anti-Semitism 2–263b
cathedral 1–429b
Caxton 3–210b
commune 3–497b
COLOMBE, JEAN 3–482a
COLOMBE, MICHEL 3–482b
Colomb family
Bordeaux 2–328a
Colonia, Juan and Simon de
See Juan and Simon de Colonia
Colonna, Egidius
Defensor pacis 4–132a
Colonna, Francis 4–248a
Colonna, Giacomo 1–148b; 2–34a; 3–95b
Colonna, Pietro 3–95b
Colonna, Sciarra 2–324a
Colonna, Stafanuccio 3–478b-479a
Colonna, Stephen 2–323b
Colonne, Guido delle 3–166b, 212a
COLONUS 3–482b
COLOPHON 3–483b

COLORS, LITURGICAL 3–484a
Coltura promiscua 1–80b
Columba 1–223b
COLUMBA, SAINT 3–485a
Adamnan, Saint 1–52b
Áedán Mac Gabráin 1–60a
Celtic church origins 3–226a,b
Clonard 3–465b
Scotland, evangelization 3–344b
Columban church
Easter controversy 1–52b
COLUMBANUS, SAINT 3–485b
Alamanni 1–117b
brewing 2–374a
Celtic church origins 3–226b, 228b, 232a
monasticism 3–344b
Columbus, Christopher 1–56a, 109a
explorations 4–555a, 558a, 559b-560b, 562a
Marco Polo 4–557a
Colum-cille
See Columba, Saint
Column Church group 3–92b
COLUMN FIGURE 3–487a
Colum of Terryglass 3–465b
Comalada, Miquel 3–168a
Combs 2–148a
Coptic art 3–587a
Comedia de Calisto y Melibea
See Celestina, La
Comedia delle ninfe fiorentine (Boccaccio) 2–281a
Comendación
See Commendatio
Comes, Vicenç 3–173b
Comestor, Peter
Chester plays 3–299b
Comic tale
See Fabliau and comic tale
COMINES (COMMYNES), PHILIPPE DE 3–487a
diplomacy 4–210a, 212a
French chronicles 3–333b
memoirs 2–237a, 240a; 3–327b
Comitatenses 3–201a
Comitatus 2–89a
Comites
Carolingian administration 3–107a-b
Comitilla, catacomb 3–155b
"Command, The" (Augustine) 1–658a
COMMANDER OF THE FAITHFUL 3–488a; 3–34b, 37b
Commandino, Federigo 1–439a,b
Commandments of Ovid, The (Chrétien de Troyes) 3–308b
Commemorations (Pere Albert) 1–413b
COMMENDA 3–489a
***COMMENDAM* 3–489b**
Commendatio animae
See Death and Burial
COMMENDATION 3–490a; 1–630a
Commentaria in quattuor libros Sententiarum (Guillaume Durand) 4–313b
Commentaries (Saint Jerome) 1–262b
Commentarii de bello gallico (Julius Caesar) 3–331b
Commentarii in Psalmos (Arnobius the Younger) 1–539b
Commentarius in Genesin (Angelomus of Luxeuil) 1–251b
Commentarius super libros quinque decretalium (Innocent IV) 3–606a
Commentary on Psalms (Odo) 2–16b
Commentary on Romans (Abelard) 3–322a
Commentary on the Apocalypse (Beatus) 1–631a; 2–143b
Commentary on the Calculus of Victurius (Abbo of Fleury) 1–12b
Commentary on the Dream of Scipio (Macrobius) 1–181a, 182a
Commentary on the Gospel of John (Cyril of Alexandria) 4–75a
"Commentator, The"
See Rushd, Ibn
Commentators
See Postglossators
Comments on Observations (Ibn al-Shāṭir) 1–622b
Commerce
See Trade
Comminges 1–410b
Common accounting 4–514a
Common Bench, court of 4–502a
Common of Saints 1–330a
COMMONPLACE BOOKS 3–492b
COMMON PLEAS, COURT OF 3–491b
Norman-Angevin England 4–470a-b
Common services 1–305a
COMMUNE 3–493a
Bruges 2–386b
class structure, Western 3–424a
Russian peasant 1–100a, 101a-b
See Also Consuls, consulate
Communia naturalium (Roger Bacon) 2–40b, 41a
Communion
See Eucharist
COMMUNION CHANT 3–504a
Agnus chant 1–73b
COMMUNION UNDER BOTH KINDS 3–504b
Commynes, Philippe de
See Comines (Commynes), Philippe de
Comneni
See Komnenoi
Compactata of Prague 3–652b
Compagni, Dino 3–196b
Compagnies d'ordonnance 3–206b
Charles VII of France 3–271b
Companies of Adventure 3–531a
Company of Saint Ursula
See Ursulines
Company of the Sons of Bonsignore
See Gran Tavola dei Bonsignori
Comparatione auctoritatis papae et concilii, De (Tommaso de Vio) 3–520b
COMPASS, MAGNETIC 3–506a
Compendia
See Encyclopedia and dictionaries
Compendiosa doctrina, De (Nonius Marcellus) 3–432a
Compendium of Theological Truth (Hugh Ripelin) 1–321b
Compendium philosophiae 4–449a
Compendium studii philosophiae (Roger Bacon) 2–35a, 37b, 40b
Compendium studii theologiae (Roger Bacon) 2–35b, 37b
Compilatio prima (Bernard of Pavia) 4–124a
***COMPLAINTE* 3–507b**
Complainte, La (Chartier) 3–275b
Complaint of the Gentleman Mataro
See Planys del cavaller Mataró
"Complaint to His Lady" (Chaucer) 3–281a
"Complaint to Pity" (Chaucer) 3–281a
Complexiones in epistolis apostolorum (Cassiodorus) 3–124a
Compline 3–67a, 230b
Divine Office 4–221b, 228, 229a
Componde of Alkemy (George Ripley) 1–139a
Composite bow 2–350b-351a,b, 352a-b
Compositio 4–107a
Compositiones Lucenses 1–135b
Compostela
See Santiago de Compostela
Compoti 4–513a, 514a
Compromise of Bec (1107) 4–422a,b
Compromise of Caspe 3–171a
COMPURGATION 3–508a
COMPUTUS 3–509a
Bede 2–154b
Byrhtferth's *Manual* 1–285b
calendars and reckoning of time 3–27b
Dionysius Exiguus 4–193a
Easter 4–365a
illustration 3–19a
Old English treatises 1–275a
Comtat Venaissin
Avignon 2–15b
COMTESSA DE DIA 3–509b
Conall Corc
Cashel 3–121a
Eóganacht 4–492b
Conall Gulban 1–52b
Conall of Tara, King
Áedán mac Gabráin 1–60a
Áed Sláne 1–60b
Conan I of Rennes
Brittany 2–379a
Concarneau 3–151b
Concejos 3–131b
Conceptu virginali et de originali peccato (Anselm of Canterbury) 1–313a, 314b
CONCEPTUALISM 3–510a
Conch church 3–378a, 380
Conciliabulum of Pisa (1511-1512) 3–643a, 655a-b
Conciliarism
See Conciliar theory
CONCILIAR THEORY 3–510b; 3–365b-366b, 642a
Conrad of Megenberg 3–539a
ecclesiology 4–373a-374a, 378a
Concilium provinciale 3–579a
CONCLAVE, PAPAL 3–523b
See Also Coronation, papal
Concordantia astronomiae cum historica veritate (Pierre d'Ailly) 1–608b
Concordantia astronomicae veritatis cum theologia (Pierre d'Ailly) 1–608b
Concordantia catholica, De (Nicholas of Cusa) 3–512b
Concordantiae
See Consonance/dissonance
CONCORDAT 3–525a
annate payments 1–304b, 305a
London (1107) 1–313b
Concordia discordantium canonum 4–127a
Gratian 4–128b
Concordia praescientiae et praedestinationis et gratiae Dei cum libero arbitrio (Anselm of Can 1–313b, 315a
Concressault Castle 3–151b
CONCUBINAGE, ISLAMIC 3–527a
See Also Family, Islamic
CONCUBINAGE, WESTERN 3–529b; 4–609a
Condet, Alice de 1–262b
CONDOTTIERI 3–531a
CONDUCTUS 3–531b
ars antiqua 1–543a,b, 544b, 545b, 546b
Bamberg manuscript 2–68b
cauda 3–196a
contrafactum 3–576b

Conductus ante evangelium 3–532a
Conductus Danielis venientis ad Regem 3–532a
Conesa, Jaume 3–166b
Conferences (John Cassian) 3–215a, 343a
Conference with Maximus the Arian Bishop (Augustine) 1–654a
Confessio 1–221b
Confessio amantis (John Gower) 3–290b
CONFESSION 3–533a
  apparellamentum 3–185b
  Burchard of Worms 2–420b
  casuistry 3–153b
  Celtic liturgy 3–230b
  last rites 4–120a
Confessional (Pseudo-Egbert) 1–286a
Confessions (Augustine of Hippo) 1–646a-b, 648a, 655a, 657b; 3–342b
CONFESSOR, ROYAL 3–534b
CONFESSOR: SAINT 3–535b
Confey, Battle of (917) 4–106a
CONFIRMATION 3–535b
  bull, papal 2–418a
  Celtic church 3–230b
  separation from baptism 2–84a, 85a
  sponsors 2–86a
Conflent 3–174b
Conflictus (lyric form) 4–122a
Conflictus de Deo Trino et Uno 1–539b
Conflictus vitiorum atque virtutum (Autpertus) 2–11a
***CONFRÉRIE* 3–536b**
Confrérie de la Passion 3–536b; 4–264a
Congal (son of Áed Sláne) 1–61a
Congalach of Knowth, King 1–61a
***CONGÉ* 3–536b**
***CONGÉ D'ÉLIRE* 3–536b**
  elections, church 4–422b, 424b
Congés (Jean Bodel) 2–290b
Congo River
  exploration 4–562a,b
Congregational Mosque of Cairo
  See Azhar, al-
Congregation of Friars Pilgrims for Christ Among the Gentiles 4–253a
Congregation of Monte Corona 3–56a
Congregation of Windesheim 2–366a-b
Coniuratio 3–493b
Coniuratio pro libertate 3–497b
Conjuge non ducenda, De 1–269b, 323b
Conláed, Bishop
  Brigit, Saint 2–376a
CONNACHT 3–537a
  Burgh, de 2–421b
Conn Cétchathach 3–537a
CONON DE BÉTHUNE 3–538a
  crusade poems 4–20a
Conques Abbey 1–145a
Conquête de Constantinople (Geoffroi de Villehardouin) 3–328a, 332a
Conrad, Constable
  Crusade of 1101 4–36b
Conrad II, Emperor
  Bohemia 2–299b
  Bruno of Würzburg, Saint 2–392a
  Burchard of Worms 2–420a
  Burgundy, County 2–424a
  Burgundy, Kingdom 2–429a
  Cambridge Songs 3–57b
  Constitutio de Feudis 3–557b
  election 4–427a
  successor 4–425b
Conrad III, Emperor 2–6b
  Bavaria 2–33b, 134b
  Byzantine empire 2–494a
  election 4–427a
  Second Crusade 4–30b, 37b-38a
Conrad IV, Emperor 4–59b, 60a
  death 1–161b
  election 4–428a
CONRAD, PRIOR 3–539a
  Christ Church Cathedral 3–83b
Conradin (son of Conrad IV) 4–60b, 95b
Conrad of Burgundy, King 2–350b, 429a; 3–114b; 4–426a
Conrad of Franconia, Duke
  See Conrad of Burgundy, King
Conrad of Gelnhausen 4–377b
  conciliar theory 3–511a,b, 514b-515a, 517a
  Western councils 3–646a
Conrad of Hildesheim, Bishop
  Berthold von Holle 2–199a
Conrad of Marburg 3–535a
Conrad of Masovia, Duke 3–306a
CONRAD OF MEGENBERG 3–539a
Conrad of Montferrat
  Fourth Crusade 2–497a
Conrad I of Salzburg, Archbishop 2–6b
Conrad of Zähringen, Duke
  Burgundy, County 2–424b
  town charters 3–494b
Conradus de Mure 2–320a
Conrois 3–204a
CONSANGUINITY 3–539b
  Alfonso I 1–160a
  Byzantine marriage 4–594a,b
Consecration, Royal
  See Kingship (Coronation), Rituals of
Consecration cross 4–9a
CONSECRATION OF CEMETERIES 3–540b
Consecration of church officers
  See Ordination
Consejo of Vivar
  Cantar de Mío Cid 3–70b
Consell de Cent 2–103b
Consideratione quintae essentiae, De (John of Rupescissa) 1–138a
Consilia (Cino da Pistoia) 3–397b
Consilium . . .de auctoritate papae et concilii (Philippus Decius) 3–520b
Consilium principis 3–541b
Consistori de la Gaya Ciència 3–170b-171a
***CONSISTORIUM* 3–541b**
  Cardinals, College of 3–93b, 94b, 95a
Consolamentum 3–181a, 185a-b
Consolat de mar 3–157b
Consolation (Ibn Ẓafar) 1–381b
Consolation des Trois Vertus, La (Alain Chartier) 3–275b
Consolation of Philosophy (Boethius) 1–182b, 186b, 188b, 280b; 2–292b
  Alfred's translation 1–166b
  Anglo-Norman translation 1–264a
  Chaucer's translation 3–283b-284a
  Old English translation 1–284a
CONSONANCE/DISSONANCE 3–541b
  Anonymous IV treatise 1–309b
  cadence 3–5b
  copula 3–596a
  diaphonia 4–172a
Consonants
  Anglo-Norman 1–259b
  Arabic 1–377a
  Celtic 3–233b
Conspiratio 3–493b
CONSTABLE, LOCAL 3–542b
CONSTABLE OF THE REALM 3–543b; 2–53a
Constance, Concordat of (1417) 3–525a
Constance, Council of (1414-1418) 1–147b; 2–16a; 3–647b-651a, 654a
  annate payments 1–305a
  d'Ailly 1–108b-109a
  deposition of rulers 4–160a
  ecclesiology 4–377b-378a
  Great Schism 3–366a
Constance, Lake 2–94b
Constance of Castile 2–94b
Constance of Hohenstaufen 1–412b
Constance of Sicily
  See Constance of Hohenstaufen
CONSTANS II, EMPEROR 3–544a; 1–478a; 3–630b; 4–418b
  Anatolia 1–241a
  Armenian church 1–500a
  Martin I, Pope 3–344a
Constantia 4–70b
Constantian Excerpts 4–446b
Constantina, Empress
  Brandeum 2–362b
Constantine
  See Cyril and Methodios, Saints
CONSTANTINE I, THE GREAT 3–545a; 1–222a, 453b
  architecture 4–331a,b, 335a, 336b-337a
  Arianism 1–633a
  Armenian saints 1–518b
  Bohemian Brethren 2–306a
  caesaropapism 3–10a-b
  church, early 2–458b, 459a,b; 3–337a-b, 338b, 339a, 340b-341a
  Constantinople 3–545b
  crusade, concept 4–15b
  dioceses 4–191b
  Donation 4–257b
  Donatism 4–259b
  economy and society 2–475b
  ecumenical councils 3–627a-b
  edict of toleration (313) 3–335b
  empire planning 2–97a
  looting 1–334b
  reign 2–484a-485a
  stepped cross 4–9b
Constantine III
  Gaul 2–96a
CONSTANTINE IV 3–546a; 3–544b
  Bulgaria 2–399b
  Third Council of Constantinople (680) 3–630b
CONSTANTINE V 3–546a; 2–488a-b
  Amorion 1–236b
  Bulgaria 2–401a
  Eclogue 4–382b
  heterodoxy 2–459a
  iconoclasm 2–462b, 463a; 3–11a, 631a
  reign 2–488a-b
Constantine VI 2–488b; 4–417b
Constantine VIII 2–118b, 491b
Constantine, Antipope 1–330a
Constantine de Born 2–201b-202a
Constantine X Doukas 1–303a; 4–263a
  Isaac I Komnenos 2–491b
Constantine Hermoniakos 2–509b, 523a
Constantine Leichoudes
  Byzantine throne 2–492a
Constantine Lips, Church of 2–455a
Constantine Maliasenos
  holdings 2–479a
Constantine Manasses 2–515b, 522a, 524b
  poetic meter 2–508a
CONSTANTINE IX MONOMACHOS 3–548a; 4–341b
  art patron 2–442a, 443a
  church schism 2–465a; 3–349b
  classical literary studies 3–431a
  Constantinople 3–553a

CONSTANTINE IX MONOMACHOS (cont.)
Mt. Athos monasteries 1–637a,b
reign 2–491b, 492a, 493a,b
Constantine III/V of Cilicia, King 3–393a
Constantine IV/VI of Cilicia, King 3–393a
Constantine of Erznka 1–511b
Constantine of Rhodes 2–507a, 524a
CONSTANTINE XI PALAIOLOGOS 3–548a; 2–503b-504a,b
CONSTANTINE VII PORPHYROGENITOS 3–546b; 1–483a
art patron 2–440b, 441a, 442a, 452b
Book of Ceremonies 2–471b
Bosnia 2–334b
boyar 2–403a
Bulgaria 2–404b-405a
church 2–461b
diplomacy 4–194b, 195a, 196a
education 3–556b
encyclopedias 4–446b
Great Moravia 2–299a
histories 2–513b-514a
regencies 2–490a
Constantine Stilbes 2–507b
CONSTANTINE THE AFRICAN 3–548b; 2–173b
CONSTANTINE (KOSTANDIN) THE **ARMENIAN 3–549a**
Constantine the Bishop
Bulgaria 2–404a
Constantine Tih 2–410a,b
art and architecture 2–413b
CONSTANTINOPLE 3–549a
administration 2–473a-b, 474b; 3–553b-554b; 4–493b
Alani 1–121a-b
Alexios I Komnenos 1–157b
altar, portable 1–225b
Amalarius of Metz 1–228a
Anatolia 1–241a,b
Andronikos I Komnenos 1–245a
Archimedes 1–434a,b
Armenian church 1–519a
Arsenius Autorianus 1–560a
art and architecture 2–417a, 437b, 457a; 4–331a, 348b, 351a, 352a-353b
Athanasius I 1–633b
Avars 2–12b
Bogomils 2–295b-296a, 297a
Book of the Eparch 4–493b
Bosporus 2–344a
Bulgaria 2–401a,b, 404b, 408b, 409a-b, 410a, 412a,b
Burgundio of Pisa 2–423b
Byzantine church 2–458b
caesaropapism 3–10a-b
Cassiodorus 3–123b
Christianity 3–631b
Council of Chalcedon 3–630a
crusades 1–158a, 636b; 2–58b; 3–357a, 431b, 639b; 4–30a, 31b, 34a, 43a, 45a,b-46b, 47b-48a, 344b-345a, 438a
currency 4–301a
Danes 4–554a
Dardanelles 4–105a
demes 3–553b-554b; 4–135a
Demetrios Kydones 4–135b
diplomacy 4–194a, 195a-b
ecumenical patriarch 2–10a,b; 4–383a
eparch 4–493b
explorations 4–556a
history 2–498a-499a, 502b-503a, 504a-b
map 3–550
Mehmed II the Conqueror 3–65a-b
Muslims 4–30a
Ottomans 2–136b; 4–56a-b
Palaiologans 1–245b, 246b
Robert II of Flanders 4–34b
traveler accounts 1–332a-333b
Turkish conquest (1453) 3–432a
Umayyads 3–38a, 41b
Constantinople, Councils of
See Councils
Anastasius Bibliothecarius 1–239a-b
Basil the Great 2–120b; 3–628b
Christian church in Persia 3–312a
Church Fathers 3–336a
clergy 3–446b
episcopal authority 3–632a
First 3–628a-b
Monophysitism 3–320a-b
Nicene creed 1–454a; 3–346a
Photios 3–632a, 633a
Second 3–630a-b
Third 3–630b
Constantinople, Histoire de la Conquêtte de
See Villehardouin, Geoffroi de
Constantinople, Latin Empire of
See Latin Empire of Constantinople
Constantinople, Second Council of (553) 3–630a-b
Constantinople Third Council of (680) 3–630b
Constantinus II 1–236a
Constantius I, Emperor
heterodoxy 2–459a
Constantius II, Emperor 1–117a, 453b
Aršak II 1–559b
Constantinople 3–551a
Ethiopia 1–32a
Nicenes 3–628a
reign 2–485a
Conste van rhetoriken, De (Mathys Casteleyn) 4–322b
***CONSTITUTIO DE FEUDIS* 3–557b**
Constitutiones Aegidianae 1–131a
Constitutiones Clementinae (Clement V, Pope) 3–438b
Constitutum Constantini
See Donation of Constantine
CONSTRUCTION: BUILDING MATERIALS 3–558a
botany 2–347b
brick 2–375a-b
castles and fortifications 3–143a, 144a-145b
cathedral 3–191b
early Christian and Byzantine architecture 4–331b, 335b
masonry 3–561a-564a
wood 3–558b-561a
CONSTRUCTION: ENGINEERING 3–564a
Brunelleschi 2–390a
centering 3–234b
Consuetudines
See Customary
Consuetudines et usus maris 3–570A
Consuetudo Bononiensis 3–21a
Consular diptych
See Diptych, consular
CONSULATE OF THE SEA 3–569b; 1–56a
Consules 4–378b
See Also Échevin
CONSULS, CONSULATE 3–570b
commune 3–500a,b, 502a-b
Consummatio 3–230b
Contadi di banco 2–75a
Contadores mayores 3–139b
"Container revolution" 2–114a
CONTE DEL LELLO ORLANDI 3–572a
Conte du Graal (Chrétien de Troyes) 3–308b
Contemplació de la Santa Quarentena (Eiximenis) 3–167b
Contemplatio (Saint Bonaventure) 3–167a
Contemplatione, De (Denis the Carthusian) 3–119a
Contemplation of Experience, The (Usāma ibn Munqidh) 1–381a
Contes moralisés (Nicole Bozon) 1–264a
CONTRACEPTION, EUROPEAN 3–572a; 4–144a
CONTRACEPTION, ISLAMIC 3–574a; 3–572b
Contracts
exchange 2–78a
notarial 2–78a
"starr" 2–81a
Contra Eunomium (Basil the Great) 2–121a
Contra Eutychen et Nestorium (Boethius) 3–321a
CONTRAFACTUM 3–575b; 3–86a
Contra Felicem (Alcuin) 1–57b
Contra haereticos (Hugh of Rouen) 4–375a
Contra Hieraclem (Eusebius of Caesarea) 1–348b
Contra Iudaeos, paganos et Arianos sermo de symbolo (Augustine) 4–371a
Contra iudices (Theodulf) 3–102b
Contra Judaeos paganos et Arianos 1–270a
Contra mendacium (Augustine) 3–153a
Contrapointamens
See Counterpoint
Contraponchamens
See Counterpoint
Contrapunctus
See Counterpoint
Contra quattuor labyrinthos Franciae (Walter of Saint Victor) 4–170a
CONTRATENOR 3–576b
ars nova 1–551a
ars subtilior 1–559a
counterpoint 3–659b
Controversia Paschali, De (Cummian) 3–228b
Contus 3–200b
Convent
See Monastery
Conversation books 1–270a, 271a
CONVERSO 3–577b
Carthusian 3–119a
Castile 3–137b, 138b, 139b
Cistercian 3–404a
Convivio (Dante) 4–99b-101a, 102b, 104b
Convocatio 3–579a
CONVOCATIONS OF CANTERBURY AND YORK 3–578a
CONWAY, PEACE OF 3–579b
COOK (COKE), **HUMPHREY 3–580b**
COOKERY, EUROPEAN 3–580b
botany 2–347a-b
bread 2–364b-365a
COOKERY, ISLAMIC 3–584a
Copernicus
astronomy, Islamic 1–621b
cosmology 1–609a
precession theory 1–615a
universe, concept of 1–615b, 616a
Cop'k' Šahuneac'
See Lesser Sophenē
Cop'k'Šahuni
See Sophenē

COPLA 3–584b
decir 4–122b
Coplas de Mingo Revulgo 3–584b
Copperplate engraving
See Engraving
COPPO DI MARCOVALDO 3–585a; 2–189a; 3–396b
Coptic alphabet 1–207b, 209b, 212a, 213a
COPTIC ART 3–585b
bronze and brass 2–384a
early Christian art 4–348b, 362b
Coptic language 1–378a
Nubian Christianity 3–315b
Copton, Agnes de (mother of Chaucer) 3–280a
COPTS AND COPTIC CHURCH 3–593b
Alexandria 1–154b
Alexandrian rite 1–155a
ankh 4–9a
art and architecture 3–585b
Cairo 3–13b
COPULA 3–595b
COPYHOLD 3–596b
Corbaccio (Boccaccio) 2–285b-286a; 3–31b
Corbeil, Treaty of (1258) 1–412b
CORBEL 3–597a
arch 1–424a
CORBEL TABLE 3–597b
Corbiac, Pierre de 3–657a
Corbie abbey
False Decretals 4–125b
Corbie Psalter 1–262b
Corbinian, Saint 1–422b; 2–134a
Corcu Baiscind 4–77a
Corcu Modruad 4–77a
Cordes 2–129a
CÓRDOBA 3–597b
agriculture 1–82a,b, 84b
Alhambra 1–170b
Asturias-León 1–625b-626a, 627a,b-628a
black slaves 2–268a
Castile 3–128a-b, 134a, 135a
Catalonia 3–175a,b
Great Mosque 1–191b, 196b; 2–31a
Umayyads 3–678a
Córdoba, Pedro de
See Pedro de Córdoba
Corfu
See Kerkyra
Corinth
Byzantine Empire 2–494a
CORIPPUS 3–601a; 1–67b
Cork 4–554b
CORMAC MAC AIRT 3–601a; 1–33a
Cormac Mac Carthaig of Munster, King 4–493a
CORMAC MAC CUILENNÁIN 3–601b
Eóganacht 4–493a
Cormont, Regnault de
See Regnault de Cormont
Cormont, Thomas de
See Thomas de Cormont
Cornaro, Caterina 4–71a
Corneille
Cid, the 3–388b
Cornelius
angel/angelology 1–249b
Cornet, Ramon de 3–170a
Cornwall
Celtic church 3–225a
Cornish dialect 3–234a
Latin church 3–344a
woodcarving 4–115b
CORONATION, PAPAL 3–602b
Coronation Gospels 4–136a
Coronation of the Virgin (Charonton) 3–274b
Coronation of the Virgin with Scenes from Her Life (Bartolo di Fredi) 2–116b
Coronation rituals
See Kingship (coronation), rituals of
Corona vault
See Vault
Coronel 1–534a
CORONER 3–605a
Corpo 2–77a
CORPORATION 3–606a
chapter 3–265a
CORPUS CHRISTI, FEAST OF 3–608a; 3–359a
altar apparatus 1–223b
Chester plays 3–298a
See Also Easter
Corpus Christi carol 2–60a
Corpus Christi plays
England 4–279a, 284b
Germany 4–268a
Corpus Gabirianum 1–141a
Corpus glossary 1–276a
Corpus iuris canonici 3–645a; 4–129a
***CORPUS IURIS CIVILIS* 3–608b**; 2–115a, 486a; 3–474a
archives 1–445b, 446a
Artašat 1–563b
Azo 2–29a,b
basilics 2–125a
Codex Theodosianus 3–475b
commentaries 2–57a
corporation 3–607a
Établissements de Saint Louis 4–515b
Correct expressions of the Persians (Shams-i-Munshī) 4–444b
Correctorium alchemiae (Richard Anglicus) 1–137a
Çorrer, Gregorio 4–424a
Čorrord Hayk' (Arm.) 1–472a
Corruption and Grace (Augustine) 1–653b
Corset (Robert of Gretham) 1–263b
Corsica
agricultural tools 1–80a
Aragon, Crown of 1–414b, 417b
Catalan language 3–157b
Genoans 4–556a
Cortebarbe 4–575b
Cortereal family 2–30a
CORTES 3–610b
Carrión 3–76b-77a
Castile 3–132a, 135a, 137a,b, 138b-139a
Cortés, Hernando
slaves 2–270a
Cortez amors
See Courtly love
CORVÉE 3–612b
Corvinus, Matthias 2–8b, 9a
Bosnia 2–339b
Corvo 2–29b
Coryphée 3–116a
Cosenza 1–71b
Coses pertenents a la conservació de la vida 3–168b
Cosimo de' Medici 2–391a
Cosimo de' Medici the Elder
art trade 1–561a
Cosmas (monk)
Ethiopia 1–30b
Cosmas (priest)
Bogomilism 2–294a
COSMAS INDICOPLEUSTES 3–613b
Christianity, Nubian 3–314a
Cosmas I of Constantinople
Bogomilism 2–294b, 295a, 296a
Cosmas II of Constantinople
Bogomilism 2–296a
COSMAS OF PRAGUE 3–614a
COSMATI WORK 3–614a
Cosmetics
See Beauty Aids, Cosmetics
Cosmographia (Bernard Silvestris) 1–183a, 607a; 2–194b-195a
Cosmographic allegory 1–182a-183b
Costa ben Luca
See Lūqā, Qusṭa ibn
COSTUME, BYZANTINE 3–614a; 3–13a
imperial and aristocratic 2–456a-b
COSTUME, ISLAMIC 3–616a; 3–13a
COSTUME, JEWISH 3–618b; 3–13a
COSTUME, WESTERN EUROPEAN 3–621b
arms and armor 1–528a, 531a
bronze and brass 2–384b
costumery law 3–622a
Costums de la mar 3–570a
Costums de Tortosa 3–157b, 570a
Cota, Rodrigo de 3–213a
Cotehardie 3–624b
Cotelette 3–624b
"Cottage-rounders" 1–651b
Cottars 4–512b
Cottian Alps 4–108a,b
COTTON 3–626b
Islamic cultivation 1–104b
Spanish cultivation 1–82a
Cotton, John
See John of Affighem
Cotton, Robert Bruce 1–286b
Cotton Genesis 1–248a
Coucy, Châtelain de
See Châtelain de Coucy
Coucy, Enguerrand de
See Enguerrand VII of Coucy
Coucy, Robert de
See Robert of Coucy
Coucy castle 3–277b
dungeon 3–148b, 150a
houxds 3–146b
Councils, Armenian
See Armenian Church, Doctrines and Councils
COUNCILS, BYZANTINE (869-1368) **3–631b**; 1–500a-501a
Bulgaria 2–403a
caesaropapism 3–11a
theology 2–466b-467a
See Also Constantinople, Councils of
COUNCILS (ECUMENICAL, 325-787) **3–627a**; 1–453b; 3–337b, 338b
Alcuin of York 1–143a
Armenian church 1–498a-500a, 502b
Athanasius of Alexandria, Saint 1–633a; 3–628a
caesaropapism 3–10b-11a
Celestine I 3–214a
Church Fathers 3–336a,b
Constantine I, the Great 3–545b
Constantine IV 3–546a
Cyril of Alexandria, Saint 4–75a
See Also Chalcedon, Council of
See Also Constantinople, Councils of
See Also Ephesus, Council of
See Also Nicea, Councils of
COUNCILS, WESTERN (869-1179) **3–632b**
Armenian church 1–501a-b
Arnold of Brescia 1–539b, 540a
Basel 2–305a; 3–23a-b, 366a,b; 4–378a
ecclesiology 4–374b, 376a
Piacenza 4–30a

COUNCILS, WESTERN (1215-1274) **3–639b**; 1–354a,b
celibacy 1–323b
confession 3–533b
COUNCILS, WESTERN (1311-1449) **3–642b**
annate payments 1–305a
Brethren of the Common Life 2–367b
Bruni 2–391a
conciliar theory 3–510b-511b, 512b, 514b, 518b, 520a, 521a
conclave, papal 3–523b, 524b
Latin church 3–336a, 361b, 362a, 364a,b, 366b, 367a
See Also Constance, Council of
Count
See County
Counteroffensive, concept of 3–146a
COUNTERPOINT 3–656b
Anonymous IV treatise 1–309b
ars antiqua 1–545b
ars nova 1–551b
Counter-Reformation
celibacy laws 3–217b
COUNTY 3–658a
escheators 4–509a-b
Courçon, Robert of
See Courson, Robert of
Cour d'amour 3–672b
Courland
See Kurland
Couronnement de Louis 3–257b-261a
Course of love, The (Dirc Potter) 4–320a
COURSON, ROBERT OF 3–659a
COURSON (COURÇON), ROBERT OF
Fifth Crusade 4–49b
COURTESY BOOKS 3–660b
courtly love 3–672b
COURT LEET 3–659b
Courtly entertainments 4–579b
COURTLY LOVE 3–667a
Albrecht von Johansdorf 1–132b
antifeminism 1–324b
Arthurian literature 1–569a
aubade 1–642a
Blancheflour et Florence 2–271a
Bussard, Der 2–434a
Cambridge songs 3–58b
Canso 3–69b
Capellanus 3–89a
Catalan narrative in verse 3–173a-b
Cavalcanti 3–196b
Celestina, La 3–212b, 213a
Chansons de malmariée 3–262b
Charles of Orléans 3–273a
Chartier, Alain 3–275b
Chastelaine de vergi, La 3–277a
Chaucer parodies 3–290b
Chrétien de Troyes 3–308b
Conon de Béthune 3–538b
débat 4–122a
der von Kürenberg 4–161a
descort 4–164a
Eleanor of Aquitaine 4–419b-420a
Fin'amor 3–70a-b, 668a, 669a
lyric 3–670a
Romance of the Rose 1–184a-185a
Court of Canterbury
See Arches, Court of
Court of Exchequer
See Exchequer, Court of
Court of the Lions 1–168b, 169b-170a
Court of the Myrtles 1–168b, 169b
***COURTOIS D'ARRAS* 3–674b**; 4–264a
Courtoisie 1–268b-269a
Courtrai, Battle of (1302) 3–204b
Courts, ecclesiastical
Court of Arches 1–433b
"Courts of love" 3–672b-673a
Coussemaker, Charles Edmond de 1–309a
Coutume réformée (1583) 4–69a
***COUTUMES DE BEAUVAISIS* 3–674b**; 2–144a-b
Coutumier
Champagne 3–249b
Couvre-feu
See Curfew
Covadonga, Battle of 1–626a
Coventry Cathedral 3–265b
Coverchief 3–623b
Covinar 4–112b, 113a
Cow 1–300a, 301b
Cowal family 3–407a
Cowter 1–525b, 534a
Cracow, University of 1–613b
Craft guilds
See Guilds and métiers
Craft of Dying, Book of the
See Ars moriendi
Craftsmen
costume 3–621b, 626a
Crakows
See Poulaines
Crane (Berthold von Holle) 2–199a,b
Cranequin 2–353b, 354a
Creation of the Angels, Book on the (Eutychios) 4–525b
Crèche
Christmas celebration 3–319a
Crécy, Battle of (1346) 3–151b, 205a-b; 4–398a, 399a
bow and arrow/crossbow 2–352b
Bradwardine 2–358b
Créd 1–34a
Credit
See Banking
Credo
See Creeds, liturgical use of
CREEDS, LITURGICAL USE OF 3–675a
baptismal sponsorship 2–86a
Caesarea 3–627b
catechumen 2–83b
Constantinople, Council of (381) 2–120b
Nicaea-Constantinople 3–628b
Nicene 3–627b-628a
Cremonensis, Jacobus 1–439a-b
Crenels 3–146a-b, 147, 149
CRESCAS, ḤASDAI 3–677a; 1–460a
Crescenzi, Pietro de' 1–87a
Crespines 3–624a
Cresques, Abraham
Azores 4–559a
Catalan Atlas 2–29b
CRETE 3–678a
Byzantine literature 2–523a
Fourth Crusade 4–48b
CRIMEA, KHANATE OF 3–678b
Black Death 2–258b; 4–142a
Byzantine church 2–461b
Caffa 3–12a
fruits and fruit trees 1–99b
Polos 4–557a
Crinet 1–529a
Çrispin, Gilbert 1–312b, 315a
Črnomen, Battle at (1371) 2–502a
CROATIA 4–1a
banus 2–82b
Bosnia 2–334b, 337a,b
Bulgaria 2–405a
Dalmatia 4–79b
map 4–3
Croce dipinta 4–13b
CROCKET 4–8b
Crocket capital 3–90b, 91a
Crònica (Ramon Muntaner) 3–165b
Crònica de Sant Joan de La Penya 3–166a
Crónica de veinte reyes 3–71a,b
Crónica general 1–161b
Crook plow 1–80a
Crops
See Agriculture and nutrition; specific crops
CROSS, FORMS OF 4–9a
altar apparatus 1–224a
Anglo-Saxon culture 1–274a
Celtic art 3–221a,b, 222a, 223a-b, 224b
chivalry, orders of 3–303b, 305b, 306a
church types 3–378a
Djvari 4–231b
Golgotha 1–236b
Greek 4–9b, 340b-341a
Latin 4–9b
Old English poetry 1–280a,b
See Also Crucifixion
CROSS, PROCESSIONAL 4–12a
Crossbow
See Bow and arrow/crossbow
Cross burning 3–358B
Cross-domed church 3–378a, 380
CROSSING 4–12a; 1–444a
Cross-in-square plans 3–378b; 4–341a-b, 344a, 345a,b, 346b, 347a
Cross of Angels 1–631a
Cross-plowing 1–89b-90a
CROSS-STAFF 4–12a; 1–613a
Cross-stone
See Xacʿkʿar
Crossword 1–46a
Crowmer, William
Cade's Rebellion 3–5a
CROWN, MURAL 4–12b
Crown of Aragon
See Aragon, Crown of
Crown pleas 3–659b
Crowns
See Regalia, temporal and religious
Croxton Play of the Sacrament 4–286a
CROZIER 4–12b
Crucifixion (Giovanni Baronzio) 2–112b
Crucifix (Coppo di Marcovaldo) 3–585a
CRUCIFIXION 4–12b
alpha and omega 1–204a
anti-Semitism 1–339a, 341a
Cimabue 3–396a-b
Crusader art and architecture 4–26a
deposition from the Cross 4–157a
Crucifixion (David) 4–114b
Crucifixion with Saints (Bernardo Daddi) 4–75b
Cruet 1–223a
Crul, Cornelis 4–322b
Cruper 1–529a
CRUSADE, CHILDREN'S 4–14a
CRUSADE, CONCEPT OF 4–15b; 4–33a
See Also Crusade propaganda
***CRUSADE AND DEATH OF RICHARD I* 4–18b**; 1–265a
CRUSADE PROPAGANDA 4–18b
Bible 2–216a
See Also Crusades: 1212 to 1272
CRUSADER ART AND ARCHITECTURE 4–21b
Byzantine 2–447a
Ephrem 4–495a
CRUSADES, POLITICAL 4–57b
Baltic countries 2–64b-67a

CRUSADES AND CRUSADER STATES 4–27a
Aleppo 1–145b
Asia, explorations 4–556a
Bohemond I 2–308a
Brittany, Duchy 2–379b
chansons de geste 3–259a
chivalry 3–302a-b
Cluny, Order of 3–470b
Constantinople 3–555b, 556a
cosmetics 2–147a
Cyprus, kingdom 4–70b
Damascus 4–81a, 82a
French chronicles 3–332a
Islamic Arabia 1–375b
Jerusalem 2–309a; 4–556a
Latin church 3–355a-356b
Louis IX of France 2–271a
song 2–18a
timber supply 3–145b
CRUSADES AND CRUSADER STATES: TO 1192 4–33a; 4–36a-37b
Adémar of Le Puy 4–30a
Albrecht von Johansdorf 1–132b-133a
Anatolia 1–241a
Ankara 1–302a,b
Antioch 1–326a
anti-Semitism 1–339b-341b; 4–371b
arms and armor 1–524a,b
art and architecture 4–21a-25a
assassins 1–590b-591a
Ayyubids 2–23b, 24a,b
Baldwin I of Jerusalem 2–58b
Bernard of Clairvaux 2–192a
Bohemond I of Sicily 4–30a
Burgundy, County 2–424b
Byzantine Empire 1–303b; 2–494b-495a
cavalry 3–203a
Cercamon 3–240b
Chanson d'Antioche 3–254b
Clermont, Council of 3–449b-450a, 635b
Cologne 3–481b
Conon de Béthune 3–538a
Danishmendids 4–91b
Edessa 4–384a
Eleanor of Aquitaine 4–419a-b
First Crusade 1–158a; 3–254b
Godfrey of Bouillon 4–30a
preachers 4–20b
propaganda 4–18b
Urban II, Pope 3–449b-450a; 4–19a
CRUSADES AND CRUSADER STATES: 1212 TO 1272 4–49a
Albigensian 3–188a-189b
Assizes of Jerusalem 1–598b-599b
Baybars al-Bunduqdārī 2–138b
Fifth Crusade 2–24a
Western councils 3–641a, 642a-b
CRUSADES AND CRUSADER STATES: FOURTH 4–41b; 2–323a
Angelos family 1–251b
Baldwin IX of Flanders 4–31b
Bulgaria 2–408b
Byzantine Empire 2–497a, 498a-499a
chronicles 3–328a
Cistercians 3–405b
Conon de Béthune 3–538a
Constantinople 1–241b, 334b; 4–438a
diplomacy 4–203b, 204a
Epiros, Despotate of 4–499a
propaganda 4–18b
Thibaut III 3–247a
Thurotte 3–277b
CRUSADES AND CRUSADER STATES: NEAR EAST 4–27a
Assizes of Jerusalem 1–598b
Beirut 2–164a
map 4–28-29
CRUSADES OF THE LATER MIDDLE AGES 4–54b
Bāyazīd I 2–136b
Enguerrand VII of Coucy 4–491a
Knights of Saint John 3–304a
Crusado 4–301b
Crux ansata 4–9a
Crux commisa 4–9a
Crux fourchette 4–9a
Crux gemina
See Double cross
Crux gemmata 4–9a
Crux hasta 4–9a
Crux patée 4–9a
CRYPT 4–62a; 1–442b
apse 1–352a
basilicas 2–124a
Crypta
See Crypt
Crypto Jews
See New Christians
Ctesibius 3–28a
CTESIPHON 4–62b
***CUADERNA VÍA* 4–63a**
Berceo 2–186b
Libro de Apolonio 1–348b
Cuba 4–561a
CUBICULUM 4–63b; 3–155a
Cuckoo and the Nightingale, The (Sir John Clanvowe) 3–408a
Cuenca 1–409a
CUERDA SECA 4–64a
Alhambra 1–171a
ceramics 3–237b
Cuffs 3–625a
Cuirass 1–529a, 531b, 532b
Cuishes
See Cuisses
Cuisses 1–525b, 534a
Cuixà
ecclesiastical culture 3–175a,b
Culdee movement 3–228a
Culemann fragment 2–142a
Culhwch and Olwen 1–566a-b, 578a
Culm 2–65a, 66a,b
Cultivo al tercio 1–83a
"Cult of carts" 1–334a
Denmark 4–149b
Cultu feminarum, De (Tertullian) 1–322b, 323a
Cuman-Kipchaks 2–131b
Cumans
See Russian nomads, Invasions of
Cumbria
Celtic population 1–290a
Durham, Treaties of 4–316a
Cumbric dialect 3–234a
Gododdin (Aneirin) 1–247a
CUMDACH 4–64b
Cummian (*De controversia Paschali*) 3–228b
Cumpoz (Philippe de Thaon) 1–262a, 271a,b
Cunedat
See Cunedda Wledig
CUNEDDA WLEDIG 4–64b
Cunes
See Conon de Béthune
CUPOLA 4–65a
Karmrawor, Church of Saint 1–601b
Cupola church
See Church, Types of
Cupper 3–400b
Cura pro mortuis gerenda, De (Augustine) 4–118b
Cur Deus Homo (Anselm of Canterbury) 1–312b, 314b
Christology 3–322a
Cure, The (Sina, Ibn) 1–458b
Cure, The
See Shifā', Al-
CURFEW 4–65a
angelus 1–252a
CURIA, LAY 4–65a
court of common pleas 3–491b
CURIA, PAPAL 4–65b
Alexander of Hales 1–148a
apostolic datary 4–106b
Avignonese papacy 3–363b, 364a
breviary 2–371b-372a
Cardinals, College of 3–95a-b
chamberlain 3–242a
clergy hierarchy 3–444b
conciliar theory 3–511a
Latin church 3–352a, 360a, 372b
Curia gratiosa 4–107a
Curial, Le (Alain Chartier) 3–275b
Curial e Guelfa 3–170a
Curia Regis 4–480b
Castile 3–132b
cortes 3–610b
CUROPALATES 4–66b
Curran
Lai d'Haveloc 1–268a
Cursing 3–231a
CURSUS 4–66b
Cursus paschalis 3–228a
Cursus velox 3–253b
Curthose, Robert 4–461b, 462a
Curtiles 4–512a
CUSP 4–68a
Custodes 3–444b
Custom
English common law 4–480a-b, 481a
CUSTOMARY 4–68a
Carthusian 3–118a,b, 119a
Custom of Paris 3–278b
Custom of the Fairs 4–592a
CUSTOS 4–68a
CUSTUMALS OF NORMANDY 4–68b
Cuthbert, Saint 2–155b, 156a
Anglo-Saxon culture 1–274a
Durham Cathedral 4–315b
Cuthbert of Jarrow 2–155b
Cuvelier, Jean
ars subtilior 1–558b
French chronicles 3–332b
Cuvier, Le 4–265b
Cuxham Manor
Black Death 2–262a, 265b
Cycle (Agathias) 1–67b
Cylinder dial 3–28b
CYNDDELW BRYDYDD MAWR 4–69b; 3–122a
Cyneheard 1–284b
Cynewulf
chronicles 1–284b
exegesis 4–550b
Old English 1–277b, 278a
Cynfeirdd 4–430b-431a
Cynghanedd 3–121b
Cyprian (metropolitan) 4–414a
Cyprian (referendary) 2–291b
CYPRIAN, SAINT 4–70a; 1–323a
altars 1–225a
church unity 3–335b
papal coronation 3–602b
CYPRUS, KINGDOM OF 4–70b
Andronikos I Komnenos 1–245a
Assizes of Jerusalem 1–599a
bishops' status 2–10a

CYPRUS, KINGDOM OF (cont.)
Byzantine Empire 2–118a
Carmelites 3–96b
chivalry 3–306b
Crusader art and architecture 4–26b
early Christian art 4–362a
exploration 4–556b
Frederick II 4–51a
Louis IX 4–52b
Cyriacus, Saint 1–520a
CYRIL AND METHODIOS, SAINTS 4–73a; 1–216a; 2–489a
Bible translation 2–215b
biblical exegesis 2–214b
Bulgaria 2–403b
Byzantine church 2–463b-464a
Moravia 2–299a-b
Nestorius 2–459b
Cyrillic alphabet 1–209b, 216a-217a
CYRIL OF ALEXANDRIA, SAINT 4–74b; 1–506a, 518b
Armenian literature 1–507b
Armenian rite 1–516b
biblical exegesis 3–336a
Christmas 3–318a
Copts and Coptic church 3–594a
divine nature of Christ 3–339b
ecumenical council 3–629b, 6291
Eutyches 4–524a
Nestorianism 3–214a, 594a
Cyril of Jerusalem
Armenian literature 1–507b
Christian dogma 3–336a
Cyrus the Younger 3–390b
Cysat, Rennward
Lucerne Passion Play 4–267b, 270a
Cywydd meter 4–76a,b
Czech Brethren
See Bohemian Brethren
Czechs
See Bohemia-Moravia

D

Dā al-wakāla 1–154a
Dabil
See Dwin
Dabiša, King 2–337b
Dach'i 3–308a
Dacia 2–90b
DADDI, BERNARDO 4–75b
Dadolwch 4–431a
Dafni, Church of
Byzantine art 2–444a-b
Dafydd ap Gruffydd 3–580a
DAFYDD AP GWILYM 4–76a; 3–233b; 4–69b
Dagh
See Ararat, Mount
Dagobert I, King 3–104b
Aquitaine 1–366b
Brittany, Duchy 2–378b
Da'ī
Abū 'Abd Allah 1–72a
Dā'i ilā'l-Ḥaqq, al-
See Ḥasan ibn Zaid, al-
Daily Office
cantor 3–88a
Daimbert, Archbishop 2–309a
Dair Balā'i izeh 1–155a
Dáirine of Corcu Loígde 3–121a
Dalassena, Anna 1–158b, 303b
D'Albano, Monreale 3–531a
DÁL CAIS 4–77a
Cashel 3–121b
DALLE MASEGNE, PIERPAOLO AND JACOBELLO 4–78b
DALMATIA 4–79b
banus 2–82b
Basil I the Macedonian 2–117b
Bogomils 2–296b, 297a
Bosnia 2–336a, 337a,b, 338a
Croatia 4–1b, 2a,b, 5b-6a, 7a-b, 8a
DALMATIC 4–80a
DALMAÚ, LUIS 4–80b
Dál nAraide 1–60a
DÁL RIATA 4–77b
Áedán Mac Gabráin 1–60a
Celtic art 3–223b, 224a
Damascene, John
See John of Damascus, Saint
Damascius 2–235b
DAMASCUS 4–80b
Ayyubid architecture 2–21a,b
Ayyubids 2–23b, 24a
Badr al-Jamālī 2–44a
crusades 4–30b, 31a, 38a, 39b, 49b
Egypt 4–52a
exilarch 4–552b
Fatimids 1–375a
Great Mosque 1–197b
Damasus I, Pope 1–348a
catacombs 3–154b
papal theory 3–341b
title of ordination 3–443b
Damasus II, Pope
papal reform 3–348b
Damian
Bulgaria 2–406b
Damian, Peter 1–111b
Alberic of Monte Cassino 1–125b
Alexander II 1–146a
Cluniac rite 3–467b
Damietta
Fifth Crusade 4–50a-51a
John of Brienne 4–31b
Kāmil, al- 4–31b-32a
Louis IX 4–52b
Saladin 4–31a
Dammartin, Drouet De
See Drouet of Dammartin
Dammartin, Guy De
See Guy of Dammartin
***DANÇA GENERAL DE LA MUERTE* 4–85b**
See Also Danse macabre
DANCE 4–86a
Italian ballata 2–60b
D'Andell (Andely), Henri 1–455b
classical literary studies 3–434b
Dandolo, Doge Enrico, of Venice
Alexios IV 4–45a
Constantinople 4–45b
death 4–48b
Fourth Crusades 4–43b, 44b
Mourtzouphlos 4–47a-b
Venice, Treaty of 4–42a
Zara conquest 4–44a
DANEGELD 4–90a
Anglo-Saxon England 4–457a
Ethelred the Unready 4–517b
Danehof 4–155a
Danelagh
See Danelaw
DANELAW 4–91a
Anglo-Saxon England 4–456b, 458a, 459a
English language 3–82b
Guthrum, treaty with 1–164a-b
map 4–92a-b
Danes
See Denmark
Daniel 1–280a
Daniel, Bishop
Armenian alphabet 1–492a
Daniel, Book of 1–249a
Daniel, Saint
Bangor monastery 2–71a
Daniel ben Moses al-Qūmisī
exegesis 4–539b
Daniel of Worcester, Bishop
Saint Boniface 2–321b
Danish language
runic alphabet 1–215b
Dānishmend
See Ghāzī Gůmůshtegin
DANISHMENDIDS 4–91b
Anatolia 1–241b
Ankara 1–302b
Armenia 1–485a
Caesarea 3–9a
Seljukid sultanate 4–27b-30a
Dānishnāma-i 'Alā'ī (Ibn Sīnā) 4–445b
Danse 4–88b
***DANSE MACABRE* 4–93a**
Dança general de la Muerte 4–86a
death and burial 4–121b
Dansse real 4–88b
DANTE ALIGHIERI 4–94a; 1–120a
allegory 1–178b, 179b-180a, 186a,b
artist, status of the 1–579a
Ascension of the Prophet 1–581b
assassins 1–590b
biography 2–240a
Boccaccio 2–285a, 286a, 289b
Bruni 2–391a
Cavalcanti 3–196a
Cecco Angiolieri 3–211b
chansons de geste 3–258a
Chaucer 3–284a, 287a
Cino da Pistoıa 3–397b
courtly love 3–669b
Divine Comedy 1–120a, 186a; 3–169b; 4–121b, 449a
Danube River 2–4b, 88b
Daoud, Ibn
See Abraham ibn Daud
Daphne
Annunciation 1–308a
Daphniaca (Agathias) 1–67b
Daphni Church 4–552b-553a
D'Aquino, Thomas
See Aquinas, Saint Thomas
Dār al-'adl 1–153b
Dār al-'Ahd
See Abode of Covenant
Dar al-bazzaziyah
See Bedestan
Dār al-Ḥarb
See Abode of Islam--Abode of War
Dār al-Islām
See Abode of Islam--Abode of War
Dār al-Khilāfah 2–46b
Dār al-tirāz 1–154a-b
Dār aṣ-Ṣulḥ
See Abode of Truce
Darazī, al-
Druze faith 4–295b-296a
Darband
See Derbent
DARDANELLES 4–105a
map 2–343a
Daredevils of Sasun
David of Sasun 4–112b
Dares Phrygius 4–496a

DARET, JACQUES 4–105b
Campin 3–60b
Darifant 2–199a,b
Darius 1–152b
Alexander the Great 1–150a,b, 151a
Daroca 1–160b, 406a, 407a
DAROKHRANITELNITSA 4–105b
Daroynk' 2–48a
***DARRAÐARLJÓÐ* 4–105b**; 4–390a,b
Darrein Presentment
See Petty Assizes, English
Darro River 1–168b
Darrynaflan paten and strainer 3–220a, 221a
Daru-banda
See Derbent
Daryal pass 3–195b
Dastagird 4–62b
Dastin, John
alchemy 1–138a
Datarius
See Datary, apostolic
DATARY, APOSTOLIC 4–106b
Date palm cultivation 1–371a
Datini, Francesco di Marco 1–446b, 562a-b; 2–77a
Dauferius
See Desiderius of Monte Cassino
Daugava River 2–64b
Daugava Valley 2–64b
DAUPHIN 4–107b; 4–109a-b
DAUPHINÉ 4–108a; 4–107b
map 4–108b
Davall, Ramon 3–171a
David (Donatello bronze) 4–257a
David (Donatello marble) 4–257a
David III
See David II (IV) the Builder
DAVID, GERARD 4–114b
David, Grand Komnenos 1–159a
David, Saint
Cadoc, Saint 3–7a
Mynyw 4–329b
David Anhołin " the Landless" 1–484b
David ben Abraham Alfasi
exegesis 4–539b
David ben Judah, He-Ḥasid
cabala 3–2b
David Hypatos 4–114b
David Kimḥi of Narbonne
biblical exegesis 2–212a
David of Dinant 1–228b
David of Garedja 4–116a
David of Georgia, King
amirspasalar 1–235b
David of Hark' 4–114b
DAVID OF SASUN 4–112a
DAVID I OF SCOTLAND 4–110b; 4–393a-b
Durham, Treaties of 4–316a
Ethelred of Rievaulx 4–516b, 517a
hunting laws 1–300b
DAVID II OF SCOTLAND 4–111a; 4–393a,b
Berwick, Treaty of 2–202b
DAVID OF TAO 4–113b
Bagratids, Georgian 2–49a
David of Tarōn 4–114b
David of Tayk' 1–483b
DAVID II (IV) THE BUILDER 4–111b; 1–485a
Ani in Širak 1–291a
Bagratids, Georgian 2–49a
DAVID THE INVINCIBLE 4–114a; 1–520a-b
David the Restorer
See David II (IV) the Builder
Davis, John 4–12b
Davis' staff 4–12b
DAW, JOHN 4–115a
Dawara 1–31b
DAWĀT 4–115b
DAWID-GAREDJA 4–116a
Dawit' Alawkayordi 1–512a
Dawit' Anyałt'
See David the Invincible
Dawlat al-atrāk 2–138a
Dawlat al-Jarkas 3–398a
Dawlat al-Turk 3–398a
Dawn of the sightless (al-Qalqashandī) 3–54a; 4–445b
Dawt'ak 4–114b
DĀWŪD IBN MARWĀN AL-MUQAM-MIṢ 4–116b
Day, divisions of 3–23b-24b
Dāya, Ibn al- 1–380b
Daylam 1–118a-b; 2–435a
Daylamites
Armenia 1–484a
Armenian Muslim emirates 1–513b
Buyids 2–435a
DAYR 4–117a
Daysam ibn Ibrahim al-Kurdi
Dwin 4–324a
Daz Anegenge 2–228a
Deacons 3–440b
DEAD, OFFICE OF THE 4–117a
All Souls' Day 1–177a
canonical hours 3–67b
death and burial 4–120a
Deadly sins
See Seven Deadly Sins
Dead Sea Scrolls 3–15b
Deans 3–444b
DEATH AND BURIAL, IN EUROPE 4–118a; 1–648a
ars moriendi 1–547b-548a
baptism 2–85a
Black Death 2–257a
Bulgaria 2–399b
catacombs 3–154a
consecration of cemeteries 3–540a
Coptic art 3–591b, 592a
danse macabre 4–93a
effigies 2–384b
Everyman 4–527b-529a
extreme unction 4–565a
Office of the Dead 4–117b
Death of the Virgin, Master of the 4–488a-b
Deaths of Oxen, On the (Endelechius) 4–451a
Death song
Ásmundar Saga Kappabana 1–587a-b
Death Song (Bede) 1–276a
***DÉBAT* 4–122a**
Debat de l'homme et de la femme (Guillaume Alexis) 1–324b
Debate between Buc and his horse
See Disputació d'En Buc ab son cavall
Debra Damo Church 2–17b-18a
Decameron (Boccaccio) 2–283b-285b, 289b; 3–211b; 4–86b
Dečani monastery 2–450b; 4–347a
Dečanski, King Stefan 2–412a, 414a
Decasyllabic Alexander 1–151a
Decimal notation 1–383a-b
***DECIR* 4–122b**
Decius, Philippus
conciliar theory 3–520b
Decius Paulinus Iunior 3–18a
Decknamen 1–139a
Decoration, early Christian 4–357a-361b
"Decreta Anastasii pape" 4–128a
DECRETALS 4–122b
Établissements de Saint Louis 4–515b
Latin church: 1054 to 1305 3–352b, 353b
Decretals (Gregory IX) 3–516b, 638a,b, 641a; 4–124a, 422b
DECRETALS, FALSE 4–124a; 2–178b-179a; 4–128a
confirmation 3–536a
Donation of Constantine 4–257b
ecclesiology 4–373a
Latin church 3–349a
DECRETISTS 4–127a
conciliar theory 3–511a
corporation 3–606a
dispensation 4–217a
Decretorum libri XX (Burchard of Worms) 4–128b
DECRETUM 4–128a
dispensation 4–217a
Spondent quas non exhibent divitias pauperes alchymistae (1317) 1–137b
Decretum (Gratian) 3–217a, 352b, 440b, 516a; 4–16b, 122b, 123a, 126b, 170a, 374a
church elections 4–421b-422a, 424a, 425a
commentaries 4–127a
Western Councils 3–635a, 636b, 637a-b
Decretum (Ivo of Chartres) 4–128b
Decretum Gelasianum 2–204a-b
Dedan 1–371a
DEDICATION OF CHURCHES 4–130a
Dedication portraits 4–262a
De' Dondi, Giovanni
clocks and reckoning of time 3–459b, 461a,b
De' Dondi, Jacopo
planetary clocks 3–464b
Deep-share ard 1–80a
Deer 1–301a
DEESIS 4–131b; 2–447b-448a,b
chin 3–301a
"Defender of the Peace"
See Defensor Pacis
Defensor civitatis
Gregory II 3–345b
***DEFENSOR PACIS* 4–132a**; 1–465a; 4–376b
DEGRADATION OF CLERICS 4–133a
Degsastán, Battle of (603) 1–60a
Deḥiyyot 3–25b-26b
Deicide
anti-Semitism 1–340b-341b
Deiniol, Saint 2–71a
Deiniolen 2–71a
Deira, Kingdom of 4–454a,b
Deir Anba Bishoi 3–587a
Deir Anba Hadra 3–586b
Deir el-Abiad 3–586b, 588a,b
Deir el-Abiad (Sohag)
Alexandrian rite 1–155a
Coptic architecture 3–586b
Deir el-Ahmar 3–586b
Deir el Muharraq 3–587a
Deir el-Shuhada 3–587a
Deir Sim'an
See Telanissus
Déisi 4–329a
Dekarchies 3–199b-200a
Delapré Chronicle 1–266a
Delft
fairs 4–586b
Deliberatio (Innocent III) 4–427b
Deliverance After Distress (al-Tanūkhī) 1–380b

DELLA ROBBIA, LUCA, ANDREA, GIOVANNI 4–134b
Brunelleschi 2–390a
Della Scala, Bartolomeo 4–99a
Della Scala, Can Signorio 2–324b
Delphi
Constantine I 1–334b
Delsoler family
Bordeaux 2–328a
Demand deposits 2–74b
Demantin (Berthold von Holle) 2–199a,b
DEMES 4–135a; 3–554a
Demesne farming
accounting 1–39a-40a
corvée 3–613a
Demetae 4–329a
Demetre I 1–235b
Demetrias
Maliasenoi 2–479a
Demetrios Chomatianos, Archbishop
Bulgaria 2–409a
DEMETRIOS KYDONES 4–135b
DEMETRIOS PRESBYTER 4–136a
Demetrius of Phalerum
fables 4–572a
Demiceint 3–625a
Demir Gapi
See Derbent
Democritus
alchemy 1–135b
DEMOGRAPHY 4–136a
Domesday Book 4–237b
Demonstrations, Book of
See Kitab al-burhān
Dendera basilica 3–586b
Dendrochronology 3–450b, 451a
Dendrophori 3–606b
Denis, Saint
Adam of Saint Victor 1–51b
Denis, Saint, Church
double-ended basilica 3–378b
Denis of Portugal, King
admirals 4–558b
Denis of Tel-Mahré
See Dionysius of Tel-Mahré
Denis the Carthusian
See Denys the Carthusian
Denis the Little
See Dionysius Exiguus
***DENKARD* 4–148A**; 1–452a
Avesta 2–14b
DENMARK 4–148b
Anglo-Saxon 1–289a,b
Anglo-Saxon England 4–455b-456b
aristocracy 4–154a-155a
Baltic countries 2–64a
bracteates 2–356a
chivalry, orders of 3–307a
Cnut the Great 3–471b
crusade of 1147 2–66a
excommunication 4–538a
explorations 4–553B, 554a
Innocent III 3–353b
map 4–150
pollen studies 3–453b
Dentifrices 2–147b-148a, 150b
Dentistry 2–150a-b
Denys the Carthusian 3–119a
conciliar theory 3–511b, 517a, 519b
Deor (Exeter Book) 1–278b
Deorham (Dyrham) 1–290a
Deorulf
Boniface, Saint 2–321b
Deotisalvi
See Diotisalvi
Deposit *a discrezione* 2–73b, 77a
Depositio martyrum
Christmas 3–317b
DEPOSITION FROM THE CROSS 4–157a
DEPOSITION OF RULERS, THEORIES OF 4–157b
Edward II 4–397b, 483a-b
DERBENT 4–162a; 1–125a; 2–26a, 27a
Dereham, Elias of
See Nicholas of Ely
Derry
See Columba, Saint
Dertusensis prima 4–123a
DERVISH 4–162b
DER VON KÜRENBERG 4–161a
Descant
Anonymous IV 1–309b
Descent into Limbo
See Anastasis
DESCHAMPS, EUSTACHE 4–163b; 1–185a, 189b
antifeminism 1–323a, 324b
ballade 2–59a
chant royal 3–263b
Des Champs, Jean
See Jean des Champs
Des Champs, Pierre
See Pierre des Champs
Desclot, Bernat 1–190b, 415b; 3–165b, 166a
DESCORT 4–164a
Description of the Western Islands of Scotland, A (Martin Martin) 2–107a
Desenzano 1–250b
Desertas
Medici Atlas (1351) 4–559a
Desert Fathers 1–204b
Deserts of Sins and Their Remission, The (Augustine) 1–653a
Desiderabile desiderium (John Dastin) 1–138a
DESIDERIUS OF MONTE CASSINO 4–164b; 2–173b, 218b
Bruno of Segni, Saint 2–392a
Constantine the African 3–548b
marble 1–333b
Pisan-Genoese expedition 3–355b
Desislava (wife of Kalojan) 2–416b
Desplá, Canon Luis 2–189b
Despoina 1–644a
DESPOT 4–165a
autocrator 2–10b
basileus 2–122b
caesar 3–9a
DESTORRENTS, RAMÓN 4–165b
Destrier 3–206a,b
Destruction de Troye, La 4–265a
Destructorium viciorum (Alexander Carpenter) 3–459b
Desvalers, Francesco
Canaries 4–559a
Dettic
Boniface, Saint 2–321b
Déu d'Amor caçador, De 3–173b
Deu le omnipotent 1–260b, 262b
DEUSDEDIT, CARDINAL 4–165b
dictatus papae 4–177b
Western councils 3–633a-b
Deusdona, Deacon
relics 1–337a
Deutenus 1–422a
Deutsche Sphaera (Conrad of Megenberg) 3–539a
Deventer
Brethren of the Common Life 2–367a
fairs 4–586b
Devil's Deceit, The (Ibn al-Jawzī) 1–380b
Devinatione, De (Cicero) 1–605a
Devon
Black Death 2–262a
woodcarving 4–115b
DEVOTIO MODERNA 4–166a; 3–369a
Augustinian canons 1–659b
Bohemian Brethren 2–306a
Brethren of the Common Life 2–366a
Groote 4–320b
religious communities 3–369a
Devout Doctor
See Bonaventure
Devshirme 2–136a, 137b
Dhāt al-Salāsil
ʿAmr ibn al-ʿĀṣ 1–236b
Dhimma
See Minorities
Dhimmis
Islamic diplomacy 4–197b
Dhū'l-Kaṣṣa, Battle of 1–25a
Dhu 'l-Nūn
Danishmendids 4–93a
Dhu 'l-Nūn al-Miṣrī 4–407a
Dhuoda
Bible 2–211b
***DIABOLUS IN MUSICA* 4–167b**
DIACONICON 4–167b; 4–343b
apse 1–352a
Diaconissa
celibacy laws 3–216a
Diagonal arch
See Arch
DIALECT 4–168a
Anglo-Norman literature 1–271b
Old English texts 1–276a
DIALECTIC 4–168a
Boethius 2–292a
Bradwardine 2–358a
Burley 2–432b
duality 4–434a
Dialectica (Abelard) 4–169b
Dialectica (Alcuin) 1–142B
Dialectica (Garlandus) 4–169b
Dialectica (Lanfranc of Bec) 4–169b
Dialectica (Petrus Ramus) 4–171a
Dialectica Alexandri
See Ars disserendi
Dialecticae disputationes (Lorenzo Valla) 4–171a
Dialogo della divina providenza (Catherine of Siena) 3–168a
Dialogue de Saint-Julien et son disciple 1–264a
Dialogue of a Philosopher with a Christian and a Jew (Abelard) 1–18a
Dialogue of the Exchequer 4–90b, 469b
Dialogue on Miracles (Caesarius of Heisterbach) 3–10a
Dialogues (Saint Gregory) 1–165a; 3–167a
translations 1–167a, 254a, 284a
Dialogus contra Judaeos (Peter Alfonso) 3–167b
Dialogus familiaris (Alain Chartier) 3–275b
Diana d'Andalo 4–248a
DIAPER PATTERN 4–171b
***DIAPHONIA* 4–172a**
Diaphragm arch
See Arch
Diarmaid Mac Muchadh of Leinster
Clonard 3–466a
Diarmait 1–61a
Diarmait mac Cerbaill
Áed Sláne 1–60b
Dias, Bartholomew 4–560b, 562b
Dias, Dinis 4–561a
DIASTEMY 4–172b
Diatessaron of Tatian 2–217b
DĪBĀJ 4–173a
Dibīr 1–488b

Dibitision 3–615a
Dicta Anselmi (Alexander of Canterbury) 1–314a
DICTAMEN 4–173b
Boncompagno 2–320a
Dictamina (Peter of Vinea) 4–174b, 176b
Dictaminis epithalamium (Juan Gil de Zamora) 4–175b
Dictaminum radii (Alberic of Monte Cassino) 4–174a
Dictates of the Pope
See Dictatus Papae
"Dictatus of Avranches" 4–177b
***DICTATUS PAPAE* 4–177a**; 3–351b, 352a, 633b; 4–374a
Deusdedit, Cardinal 4–165b
Dictionaries
See Encyclopedias and Dictionaries
Dictionaries, Hebrew
See Hebrew language, study of
Dictionarium Saxonico-Latino-Anglicum (William Somner) 1–287a
Dictum of Kenilworth (1266) 2–112b; 4–396a
DICUIL 4–178a
geography 4–553b
Didache 1–605a
Church Fathers 3–334b
Didascalia
apostolic constitutions 1–349b
Didascalicon (Hugh of Saint Victor) 1–607b; 4–448b
Didgori, Battle of (1121) 4–112a
Di Dia, Comtessa 4–110a
Didymotichon 2–480b
Didymus the Blind, Saint
Athanasian doctrine 3–336a
Diego de Azevedo of Osma, Bishop
Albigensian heresy 4–239b
Dominican nuns 4–254a
Diego Laínez 3–383b
Die judicii, De (Bede) 1–280a
Die natali, De (Censorinus) 1–605a
Diet
See Representative Assembly
Dietari 3–166b
Dietari del capella d'Alfons el Magnanim (Melcior Miralles) 3–166b
Dietary laws, European 1–300a
DIETARY LAWS, ISLAMIC 4–178b
beverages 2–208b
cookery 3–584a
horsemeat 1–300a
DIETARY LAWS, JEWISH 4–180a
See Also Cookery, European
DIETMAR VON AIST 4–184a
Dietrich of Freiberg
Albertus Magnus 1–129b
Dietrich of Nieheim 4–377b
conciliar theory 3–511a, 512b, 515b, 517a
Dietrichs Flucht
See Buch von Bern, Das
Dietrich von Bern
See Theodoric the Great
Dietricus 1–545a
Diez, Manual 3–168b
DIFFERENTIA 4–185a
Evovae 4–529a
Differentia animae et spiritus, De 1–458a, 461a-b
Difnar 1–155b
***DIGENIS AKRITAS* 4–185a**; 2–508b, 521b, 524b
akritai 1–116a
Digest
See Corpus Iuris Civilis
Digest (Tribonian) 3–608b, 609a
Digestum novum 3–609b
Digestum vetus 3–609b
Dignity of the Church of Liège, On the (Alger of Liège) 1–167b
DIJON, CHARTREUSE DE CHAMPMOL 4–186a
Broederlam 2–383a
construction 4–295a
establishment 3–118b
Sluter, Claus 2–428a
Dijonnais 2–427a
Dilectione Dei et proximi, De (Brescia) 3–671a
Dimashq
See Damascus
Dimma, Book of 3–230b
Dīn, Khwarazm-shāh Jalāl al- 1–485b
DINANDERIE 4–186b; 2–384a
Dinant 2–384a
DINAR 4–187a; 4–301b
dirham 4–215b
Dinas Powys
Celtic art 3–219a
DĪNAWARĪ, ABŪ ḤANĪFA AḤMAD IBN DĀWŪD, AL 4–187b; 2–50a
***DINDSHENCHAS* 4–188b**; 1–33b
Din Eidyn 4–392b
DINIS 4–189b; 3–87a, 306b
Dinnshenchas
See Dindshenchas
DIOCESE, ECCLESIASTICAL 4–191a
Burgundy, Duchy of 2–427b
cathedral 3–192a
church organization 3–372b
DIOCESE, SECULAR 4–191b
Diocletian, Emperor
Byzantine economy and society 2–475b
Constantine I 3–545b
dioceses 4–191b
Donatism 4–259b
empire planning 2–97a
era 3–18b
Diodorus of Tarsus
Antiochene School 3–336a
Diodorus Siculus
bards 2–105b
bestiary 2–203b
Diogenes
barrel 2–114a
Diogo Cão 4–562a
Diogo de Azambuja 4–562a
Dionigi da Borgo San Sepolcro
Boccaccio 2–278a
Dionysiana 3–229b
Dionysia of Munchensy 1–270b
Dionysio-Hadriana (Pope Adrian I) 3–349a; 4–124b, 373a
DIONYSIOS OF FOURNA 4–191b
DIONYSIOS THE GREEK 4–192a
Dionysiou monastery 1–637a, 638a
Dionysius Cato 3–193b
Dionysius Colle
plague 2–264b
DIONYSIUS EXIGUUS 4–192b; 4–365a
apostolic constitutions 1–350a
calendars 3–18b-19b, 22a
canon law 3–216a, 348b
DIONYSIUS OF TEL-MAHRÉ 4–193a
Dionysius the Areopagite, Saint 4–63b
Alan of Lille 1–119b-120a
Denis, Saint 1–51b
Dionysius the Pseudo-Areopagite
See Pseudo-Dionysios the Areopagite
Dionysius Thrax
Armenian Hellenizing School 1–505b
Dioscorides
botany 2–245a,b, 246a, 345a
pharmacology 2–250b
Dioscoros of Alexandria
Chalcedon, Council of (451) 2–459b
Ephesus, Second Council of (449) 3–594a, 629b; 4–524a
Dioscorus, Antipope 1–330a
Dioskoros 2–506a
DIOTISALVI (DEOTOSALVI) **4–193b**
DIPLOMACY, BYZANTINE 4–193b
chancery 3–254a
DIPLOMACY, ISLAMIC 4–197a
DIPLOMACY, WESTERN EUROPEAN 4–201b
chancery 3–252a-b
Diplomatic immunity 4–211a-b
DIPTYCH 4–214b
DIPTYCH, CONSULAR 4–215a
Direct
See Custos
DIRHAM 4–215b
Dirhem
See Dirham
Dirige 4–117b
Dirk of Herxen
Brethren of the Common Life 2–367a, 368a
"Disappearing Christ" 1–273b
Discant
See Notre Dame School
DISCANTOR 4–216a
clausula 3–437a
diaphonia 4–172a
***DISCIPLINA CLERICALIS* 4–216b**; 1–264a; 3–167b
Disciplinants of Santa Maria della Scala 2–195b-196b
Disciplines (Varro) 4–447b
Discourses Against the Arians (Athanasius) 1–633b
Discours politique des diverses puissances 3–522a
Discussion Between the Heretic and the Christian (Eutychios) 4–525b
DISPENSATION 4–216b
apostolic datary 4–107a
Disputació d'En Buc ab son cavall 3–170b, 173b
Disputatio contra mathematicos (Hélinand of Froidmont) 1–607b
Disputatio de auctoritate concilii supra pontificem maximum (John Major) 3–521a
***DISPUTATIO INTER CLERICUM ET MILITEM* 4–218a**
Disputationes adversus astrologos (Pico della Mirandola) 1–609a
Disputations
See Polemics
Disputatio Pippini cum Albin (Alcuin) 1–142b
Disputed Questions on Evil (Thomas Aquinas) 1–363b
Disputed Questions on Truth (Thomas Aquinas) 1–361a, 363b
Dispute with Lady Hope
See Raonament entre Francesc Alegre i Esperança
Disseisin
See Seisin, disseisin
Dissonances, musical
Anonymous IV 1–310a
Disticha (Dionysius Cato) 1–264a
Disticha Catonis
See Cato's Distichs (Latin)
DISTILLED LIQUORS 4–219a
Distinctiones (Alan of Lille) 1–120a
glosses 4–127b

Distraint
See Distress
DISTRESS 4–220b
Districtus 2–69a
Disūq
fairs 4–589b
***DIT* 4–221a**
Dit des trois mors et des trois vifs, Le 4–121b
Ditié (Christine de Pizan) 3–317a
Ditié (d'Urbain)
See *Urbain le courtois*
Ditmarus de Agasta
See Dietmar von Aist
Diu Urstende 2–228b
Diversis artibus, De (Theophilus) 4–438b
Divination
astrology 1–604a, 617a
Divine Comedy (Dante) 4–94a-95b, 97a, 98b, 100a-b, 101a-b
Divine Comedy
See Also Dante Alighieri
DIVINE OFFICE 4–221b
breviary 2–326a, 370b, 371b
canonical hours 3–67a
Carthusian rite 3–118a
Celtic liturgy 3–230a, 239b
Cistercian rite 3–406a
Cluny, Order of 3–468b
collectarium 3–479b
Office of the Dead 4–117b, 121a
Divine right principle
Abbasid caliphate 3–46a-47b
Divorce
See Family
Diwan 1–168b
Dīwān (registry system) 3–34a, 37b, 39b
Abbasids 3–44a
Dīwānī (script style) 3–54b
Ḍiyā' al-Dīn Abū 'L-Fatḥ Naṣr Allāh 1–634b-635a
Diyala Plains 2–45b, 47a
DIYARBAKIR 4–231b; 2–24a
Aq Qoyunlu confederation 1–352a
architecture 1–6a
Diyar Mudar 2–24a
Djābir ibn Ḥayyān 1–141a
Djabrā'īl 1–248b
Djahḥāfids 1–513a
Djed
Bosnian church 2–342a,b
Djime (Medinet Habu)
architecture 3–586b
DJVARI 4–231b
Djvari Church 1–632b
Dmitar Zvonimir, King 4–79b
Dmitri Donskoy, Prince 1–159b
DMITRII IVANOVICH DONSKOI 4–232a
boyars 4–306a
Dnieper River 1–96b
Crimea, Khanate of 3–678b
Danes 4–554a
trade 4–588a
Dnieper Valley
Goths 2–90a
Dobla 3–185b
Dobriner Order
Baltic countries 2–66b
Dobrotica 2–412b
Dobrudja 2–409b
Dobruja
See "Scythia Minor"
Doccioni
See Gargoyle
DOCETISM 4–233a
church, early 3–339b
Docheiariou monastery 1–636b
DOCTOR 4–233b
Doctor and Student (Christopher Saint German) 4–503a
DOCTORS OF THE CHURCH 4–234a
Church Fathers 3–334b
Doctor subtilis
Duns Scotus 4–308a,b
Doctrina Christiana, De (Saint Augustine) 3–432a
Doctrina compendiosa (Eiximensis) 4–416b
Doctrina de compondre dictats (Ramon Vidal de Besalú) 3–69b, 164b
Doctrina de dictatz 4–87a
Doctrinal de trobar (Ramon de Cornet) 3–170a
Doctrinale puerorum (Alexander de Villa Dei) 3–434b
Doctrinal sauvage 1–264a
Documenti d'amore (Francesco da Barberino) 3–665b
Dodici avvertimenti che deve dare la madre alla figliuola quando la manda a marito 3–663a
Dodos Rka monastery 4–116a
Dog
charms, old High German 3–274a
food animal 1–300a
Doge's Palace
Buon, Giovanni and Bartolomeo 2–419b
Dogmatic Panoply (Euthymois Zigabenos) 1–303b
Dol
Baudri of Bourgueil 2–132a
Celtic church 2–381b
Dolça of Provence 3–178a
Dolce stil nuovo
Cecco Angiolieri 3–211b-212a
Dôle, University of 2–426b
Dolgorukii, Iuri 2–203b
Domagoj, Prince 4–2b
Dombelay, John
alchemy 1–138a
DOME 4–234b
Armenian architecture 1–493b
Bulgarian art and architecture 2–417a
Justinianic 4–338a-339b
Domed octagon plan 3–378b, 380; 4–341b-343a
Domenec, Jaume 3–166b
Domenichi, Domenico de'
conciliar theory 3–519b
Domenico, San
Cimabue 3–396a
Domenico di Cambio
art trade 1–562b
DOME OF HEAVEN 4–236b; 4–359a
DOME OF THE ROCK 4–237a; 3–40b; 4–24a, 359b
calligraphy 3–52a
DOMESDAY BOOK 4–237b; 1–212b
accounting 1–38b
agriculture 1–91a
boroughs 2–330a-b
brewing 2–374b
Celtic languages 3–234a
Danelaw 4–91a
demography 4–137b, 139b
king's dues 4–533b
Norman-Angevin England 4–461b
DOMESTIC 4–239a
Domestication of animals 1–293a
DOMINIC, SAINT 4–239b; 1–127a; 3–183b
Dominicans 4–242a
mysticism 4–248a
nuns 4–254a
Dominica in albis 4–364b-365a
Dominical letter of year 3–23b
DOMINICAN CHANT 4–240a
DOMINICAN RITE 4–241b
DOMINICANS 4–242b
Albertus Magnus 1–126b
alchemy 1–137b
Antoninus, Saint 1–342a
Aquinas 1–353b
Aragon, Crown of 1–413b
Aristotelianism 1–461b-462a, 465a
Armagh 1–470a
astrology 1–607b
Bacon 2–37a
Barcelona 2–104a
beguines and beghards 2–159a, 161a
biblical exegesis 2–214a; 4–544a
canonical hours 3–67a-b
Carmelites 3–96b
Cathars 3–189b-190a,b
Christian Hebraists 3–314a
church, Latin 3–353a-b, 368a,b
Cilician-Roman church union 3–394b
confessor, royal 3–534b
crusade propaganda 4–20b
Cyprus 4–72b
Dominic, Saint 4–239b
Eckhart 4–380b
education of laity 3–359a
exempla 4–551a
Lyons, Council of (1274) 3–641b
trination 1–177a
Dominici, Cardinal John 3–649a
Dominic of Sora, Saint 1–125b
DOMINICUS 4–255b
Dominicus Dominici Visentinus
dictamen 4–175b, 176b
Dom Leclercq
Marian office 2–274a
Domnal Brecc 4–78b
Domnes of Antioch 3–629b
Domnizo
See Donizo
Domnonia 1–144a
Dömös Abbey 1–298b
Dom Pedro
Arthurian literature 1–576a
***DOMUS ECCLESIAE* 4–256a**
Dura Europos 4–313a
Donait français 1–270b
DONALD III (DONALDBANE) **4–256a**; 4–110b
Donaldbane
See Donald III
DONATELLO 4–256b
Brunelleschi 2–388b
frescoes 1–226b
Donati, Corso 4–99a
banishment 4–98a
Cavalcanti's feud 3–196b
Donati, Gemma (wife of Dante) 4–96a
DONATION OF CONSTANTINE 4–257b; 3–346a
Adrian 3–110a
Augustinus Triumphus 2–1a
Decretals, False 4–124b-125a
ecclesiology 4–373a
See Also Constantine I, the Great
Donation of Pepin
See Pepin
DONATISM 4–259b
Augustine of Hippo 1–651b-652a
Bohemian Brethren 2–306a
canonization 3–67b
Constantine I 3–545b
Donato Albanzani
Boccaccio 2–280b

Donato Bramante
astrarium 3–462a
Donato di Niccolò di Betto de' Bardi
See Donatello
DONATUS OF FIESOLE 4–260a
Auraicept na nÉces 2–2a
Brigit, Saint 2–377a
grammars 2–107b; 3–432a
Donaustauff castle 1–128b
Doncaster
Black Death 2–262b
DONDI, GIOVANNI DE' 4–260b
Dondi, Jacopo de'
astronomical clock 3–29b
Doneldey, Arnold 4–579b
Dongola 4–404a
DONIZO (DOMNIZO) **4–261a**
Donji Kraji 2–334a, 335a, 336b, 337b, 338b
Donjon
See Dungeons
Donjon-coquille 3–144a
"Donna me prega" (Cavalcanti) 3–196b
Donnchadh Mór ó Dálaigh 1–111b
Donnchad of Munster, King 4–77b
***DONNEI DES AMANTS* 4–261b**; 1–268b
DONOR PORTRAIT 4–261b
"Do Not Take a Wife" 1–323b
Don Quixote (Cervantes) 3–212b, 258a
Don River
Crimea, Khanate of 3–678b
exploration 4–556b
Donskoi, Dmitrii Ivanovich
See Dmitrii Ivanovich Donskoi
Doomsday, Signs of
Airdena Brátha 1–111a
Doon de Mayence 1–267a; 2–201b; 3–258b
Dormition (Baronzio) 2–112b
Dormition at Nicaea, Monastery of the
mosaics 2–439a
Dormition of the Virgin
See Koimesis
Dorotea, La (Vega) 3–212b
Dorotheus of Sidon 1–617a
Dorothy, Saint
miracle plays 4–268b
Dorylaeum
crusades 2–309a, 495a; 4–30a, 35a
Dotzé (Eiximenis) 3–168b
Doubios
See Dwin
Double cathedral
See Church, Types of
Double cross
See Cross, Forms of
Double-enceinte fortification 4–333b-334a
Double-ended church
See Church, Types of
Double-entry accounting 1–40b-42b
Double-shell dome 4–235a, 236a
DOUGLAS, GAVIN 4–262a
DOUKAS 4–263a; 2–517b
Byzantine Empire 2–496a
Constantine 1–303a
Irene 1–303a; 2–495b
Romanos IV 2–493a
Douro region 1–626a,b, 627a
pressura system 1–629a-b
Dove's neck ring (Ibn Ḥazm) 3–672a
Dower, Dowry
See Family
DOWN, ROGER 4–263a
Doxompous
agriculture 1–79a
Drač
See Dyrrachium
Dragalevci
frescoes 2–417b
Dragmaticon philosophiae (Guillaume de Conches) 3–168b-169a
Dragometia
See Dragovitsa
Dragon
animal style 1–293a
Dragon, Order of (Hungary) 3–306b
Dragovitsa 3–183b, 184a
Dragutin
Braničevo 2–411a
DRAMA, FRENCH 4–263b
Courtois d'Arras 3–674b
DRAMA, GERMAN 4–266b
DRAMA, LITURGICAL 4–272b
confrérie 3–536b
Dutch 4–321b-322a
Easter 4–366a-368a
French 4–263b-264a
German 4–267a-270b
Latin 4–280b-282b
terminology 4–278b-279a
DRAMA, WESTERN EUROPEAN 4–277b
Anglo-Norman 1–269b-270a
Bodel, Jean 2–290b
Castle of Perserverance 3–142b
Celestina, La 3–212a
Chester plays 3–298a
Dutch 4–321a
Everyman 4–526b
French 4–263a
Germany 4–266b
Drang nach dem Osten 2–66a
Dráp Niflunga 4–386a
Drassanes 2–104b
Drastamat 1–560a
***DRAUMA-JÓNS SAGA* 4–289b**
***DRAUMKVÆDE* 4–290a**
Drava River 2–4b; 4–4a
Drawbridge 3–148a, 149, 150b
DRAWINGS AND MODEL BOOKS 4–290b
Draživojevići 2–336b, 337b, 340a
Sanković family 2–340a
Dream of Hell (Houdenc) 1–185b
Dream of Rhonabwy, The 1–566a,b, 578a
Dream of Scipio 1–181a
Dream of the Rood 1–279a, 280a,b
Drepana
See Sickles
***DRESDENER HELDENBUCH* 4–292b**
Eckenlied 4–380a
Dress
See Costume
Dreus, Jean
See Girart de Roussillon, Master of the
Dreyfaltigkeit (Ulmannus) 1–138b
Drina River 2–70a, 337a
Drogo of Laon
Divine Office 4–223a
Drogo of Metz, Bishop 4–371b
Drogo Sacramentary 1–224b
DROLLERY 4–293b
DROLLERY 4–294a
Dromedary
See Camel
***DROPLAUGARSONA SAGA* 4–294a**; 4–612b, 613b
***DRÓTTKVÆTT* 4–294b**; 4–401a
Bragi Boddason the Old 2–359b
Einarr Helgason Skálaglamm 4–410b
Einarr Skúlason 4–411b
Drouart La Vache 1–189a
DROUET OF DAMMARTIN 4–295a
Chartreuse de Champmol 4–186a
Droungos 3–199b
Druim Cett convention (575) 4–78a
Drummond, Margaret 4–111b
***DRUNGARIOS* 4–295b**
Druthmarus, Christianus 3–311b
DRUZES 4–295b
Dry-farming regime 1–80b
Držić, Marin 4–300b
Držislav, Stjepan 4–5a-b
DUALISM 4–297a
Bogomils 2–294a
Bosnian church 2–343a-b
Cathars 3–182b, 183a, 184b, 187a
church, early 3–339b-340b
Docetism 4–233a
Duarte, King
Madeiras 4–559a
***DUBIIS NOMINIBUS, DE* 4–298b**
DUBLIN 4–298b; 1–470a
Norwegians 4–554b
Dublin Castle 4–299b
Dubricius
See Dyfrig, Saint
DUBROVNIK 4–300a
Arabs 2–117b
Bosnia 2–335a, 336a,b-337a, 338a, 339a-b, 340a-341a,b, 341b
city walls 3–151b
Croatia 4–1b, 3
Dalmatia 4–79b
DUCAT 4–301a
Ducato 4–301b
DUCCIO DI BUONINSEGNA 4–301b; 2–448a
Chairete 3–241a
influence 2–111a
Duces 1–117b
DUCHY 4–303b
Duck 3–581b
Ductia 4–87a-88b
DUDO OF SAINT QUENTIN 4–304a
French chronicles 3–331a
Du droit des magistrats (Theodore Beza) 3–521b
Dudum sacrum 3–653a
Duecento art
See Dugento (Duecento) art
Duelo de la Virgen (Gonzalo de Berceo) 2–187b
Duels
champions 3–250b
Duesmois 2–427a
Dufay 3–256b
Dufnal (Dumnail)
Chester, Treaty of 3–300a
DUGENTO (DUECENTO) **ART 4–304a**
Duke
See Duchy
Duklja
Bosnia 2–334b
Bulgaria 2–406b
***DUKUS HORANT* 4–304b**
Dulgadir
Caesarea 3–9b
Dulmo, Fernão
Azores capitan 2–30a
Seven Cities, island of the 4–559b-560a
DUMA 4–305b
See Also Boyar
Dumbleton, John 3–59b
Bradwardine 2–358a
Dumnail
Chester, Treaty of 3–300a
Dunadd
ornamented molds 3–224a
Dunash ben Labrat
biblical exegesis 2–212a

DUNATOI **4–306b**
Constantine VII Porphyrogenitos 3–547a
DUNBAR, WILLIAM 4–307a; 4–394a
DUNCAN I OF SCOTLAND 4–308a
Duncan II of Scotland 4–256a
DUNGEON 4–308a; 3–148b-150b
Dunois, Jean
Charles of Orléans 3–273a
DUNS SCOTUS, JOHN 4–308b
adoptionism 1–58a
angel/angelology 1–250a,b
Aristotelianism 1–463b-464a, 466b-467a
Burley 2–433a
Christology 3–323b, 324a
plurality of forms 1–660b
predestination 3–371a
Dunstable Priory
clock 3–460a
***DUNSTAN, LIFE OF* 4–311b**
Canterbury 3–82a-b
Dunstan, Saint
Aelfric 1–61b
biographies 4–311b-312b
church reforms 3–347b
Ethelwold 4–517b
liturgy 2–172b
monastic reform 1–273a; 3–375a; 4–457a
***DUNSTANUS SAGA* 4–311b**
***DUODECIM ABUSIVIS SAECULI, DE* 4–312a**
Duomo
Brunelleschi 2–388a,b
Buscheto of Pisa 2–433b
Ciuffagni 3–406b
Conte del Lello Orlandi 3–572a
DUPLUM 4–312b
motet 1–546b
Dupsing 1–528a
Duqāq of Damascus
Riḍwān of Aleppo 4–27b
DURA EUROPOS 4–313a; 4–349b, 350a
baptistery 2–87b
early Christian art and architecture 4–335a, 358a
Durance Valley 4–110a
DURAND, GUILLAUME 4–314a; 3–624a; 4–120b, 367a
Advent 1–59b
Christmas celebration 3–318a
consecration of cemeteries 3–541a
Divine Office 4–223a
liturgical colors 3–484b
Western councils 3–645b
Durand, Guillaume, the Younger 2–178b; 3–517b
DURAND OF SAINT POURÇAIN 4–313b
Christology 3–324a
DURANDUS 4–315b; 1–58a
Durandus, Gulielmus
See Durand, Guillaume
Durayd, Ibn 4–444a
Durazzo
See Dyrrachium
Durben, Battle of (1260) 2–66b-67a
Dürer, Albrecht
Brant 2–363b
engraving 4–487b, 489a, 490a
etching 4–516b
Durham
Anglo-Saxon art 1–272b
estates 4–512b
scriptoria 1–276a
DURHAM, TREATIES OF 4–316a
DURHAM CATHEDRAL 4–315b
Anglo-Saxon culture 1–274a
architecture 1–226a, 255b, 256a; 2–125a; 3–90b
Benedictine monastery 3–265b
Durovernum
See Canterbury
Durrës
See Dyrrachium
DURROW, BOOK OF 4–316b; 2–220a
Celtic art 3–219a
Dust boards
Arabic numerals 3–383b-384a,b
Dūst Muḥammad 1–106b
DUTCH LITERATURE 4–318a
Arthurian literature 1–572a
beast epic 2–140b
chansons de geste 3–258a
Elckerlijc 4–419a
Duwil, al-
See Dwin
***DUX* 4–323a**
barbarian invasion 2–88b, 89a
Dvina River 4–554a
DWIN 4–323a; 1–124b-125a, 450b, 473b, 481a; 2–20a
Artašat 1–563b
councils 1–123b, 499a, 501b
Muslim emirates 1–513a,b
Shaddādid emir 1–290b
DYES AND DYEING 4–325a; 2–347b
Dyfalu 4–69b
DYFED 4–329a
Dyfrig, Saint
Deiniol, Saint 2–71a
Dynastic succession 3–37a, 38b-39a, 42b-43a
Armenia 1–489b-490a
Dyrham 1–290a
DYRRACHIUM 4–329b
Basil II 2–119a
Bohemond 1–158b
Bulgaria 2–406b, 407b
Guiscard 1–158a
Normans of Sicily 4–27b
Dysmus
crucifixion 4–12b

E

EADMER OF CANTERBURY 4–330b; 1–311b
Eadwine Psalter 2–218b; 3–56b, 57a
Ealhwine
See Alcuin of York
Eanbald I 1–142a
Eanbald II of York 1–142b
Eanes, Gonçalves
Africa 4–562a
EARLY CHRISTIAN AND BYZANTINE ARCHITECTURE 4–331a
Aachen palace chapel 1–3a
arch 1–423b
baptistery 2–87b
Bulgarian 2–414b
Cappadocia 3–92a
church types 3–378a-b, 379a
diaconicon 4–167b
dome 4–234b
dome of heaven 4–236b
domus ecclesiae 4–256a
Dura Europos 4–313a
liturgical aspects 1–441b
See Also Byzantine art
EARLY CHRISTIAN ART 4–348a
alpha and omega 1–204a
altarpiece 1–225b
andachtsbild 1–243b
Armenian 1–493a-497b
baptism of Christ 2–86b
Coptic art 3–585b
See Also Byzantine art
Early English architecture 4–472a
Earth, rammed 3–561a
Earthenware 3–237a,b, 238b
Earthquake of 1319
Ani in Širak 1–291a
East Anglia
Black Death 2–261b, 262b
Danelaw 1–164a; 4–91b
Danish invasions 4–456a
emergence 2–96b; 4–454a
East Antiochene rites
See Antiochene rite
EASTER 4–364b
Ascension, Feast of the 1–582a
baptism 2–85b, 86a
Byzantine liturgy 2–468b
calendars 3–18b, 20a, 30b
Celtic church 2–381b
Cluniac rite 3–468a
dance 4–86a
dating 1–52b, 144a; 3–17b, 21b-22b, 23b, 228a,b, 465b, 486a, 628a
Dionysius Exiguus 3–18b
Elfoddw 2–71b
Entry into Jerusalem 4–491b
fast of Lent 3–99b
liturgical colors 3–484b
Eastern March 2–132b, 134b
Eastern Orthodox church
See Byzantine church
Easter Song (Saint Peter Damian) 4–63a
East Indies
Arabic language 1–378b
East Saxons 4–454a
East Slavs
See Slavs
East Syrian rites
See Syrian rites
Ebarcius of Saint Amand 4–368a
Ebbo
See Ebo of Rheims
Eberhard of Bamberg, Bishop
Eutychianism 1–58a
Ebinor, Lake
exploration 4–556b
Eble of Ventadorn 2–197a
EBO OF RHEIMS 4–368a; 3–112b
Denmark 4–151a
False Decretals 4–125b
Physiologus 4–368b
Ebreo, Guglielmo 4–89a
Ebro River 1–406a
agriculture 1–84a
Castilian fortifications 3–128a
Ebro Valley 1–403b, 407a
Alfonso I 1–160b
Ebsham, William 1–320a
***ECBASIS CAPTIVI* 4–369a**; 2–141a
Ecbasis cuiusdam captivi per tropologiam
See Ecbasis Captivi
ECCE HOMO 4–370a
Ecchellensis, Abraham 4–525b
Ecclesia, De (Hus) 4–377a
ECCLESIA AND SYNAGOGA 4–370b
architecture 1–442a
Auto de los Reyes Magos 2–9a

Ecclesia Primitiva
See Primitive Church, Concept of
Ecclesia Sclavoniae 2–296b
Ecclesiastical estates 4–511b, 512b
Ecclesiastical Hierarchy (Pseudo-Dionysius the Areopagite)
angel/angelology 1–250b
Ecclesiastical History (Eusebius of Caesarea) 4–523b
Ecclesiastical History of the English Nation (Bede) 1–165a, 275b, 277b, 284a, 645a; 2–154a, 155a-b; 3–228b, 485a; 4–454b
Easter 3–228b
Ecclesiastica potestate, De (Egidius) 4–400a
Ecclesiasticis disciplinis, De (Regino of Prúm) 3–572b
Ecclesiasticus 4–67a
ECCLESIOLOGY 4–372a
Egidius Colonna 4–400b
Ecclesius, Bishop
donor portrait 4–261b
Ecgfrith of Mercia 4–455a
ÉCHEVIN 4–378b; 3–570b
Bruges 2–386b
communes 3–502a
ÉCHOPPE 4–379b
Eck, Johann
Biel 2–234a
Eckbert of Schönau
Cathars 3–181b, 183b, 184a
***ECKENLEID* 4–380a**
Eckenstrophe 4–380a
ECKHART, MEISTER (ECKHART VON HOCHHEIM) **4–380b**; 3–368b
Albertus Magnus 1–129b
Dominican mysticism 4–248b
Eckhart von Hochheim
See Eckhart, Meister
Ecliptic 3–17b-18a
Ecloga duarum sanctimonialium (Paschasius Radbertus) 1–72b
Ecloga Theoduli
See Gottschalk of Orbais
***ECLOGUE* 4–382b**; 4–594a
Calpurnius Siculus Titus 3–55b
Leo III 2–117b
Eclogues (Vergil) 1–72b
Economy
See Byzantine economy and society; specific countries
Écry Castle 4–41b
Ecthesis
See Ekthesis
Ecuens 2–424a
Ecumenical councils
See Councils (Ecumenical)
ECUMENICAL PATRIARCH 4–383a; 2–10a
Athos, Mount 1–637a
Edda (Snorri Sturluson) 1–63a; 4–403a
Eddica minora 4–388a
EDDIC METERS 4–384a; 4–388a-389a
Breta Sǫgur 2–366a
EDDIC POETRY 4–385a
Atlakviđa 1–638a
Atlamál 1–638b
Baldr 2–55a
Baldrs Draumar 2–56a
Bjarkamál 2–254a
Brynhild 2–394b
Egill Skallagrímsson 4–400b
Eiríksmál and Hákonarmál 4–414b
Eyrbyggja saga 4–568a
Eyvindr 4–570a
meter 4–384a
Eddius Stephanus
See Aeddi
Edelsi, King
Lai d'Haveloc 1–268a
EDESSA 4–384a
EDESSA 4–392
Baldwin I 2–58b; 4–30a
Byzantine empire 2–493a
crusades 4–30b-31a, 35a, 37a-b, 38a
Zangī 4–30b
Edgar of Scotland 4–256a
Edgar the Peaceable, King 1–264b, 273a; 4–456b-457a, 459a
Anglo-Saxon poetry 1–278b
Chester, Treaty of 3–299b
church reforms 3–347b
coronation 3–82b
Edict of Milan (313) 4–348a, 351a, 358a
EDINBURGH 4–392b
Aneirin 1–247a
Edington, Battle at (878) 1–164a
Edirne
See Adrianople
Edmund, Prince 1–278b
Edmund, Saint
See Passiun Seint Edmund, La; *Vie Seint Edmund le Rei, La*
Edmund Ironside 4–472b
Cnut the Great 3–471b
Edmund of Abingdon, Saint 1–261a,b
Edmund of Scotland 4–256a
Edmund of Sweden, King 1–47a
Edmund the Martyr, King 4–456a
Wilton Diptych 4–476a
Edmund the Martyr, Saint 1–263a
Ednyfed Fychan 4–430b
Edouard le Confesseur, vie d'
See Vie d'Edouard le Confesseur
Education
See Schools; Universities
Edward (courtesy book) 3–661a
Edward (son of Alfred the Great) 4–456b
EDWARD I OF ENGLAND 4–395b; 1–453a
admiralty 1–56a
Aquitaine 1–367b-369a
archeological excavations 1–337b
Baron's War 2–112a-b
bastides 2–128b
boroughs 2–331a
Burgh, de 2–421b
clericis laicos 3–448a
common pleas court 3–492a
convocations of Canterbury and York 3–578b
Conway, Peace of 3–579b
court leet 3–660a
crusades 4–53b, 54a
diplomacy 4–204b
Edinburgh 4–393a
Edward III 4–397a
Exchequer 4–534a
finances 4–532b
Jews, expulsion of 2–81a; 4–564a
longbow use 3–205a
parliament, rise 4–481b-483a
right to kingship 4–475a-b
Wales, prince of 4–108a
EDWARD II OF ENGLAND 4–397a
assize 1–595b
Bannockburn, Battle of 2–102a
baptism 2–72a
convocations of Canterbury and York 3–578b
deposition 4–160b, 483a-b
diplomacy 4–208a
Edward III 4–398a
Exchequer 4–534b
finances 4–532b
parliament 4–483a
right to kingship 4–475b
Wilton Diptych 4–476b
EDWARD III OF ENGLAND 4–398a; 3–333a
admiralty 1–56a,b
Anglo-Norman lyric poetry 1–269a
Aquitaine 1–368a
Bedlam 2–157a
Bradwardine 2–358b
Brittany, Duchy 2–380a
Burley 2–432b
Calais 3–64b
Clanvowe 3–408a
convocations of Canterbury and York 3–578b
Crécy, Battle of 3–205b
David II of Scotland 2–202b; 4–111a
death 3–283a
diplomacy 4–210a
Edward the Black Prince 4–398b
Enguerrand VII of Coucy 4–490b
Florentine debts 2–287a
Garter, Order of the 3–307a
parliament 4–485a
right to kingship 4–475b-476a
Wilton Diptych 4–476b
Edward IV of England
right to kingship 4–478a-b
Edward V of England
contention over throne 4–478b
deposition of rulers 4–160b
Edward VI of England
asylum system 1–632b
Edward the Atheling 4–395a
EDWARD THE BLACK PRINCE 4–398b; 4–398a
Aquitaine 1–368a
arms and armor 1–525a
Burley 2–432b
Castilian civil war 3–137a
EDWARD THE CONFESSOR, SAINT 4–394a; 1–261a; 2–434b; 4–452b, 457a
ancestral romances 1–267b
Anglo-Norman literature 1–261a
Anglo-Saxon poetry 1–278b
canonization 4–475a
confessor title 3–535b
death 4–461a
documents 1–286b
Godwin 3–82b
taxation 4–90b
Westminster Abbey 1–255b, 286b
Wilton Diptych 4–476b
Edward the Martyr
murder 4–457a
Edwin of Northumbria, King 1–107a
Eerste bliscap van Maria, De 4–322a
Effects of Good Government, The (fresco) 4–86b
Egbert Codex 4–399b
Egbert of England, King 4–455a-b
EGBERT OF LIÈGE 4–399b
EGBERT OF TRIER 4–399b; 4–262a
Egbert of York, Archbishop
All Saints' Day 1–176b
Bede 2–155b
consecration of cemeteries 3–540b
Eggeling Becker of Braunschweig
Biel, Gabriel 2–233b
Eghri
See Ararat, Mount
Egidio da Viterbo 3–3b
EGIDIUS COLONNA 4–400a; 2–1a
Augustinian friars 1–660a
EGILL SKALLAGRÍMSSON 4–400b; 4–402a

EGILS SAGA EINHENDA OK ÁSMUNDAR BERSERKJABANA 4–401b
EGILS SAGA SKALLAGRÍMSSONAR 4–402a; 1–311a; 4–161a, 400b, 612b, 614a
berserks 2–198b
Eginhard
See Einhard
Eginhartus
See Einhard
Egla
See Egils Saga Skallagrímssonar
Egmond Abbey 4–399b
Egrisi
See Georgia: Geography
EGYPT, ISLAMIC 4–403b; 2–487a
Abbasid art and architecture 1–5b
Abbasids 1–9b, 12a; 3–49a
Aghlabids 1–72a
agriculture 1–105a
alchemy 1–135a-136a, 140b
Aleppo, rule of 1–145a
Alexandria 1–153a
alphabetization 1–204a
alphabets 1–212a, 218a
Amalric I 4–38b
ʿAmr ibn al-ʿĀṣ 1–236b
animals, draft 1–298a
Aragon, Crown of 1–414b-415a
art 1–5b
Axum, kingdom 2–17a-b
Ayyubid art and architecture 2–20b, 21b
Ayyubid rule 2–23a-b, 24a, 25a
ʿAzīz, al- 2–28a
Barqūq 2–113a
Baybars al-Bunduqdārī 2–138a
Byzantine church 2–462a
Cairo 3–13a
cavalry 3–209a,b
ceramics 1–5b; 3–238b
Christianity, Nubian 3–314a
church, early 3–339a, 340a
church, Latin 3–344a
church types 3–378a
Circassians 3–398a, 399a
Coptic art 3–585b
Copts and Coptic church 3–593b
cotton 3–626b
crusader art and architecture 4–26b
crusades 4–27a, 32a, 38b, 39a, 52a, 53b
Damascus 4–82b
dervish 4–163a
dinar 4–187a
Druzes 4–295b
exploration 4–553b
fairs 4–589b
Fatimids 1–11b, 375a; 2–44b; 3–50b
Jewish marriage and divorce 4–605b, 606b
map 4–404
monastic tradition 2–170a
Muʿāwiya 1–173a
Ottoman Empire 1–145b-146a
slavery 2–268a
Umayyads 1–16a
See Also Roman Egypt, Late
Egypt in the Late Empire
See Roman Egypt, Late
Eichstätt
Saint Boniface 2–322a
Eidyn
See Edinburgh
EIGEL 4–408b
Eight Tombs, The 1–135b
EIKE VON REPGOWE 4–408b; 2–144b
elections, royal 4–428a
Eilhart von Oberg
See Tristrant
EILÍFR GOÐRÚNARSON 4–409b
Einarm 3–179b-180a
EINARR HELGASON SKÁLAGLAMM 4–410b
EINARR SKÚLASON 4–411a
EINHARD 4–412a; 1–143a; 2–173b
biographical writing 2–239b
Carolingian empire 3–110b, 111a, 112a
Carolingian Latin poetry 3–101b
Translatio et miracula sanctorum Marcelli et Petri 1–337a
Vita Karoli 2–236a
Einhartus
See Einhard
Ein neues unvollendetes Werk des hl. Anselm von Canterbury 1–314a
EINON AP GWALCHMAI 4–413a; 4–431a
Einsiedeln Madonna (E.S.) 4–330a
Eire
archives 1–448b
Eiríkr Bloodaxe
See Eric Bloodaxe
EIRÍKR ODDSSON 4–413b
EIRÍKSMÁL AND HÁKONARMÁL 4–414b
Eddic poetry 4–389a
Eyvindr 4–570a
Eiríks Saga Rauda
See Vinland Sagas
Eis, Gerhard
Fachschrifttum 4–577b
EISTEDDFOD 4–415a
EIXIMENIS, FRANCESC 4–416a; 1–420a; 3–57b
Catalan literature 3–167a, 168b
Eiximenis, Joan 3–167b
ĒJMIACIN 4–417a
Ekeleacʿ (Arm.) 4–508b
EKKEHARD OF AURA 4–417b
EKKEHARD I OF SAINT GALL 4–418a; 4–418b
Ekkehard III of Saint Gall 4–418a
EKKEHARD IV OF SAINT GALL 4–418a
Ekkehard II Palatinus 4–418a
Ekklesia
early church 3–338a
Nicaea, Council of 3–341a
Ekloga
See Eclogue
EKTHESIS 4–418b
caesaropapism 3–10b
ecumenical councils 3–630b
El-Ashmunein Church (Hermapolis) 3–586a
Elazar ben Natan 4–607b
Elbe River 2–297b
Lombard settlement 2–95a
Elbow-cops
See Cowters
Elbrus, Mount 3–195a, 196a
Elburz Mountains
Alamūt 1–118a
ELCKERLIJC 4–419a; 4–286b, 322a
Everyman 4–527a-b
Eldad ha-Dani 1–346a,b
Elders
early church 3–338b
Eldigüz
See Ildiguizid (Eldigüz)
ELEANOR OF AQUITAINE 4–419a; 1–367b
Benoît de Sainte-Maure 2–182a
Bernart de Ventadorn 2–197a
Brut, The 2–393b
Cercamon 3–240b
courtly love 3–673a
crusades 4–37b, 40b
marriage 2–126b; 3–245a
Norman-Angevin England 4–463a, 467b, 468a, 471b
Oléron, laws of 1–56b
vase collection 1–335b
Eleanor of Castile, Queen 1–264a, 412a; 4–419b
Edward II 4–397a
Eleanor of Provence 1–262b
Edward I 4–395b
Eleanor of Sicily 1–416a
ELEAZAR BEN JUDAH OF WORMS 4–420b
Electione romani pontificis, De (Gozzadini) 3–520a,b
ELECTIONS, CHURCH 4–421a
chapter 3–265b
pope 3–351a
ELECTIONS, ROYAL 4–425a
acclamations 1–35b
kingship, evolution of 4–473b
parliament 4–485a
Elegia di Madonna Fiammetta (Boccaccio) 2–282a-b
Elegies
Arabic poetry 1–401b
Elementarium erudimentum doctrine (Papias) 4–449b
Elementorum philosophiae libri IV (William of Conches) 1–607a
Elements (Euclid) 1–53b, 433b, 436b
Elements of Astrology (Bīrūnī) 2–250a-b
Elements of Theology 1–457b
Elene (Cynewulf) 1–277a, 278a, 279a
ELEONORE OF AUSTRIA 4–429a
ELEOUSA 4–429b
Elephant, Philip
alchemy 1–138a
Elephants 2–243a
ELEVATION OF THE HOLY CROSS 4–430a
Elfgifu of Northampton 3–471b
Elfheah, Bishop 4–517b
Elfodd
See Elfoddw
Elfoddw, Bishop 2–71a
Elias of Cortona
alchemy 1–137a
Elias of Dereham
See Nicholas of Ely
Elicsenda de Montcada 1–415b
ELIDIR SAIS 4–430b
Einon ap Gwalchmai 4–413a
Élie de Saint Gille 4–431b
Elie de Wincestre
Cato's Distichs 3–193b
Elie de Winchester 1–264a
Eliezer ben Yose ha-Gelili
exegesis 4–539a
Eliezer of Beaugency
biblical exegesis 2–212b; 4–541a
Eligius, Saint
cloisonné enamel 4–437b
Elijah
Antichrist 1–322a
Elipandus, Archbishop 1–630b
adoptionism 1–57b; 3–321b
ELISABETH OF NASSAU-SAARBRÜCKEN 4–432b
Eleonore of Austria 4–429a

Elisaeus Libaerts
arms and armor 1–536b
ELIŠE 4–433a; 1–509a; 3–199a
Armenian Saints 1–518b, 520a-b
Elise ab Iorwerth
Conway, Peace of 3–580a
***ELIS SAGA OK ROSAMUNDU* 4–431b**
Elixir 1–134a, 141b
Elizabeth, Countess of Ulster
Chaucer 3–280a
Elizabeth of Hungary
perfume 2–147a
royal confessor 3–535a
Elizabeth of Hungary, Saint 1–261b
Elk 1–301a
Ellandun Wroughton, Battle of (825) 4–455b
Ellebaut 1–120a
Elmina
exploration 4–561b
trade 4–562a
Elmiram mommini 3–489a
El Muzeirib
fairs 4–589a
Elnatan ben Moses Kalkis
cabala 3–3a
Elpidus Rusticus 4–358b
***ELUCIDARIUM* AND SPANISH *LUCIDARIO* 4–434a**; 1–263b; 2–226b
Elucidarius (Christopher of Paris) 1–138b
Elvira, Council of (300) 4–349a
Ely Cathedral 1–423b
architecture 1–255b
Benedictine monastery 3–265b
bishop's jurisdiction 3–59b
Lady Chapel 3–264a
ÉMAIL BRUN 4–435b
Emanuel I of Portugal, King
Jews, expulsion of 4–564b
Embalming 4–120a-b
See Also Death and Burial, in Europe
Embassies 4–206b
EMBER DAYS 4–435b
Embossing 1–536a-b
EMBRICHO OF MAINZ 4–436b
Embroidery
Anglo-Saxon 1–272b
See Also Tapestry; Textiles
Emerald table 1–136a, 141b
EMETERIUS OF TÁBARA 4–436b
Emhain Macha
See Ulster
Emich of Leisingen
Peasants' Crusade 4–34a
Emilia 1–131a
Emilian, Saint
Braulio of Saragossa, Saint 2–364b
EMIR 4–437a
Abbasid 3–44b
caliphate 3–34b, 43a, 49b, 50a
Emly Church 3–121b
EMMANUEL 4–437a
Emma of Normandy, Queen 3–471b
Edward the Confessor 4–394a,b
Emmeram, Saint 1–422b, 540b; 2–134a
Emphyteutic law
Bohemia 2–302a
Empordà 1–414a
Empúries 1–415a
Ems, Rudolf von
Alexander romances 1–151b
ENAMEL 4–437b
Anglo-Saxon 1–273b
art trade 1–562b
bronze and brass 2–384b
Byzantine 2–455a
Celtic art 3–218b, 219a-b, 220b, 221a
Deesis 4–131b
ENAMEL, BASSE-TAILLE 4–441a; 4–438a, 439a, 440a
ENAMEL, CHAMPLEVÉ 4–441a; 4–438a,b, 439a, 440a
Celtic art 3–218b
vermiculé enamel 4–442a
ENAMEL, CLOISONNÉ 4–441a; 4–437b-438a,b, 440b
Celtic art 3–219b
ENAMEL, LIMOGES 4–441b; 4–438b, 439a-b, 440b, 442a
ENAMEL, MILLEFIORI 4–441b
Celtic art 3–218b-219b
ENAMEL, VERMICULÉ 4–441b; 4–438b
Enarrationes in Psalmos (Augustine) 3–123b
Enarrationes in quattuor libros regum (Angelomus of Luxeuil) 1–251b
ENCAUSTIC 4–442a
Encheiridion (Alfred the Great) 1–165a
Encina, Juan del 3–584b
Encolpion
See Encolpium
ENCOLPIUM 4–442a
Encomendación
See Commendatio
Encomienda
See Commendatio
ENCYCLOPEDIAS AND DICTIONARIES, ARABIC AND PERSIAN 4–442b
ENCYCLOPEDIAS AND DICTIONARIES, BYZANTINE 4–446b
Constantine VIII Porphyrogenitos 3–547a-b
ENCYCLOPEDIAS AND DICTIONARIES, WESTERN EUROPEAN 4–447b
alchemy 1–137a
animals 2–242b-243a
Apocalypse 1–344a
Boccaccio 2–286b
botany 2–345b
codex 3–474a
Elucidarium and Spanish *Lucidario* 4–434a
Fachschrifttum 4–577b
Genealogy of the Pagan Gods 2–283a-286b
indexes 1–207a
Old English scholarship 1–287a
ENDE 4–450b
ENDELECHIUS 4–451a
Endowments
See Waqf
Endura 3–181b, 185b
Eneados (Gavin Douglas) 4–262b
ENÉAS, ROMAN D' 4–451a
Enechelon plan
See Apse Echelon
Enfances Ogier, Les (Adenet le Roi) 1–55a
Enfants de Maintenant, Les 4–265a
ENGELBERT OF ADMONT 4–451b
ENGELMODUS 4–452a
Engineers
castle building 3–150b-151a
ENGLAND 4–452b
accounting 1–37b-38a,b
admirals 1–55b
Admiralty, Court of 1–56a; 3–570a
agriculture 1–91a
annate payments 1–305a
arch 1–423b
archives 1–448b
Augustinian canons 1–659b
bailiffs 2–52a
banking 2–74a, 77b
banking, Jewish 2–80b-81a,b
bannerets 2–82a
barons 2–111a
bastides 2–129a
borough 2–329b
butler 2–434b
castles and fortifications 3–125a, 143b-146a
Cathars 3–186b
cathedral monasteries 3–265b
ceramics 3–236a,b-237a
chaplains 3–264b
cheeses 1–95b-96a
chivalry, orders of 3–307a
chronicles, clerical 3–327a
church, Latin 3–373b, 375a,b-376a
Cistercian Order 3–404a
classical literary studies 3–432b, 433b
clockwork, planetary 3–464b
clove 3–466b
coal mining 3–472b, 473a
communes 3–498a-499a, 501b, 502a,b
constable of the realm 3–543b
coroner 3–605a
deposition of rulers 4–160b
dictamen 4–175a
earls 3–659a
excommunication 4–538a
fairs 4–586b-587a
food animals 1–95b, 298b, 300a
Franciscan Order 1–73a
inheritance laws 3–414a
justice administration 3–659b-660a
manorial court records 4–138b
physicians 2–98b
serfs, legal status 3–415b
verse anthologies 1–319a,b
weights and measures 2–113a-114b, 241a-b, 310b
ENGLAND: ANGLO-SAXON 4–452b
Alfred the Great 1–163b
angelus 1–252a
Augustine of Canterbury 1–645a
Aurelianus 2–2b
Canterbury 3–81a-82b
Celtic art 3–218a-223a
Celtic church 3–225b, 226a,b, 228b, 229b, 232a
Celtic languages 3–232a-233a
church, Latin 2–10a; 3–351b, 355a
Cnut the Great 3–471b
county 3–658a
Danelaw 4–91a
Edward the Confessor 4–394a
elections, church 4–424b-425a
Ethelred the Unready 4–517b
Germanic invasions 2–96a-97a
horse breeding 1–294b
households 4–600a-b
map 4–453
monasteries 2–172a
Norman conquest 4–459b-461a
origins and migration 1–288b
poetry 1–254b
Roman abandonment 2–96a
Vikings 4–151b, 554a
ENGLAND: NORMAN-ANGEVIN 4–459b
Becket 2–151a
church, Latin 3–353b
Clarendon, Assize of 3–408b
Clarendon, Constitutions of 3–409b
diplomacy 4–202b
Domesday Book 4–237b
Dublin 4–299a-b
Edward I 4–395b

ENGLAND: NORMAN-ANGEVIN (cont.)
Eleanor of Aquitaine 4–419a
Englishry, presentment of 4–487a
estate management 4–512a-513a
Exchequer 4–530b-532a
Exchequer, Court of 4–533a-b
map 4–460
monasteries 2–173b
ENGLAND (1216-1485) **4–472b**
anti-Semitism 1–340a-b; 2–263b; 4–564a
Black Death 1–142a; 2–261b-262b
Cade's Rebellion 3–4b
cavalry 3–205a-206b
Clericis laicos 3–447b
constitutional crisis 2–112a
diplomacy 4–202b, 205a,b
duchies 4–304a
Edward I 4–395b
Edward II 4–397a, 398a
Edward the Black Prince 4–398b
estate management 4–513a-b, 514a-b
Exchequer 4–532a-533a
Exchequer, Court of 4–533b-535a
map 4–474
Portuguese trade 4–558a
Scottish wars 4–111a
theater 4–284b-288a
Western councils 3–650b
English language and literature
See Anglo-Saxon Literature; Middle English
English longbow 2–350b, 351b, 352b
English Nation of Merchant Adventurers 3–210a
English Peasants' Rising (1381) 3–428b
ENGLISHRY, PRESENTMENT OF 4–487a
Englyn 3–121b
ENGRAVING 4–487b
art trade 1–561a
bronze and brass 2–384b
Burin 2–432a
échoppe 4–379b
etching 4–516a
Master E.S. 4–330a
Enguerrand de Marigny 3–124b
ENGUERRAND VII OF COUCY 4–490b
Coucy castel 3–148b, 150a
Enguerrand Quarton
See Charonton (Quarton), Enguerrand
Enlevage 4–439b
Enna
See Castrogiovanni
Enneads (Augustine) 1–651a
ENNODIUS, MAGNUS FELIX 4–491b; 1–422a
Enns River 2–4b
Enoch
Antichrist 1–322a
Enquête par turbe 3–279b
Enravota of Bulgaria 2–402a
En Santa Gadea de Burgos 3–388b
Enseignemens à son filz Jean de Castel (Christine de Pizan) 3–662a
Enseignement des princes (Robert de Blois) 3–665b
Enseignements Trebor (Robert de Ho) 1–264a
Ensenhamen (Arnaut de Mareuil) 3–664b-665a
Ensenhamen de la donzela (En Amanieu de Sescas) 3–663b, 672b
Ensenhamen d'onor (Sordello) 3–665a
Ensenhamen (En Amanieu De Sescas) 3–665b
Ensenhamen (Garin lo Brun) 3–664a, 672B
Ensenhamen (Guilhem de Marsan) 3–665a-b
Ensenyament (Guerau de Cabrera) 3–164a
Ente et essentia, De (Aquinas) 2–36a; 4–510a
Entica
See Commenda
Entremets 3–582b
ENTRY INTO JERUSALEM 4–491b
ENVOI 4–492a
chant royal 3–263b
EÓGANACHT 4–492b
Cashel 3–121a
Dál Cais 4–77a
Eodem et diverso, De (Adelard of Bath) 1–53b-54a
Eormanric 1–278b
***EPANAGOGE* 4–493a**
Basil I the Macedonian 2–117b
Constantinople 3–556a
ecumenical patriarch 4–383b
EPARCH 4–493b
Constantinople 3–553b, 554b
***EPARCH, BOOK OF THE* 4–493b**; 2–453a
Épernay
fairs 4–590b, 591a
EPHESUS 4–494b
Anatolia 1–239b
Ephesus, Council of 3–214a, 628b-629a,b; 4–75a
Christology 3–320a
Mary, doctrine of 3–318b
Nestorianism 2–485b; 3–339b
Ephraim
See Ephrem
Ephraim the Syrian 1–508a; 2–524b
EPHREM (EPHRAIM) 4–495a
Church of the Nativity 4–24b
Ephthalites of Turkestan 2–12a
***EPIBOLÉ* 4–495b**
Epic, cosmographic 1–183b
Epic, courtly 1–132a
Epic, French
See Chansons de Geste
EPIC, LATIN 4–495b
Eupolemius 4–523a
Gautier de Châtillon 1–150a, 151a
Epiclesis 1–156a-b
Epidamnos
See Dyrrachium
Epieikeia
See Equity
Epigonation 3–616a
Epigraphic studies 1–336a,b
Epila 1–416a
Epimanikia 3–615b
Epinal glossary 1–276a
Epiphanius of Pavia, Bishop 4–491b
Epiphanius of Salamis 1–507b
bestiary 2–204a
EPIPHANY, FEAST OF 4–496b
altar apparatus 1–222b
Christmas celebration 3–317b
EPIPHANY IN ART 4–497b
EPIROS, DESPOTATE OF 4–499a
Bulgaria 2–406b, 409a, 410a
Byzantine empire 2–498a, 500a, 501a
Dyrrachium 4–330a
family 4–595b
marriage 4–594b
Palaiologans 1–246a,b
Visigoths 2–90b
Episcopa 3–216a
Episcopal consecration
Celtic church 3–229a
Episkopoi 3–338b
Epistle Against Jovinian (Saint Jerome) 1–323a
Epistle of Barnabas 3–334b
Epistle of Forgiveness (al-Maʿarrī) 1–381b
Epistles (Basil the Great) 2–121a
Epistles of Paul 3–338a
Epistle to the Laodiceans 1–347a
Epistola ad Berengarium magistrum (Eusebius Bruno) 4–523b
Epistola ad Bonifatium Papam (Arnald of Villamona) 1–138a
Epistola ad Elipantum 1–143a
Epistola ad Hasen regem 1–136b
Epistola ad papam Joannem XXII (John Dastin) 1–138a
Epistola ad regem neapolitanum (Arnald of Villanova) 1–138a
Epistola Alexandri Macedonis ad Aristotelem 1–149b-150a
Epistola concilii pacis (Henry of Langenstein) 3–511b, 518a
Epistola concordiae (Conrad of Gelnhausen) 3–511a,b, 514b
Epistola consolatoria a messer Pino de' Rossi (Boccaccio) 2–287b
Epistola de sacramentis ecclesiae (Anselm of Canterbury) 1–313b, 315a
Epistola de sacrificio azimi et fermentati (Anselm of Canterbury) 1–313b, 314b
Epistola diaboli Leviathan (Pierre d'Ailly) 1–108b; 3–518a
Epistolae heroidum (Ovid) 3–169a
Epistolae sine nomine 2–34b
Epistolare dictamen (Henry of Isernia) 4–176a
Epistolarium (Matthew of Vendôme) 4–175a
Epístoles farcides 3–164a
Epistolography
Byzantine 2–519b-520a
Epistre au dieu d'amours (Christine de Pizan) 3–316b
Epistre d'Othéa (Christine de Pizan) 3–316b, 665b-666a
Epistula ad Nepotianum (Saint Jerome) 3–440a
Epistula ad Vigilium (Arator) 1–422a-b
Epistula longior (Augustine) 1–658a
Epistula longissima (Augustine) 1–658a
Epitaphios 1–243b
Epitome (Julius Valerius) 1–152b
Epitome Almagesti 1–613b
Epitome of Popes' Lives Down to Gregory I (Abbo of Fleury) 1–13a
Epitrachelion
See Epitrakhil
***EPITRAKHIL* 4–500a**; 3–615b-616a
Equal hours, time reckoning by 3–24a-b, 29b
Equatorie of the Planetis (Chaucer) 3–290b
EQUATORIUM 4–500b; 1–622b-623a
Equilateral arch 1–423b, 424
Equinoxes, precession 3–17b
EQUITY 4–501a
Er, Myth of (Plato) 1–180b-181a, 185b
Eraclius (Otte) 1–635b
Era of Martyrs 3–18b
Erard mac Coise 1–110b
Erard of Brienne 3–247b
Eras
Islamic calendar 3–27a-b
Jewish calendar 3–24b-25a

Julian calendar 3–18a-19b
Erasmus, Desiderius
Bohemian Brethren 2–307b
Devotio Moderna 4–167a
Erasmus of Rotterdam
Brethren of the Common Life 2–369a
Erašx
See Araks River
Erasxajor 2–20a
Eratosthenes 1–370a
Erbil
See Arbela
ERCHAMBERT OF FREISING 4–504a
Erchanbert
See Erchambert of Freising
Erchempert
See Erchenbert of Monte Cassino
ERCHENBERT OF MONTE CASSINO 4–504a
Erçiş
See Arčēš
Erec (Hartmann von Aue) 1–229b
Érec et Énide (Chrétien de Troyes) 1–643b; 3–308b; 4–504b
Eremiticae regulae 3–56a
Eremiticism
Celtic 3–231b
church, Latin 3–354b
EREROYKʿ 4–504b
Aštarak 1–601a
Eretnids
Ankara 1–302b
Erevan
See Ałc
***EREX SAGA* 4–504b**
Erez
See Erzincan
Erezawan
See Erzincan
Erfurt
Boniface, Saint 2–322a
Erfurter Moralität 4–269a
Erfurt glossary 1–276a
Ergasterion 4–494a
Ergotism 2–365a
Eric Bloodaxe 4–401a, 403a, 414b, 456b
Eric I of Denmark, King 4–152b
Eric V of Denmark, King 4–154b
Eric of Pomerania
Nordic Union 4–156a
Eric the Red 4–554b
Erigena
See John Scottus Eriugena
Erik of Sweden, King
Saint Birgitta 2–247a
***ERIKSKRÖNIKAN* 4–505b**
Erill, Arnau d' 3–171a
Eris-mtʿavari
See Eristʿaw
Erispoë
Brittany, Duchy 2–379a
Eristavt-mtʿavari
See Eristʿaw
ERISTʿAW 4–506a
Eritrea 1–30b
Erlandsen, Archbishop Jakob 4–154b
Erlösung, Die 2–229b, 231a, 232b
Ermanaric
See Ermanrich
Ermanrich, Emperor 1–219a
Ermbert of Freising 1–422b
Ermenberga 1–311b
ERMENGAUD, MATFRE 4–506b; 3–169a
courtly love 3–672b
Ermengol X 1–413b
Ermengol VI of Urgell 1–408a
ERMENRICH OF ELLWANGEN 4–507a
***ERMENRÎKES DÔT* 4–507a**
Ermolao Barbar, Bishop 4–424a
Ermold the Black
See Ermodus Nigellus
ERMOLDUS NIGELLUS 4–507b; 2–102b; 3–103a
Louis the Pious 2–236a-b
Ernest of Austria 2–8b-9a
Ernest of Pardubice, Archbishop
Bohemian church 2–304a; 3–368a
Ernst, Herzog
See Herzog Ernst
ERNULF 4–508a
Errationes in cantica canticorum (Angelomus of Luxeuil) 1–251b
Ertanids
Caesarea 3–9b
ERWIN, MASTER 4–508a
Erwin of Minden
See Erwin, Master
ERZINCAN (ERZINJAN) **4–508b**
Erzinjan
See Erzincan
Erznka
See Erzincan
Erzurum
See Theodosiopolis
E.S., MASTER 4–330a
engraving 4–488b, 489a,b
Esai Nčʿecʿi 1–512a
Escape of a certain captive told in a figurative manner
See Ecbasis Captivi
Eschatocol
chancery documents 3–253a
charter 3–275a
Eschatology
Apocalypse illustration 1–343b-344a
apocrypha, Irish 1–347b
Eschaton 1–180a
ESCHEAT, ESCHEATOR 4–508b
Escouchy, Mathieu d' 3–333b
Escrivà, Bernat
See Desclot, Bernat
Escutcheon mold 3–219b
Esdras, books of 1–110b
Eski Gümüş Church (Cappadocia) 3–92b
Eskil, Archbishop 4–153a,b
Eskişehir
See Dorylaeum
Esmoreit 4–321a-b
España del Cid, La (Ramón Menéndez Pidal) 3–386a
Esphigmenou Monastery 1–638a
Espingale 3–180a
Espinosa de los Monteros 3–125b
Esplandián 1–227b
***ESPURGATOIRE SAINT PATRICE* 4–509b**
Essais historiques sur les bardes, les jongleurs et les trouvères normands 1–271a
ESSENCE AND EXISTENCE 4–510a
Essex
Anglo-Saxon 4–454a
Black Death 2–262b
emergence of kingdom 2–96b
ESSEX, JOHN 4–510b
Establishment of Port 2–155a
Estada 1–405b
Estampie
See Dance
ESTATE MANAGEMENT 4–511a
Estates, legal and social
See Class Structure
Estates, political
See Representative Assembly
Estates General, Dauphiné 4–109b
Este, Nicolò II d' 2–114b
Estevam da Guarda 4–190a,b
Estienne, Robert 4–450a
Estinnes
See Liftina
Estoire des Engleis (Geffroy Gaimar) 1–261a
Estoire de Griseldis 4–287b
Estoire de la Guerre Sainte (Ambroise d'Evreux) 3–331a
Estoire des Bretuns (Geffroy Gaimar) 1–264b
Estoire des Engleis (Geffroy Gaimar) 1–264b, 268a; 3–331a
Estoire des rois d'Angleterre et de Normandie 3–332a
Estoire des rois de France 3–332a
Estoire de Waldef 1–267a
Estoire d'outre-mer (William of Tyre) 3–331b
Estonia 2–61b, 64a, 67b
crusades 2–65a-b
cultivation 1–97a
German culture 2–68a
Roman church missions 2–64b
Teutonic Order 2–65b
Universal History 1–166b
Estoria de España (chronicle) 3–71b
Estoria del Cid 3–71b
***ESTRABOT* 4–515a**
Estrambote
See Estrabot
Estrangela
See Syriac alphabet
Estreito 4–560a
Estremadura
agriculture 1–85a
Alfonso IX 3–133b
Estribotz
See Estrabot
Estrithson, Sweyn, King 1–49b, 50b
***ÉTABLISSEMENTS DE SAINT LOUIS* 4–515a**
ETCHING 4–516a
arms and armor 1–536a
Ethelbald of England 4–455a
Ethelbert of England, King 4–453a-b
Augustine of Canterbury 1–645a-b
Canterbury 3–81a-b
ETHELRED OF RIEVAULX, SAINT 4–516b; 1–261b
Cistercian order 3–405a
sermons 4–278b
ETHELRED THE UNREADY 4–517b; 3–471b; 4–457a, 459a
Albans, Saint 1–335b
danegeld 4–90a,b
Edward the Confessor 4–394a,b
ETHELWOLD AND THE BENEDICTINE RULE 4–517b; 4–457a
Aelfric 1–61b
Aldhelm 1–144b
church organization 3–375a
liturgy 2–172b
Marion office 2–273b
Ethelwulf 1–254b
Etheria
Ascension 1–582a
Christmas 3–318a
Ethica (Abelard) 1–18a, 19a
Ethics (Aristotle) 1–127b
Ethics, study of 2–241a
Ethiopia
See Abyssinia

Ethiopian language
See Also Arabic language
Ethiopic alphabet 1–207b, 209b, 210a
Étienne II, Count
Burgundy, County 2–424b
Étienne, Saint, Abbey 3–8b
Étienne du Castel 3–316a
Étienne-Henri, Count
fairs 4–591a
Etiquette
See Courtesy books
Etiquettes
Arabic prose literature 1–380a
Etruscans
alphabet 1–212b, 215a
arch 1–423b
Etsi de statu 3–448a
Étude sur le dialecte anglo-normand du XII siècle (Johan Vising) 1–271b
Etymologiae (Isidore of Seville) 1–46a, 52a, 606a, 610a, 612a; 2–204b, 242b; 3–440b; 4–447b, 448a
Euboea
agriculture and nutrition 1–77b-78a
Eucharist
See Mass
Eucherius of Lyons 4–356a
Euclid 1–53b, 433b, 435a
Boethius 2–291b
Eudes III, Count
fairs 4–590b-591a
Eudes IV, Count
Burgundy, County 2–426a
EUDES OF MONTREUIL 4–518b
EUDES RIGAUD 4–519a
Bonaventure, Saint 2–313a, 315b
Eudokia 2–491b
Eudusii 1–117a
Eufemia of Norway, Queen 4–519b, 520a
***EUFEMIAVISOR* 4–519b**
Eugene IV, Antipope 1–331b
Eugene III, Pope 1–52a
Alexander III, Pope 1–146b
Arnold of Brescia 1–540a
EUGENIUS II OF TOLEDO 4–520b; 3–58a
Eugenius II, Pope
crusade propaganda 4–20b
Eugenius III, Pope
Adrian IV 1–58a
Aragon, Crown of 1–408a
Bernard of Clairvaux 2–191a, 192a
Bernard Silvester 2–195a
Cistercian order 3–405b
councils 3–637b
decretum 4–129b
papal bull 4–19b
papal canonization 3–68a
papal reform 3–352b
Second Crusade 3–356b; 4–37b
tournaments 3–638b
Eugenius IV, Pope
Alberti 1–126a
Basel, Council of 3–651b, 652b-654a
church schism 2–465b-466a
conciliar theory 3–366a,b, 367a, 512b, 519a, 520b
crusades 4–56a
ecclesiology 4–377b, 378a
papal conclave 3–524b
Eugenius, Admiral 1–55b
EUGENIUS VULGARIUS 4–520b
EUGIPPIUS 4–521a
***EULALIE, LA SÉQUENCE DE SAINTE* 4–521a**
assonance 1–600b
Eulalios 2–438b
Eulalius, Antipope 1–330a
Eulogius of Alexandria
Christology 3–320b
Gregory I 1–645a
EULOGIUS OF CÓRDOBA 4–521b; 3–598b
Eunuchs
Byzantine bureaucracy 2–472b-473a, 474a,b
Euouae
See EVOVAE
EUPHRATES RIVER 4–521b; 1–470a
Anatolia 1–239b, 240
map 4–522
Euphrosyne, Saint
Aelfric 1–285a
EUPOLEMIUS 4–523a
Latin epic 4–496b
Euric, King of the Visigoths 2–102b
Europe
agriculture and nutrition 1–89a-96a
climatic zones 3–451b, 452a
population estimation 4–140a
See Also specific countries
EUSEBIUS BRUNO 4–523b
EUSEBIUS OF CAESAREA 4–523b; 1–162a, 348b, 475b, 483a; 2–512b
altar apparatus 1–221b
Armenian literature 1–507b
Bible interpretation 2–211a
Byzantine church 2–459a
Canon Table compilation 3–66a
Christian dogma 3–336a
Eusebius of Emessa
Armenian literature 1–507b
Eusebius of Nicomedia, Archbishop 1–453b
Eusebius of Vercelli
canon community 1–659a
Eustace, Saint
Aelfric 1–285a
Eustace de la Fosse
slaves 2–269a
Eustache Deschamps
See Deschamps, Eustache
Eustathios, Archbishop
agriculture 1–78a
bestiary 2–204a
classical literary studies 3–431b
Eustathios Boilas
Byzantine minor arts 2–455a
Eustathios Kataphloros 2–516a
Eustathios Makrembolites 2–508a, 522a
Eustathius of Sebaste
Arianism 2–121a
asceticism 2–120a
Eustratios of Nicaea, Bishop
Byzantine councils 3–632a
Euthymios 2–413b
Euthymius of Iviron 2–54b
Euthymius of Peribleptos
Bogomilism 2–295b
Euthymius Zigabenus
Bogomilism 2–295b-296a
Eutihije
See Eutychios
Eutocius of Ascalon 1–434a,b, 435b, 437b
EUTYCHES 4–523b
Christology 3–320a
church, early 3–339b
ecumenical councils 3–629a-b
See Also Monophysitism
Eutychianism
See Monophysitism
Eutychii Aegyptii, patriarchae orthodoxorum Alexandrini...ecclesiae suae origines (Selden) 4–525a
EUTYCHIOS 4–524b
church decoration 2–448a
EUTYCHIOS THE MELCHITE 4–525a
Eutychius
Armenian Hellenizing School 1–505b
Eutychius, patriarcha Alexandrinus, vindicatus (Abraham Ecchellensis) 4–525b
Evagrius of Pontus 2–513a
Armenian literature 1–507b
early church theology 3–342b
EVANGELIARY 4–525b
altar apparatus 1–224a
Evangelienbuch
See *Liber evangeliorum*
EVANGELIST SYMBOLS 4–526a
early Christian art 4–349b-350b
Evangelorum libri IV (Juvencus) 4–496a
Evangiles des domnees (Robert of Gretham) 1–262b
Everaert, Cornelis 4–322b
Everard the German 1–553b
Everart
Cato's Distichs 1–264a; 3–193b
Everhard of Wampen 4–579b
Evernew Tongue, The 1–111a,b, 112a
***EVERYMAN* 4–526b**; 4–286b
allegory 1–186a
Elckerlijc 4–419a
Evesham, Battle of (1265) 4–396a
Evil, nature of
early church 3–340a-b
Evodius, Bishop
Augustine of Hippo 1–653b
EVOVAE 4–529a
differentia 4–185a
Evrard of Béthune
classical literary studies 3–434b
Evreux, Ambroise d' 3–331a
Ewert, Alfred 1–271b
Examenis
See Eiximenis, Francesc
EXARCHATE 4–529b
EXCALIBUR 4–530a
Excerpts from the Fathers (Abbo of Fleury) 1–13a
Excerpts from the Works of Saint Augustine (Eugippius) 4–521a
"Exchange Bank of Barcelona"
See Taula de Canvi de Barcelona
Exchange banks 2–73b-75b
Exchange contract 2–78a
Exchanger, Royal 2–74a
EXCHEQUER 4–530b; 1–37b-38a,b
archives 1–446a
banking, European 2–75b-76a
banking, Jewish 2–81a
Caen 3–8b
chamberlain 3–242a
equity 4–502b
escheat 4–509a
lay curia 4–65b
Norman-Angevin England 4–464a, 469b
EXCHEQUER, COURT OF 4–533a
Caen 3–8b
Jews 4–535a
lay curia 4–65b
Norman-Angevin England 4–470a-b
EXCHEQUER OF THE JEWS 4–535a
Excidio Troiae, De (Josephus Iscanus) 4–496a
Excidis et Conquestu Brittainiae, De
See Gildas
Excitatori de la pensa a Déu (Bernat Oliver) 3–168a
EXCOMMUNICATION 4–536a
bull, papal 2–418a
Execrabilis (Pius II) 3–366b, 518b, 654b
EXEDRA 4–538b

EXEGESIS, ANGLO-NORMAN
Andrew of Saint Victor 1–244b
EXEGESIS, JEWISH 4–538b
EXEGESIS, LATIN 4–542a; 2–212a-215a, 223b-224b; 4–545a-b, 546a, 550b
allegory 1–180a-b, 186a
Augustine of Hippo 1–656b, 660b
Autpertus 2–11a
Cassiodorus 3–123b
Ireland 2–220a-b
EXEGESIS, MIDDLE ENGLISH 4–545a
EXEGESIS, OLD ENGLISH 4–548b
Exempla honestae vitae (John of Garland) 1–255a
EXEMPLUM 4–551a
ars praedicandi 1–557a
Exeter Book 2–204b
alliterative patterns 1–277a
Cynewulf 1–278a
Old English poetry 1–278b-281a, 318a, 319a
Exeter Cathedral
Anglo-Norman architecture 1–256a
Bracton 2–356b
clocks and reckoning of time 3–29b, 460a
Old English poetry 1–277a
Old English scriptoria 1–276a
Exeter Madonna (Petrus Christus) 3–324b
EXILARCH 4–551b
Eximenis, Francesc
See Eiximenis, Francesc
Existence
See Essence and existence
Exivi de paradiso 3–645a
Exodus 1–279b
EXONARTHEX 4–552b; 3–389a
Exorcism
baptism rite 2–83b, 84a
Celtic liturgy 3–231a
clergy 3–441a, 442a
oils 2–177b
Explanation of 84 Propositions on the Epistle to the romans (Augustine) 1–649a
Explanation of the Epistle to the Galatians (Augustine) 1–649a
EXPLORATION BY WESTERN EUROPEANS 4–553a
Azores 2–29b
Canary Islands and Béthencourt 3–61b
Expositionis in apocalypsin (Autpertus) 2–11a
Expositio Psalmorum (Cassiodorus) 3–123b
Expositiunculae in Evangelium (Arnobius the Younger) 1–539b
EXPULSION OF JEWS 4–563b; 1–586a
EXTREME UNCTION 4–565a
anointing 1–308a
Celtic liturgy 3–230b
Exultabunt 4–117b
EXULTET ROLL 4–565b; 4–566a
EX VOTO 4–529b
Eyalet 3–678b
EYCK, JAN VAN AND HUBERT VAN 4–566a
Campin 3–61b
Eyeslit 1–524a, 526a, 530a, 534a
Eymeric, Nicholas 4–247b
***EYRBYGGJA SAGA* 4–568a**; 4–613b, 614a
Bandamanna Saga 2–70b
Eyrr clan 4–568a
EYSTEINN ÁSGRÍMSSON 4–568b
Eysteinn Beli 2–359a
***EYVĀN* 4–569b**; 4–408a
bayt 2–140a
EYVINDR FINNSSON SKÁLDASPILLIR 4–570a; 4–415a
Ezana, Emperor 1–30b, 32a
Eznak the Priest 4–417a
EZNIK OF KOŁB 4–570b; 1–508a; 2–217a
Ezra, Ibn
See Abraham ben Meïr ibn Ezra
Ezzo 2–226b; 4–571b
***EZZOLIED* 4–571b**; 2–226b
Ezzos Gesarg
See Ezzolied

F

Faba, Guido 4–174b, 175a
Fabian, Pope
election 3–602b
FABLES 4–572a
allegory 1–188a
Avianus 2–15b
Bozon, Nicole 1–264a
Byzantine 2–523a
Calila e digna 3–31b
Ecbasis captivi 4–369a
Everyman 4–528a
FABLES, FRENCH 4–573a; 4–572a,b
FABLIAU AND COMIC TALE 4–574a
Anglo-Norman poetry 1–269b
Canterbury Tales 3–292b-294a
Fabri, Felix 4–246b
"Fabric fund" 3–191b
Fabrics
See Textiles
Fabulae
See Fables
Fachprosa 4–577b
***FACHSCHRIFTTUM* 4–577b**
Factor 1–40b
"Faculty of regress" 1–305b
Fadak 1–25a
Fadlan, Ibn
See Scandinavia, Arabic sources in
Faḍl ibn Yaḥyā, al- 2–110b
Faenza
art trade 1–561b
FAENZA CODEX 4–580a
ars nova 1–553a
***FÆREYINGA SAGA* 4–580b**
Faerie Queene, The (Spenser) 1–183b, 186a
Faeroe Islands
See Faroe Islands
Faeroese ballads
See Faroese Ballads
Fáfila 1–626a
FÁFNIR 4–581a
Fáfnismál
See Reginsmál and Fáfnismál
Fagrskinna 4–410b, 413b, 415a
Faial
Flemings 2–29b, 30a; 4–559b
FAIENCE 4–582a
European 3–237b
Islamic 3–238b
Fairfax Manuscript 1–320a
Fair of the Holy Innocents 4–592a
FAIRS 4–582b
banking 2–78a-b
Burgundy, County of 2–426a
Castilian 3–139b
FAIRS OF CHAMPAGNE 4–590b; 3–245b; 4–583a, 584a, 585a, 587a
Burgundy, County of 2–426a
Fais et bonnes meurs du sage roy Charles V (Christine de Pizan) 3–333a
Faits des Romains
See Fet des Romains, Li
Fakhkh massacre (786) 1–174b
Fakhr al-Dīn al-Rāzī 4–445b
Fakhr al-Dīn ibn Ma'n 2–164b
Fākihat al-khulafā' (Ibn 'Arabshah) 1–381b
Falaise
church 1–256a
fairs 4–586a
Falak books 1–620a-b
FALCHION 4–593b
Falconry 1–98b
Arte venandi cum avibus, De 2–244b
"Falcon Song" (Der von Kürenberg) 4–161a
Falkenlied 4–387a
Falkirk, Battle of (1298) 3–205a; 4–396b
Fall of the Devil, The (Anselm of Canterbury) 1–312a, 314b
"Fall of Troy"
See Excidio Troiae, De
False Decretals
See Decretals, False
Falsis deis, De (Aelfric) 1–284b
FAMILY, BYZANTINE 4–593b
FAMILY, ISLAMIC 4–596b
concubinage 3–527a
contraception 3–574a
FAMILY, WESTERN EUROPEAN 4–599a
celibacy 3–216a-217a; 4–443b
class structure 3–412b
concubinage 3–529b
consanguinity 3–539b
contraception 3–572a
courtesy books 3–661b-664b
courtly love 3–672a-b, 673b, 668b
demography 3–137b, 138a, 143b, 144a-146b
dowager rights 3–426a
dowry 2–207b
FAMILY AND FAMILY LAW, JEWISH 4–605b
circumcision 3–401a
FAMILY AND MARRIAGE, WESTERN EUROPEAN 4–608a
annulment 1–306a
antifeminism 1–323b-324a, 325a
betrothal 2–207b
Celtic liturgy 3–231a
chansons de malmariée 3–262b
decretum 4–129a
dispensation 4–217a
kingship theories 4–473b-475a
Family of the kings 4–194a
FAMILY SAGAS, ICELANDIC 4–612a
Bjarnar saga 2–255a
Droplaugarsona saga 4–294a
FAMINE IN THE ISLAMIC WORLD 5–1a
agriculture and nutrition 1–79b
FAMINE IN WESTERN EUROPE 5–3a
climate 1–94b
demography 4–137a, 142a
three-field rotation system 1–92b

Fan
altar apparatus 1–224b-225a
See Also Flabellum
Fantosme, Jordan
Anglo-Norman chronicles 1–265a
Fan vault
See Vault
Faqīr 4–163a
FARĀBĪ, AL- 5–9b; 1–458b
alchemy 1–141b
astrology 1–617b
encyclopedias 4–445a
Farahnāma (Abū Bakr al-Muṭahhar Jamālī) 4–445b
Faraj 3–399b, 400a
Faras (Pachoras) 3–315a
FARAZDAQ, AL- 5–12a; 1–115a
qaṣīda 1–400a
Farce de Maître Trubert et d'Antroignart (Eustache Deschamps) 4–163b
FARCES 5–13b
Dutch 4–321b
French 4–264b, 265a,b, 266a
German 4–271a
FARCING 5–13b
FARDALFUS ABBAS 5–14a
"Farewell to His Cell" (Alcuin) 3–100b
FARGHĀNA (FERGANA) **5–14a**
Farghānī, al- 1–612a
Fāriḍ, Ibn al- 1–402a
Farlati 4–5a
Farmers
costume 3–626a
FARMERS' LAW 5–15a; 1–77b, 78a,b
Slavic translation 1–99a
Faroe Islanders, Saga of
See Færeyinga saga
Faroe Islands
Vikings 4–554a
FAROESE BALLADS 5–15b
Færeyinga saga 4–580b
Farrukhān, Ibn al- 1–617a
FĀRS 5–17b
Buyids 2–435b, 436a
Fasciculus de superioritate maris 1–56b
Fashion
See Costume
FASTING, CHRISTIAN 5–18a
Anglo-Saxons 1–285b
carnival 3–99a
Cathars 3–185a,b
cookery 3–580b-581a
ember days 4–435b
FASTING, ISLAMIC 5–19b
Fastoul, Baude 3–536b
Fate
See Fortune
Fates of the Apostles, The (Cynewulf) 1–278a, 281a
Fāṭima al-Zuhrā' 1–25a, 112b; 2–27b
caliph 1–374a
Fatimids 1–375a
marriage 1–171b
FATIMID ART 5–21a
ceramics 1–5b
FATIMIDS 5–24a
Abbasids 1–9a
Aleppo 1–145a
Alexandria 1–153b
Atlas Mountains 1–641a
Ayyubids 1–375b; 2–23a
Azhar, Al- 2–27a
'Azīz, al- 2–28a
Bāb al-Mandab 2–33a
Badr al-Jamālī 2–44a
Basil II 2–119a
Beirut 2–164a
Buyids 2–436b
cavalry 3–209a
costume 3–618a
Damascus 4–81b, 82a, 83a, 84b
Egypt 1–11b; 3–13b-14a; 4–405b-406a, 407a, 408a
Fāṭima 1–375a
Ismailis 1–590a; 3–50a-b
Jerusalem 4–33b
Nūr al-Dīn 4–31a
origin 1–175a, 375a
Saladin 4–31a
Seljuks 1–203a,b
Syria 4–27b
'Ubayd Allāh 1–72a
FATWĀ 5–30a; 1–199b
Faula, La (Torroella) 3–173a
Faustus of Byzantium
See P'awstos Buzand
FAUSTUS OF RIEZ 5–32b
Faustus the Manichaean 1–647a, 651a
***FAUVEL, ROMAN DE* 5–32b**; 1–545b, 548b, 549b, 553a
allegory 1–189b
Fava, Guido 2–312b
Feast of Herod (Donatello) 4–257a
Feast of Tara, The 1–34a
Feast of the moles (Anthonis de Roovere) 4–322b
FEASTS AND FESTIVALS, EUROPEAN 5–33b
Ascension 1–582a-b
Circumcision 1–347a; 3–20b
Holy Cross, elevation of 4–430a
Nativity 3–394b
FEASTS AND FESTIVALS, ISLAMIC 5–38a
Feasts and festivals, Jewish
calendar 3–27a,b
Feathers
bow and arrow 2–351a-b
Febrer, Andreu 3–169b, 171a
Fecunda ratis (Egbert of Liège) 4–399b
Federigo da Montefeltro
palace 2–198a
FEET, WASHING OF 5–41a; 2–83b
Celtic church 3–230b
Feidlimid mac Crimthainn, King 4–493a
Feis Temrach 1–34a
Felire Oengusso Celi De
See Martyrology, Irish
Felix II, Antipope 1–330a
caesaropapism 3–11a
Felix V, Antipope 1–330b
Basel, Council of 3–653b-654a
concordats 3–526a
Great Schism 3–366b
papal conclave 3–524b
Felix of Crowland 1–279a
Félix of Urgel 1–630b
adoptionism dispute 1–57b; 3–321b
Nicene-Constantinopolitan Creed 3–677a
Felix Vita Guthlaci
See Guthlac, Saint
FELONY 5–42b
Femme et de la pye, De la (Bozon) 1–269b
Fenari Isa Camii
See Constantine Lips, Church of
Fencing 4–579b
Fenestellae 1–221b
FENIAN POETRY 5–43b
Fenollar, Mossèn Bernat 3–171b
Fenollet, Lluís de 3–166b
FENRIS WOLF 5–47b
Feoda Campanie 3–245b
Feodosiya
See Caffa
Feral 3–625a
Ferdinand I de Antequera 1–417b; 3–138a, 170b-171a
Ferdinand de la Cerda 3–134a
Ferdinand III el Santo of Castile 3–133b-134a
Alfonso X 1–161a
Castilian court 3–87a
Castilian language 3–142a
commerce 4–557b
Córdoba 3–600a
cortes 3–610b
elections, church 4–423b
Ferdinand II of Aragon
See Ferdinand V of Castile
Ferdinand I the Great of Castile 1–628b; 2–126b; 3–128b-129a
Cid 3–383b
Ferdinand II of Castile 1–628b; 3–130b
Ferdinand IV of Castile 3–134b
cortes 3–610b
Ferdinand V of Castile
Abrabanel 1–21b
ascension 1–419a
Calatrava, Order of 3–17a
church reform 3–139b-140a
conciliar theory 3–520a
government 3–139a
Jews, expulsion of 4–564a
marriage 3–138b
Ferdinand of Peñafiel
See Ferdinand I de Antequera
Ferdinand I of Portugal
death 3–137b
Ferdinand of Portugal, Prince
Azores 2–29b; 4–559b
Ferdinand van Olmen
See Dulmo, Fernão
Fergana
See Farghānā
Fergus 1–260b, 267b
Fergus Mór mac Eirc 4–78a
Fernández, Garcí 3–128a
Fernández de Constantina, Juan 3–63b
Fernandez Torneol, Nuno 3–87a
Fernando de Rojas
See Celestina, La
La Celestina 3–212a
Fernando I of Castile
See Ferdinand I the Great
Fernando II of León
See Ferdinand II of Castile
***FERNAN GONZALEZ, POEMA DE* 5–48a**
Fernão do Po 4–561b
Ferraginers
See Herrenales
Ferrand, Jacques 3–196b
Ferrara
fairs 4–587a
FERRARA-FLORENCE, COUNCIL OF 5–48b; 3–366b; 4–56a
attendance 3–653a-654b
Byzantine church 2–469b-470a
Cilician-Roman church union 3–395b
Ethiopia 1–32b
John VIII Palaiologos 2–504a
Laetentur coeli 3–653b; 4–378a
FERRER I (THE ELDER), **JAIME 5–49b**
Ferrer, Boniface
Bible translation 2–215b; 3–167a
Ferrer, Francesc 3–171b, 173b
Ferrer, Vincent, Saint 1–419b, 420a; 3–159b, 161b-162a
Ferrer Bassa
See Bassa, Ferrer

Ferreri, Zacharia
  conciliar theory 3–520b
Ferretti, Paolo 3–235b
Ferruç, Gabriel 3–171a
Fertile Crescent
  Athīr, Ibn al- 1–634a
  Mamlūk cavalry 3–209b
Fertilizer 1–98a
  Islamic agriculture 1–105a
Ferula 3–604a
FĒS 5–50a
  Almohads 1–194a
Festivals
  See Feasts and Festivals
***FET DES ROMAINS, LI* 5–51b**
FEUDALISM 5–52a
  antrustiones 1–343a
  Armenia 1–489a, 504b
  assizes 1–596b, 599a, 600a
  Asturias-León 1–629a
  aznauri 2–29a
  ban 2–69a
  bastide 2–128a
  Brittany 2–379b, 382a
  Buch von Bern, Das 2–396a
  charistikion 3–268a
  class structure 3–411b-416a, 419b, 424a,b
  commendation 3–490a
  communes 3–493b, 494a, 495a,b
  Constitutio de Feudis 3–557b
  courtly love 3–668b
  Croatia 4–8a
  escheat 4–508b
  estate management 4–511b-512a
  Latin states 4–37a
  military 4–480a
  Norman-Angevin England 4–463b-465a, 470a
Feudorum liber 3–609b
Feud sagas 4–613b-614a
Fez
  See Fēs
Fiana 1–33b-34a
Fibonacci, Leonardo 1–38b, 395b, 396a, 436a
FIBULA 5–57a
Fichtelgebirge Mountains 2–132b
Fiction du lion, La (E. Deschamps) 4–163b
Fide ad Petrum, De (Fulgentius of Ruspe) 3–321a
Fi del comte d'Urgell, La 3–166b
Fidolio (Saint Columbanus) 3–486b
FIEF 5–57b
  benefice, lay 2–179b
  Bulgaria 2–407b
  Catalonia 3–176b
  estate management 4–511a
FIEF, MONEY 5–59b
  estate management 4–511a
FIELD SYSTEMS 5–60b
  Byzantine 1–77a, 78a
  estate management 4–511b
  European 1–91a-b
  Italy 1–86a
  Midi 1–85a-86a
  open-field 1–91b
  Sardinia 1–88a
  Slavic 1–96b, 97a-b, 99b
  Spain 1–80b-81a, 82a, 83a-84b
  three-field rotation 1–92a-93a
Fière Pucelle, La 1–266b
Fieschi reliquary 1–239a
Fiesole, Andrea da
  See Andrea da Firenze
Fifteen Signs Before Doomsday 1–347b
Fight at Finnsburh, The 1–278a,b
Fihrist (Ibn al-Nadīm) 1–384a
Filae 1–223a
Filastrius of Brescia 3–318a
Fili 2–105b
Filigree
  Celtic art 3–220a
***FILIOQUE* 5–62b**
  Armenian church 1–501a
  Byzantine church 2–464b-465a; 3–632a,b
  exegesis 2–214b
  Latin church 3–349a, 351a
  Latin creed 3–346a, 677a
  Western Councils 3–642a
Filius adoptivus 3–321b
FILLASTRE, GUILLAUME 5–63a; 3–647a, 648a,b
Fillet 3–624a
Filocolo (Boccaccio) 2–279a-280a
  Chaucer 3–282b, 290b, 292a
Filostrato (Boccaccio) 2–278b-279a
  Chaucer 3–282b, 287b
FIMBUL WINTER 5–63b
Fin'amor
  See Courtly love
Fine, Oronce 1–439a
Fingal 1–60b
FINIAL 5–64a
***FINNBOGA SAGA* 5–64a**; 1–116b
Finnboga saga ramma
  See Finnboga Saga
Finnian, Saint 3–465b
Finn mac Cumaill 1–33a
FIORAVANTI, ARISTOTELE 5–65a
Fiore (Dante) 4–101b
Firdause
  See Firdawsī
Firdaws, Al- (Aleppo) 2–21b
Firdawsī 2–50b
Firearms
  arms and armor 1–531b-532a
  texts 4–579a
Fír flathemon 3–601a
FIRMICUS MATERNUS, JULIUS 5–65b
Firmin de Belleval 3–23a
Firmiter credimus 3–640b
First Civil War 3–35b-36b
FIRST ROMANESQUE 5–65b
Firth of Forth 4–392b
Firuz 4–35a-b
FIRŪZĀBĀD 5–66a
Firūzābādī, al- 4–444a
Fís 1–347b
Fís Adamnáin 1–347b
Fiscal surveys
  demography 4–137b, 138a
Fisco barcinonensi, De 2–102b
Fish 1–301a; 3–584a
Fishacre, Richard 2–36a
  Dominican theology 4–246b
FISHERIES, MARINE 5–66a
  Baḥrayn, Al- 2–51a
  Cistercians 3–404a
  Kievan Rus 1–100a,b
Fish fairs 4–587b
Fishlake Church 1–256b
Fishmongers Guild 3–607a
FISHPONDS 5–73a
  Byzantine agriculture and nutrition 1–79a
Fistula 1–222b
Fithir and Dáirine 1–34a
Fitna
  See First Civil War
Fitzcount, Brian
  ancestral romances 1–268a
FITZGERALDS 5–74b
Fitz-Gislebert, Robert 3–331a
Fitz Mary, Simon 2–157a
Fitzneale, Richard 1–37b; 4–469b
  exchequer 4–530b
FitzRalph, Richard
  Summa in quaestionibus armenorum 4–548a
Fitz Waryn, Foukes
  See Foukes le Fitzwarin
Five Books on Consideration (Bernard of Clairvaux) 2–191a,b
Five Boroughs capture (942) 1–278b
Five Hundred Books (Jābir ibn Ḥayyān) 1–136a
***FLABELLUM* 5–76b**; 1–224b; 3–298a
  early Christian art 4–361b
Flaccus
  See Alcuin of York
FLAGELLANTS 5–76b
  Black Death 2–263a
  Celtic mortifications 3–231b
  Clement VI 3–439b
Flagellation (Master of 1446) 4–488b
Flagellation of Christ (Antonio Veneziano) 1–343a
***FLAMENCA, ROMANCE OF* 5–77b**
Flancards 1–529a
FLANDERS AND THE LOW COUNTRIES 5–77b
  agriculture 1–96a
  altarpieces 1–225b
  anti-Semitism 2–263b
  Azores 2–29b; 4–559a-b
  bailli 2–52b
  Baldwin I of Flanders 2–58a,b
  Baldwin I of the Latin Empire 2–58b
  Black Death 2–261a
  brick 2–375b
  Bruges 2–386a-388a
  county 3–658b
  crusades 4–49b-50a
  Dutch literature 4–318a
  dye industry 4–328b
  échevins 4–379a
  fairs 4–583b, 584b, 585a-b, 586b, 592a, 593a
  financial system 4–532a
  flagellants 2–263a
  Oliver of Paderborn 4–49b
  trade 2–78a; 3–135b; 4–558a
Flann Sinna mac Máel Sechnaill 4–64b
  Cormac 3–602a
Flateyjarbók 4–387b
Flavian, Emperor 3–321a
Flavian, Patriarch
  Chalcedon, Council of 3–629a,b
  Eutyches 4–524a
Flavian Tome
  See Tome of Leo
Flavius Basilius Iunior 3–18a
Flavius Josephus 1–605a
Flavius Mithridates 3–3b
FLAX 5–83b
  canvas 3–88a
FLÈCHE 5–84a
FLECK, KONRAD 5–84a
Flemalle, Master of
  See Campin, Robert
FLEMISH PAINTING 5–85a
  Broederlam, Melchior 2–383a
  Bruges 2–387b
  Christus, Petrus 3–324b
  Daret, Jacques 4–105b
  David, Gerard 4–114b
  Ecce Homo 4–370b
  influence 2–35a
  van Eycks 4–568a

Flemish River
See Ribeira dos Flamengos
***FLETA* 5–55a**
parliaments 4–483a
Seneschaucy 4–513b
Fletchings 2–351a, 353b
FLEURON 5–88a
***FLEURY PLAYBOOK* 5–88b**
***FLEXA* 5–89a**
***FLJÓTSDÆLA SAGA* 5–89a**; 4–613b
***FLÓAMANNA SAGA* 5–89b**
FLODOARD OF RHEIMS 5–90b
Floire et Blancheflor 1–643b
FLOKKR 5–91a
Floral Borders, Master of the 4–489a
Florarium (Johannes de Mirfeld) 1–206a
FLORENCE 5–91b; 3–500a
Andrea da Firenze 1–244a
Angelo da Orvieto 1–251a
Antoninus, Saint 1–342a,b
art trade 1–562b
banking 2–72b
barbers' guild 2–99b
Black Death 2–259a-260a
Brunelleschi, Filippo 2–388a-390b
Bruni, Leonardo 2–390b
campanile 3–60b
carroccio 3–117a
Cavalcanti, Guido 3–196a
Ciuffagni, Bernardo 3–406b
currency 4–301a
Dante 4–96a, 97b, 98b-99a, 102a, 103b-104a
Della Robbia art 4–134b
dye industry 4–328a,b, 329a
engravings 4–488b, 489a
fiscal surveys 4–138a
Henry VII of Germany 4–102a
trade 4–557b
urban chronicles 3–329b
Veneziano, Antonio 1–342b
FLORENCE, BIBLIOTHECA MEDICEO-LAURENZIANA, MS PLUTEUS 29.1 5–104a
Florence, Council of
See Ferrara-Florence, Council of
Florence Antiphonary 1–319a
Florence Cathedral
Arnoldi, Alberto 1–540b
Arnolfo di Cambio 1–541a
Brunelleschi, Filippo 2–389a
Florence de Rome 3–77a, 259a
Florence et Blancheflor (Brykhulle) 1–268b
Florence-Ferrara, Council of
See Ferrara-Florence, Council of
Florence of Holland, Count
diplomacy 4–209b
Florence of Worcester 3–299b, 300a
Florent de Hesdin 1–128a; 4–245b
Florentine style calendar 3–20a
FLORENTIUS 5–107a
FLORES, JUAN DE 5–107a
Flores dictaminum (Bernard of Meun) 4–175a
Flores Island 2–29b
Flores och Blanzeflor 4–519b, 520a
***FLÓRES SAGA KONUNGS OK SONA HANS* 5–108a**
***FLÓRES SAGA OK BLANKIFLÚR* 5–108b**
Flores sanctorum 3–167a
Floriacensis
See Abbo of Fleury
Florian, Abbot 1–422a
Floridus aspectus (Petrus Riga) 1–319a
FLORILEGIA 5–109b; 1–317b-318a; 2–211b
alphabetization 1–204b
Byzantine 2–523b
Florilegium Angelicum 1–317b
Florilegium Gallicum 1–318a
FLORIN 5–110b; 4–301a
FLORIS 5–110b; 4–318b, 520a
Floris V of Holland 4–319b
FLORUS OF LYONS 5–111b; 3–112a; 4–373a
Divine Office 4–223a
Latin exegesis 4–542b
Flos florum (Arnald of Villanova) 1–138a
Flos mundi 3–166b
Flowery gardens in the realities of secrets (Fakhr al-Dīn al-Rāzī) 4–445b
Floyris
See Floris
FLUSHWORK 5–112a
Fluting 1–531a
Flying buttress
See Buttress
Foča 2–341a
Fodrum 3–557b, 558a
Foederati 2–91a
Fogassot, Joan 3–171b
Foi, Sainte, Church (Conques) 3–379b
Foillan 3–226b
Foix 1–410a,b, 412b, 413b
Fojnica 2–334a
Folchino de' Schizzi 2–324b
FOLCWIN OF LOBBES 5–112a
***FOLIES TRISTAN* 5–112b**; 1–266a, 643b
See Folies Tristan
Folie Tristan de Berne
See Folies Tristan
FOLIO 5–113a
Foliot, Gilbert
Becket, Thomas 2–151b
Folklore and magic
See Magic and Folklore
Folk plays 4–283b
Folle Bobance 4–265b
FOLQUET DE MARSEILLES 5–113a
Folquet de Romans 4–110a
FOLZ, HANS 5–113b; 4–271b
Fonsadera 3–132b
Fons memorabilium universa (Domenico Bandini) 4–449a-b
Fons vitae
See Fountain of Life
Font, baptismal 2–85b-86a, 87b
Calbulus 3–17a
Fontaine, Jean de la 1–138b
Fontaine des amoureux de science (Jean de la Fontaine) 1–138b
Fontana, Giovanni 1–437b
FONTENAY ABBEY 5–114b
Fontenoy, Battle of (841) 3–112b, 202b
Fontes 1–223a
Fontevrault
See Robert d'Arbrissel
Food
agriculture and nutrition 1–76b
animals, food 1–299a
blessing of 2–178a
cookery 3–580b-584b
dietary laws 4–178b-183b
See Also Famine
Food for Entertainment (al-Tanūkhī) 1–380b
FOOD TRADES 5–115a
bread 2–365a
Fools and Gullible People (Ibn al-Jawzī) 1–380b
Fool's cap 3–624b
Footgear
See Shoes and shoemakers
Forcadel, Pierre 1–439b
Forest, Jacos 3–331b
FOREST LAW 5–127b
FORESTS, EUROPEAN 5–131a
building materials 3–560b
Burgundy 2–426a-b, 428a
food animals 1–299b
hunting laws 1–300b, 301a
Forgaill, Dallan 3–233a, 485a
FORGERY 5–136b
decretals, false 4–124a
epigraphic studies 1–336a,b
Forlì 4–99a
Forma compoti 4–513b
Forma dictandi (Albert of Morra) 4–67a-b
Formae 3–155a
"Former Age" (Chaucer) 3–286a
FORMERET 5–137a
Formigny, Battle of (1450) 3–66a
Formosus, Pope
Arnulf 1–541b; 3–114a
Bulgaria 2–403a
election 2–11b
Eugenius Vulgarius 4–520b
Formularies
See Cartulary
Formularium spiritualis (Eucherius of Lyons) 4–356a
Formularius de modo prosandi 4–175b
Formulary of Marculf
alod 1–190a
chancery 3–253a
***FORNALDARSÖGUR* 5–137b**; 4–612b, 618a
Bósa saga 2–333b
Brut, The 2–393a
Egils Saga 4–401b
Fornaldar Sögur Norðurlanda 1–310b
Fornyrðislag 4–105b, 384a-b, 388b, 389a
Fors
See Fueros
FORTESCUE, SIR JOHN 5–143b
Forth River 1–60a
Fortifications
See Castles and fortifications
Fortunate Islands
See Canary Islands and Béthencourt
Fortunatianus, Bishop 1–352b
FORTUNE 5–145b
Alexander romances 1–151a
"Fortune" (Chaucer) 3–286a
FORTUNE, OLD SPANISH 5–147b
Forum Boarium 1–333B
Forum judicum
Catalan translation 3–164b
Forum Romanum 1–333b
Fossarii 4–121a
Fosse 3–278b
***FÓSTBRŒÐRA SAGA* 5–148a**; 2–254a; 4–612b-613a
Fotharta Airbrech 2–376a
Fouage 3–269b, 270a
***FOUKES LE FITZWARIN (FITZ WARYN)* 5–149a**; 1–267b, 268a
Fountain of Knowledge
See Fountain of Wisdom
FOUNTAIN OF LIFE 5–149a; 1–459b-460a
Fountain of Wisdom (John of Damascus) 3–320b, 336b
FOUQUET, JEAN 5–149b
Fourcès 2–129a
Four-column plan
See Cross-in-square plans

Four Homilies in Praise of the Blessed Virgin (Bernard of Clairvaux) 2–191a
Fournival, Richard de 1–188b
Fourth Armenia
See Armenian Pentarchy
FOWL, DOMESTIC 5–150a; 1–301a
FOWLING 5–151b
Fox
beast epic 2–140b
Foy, Saint 1–261b
Fra Angelico
See Giovanni da Fiesole
Frá dauða Sinfjǫtla 4–386a
Fraga, Battle of (1134) 1–160b-161a, 406a-b
France
accounting 1–38b-39a
Admiralty, Court of 1–55b, 56a-b
agriculture and nutrition 1–85a-86a
alodial tenure 1–190b
Angevins 1–253a
Apocalypse illustration 1–344a
appanages 1–351a
Aquitaine 1–366a
architecture 1–423b
archives 1–447a
bailli 2–52a
banalité 2–69a
banneret 2–82a
barrels 2–114a
bastide 2–128a
boisseau 2–310b
Bordeaux 2–327b
Brittany 2–377b-382b
Burgundy, County of 2–424a
Burgundy, Kingdom of 2–428b
castellans 3–124b, 125a
castles and fortifications 3–144b-145b, 146b, 148b-150a, 152a
Catalonian ties 3–164a
Cathars 3–181b
cattle breeding 1–293b
ceramics 3–236a,b-237a
chamberlain 3–242a
Champagne fairs 4–590b
Cistercian order 3–403a
classical literary studies 3–433b
climatology 3–454a
coal mining 3–473a
communes 3–495b-497b, 500b, 502a,b, 503a
conciliar theory 3–520b
constable of the realm 3–543b
consulate 3–570b, 571b
coronation rites 1–308b
counties 3–658b-659a
dance 4–88a,b-89a
dauphin 4–107b
Dauphiné 4–108a
demographics 4–140a, 141b
dualism 2–296b-297a
dye industry 4–328a,b
elections, church 4–421b
fairs 4–583b, 585a,b-586a
inheritance laws 3–414a; 4–607a
Knights Templars 3–304b
Latin church 3–351a,b, 354a, 355a
marriage annulment 1–307a
planetary clockwork 3–464b
water buffalo 1–298b
weights and measures 1–542a; 2–310b
FRANCE: TO 987 5–152b
barbarian invasions 2–94a-b
Capetian family 3–89a
Carolingians 3–104a
cavalry 3–201a-202b
Charlemagne 3–268a
Clovis 3–466b
Colonus 3–482b
map 5–153
monasteries 2–172a
FRANCE: 987-1223 5–154b
Albigensian heretics 4–17b
anti-Semitism 4–563b-564a
Blanche of Castile 2–270b
Children's Crusade 4–14a
church reforms 3–347b, 355a
Crusade, Fifth 4–49b
diplomacy 4–202b
duchies 4–303b-304a
financial system 4–532a
Innocent III 3–353b
Jewish exegesis 4–540b-541b
map 5–155
FRANCE: 1223-1328 5–166a
Alexander of Roes 1–148b-149a
anti-Semitism 2–81b, 263b
Blanche of Castile 2–270b
Boniface VIII 2–323b, 324a
Clericis laicos 3–448a
crusades, political 4–59a-61b
crusades of the later Middle Ages 4–55a
Dante 4–101b
diplomacy 4–202b
Edward I of England 4–396a-b
Eudes Rigaud 4–519a
map 5–167
FRANCE: 1314-1494 5–176b
Agincourt, Battle of (1415) 1–72b
Black Death 2–260b-261b; 4–142a
Cabochien riots 3–3b
cavalry 3–205a-206b
Charles V 3–269a
Charles VII 3–270b
diplomacy 4–202b, 205b
Enguerrand VII of Coucy 4–490b
Hundred Years War 4–398a
map 5–177
slaves 2–268b, 269b
Western Councils 3–650b
Francesc de Verntallat 1–418b
Francesc Eiximenis
See Eiximenis, Francesc
Francesco da Buti 1–590b
Francesco da Carrara of Padua 4–260b
FRANCESCO DA RIMINI 5–190b
Francesco del Tuppo
Romulus 4–572b
FRANCESCO DI VALDAMBRINO 5–190b
Francesco of Rome 2–100b
Francescuolo da Brossano 2–289b
Franch, Narcis 3–169b
Franche-Comté
See Burgundy, County of
Francia
bailli 2–52b-53b
See Also Carolingians and the Carolingian Empire
Francien
See French language
FRANCISCAN RITE 5–192b
FRANCISCANS 5–194b
Agnellus of Pisa 1–72b
alchemy 1–137b
Alexander of Hales 1–148a
Anglo-Latin poetry 1–255a
Anthony of Padua, Saint 1–320b
Aragon, Crown of 1–413b
Aristotelianism 1–460a, 461b, 465a,b
Armagh 1–470a
Bacon, Roger 2–35a
Barcelona 2–104a
beguines and beghards 2–159a, 161a, 162b-163a
Bernard Silvester 2–196a-b
Bonaventure, Saint 2–313a
Bosnia 2–334b, 336b, 338b
breviary 2–372a-b
Bulgaria 2–412b
canonical hours 3–67a-b
Cathars 3–190b
Celestines 3–215a
Christian Hebraists 3–314a
Christology 3–323b
church, Latin 3–353a, 355b, 359a,b, 363b, 364b, 368a, 369a
Cilician-Roman church union 3–394b
crusade propaganda 4–20b
Cyprus 4–72b
Divine Office 4–231a
ecclesiology 4–375a,b, 376b
Elias of Cortona 1–137a
Eudes Rigaud 4–519a
exegesis 2–214a
exempla 4–551a
Peter of Candia 1–147a
Western Councils 3–641b, 644b-645a
Francisco de Mello 1–439b
Francisco de Quiñones 2–373a
FRANCIS OF ASSISI, SAINT 5–191a; 1–261a; 2–24a; 3–183b
Agnellus of Pisa 1–72b
Angela of Foligno 1–251a
Anthony of Padua, Saint 1–321a
Bonaventure, Saint 2–313a
Church of San Francesco (Assisi) 1–593b
crusades 4–50a
ecclesiology 4–375a,b
Egypt journey 3–357a
Muslims 4–50a
Francis I of France, King
arms and armor 1–529b
Francis II of France, King
Brittany 2–380b
Franco-Flemish chanson 3–256b
Francoforte Castle 2–269b
Franconia
Babenberg family 2–33a-b
FRANCONIAN MOTET 5–208b
FRANCO OF COLOGNE 5–206b
ars antiqua 1–542b, 543b, 544b
ars nova 1–549a
copula 3–596a
counterpoint 3–657a
motet manuscripts 1–545b
FRANCO OF LIÈGE 5–207b
Franco-Provençal
See French language
FRANCO-SAXON SCHOOL 5–208a
FRANKALMOIN 5–209b
FRANKE, MEISTER 5–210b
Frankfurt, Council of (794) 1–143a
Christology 3–321b
iconoclasm 3–346b
Frankfurt am Main
anti-Semitism 2–263b
exchange banks 2–74a,b
fairs 2–78b; 4–583a, 586a
Frankfurt an der Oder 2–360b
Frankfurt Capitulary (794) 3–91b
Frankfurt *Paradise Garden*, Master of 4–489b
Frankfurt Passion 4–270a, 284b
Frankincense 1–370a
Frankish states in Greece
See Latin principalities and Frankish states in Greece
Frankpledge 3–659b, 660a
Franks
Alamanni 1–117a; 2–94b-95a

FRANKS (cont.)
Aquitaine 2–91a
Aragon 1–403b
arms and armor 1–522a
Bavaria 2–94b-95a, 133b
Baybars al-Bunduqdārī 2–138b
Bulgaria 2–401b, 402a-b
Burgundy, County of 2–423a, 424a
capitularies 3–91a
Catalonia 3–174a
cavalry 3–201a, 202a
Charlemagne 3–268a
Croatia 4–1b-2a,b
Cyprus 4–72b
Dalmatia 4–2b
Gaul 2–89b
Historia (Gesta) Francorum 1–109b
Leo IV 4–18b
Lombards 2–95b, 96a
Merovingians 3–104a
Saladin 4–39a
taxation 2–423a
vernacular liturgy 4–73b-74a
Franks Casket 1–276a, 281a
Frater
See Refectory
Frater Albertus Teutonicus
See Albertus Magnus
Fratres Militae Christi
See Brethren of the Sword
Fratres Unitores
Cilician-Roman church union 3–395b
FRAU AVA 5–210b; 2–228a,b
"Frauendienst" (Ulrich von Lichtenstein) 1–230a
***FRAUENLIST* 5–211b**
Frauenlob
See Heinrich von Meissen
Frawenpreiss 1–529b
Fraw Eren hof 1–133b
Frayre de Joy e Sor de Plaser 3–173a
FRECHULF (FREUCHULPH) 5–212a
FREDEGARIUS 5–212b
Fredegisus
Charlemagne 3–109b
FREDERICK I BARBAROSSA 5–212b; 1–449b; 4–467b
Aachen 1–1b, 2a
Adrian IV 1–58b
Alexander III 1–146b
Antichrist plays 4–282a
Aragon, Crown of 1–408b
Arnold of Brescia 1–540a
Bavaria 2–6b, 33b, 134b
Bohemia 2–300a
Bulgarus 2–418a
Burgundio of Pisa 2–423b
Burgundy 2–424b, 429a
Byzantines 2–494a-b, 496b
camels 1–296b
carroccio 3–117b
communes 3–497b
consulate 3–571a
Crusade, Third 4–31b, 40a
Danes 4–153b, 154a
diplomacy 4–203b, 209a
elections, church 4–422a
elections, royal 4–427a,b
Henry II the Lion 2–6b, 33b
inheritance laws 3–414a
lay benefices 2–180a
papacy 3–353a
Welfs 2–6b, 33b
Western Councils 3–637b-638a
Frederick II Barbarossa 2–240a
Frederick II Hohenstaufen
See Frederick II of the Holy Roman Empire, King of Sicily
Frederick II of Aragon 1–414b
Catalan Company 3–157a
medical legislation 2–98b
Frederick I of Austria 2–7a, 33b
Frederick II of Austria, duke 2–7a-b, 33b
Frederick III the Fair of Austria 2–7b-8a
Avignonese papacy 3–363b
Frederick IV of Austria 2–8b-9a
Frederick V of Austria
See Frederick III of the Holy Roman Empire
Frederick I of Brandenburg 2–362a
Frederick II of Brandenburg 2–362a
Frederick I of Denmark 4–156b
Frederick III of Denmark 4–385a
Frederick of Lorraine
See Stephen IX, Pope
Frederick V of Lorraine 4–432b
Frederick III of Sicily
Arnald of Villanova 1–538a
Frederick I of Swabia 2–6b
Frederick II of Swabia 4–427a
Frederick III of Swabia
See Frederick I Barbarossa
Frederick V of Swabia
Third Crusade 4–40a
FREDERICK II OF THE HOLY ROMAN EMPIRE, KING OF SICILY 5–214a; 2–7a-b, 24a
Bavaria 2–134b-135a
Bohemia 2–300a
Burgundy Kingdom 2–429b
Cathars 3–190b
ceramics 3–237b
church, Latin 3–353a,b
consuls, consulate 3–571a
crusader art and architecture 4–25b
crusades 3–357a; 4–50a, 51a-b, 52a, 58b
Cyprus 4–70b-71a
Dante 4–101b-102a
De arte venandi cum avibus 2–242b, 244b
diplomacy 4–204b, 211b
excommunication 4–32a, 537b
Gregory IX 4–32a
horse care manual 4–579b
Jews 1–340b
Kāmil, al- 4–32a
Palestine 4–32a
Western Councils 3–640b, 641a-b
Frederick III of the Holy Roman Empire 2–9a
Eugenius IV 3–654a
Frederick I the Victorious
arms and armor 1–528b
Free Choice (Augustine) 1–565b, 648b, 651a, 653a
Freedom of Choice (Anselm of Canterbury) 1–312a, 314b
Freeman 3–424a
FREE SPIRIT, HERESY OF 5–216a
beguines and beghards 2–157b
FREIDANK 5–220a; 2–363b
Freising 1–422b
bishoprics 2–134a
Boniface, Saint 2–322a
Erchambert 4–504a
"French Donatus" 1–270b
French drama
See Drama, French
FRENCH LANGUAGE 5–220b
aubade 1–123a
Cilician court 3–393a
French-English vocabularies 1–270b
influence on Castilian 3–142a
French Laws of Oléron 3–570a
FRENCH LITERATURE: TO 1200 5–232a
Bodel, Jean 2–290b
Bussard, Der 2–434a
Capellanus, Andreas 3–88b
chansons de geste 3–257a-262b
Chrétien de Troyes 3–308b
dictamen 4–175a
Eleanor of Aquitaine 4–419b-420a
Séquence de Ste. Eulalie 4–521a
FRENCH LITERATURE: AFTER 1200 5–254a
Anglo-Norman literature 1–259a
Beaumanoir 2–144b
Bible translations 2–218b
Brittany 2–370a-b
Cent nouvelles nouvelles 3–235a
Cercamon 3–240a
chansons de geste 3–257a-262b
chant royal 3–263b
Charles of Orléans 3–272b
Chartier, Alain 3–275a
Chastelaine de vergi, La 3–277a
Christine de Pizan 3–315b
chronicles 3–327a-329a
congé 3–536b
courtly love 3–668a-b
Deschamps, Eustache 4–163b
drama 4–263a
encyclopedias 4–449a
fabliaux 4–574a
histories 2–236b
FRENCH LITERATURE: DIDACTIC 5–281a
allegory 1–184a, 185a,b, 188a
beast epic 2–140b
cantefable 1–642b
dit 4–221a
exempla 4–551b
FRENCH LITERATURE: LYRIC 5–281b
ars antiqua 1–542b
ars nova 1–550b-552b
ars subtilior 1–558a-559a
assonance 1–600b
aubade 1–642a
Aucassin et Nicolette 1–642b
ballade 2–59a
cantilène 3–87b
chansons de geste 3–257b
chansons de malmariée 3–262b
débat 4–122a
dit 4–221a
FRENCH LITERATURE: ROMANCES 5–283b
Albrecht von Scharfenberg 1–134b
Arthurian 1–567b-571b, 568b-571b, 575b
Châtelain de Couci 3–277b
Eleanor of Aquitaine 4–419b-420a
FRENCH LITERATURE: TRANSLATIONS 5–288a
Bible translations 2–218b
Frequens (1417) 3–650b, 651a, 652a, 653a, 654a; 4–377b
conciliar theory 3–511a
Council of Constance 3–366a
Frescobaldi, Lionardo 1–154b
Frescobaldi company 2–77b
FRESCO BUONO 5–291b
FRESCO PAINTING 5–291b
Alt'amar 1–220b
Altichiero 1–226b
Andrea da Firenze 1–244a
Anglo-Saxon 1–273b
Annunciation (Giotto) 1–308a
Armenian 1–496a
Arriccio 1–542b

Barna da Siena 2–111a
Bartolo di Fredi 2–116b
Bulgaria 2–413b, 417b
Cavallini, Pietro 3–198a
Cennini 3–234a
Church of San Francesco (Assisi) 1–593b
Church of San Grigor Lusaworičʿ (Ani) 1–292a
Cimabue 3–396a
death and burial 4–121b
Eutychios 4–524b
model books 4–292b
San Clemente (Rome) 1–224b
Veneziano, Antonio 1–342b, 343a
FRESCO SECCO 5–296b
FRESSANT, HERMANN 5–296b
Frets 3–624a
Freyja
Æsir 1–63a
FREYR 5–296b
Æsir 1–63a
FRIARS 5–297b
Augustinian 1–659b
Friars Preachers, Order of
See Dominicans
Friday Mosque (Basra) 2–127a
FRIDAY PRAYER 5–298b
Fridegodus
See Frithegod
Fridigus 1–142b, 143a
FRIDUGISUS OF TOURS 5–299b
Friedberg
fairs 4–586a
FRIEDRICH VON HAUSEN 5–300a
FRIGG 5–301a; 1–63a
Baldr 2–55a-b
FRIK 5–301a; 1–512a
Frisians 1–50b
Anglo-Saxons 1–289a,b
Boniface, Saint 2–321a,b, 322b
ceramics 3–236b
Crusade, Fifth 4–49b-50a
Kent settlement 4–452b
kinship group 4–599b
missionaries 3–344b
Oliver of Paderborn 4–49b
FRITHEGOD 5–302a
Frithestan of Winchester 1–272b
Fritigern, King 2–90b
Fritzlar, Battle of (906) 3–202b
Friuli 2–132b
Lombards 2–95b
FROISSART, JEHAN 5–302b; 1–185a
ballade 2–59a
chronicles 2–237a; 3–325a, 332b, 333a
flagellants 2–263a
FROMENT, NICOLAS 5–304a
From the life of Our Lord 4–320a
FROMUND OF TEGERNSEE 5–304b
Frontal 1–222a, 224a
Frontinus 3–77a
FRUCTUOSUS 5–304b
Fructus primi anni
See Annate
Fruela 1–627a
FRUITS AND NUTS 5–305a
botany 2–347a-b
Byzantine Empire 1–78a
Cistercians 3–404a
Europe 1–96a; 3–581b
Islam 1–81a,b, 82b, 104b; 3–584a
Italy 1–86b-87a
Midi 1–85b
Portugal 1–85a
Sardinia 1–88a
Sicily 1–87b
Slavs 1–98b, 99b
Spain 1–83b-84a
Frumentius 1–31b-32a; 3–595b
FRUTOLF OF MICHELSBERG 5–307b
Ekkehard of Aura 4–417b
Frych, Merfyn 4–64b
***FUERO* 5–308b**
ARagon 1–417b
Basque 2–126b
Castile 3–131b
Latin 3–142a
Fuero general 3–611b
Fuero general de Navarra 1–576a
Fuerre de Gadres (Alexandre de Paris) 1–151a
Fuerteventura 3–62a-b
Füetrer, Ulrich 1–133a
FULBERT OF CHARTRES 5–310a
Abbo of Fleury 1–13a
Adelman of Liège 1–54b
Angelram of St. Riquier 1–252a
exegesis 2–213a
poetry 3–58a
FULCHER OF CHARTRES 5–311a
crusades 3–356a; 4–20a
travel accounts 1–332b
FULDA 5–311b
Boniface, Saint 2–322a
Candidus 3–63b
double-ended basilica 2–124b; 3–378b, 381
Eigel 4–408b
Fulgens and Lucrece 4–287b
Fulgentius metaphoralis (John of Ridewall) 1–183b
Fulgentius of Ruspe 3–321a
Fulk of Neuilly
crusades 4–41b
French chronicles 3–332a
Fulk V the Young
coronation 4–22b
Fulnek 2–306b
Fulrad of Saint Denis 3–106b
Fundamentals of eloquence (Al-Zamakhsharī) 4–443b
***FUNDUQ* 5–312b**; 1–154a
Funerary practice
See Death and burial
Furniture, Coptic 2–587a
FURNITURE, ISLAMIC 5–313a
FURNITURE, LITURGICAL 5–316b
early Christian art 4–357a-361b
FURNITURE, WESTERN EUROPEAN 5–321a; 2–347b
FURS, FUR TRADE 5–325b
Champagne fairs 3–621b, 623b; 4–592a
Russia 4–588a
Fursa 3–226a-b
Furs de València 3–157b
Fusee clock 3–29b
FUSORIS, JEAN 5–335a; 1–439a
astronomical clock 1–612b; 3–459b, 462b
Fusṭāṭ, Al-
See Cairo
Fūta 3–618a
Futūḥ al-Buldān (al- Balādhurī) 2–54a
FYLGJA 5–335a

G

GABELLE 5–336a
Gabirol, Ibn
See Solomon ben Judah ibn Gabirol
Gableboard
See Bargeboard
Gabriel (archangel) 1–248b, 249a, 433a
Annuciation 1–307b
Gabriel Biel
See Biel, Gabriel
Gabriel de Mussis 2–258b
Gabriel of Melitene 1–484b
Gabrielopouloi family 2–479a
Gabriel Radomir 2–406b-407a
GABRI WARE 5–337a
GACE BRULÉ 5–337b; 1–123a
Gacka 4–4a
GADDI, AGNOLO 5–337b; 3–234b
GADDI, GADDO 5–338a
GADDI, TADDEO 5–338a; 1–343a; 3–234b
Gaelic
See Celtic languages
Gaetani, Benedict
See Boniface VIII, Pope
Gageure, La 1–269b
GAGIK I 5–338b; 1–482a,b, 483a, 511b; 4–113b
Armenian sculpture 1–495b
Church of S. Grigor Lusaworičʿ (Ani) 1–292a
Dwin 4–324a
GAGIK II 5–339a; 1–290b, 484a, 485a
Byzantine Empire 2–493a
Gagik Arcruni, King 1–449b, 481b-482a
Ałtʿamar 1–220a
GAGIK OF KARS 5–340a; 1–484b, 485a
GAGIK/XAČʿIK-GAGIK 5–339b
GAGIK/XAČʿIK-GAKIK 1–451a
Gahnamak 1–489a
Gaia 4–13b
Gaia festa 3–171a
Gaianites 4–524b
Docetism 4–233a
GAIMAR, GEFFREI 5–340b; 1–264b
Anglo-Norman literature 1–261a
Arthurian Literature 1–565a
patronage 3–33a
Gaiseric
See Genseric, King
Galata
See Pera-Galata
Galata, Tower of 4–45a-b
Galatia
Anatolikon theme 1–242a
civil government 1–240a
Galbert de Bruges 2–386b; 3–497a
Galceran de Requesens 1–418a
Galdralag 4–348b, 384a, 388b
Galen
medical theory 4–579b
plague 2–264a
GALERAN DE BRETAGNE 5–341a
Galicia
agriculture 1–80a, 83b
Muslim abandonment 1–626a
Galician clergy, Declaration of 3–521b
Galician-Portuguese dialects 3–141b

GALICIAN-PORTUGUESE POETRY 5–341b
Galilee
  Fourth Crusade 4–32a
Galindo Aznar I 1–404a
Galindo Aznar II 1–404a
Galiot 1–558b
GALL, SAINT 5–342b; 2–2a
  Benedictine Rule 2–170b
  Columbanus, Saint 3–486a
  See Also Saint Gall, Church of
Galla Placidia 2–91a
  mausoleum 4–352a, 358a, 359a
GALLEGO, FERNANDO 5–343a
Gallego River 1–406a
GALLERY 5–343a
  Aachen palace chapel 1–2b-3a
  basilica 2–125a
GALLICAN CHANT 5–343b
Gallican Psalter 4–223b
GALLICAN RITE 5–344a
  Advent 1–59a
  Arundel Psalter 1–580b
  dedication of churches 4–131a
Gallican Vulgate 2–211b
Gallic Wars(Julius Caesar) 2–89a
Gallienus
  cavalry 3–201a
Gallipoli 4–105a
  Byzantine Empire 2–501b, 502a
  Ottoman capture 4–55b
Gallnuts 4–326a
GALLON 5–345b
Galluzo priory (Florence) 3–118b
GALUT 5–346a
Gama, Vasco da 4–563a
Game
  See Fowling
  See Hunting
Game and Playe of the Chesse, The 3–210b
GAMES, ISLAMIC 5–353a
GAMES AND PASTIMES 5–347a
  arms and armor 1–526a, 532b-533a
  bow and arrow/crossbow 2–352b-353a
  cavalry 3–202b-203a, 204a
  See Also Chivalry
GAMLI, KANÓKI 5–354b
Gammadion 4–9b
Gamrakeli 1–235b
Gandersheim convent
  Hathumoda 1–72b
Gandulf of Rochester 2–274a
Gandzha
  See Ganja
Gangra
  synods 2–121b; 3–607a
Ganja 1–125a, 521a
GANJAK 5–355b; 2–107a
  Armenian Muslim Emirates 1–513b
GANJAK OF ATROPATENE 5–356a
GANO DA SIENA 5–356b
Gansfort, Johann Wessel 4–167a
Gaol Delivery
  See Jail delivery
Gaon
  See Schools, Jewish
GAONIC PERIOD 5–356b
  exegesis 2–212a; 4–539a
Gapugh
  See Derbent
Garattus, Bishop 3–185b
Garbo, Dino del 3–196b
Garcia, Martí 3–171b
García, Sancho 3–128b
Garcia de Resende 1–576a
García Iñiguez, King 1–404a
García of León, King 1–627a
García of Navarre 3–128b
***GARÇON ET L'AVEUGLE* 5–358a**; 4–264a
Garde de la prévôté de Paris 3–278b
Garden of Fragrant Plants (al-Yāfi'i) 1–380b
Garden of Paradise, Islamic 2–147a
GARDENS, EUROPEAN 5–358a
  kitchen 2–347b-348a
Gardens, Islamic
  See Rauḍa
Gardman 1–123b, 124a, 125a
GARGOYLE 5–365b
Garin de Monglane 3–258b
Garin le Loherain 3–261b
Garin lo Brun 3–664a, 672b
Garlandia, Johannes de
  See John of Garland
Garlandus 4–169b
Garniture 1–533a
Garter, Order of the 3–307a; 4–398a
Garvan (Dinogetia)
  asses 1–295b
Gascon War (1294-1303) 4–396b
  Bordeaux 2–328b
Gascony 1–407a; 2–126b
  Aquitaine 1–366b
  bastides 2–129a
  Bordeaux 2–327b
  commune 3–497a
  Jewish expulsion 4–564a
Gastaphretes 2–354b
Gaston III of Foix 3–333a
Gaston VII of Foix 1–412b
Gasull, Jaume 3–171b
Gate of Justice (Alhambra) 1–168b
GATHAS 5–366a
  Avesta 2–14b
Gattamelata (Donatello) 4–257a
GATTAPONI, MATTEO 5–367a
GAUCHIER DE DOURDAN 5–367b
Gaue 3–658a
Gaufredi, Raymond 2–41a
GAUFRID (GAUDFRED) MALATERRA 5–367b
Gaufridus Anglicus 2–320a
Gaul
  Alamanni 2–94b
  Alani 1–121a
  baptismal rites 2–83a,b
  barrel 2–114a
  Benedictine Rule 2–170a
  Burgundians 2–92a,b
  Caesar 2–88b
  Celtic church 3–225b
  Christmas 3–318a
  counts 3–658b
  dioceses 4–191b
  fairs 4–583b
  Franks 2–89b, 94a
  Huns 2–92b
  Merovingians 1–190a
  Romano-Britons 2–96a
  Vikings 4–554a
  Visigoths 2–91a
Gauntlet 1–534a
GAUTIER D'ARRAS 5–368a; 1–189a; 3–246b
Gautier de Châtillon
  See Walter of Châtillon
GAUTIER DE COINCI 5–368a; 4–574a, 576b
  contrafactum 3–576a
***GAUTREKS SAGA KONUNGS* 5–368a**
Gauzlin of Fleury 1–244a
Gauzlin of Jumièges 2–173b
Gavelkind 3–424b
Gaveston, Piers 4–397a
***GAWAIN AND THE GREEN KNIGHT, SIR* 5–369a**; 1–570a
  arms and armor 1–526a
  Excalibur 4–530a
***GAWIT'* 5–371a**
GAYIANĒ, CHURCH OF (VAŁARŠAPAT) **5–371b**; 1–493b
Gayianē, Saint 1–517b, 518a
GAYRARD, RAYMOND 5–371b
Gaza 4–52b
Geber
  See Jābir ibn Ḥayyān
Gedimin of Lithuania 2–67a
GEERTGEN TOT SINT JANS 5–372a; 4–114b
Geffrei Gaimar
  See Gaimar, Geffrei
GEFJON 5–372a
Geisli 4–411a-b
GEŁARD 5–373a
Gelasian Sacramentary 3–676a; 4–120b
GELASIUS I, POPE 5–374a; 4–374a
  Bible 2–211b
  caesaropapism 3–11a,b
  Decretals, False 4–128a
  papal theory 3–342a
Gelasius II, Pope 3–636a
  cursus 4–67a
  papal documents 3–253b
GELAT'I 5–374a
  David II (IV) the Builder 4–112a
Geld system 4–90b
Gellius, Aulus 1–52a
Gelmírez, Diego 3–130a
GEMISTOS PLETHON, GEORGIOS 5–375a
  classical literary studies 3–432a
  portable clocks 3–464a
Gemma Tiberiana 1–335a
GEMS AND JEWELRY 5–375a
  Bīrūnī, al- 2–250b
  collections 1–335a,b
Genealogies (Boccaccio) 1–183b
Genealogies of the Nobles Among the Arabs
  See Ansāb al-Ashrāf
Genealogy of the Kings of England (Saint Ethelred) 4–517a
Genealogy of the Pagan Gods (Boccaccio) 1–180b; 2–283a-b, 288b
General Admonition (789) 3–91b, 108b, 109b
Generalife (Alhambra) 1–170b
General Rule to Teche Every Man . . . to Serve a Lorde . . . 3–661b
Gènesi de Scriptura 3–167a
GENESIOS, JOSEPH 5–382a; 2–514a
  Constantine VII Porphyrogenitos 3–547b
Genesis 1–279b
  Cotton MS 4–356b
  Vienna MS 4–356b
Genesis According to the Text (Augustine) 1–655b, 656a
Genesis and Exodus 2–221b
Genesis Through Judges (Aelfric) 2–221a
Genethliac horoscope 1–604a, 619a-b
Geneva
  Burgundians 2–92a, 422b
  fairs 2–78b; 4–585b
Genever 4–220a
Genghisids 2–131b
GENGHIS KHAN 5–382a; 2–131a
Genizah
  See Cairo Genizah
Genja
  See Ganjak of Atropatene

Gennadius II, Patriarch
See George Scholarios
Gennadius of Marseilles 2–180a
biographical writing 2–239a
Statuta ecclesiae antiqua 3–441a
GENOA 5–383b
Aragon, Crown of 1–412a, 416a,b, 417b, 419b
banking 2–73a-b, 74a, 75b-76a, 78b
Black Death 2–259a
Bosporus 2–344a
Byzantine Empire 2–494b, 496a, 499a, 501b
Caffa 3–12a
commune 3–500a
Cyprus 4–71a
maritime law 3–570a
Palaiologoi 1–246a,b
Pisa 4–59a
slaves 2–269b
Tortosa 1–408a
trade 4–557b, 558a
Genseric, King 2–91b
Gens nouveaus, Les 4–265b
GENTILE DA FABRIANO 5–387a
Bellini, Jacopo 2–165a
"Gentilesse" (Chaucer) 3–286a
Geoffrey de Mandeville 3–498b
Geoffrey Le Tor 1–599a
Geoffrey of Anjou, Count
Angevins 1–253a
Brittany 2–379b
Geoffrey of Auxerre
Bernard of Clairvaux 2–192a
Carthusians 3–119a
Geoffrey of Charni 3–666a
Geoffrey of Eversley 4–175b
GEOFFREY OF MONMOUTH 5–387b; 1–264b; 2–3a
Arthurian literature 1–565a, 576b
Breta Sǫgur 2–365b
Brut, The 2–393a-b
Canterbury 3–81a
Historia regum Britanniae 1–264b, 565a, 576b; 2–236b; 3–327a, 331a; 4–431a, 471b
Norman-Angevin England 4–471b
Wace 3–331a
GEOFFREY OF NOYERS 5–390b
GEOFFREY OF VINSAUF 5–390b; 1–452b
ars poetica 1–553b, 554a-555a
Poetria nova 1–255a
GEOFFROI D'AINAI 5–391b
Geoffroi de Fontaines
See Godfrey of Fontaines
Geoffroi de Paris
chronicles 3–332b
Geoffroy de Vigeois
Council of Clermont 2–274a
Geography (Vardan Vardapet) 2–20b
GEOGRAPHY AND CARTOGRAPHY, ISLAMIC 5–391b
Bāb al-Mandab 2–32a
Baḥr al-MuḤīt 2–49b
casbahs 3–121a
GEOGRAPHY AND CARTOGRAPHY, WESTERN EUROPEAN 5–395a
Airbertach mac Coisse 1–110a-b
Andalusia 1–243b
Anglo-Saxons 1–288b
antiquarianism and archaeology 1–332a-333a
Bacon, Roger 2–38b
Celtic church 3–225b
Champagne 3–243a
Old English texts 1–275a, 285b, 286a
Geography of the World
See Ašχarhac'oyc'
Geonim
See Gaonic period
***GEOPONICA* 5–399b**; 1–77a; 4–446b
estate management 4–511a-b
George II, *Kat'ołikos* 1–480b
George, Saint 1–520a
Alaverdi 1–122b
Anglo-Norman life of 1–261a
Bulgarian art 2–416b, 417b
miracle play 4–268b
George, Saint, Bank of
Caffa 3–12b
George Akropolites 2–516a
GEORGE KALLIERGIS 5–399b
George Maniakes 2–492a, 493a
GEORGE OF CYPRUS 5–399b
George of Laodicea, Bishop 1–348a
George of Ostia 3–109a
GEORGE OF PISIDIA 5–400a; 1–506a; 2–513a, 524a
George of Poděbrady 2–8b, 306b
GEORGE OF TREBIZOND 5–400b
George Pachymeres 2–516b
George Phrantzes
See George Sphrantzes
Georges Chastellain
See Rhétoriqueurs
GEORGE SCHOLARIOS 5–401a; 4–529b
Classical literary studies 3–432a
GEORGES DE LA SONNETTE 5–402a
George Sphrantzes 2–517a
George Sursuval 2–405a
George Synkellos 2–513a
George Terter, Czar 2–411a
GEORGE THE MONK 5–401a; 2–513b
GEORGIA: GEOGRAPHY AND ETHNOLOGY 5–402a; 3–193b-195a
Armenia 1–473b, 485a-b
Caucasia 3–193b-195a,b
Colchis 3–195b
Kartli 1–632b; 2–49a
GEORGIAN ART AND ARCHITECTURE 5–407b
Alaverdi 1–122b
Atenis Sioni 1–632b
Bagrat's cathedral 2–47b
Bana 2–70a
Bitshvinta 2–253b
Bolnisi Sioni 2–311a
Dawid-Garedja 4–116a
Djvari 4–231b
silversmiths 2–164b
Georgian Chronicle
See K'art'lis C'χovreba
GEORGIAN CHURCH AND SAINTS 5–412b
Antiochene rite 1–326b
Armenian church 1–499b
autocephalos 2–10a
Byzantine church 2–460a
Dawid-Garedja 4–116a
GEORGIAN LANGUAGE 5–414b
alphabet 1–207b, 214a-215a
GEORGIAN LITERATURE 5–416a
Balavariani 2–54b
GEORGIANS (IBERIANS) 5–419a
GEORGIA: POLITICAL HISTORY 5–404b
amirspasalar 1–235b
Arcrunis 1–451b
aznauri 2–28b
Bagratids 2–47b, 48b
Byzantine annexation 2–118b
Chosroids 3–307b
David II (IV) the Builder 4–112a
David of Tao 4–113b
erist'aw 4–506a
Seljuks 1–203b
vazir 1–632a
Georgius of Cracow 4–176a
Georg of Ehingen 4–579a
***GEORGSLIED* 5–420b**; 3–325a
Gepids 2–12b
Geraint of Domnonia, King 1–144a
Geraldines
Maurice fitz Maurice 2–421b
Gerald of Cabrera 1–411b
GERALD OF WALES 5–420b; 1–317a, 337a,b; 4–466b
biographical writing 2–240a
Brigit, Saint 2–376a
crusade propaganda 4–20b
Speculum duorum 1–260a
Gerard II of Cambrai, Bishop 3–496a
Gerard of Abbeville 2–318a
Gerard of Borgo San Donnino 2–315a
Gerard of Brussels 1–435a, 436b
GÉRARD OF CLAIRVAUX, SAINT 5–421b
GERARD OF CREMONA 5–422a; 1–461a
Archimedes 1–435a, 437a, 438a,b
astronomy 1–612a
GERARD OF CSANÁD, SAINT 5–422a
Marian offices 2–274a
GERBERT DE MONTREUIL 5–423a
Gerbert of Aurillac
See Sylvester II, Pope
Gerefa 1–286a
Gereint Son of Erbin 1–566b, 578a
Gerfrid, Bishop 1–226a
GERHAERT, NIKOLAUS 5–423b
GERHARDO DI JACOPO STARNINA 5–424b
GERHARD OF AUGSBURG 5–424a
GERHARD OF COLOGNE 5–424a
Gerhard of Holstein 4–155a
GERHARD OF SOISSONS 5–424b
GERHOH OF REICHERSBERG 5–424b
plays 4–268b, 282a
Geribert, Mir 3–176a-b
Gerland 1–262a
German drama
See Drama, German
Germania (Tacitus) 2–61b-62a, 89a
Germanic tribes
Alamanni 1–117a
Anglo-Saxons 1–288b
family 4–599b, 600a
marriage annulment 1–306b
GERMAN LANGUAGE 5–425b
baptismal vows 2–87a
chansons de geste 3–258a
Latin alphabet 1–212b
runic alphabet 1–215a,b
GERMAN LITERATURE 5–427a
Bible translations 2–215a-b
biblical poetry 2–224b
Cambridge Songs 3–57a, 58a
See Also Middle High German Literature
See Also Old High German Literature
GERMAN LITERATURE: ALLEGORY 5–427b
Ackermann aus Böhmen, Der 1–44b
beast epic 2–140b
GERMAN LITERATURE: LYRIC 5–433a
Albrecht von Johansdorf 1–132b
assonance 1–600a
Bruder Hans 2–385a-b
Brynhild 2–394b-395a

GERMAN LITERATURE: LYRIC (cont.)
charms 3–273a
Der von Kürenberg 4–161a
Dietmar von Aist 4–184a
Elisabeth of Nassau-Saarbrücken 4–432b
Ezzolied 4–571b
GERMAN LITERATURE: ROMANCE 5–444a
Alexander romances 1–150a
Atis und Prophilias 1–635b
Biterolf 2–253a
Eleonore of Austria 4–429a
Germanos
Nikephoros III 2–492a
GERMANOS I, PATRIARCH 5–471B
Armenian church 1–500a
iconoclasm 2–462b
letters 2–520a
GERMAN TOWNS 5–457b
development 3–416b
GERMANUS OF AUXERRE, SAINT 5–471b
Celestine I 3–214a
Celtic church 3–225b
Germanus of Bethlehem 3–122a,b
GERMANUS OF PARIS, SAINT 5–472a
liturgical colors 3–484b
Germanus of Ramsey 1–12b
GERMANY 5–472b
Aachen 1–1a
agricultural products 1–96a
Alamanni 1–117b
alodial tenure 1–190b
altarpieces 1–225b
animals, draft 1–293b, 294b, 296b, 298a
archives 1–448b
Ashkenaz 1–585b
Balts 2–64a, 68a
Barbarian invasions 2–88a, 94a
Bavaria 2–132b
Burgundy, County of 2–426a
calendar 3–20b
Celtic church 3–225b
ceramics 3–237a
church organization 3–375a
church reforms 3–347b
classical literary studies 3–433b
climatology 3–453b, 454a
coal mining 3–473a
Cologne 3–480b
colonus 3–482b
communes 3–497a-498a, 500b, 502a
consulate 3–570b
demography 4–140a
deposition of rulers 4–157b
dictamen 4–175b
distilled liquors 4–220a
dye industry 4–325b
elections, royal 4–425a
excommunication 4–538a
fairs 4–583a,b, 586a
hall church style 3–379a
Holy Roman Empire 1–148b-149a
inheritance 4–607a
Jewish family 4–605b, 606a,b
margraves 3–659a
monasteries 2–172a
noble class 3–414b
Old English literature 1–274b
peasant life 1–94a-b
planetary clockwork 3–464b
Slavic colonies 1–96b-98a
Teutonic Knights 3–306a
urban chronicles 3–328b-329b
GERMANY: 843-1137 5–473a
Boniface, Saint 2–321a
Brandenburg 2–360a-b
Burgundy, Kingdom of 2–429a
Byzantine Empire 2–494a
canonical reform 3–355a
Capetians 3–89a
Carolingians 3–112a-b
Constitutio de feudis 3–557b
GERMANY: 1137-1254 5–478b
Brandenburg 2–360b
Burgundy, Kingdom of 2–429a-b
Children's Crusade 4–14a
Cistercians 3–404a
Crusade of 1147 2–66a
Fifth Crusade 4–49b-50a,b
Innocent III 3–353b
political crusades 4–58a-60a, 61b
GERMANY: 1254-1493 5–485b
Alexander of Roes 1–148b
angelus 1–252a
anti-Semitism 2–263b
arms and armor 1–526b, 528a
Black Death 2–262b-263a; 4–142a
block books 2–274a
Brandenburg 2–360b-362a
Burgundy, Kingdom of 2–429b
diplomacy 4–205b, 206a
flagellism 2–263a
Hungary 2–300b
Lithuania 2–67a
GERMANY: ELECTORS 5–491a
GERMANY: IDEA OF EMPIRE 5–493b
GERMANY: IMPERIAL KNIGHTS 5–497a
GERMANY: PRINCIPALITIES 5–498b
GERMANY: STEM DUCHIES 5–505a; 4–303b
Germigny des Prés 3–378b
Gero Codex 1–306a
Gerona 1–414a, 418b; 3–174b
Charlemagne 3–174a
Council of 1077 3–177b
French seige (1285) 4–61a
Gero of Brandenburg 2–360a
GERSHOM BEN JUDAH 5–511b
divorce 4–607a
GERSON, JOHN 5–512a
ars moriendi 1–547b
Birgitta, Saint 2–247a
Christine de Pizan 3–316b
Collège de Navarre 1–108a
conciliar movement 3–365b
contraception 3–573a
Council of Constance 3–648a-b, 650a
ecclesiology 4–377b
Hebrew 3–314a
Latin exegesis 4–544b
Gersonides
See Levi ben Gerson
Gertrude, Saint 4–248a
Gervais de La Rue 1–271a
Gervais du Bus 1–189b
Gervase, Saint
tomb 1–254b
GERVASE OF CANTERBURY 5–513b; 1–426a
Canterbury Cathedral 3–84a
Gervase of Melkley
ars poetica 1–554a
dictamen 4–175b
Geschlechter
Cologne 3–481b, 482a
GESSO 5–513b
***GESTA APOLLONII* 5–514a**
Gesta Archiepiscoporum Mediolanensium (Arnulf of Milan) 1–541b
Gesta comitum barcinonensium 3–164a
Gesta Danorum (Saxo Grammaticus) 1–310b; 3–327a; 4–152a, 414a
Baldr 2–55a
Gesta de las mocedades de Rodrigo 3–71b, 388b, 389a
Gesta episoporum Tungrensium, Trajectensium et Leodiensium (Anselm of Liège) 1–316b
***GESTA FRANCORUM ET ALIORUM HIEROSOLIMITANORUM* 5–514a**; 4–20a
Gesta Hammaburgensis ecclesiae pontificum 1–49b-50b; 4–152a
Gesta Ludovici IX (Guillaume de Nangis) 3–332a
Gesta Philippi III (Guillaume de Nangis) 3–332a
Gestas 4–12a
Geste de Burch 1–265b
Gestes des Chiprois 4–73a
Gestis regum Anglorum, De (William of Malmesbury) 2–3a
Geta 4–283a
translation 4–163b
Getadarj, Peter 1–290b
Getica (Jordanes) 1–638a; 3–123a
Gévaudan 1–410a
Geza I of Hungary, King 4–437b
Gharīb al-muṣannaf, al- (Abū 'Ubayd) 4–443a
Gharīb al-Qur'ān 4–442b
GHASSANIDS 5–514b
origins 1–371b
Ghazāl, al-
fig trees 1–82b
GHAZĀLĪ, AL- 5–515b; 3–381a
Aristotelianism 1–459a
Ash'arī, al- 1–585a
astrology/astronomy 1–618a-b
caliphate literature 3–50b
contraception 3–575a
encyclopedias and dictionaries 4–445a-b
law 1–193b
GHĀZĀN (KHAN), MAḤMŪD 5–517b
GHĀZĪ 5–518a
Bāyazīd I 2–136a
Ghāzī Gümüshtegin 4–91b
Bohemond I of Jerusalem 4–36b
Ghazna
See Ghazni
GHAZNAVID ART AND ARCHITECTURE 5–518b
GHAZNAVIDS 5–520a
Afghanistan 1–64b-65a
Alptigin 1–219b
Buyids 2–436a-b
Ghazni 1–65a, 219b, 220a
GHENT 5–520b
échevinages 4–379b
GHENT ALTARPIECE 5–523b; 4–566b
Deesis 4–131b
Gherardello da Firenze 2–61a
Ghibellines
See Guelphs and Ghibellines
GHIBERTI, LORENZO 5–524b
Brunelleschi 2–388a,b
Ciuffagni 3–406a
Donatello 4–256b
GHISLEBERT OF SAINT AMAND 5–526a
Ghiyār 3–616b, 619b, 620b
Ghiyāth ibn Ghawth ibn al-Ṣalt
See Akhṭal, al-
Ghubār
See Arabic numerals
GHURIDS 5–526a; 1–65a,b

Ghūṭa (Damascus) 4–81a, 83a-b
GIACOMO DA CAMPIONE 5–527b
Giacomo da Lentino
  See Iacopo da Lentini
Giacomo di Maiorca 2–289b
Gibecière 3–625b
Gibert, Guillem 3–171b
Gibraltar
  siege (1350) 3–135a
GIBUIN OF LANGRES 5–527b
Gikatilla, Joseph 3–2a,b
Gilan
  See Daylam
Gilbert Crispin
  Bible gloss 2–213a
Gilbert de la Porrée
  See Gilbert of Poitiers
GILBERTINE RITE 5–528A
Gilbert of Clare 2–112b
Gilbert of Fresney 4–244a
Gilbert of Limerick
  Celtic church reforms 3–232a
GILBERT OF POITIERS 5–528a
  Alan of Lille 1–119a, 120a
  Bernard of Chartres 2–190a
  Bernard of Clairvaux 2–192a
  Christology 3–322b
  dialectic 4–170a
  exegesis 4–543b, 547b
  Synod of Rheims (1148) 3–94b
Gilbert of Sempringham
  canonization 3–68b
Gilbert the Universal 4–543b
GILDAS, SAINT 5–528b
  Ambrosianus Aurelianus 2–2b
  Arthurian literature 1–564a, 578a
  Celtic intellectual life 3–232a
  David, Saint 3–7a
Giles of Lessines 1–129b
Giles of Rome
  See Egidius Colonna
Giles of Viterbo 3–655a
Gilim
  See Kilim
Gilimot 1–266b
Gin 4–220a
Giorgi II 4–112a
GIORGI III 5–529b; 1–291a; 2–207a
Giorgi, Francesco 3–3b
GIOTTO DI BONDONE 5–530a;
  1–343a; 2–113a; 3–234b
  Annunciation fresco 1–308a
  Arena Chapel 1–226b, 453a
  Boccaccio 2–278a
  Cavallini 3–198b
  Church of San Francesco (Assisi) 1–593b
  Cimabue 3–395a
  Daddi, Bernardo 4–75b
  Duccio 4–302b
Giovanna of Naples, Queen 1–417b
  Boccaccio 2–288b, 289b
Giovanni Buon
  See Buon, Giovanni and Bartolomeo
GIOVANNI DA CAMPIONE 5–532b;
  2–324b
GIOVANNI DA FIESOLE 5–532b
Giovanni da Imola 2–57a
Giovanni da Legnano
  laws of war 2–312a
GIOVANNI D'AMBROGIO 5–532b
GIOVANNI DA MILANO 5–535a
GIOVANNI (NANNI) **DE BARTOLO 5–536a**; 2–419b
GIOVANNI (GIOVANNINO) **DE' GRASSI 5–535b**
  sketchbook 4–292a
Giovanni del Biondo 2–266b
Giovanni del Virgilio 4–104a
GIOVANNI DI BALDUCCIO 5–535b
Giovanni di Bartolo 2–419b
GIOVANNI DI BENEDETTO DA COMO 5–536b
Giovanni di Bonandrea 4–174b
Giovanni di Castro 4–327a
GIOVANNI DI CECCO 5–537a
GIOVANNI DI PAOLO 5–537a
Giovanni Dominici 1–561b
Giovanni Mazzuoli da Strada 2–277b
Giovanni of Arcoli 2–150a
Giovanni of Pian de Carpine
  See John of Plano Carpini
GIOVANNI PISANO 5–537b
  artist's status 1–579b
Giralda (Seville) 1–193a
Giraldes, Afonso 1–163a
Giraldus Cambrensis
  See Gerald of Wales
Girart de Roussillon 3–330b; 4–419b
Girart de Roussillon, Master of the
  See Jean, Dreux
GIRAUT DE BORNELH 5–539b
  alba 1–123a
Giray II, Gazi 3–679b
Giray III, Islam 3–679b
Giray I, Muḥammad 3–679b
Giray III, Muḥammad 3–679a
Giray IV, Muḥammad 3–679a
Giray II "Semiz" (the Fat) 3–679a
Giray, Devlet 3–679b
Giray, Haji 3–678b
Giray, Inayet 3–679a
Giray, Krim 3–679a
Giray, Mengli 3–678b
Giray, Saadet 3–680a
Giray, Sahib 3–680a
GIRDLED PATRICIAN 5–539b
***GIRK TŁTʻOCʻ* 5–540a**
Girolami, Remigio de' 4–101a
Girona
  See Gerona
Gironde River 2–327b
Gironès 1–418a
***GÍSLA SAGA SÚRSSONAR* 5–540b**;
  4–294b, 613a, 616a
GISLEBERTUS 5–541b
GIULIANO DA RIMINI 5–542a
Giustiniani, Blessed Paul 3–56a-b
Giustiniani, Tommaso 3–655a
  conciliar theory 3–520b
GIUSTO DE MENABUOI 5–542a
Givry 2–261a
Gjubār numerals 1–387b-395a
Glacier movement 3–451b, 453a,b, 454a,b, 455a,b
Glagolitic alphabet 1–216a-217a; 4–73b
GLAGOLITIC RITE 5–542b
  Cyril and Methodios, Saints 4–73b
GLAJOR 5–543b
GLANVILLE, RANULF DE 5–544a
  common law 4–470a-b, 471b
  kingship 4–473b
Glarus 2–8a
GLASS, ISLAMIC 5–545a
GLASS, STAINED 5–548a
GLASS, WESTERN EUROPEAN 5–554a
  Cennini 3–234a
Glastonbury
  abbey 1–256b; 4–512b
  Anglo-Saxon art 1–273a
  archeological excavations 1–337a,b
  King Arthur's grave 4–475a
  monastic reform 1–273a
Glastonbury Miscellany 3–493a
Glaž 2–334a
Glazing
  See Ceramics
Glendamain 4–492b
Gleoman 2–106a
***GLOBUS CRUCIGER* 5–564a**
GLORIA 5–564a
Glòria d'amor (Bernat Hug de Rocabertí) 3–169b, 172a
Gloriant 4–321a,b
GLOSS 5–564b
  Anselm of Laon 1–315b
  Bukhārī, al- 2–398b
  Celtic languages 3–233a,b
  decretists 4–127a
  English Bible 2–221a
  exegesis 4–543b, 544b, 545b-548a, 548b-549a
  Irish Bible 2–220b
  Old English texts 1–275a
  See Also Glossators
Glossa ordinaria (Accursius) 2–29a
Glossa ordinaria (Anselm) 2–213a, 219a; 4–543b, 546a
Glossa ordinaria (Johannes Teutonicus) 3–516a
Glossaries
  alphabetization 1–204a,b
  Anglo-Saxon literature 1–276a,b, 285b, 287a
  Cormac mac Cuilennáin 3–602a
GLOSSATORS 5–565b
  Azo 2–29a
  cross-references 4–515b
  University of Bologna 2–312a
Glossators, Jewish
  See Talmud exegesis and study of
Glossed Gospels 2–222a
Gloucester, Statute of (1278) 4–396b
GLOUCESTER CATHEDRAL 5–568a;
  1–255b
Glycerius, Emperor 2–422b
***GLYKOPHILOUSA* 5–568b**
Gnel 1–560a
GNOMIC LITERATURE 5–568b
  Exeter Book 1–281a
Gnosticism
  See Mysticism
Gnunis 1–423a, 489a
Goa
  exploration 4–563a
Goar, King 1–121a
Goat 1–299a, 302a
Goat-foot lever 2–353a, 354a
Godeffroi de Saint Omer
  Knights Templars 3–304a
Godefroid de Claire
  See Godefroid of Huy
GODEFROID OF HUY 5–569b; 4–438b
Godegisel 2–423a
Godescalc of Aix 3–97a
Godfred of Denmark, King 4–151b
Godfrey of Bouillon 2–58b
  First Crusade 3–303a; 4–30a,b, 33b-36a
  French chronicles 3–331a
Godfrey of Cambrai 1–254b
GODFREY OF FONTAINES 5–570b;
  1–463b
GODFREY OF RHEIMS 5–570b
GODFREY OF WINCHESTER 5–571a
Gododdin 1–247b
Godric of Finchale, Saint 3–416a
Gods, Germanic
  Anglo-Saxon worship 1–289a
Godwin of Wessex, Earl 4–394b-395a
  Edward the Confessor 3–82b
Godwinson, Harold 1–265a
GODZIN OF MAINZ 5–571a

GOES, HUGO VAN DER 5–571b
GOFFREDO DA VITERBO 5–572a
Arthurian literature 1–572b
Gogarenē
See Gugark'
Gogynfeirdd 2–106a; 4–69b, 430b-431a
Goharinos of Sebastia 1–521a
Gojislav 4–5b
Gök Su
See Salef River
Gold
See Metalsmiths, gold and silver
Gold Coast
exploration 4–561b
***GOLDEMAR* 5–572b**
Golden Ass, The (Apuleius) 1–651b
Golden Book on Marriage (Theophrastus) 1–323a
Golden Bull of 1356 2–8a; 3–334a; 4–425b, 428b
Brandenburg 2–361b
Golden Fleece, Order of 3–307a
GOLDEN HORDE 5–572b
Armenia 1–486a
Batu 2–131a
Bulgaria 2–411b
Caffa 3–12a
Caucasia 3–195b
Crimea, khanate of 3–678b
Muscovy 4–232a-b
GOLDEN HORN 5–573b
Fourth Crusades 4–45a-b, 47b
GOLDEN HORN WARE 5–574a
***GOLDEN LEGEND* 5–574a**; 2–236a; 4–547a
Chaucer translation 3–286a
Chester plays 3–299b
Dominicans 4–247b
exegesis 4–547a
Helena, Saint 1–336b-337a
Irish apocrypha 1–347b
Golden Meadows (al-Mas'ūdī) 1–381a
Golden Octagon (Antioch) 4–332a, 337a, 339a, 378a
Golden Psalter of Saint Gall 3–202b
GOLDEN SECTION 5–574b
Golden Spurs, Battle of (1302) 2–387b
Goldsmiths
See Metalsmiths, gold and silver
Goldsmiths Guild 3–607a
GOLIARDS 5–574b; 4–576b
Archpoet 1–449b, 450a
Carmina Burana 3–97b
Göllheim, Battle of (1298) 2–7b
***GOLOSNIKI* 5–576a**
Gołt'n
Muslim emirate 1–513a
Goł Vasil 1–484b
Gomatou 2–480a
Gomera Island
exploration 4–558b
map 3–62a-b
Gomes, Fernão 4–561b
Gonçalves, Antão 4–561a
Gonçalves, Fernán 3–87a
Gondi Chapel (Florence)
Brunelleschi, Filippo 2–388a
***GQNGU-HRÓLFS SAGA* 5–576a**
GONSALVES, NUÑO 5–577a
Gonzaga, Francesco 2–114b
González01an, count
Asturias-León 1–627b
Castile 3–128a
GONZÁLEZ DE CLAVIJO, RUY 5–577a
Good Friday 4–366a-b
Cluniac rite 3–468a
Good of Marriage, The (Augustine) 1–651a
Good Parliament (1376) 2–34a; 4–398a
Anonimalle chronicle 1–265b
GOOD SHEPHERD 5–577b
crozier 4–12b
Good Wife Taught Her Daughter, The 3–662b
Good Wyfe Wold a Pylgremage, The 3–663a
Goose 3–581b
Gorcakal 1–489a, 490b
Gorchanau 1–247a
Gordyenē
See Korčēk'
Göreme Valley 3–92a
Gormont, King
Anglo-Norman chronicles 1–264b
Gormont et Isembart 3–258b, 259b
Gorm the Old of Denmark 4–151b
GORO DI GREGORIO 5–578a
GORZE 5–578b
monastic reform 3–348a
GOŞAN 5–579b
GOŠAVANK' 5–579b
Goscalcus 3–657b
Gospel According to the Hebrews 1–347a
Gospel According to the Mark of Silver 3–352b
GOSPELBOOK 5–579b
Anglo-Norman art 1–258a
Book of Durrow 4–316b
carpet page 3–117a
Codex Aureus 3–474b
manuscript illuminations 1–496b-497b
Gospel of Goslar 4–292a
Gospel of John
chairete 3–241a
Gospel of Nicodemus 1–285b
Gospel of Pseudo-Matthew
Old English translation 1–285b
Gospels
altar apparatus 1–224a
catechumen ceremonies 2–83b
Gospels of Saint Augustine 4–357a
Gossouin
ars antiqua 1–544a
Gost 2–342a
Gotenhof
fairs 4–588a
GOTHIC, DECORATED 5–626b
ball-flower 2–61b
GOTHIC, FLAMBOYANT 5–627a
GOTHIC, INTERNATIONAL STYLE 5–627a
Melchior Broederlam 2–383a
GOTHIC, MANUELINE 5–630a
GOTHIC, PERPENDICULAR 5–630b
GOTHIC, RAYONNANT 5–631b
Gothic alphabet 1–207b, 209b, 212a-213b
GOTHIC ARCHITECTURE 5–580b; 1–427a, 429b, 449a
Amiens Cathedral 1–234b
arch 1–423b, 425a
architect's status 1–440a
arms and armor 1–529b-530a
Barcelona 2–104a
bar tracery 2–116b
bay system 2–139b
Benedictines 2–175a
boss 2–344b
brattishing 2–364a
brick 2–375b
Brunsberg, Hinrich von 2–392b
Burghausen, Hanns von 2–422a
buttress 2–434b-435a
capital 3–90b
Chartres Cathedral 3–276a
church types 2–124b, 125a, 192a-b; 3–379a-b
clerestory 3–440a
construction materials 3–558b, 562a-b, 563a-564a
cusp 4–68a
Drouet of Dammartin 4–295a
GOTHIC ART: PAINTING AND MANUSCRIPT ILLUMINATION 5–603a
Campin 3–61a
Ecce Homo 4–370a
GOTHIC ART: SCULPTURE 5–616b
Arnoldi, Alberto 1–540b
Arnolfo di Cambio 1–541a
Buon, Giovanni and Bartolomeo 2–419a-b
Gothic Bible translation 2–211b-212a
Goths
See Ostrogoths; Visigoths
GOTLAND 5–631b
Muslim coins 4–555b
trade center 2–62b
Gottesgeburt in der Seele (Meister Eckhart) 4–382a
Gottes Zukunft (Heinrich von Neustadt) 2–230b
GOTTFRIED VON NEIFEN 5–633b
GOTTFRIED VON STRASSBURG 5–634a; 1–133a, 455b
Anglo-Norman romances 1–266a
Arthurian literature 1–571b-572a, 573b
Bligger von Steinach 2–274b
courtly love 3–669b
Gottschalk
Peasants' Crusade 4–34a
Gottschalk, Prince 1–47a, 50a
GOTTSCHALK OF ORBAIS 5–638a
"double predestination" 1–660b
Gourdaine 3–278b
Government administration
See Chancery
Government of the City-State, On the (Bartolo da Sassoferrato) 2–115a
GOWER, JOHN 5–639b; 1–263b
Anglo-Latin poetry 1–255a
Anglo-Norman lyric poetry 1–269a
ballade 2–59a
Confessio amantis 3–290b
courtly love 3–669b
exempla 4–551b
Göyük, Khan 2–131b
GOZBERTUS 5–643a
Gozzadini, Giovanni
conciliar theory 3–520a,b
Grabow, Matthew 3–649a
Grabow Altarpiece 2–201a
Gračanica 4–347a
Gracial (Adgar) 1–55b
GRADUAL 5–643b
cantatorium 3–80b
Gradual of Monza 3–80b
Graecismus (Evrard of Béthune) 3–434b
Graelent 3–277b
Graf, Urs 4–516b
Graffiti, pre-Islamic 1–376b
***GRAF RUDOLF* 5–644a**
GRAIL, LEGEND OF 5–645a; 1–570b-571a
Grain crops
Arab Green Revolution 1–81a, 82a-b
Byzantium 1–76b, 77b-78a
cookery, Islamic 3–584a
Islamic lands 1–82a-b, 104b
northern Europe 1–89a-b, 92a, 94b-95a
Slavic lands 1–97b, 99b

GRAIN CROPS, WESTERN EURO-PEAN 5–645b
bread 2–364b-365a
brewing 2–374a
bushel 2–433b
distilled liquors 4–220a
Italy 1–80b, 86a-b, 87b
Midi 1–85a-b
Portugal 1–84b-85a
Sicily 1–87b-88a
Spain 1–82a-84a
three-field rotation systems 1–92a, 93a
Graindor de Douai
Chanson d'Antioche 3–254b
French chronicles 3–331a
Gramadegau'r Penceirddiaid
See Bardic grammars (Irish, Welsh)
GRAMMAR 5–648a
Anglo-Norman 1–259b, 270a,b
Arabic language 1–377b
Bacon, Roger 2–37b-38a
bardic 2–107a
Cato's Distichs 3–193a
classical literary studies 3–434b
dictamen 4–173b
Erchambert of Freising 4–504a
Old English 1–275a, 281b, 285b, 287a
Grammar (Dionysius Thrax) 4–114a
Grammatica, De (Alcuin) 1–142b
Grammatico, De (Anselm of Canterbury) 1–311b, 314a; 4–169b
GRANADA 5–651b; 1–407a
agriculture 1–81b
Alfonso I 1–160b
Alhambra 1–168a
Aragon, Crown of 1–413b, 415b
Castile 3–134a,b, 138a-b
Granada, Battle of (1319) 1–162b
Gran Crónica 1–162b
Grand, Jens 4–154b
Grand Assize
See Assize
Grand baillis 2–53a-b
Grand Council of Venice 2–99b
Grand coutumier
See Summa de legibus
Grande Chartreuse 4–109b
Grande e general estoria 1–161b-162a
***GRANDES CHRONIQUES DE FRANCE* 5–653b**; 2–236b; 3–327a,b, 331b
monastic chronicles 3–326b
source 1–109b
Grandguard 1–534a
Grand jury 4–470b
Grandmont 4–438b
GRANDMONT, ORDER OF 5–654b
Burgundy, Duchy of 2–428a
Grandson, Battle of (1476) 2–352b
Grand Union of 1256 1–659b
Granson, Oton de 1–185a
Gran Tavola dei Bonsignori 2–76b
Grant Mal Fist Adam 1–260b
Grants geanz 1–265b
GRASSER, ERASMUS 5–656b
Grasshoppers
Jewish dietary laws 4–181b
Gratiam tuam
angelus 1–252a
GRATIAN 5–656b; 1–117a, 121a
Alger of Liège 1–167b
Ammianus Marcellinus 1–235b
astrology 1–607a
canon law 2–312a
crusade concept 4–16b
Decretum 2–217a; 3–440b, 635a; 4–122b, 123a, 127a, 128b, 129a,b, 130a, 170a
dispensation 4–217a
Divine Office 4–222b
elections, church 4–421b-422a,b
Graver
See Échoppe
Gravity 1–615b
Gray, Thomas, of Heton 1–265b
Great Arbitration of 1258 3–481b
Great Bank of the Bonsignori
See Gran Tavola dei Bonsignori
"Great Book of Fiefs" 1–411a
Great Companies 3–206a
condottieri 3–531a
Great Council of Union 3–632a
Great Domesday
See Domesday Book
Great Entrance 4–335b
Greater Armenia/Armenia Major
See Armenia: Geography
Greater Armenian Era 3–30b-31a
Greater Privilege (Rudolf IV Habsburg) 2–8a
Greater Sophenē 1–515a
Great Fish River 4–562b, 563a
Great heaume 1–526a, 527a, 532b, 534b
Great Hippodrome (Constantinople) 3–554a
Great Lavra Monastery 1–637b-638a
altar cross 4–9a
GREAT (OR OLD) MORAVIA 5–658a; 2–299a-b
Great Mosque (Qayrawān) 1–5b
Great Mosque (Samarra) 1–5b
Great Mosque (Córdoba) 3–598a, 599b, 600b
Great Palace (Constantinople) 4–334b, 343a,b, 344a
Great Pigeon House of Çavuşin 3–92b
Great Saint Bernard Hospice 1–659b
Great Yarmouth
Black Death 2–261b
Greaves 1–525b, 534a
GRÉBAN, ARNOUL 5–659a
passion plays 4–264b
Greco-Roman art 4–350b-353b
Greece 2–481b
Alaric 1–122a
alchemy 1–135a-136a, 140b
animals, draft 1–295b, 296a,b, 298a
Aragon, Crown of 1–415a
Catalan Company 3–156a, 157b
classical literary studies 3–430a,b, 431a,b, 432a
clocks and reckoning of time 3–457b
crusader art and architecture 4–26b
crusades 4–34a,b, 55b
Cyprus, Kingdom of 4–72a,b
demography 4–140a
Dominicans 4–252b
early Christian and Byzantine architecture 4–337b
Epiros, Despotate of 4–499a
fairs 4–588a
just war concept 4–15b
marriage 4–594b
Mount Athos 1–636b
Nūr al-Dīn 4–39a
See Also Byzantine Empire: History
Greek alphabet 1–204a,b, 207b, 209b, 212a,b, 214a,b, 217b, 218a
alpha and omega 1–204a
Greek Book of Agriculture (Qusṭūs) 1–106a
Greek cross 4–9b, 10
Greek cross church 3–379a, 381
Greek-cross domed octagon 3–379a
GREEK FIRE 5–659b; 3–145a
Bosporus 2–344a
catapults 3–180a
GREEK LANGUAGE, BYZANTINE 5–659b; 3–345a
alchemical 1–140b
Alexander romances 1–149b
Alexandrian rite 1–155b-156a
Arabic literature 1–379a
Arabic loanwords 1–377a
Bible translations 2–211a
Bulgaria 2–401b, 407a
Burgundio of Pisa 2–423b
Nubian Christianity 3–315b
scientific language 1–610a
Greek Orthodox
See Byzantine church; Russian church
Greenland
Black Death 2–261b
colonization 3–454a
Eyrbyggja saga 4–568a
Leif Ericsson 4–555a
Vikings 4–554a,b
Green Sea
See Baḥr al-Muḥīt
Greenwich
arms and armor 1–529b
Greeting of Love
See Salut d'Amor
Gregoras, Nikephoros 3–556b
Andronikos II Palaiologos 1–246a
calendar reform 1–614a
GREGORIAN CHANT 5–661a
cadence 3–5b
Gregorian code
See Codex Theodosianus
Gregorian Decretals 2–57a
Gregorian offertory
Ave Maria 2–13a
Gregorian reform
Amatus of Monte Cassino 1–229a
Anselm II of Lucca 1–311a
Augustinian canons 1–659a
celibacy, clerical 3–443b
crusades 4–17b
Danish church 4–153b, 154a
Deusdedit 4–165b
Gregorian Sacramentary
confirmation 3–536a
GREGORIDS 5–665a
social structure 1–489a
Gregoriou monastery 1–638a
Gregorius
See Bar Hebraeus
Gregory I, Katholikos
Christian church in Persia 3–312b
GREGORY I THE GREAT, POPE 5–668b; 1–261b, 274b, 276a; 3–167a, 343a; 4–383a
Advent 1–59a
Alfred the Great 1–164b, 165a,b-166a
angelology 1–250b
ars praedicandi 1–556b
Asser 1–593a
Augustine of Canterbury and 1–644b
Benedictines 2–171a
Benedict of Nursia 2–168b, 169a, 170a
brandeum 2–362b
Byzantine Church 2–461a-b
Christmas Mass 3–318a
Christology 3–321a
church fathers 3–336b
churching of women 3–383a
church policies 3–343b
conversion of England 3–81b; 4–458a
crusade concept 4–15b
dedication of churches 4–130b
deposition of rulers 4–158a
Dialogues 1–254a

GREGORY I THE GREAT, POPE (cont.)
doctors of the church 4–234a
early Christian art 4–357b-358a
early church theology 3–342b
Easter dating 3–228b
Ecclesia and Synogoga 4–371a-b
ecclesiology 4–372a,b
excommunication 4–536b
exegesis 2–224a; 4–542b, 550a
exempla 4–551a
homilies 1–284b
Moralia 1–364a
papal coronation 3–603a
vices, list of 3–122b
Gregory II, Pope
Boniface, Saint 2–321b
Charles Martel 3–272b
iconoclasm 2–462b-463a
papal power 3–345a,b
Gregory III, Pope
All Saints' Day 1–176b
Boniface, Saint 2–322a
dietary prohibition 1–300a
papal policies 3–345b
Gregory IV, Pope
All Saints' Day 1–176b
Divine Office 4–230a
Gregory V, Pope 1–13a
GREGORY VII, POPE 5–669b; 1–218b; 3–129a
Alexander II 1–146a
Bernold of Constance 2–197b
breviary 2–371b
Bruno the Carthusian, Saint 2–392a
Byzantine Empire 2–494a
Camaldolese Order 3–56a
Canossa 3–69a
Castile 3–133a
chamberlain 3–242a
church councils 3–633b, 634b-635a
Cilician-Roman church union 3–394a
clerical celibacy 3–217a
Clermont, Council of 3–449a
crusade concept 4–16a
deposition of rulers 4–159a,b
Desiderius of Monte Cassino 4–164b
dictatus papae 4–177a
Donation of Constantine 4–258b
elections, church 4–421a
ember days 4–435b
Guiscard, Robert 1–158a
Henry IV of Germany 2–182b, 299b
Norman invasion of Balkans 3–356a
papal monarchy 4–374b
reforms 3–348b, 351a,b, 352a, 355a; 4–465b, 473b
Gregory VIII, Pope 1–296b, 330a
Forma dictandi 4–67a-b
Lateran Synod 3–636b
GREGORY IX, POPE 5–671a; 1–461a
angelus 1–252b
Anthony of Padua 1–321a
Audivimus (1234) 3–68b
bells 2–166a
blasphemy 2–272a
Bogomils 2–294b
breviary 2–372a
Cathars 3–189b, 190a
Church of San Francesco (Assisi) 1–593b
clerics, degradation of 4–134a
College of Cardinals 3–94a
crusades 4–51b-52b, 58b-59a
decretals 4–124a
elections, church 4–423a
excommunication 4–537b
Franciscan dispute 3–645a
Frederick II of the Holy Roman Empire 4–32a
Inquisition 3–353b
papal conclave 3–523b
Gregory X, Pope
Bonaventure, Saint 2–318a,b-319a
Celestines 3–214b
Dominicans 4–251a
Durand, Guillaume 4–314a
Lyons, Council of 3–641b
papal conclave 3–523b
papal power 3–354a
Ubi periculum 3–94b
Gregory XI, Pope
Baldus 2–57a
Cilician-Roman church union 3–395a,b
death 2–16a
papal residence 3–362a, 365a
Sachenspiegel 4–409b
Gregory XII, Pope
Constance, Council of 3–648b-649a
Great Schism 3–365b, 366a, 645b, 646a-647a
papal conclave 3–524b
Pisa, Council of 1–147b
Gregory XIII, Pope
calendar reform 3–23b
Gregory XV, Pope
Albertus Magnus 1–129a
Gregory, Antipope 1–330b
Gregory Manikonean 1–478b
Gregory of Akanc
See Grigor Akanc'i
Gregory of Anawarza
Armenian saints 1–521a
Gregory II of Cyprus, Patriarch 2–518a; 3–632b
Filioque 2–465b
Gregory of Montelongo 4–59b
Gregory of Narek
See Grigor Narekac'i, Saint
GREGORY OF NAZIANZUS, SAINT 5–665b; 2–120b, 510a-b
Apollinarius 1–348a
Arianism 1–454a
Armenian literature 1–508b
Armenian Rite 1–516b
Catechetical School of Alexandria 3–594a
Christmas 3–318a
church fathers 3–336a
classical literary studies 3–430b
doctor of the church 4–234a
Homilies 2–440a,b, 454b
patriarch 2–461b
poetry 2–524b
salvation theory 3–342a
GREGORY OF NYSSA, SAINT 5–666b; 1–506a
Apollinarius 1–348a
Arianism 1–454a
Ascension the 1–582a
Byzantine theology 2–466b
Christian dogma 3–336a
Christmas 3–318a
church fathers 3–335b, 336a
salvation theory 3–342a
translations 4–193a
Gregory of Prague 2–306b
GREGORY OF RIMINI 5–671b
Augustinism 1–660a
predestination 3–371a
Gregory of Sinai
Bulgaria 2–413b
kellia 1–637b
Gregory of Tat'ew
See Grigor Tat'ewac'i
GREGORY OF TOURS, SAINT 5–667a
biographical writing 2–239b
brandeum 2–362b
chamberlain 3–242a
Champagne 3–243b
climatology 3–453b
Ecclesia and Synagoga 4–371a
Historia Francorum 1–336b
Liber in gloria confessorum 3–540b
liturgical colors 3–484a
Gregory of Visoki Dečani 2–414a
Gregory of Xlat'
See Grigor Xlat'ec'i
GREGORY PALAMAS 5–672a
Barlaam of Calabria 2–109b
hesychasm 2–501b
letters 2–520a
Gregory Thaumaturgus 1–507b; 2–120a
Apollinarius 1–348a
Gregory the Englishman
antiquarianism 1–333a
GREGORY THE ILLUMINATOR, SAINT 5–668a; 1–475b, 517b-518a, 519a,b; 4–417a
Armenian church 1–503a
History of the Armenians 1–66a-67a
Gregory the Martyrophil 1–520a
Grey, John de 4–423a
Gremi 2–104a
Grenade-sur-Garonne 2–129a
Grenoble
Carthusians 3–118a
monasticism 4–109b
university 4–110a
"Grete Boke" (Sir John Paston) 1–320a
***GRETTIS SAGA ÁSMUNDARSONAR* 5–673a**; 2–184b; 4–612b, 613a
Bandamanna Saga 2–70b
Grgur, bishop 4–4b-5a
Griffin 2–206a
Grigor Abasean 1–512a
GRIGOR AKNERC'I 5–674a; 1–511b
Grigoris, Saint 1–518a
Grigoris Alt'amarc'i 1–511b
Grigoris of Aršarunik' 1–509b-510a
GRIGOR MAGISTROS 5–675a
literature 1–510b, 511a
GRIGOR NAREKAC'I, SAINT 5–673b; 1–520a-b
literature 1–510b, 511a
Grigor Tat'ewac'i 1–520b
literature 1–512a
Grigor the Priest 1–511b
Grigor Tłay 1–511b
GRIGOR II VKAYASĒR 5–675b
Grigor Xlat'ec'i 1–511b, 521a
Grimace
ars subtilior 1–558b
Grimestone, John
commonplace books 3–493a
***GRÍMNISMÁL* 5–676a**; 4–385b, 386b, 390a, 391a
Grimoald of Austrasia 3–104b
***GRÍMS SAGA LOÐINKINNA* 5–677a**; 1–310b
Gringore, Pierre
Jeu du Prince des Sots 4–265b
***GRÍPISSPÁ* 5–678a**; 4–386a, 390a,b
GRISAILLE 5–678b
Grisone, Federico 3–206b
GROAT 5–679a; 4–301a
Grocheio, Johannes de
dance 4–87a-88b
Groenlendinga saga
See Vinland sagas
Groined vault
See Vault

GROOTE, GEERT 5–680b; 4–320b
  Brethren of the Common Life 2–366b
  Devotio Moderna 1–659b; 4–166a
  religious communities 3–368b
Grosse Heidelberger Liederhandschrift 2–274b
GROSSETESTE, ROBERT 6–0; 1–263b, 461a,b
  Agnellus of Pisa 1–73a
  Aristotle 1–53b
  ars antiqua 1–544a
  ars praedicandi 1–556a
  astronomy 1–612a
  Bacon, Roger 2–38a, 39a, 40a, 41a
  beguines 2–159b
  Bradwardine, Thomas 2–358a
  Christian Hebraists 3–314a
  dialectic 4–170b
  estate management 4–513b
  excommunication 4–537b
  exegesis 2–214a; 4–544a
  mathematics 1–396b
  translations 1–127b
Grosso
  See Groat
GROTESQUE 6–0
Grottaferrata Abbey
  monastic reform 3–348a
***GROTTASQNGR* 6–0**; 4–387b, 390a
Grue, La 1–269b
GRUFFUDD AB YR YNAD COCH 6–0
Gruffudd ap Adda 4–76b
GRUFFUDD AP CYNAN 6–0; 2–71b
  eisteddfod 4–415b
Gruffudd ap Nicolas
  eisteddfod 4–415b
Gruffudd Gryg 4–76b
Gruuthuse manuscript 4–320b
Guadalquivir River
  admirals 1–55b
  agriculture 1–81b
Guadiana River 3–16b
Gual, Domingo 4–559a
Gualberti, John 3–354b
Gualbes, Melchior de 3–171a
Gualterus Anglicus
  See Walter the Englishman
Guaram, King
  Djvari 4–231b
Guaramids 2–48b
GUARIENTO DI ARPO 6–0
Guarino da Verona
  dictamen 4–176b
GUAS, JUAN AND PEDRO 6–0
Guccio de Manmaia 4–439a
Gudmarsson, Catherine 2–247a
Gudmarsson, Ulf 2–246b
Gudmod 1–266b
GUELPHS AND GHIBELLINES 6–0
  Albornoz, Gil 1–131a
  Andronikos II Palaiologos 1–246a
  Cavalcanti, Guido 3–196a
  Cecco Angiolieri 3–211b
  Cino da Pistoia 3–397a
  Dante 4–95b-96a, 97b, 98a-99b, 101b, 102a, 103b-104a
Guelphs and Ghibellines, On (Bartolo da Sassoferrato) 2–115a
Guénolé, Saint 2–377b
Guérande, Treaty of (1365) 2–380a
Guerau de Cabrera 3–164a
Guerilla warfare
  Hundred Years War 3–206a
GUERNES DE PONT-SAINTE-MAXENCE 6–0
  Anglo-Norman literature 1–260b
  Becket, Thomas 2–236a
  dialect 4–168a
Guerric of Igny 3–405a
Guesclin, Bertrand du
  Castilian civil war 3–137a, 270a
  Charles V of France 3–269b-270a
  chivalry 3–303a
  guerilla warfare 3–206a
Guesnes de Béthune
  See Conon de Béthune
Gugark' 1–472b, 473b; 2–140b
GUGLIELMO, FRA 6–0
GUGLIELMO DA VERONA 6–0
Guḥadset 3–25a
Guiart, Guillaume 3–332b
GUIBERT OF NOGENT 6–0
  communes 3–496a
  exegesis 2–224a
  memoirs 2–237a
Guibert of Ravenna 3–635a
Guichard de Beaulieu
  See Guischart de Beaulieu
Gui de Cambrai 1–151a
Gui de Nanteuil 3–166a
Guide of the Perplexed (Maimonides) 1–460a; 4–381b
***GUI DE WAREWIC* 6–0**; 1–267b, 271b
Guido Cavalcanti
  See Cavalcanti, Guido
GUIDO DA COMO 6–0
GUIDO DA SIENA 6–0; 2–189a
GUIDO DA VIGEVANO 6–0
GUIDO OF AMIENS 6–0
GUIDO OF AREZZO 6–0
  Cistercian chant 3–402b
  clef 3–438a
  consonance/dissonance 3–542a,b
  surgery 2–98b
Guido I of the Chartreuse 3–118a,b, 119a
Guido II of the Chartreuse 3–119a
Guienne 1–367b
Guifred I the Hairy
  Catalonia 3–174b-175a
Guifred II 3–175a
Guigemar 3–277b
Guigues 4–107b, 109a
Guilds, Armenian 1–491a
GUILDS, BYZANTINE 6–0; 2–476a, 478a-b
  bakers 2–478a
  Book of the Eparch 4–494a-b
  shipowners 2–477b
Guilds, Islamic
  See Ṣinf
GUILDS AND MÉTIERS 6–0
  Ankara 1–302b
  barbers 2–98a, 99a-100a
  Barcelona 2–104a
  Cologne 3–481a, 482a
  commune 3–501a
  confrérie 3–536b
  corporation 3–606a
  échevins 4–379b
  gremi 2–104a
  hemp production 3–88b
  Norman-Angevin England 4–465a-b
  Western European 4–602b-603a
GUILDS OF ARTISTS 6–0
  arms and armor 1–529b
  Bottega 2–349a
  Chester plays 3–299a
GUILHEM DE TUDELA 6–0
  Chanson de la Croisade contre les Albigeois 3–255a
Guillaume d'Angleterre (Chrétien de Troyes) 1–260b, 267b; 3–308b
Guillaume da Volpiano 2–428a
Guillaume de Conches
  See William of Conches
Guillaume de Deguileville 1–185b, 186a, 189b; 3–281a
***GUILLAUME DE DOLE* 6–0**
  chansons de toile 3–263a
GUILLAUME DE LORRIS 6–0; 1–184a-185b
  Chrétien de Troyes 3–311a
  fabliau 4–574b
Guillaume de Machaut
  See Machaut, Guillaume de
Guillaume de Nangis
  chronicles 3–332a
Guillaume de Nogaret
  See Nogaret, Guillaume de
Guillaume de Normandie 1–188b
Guillaume de Sens
  See William of Sens
Guillaume de Villehardouin
  Michael VIII Palaiologos 2–498b, 499a
Guillaume Fillastre
  See Fillastre, Guillaume
GUILLAUME LE BRETON 6–0
  Philip Augustus 2–236b, 240a
Guillaume le Clerc de Normandie 1–260b, 264a
  bestiary 2–205b
Guillaume le Grand 2–424b
Guillaume le Maréchal
  See William Marshal
Guillaume IX of Aquitaine 4–419a
Guillaume X of Aquitaine 1–367b
Guillaume of Bourges
  conductus 3–532b
Guillaume of Châteauneuf
  ¿Ay, Iherusalem! 2–18b
Guillaume-Sanche of Bordeaux 2–327b
Guillem de Cabestany 3–164b
Guillem de Cervera 3–164b
Guillem de Torroella 1–576a
Guillem VII of Montpellier 1–410a, 412a
Guillem Ramon de Montcada 1–408a
Guilleville, Guillaume de
  See Guillaume de Deguileville
Guinea
  Portugal 4–562a
  slaves 4–561a
Guinea fowl 1–301a
Guinefort, Saint 3–360a
Guinevere 1–337a,b
  See Also Arthurian Literature
GUINIZZELLI, GUIDO 6–0
GUIOT DE PROVINS 6–0
Guipúzcoa
  Basques 2–126a
  Castilian expansion 3–130b
GUIRAUT RIQUIER 6–0; 3–255b
Guirlanda esmaltada de galanes (Fernández de Constantina) 3–63b
Guiscard, Robert
  See Robert Guiscard
GUISCHART DE BEAULIEU 6–0; 1–261b, 262b
Guitmund of Aversa 2–188a
Gül Camii (Constantinople) 4–344b
Gulf of Alexandretta 3–391a, 392; 4–556b
Gulf of ʿAqaba 4–30b
Gulf of Guinea
  exploration 4–561b
Gulf of Roses 1–414a
Gulielmus Durandus of Mende
  See Durand, Guillaume, the Younger
GULISTĀN 6–0
***GULL-ÞÓRIS SAGA* 6–0**
GUMPOLD 6–0
GUNBADH 6–0
Gundacker von Judenburg 2–230a-b

Gundahar of Burgundy, King 2–422b
GUNDEŠAPUR 6–0
Gundisalvo, Domingo
philosophy 2–241b
Gundobad of Burgundy, King 2–92b, 423a
GUNDULF (BISHOP OF ROCHESTER) 6–0; 1–311b
Gundulf (father of Anselm of Canterbury) 1–311b
Gundulić, Djivo 4–300b
Gunnhild of Norway, Queen 4–415a
Gunnlaugr Leifsson 2–365b
***GUNNLAUGS SAGA ORMSTUNGU* 6–0**; 2–255b; 4–402b, 612b-613a
Gunpowder
cavalry 3–205a, 206b
fortifications 3–151a,b-152a
Gunter of Denmark, King
Lai d'Haveloc 1–268a
Gunther of Bamberg
Ezzolied 2–226b; 4–571b
Guntram of Burgundy, King 3–486a
Gunzo de Baume 3–468a-b
GUNZO OF NOVARA 6–0
"Guote liute, holt" (Albrecht von Johansdorf) 1–133a
Gurgeni of Iberia, King 2–49a; 4–113b
Chosroids 3–307b
Gurgēn of Armenia 1–483a
Gusir of Finland, King 1–311a
Gusisnautar 1–311a
Gustavus I of Sweden, King 4–156b
***GUTE FRAU, DIE* 6–0**
GUTENBERG, JOHANNES 6–0; 3–210b
Guthlac 1–279a
GUTHLAC, SAINT 6–0; 1–279a
bell 2–166a
Vercelli Book 1–285a
***GUÐMUNDAR SAGA BISKUPS* 6–0**; 2–252a
GUÐMUNDR ARASON 6–0
Guthrum of East Anglia, King
baptism 1–164a
Danelaw 1–64a; 4–91a, 456a
***GUÐRÚNARHVQT* 6–0**; 4–386b
GUÐRÚNARKVIÐA I 6–0; 4–386a, 391b
GUÐRÚNARKVIÐA II 6–0; 4–386a-b, 391b
GUÐRÚNARKVIÐA III 6–0; 2–199a,b; 4–386b
Guy, Brother
heresy 3–187b
Guyart des Moulins
Bible translation 2–219a-b
exegesis 4–547b
Guy de Chauliac
plague 2–264a
Guy de Thourotte
See Châtelain de Coucy
Guy of Blois 3–333a
GUY OF DAMMARTIN 6–0; 4–295b
Guy of Dampierre
Adenet le Roi 1–55a
Bruges 2–387a
Guy of Hampton
Boeve de Haumtone 1–267a
Guy of Lusignan (late 12th century) 4–70b, 71b
Saladin 4–31a
GUY OF LUSIGNAN 6–0
Cilicia 3–393a, 395a
Guy of Vaux-de-Cernay 3–405b
Guy of Vienne
See Calixtus II, Pope
Guy of Warwick 3–170a
Guzmán, Dominic 3–187b
Guzmán, Leonor de 1–163a
Guzzūla
fair 4–589a
GWALCHMAI AP MEILYR 6–0; 3–122a; 4–413a, 431a
Gwenllïant 3–121b
Gwion, Bishop 2–71b
Gwynedd
Cunedda Wledig 4–64b
GYLFAGINNING 6–0
GYPSIES 6–0
***GYÐINGA SAGA* 6–0**

H

Haakon Hákonarson
See Hákon Hákonarson of Norway
Haakon VI Magnusson of Norway, King
See Hákon VI Magnusson of Norway, King
Ḥabashat 1–370b
Ḥabbs 2–101a,b
Ḥabīb ibn Maslama 1–478b; 4–323b
Habitus theory 3–322b, 323a
Habrecht, Isaac
clocks 3–465a
Ḥabr qawmih 1–617a
HABSBURG DYNASTY 6–0
archives 1–448b
Austria 2–7b-9a
Burgundy, County of 2–424b, 426a
Ḥada' iqu'l-anvār fī ḥaqā'iqi'l-asrār (Fakhr al-Dīn al-Rāzī) 4–445b
HADAMAR VON LABER 6–0
Hadermod 1–266b
HADEWIJCH OF ANTWERP 6–0; 2–160b; 4–319b
Hadhramaut 1–370a,b
Hādī, al- 2–46a
Alid rebellion 1–174b
Hārūn 2–110a-b
HADĪTH 6–0; 1–634a
biographies 2–237b
Bukhārī, al- 2–397b
circumcision 3–400b
contraception 3–575a
dietary laws 4–179a-b
prose literature 1–379a
HADOARDUS 6–0
HADRAMAWT 6–0
Hadrian I, Pope
See Adrian I
Hadrian IV, Pope
See Adrian IV
Hadrian, Emperor 1–426a
cavalry 3–200a
Córdoba 3–597b
Hadrian of Canterbury
See Hadrian of Niridanum
Hadrian of Niridanum 2–153b
Canterbury school 3–82a
mass book 2–180b
Hadrian's Wall 3–143b
Hadya 1–31b
Haec sancta synodus 3–648b, 652a, 653a,b, 654a, 655a; 4–377b-378a
conciliar theory 3–366a,b, 511a, 513a
Haegen, Willem van der
Azores 2–29b; 4–559b
Hæsten 1–163b, 164a
ḤAFIẒ 6–0; 2–28a
Ḥafṣa
ʿĀ'isha 1–112b
HAFSIDS 6–0; 1–201a
Almohads 1–195b
commander of the faithful 3–488b
Hagenau
Constantinople 4–43a
HAGENAUER, NICHOLAS 6–0
Haggada
Bible 2–216a
Hagia Irene church 4–339a
Hagia Katherini church 4–345a
Hagia Sofia (Bizye) 4–340a
HAGIA SOPHIA (CONSTANTINOPLE) 6–0; 3–632a; 4–338, 340, 342, 344, 359a,b
Andronikos I Komnenos 1–245a
Anthemios of Tralles 1–317a
architecture 4–339a-b
Asmatikon 1–586b
Baldwin I 2–58b
Constantine 2–443a
construction 2–461a, 486a
Deesis 4–131b
ecumenical patriarchate 4–383b
Fourth Crusade 4–46a
furnishings 4–361a
liturgies 2–468a; 4–333a, 430a
mosaics 2–439a-440a, 447b
mosque 2–470a
restoration 2–442a
Hagia Sophia (Edessa)
dome of heaven 4–236b-237a
HAGIA SOPHIA (KIEV) 6–0
architectural type 3–378b
mosaics 2–443a
Hagia Sophia (Ochrid)
paintings 2–443b
Hagia Sophia (Thessaloniki) 4–340a
Hagia Sophia (Trebizond)
restoration 2–447a
Hagiography
angel/angelology 1–249b
Annolied 1–306a
Bulgaria 2–413b
canonization 3–67b
Eigel 4–408b
HAGIOGRAPHY, BYZANTINE 6–0; 2–518a-519a
Armenian saints 1–519a
HAGIOGRAPHY, FRENCH 6–0; 2–235b-236a
Aimoin de Fleury 1–109b
André de Fleury 1–244a
Séquence de Ste. Eulalie 4–521b
HAGIOGRAPHY, GEORGIAN 6–0
HAGIOGRAPHY, MIDDLE ENGLISH 6–0
Bede 2–155a
HAGIOGRAPHY, WESTERN EUROPEAN 6–0
Alcuin of York 1–143b
bishops' sagas 2–252b
Brendan voyage 1–262a
Brigit, Saint 2–376a-377a
Candidus of Fulda 3–63b
Catalan texts 3–167a, 168a
chansons de geste 3–259a-b
Cistercian Order 3–405a
Clonard 3–465b
Dunstan, Saint 4–311b-312b
Duth literature 4–320a
Eadmer of Canterbury 4–330b
funeral rites 3–231a
kings' saga 4–414a
Latin church 3–373a

Hagioi, Church of 4–338b
Hagion oron
See Athos, Mount
Hagios Demetrios
ex voto images 4–529b
Hague, The
archives 1–448a
HAGUE FRAGMENT 6–0
Ḥaḥuli
See χaχuli
Hai ben Mekiẓ (Ibn Ezra) 1–23a
Haikal
Coptic architecture 3–587a
HAIMO OF AUXERRE 6–0
Antichrist doctrine 1–321b
patristic exegesis 4–542b
Hainaut
fairs 4–592a
Hair
care 2–148b-150a
tonsure 2–381b; 3–228b-229a
Haiti
Columbus 4–561a
Ḥājib 3–37a
Hajj 3–27b
Ḥajjāj, Muslim ibn al-Bukhārī, al- 2–399a
Ḥajjāj ibn Maṭar, al- 1–620a
ḤAJJĀJ IBN YŪSUF, AL- 6–0
ʿAbd Allāh 1–16a
Iraq 3–39b
Ḥajjī 3–398b
death 1–628a
Ḥakam I
Córdoba 3–598b
Ḥakam II
Córdoba mosque 1–197a
ḤĀKIM BI-AMR ALLĀH, AL- 6–0
ʿAzīz, al- 2–28a,b
Copts and Coptic church 3–594b
Druzes 4–295b-296b
mosque of 1–196b
persecution of Jews and Christians 3–15a
Hákonarmál 4–389a
See Eiríksmál and Hákonarmaál
***HÁKONAR SAGA HÁKONARSONAR* 6–0**
***HÁKONAR SAGA ÍVARSSONAR* 6–0**
Hákon V Magnússon
Eufemia 4–519b, 520a
Hákon IV Hákonarson 4–504b
Elis Saga Ok Rosamundu 4–431b
Hákon I the Good 4–414b
Eyvindr 4–570a
Hákon the Great, Earl 4–409b-410b
Eyvindr 4–570a
Ḥakw 3–616b
Halakha
See Law, Jewish
Ḥalakim 3–24b
HAŁARCIN 6–0
HAŁBAT 6–0; 1–589b
Halberd 3–204b
Halberstadt, Albrecht von
See Albrecht von Halberstadt
Halevi, Judah 1–22a
Cairo Genizah 3–16a
Ha-Levi Abulafia, Samuel
time measurements 3–458a
Háleygjatal (Eyvindr Finnsson Skáldaspillir) 4–570a-b
Half-Bracteates
See Bracteates
Halfdan
See Healfdene
***HÁLFDANAR SAGA BRÖNUFÓSTRA* 6–0**
***HÁLFDANAR SAGA EYSTEINSSONAR* 6–0**
***HÁLFS SAGA OK HÁLFSREKKA* 6–0**
HALF-TIMBER 6–0
Halich
Byzantine church 2–469b
ḤALLĀJ, AL- 6–0
Hall church (Hallenkirche) 3–379a, 381
Halldórsson, Jón 4–289b
***HALLFREÐAR SAGA* 6–0**; 2–255b; 4–612b-613a
Hall of Justice, Alhambra 1–171a
Hall of the Abencerrajes, Alhambra 1–168b, 170a
Hall of the Ambassadors, Alhambra 1–170a
Hall of the Two Sisters, Alhambra 1–168b, 170a
Hallstatt culture
Celtic languages 3–232b
Halo
See Nimbus
Ḥalūg 3–618b
Haly 2–38b
ḤAMA 6–0
Ayyubids 2–23b, 24a
Saladin 4–39b
Hamadhānī, al- 1–381b
ḤAMAʾIL 6–0
Hamam Bagratuni, Prince
literature 1–511a
Hamartigenia (Prudentius) 1–181a-b
Hamazasp Acruni, Prince
martyrdom 1–479b, 519a
Hamazasp Mamikonean 1–478b
Hamburg-Bremen
Adalbert 1–47a
archbishops 1–50a
Ham castle 3–152a
Hamdānī, al- 2–32b
HAMDANIDS 6–0; 1–513b
Antioch 1–326a
Armenia 1–482a-b
Ḥammād ibn Abī Sulaymān
Abū Ḥanīfa 1–26a
Hammadid dynasty 1–194a
ḤAMMĀM 6–0
HAMMER BEAM 6–0
***HAMÐISMÁL* 6–0**; 4–386b, 390a
Ḥamza
Muḥammad 1–15a
Ḥamza ibn ÆAlī
Druzes 4–296a-b
Hamzić, Mihajlo 4–300b
ḤĀN 6–0
Hanafi school of religious law 1–26a
ḤANBAL, AḤMAD IBN MUḤAMMAD IBN 6–0
Ashʿarī, al- 1–583b, 585b
Hanbali scholars 4–84b-85a
Handboc (Byrhtferth of Ramsey) 1–284a, 285b
Handfaestning 4–155a
Handlyng Synne
See Mannyng, Robert
Handlyng Synne (Mannyng) 1–263a; 3–662a
Hand of God 4–13b
Handy Table (Ptolemy) 1–620b, 621b-622a
Haneron, Anthony
dictamen 4–176b
Hangchow
See Kinsai
HANGING BOWL 6–0
Celtic art 3–219a
Ḥanīfa 1–16a
Hanjit
See Ingilene-Anzitenē
Hankey, John
Chester plays 3–298b
Hanneken Leckertant (Jan van den Berghe) 4–322b
Hanover, Kingdom of
Billungs 2–235b
Hans, Bruder
See Bruder Hans
HANSEATIC LEAGUE 6–0
Denmark 4–155b
fairs 4–587b
maritime law 3–570a
Hanukkah 3–27a
Happy Adventure
See Una ventura
Harald Bluetooth 3–300a; 4–151b
Christianity 4–151a
Harald Gilli, King 4–414a
Haraldr gráfeldr
Eyvindr 4–570a
Haraldr Hárfagri of Norway, King
See Harold I of Norway
***HARALDSKVÆÐI* 6–0**; 1–638b; 4–389a
Ḥaram
Dome of the Rock 4–24a
HÁRBARÐSLJÓÐ 6–0; 4–386b, 390a, 391a
Harbaville Triptych
Deesis 4–131b
Ḥarb ibn Umayya
ʿAbd al-Muṭṭalib 1–14b
Hardecnut 3–472a; 4–394b
HARDING, STEPHEN 6–0
Cistercian Order 3–403b
Cîteaux Bible 2–213b, 218a
Hare, 1–301a
HAREM 6–0
Abbasid caliphate 3–45a
Alhambra 1–168b
See Also Concubinage, Islamic
Harǧa
See Kharja
Harim
siege (1164) 4–38b-39a
See Harem
Hariolf of Langres
Ermenrich of Ellwangen 4–507a
Ḥarīrī, al- 1–381b; 2–22b
HARIULF 6
Angelram of Saint Riquier 1–252a
Harley Lyrics 1–318a, 319b
Harley Psalter 1–273b
HARMENOPOULOS, CONSTANTINE 6–0
Harmonica institutione, De (Hucbald of Saint Amand) 3–542a
HARMONY 6–0
ars nova 1–551b
counterpoint 3–656b
Harmony of the Foreknowledge, the Predestination, and the Grace of God with Free Choice (Ansel 1–313b, 315a
Harmsól
See Gamli Kanóki
Harness
See Tools, Agricultural
Haro, Lope Díaz de, Lord 3–134b
Harold II of England 4–395a, 452b, 457a-b, 461a
Bayeux Tapestry 2–139a
Harold I of Norway
saga 4–402b, 414b
Harold III of Norway, King 1–47a
Harold III Hardrada of Norway 4–395a

Harran
 Islamic alchemy 1–136a
Harrow
 See Tools, Agricultural
Harrowing of Hell
 See Anastasis
Harry, Blind
 See Henry the Minstrel
HARÐAR SAGA GRÍMKELSSONAR 6–0
HARTMANN VON AUE 6–0
 Ambraser Heldenbuch 1–229b
 Arthurian literature 1–571b
 biblical poetry 2–228b
 Bussard, Der 2–434a
HĀRŪN AL-RASHĪD 6–0; 1–9a-10a, 27b, 115a, 141a, 174b, 374a
 Baghdad 2–46a-b
 Barmakids 2–110a-111a
 caliphate 3–43a, 44a, 48a
 diplomacy 4–200b
 Ibrāhīm ibn al-Aghlab 1–70a
 perfume 2–147a
Hārūt 1–248b
Harvesting
 See Agriculture and Nutrition
Harzburg
 siege (1073) 3–97a
Hasa, al-
 See Baḥrayn, al-
Ḥasan 1–171b, 173b, 374a,b
 descendants 1–174b-175b
Ḥasan, Sultan 4–408a
ḤASAN IBN ʿALĪ IBN ABĪ ṬALIB, AL- 6–0
Ḥasan ibn-al-Sabbah
 Alamūt 1–118b
Ḥasan ibn Hāni', Al-
 See Abū Nuwās
Ḥasan ibn Zaid, Al-
 Alamūt 1–118b
Ḥasan-i Ṣabbāḥ
 Nizārī Ismailis 1–590a
Hasdai Crescas
 See Crescas, Hasdai
Hāshim 1–172a
 ʿAbbās, al- 1–4a,b
 ʿAbd al-Muṭṭalib 1–14a-b
 Abū Ṭalib 1–29b-30a
 boycott 1–28b
HĀSHIM IBN ʿABD MANĀF 6–0
Hāshimiyya
 Abbasids 1–7a
Hāshimiyyah, al- 2–45a,b
Hashīshiyya 1–592a-b
HASIDEI ASHKENAZ 6–0
 Eleazar Ben Judah of Worms 4–421a
Ḥasidim
 Jewish apocalyptic literature 1–345b
HÄSLEIN, DAS 6–0
Hassagot
 Rabad 1–22b-23a
Ḥassān Mosque, Rabat 1–191b
Ḥaštean' 1–472b, 515a
HASTINGS, BATTLE OF (1066) **6–0**; 2–139a; 4–461a
 Anglo-Norman chronicles 1–265a
 bow and arrow/crossbow 2–352b
 feigned retreat 3–203b
Hathumoda, abbess
 Agius of Corvey 1–72b
Hats, headdress
 Islamic 3–616b
 Jewish 3–619b, 620b
 Western European 3–623a-624b
HÁTTALYKILL 6–0
HÁTTATAL 6–0
Ḥattīn, Battle of (1187) 2–23a
Hatton manuscript of West Saxon Gospels 1–275b
HÄTZLERIN, KLARA 6–0
Hauberk 1–524b
Haukr Erlendsson
 Breta Sǫgur 2–365b
HAUKR VALDÍSARSON 6–0; 4–294b
Ḥaurān plateau 4–81a
Hausbrand 4–220a
Hautefort Castle 2–201b-202a
Hauteville family 2–492b
Hautvillers abbey
 fairs 4–591a
***HÁVAMÁL* 6–0**; 4–386b, 390a, 391a
***HÁVARÐAR SAGA ÍSFIRÐINGS* 6–0**; 4–612b
Havelberg
 bishopric 2–360a-b
HAVELOK THE DANE 6–0
 chronicles 1–264b; 3–325b
Ḥawāla 2–79b
Hawāra
 See Berbers
Hawāzin 1–24b
Hawking 4–579b
Hawkwood, John 3–531a
Ḥawqal, Ibn 1–485a
 Baylakān 2–139b
Hay, John
 See Moulins, Master of
HAY, SIR GILBERT 6–0; 1–151b; 3–666b
Hay'ah 1–616b, 622a
Ḥaydara
 See ʿAlī Ibn Abī Ṭālib
Hayk 2–47b; 3–30b
Haymo of Auxerre
 homilies 1–284b
Haymo of Faversham
 breviary 2–372a
Haytham, Ibn al- 1–436a, 437a, 438b; 4–407b
 Bacon's optics 2–39a
 Ptolemy 1–621a
Hayyat, Juda
 cabala 3–3a
HAZĀRABAD 6–0
Hazarapet 1–489a
ḤAZM, IBN 6–0; 1–401a; 3–599a-b, 672a
 astrology/astronomy 1–618a
 love poetry 1–381b, 401a
Headdress
 See Hats, headdress
Head of the Jews
 See Nagid
Headrail 3–623b
Healfdene of Denmark 4–456a
 Alfred the Great 1–163b, 164a
Hearth lists 4–138a
HEATING 6–0
 fuels 2–347b
Heaume Topfhelm 1–527a
HEAVENLY JERUSALEM 6–0
 Entry into Jerusalem 4–491b
Hebdomada alba 4–364b
Hebdomadibus, De (Boethius) 2–36a
 Aquinas 1–357b
HEBREW BELLES LETTRES 6–0
HEBREW LANGUAGE, STUDY OF 6–0
 alphabet 1–207b-209a, 217b, 218a
 Christian Hebraists 3–313b
 exegesis 4–538b-539a
 Semitic linguistic family 1–376b
Hebrew literature
 Alexander romances 1–150a
 Arthurian literature 1–572b
HEBREW POETRY 6–0
 Cairo Genizah 3–15b
Hebrides
 exploration 4–554a
HEDEBY 6–0
 bracteates 2–355b
Hegesippus
 apostolic succession 3–338b
Hegira 1–112b
 Badr, Battle of 2–42b
 Islamic era 3–27a
Hegoumenos 3–447a
Hegyon ha-Nefesh (Abraham bar Ḥiyya) 1–22a
HEIDIN, DIE 6–0
Heikhalot rabbati 1–344b
Heilagra manna sǫgur
 See Saints' sagas
Heilige Kreuz 1–127b
Heilig Geist church
 Burghausen 2–422a
Heimdalargaldr 4–387b
HEIMDALLR 6–0
Heimericus de Campo
 See Van den Velde, Heymerich
Heimskringla (Snorri Sturluson) 1–310b; 4–403a, 410b, 411a, 413b, 414a, 415a
Heinhardus
 See Einhard
HEINRICH VI 6–0
Heinrich der Glîchezaere
 beast epic 2–141b
HEINRICH DER TEICHNER 6–0
Heinrich der Vogler
 Buch von Bern, Das 2–396a
HEINRICH OF AUGSBURG 6–0
Heinrich Suso
 See Suso (Seuse), Heinrich
HEINRICH VON DEM TÜRLIN 6–0
 Ambraser Heldenbuch 1–229b
HEINRICH VON FREIBERG 6–0; 1–636a
 Arthurian literature 1–572a
HEINRICH VON MEISSEN 6–0; 1–229b
HEINRICH VON MELK 6–0
HEINRICH VON MORUNGEN 6–0
HEINRICH VON MÜGELN 6–0
Heinrich von München
 biblical poetry 2–229a
HEINRICH VON NEUSTADT 6–0
 biblical poetry 2–230b
HEINRICH VON RUGGE 6–0
HEINRICH VON VELDEKE 6–0
***HEINRICO, DE* 6–0**
Heiric of Auxerre
 classical literary studies 3–433a
 Latin exegesis 4–542b
HEIRMOS 6–0
***HEIÐARVÍGA SAGA* 6–0**; 4–613b, 614a
HEJAZ 6–0; 1–16a, 25a
HEL 6–0
Helena, Saint
 archaeological excavations 1–336b, 337a
 crux gemmata 4–9a
 Elene 1–279a
 elevation of the Holy Cross 4–430a
Helgafell monastery 4–568a
Helgakviða Hjǫrvarðssonar 4–386a, 390a
Helgakviða Hundingsbana I 2–56a; 4–386a, 389a, 390a
Helgakviða Hundingsbana II 4–386a, 390a,b
HELGA ÞÁTTR ÞÓRISSONAR 6–0
HELGAUD 6–0

HELGI POEMS 6–0
Droplaugarsona saga 4–294a
***HELIAND* 6–0**; 1–280a; 2–225a
Hélinandus de Froidmont 1–264a
astrology 1–607b
Heliopolis, Battle of (640) 4–403b
Hellenism
Basil the Great 2–120a
Hellespont
See Dardanelles
Helluland
discovery 4–555a
Helmbrecht (Wernher der Gartenaere) 1–230a
Helmet 1–526a, 527, 530a, 534a
barbarian 1–522a
Norman 1–524a, 527
Saxon 1–523a
Viking 1–522b-523a
HELMOLD OF BOSAU 6–0
Helmschmied 1–529b
Heloise
See Abelard, Peter
HELPERIC OF AUXERRE 6–0; 1–262a
***HELREIÐ BRYNHILDAR* 6–0**; 2–395a; 4–386a, 390a,b
Hemerken, Thomas
See Thomas à Kempis
HEMMEL, PETER 6–0
HEMP 6–0
canvas production 3–88a
Hendrik van Veldeke
See Heinrich von Veldeke
Henna dye 4–326a,b
Hennequin de Bruges
See Bondol, Jean
Hennin 3–623b-624a
***HENOTIKON* 6–0**; 1–499a, 508b
caesaropapism 3–10b
Henricho 3–463b
Henricus Aristippus 1–136b
Henri d'Andeli
fabliau 4–575a
Henri de Ferrières 1–189b
Henry Beauclerc
See Henry I of England
HENRY DE MONDEVILLE 6–0
Henry II Jasomirgott 2–6b
Bavarian rule 2–33b, 134b
Henry of Ahaus
Brethren of the Common Life 2–367a
Henry of Almain
Baron's War 2–112a
Henry of Avranches 1–450a
Henry IX of Bavaria the Black
Saxony 2–235b
Henry X of Bavaria the Proud 2–134b
Henry of Blois
antiquarianism 1–335a
Henry of Bolingbroke
See Henry IV of England
Henry III of Brabant
Adenet le Roi 1–55a
Henry of Burgundy, Count
Portugal 3–129b, 130a
Henry I of Castile 3–133b
Henry II of Castile 1–416b; 3–136b, 137a-b, 270a
Henry III of Castile 3–137b-138a
Canary Islands expedition 3–61b
Henry IV of Castile 1–418b, 419a; 3–138a-b
taxation 3–612a
Henry II of Champagne 3–247a
Henry III of Champagne 3–249b
Henry I of Champagne the Liberal 3–245a
fairs 4–591b
Henry of Cîteaux
Cathars 3–187a
Henry of Clairvaux
Cistercian Order 3–405b
Henry of Cologne
Dominican mysticism 4–248a
HENRY OF CREMONA 6–0
Henry I of Cyprus 4–71a
HENRY I OF ENGLAND 6–0; 4–462a-463a
Angevins 1–253a
Anselm of Canterbury 1–313a,b; 4–466a-b, 470b
Bec 4–422a
boroughs 2–330b
Brandenburg 2–360a
Clarendon, Constitutions of 3–409b
communes 3–497a, 498a,b
court of common pleas 3–491b
Durham treaties 4–316a,b
Exchequer 4–530b
fairs 4–586b
Fantosme, jORDAN 1–265a
gem collection 1–335b
law 4–464b
town charters 3–494b
HENRY II OF ENGLAND 6–0; 4–466b-467b
Angevins 1–253a
Aragon, Crown of 1–408b-409b
Assize 1–594b, 596a-b, 598a
Assize of Clarendon 3–408b
Becket 1–147a; 2–151a, 152a-b
Bertran de Born 2–201b-202a
boroughs 2–330b
brewing 2–375a
Brittany, Duchy 2–379b
Cambridge Songs 3–57b
Canterbury 3–83a,b
church-state relations 4–471a
coinage 4–531b
communes 3–497a, 498b
court leet 3–659b
court of common pleas 3–491b
culture and learning 4–471b
death 4–40a
Eleanor of Aquitaine 1–367b; 2–126b; 4–419b-420a, 471b
elections, church 4–423a, 424b
Ethelred of Rievaulx, Saint 4–517a
Fantosme, Jordan 1–265a
government 4–469a-470b
Ireland 1–58b
legitimacy of royal rights 4–475a
Stephen and Matilda 4–463a,b
Third Crusade 4–40a
HENRY III OF ENGLAND 6–0
Agnellus of Pisa 1–73a
Aquitaine 1–367b, 369a
ascendance to throne 4–469a, 472b-473a, 475a
Baron's War 2–111b
bastides 2–128b
Blanche of Castile 2–270b
Bordeaux 2–328a
boroughs 2–331a
Burgh, de 2–421b
Burgundy, Kingdom of 2–429a
Cambridge Songs 3–57b
church-state relations 4–471b
deposition 4–160b
diplomacy 4–209a
Edward I 4–396a
elections, church 4–423b
Louis IX 1–148a
parliament 4–481a,b
provincial synods 3–578a
Sicily 4–60a
HENRY IV OF ENGLAND 6–0
Admiralty, Court of 1–57a
anointing of kings 1–309a
Bedlam 2–157b
Broun, Robert 2–385a
Burgundy, County of 2–424b
Byzantine Empire 2–503a
corporation 3–607b
English language 1–259a
papacy 1–146b
parliament 4–484b-485b
right to kingship 4–476b-478a
HENRY V OF ENGLAND 6–0
Agincourt 1–72a
biographies 3–328a
Caen 3–8b
Catherine 3–271a
death 3–271a
diplomacy 4–208b
rights to kingship 4–477a
HENRY VI OF ENGLAND 6–0
Byzantine Empire 2–497a
Cade's Rebellion 3–4b
Charles VII 3–65a
diplomacy 4–209b
parliament 4–485b
rights to kingship 4–477a
tomb 4–510b
Henry VII of England
financial system 4–533a
rights to kingship 4–472b-473a, 478b-479b
Henry VIII of England
Admiralty, Court of 1–57a
arms and armor 1–529b
asylum system 1–632b
caesaropapism 3–11b
parliamentary 4–485b
Henry of Flanders
Bulgaria 2–409a
Henry I of France
Council of Rheims 3–634a
Henry II of France
arms and armor 1–529b
art 1–258b
Henry IV of France 3–351b
Anglo-Norman art 1–258b
Henry I of Germany 3–115a
Henry II of Germany the Wrangler 2–6a
Bebo 2–150b
Billungs 2–235a
Burchard of Worms 2–420a
Burgundy, Kingdom of 2–429a
election 4–426b
HENRY III OF GERMANY 6–0; 1–47a, 228b, 311b; 2–6a, 392a; 4–427a
Billungs 2–235a
election 4–425b
Leo IX 3–351a
papal coronation 3–604a
papal reform 3–348b
HENRY IV OF GERMANY 6–0; 1–158a; 2–494a; 3–634b, 635a; 4–427a
Adalbert of Bremen 1–47a
Billungs 2–235b
Bruno of Magdeburg 2–391b
Byzantine Empire 2–494a
Canossa 3–69a
Carmen de Bello Saxonico 3–97a
excommunication 4–374b
Gregory VII 2–182b; 4–159a
martial spirit 4–33a
Vratislav II 2–299b
Henry V of Germany 2–6b
Bohemia 2–299b
Cologne 3–481a
Concordat of Worms 4–422a
Matilda 4–462b

HENRY V OF GERMANY (cont.)
Paschal II 3–635b
Henry VI of Germany 4–427b
Constance 4–58a
consuls, consulate 3–571a
Cyprus 4–70b
papacy 3–353a
Richard I the Lionhearted 4–467b
Henry VII of Germany 4–101b-103a,b
Bartolo da Sassoferrato 2–115a-b
Bohemia 2–300b
Cino da Pistoia 3–397b
Clement V 3–439a
Henry I of Germany the Fowler
election 4–426a-b
HENRY OF GHENT 6–0; 1–463b-464a
Henry of Halle
Gertrude, Saint 4–248a
Henry of Harclay
Bradwardine, Thomas 2–358a
Henry of Hesse
See Henry of Langenstein
Henry of Isernia
dictamen 4–176a
Henry of Kirkestede 1–206b
Henry of Lancaster, Duke 1–263b
HENRY OF LANGENSTEIN 6–0; 1–438a
astronomy 1–613b
conciliar theory 3–511a, 514b, 518b
Western councils 3–646a
Henry of Lausanne 3–359a
Henry II of Lusignan
crusader art and architecture 4–26a
Henry of Luxembourg
See Henry VII of Germany
Henry of Portugal, Prince
Azores 2–29b; 4–559a,b
Canary Islands 3–63a; 4–561a
Cape Verde Islands 4–561b
Ethiopia 1–32b
HENRY OF REYNES 6–0
Henry of Silesia
See Henry the Pious
Henry of Sully
archealogical excavations 1–337a
Henry of Susa
See Hostiensis
Henry of Trastámara
See Henry II of Castile, King
HENRYSON, ROBERT 6–0
Henry III the Black
See Henry III of Germany
HENRY THE LION 6–0
Bavaria 2–6b, 134b
Billung duchy 2–235b
Philip of Heinsberg 3–481a
HENRY THE MINSTREL 6–0
Henry the Navigator
See Henry of Portugal, Prince
Henry the Pious
Mongol invasions 2–131b
Henry the Young King
See Henry II of England
HEPHTHALITES 6–0
Afghanistan 1–64a
Hephzi-bah (mother of Messiah) 1–345a
Heptaméron (Marie d'Angoulême) 3–277b
HEPTAMÉRON, L' 6–0
Heptateuch (Aelfric) 2–221a
Heraclea
Anatolia 1–239b
Heracles Papyrus 4–292a
HERAKLIDS 6–0
HERAKLIOS 6–0; 1–123b-124a, 478a
Antioch 1–325b
Byzantine church 2–462a
dinar 4–187a
Dwin 4–323b
early Christian art 4–353a, 362a
economy and society 2–477b
Ekthesis 4–418b
reign 2–487a,b
HERALDRY 6–0
arms and armor 1–524a
chivalry 3–302a
Herat 1–65a,b
Herbals
botany 2–244b-246a, 345b
HERBALS: ARABIC AND BYZANTINE 6–0
HERBALS: WESTERN EUROPEAN 6–0
allegory 1–188b
Catalan 3–168b
cookery 3–581b
Herbarium (Pseudo-Apuleius) 1–286a
Herbert of Bosham
biblical exegesis 2–213b; 3–313b
Herbert II of Vermandois 3–243b
Herbert the Younger of Champagne 3–243b
HERBORT VON FRITZLAR 6–0; 1–635b
HERBS 6–0
brewing 2–374b
cookery 3–581b
HERBS, ISLAMIC 6–0
Hercegovina 2–339a,b, 340a
gravestones 2–341a
Hereford, Nicholas
Wycliffe Bible 2–222a
Hereford Cathedral Library
chained books 3–240b
HEREFORD RITE 6–0
Heregeld 4–90b
HERESIES, ARMENIAN 6–0
HERESIES, BYZANTINE 6–0
Bogomils 2–294a
HERESIES, WESTERN EUROPEAN 6–0
Amalric of Bène 1–228a
Berengar 2–188a
Bogomils 2–294a
Cathars 3–181a,b
HERESY 6–0
adoptionism 1–57b
beguines and beghards 2–159a
blasphemy 2–27a,b
clerics' degradation 4–133a
convocations, Canterbury and York 3–579b
crusades 4–17a
Docetism 4–233a
Latin church 3–367b-371b
HERESY, ISLAMIC 6–0
Afghanistan 1–65a-b
Alamūt 1–118a
Azhar, al- 2–27b
ʿAzīz, al- 2–28b
Buyids 2–436b
Corpus Gabirianum 1–141a
Druzes 4–295b
Ismailism 3–50a
Herger
See Spervogel
Heribert of Antimiano
See Aribert II of Milan
Heribert of Cologne, Archbishop
Cambridge Songs 3–57b
HERIBERT OF EICHSTADT 6–0
Heribert of Rothenburg 3–58a
HERIGER OF LOBBES 6–0
Heriger of Mainz, Archbishop 4–426a
Herimar, Abbot 3–634a
HERIOT 6–0
HERLAND, HUGH 6–0
***HERMANDADES* 6–0**
Castile 3–134b, 137b, 139a
HERMANN OF CARINTHIA 6–0; 1–393b
Hermann of Dalmatia 1–611b
HERMANN OF REICHENAU 6–0
astrolabe 3–29a
cylinder dial 3–28b
Hermann of Saxony 2–235a
See Billungs
Hermannus Contractus
astrolabe 1–611a
HERMANN VON SACHSENHEIM 6–0
Hermann von Salva
Teutonic Knights 3–306a
Herman of Valenciennes
Bible version 2–215a
HERMAN THE GERMAN 6–0
Hermeneia (Dionysios of Fourna) 4–191b
Hermes Trismegistus 1–605a
Hermine, King
Boeve de Haumtone 1–267b
HERMITS, EREMITISM 6–0
anchorites 1–242b
Ancrene Riwle 1–243a
Celtic spirituality 3–231b
Hermits of Morrone
See Celestines
Hermits of Saint Augustine
See Augustinian Friars
Hermits of Saint Damian
See Celestines
Hermogenian code
See Codex Theodosianus
Hermoldus, Abbot
See Ermoldus Nigellus
Hermóðr 2–55b; 4–414b
Hernando del Castillo 3–63a
Herod 4–22a
Heroic poetry
eddic poetry 4–390a-b
Heroides (Ovid) 1–184a
Héron, Le (La fille mal gardée) 1–269b
Heron Island
See Ilha das Garcas
Herpin
See Lion de Bourges
Herrad of Hohenburg, Abbess 4–448b
HERRAND VON WILDONIE 6–0
Ambraser Heldenbuch 1–230a
Herrenales 1–83b
Herrera, Gabriel Alonso de 1–81b
Herring
Denmark 4–149b
Herr Ivan Lejonriddaren 4–519b, 520a
Herrnhut
Bohemian Brethren 2–305b
Hersant the She-Wolf 2–140b
Herstal, Capitulary of (779) 3–91b, 108b, 109a
Hertford, Council of (672 or 673) 1–144a
Hertig Fredrik av Normandie 4–519b, 520a
***HERVARAR SAGA OK HEIÐREKS KONUNGS* 6–0**; 4–387b, 388a
Hervé, Bishop 2–71b, 72a
Hervey
See Hervé
HERZOG ERNST 6–0
Hesler, Heinrich von
biblical poetry 2–231a, 232a
Hesse
Boniface, Saint 2–321b
HESYCHASM 6–0; 2–501b
Barlaam of Calabria 2–109b

Bulgaria 2–413b-414a
Hesychios the Illustrious of Miletos 4–447a
Hesychius 1–508b
Heteroousians
See Anomoeans
HETOIMASIA 6–0
Het spel vanden heilighen sacramente vander Nyeuwervaert 4–322a
HET'UM I 6–0
Ayās 2–19a
HET'UMIDS 6–0
Cilician kingdom 3–341a
HET'UM II 6–0
death 3–391b-392a
Het'um Korikosc'i 1–511b
Hexabiblos
See Harmenopoulos, Constantine
HEXAEMERON 6–0
Hexaemeron (Abelard) 1–17b
Hexaemeron (Basil the Great) 2–121a, 122a
Hexameron (Aelfric) 1–61b, 285b
Hexapla 2–211a
Heytesbury, William 1–464b
Bradwardine, Thomas 2–358a
HEZELON OF LIÈGE 6–0
Cluny Abbey Church 3–468b
Hibernensis
funeral rites 3–231a
HIBERNO-LATIN 6–0
apocrypha 1–347a
Hiberno-Saxon Art
See Migration and Hiberno-Saxon Art
Hickes, George 1–286b, 287a
Old English poetry 1–278a,b
HICKLING, ROBERT 6–0
Hidāya 'ilā farā'iḍ al-qulūb, Al- (Baḥya ben Joseph ibn Paquda) 1–23a; 2–51a-b
HIDE 6–0
HIEREIA, COUNCIL OF 6–0
Constantine V 3–546a
HIEROKLES 6–0
Hierro Island 3–62b
HIGDEN, RANULF 6–0; 3–325a
Chester plays 3–298b
Middle English exegesis 4–547a
High Atlas Mountains 1–193b, 639b
HIGH CROSSES, CELTIC 6–0
High Gothic churches
arches 1–423b
Ḥijāz
See Hejaz
'Amr ibn al-'Āṣ 1–236b
Hilarion, Saint, Fort 4–70b
Hilarion of Moglen, Bishop
Bogomils 2–294b, 296a
Hilarius
plays 4–281b
refrains 4–263b
HILARY OF POITIERS, SAINT 6–0
adoptionism 1–57b
biblical exegesis 2–224a
Western church 3–336a
Hilda of Hartlepool, Abbess 1–107b
Hilda of Wearmouth-Jarrow
Celtic monasteries 3–227b
HILDEBERT OF LAVARDIN 6–0
Hildebert of Le Mans 1–318b, 319a
Hildebert of Mainz
Otto I the Great 4–426b
Hildebrand
See Gregory VII, Pope
***HILDEBRANDSLIED* 6–0**; 1–587b
Hildegaersberch, Willem van 4–320a
HILDEGARD OF BINGEN, SAINT 6–0
biblical exegesis 2–213b
botanical writings 2–245a
brewing 2–374b
man as microcosm idea 1–607a
Hildegard of Rupertsberg 2–173b
Hildgard of Hürnheim
encyclopedia 4–578b
HILDUIN OF SAINT DENIS 6–0
angel/angelology 1–250b
Hilduin of Saint Médard, Abbot
altar relic 1–337a
Hill, Richard 2–60a
commonplace books 3–493a
Hillel II
Jewish calendar 3–24b-25a
Hilton, Walter
See Mystical writings, Middle English
Hilton of Cadboll
stone monuments 3–223b
Ḥimā 1–103b
Himerius of Tarragona 3–318a
Himmerod church 1–43a
HIMṢ 6–0
Himyarites 1–370a,b
Hincmar of Laon
Decretals, False 4–126b
HINCMAR OF RHEIMS 6–0
Charles the Bald 3–114b
Decretals, False 4–125b, 126b
dioceses 4–191a
ecclesiology 4–373a-b
Hindu-Arabic numerals
See Arabic numerals
Hindu Kush massif 1–65a
Hindu Reckoning (Kūshyār) 1–385b
Hindu-Shahids 1–64a, 65a
Hingston Down, Battle of (838) 4–455b
"Hinnen varn, Die" (Albrecht von Johansdorf) 1–132b
Hinrich von Brunsberg
See Brunsberg, H(e)inrich von
Hintāta tribe 1–194a
Hinton
Carthusian priories 3–118b
Hipparchus
anaphoric clock 3–457b
precession phenomenon 3–22b
Hippiatrika 4–446b-447a
Hippocrates
medical theory 4–579b
Hippolytus (writ.)
Antichrist doctrine 1–321b
Armenian literature 1–507b
creeds, liturgical use 3–675b, 676a
Docetism 4–233a
holy oils 2–177a
papal coronation 3–602b
Philosophumena 3–335a
Hippolytus, Antipope 1–330a
Hira
barbotine 2–101a
HIRA, AL- 6–0
HIRSAU 6–0
Benedictines 3–404a
Ḥisāb al-hind 1–383a
Ḥisāb al-nīm 1–385a
Ḥisdai ibn Shaprut
Córdoba 3–600a
Hishām III
Córdoba 3–600a
HISHĀM IBN 'ABD AL-MALIK 6–0; 3–40b, 41b
Ḥiṣn Kaifa
Ayyubids principality 2–23b
Hispana 3–229b; 4–124b
Hispanic Latin
Celtic intellectual life 3–231b
Hispaniola
Columbus 4–561a
HISPANO-ARABIC LANGUAGE AND LITERATURE 6–0
courtly love 3–671b-672a
HISPANO-MAURESQUE ART 6–0
Hispanus, Petrus 3–168b
HISPERIC LATIN 6–0
Brittany, Duchy 2–379a
Histoire de Guillaume le Maréchal 1–266a
Histoire universelle 4–26a
Historia ad Christi nativitatem (Nicholas Trivet) 1–265b
Historia Apolonii Regis Tyri 1–349a
***HISTORIA BRITTONUM* 6–0**; 2–71b; 4–64b
Historia calamitatum (Abelard) 1–16b, 17b, 19b, 323b
Historia crítica de España (Juan Francisco Masdeu) 3–386a
Històrìa de Jacob Xalabín 3–170a
Històrìa del cavaller Partinobles de Bles 3–170a
Historia de los amores de París y Viana 1–176a
Historia de Preliis (Leo of Naples) 1–152b
Historia de rebus gestis Glastoniensibus (Giraldus Cambrensis and Adam of Domerham) 1–337a
Historia destructionis Troiae (Guido delle Colonne) 3–166b, 212a
Historiae Alexandri (Quintus Curtius Rufus) 1–149b
Historia ecclesiastica gentis Anglorum (Bede) 1–155a-b
Historia (Gesta) Francorum (Aimoin de Fleury) 1–109b
Historia Francorum (Gregory of Tours) 1–336b
Historia Hierosolimitana (Baudri of Bourgueil) 2–132a
Historia Hierosolymitana (Fulcher of Chartres) 1–333a; 4–20a
Historia Karoli Magni et Rotholandi (Pseudo-Turpin) 3–331b
Historia (Michael Attaleiates) 1–641b
Historia naturalis (Pliny)
medieval copies 1–335b
Historia Normannorum (Amatus of Monte Cassino) 1–229a
Historia novorum (Eadmer of Canterbury) 4–331a
Històrìa (Pere Tomich) 3–166b
Historia Regum Britanniae
See Geoffrey of Monmouth
HISTORIA REGUM FRANCORUM 6–0; 2–236b; 3–332a
Historia rerum in partibus transmarinis gestorum
See William of Tyre
Historia Roderici 3–76b
Cid legend 3–387a
Historia Salonitana Maior 4–4b
Historia scholastica (Peter Comestor) 3–299b
Historia troyana polimétrica 1–162b-163a
Historica ecclesiastica tripartita 3–124a
Historical Library (Diodorus Siculus) 3–325a, 330a
Historical societies
Anglo-Norman literature 1–271a
Historien der alden é 2–232a
Histories (Agathias) 1–67b-68a

Historie van Troyen (Jacob van Maerlant) 4–318b
HISTORIOGRAPHY, ARMENIAN 6–0
HISTORIOGRAPHY, BYZANTINE 6–0; 2–511b-517b
Bar Hebraeus 2–108a
Corippus 3–601a
Dionysius of Tel-Mahré 4–193a
poems 2–508a-b
HISTORIOGRAPHY, IRISH 6–0
HISTORIOGRAPHY, ISLAMIC 6–0
Arabic prose literature 1–379a
Balādhurī 2–54a
Dīnawarī, al- 4–188a-b
Egypt 4–407b
HISTORIOGRAPHY, JEWISH 6–0
HISTORIOGRAPHY, SCOTTISH 6–0
HISTORIOGRAPHY, WESTERN EUROPEAN 6–0
Aimoin de Fleury 1–109b
André de Fleury 1–244a
Bede 2–155a
Bruni 2–390b
Catalan literature 3–164a-b, 165a-166b
chronicles 3–325a-334a
Eadmer of Canterbury 4–330b
Erchenbert of Monte Cassino 4–504a
History of His Own Time (Procopius) 3–199b
History of Taron
See Patmut'iwn (Yerkrin) Taronoy
History of the Armenians (Agat'angełos) 1–66a
History of the Bishops of the Church of Hamburg 1–49b-50b
History of the British Kings
See Geoffrey of Monmouth
History of the English Church and People (Bede) 1–155a-b
History of the Foundation of Wigmore Abbey 1–266a
History of the Lombards (Erchenbert of Monte Cassino) 4–504a
History of the Lombards (Paul the Deacon) 3–101b
History of the Muslim Conquests
See Futūḥ al-Buldān
History of the Patriarchs of Alexandria (Sawīrus ibn al-Muqaffa') 4–525a
History of the World, The (Orosius) 1–284a
History of Vardan and the Armenian War (Ełišē) 4–433a
History Regarding the Sufferings Occasioned by Foreign Peoples Living Around Us (Aristakēs 1–454b-455a
Hit 4–522a
ḤIṬṬĪN 6–0
crusades 4–31a
Hittites
Aleppo 1–145a
HJÁLMÞERS SAGA OK ÖLVIS 6–0
HJAÐNINGAVÍG 6–0
Hjǫrungavágr, Battle of (985) 4–410b
HLǪÐSKVIÐA 6–0; 4–387b, 390a
HOCCLEVE (OCCLEVE), **THOMAS 6–0**
Letter of Cupid 1–324a
Middle English exegesis 4–545b
Hochstaden, Conrad von, Archbishop 1–127b
HOCKET 6–0; 1–547a, 551b
Bamberg manuscript 2–68b
HODEGETRIA 6–0
Eleousa 4–429b
Hodegitria of Aphendiko, Church of the 4–345a
Hodna chain of Atlas Mountains 1–639b
Hoël, Count 2–379a
HŒNIR 6–0
Fáfnir 4–581a
***HŒNSA-ÞÓRIS SAGA* 6–0**; 4–613b, 614a
Hofer Bestiary 2–206a
Hǫfuðlausn 4–401a, 403a
Hoguine 1–533a
Hohe Minne
See Courtly Love
HOHENFURTH, MASTER OF 6–0
HOHENSTAUFEN DYNASTY 6–0; 1–127a, 413b, 418a
Angevins 1–253b
Babenberg family 2–6b, 33b
Burgundy, County of 2–424b
elections, royal 4–427a-b
Fourth Crusade 3–357a
papacy 1–58b; 4–17b
Richard of Cornwall 4–51b
Hohenzeuggestech 1–533a
Hólar
historiography 4–618a
sagas 2–252a-b
Holbein the Younger 4–93a
HOLCOT, ROBERT 6–0
Latin exegesis 4–544b
nominalist theology 3–371a
HOLEWELL, THOMAS 6–0
HOLGER DANSKE 6–0
Holinshed
Arthurian literature 1–565b
***HOLKHAM BIBLE PICTURE BOOK* 6–0**; 1–262b
Holland
Devotio Moderna 4–166a
Teutonic Knights 3–306a
Holland, John
admiralty jurisdiction 1–57a
Holmgard
See Novgorod
Holy Apostles Church at Constantinople 4–332a, 339a, 344a
Holy Apostles Church at Paris 3–467a
Holy Apostles Church at Thessaloniki 2–450a; 4–345a
Holy Cross Abbey at Holyrood 4–393a
Holy Cross, Church of the (Ałt'amar) 1–495b
Holy Ējmiacin 4–417a
Holy Grail, Knights of 3–307a
Holy Grail legend
Albrecht of Scharfenberg 1–133b-134a
Chrétien de Troyes 3–308b
Holy Innocents, Church of the (Paris) 4–93a
Holy Lance
Peter Bartholomew 4–35b
Holy Land
See Crusades
Holy monogram 2–196a-b
Holy Mountain
See Athos, Mount
Holy orders
See Ordination
Holy River, Battle of the
Cnut the Great 3–472a
HOLY ROMAN EMPIRE 6–0
Aachen 1–1a-b
Alfonso X 1–161a; 3–134a
annate payments 1–305a
archives 1–446a, 448b
Bavaria 2–133a
Burgundy Kingdom 2–428b
Butler 2–434b
church, Latin 3–343a
German 1–148b-149a
HOLYROOD 6–0
Holy Sepulcher, Church of the 4–336b
completion 4–23b
crusader art and architecture 4–25a
crusades 4–36a, 37a
dedication 4–24a
restoration 2–443a
Urban II 4–33b
Holy Sepulcher, Knights of 3–306b
Holy Spirit of Maiella Abbey 3–214b
Holy Thursday 4–366a
altar apparatus 1–222b
anointing 1–308a
Cluniac rite 3–468a
Holy Translators
Armenian saints 1–520a-b
Holy war, European
See Crusade, Concept of
Holy war, Islamic
See Jihād
HOLY WEEK 6–0
Cluniac rite 3–468a
HOLY YEAR 6–0
HOMAGE 6–0
Armenia 1–489a
Assizes of Jerusalem 1–599a
commendation 3–490b
HOMICIDE 6–0
HOMICIDE, ISLAMIC LAW 6–0
blood money 2–276b
Homiletic texts 1–262b-264a
Homiliaries 4–224b
Homilies (Basil the Great) 2–121a
Homilies d'Organyà 3–159b, 160b, 164b
Homily, Homilarium
See Preaching and Sermon Literature
Homme Juste et l'Homme Mondain, L' 4–265a
Homme Pécheur, L' 4–265a
Homoeans 1–454a
Homs
See Ḥimṣ
Honenc', Tigran 1–291a, 292a
HONEY 6–0
cookery, Islamic 3–584a
Honeycomb Vault
See Vault
HONORÉ, MASTER 6–0
Honoré of Autun
See Honorius Augustodunensis
Honorius II, Antipope 1–330a
Alexander II 1–146a,b
Benzo of Alba 2–182b
biblical interpretation 2–231b
death 3–636b
Knights Templars 3–304b
Honorius I, Pope
Easter dating 3–228b
Ekthesis 4–418b
Monothelitism 3–630b
Honorius III, Pope 4–375b
beguines 2–158b
Carmelite Rite 3–96b
Divine Office 4–223a
Dominicans 4–239b
Fifth Crusade 4–49b
Frederick II of Sicily 4–58b
papal power 3–353b
Honorius IV, Pope 1–453a
Honorius, Flavius, Emperor 1–653b
reign 2–485b
Visigoths 2–90b
HONORIUS AUGUSTODUNENSIS 6–0; 1–263b, 610b
Anselm of Canterbury 1–315a
biblical poetry 2–226b

biographical writing 2–239b
Divine Office 4–223a
Donation of 4–258b
Elucidarium and Spanish *Lucidario* 4–434a
encyclopedias 4–448a, 577b
Ermengaud 4–506b
Marian offices 2–274a
Honor of Louis, the Most Christian Caesar Augustus, In (Ermoldus Nigellus) 4–507b
Honrado Concejo de la Mesta
See Mesta
Hood molding
See Molding
Hoods 3–623b
Hopfer family 4–516b
Hopkins, Gerard Manley 1–287b
Hora nona 3–24a
Hormisdas, Pope
Brandeum 2–362b
Hormizd IV, King 2–50a
Horn et Rimenhild 4–429a
Horns of Hamma, Battle of (1175) 4–39b
Horns of Ḥiṭṭīn
Jerusalem 4–39b
See Also Ḥiṭṭīn
Horologia
Norwich Cathedral 3–460b
production 3–460a
Horologion 1–155b; 2–468b
canonical hours 3–67a
Horologium mirabile Lundense 3–465a
HOROMOS 6–0
Horoscope
genethliac 1–604a, 619a-b
nativities 1–605b
Horse
agriculture 1–93a-b
breeding 3–404a
draft animal 1–294a-295b
food animal 1–95b, 299a
text 4–579b
war 3–204b, 206a,b
Horseshoe
coldblood horse 1–295a
Horseshoe Arch
See Arch
Hortensius (Cicero) 1–646b, 647a
Horticulture
botany 2–347b-348a
Hortus conclusus 1–184b; 4–330a
Hortus deliciarum (Herrad) 4–448b
Apocalypse illustration 1–344a
HOSE 6–0
costume, Western European 3–622b-623a, 625a, 626a
Hoshana Rabba 3–27a
Hosios David
Christ enthroned depiction 4–358b
evangelist symbols 4–526a
Greek cross style 3–379a
hierarchical compositions 4–354b
HOSIOS LUKAS 6–0
architecture 4–341b
mosaics 2–442a-443a, 444a
Hosius of Códoba, Bishop 3–597b, 628a
Hospices de Beaune
Rolin 2–427b
Hospicia 4–512a
Hospital de Santa Cruz 1–20a
Hospitalers, Knights 3–303b-304a
Aragon, Crown of 1–410b, 415a
bastides 2–128b
Bernard, Saint 3–356b
Clement VI 3–439b
crusader art and architecture 4–21b
crusades 4–32a
funding 4–109b
papal funds 2–77b
Severin 2–70a
Templars 3–644b; 4–52a,b
Vienne, Council of 3–644b
HOSPITALS AND POOR RELIEF, BYZANTINE 6–0
HOSPITALS AND POOR RELIEF, ISLAMIC 6–0
HOSPITALS AND POOR RELIEF, WESTERN EUROPEAN 6–0
Bedlam 2–157a
HOST DESECRATION LIBEL 6–0
HOSTIENSIS 6–0
conciliar theory 3–517a,b
contraception 3–573a
Hôtel de Nesle
construction 4–295a
Hǫðr 2–55b, 56a
Houdenc, Raoul de 1–185b, 188b
Houppelande 3–625a-b
Hour, divisions of 3–24b
Hours, canonical
See Canonical hours
Hours of Anne of Brittany 2–350a
Hours of Frederick of Aragon 2–350a
Hours of the Virgin
See Blessed Virgin Mary, Little Office of
HOUSEBOOK, MASTER OF THE 6–0; 4–490a
engraving 4–487b
HOUSEHOLD, CHAMBER, AND WARDROBE 6–0
blessing 2–178a
butler 2–434a-b
Byzantine bureaucracy 2–472a, 474a
charms, old High German 3–274a
courtesy books 3–661b
housekeeping manual 4–579a
House of Fame (Chaucer) 3–284a,b
House of Wisdom
See Bayt al-Ḥikma
Houwaert, Jan Baptist 4–322b
Houxds 3–146b
Hoviv Chapel
architecture 1–292a
Ḥovot ha-Levavot
See al-Hidāya 'ilā farā'iḍ al-qulūb
Howden, Roger 1–265a
How the Wise Man Taught His Son 3–662a
HRABANUS MAURUS 6–0; 3–64a; 4–412b
animal studies 2–242b
ars praedicandi 1–556b
astrology 1–606b
Calpurnius Siculus Titus 3–55b
Cassiodorus 3–124a
Divine Office 4–223a
Eigel 4–408b
encyclopedias 4–447a, 577b
exegesis 2–213a; 4–542b
plant studies 2–245a
poetry 2–226a; 3–103a
Hrabr' 2–404a
Hrafnista sagas 1–310b
***HRAFNKELS SAGA FREYSGODA* 6–0**; 4–613b, 614a
Hrafn Sveinbjarnarson 2–256a
Hrak'ot-Perož 2–139a
Hṙip'simē 1–517b
Trdat 1–66b
HRIP'SIMĒ, CHURCH OF SAINT 6–0; 1–493b
Hrólf Kraki, King 4–388a
***HRÓLFS SAGA GAUTREKSSONAR* 6–0**; 4–402a
***HRÓLFS SAGA KRAKA* 6–0**; 2–254a,b; 4–388a
HROMKLAY 6–0
Armenian council 1–500b
***HRÓMUNDAR SAGA GRIPSSONAR* 6–0**
HROTSVITHA VON GANDERSHEIM 6–0
comedies 4–282b
Córdoba 3–599a
Hrvatinić family 2–336b, 337a, 338a,b
Hryggjarstykki (Eiríkr Oddsson) 4–413b-414a
Hsiung-nu
See Huns
Hsüan Tsang
Bukhara 2–397a
Hubert I, Duke
Boniface, Saint 2–322a
Huc, Bernard
Cathars 3–190a
HUCBALD OF SAINT AMAND 6–0
consonance/dissonance 3–542a
Ḥudaybiya, al-, Treaty of (628) 1–4b
HUE DE ROTELANDE 6–0; 1–266b
HUELGAS MS, LAS 6–0
Huerta cultivation 1–86b-87a
Huesca 1–404a,b, 405a,b, 406b, 407a,b, 417a
Aragon, Crown of 1–411b
Huge Scheppel (Elisabeth of Nassau: Saarbrücken) 4–432b-433a
Hugh Capet 3–89b
Hugh de Salins, Archbishop
Burgundy, County of 2–424b
Hugh le Despenser 4–397b
Hugh le Grand
See Hugh the Great of Burgundy
Hugh le Noir of Burgundy, Duke 2–427a
Hugh Le Puiset, Lord 3–145a
Hugh of Antioch, King 4–71a
Hugh of Arles, King 2–429a
Hugh of Avalon 4–423a
Hugh of Breboble, Saint
Carthusians 3–118a
Hugh III of Burgundy, Duke 4–109a
Hugh IV of Burgundy, Duke 2–424b; 4–71a
Hugh of Cluny 2–173b
First Crusade 3–356b
Henry IV 3–69b
Hugh II of Cyprus, King 4–71a
HUGH OF FLEURY 6–0
André de Fleury 1–244a
Hugh of Folieto
bestiary 2–205a
Hugh of La Marche, Count 4–468a
Hugh of Lusignan
death 4–37a
Hugh of Lyons, Archbishop 1–312b
Hugh of Novocastro
Antichrist theology 1–322a
HUGH (PRIMAS) OF ORLÉANS 6–0
Hugh of Payns
Knights Templar 3–244b
Hugh of Pisa
conciliar theory 3–516b
Hugh of Rouen, Archbishop 4–375a
HUGH OF SAINT ALBANS 6–0
HUGH OF SAINT CHER 6–0; 1–462a; 2–36a
Albertus Magnus 1–127b
exegesis 2–22b; 4–544a, 546a
vulgate 4–246a
Hugh of Saint Pol, Count
Fourth Crusade 4–42a
Pseudo-Turpin Chronicle translations 3–331b

HUGH OF SAINT VICTOR 6–0; 1–188b; 3–167b
Adam of Saint Victor 1–51b
astrology 1–607b
Augustinian canons 1–659b
baptism 2–84a
biblical exegesis 2–213b, 224a; 4–543b-544a
Christology 3–322b
encyclopedias 4–448b, 577b
physics 2–241b
Hugh of Santalla 1–136b
HUGH OF SEMUR, SAINT 6–0
Cluny Abbey Church 3–468a, 469a
Rome 3–470a
Hugh of Strassburg 1–129a
Hugh of Troyes, Count
Champagne 3–244a
Hugh of Vermandois
crusades 4–34a,b, 36a
death 4–36b
Hugh Ripelin
Antichrist doctrine 1–321b
Hugh the Great of Burgundy, Duke 2–427a; 3–89b
Carolingian Empire 3–115a
Hugh the White
See Hugh the Great of Burgundy
HUGINN AND MUNINN 6–0
HUGO 6–0
Corpus iuris civilis 3–609b
Hugo de Porta Ravennate 2–417b
HUGOLINUS 6–0
HUGO OF BURY SAINT EDMUNDS 6–0
Hugo IV of Lusignan
Boccaccio 2–283b
HUGO VON MONTFORT 6–0
HUGO VON TRIMBERG 6–0
HUGUCCIO 6–0
conciliar theory 3–516b
summary of *Decretum* 4–127b
Hugues of Saint Cher
See Hugh of Saint Cher
HUGUET, JAIME 6–0
Huguet de Mataplana 3–164b
Hugutio of Pisa
encyclopedias 4–449b-450a
HULAGU 6–0
Alamūt 1–118b
Ayyubids 2–23b
Baghdad conquest (1258) 2–47a
Christian church in Persia 3–313a
Hulthem manuscript 4–321a
Hum 2–335a-336a,b, 338b, 339a,b, 340a
Humanism
astrology 1–609a
classical literary studies 3–430b
Humanum Genus
Castle of Perserverance 3–142b
Humber, England 4–454a-b
Humbert II 4–107b-108a, 109a,b, 110a
Humbert de La Tour du Pin 4–109a
Humbert de Miribel
Carthusians 3–118a
Humbert of Moyenmoutier 3–351a
Humbert of Romans
Albertus Magnus 1–128a,b
Dominicans 4–241b-242a, 245a, 254b
preaching 4–20b, 250a-b
HUMBERT OF SILVA CANDIDA 6–0
Donation of 4–258b
reforms 3–348b; 4–374a
schism Eastern-Western church 3–349a
Western councils 3–634b, 635a
Humbert of Vienne
crusade 4–55b
Humbert White Hands, Count 4–108b
Humphrey of Gloucester, Duke
biographies 3–328b
Humphreys, Bishop 2–72a
Hunaldo (Saint Columbanus) 3–486b
Ḥunayn, Battle of
Abū Bakr 1–24b
Abū Sufyān 1–29a
Ḥunayn ibn Isḥāq al-ʿIbādī 1–391b, 458a; 3–313a
Hundingsbani, Helgi 2–56b
HUNDRED (LAND DIVISION) **6–0**
Anglo-Saxon period 4–457b
constable, local 3–543b
court leet 3–659b
Englishry, presentment of 4–487a
Norman-Angevin period 4–464b
HUNDRED AND HUNDREDWEIGHT 6–0
Hundred Tales
See Decameron (Boccaccio)
HUNDRED YEARS WAR 6–0
Agincourt, Battle of 1–72a
Aquitaine 1–368a
Avignonese papacy 2–16a; 3–362b
bow and arrow/crossbow 2–352b
Brittany, Duchy of 2–380a
Bruges 2–387b
Burgundy, Duchy of 2–427b
cannon usage 3–65a,b-66a, 151b
cavalry 3–205a-206b
celibacy laws 3–217b
Champagne 3–250a
Charles of Orléans 3–272a
Charles V 3–269a
Charles VII 3–270a
Chartier, Alain 3–275a
chronicles, French 3–333a
Cistercian Order 3–405b
Clanvowe, Sir John 3–408a
Clement VI 3–439b
demographics 4–142a
Edward II 4–398a
Edward the Black Prince 4–398b
Enguerrand VII of Coucy 4–490b
parliament, English 4–484a
HUNGARIAN DIET 6–0
HUNGARIAN LANGUAGE 6–0
Latin alphabet 1–212b
HUNGARY 6–0
Andronikos I Komnenos 1–245a
Angevins 1–253b
animals, food and draft 1–293b, 296b, 298a, 299b-301b
archives 1–448b-449a
banat 2–70a
banus 2–82b
Bosnia 2–334b-340a
Bosnian church 2–342a
Buda 2–396b
Bulgaria 2–409a, 410a-b, 412b
Byzantine Empire 2–492b-493a, 494a, 504a
chivalric orders 3–306b
Croatia, 4–6b-8a
dictamen 4–176a
Dominicans 4–252b
Dubrovnik 4–300b
monasteries 2–172a
Mongol invasions 2–131b
Ottoman conquest 4–56a
Peasants' Crusade 4–34a
Hungary Water 2–147a
***HUNGRVAKA* 6–0**; 2–252a,b
Hunlaf, King
Romance of Horn (Master Thomas) 1–266b
HUNS 6–0
Alani 1–121a,b
arms and armor 1–522a; 2–352a
Austria 2–4b
Avars 2–12a
Burgundians 1–638a-639a; 2–92a, 422b
Byzantine Empire 2–485a,b
cavalry, Roman 3–201a
empire 2–92b-93a
Franks 2–92b, 94a
Vandals 2–91b
Hunter god of Lover 3–173b
Hunterston brooch 3–224a
HUNTING, IRANIAN 6–0
HUNTING AND FOWLING, ISLAMIC 6–0
dietary laws 4–179a,b
HUNTING AND FOWLING, WESTERN EUROPEAN 6–0
agriculture 1–299a
bow and arrow/crossbow 2–353a
Kievans 1–100a
laws 1–300b-301a
manuals 2–242b, 244b; 4–579a-b
Slavs 1–98b, 99b
Huntingdon
Treaties of Durham 4–316b
Huntington, Ellsworth
climatology 3–452b
Hunyadi, John 3–170a
crusades 4–56a
Hungary 2–8b
Huon de Bordeaux 3–259a
Huon III d'Oisi
Conon de Béthune 3–538b
Huosi family 1–422b
HURLEY, WILLIAM 6–0
Ḥurr ibn ʿAbd al-Raḥmān al-Thaqafī, al- 3–598a
Hurtere, Josse de
Azores 2–29b
Ḥurūf al-ghubār 1–389b
HUS, JOHN 6–0
Bohemian church 3–368a
ecclesiology 4–377a-b
execution 3–366a
heretical dissent 3–370a-b
Western councils 1–109a; 3–649b-650a, 652b
Husayn Bayqara
Afghanistan 1–65b
ḤUSAYN IBN ʿALĪ, AL- 6–0; 1–171b, 173b, 374a
descendants 1–174b, 175a-b
Ḥusayn ibn Manṣūr
See Ḥallāj, al-
Ḥusaynīya, Al- 3–15a
Husbandry 4–513b, 514a
Husband's Message, The 1–281a
Husdent
Tristan romance 1–266a
Hussite church 2–306a
HUSSITES 6–0
artillery tactic 3–65b
Bohemian Brethren 3–305b
military successes 2–304b-305a
Husting court 1–144a
Hyacinth, Saint
Dominicans 4–244a
Hylāj 1–619b
Hyle Historias (Nikephoros Bryennios) 1–303b-304a
HYLL, JOHN 6–0
Atherington screen 4–263a-b
Hylomorphism
Aquinas 1–358b-360b
Bacon 2–35b-36b

Hymiskviđa 4–386b, 390a,b, 391a,b
Hymn (Caedmon) 1–275b
Northumbrian dialect 1–276a
Hymn Against the Donatists (Saint Augustine) 4–63a
Hymns
hymnaries 4–224b
HYMNS, BYZANTINE 6–0; 2–468b-469a
Akathistos 1–114b
Ephrem, Saint 1–327a
Komitas 1–509a-b
HYMNS, LATIN 6–0
Ambrosian chant 1–232a
Ambrosiani 1–231a
HYNDLULJÓĐ 6–0; 4–387b, 390a,b, 391a,b
Hypatia 4–74b
HYPERPYRON 6–0
HYPOGEUM 6–0
Ałc 1–134a
Hypostasis
Basil the Great 2–121b
Hystoire de Julius Cesar (Jean de Thuim) 3–331b
HYWEL AB OWAIN GWYNEDD 6–0
Hywel ap Ieuaf 3–300a
Hywel Da
See Law, Welsh
Hywel Dda, King 4–329b
bards 2–106a
Chester treaty 3–300a

I

IACOPO DA LENTINI 6–0
Iago, King 3–299b-300a
Iamblichus, Bishop 2–4a
IAM OF ZWOLLE, MASTER 6–0
Iatrika (Theophanes Nonnos) 4–446b
Ibadism 1–374b
Ifrīqiya 1–70a
Ibāna 1–583a
Ibas of Edessa
Second Council of Constantinople (553) 3–630a
IBELIN, JEAN D' (OF BEIRUT) 6–0
IBELIN, JEAN D' (OF JAFFA) 6–0
Iberia
See Georgia: Geography
Iberian/Georgian March 2–140b
Iberian Peninsula
Andalusia 1–244a
Basques 2–126a
Black Death 2–263b
casbah 3–121a
Crónica general 1–161b
Islamic conquests (711) 1–625b
trade 4–557b
Ibiza 1–412a
Catalan language 3–157b
IBLĪS 6–0
Ibn
See next element of name
IBRĀHĪM IBN AL-AGHLAB 6–0
Aghlabids 1–70a
Ibrāhīm II 1–71b
Great Mosque of Qayrawān 1–69a
ʿIbrī, ibn al-
See Bar Hebraeus
Ibshīhī, al- 1–380b; 4–445a
Icart, Lluís 3–171a
Içe de Gebir 1–176a
ICELAND 6–0
bishops' sagas 1–537a; 2–252a
Black Death 2–261b
Bósa saga 2–333b
Codex Regius 4–385a
colonization 3–454a,b
Faereyinga saga 4–580b
family sagas 4–612a
Old English literature 1–274b
poetry 1–319b; 4–568b
settlement 4–402b
Vikings 4–554a,b-555a
Icelandic calendar 3–20b
Icelandic literature
Ála flekks saga 1–116b
Arthurian literature 1–572a
chansons de geste adaptations 3–258a
"Ich unde ein wip, wir haben gestriten" (Albrecht von Johansdorf) 1–132b
"Ich vant si ane huote" (Albrecht von Johansdorf) 1–132b
Icknield Way 4–454a
Icocedron (Walter of Odington) 1–138a
ICON, THEOLOGY OF 6–0
Iconium
See Ikonion
ICONOCLASM, CHRISTIAN 6–0
Alcuin of York 1–143a
Amorians 1–236a
Anatolia 1–241a
Bulgaria 2–402a
Byzantine church 2–462b-463a
Byzantine Empire 2–487b, 489a
caesaropapism 3–10b-11a
Constantine V 3–546a
Constantinople 3–555b, 556a
early Christian and Byzantine art and architecture 2–439a, 440a; 4–331a, 340a, 348a, 353b, 362b-363a
ecumenical councils 3–320b, 346b, 627b, 631a
Latin church 3–345a, 346a, 349a
ICONOCLASM, ISLAMIC 6–0; 3–53a
ICONODULE 6–0
ICONOGRAPHY 6–0
Anglo-Saxon 1–273a
arma Christi 1–469b
Armenian 1–495a-b, 502a
Ascension 1–580b
baptism of Christ 2–86b
Blachernitissa 2–256b
botany 2–346a, 348b
Brittany, Celtic 2–382b
Bulgarian 2–417a,b
Burāq 2–419b
Christogram 1–319b
Cilician 1–497b
Crucifixion 4–12b
early Christian 4–362b-363a
Ecce Homo 4–370a
evangelist symbols 4–526a
ICONOLOGY, ISLAMIC 6–0
ICONOSTASIS 6–0; 1–444a
chin 3–301a
Coptic and Ethiopian churches 1–157a
early Christian and Byzantine architecture 4–344a
ICONS, MANUFACTURE OF 6–0
art trade 1–561b
Basmenoye delo 2–125b
ICONS, RUSSIAN 6–0
Alempi 1–175b
Idalius, Bishop 2–102b
Ida of Austria
Crusade of 1101 4–36a,b
Ida of Louvain 2–13b
Ida of Saint Cecilia 1–316b
Iden, Alexander
Cade's Rebellion 3–5a
Ides 3–20b-21a
Idley, Peter
courtesy books 3–662a
IDRĪSĪ, AL- 6–0; 1–82b
Idrīs ibn ʿAbdullāh 1–174b
IDRISIDS 6–0
Abbasids 3–49a
Aghlabids 1–70a, 71a
founding 1–174b
Iewan 3–224a
Ifat 1–31b
Iffley Church
Anglo-Norman sculpture 1–256a
Ifor Hael 4–76a,b
IFRĪQIYA 6–0
Almohad empire 1–194a, 195a
Ibrāhīm ibn al-Aghlab 1–70a
trade routes 1–70b
IGNATIOS, PATRIARCH 6–0
Basil I the Macedonian 2–117b
Byzantine councils 3–631b-632a
Ignatius of Antioch, Saint
apostolic succession 1–350b
astrology 1–605a-b
postapostolic writing 3–334b
Iguácel 1–404b
IHRAM 6–0
Iḥṣā' al-ʿulūm (al-Fārābī) 4–445a
Iḥyā' ʿulūm al-dīn (al-Ghazālī) 4–445a-b
Ijmāʿ, concept 3–40a, 41a
Ikasia
See Kasia
Ikhshīd 4–405b
IKHSHIDIDS 6–0
Aleppo capture (936-937) 1–145a
Copts 3–594b
Damascus 4–81b, 82a
emirs 4–437a
Islamic Egypt 4–405b-406a
ʾIkhtiyārāt 1–619a
Ikhwān al-Ṣafā 4–445a
IKONION 6–0
Anatolia 1–241b
Byzantine Empire 2–493a
Seljukid sultanate 4–27b
William of Nevers 4–36b
IKONOPISNYI PODLINNIK 6–0
Iksīr, al- 1–141b
Ikskile
See Uxküll
ILARION 6–0
ILDEFONSUS, SAINT 6–0
biographical writing 2–239a
Ildenizids 1–514a; 2–27a
atabeg state 1–632a
ILDIGUIZID (ELDIGÜZ) **6–0**
Dwin 4–324b
Ilha das Garcas
slaves 4–561a
Ilias Latina (Pseudo-Pindarus Thebanus) 1–152b
Ili Valley
exploration 4–556b
ILKHANIDS 6–0
Ankara occupation 1–302b
Armenia 1–486a
Azerbaijan 2–27a
Erzincan 4–508b
"Ill-cut Coat, The" 1–268a
Ille et Galeron (Gautier d'Arras) 1–189a
Illegitimacy
apostolic datary 4–107a

ILLUGA SAGA GRÍÐARFÓSTRA 6–0
Illuminationism 1–656b, 660b
Illustribus Henricis, De (Capgrave) 3–90a
Illyria
Alaric as *magister militum* 1–122a
Bosnia 2–334b
Croatia 4–1b
Ostrogoth settlement 2–93a
prelates status 2–10a
ILLYRICUM 6–0
Byzantine Church 2–461b, 463a
dioceses 4–191b
'Ilm' aḥkām al-nujūm
See Astrology/Astronomy, Islamic
'Ilm al' aḥkām
See Astrology/Astronomy, Islamic
'Ilm al-falak
See Astrology/Astronomy, Islamic
'Ilm al-hay'ah
See Astrology/Astronomy, Islamic
'Ilm al-Ḥurūf (science of letters) 3–55a
'Ilm al-nujūm
See Astrology/Astronomy, Islamic
'Imād, ibn al-
biographies 2–238b
'IMĀD AL-DAWLA 6–0
Buyids 2–435b
'Imād al-Dīn Zangī (Zengī)
Aleppo 4–37a
Mosul 4–37a-b
Image of the World (Honorius Augustodunensis) 4–448a
Imagine Dei, De (Candidus Wizo) 3–64a
Imagine mundi, De (Augustodunensis) 1–610b
Imago Clipeatus
See Clipeus (Clipeatus)
Imago mundi (Pierre d'Ailly) 1–109a, 263b
***IMAGO PIETATIS* 6–0**; 1–469b
IMAM 6–0
Alids 1–175a
caliphate 3–46b
Shiite 1–171b, 173b
'Imāma 3–616b, 619b
Imamite Shiite sect
See Twelver Shiite sect
Imām Yaḥyā (shrine) 2–43b
IMĀMZĀDE 6–0
Imbach church 3–379a
Imereti kingdom 2–49a
Imerithia
See Georgia: Geography
Imitatio Jesucristi 3–168a
Imitation of Christ, The (Thomas à Kempis) 1–659b; 3–369a; 4–166b
Īmiyā', al-
See Alchemy, Islamic
Immanuel ben Solomon of Rome
exegesis 4–541b
Immersion, ascetic
Celtic mortifications 3–231b
Immortality of the Soul (Augustine) 1–648a, 656a
Immram 1–262a
Imotska *župas* 4–4a
IMPEACHMENT AND ATTAINDER 6–0
Imperator (title) 2–122b
IMPERIAL, FRANCISCO 6–0
Imperial art 4–353b-355b
Imperial Histories (Genesios) 3–547b
Imperial Palace at Constantinople 4–362b
Impilāyōt 3–619a
IMRU' AL-QAYS 6–0; 1–399a
Incarnatione Verbi, De (Anselm of Canterbury) 1–312b, 314b
Incarnation, feast of 4–497b
Incarnation of the Word, The (Anselm of Canterbury) 1–312b, 314b
Ince Hall Madonna (Jan van Eyck) 4–567a
INCENSE 6–0
Incomplete Work Against Julian (Augustine) 1–650b
Incunabula
dictamen 4–176b
In Déis 4–77a
Indexes
alphabetization 1–205b-206a
Index of Prohibited Books 1–76a
India
Arabic language 1–378b
Arabic numerals 1–382a
Bīrūnī 2–249a
fabliau 4–576a
Marco Polo 4–557a,b
routes 4–558a-b, 562a,b
sugar cane 1–81b
traveler accounts 1–332b
Indian Ocean
Bab al-Mandab 2–32a
exploration 4–562b, 563a
INDICTION 6–0; 3–18b
Indigo (*Indigofera tinctoria*) 4–325b
Indochina
Marco Polo 4–557a
INDO-EUROPEAN LANGUAGES, DEVELOPMENT OF 6–0
Armenian 1–506a-507b
Caucasia 3–195a
Celtic 3–232a
INDULGENCES 6–0
crusades 4–19a, 34a, 58b
Ine of Wessex, King 1–90b; 4–455a
Boniface, Saint 2–321a
Infancy Gospel of Thomas 1–347a
Infanta Leonora of Aragon 1–416b
Infantes de la Cerda 1–413b
Infanticide
Europe 4–599b
Infantry
arms and armor 1–531b; 3–209b
development 3–204b-206a
Infanzones 1–629b
Inferno (Dante) 3–197b; 4–94b, 95b, 97a, 98a,b, 99a, 100b, 101a, 102a-b, 103b
Bertran de Born 2–202a
Inflation
Castile 3–135a-b
Infortiatum 3–609b
Ingalawa
See Karkathiokerta
Ingelard of Saint Riquier 1–252a
Ingerina, Eudokia 2–118a
marriage 2–117a
Ingilenē, Armenia 1–472b, 515a
Ingjaldr of Naumdælafylki 1–310b
INGLÉS, JORGE 6–0
Inheritance
Jewish law 4–607a
INHERITANCE, BYZANTINE 6–0
Armenian 1–490a-b
family 4–594a, 595a-b
INHERITANCE, ISLAMIC 6–0
concubinage 3–527a
family 4–598b-599a
INHERITANCE, WESTERN EUROPEAN 6–0; 4–600b-601a
appanages 1–351a
borough-English 2–332a
Brittany, Celtic 2–382a
class structure 3–410b-411a
clerical celibacy 3–417b
consanguinity 3–539b
death and burial 1–120a
family 4–600b-601a
marriage 3–425b-426a
nobility 3–413a, 414a-b, 420b
peasant 3–415a, 424a-b
serfdom 3–424a-b
In I librum Sententiarum (Aquinas) 4–510a
Inishbofin
See Colman, Bishop of Lindisfarne
INITIALS, DECORATED AND HISTORIATED 6–0
Initiation
Cathar liturgy 3–181a
INK 6–0
In mulieres (Saint Columbanus) 3–486b
Inner Armenia
See Armenia: Geography
Innocent I, Pope
papal theory 3–341b
Pelagius 1–653A
Innocent II, Pope 1–17b, 330b
Abelard 1–18a
Anacletus II 3–637a
Arnold of Brescia 1–540a
Bernard of Clairvaux 2–191b
Consuetudines 3–118b
reform 3–352a
tournaments 3–638b
volume of business 3–353b
Western councils 3–636b-637a
INNOCENT III, POPE 6–0; 1–224b, 228a, 330a, 446a, 448a; 3–638a
Albigensian heresy 4–376a
anointing of kings 1–308b
Aragon, Crown of 1–410a-b, 411a
Bible 2–215a, 218b
Bohemia 2–300a
Boniface of Montferrat 2–323a
breviary 2–371b-372a
Brittany, Duchy 2–379a
Cathars 3–187a-188a, 189a,b
celibacy laws 3–216a
Celtic church 2–381b
Cistercians 3–405a
clerical dress 3–444b
commentaries 3–167a
Constantinople 1–334b
coronation 3–604b
Corpus iuris civilis 3–610a
Courson appointment 3–659a
crusades 2–497a; 3–247a, 405a; 4–16b, 20b, 41b, 42a, 43a, 44a,b, 49a-b, 58a-b
decretals 4–124a
dispensation 4–217a-b
Divine Office 4–231a
Dominicans 4–243b
Donation 4–259a
elections, church 3–265b; 4–423a, 424a,b
elections, royal 4–425b, 427b
excommunication 4–537b
"fullness of power" 3–353a
Kunigunde, Saint 3–68b
Leo I/II of Cilicia 3–391b
liturgical colors 3–484b
Norman-Angevin England 4–468b, 471b
papal documents 3–253b
power 3–353b
title of ordination 3–444a
vicar of Christ 4–374b
volume of business 3–353b
Western councils 3–639b-641a
INNOCENT IV, POPE 6–0; 1–501a; 2–7b; 4–71a
Albertus Magnus 1–127b
art 1–335b

Bosnian church 2–342a
Cathars 3–190a
College of Cardinals 3–94a
corporation 3–606a
crusades 4–31b, 59a-60a
Cyprian church 4–72b
Defensor pacis 4–132a
deposition of rulers 4–160a
diplomacy 4–209a
Dominicans 4–251b
Donation of Constantine 4–259a
elections, church 4–423b
Franciscans 3–645a
Louis IX 4–52b
Mongol aid 4–556b
papal bankers 2–76b
volume of business 3–353b
Western councils 3–641a
Innocent V, Pope 1–128a; 3–641b
Bonaventure, Saint 2–319a
Dominican studies 4–245b
Innocent VI, Pope
Avignonese papacy 3–362a
College of Cardinals 3–95b
conclave 3–524b
policies 1–130b-131a
Innocent VII, Pope
Bruni 2–390b-391a
Dominican laity 4–254b
Great Schism 3–365b, 645b
Innocent VIII, Pope
Africa exploration 4–562a
Innocentian-Anacletian schisms
See Schisms, Innocentian-Anacletian
INNS AND TAVERNS 6–0
Innsbruck
arms and armor 1–529a
INNS OF COURT 6–0
corporation 3–606b
INQUEST, CANONICAL AND FRENCH 6–0
INQUEST, ENGLISH 6–0; 4–464a, 470b
INQUISITION 6–0
Cathars 3–182a,b, 186a, 189b-190b
Converso 3–577b
Gregory IX 3–353b
Waldensians 3–370a
INSANITY, TREATMENT OF 6–0
Bedlam 2–157a
Inscribed cross plan 4–341a-b
Inscriptions
Arabic language 1–376b
bedouins 1–370b, 371a
Celtic 3–233a,b-234a
Insignia
basileus 2–123a-b
Insolentia Judaeorum, De 3–620b
Institutes
See Corpus iuris civilis
Institutes (John Cassian) 3–343a
Institutes of Polity (Wulfstan) 1–286a
Institutio canonicorum
Office of the Dead 4–117b
Institutione arithmetica, De (Boethius) 2–291b
Institutione morum, De 1–317a
Institutione musica, De (Boethius) 2–291b
Institutiones (John Cassian) 3–122b
Institutiones (Cassiodorus) 3–124a, 432b; 4–447b
Institutiones (Justinian)
Corpus iuris civilis 3–609a
Instruction of the Uneducated (Augustine) 1–655a
Instructions for Christians 1–281a
Instructions to His Son (Peter Idley) 3–662a
Instrumentation, surgical 2–99a
Instruments of the Passion
See Arma Christi
Instrumentum ex causa cambii 2–78a
Insular group
See Celtic languages
INTAGLIO 6–0
medieval collections 1–335a,b
INTARSIA 6–0
Integumenta Ovidii (John of Garland) 1–183b
Intercession, Church of the 2–293b
Intercultivation 1–80b
Interculture
See Polyculture
INTERDICT 6–0
Interest rates 2–73a-b, 81a-b
INTERLACE 6–0
Celtic art 3–220, 221a, 223a
Interlacing Arch
See Arch
Interlocucyon with an Argument betwyxt Man and Woman (Guillaume Alexis) 1–324b
International banking 2–76a-78b
International Relations
See Diplomacy
International Style, Gothic
See Gothic, International Style
Interpolated Quintus Curtius 1–149b
Interpretations of Hebrew Names 1–205b
Interrogatio Johannis 2–294b, 297b
Interrogationes 1–619a
Interrogationes Sigewulfi in Genesin (Aelfric) 1–285b
Inter sollicitudines 3–644b
Interstices 3–442b, 443a
Intervals, musical
Anonymous IV treatise 1–309b
Inthronizatio 3–604a
INTONACO 6–0
INTONATIO 6–0
INTRADOS 6–0
Introduction(Muḥammad ibn Mūsā al-Khwārizmī) 1–53b
Introductiones in Logicam (William of Sherwood) 4–170b
Introductiones prosaici dictaminis (Bernard of Bologna) 4–175a
Introduction to Astrology (Abū Ma'shar) 1–618b
Introduction to knowledge (al-Zamakhsharī) 4–44b, 444b
Introduction to knowledge
See Muqaddimat al-adab
Introductorium in astronomiam (Abū Ma'shar) 1–606b
Introductorius Liber qui et pulveris dicitus in mathematicam disciplinam 1–389a
INTROIT 6–0
antiphon 1–328b
Invasions, barbarian
See Barbarian Invasions
Inventione dialectica, De (Rodolphus Agricola) 4–171a
Investigatione perfectionis, De (Geber) 1–138a
INVESTITURE AND INVESTITURE CONTROVERSY 6–0
Alberic of Monte Cassino 1–125b
Anselm of Bec 4–466a-b
Babenbergs 2–6b
benefices 2–179a
Benzo of Alba 2–182b
Burgundy, County of 2–424b
Burgundy, Kingdom of 2–429a
caesaropapism 3–11b
Canossa 3–69a
cardinal's power 4–65b
church governance 3–352b
Congé d'élire 3–536b
ecclesiology 4–374a
elections, church 4–421a
history 2–197b
Western councils 3–634b-635a, 636b
Investments
European banking 2–73b, 75b
Invitatio amicae 3–58a
Invitatories 1–328b
Ioane, Bishop 2–164b
IOANNES LAURENTII LYDUS 6–0
Ioannina 4–499a
Ioasaph
See John Kantakouzenos
Ioland of Hungary 1–412a
IOLO GOCH 6–0
Dafydd ap Gwilym 4–77a
Iona
See Columba, Saint
Iona monastery 3–227b, 485a
Ionia 1–241a
Ipomedon (Hue de Rotelande) 1–266b
Ipswich
commune 3–499a, 501b
IQĀ' 6–0
IQALTO 6–0
'Iqd (Ibn 'Abd Rabbih) 4–445a
'Iqd al-farīd (Ibn 'Abd Rabbih) 1–380b
Iqṭā' 2–25a; 4–406a
Buyids 2–437a
Ira, De (Seneca) 2–40a
Iran, History: Before 650
See Sasanians
IRAN, HISTORY: AFTER 650 6–0
Abbasids 1–8b
Achaemenid Empire 3–195b
Aghkand ware 1–68a
Albania 1–123b
Arabic language 1–378a
Araks River 1–421b
Armenia 1–482b
art 1–5b
assassins 1–591b
Avesta of Zorastrianism 2–14a
Azerbaijan 2–25b
Barmakids 2–109b
Bishapur 2–251b
Buyids 2–435a
ceramics 3–238b, 240a
Christian church 3–312a
Crusades: Fourth 4–31b
Saffarids 1–64b
Turks 2–493a
Iranian architecture
eyvān 4–569b
IRANIAN LANGUAGES 6–0
Arabic loanwords 1–377a
IRANIAN LITERATURE 6–0
IRAQ 6–0
Abbasids 1–8a,b, 9a, 10a, 11a,b, 12a; 3–42a
'Abd Allāh 1–16a
Abū Bakr 1–25b
Baghdad 2–44b
Basra 2–127a
Buyids 2–435b, 436a
caliphate 3–42a, 50a-b
ceramics 3–239b
conquest 1–4b
dyes and dyeing 4–325b
exilarch 4–551b
Jewish family 4–606b, 607a,b
revolutionary movement 1–7a-b
Umayyads 3–39b

IRAQ (cont.)
Zanj slave rebellion 3–49a
Ireland
apocrypha 1–346b
butler 2–434b
classical literary studies 3–432b
coroner 3–605b
food animals 1–300a,b
IRELAND: EARLY HISTORY 6–0
Anglo Saxon literature 1–274b
Brigit, Saint 2–376a-377a
Celtic art 3–218a
Celtic church 3–225a
Celtic language 3–232b
Cinéal Eóghain 3–396b
Clonard 3–465b
Columba, Saint 3–465a
Columbanus, Saint 3–465b
Connacht 3–537a
Copts and Coptic church 3–595b
Cormac Mac Airt 3–601a
Cormac Mac Cuilennáin 3–601b
Dál Cais 4–77a
Dál Riata 1–60a; 4–77b
Dublin 4–298b-299a
Eóganacht 4–492b
Latin church organization 3–373b
missionaries 3–344a-b
Nicene-Constantinople Creed 3–676b
Stowe Missal 2–83b
Uí Néill power 1–60b
Vikings 4–554a
IRELAND: AFTER 1155 6–0
Burgh, de 2–421b-422a
Dublin 4–299a-b
Henry II of England 4–467a
Ireland, John
conciliar theory 3–520b
Irenaeus
angel/angelology 1–249b
apostolic succession 1–350b, 351a
Armenian Hellenizing School 1–505b
Christian doctrine 3–342a
evangelist symbols 4–526a
Gnosticism 3–335a
IRENE, EMPRESS 6–0; 1–303a; 2–463a; 3–110a
reign 2–488b
Irene Doukaina
Alexios I Komnenos 1–157b, 158b
Irene of Montferrat 2–499b
Irene Palaiologos
Bulgaria 2–410b
I'r Grawys (Elidir Sais) 4–431b
Irish alphabets 1–212b, 215a
Irish church
See Celtic church
Irish language
See Celtic languages
IRISH LITERATURE 6–0
Acallam na Senórach 1–33a
Aislinge meic Con-Glinne 1–113b
Arthurian literature 1–567a-b
Auraicept na nÉces 2–2a
Carolingian court 3–103a
Celtic languages 3–233a-b
Cormac Mac Cuilennáin 3–602a
darraðarljóð 4–106a
Dindshenchas 4–188b
IRISH LITERATURE: BARDIC POETRY 6–0; 2–105b, 107a
IRISH LITERATURE: HISTORICAL COMPOSITIONS 6–0
Bansenchas 2–82b
IRISH LITERATURE: RELIGIOUS 6–0
Airdena Brátha 1–111a
Bible glosses and commentaries 2–220a
Brigit, Saint 2–376b-377a
Duodecim, De 4–312a
IRISH LITERATURE: SAGA 6–0
IRISH LITERATURE: VOYAGE TALES 6–0
Espurgatoire Saint Patrice 4–509b
Voyage de Sainte Brendan 1–262a
Irish Missionaries
See Missions and Missionaries, Christian
IRISH SOCIETY 6–0
Irish whiskey 4–219b, 220a
Irminon of Saint Germain-des-Prés 4–511b
demography 4–137b
IRNERIUS 6–0; 4–501B
Bologna University 2–312a
Bulgarus 2–417b
Corpus iuris civilis 3–609b
Iron Age
Celtic art 3–218a
food animals 1–299a
Iron Arm
See Baldwin I of Flanders
Ironworking
charcoal 3–267b
IRREGANG UND GIRREGAR 6–0
IRRIGATION 6–0
cotton production 3–626b
Islamic 1–80b, 81a, 103b, 104a-b
Isaac, Rabbi Solomon ben
See Rashi (Rabbi Solomon ben Isaac)
Isaac Abu Ibrahim ibn Yashush
exegesis 4–539b
Isaac Alfasi
biblical exegesis 2–212a
Isaac Angelos
Andronikos I Komnenos 1–244a
ISAAC II ANGELOS 6–0; 1–251b
Boniface of Montferrat 2–323a
Bulgaria 2–407b-408a
Crusades: Fourth 4–46a
French chronicles 3–332a
reign 2–496a,b, 497a
Isaac ben Jacob Ha-Cohen
cabala 1–346a; 3–2a
Isaac ben Judah Abrabanel
exegesis 4–540a
ISAAC BEN MOSES ARAMA 6–0
Isaac ben Sid
time measurements 3–458a
Isaac ben Todros
cabala 3–1b-2a
Isaac I Doukas 4–263a
Isaac ibn Latif
cabala 3–2a
Isaac I Komnenos 1–157a
Byzantine throne 2–491b, 492b
Isaac Komnenos of Cyprus 4–70b
Andronikos I Komnenos 1–245a
Byzantine Empire 2–496b
Richard I 4–40b
Isaac Moḥeb ibn Ephraim
Córdoba 3–600b
Isaac of Stella
Cistercian sermons 3–405a
Isaac Saggi Nehor
cabala 3–1b
Isaac the Blind
See Isaac Saggi Nehor
Isabella, Abbess of Longchamp 2–316a
Isabella, Princess 4–25b
Isabella of Angoulême
John 4–468a
Isabella of Bavaria 3–270b
Isabella I of Castile 1–419a
Abrabanel 1–21b
Calatrava Order 1–17a
church reform 3–139b-140a
Columbus 1–56a; 4–560b
government 3–139a
Jews, explusion of 4–564b
marriage 3–138b
Isabella of France 4–397b
Edward II 4–475b, 483a-b
Edward III 4–398a
Isabella of Portugal 3–138a
portrait 4–566a
Isabelle, Blessed 2–270b
Isabelle of Valois 3–272b
Isabellian Style
See Plateresque Style
Isabel of Gloucester 4–468a
ʿIsā de Gebir
See Içe de Gebir
Isagoge (Boncompagno of Signa) 2–320b
Isagoge (Porphyry) 4–168b
Isagogen Porphyrii commenta, In (Boethius) 1–34b
Isaiah, Prophet
Annunciation 1–308a
Isaiah ben Elijah di Trani "the Younger"
exegesis 4–541b
ʿĪsā ibn Manṣūr
Córdoba 3–600a
Isak-Beg
Bosnia 2–338a,b
ISAPOSTOLOS 6–0
ISAURIANS 6–0
Isengrim the Wolf 2–140b, 141b, 142a
Isengrimus
See Ysengrimus
ISENMANN, CASPAR 6–0
Isère Valley 4–110a
Iseut aux Blanches Mains
Anglo-Norman romances 1–266a
ISFAHAN 6–0
Isḥāq 1–200b
Isḥāq ibn Ḥunayan 1–434b, 620a
Isḥāq ibn Muḥammad ibn ʿAlī ibn Yusuf ibn Ghāniya 1–200b
Ishmael ben Elisha
Jewish apocalyptic literature 1–344b
ʿIshrūn Maqālāt (Dāwūd ibn Marwān al-Muqammiṣ) 4–116b
Ishtar Gate
ceramics 3–238a
ISIDORE 6–0
ISIDORE OF SEVILLE, SAINT 6–0; 1–22a, 52a, 152b, 445b
acrostics 1–46a
Adoptionism 1–57b
allegory 1–188a
animal studies 2–242b, 243a
astronomy and astrology 1–606a, 610b
bestiary 2–204b-205a
Bible 2–211b, 212b
biographical writing 2–239a
botany 2–245a, 345a
Braulio of Saragossa, Saint 2–364b
Cassiodorus 3–124a
Christian theology 3–336b
Christology 3–321a
church father 3–334b
clergy 3–440b
deposition of rulers 4–158a
dialectic 4–169a
diaphonia 4–172a
Divine Office 4–222b, 229b
ecclesiology 4–372b
encyclopedias and dictionaries 4–447b, 448a, 449a, 577b
exegesis 2–216b; 4–542b
exempla 4–551a

Greek alphabet 1–217b
influence 2–2a
philosophy 2–241b
ISIDOROS OF MILETOS 6–0
Archimedes 1–434a
Constantinople 3–555b
Hagia Sophia 1–317a
"Isidorus Mercator"
False Decretals 4–124a, 128a, 373a
Iskenderun, Gulf of
Ayās 2–19a
Islam
agriculture and nutrition 1–103a-106b
Arabic poetry 3–400a-402b
banking 2–79a
cosmetics 2–147a
crusades 4–16a, 33b
ISLAM, CONQUESTS OF 6–0
Abu Bakr 1–25a-b
Afghanistan 1–64a-65a
Africa 1–199a, 200b
Arabic language 1–376a
Asturias-León 1–625b
Berbers 2–186a,b
Charles Martel 3–272a
Córdoba 3–598a-599b
Damascus 4–81b-82b
Egypt 4–403b
Futūḥ al-Buldān 2–54a
ISLAM, RELIGION 6–0
ʿAbbās, al- 1–4a
Adoptionism 1–57b
Albania 1–125a
Aleppo 1–145b
Allah 1–177a
Almoravids 1–198a-b
Armenian Saints 1–519a
Ascension of the Prophet 1–581a-b
Ashʿarī, al- 1–582b-585b
Badr, Battle of 2–43a
Bukhārī, al- 2–397b
Buyids 2–435b
calligraphy 3–52a-b
circumcision 3–400b
Damascus 4–84b-85a
Druzes 4–295b
Egypt 4–405a-b, 407a
Ethiopia 1–31a-b
food prohibitions 1–300a
Ismailis 1–590a
Latin church relations 3–355b-357a
Umayyad caliphate 3–40b
Islam, Sects
See Sects, Islamic
ISLAMIC ADMINISTRATION 6–0
Abbasids 1–6b; 3–44a,b-45a,b
agriculture and nutrition 1–81b
alms tax 1–201b
caliphate 3–32a, 34a-b, 40a-b, 45b-48b, 49a-b
Damascus 4–84a-b
diplomacy 4–197a
emirs 4–437a
Futūḥ al-Buldān 2–54a
Ghazni 1–65a
scribes 3–53b-54a
Islamic alchemy
See Alchemy, Islamic
ISLAMIC ARCHITECTURE 6–0
Abbasid 1–5a
ajímez 1–114b
Alhambra 1–168a
Almohad 1–191b
arch 1–423b
bāb 2–32a
Bādgīr 2–42a
Bādiya 2–42b
bay 2–140a
bedestan 2–156b
crusader art and architecture 4–22a
Dome of the Rock 4–237a
Egypt 4–408a
eyvān 4–569b
ISLAMIC ART 6–0
Abbasid 1–5a
Aghkand ware 1–68a
Alhambra 1–168a
Ayyubid 2–20b
Azulejo 2–30b
Badr al-Dīn 2–43b
barbotine 2–101a
Burāq 2–419b
ceramics 3–238a
Dome of the Rock 4–237a
Islamic astrolabes 1–602b, 603a-b
Islamic astrology 1–606b-607a
Islamic calendar 3–28a-b
ʿUmar ibn al Khaṭṭāb 3–34b
Islamic dietary laws
See Dietary laws, Islamic
Islamic law
See Law, Islamic
Island Magee
See Rinn Seimne
Íslendingabók 4–618a
Íslendingadrápa
See Haukr Valdísarson
Íslendinga sǫgur
See Family sagas, Icelandic
Isle of Man
Áedán 1–60a
Isle of Thanet 3–82a
Ismāʿīl ibn Jaʿfar al-Ṣdiq
Fatimids 1–175a
Ismailis 1–374b-376a
Ismailism
See Sects, Islamic
ISMĀʿĪLĪYA 6–0
assassins 1–589b-590b
Isopets
See Fables, French
ISORHYTHM 6–0
ars nova 1–551a-b
Isperikh
migration 2–399a-b
ISRAELI, ISAAC 6–0; 1–459b
Isrāfīl 1–248b
ISRAHEL VAN MECKENEM 6–0
engraving 4–488b-489a
Issus, Battle of 1–150b
Istanbul manuscripts
Arabic numerals 1–385b, 386a
Istanpitte 4–88a
Isṭōla 3–618b, 619a
Istria
Ravenna exarchate 4–529b
István V of Hungary
hunting laws 1–301a
IŠXANI 6–0; 1–488b, 490b
Isχan Isχanacʿ
See Archon ton Archonton
Italian architecture
Angelo Da Orvieto 1–251a
arches 1–423b
ITALIAN LANGUAGE 6–0
ars nova 1–552b
Bible translations 2–215b
chansons de geste 3–258a
Dante 4–95a, 100a-b
ITALIAN LITERATURE: ALLEGORICAL AND DIDACTIC 6–0
Dante 4–94a
ITALIAN LITERATURE: CHRONICLES 6–0; 3–330a
urban 3–328b
ITALIAN LITERATURE: DRAMA 6–0
ITALIAN LITERATURE: EPIC AND CHIVALRIC 6–0
Arthurian literature 1–572b-573a
ITALIAN LITERATURE: LYRIC POETRY 6–0
ars nova 1–550a-b, 552b-553a
Cecco Angiolieri 3–211b
Cino da Pistoia 3–397a
ITALIAN LITERATURE: POPULAR POETRY 6–0
ITALIAN LITERATURE: PROSE 6–0
Boccaccio 2–277b
ITALIAN LITERATURE: RELIGIOUS POETRY 6–0
Dante 4–96b-97a
ITALIAN LITERATURE: SERMONS 6–0
ITALIAN LITERATURE: THIRTEENTH-CENTURY POETRY 6–0
assonance 1–600b
Cavalcanti 3–196b
ITALIAN LITERATURE: VERSIFICATION AND PROSODY 6–0
Italian Renaissance
Augustinians 1–660a
Castilian language 3–142a
ITALIAN RENAISSANCE, BYZANTINE INFLUENCE ON 7–0
Italos, John
Alexios I 1–158b
Byzantine councils 3–632a
Italy
accounting 1–41a-42a
agriculture and nutrition 1–78a, 80a, 86a-87b, 95b; 3–626b
Alamanni settlement 2–94b
Alaric 1–122a
altarpieces 1–225b
Angevins 1–253b
Anglo-Norman architecture 1–256a
archives 1–448a
Balkans 4–3a
banking 1–41b; 2–72b, 74b, 76a-78b
barbarian invasions 2–88a
basilicas 2–124a
Byzantine church 2–461b, 463a
calendar 3–21a
canonical reform 3–355a
Cathars 3–181b
Celtic church 3–225b
ceramics 3–237b-238a
Christmas celebration 3–318a
classical literary studies 3–433a, 435a
conciliar theory 3–520b
crusades 4–27b, 31b, 51a
dance 4–88a-89b
dictamen 4–174b
dioceses 4–191b
distilled liquors 4–220a
draft animals 1–296a, 298a
Dugento art 4–304a
elections, church 4–424a
excommunication 4–538a
Gothic rule 3–123a
hairstyles 3–624a
Jewish exegesis 4–541b
Lombards 2–95a-96a
medical profession 2–98b
monasteries 2–172a
monasticism 3–343a
Norwegians 4–554b
papal vs. imperial allegiances 4–58a-b
pawnbroking 2–76a
population demographics 4–140a, 141b
time keeping 3–24b

ITALY, BYZANTINE AREAS OF 7–0; 2–95a
Bari 2–108b
exarchate 4–529b-530a
See Also Ravenna
ITALY, FOURTEENTH AND FIFTEENTH CENTURIES 7–0
Black Death 2–258b-260b; 4–142a
condottieri 3–531a
Dante 4–95b-104b
diplomacy 4–202b
exploration 4–557b, 558b-559a, 561b
slaves 2–268b, 269b
Italy, Muslims in
See Sicily, Islamic
Italy, Normans in
See Sicily, Kingdom of
ITALY, RISE OF TOWNS IN 7–0; 3–416b
commercial expansion 2–73a
communes 3–499a-500a, 502a, 503a
consuls 3–570b
fairs 4–583b, 585b, 587a
merchants 4–592b, 593a
Ita of Killeedy
Celtic monasteries 3–227b
ITE CHANT 7–0
Iter ad Paradisum 1–150a, 151a
Ithael 3–224a
IÐUNN 6–0
Itinerant justices
Norman-Angevin England 4–470b
Itinerarium (Baudri of Bourgueil) 2–132a
Itinerarium Burdigalense (Pilgrim of Bordeaux) 1–332a
***ITINERARIUM EGERIAE* 7–0**
Itinerarium einsidelense 1–333b, 336b
Itinerarium mentis in Deum (Saint Bonaventure) 2–315b-316a
Iudica Dei
See Ordeals
Ivajlo
Bulgaria 2–410b-411a
Īvān
See Eyvān
Ivanē Mχargrzeli
See Zak'arids
Ivanko
Bulgaria 2–408a
IVAN III OF MUSCOVY 7–0; 1–101b
art 4–192a
Byzantine church 2–470a
duma 4–306b
Ivan of Ochrid, Archbishop 2–407a
Ivanovo 2–417b
Ivan Rilski, Saint 2–417b
Ivar the Boneless 1–163b
***ÍVENS SAGA* 7–0;** 1–571b
Erex Saga 4–504b
Iviron Monastery 1–636b, 638a
IVO OF CHARTRES, SAINT 7–0
astrology 1–607a
Decretum 4–128b
dispensation 4–217a-b
Divine Office 4–230b
IVORY CARVING 7–0
Byzantine 2–454a-b, 457b-458a
Coptic 3–587b
Deesis 4–131b
diptych 4–214b
IVORY CARVING, ISLAMIC 7–0
Córdoba 3–599b
Ivory Coast 4–561b
Iwan
See Eyvān
Iwanē MXargrzeli
See Zak'arids
Iwein (Hartmann von Aue) 1–229b
Iyās, Ibn 4–407b
Izār 3–616b
Izmir
See Smyrna
Izmit
See Also Nicomedia
Iznik
See Nicaea
'Izz al-Dīn Abū 'L-Ḥasan 1–634a-b
'Izz al-Dīn Ma'sūd 1–635a

J

Jabala ibn-Sālim 2–50b
Jabal al-Alsun
See Caucasus Mountains
Jabal al-Qarn, Battle of (1159) 1–194a
Jābir 2–54a
Jābir Ibn Aflaḥ
Ptolemy 1–621a
Jābir ibn Ḥayyān
Islamic alchemy 1–136a, 139b
Jābiya, al- 4–83a
Jablanić, Raden 2–337b
Jabrids 2–51a
Jaca
James I 1–411b
Jacob, King
Chester, Treaty of 3–300a
Jacob al-Qirqisānī
exegesis 4–539b
Jacob and Joseph 2–221b
Jacob ben Asher
exegesis 4–540a
Jacob ben Jacob Ha-Cohen
cabala 3–2a
JACOB BEN MEIR (RABBENU TAM) **7–0**
Jacob ben Nissim
biblical exegesis 2–212b
Jacob ben Reuben ha-Sepharadi
exegesis 4–539b
Jacob ben Sheshet
cabala 3–1b
Jacob de Senleches
ars subtilior 1–558b
Jacobite alphabet 1–208a, 209a
Jacobite church
See Monophysitism
Jacob's Staff
See Cross-staff
Jacob's Well 3–572b
JACOBUS 7–0
Jacobus Cremonensis 1–439a,b
Jacobus de Cessolis 3–169a
Jacobus de Voragine
See Golden Legend
JACOBUS OF BOLOGNA 7–0
Jacobus of Liège
See Jacques de Liège
Jacob van Maerlant
Arthurian literature 1–572a
Jacomart Master
See Baçó, Jaime
Jacopo d'Avanzi
See Avanzo, Jacopo
Jacopo da Voragine
See Golden Legend
JACOPO DELLA QUERCIA 7–0
JACOPO DI CIONE 7–0
art trade 1–562b
JACOPO DI PIERO GUIDI 7–0
Jacopo Franchi, Rosello di
See Rosello di Jacopo Franchi
JACOPONE DA TODI 7–0
JACQUEMART D'HESDIN 7–0
JACQUERIE 7–0
Bruges 2–387b
Champagne 3–250a
Charles V of France 3–269b
Enguerrand VII of Coucy 4–491a
Jacques Coene
See Coene, Jacques
JACQUES COEUR 7–0
Jacques d' Amiens 1–189a; 3–672b
JACQUES DE BAERZE 7–0
Broederlam, Melchior 2–383a
Jacques de Bruges
Azores 4–559b
Jacques de Lalaing
Burgundy, Duchy of 2–428a
JACQUES DE LIÈGE 7–0; 1–542b, 544b, 545a
ars antiqua 1–548b
Jacques de Neuilly
Chartreuse de Champmol 4–186a
JACQUES DE VITRY 7–0; 1–455b
assassins 1–591a
beguines 2–158b
crusades 4–49b
exempla 4–551a
Jaén
Ferdinand III 3–134a
Ja'far al-Ṣādiq 1–175a
Ja'far ibn Khālid 2–110b
Ja'far ibn Muḥammad 1–175a
Jaffa
Baybars 2–138b
Louis IX 4–25b
JAGIEŁŁO DYNASTY 7–0
Jāhiliyya 3–52b
JĀḤIẒ, AL- 7–0
Arabic prose literature 1–379a,b
Islamic contraception 3–574b
Jahm ibn Ṣafwān
Ash'arī, al- 1–584a
Jahwarid family
Córdoba 3–600a
JAIL DELIVERY 7–0
assize 1–595a
Jaime I
See James the Conqueror
Jaime Baçó
See Baçó, Jaime
Jaime Ferrer the Elder
See Ferrer the Elder, Jaime
Jaime Serra
See Serra, Pedro and Jaime
Jajca 2–70a, 338b, 339b, 340a
Jajce
See Jajca
Jakemes
Châtelain de Coucy 3–277b
Jakov Svetoslav
Bulgaria 2–410a-b
Jalāl al-Dīn 1–634a, 635a
Dwin 4–324b
Jalāyirids 2–27a
Jālūt 2–185b
Jamal, al-
See Camel, Battle of
Jamāl al-Dawla ibn 'Ammār 2–44a
JAMB 7–0
James I
See James the Conqueror
James, Saint 2–13a
Compostela shrine 1–626b, 627a, 629b

liturgy 2–468a
See Also Santiago de Compostela
James II of Aragon 3–164b
Arnald of Villanova 1–537b
cortes 3–611a
James I of Cyprus 4–71a
James I of England
asylum system 1–632b
James of Majorca 1–413b, 414a
James III of Majorca 1–416a
James IV of Majorca 1–416b
James of Nisibis, Saint 1–520a
James I of Scotland
Eleonore of Austria 4–429a
James II of Scotland 4–393a
Edinburgh 4–393a
James IV of Scotland
Dunbar, William 4–307a
Edinburgh 4–393a
James of Urgell 1–417a,b
James of Venice 1–460b
JAMES OF VITERBO 7–0; 1–660a
Augustinians 1–660a
James the Conqueror 1–411a-413b; 3–168a
Barcelona 2–103b
Bible translations 2–215b
chronicles 3–165a-b
Code of Huesca 3–611b
consuls 3–571b
court 3–164b
inheritance laws 3–414a
Spain reconquest 1–161a
Valencia 1–190b
See Also Aragon, Crown of (1137-1479)
JAMES THE MONK (KOKKINOBAPHOS) **7–0**; 2–445a
James the Stewart of Scotland
Burgh, de 2–421b
Jāmi' al-bayān fī tafsīr al-Qur'ān (Muḥammad ibn Jarīr al-Ṭabar? 4–442b
Jāmi' al-Qāhira
See Azhar, al-
Jamīl 1–400b
Jancelin, Prior 3–118a
Jandun
See Jean de Jandun
Janiberg
Caffa siege 3–12a-b
JANISSARY 7–0
Jans Enikel
German biblical poetry 2–229a
Janus of Cyprus, King 4–71a
Japan
See Also Cipangu
Japhet ben Ali ha-Levi
exegesis 4–539b
Jarcha
See Kharja
JARĪR 7–0; 1–115a, 400a
***JARLMANNS SAGA OK HERMANNS* 7–0**
Jarrow Monastery 4–458b
Játiva 1–412a, 418a
Jaufré 1–575b; 3–164b, 173a
JAUFRE RUDEL 7–0
Jauhari, al- 4–444a
Jaume I of Catalonia
See James the Conqueror
Jaume II of Catalonia
See James II of Aragon
Jaume Sarroca 3–165a
Jawālīqī, al- 4–443b
Jawsaq al-Khāqānī, al- 1–5b
Jawzī, Ibn al- 1–380b
Jawziyyah, al-
Islamic alchemy 1–141b
JAXARTES 7–0
Jazīrat ibn 'Umar 2–43b
Ibn al-Athīr family 1–634a
JEAN, DREUX 7–0
JEAN, DUKE OF BERRY 7–0
book of hours 2–326b, 327a
manuscript collections 1–336a
patronage 2–145a; 4–295a
Jean à la Barbe 1–332b
Jean Boucicaut
See Boucicaut, Jean
Jean d'Acre, Saint 4–25b
JEAN (JEHAN) D'ANDELI 7–0
Jean de Beauce
See Texier, Jean
Jean de Béthencourt
Canaries 4–559a
JEAN DE BRIENNE 7–0
Jean I de Chalon-Arlay
Burgundy, County of 2–424b, 426a
JEAN (JEHAN) DE CHELLES 7–0
Jean de Griffemont 3–119a
JEAN DE JANDUN 7–0; 1–465a
Jean de Joinville
Louis, Saint 2–236a, 240a
Jean de la Loupe
See Le Loup, Jean
JEAN DE LIÈGE 7–0
Jean de Maisonneuve
Albertist school 1–129b
Jean de Marville
Chartreuse de Champmol 4–186a
JEAN DE MEUN (MEUNG) 7–0
allegory 1–183b, 184b-185a,b, 188b, 189a
beguines 2–159b
dialect 4–168a
L'art de chevalerie 3–302a
Romance of the Rose, The 1–324a
JEAN DE MIREMONT 7–0
Jean de Montreuil
Collège de Navarre 1–108a
Jean II de Nesle 2–276a
Jean de Palmis 1–37a
Jean de Paris
See John of Paris
JEAN DE RAVI 7–0
JEAN DES CHAMPS 7–0
Jean de Sy 2–219b
Bible 2–321a
JEAN DE THUIM 7–0
French chronicles 3–331b
Jean de Vitry
Burgundy, County of 2–426b
Jean D'Ibelin of Beirut
Assizes of Jerusalem 1–599a
Jean D'Ibelin of Jaffa and Ascalon, Count
Assizes of Jerusalem 1–598b-599a
Cyprus 4–70b-71a
JEAN D'ORBAIS 7–0
Jean "l'Antique" (or "le Sage")
Burgundy, County of 2–424b
Jean le Bon
manuscript collections 1–336a
JEAN LEMAIRE DE BELGES 7–0
Jean Le Meingre II
Boucicaut Master 2–349b
JEAN LE TAVERNIER 7–0
Jean le Teinturier) 1–188b
JEAN MICHEL 7–0
JEAN MIÉLOT 7–0
Jeanne de Penthièvre
Brittany, Duchy 2–380a
Jeanne of Burgundy
fables 4–573b
Jeanne of Champagne 3–249b
Jean Quidort
See John of Paris
JEAU D'ADAM 1–269b
Jechaburg, Thuringia 1–131b
Jehan
See Also Jean
Jehan de Brie 4–513a
Jehan de Brugis
See Bondol, Jean
Jehan de Chastelet 3–193b
Jehan de l'Escurel
See Jehannot de l'Escurel
JEHAN DES MURS 7–0; 1–437a-b, 542b
Alfonsine Tables canons 1–159b, 160a, 612b
ars nova 1–548a
calendars and reckoning of time 3–23a
Jehan et Blonde (Philippe de Beaumanoir) 2–145a
Jehannot de L'Escurel
ars antiqua 1–547a
ballade 2–59a
Jelena of Bosnia 2–337b
JELLING STYLE 7–0
Jem Sultan
Bāyazīd II 2–137a
Jerarchie (John Peckham) 1–264a
Jeremiah Monastery
Coptic architecture 3–586b
Jeremiel 1–249b
Jerez
commerce 4–558a
JEROME, SAINT 7–0
allegorical interpretations 1–188a
Antichrist doctrine 1–321b
Arnobius the Elder 1–539a
Augustine of Hippo 1–653a
bestiary 2–204a
Bible translation 2–211a
biographical writing 2–239a
Canon Table 3–66a
Catechetical School of Alexandria 3–594a
doctor of the church 4–234a
early church theology 3–336a, 342a
exegesis 2–224a
hagiography 2–236a
manuscript illumination 4–355b
psalters 4–223b
virginity 1–323a
vulgate 2–220a
Jerome of Ascoli
Bacon 2–35a-b
Bonaventure, Saint 2–319a
Jerome of Moravia
ars antiqua 1–544b
Dominican studies 4–247b
Jerome of Prague 3–649b, 652b
Jerónimo of Valencia 3–75b
JERUSALEM 7–0
Alexander the Great 1–150a,b
Antiochene rite 1–326b
Armenian church 1–504a
Ascension of the Prophet 1–581a
Baldwin I 2–58b
Byzantine church 2–462b
church of 2–460b-461a
Dome of the Rock 4–237a
early Christian and Byzantine architecture 4–332a, 335a
Easter rites 4–367a
Ethiopian monks 1–32a
exploration 4–553a-b
fairs 4–589a
Kāmil, al- 4–31b-32a
Muslims 4–50a
patriarchal see 3–340b, 346a
Saladin 4–31a

Jerusalem, Assizes of
See Assizes of Jerusalem
Jerusalem, Church of
Ambrosian chant 1–232b
Jerusalem, Entry into
See Entry into Jerusalem
Jerusalem, Kingdom of
See Crusades and Crusader States
Jeshuah ben Judah
exegesis 4–539b
Jesus College, Cambridge 3–59b
Jethro 4–296b
JEU 7–0
***JEU D'ADAM* 7–0**; 1–269b; 4–264a, 282b
***JEU DE LA FEUILLÉE, LE* (ADAM DE LA HALLE) 7–0**; 1–48b, 49a
***JEU DE ROBIN ET MARION, LE* (ADAM DE LA HALLE) 7–0**; 1–49a; 4–264a, 283b
Jeu de Saint Nicolas (Jean Bodel) 2–290b; 4–264a
Jeu du pèlerin, Le (Adam de la Halle) 1–48b
Jeu du Prince des Sots (Pierre Gringore) 4–265b
***JEU-PARTI* 7–0**; 4–122a
Jevington
Anglo-Norman sculpture 1–256a
Jeweled necklace, The (Ibn ʿAbd Rabbih) 4–445a
Jewelry
Celtic 3–219b, 220b, 221a, 222
European banking 2–75a-b
Sutton Hoo 1–274a
Jewish Antiquities (Josephus) 3–124a
JEWISH ART 7–0
Dura Europos 4–313a
Jewish calendar 3–24b-27a
JEWISH COMMUNAL SELF-GOVERNMENT: EUROPE 7–0
archives 1–446b
JEWISH COMMUNAL SELF-GOVERNMENT: ISLAM 7–0
Cairo Genizah 3–15b
Jewish dietary laws
See Dietary laws, Jewish
Jewish Gate 3–600b
Jewish Khazars
See Khazars, Jewish
Jewish literature
See Judeo-Arabic Literature
Jewish New Year 3–26b
Jewish Oath
See Oath More Judaico
Jewish Science
See Science, Jewish
Jews
anti-Semitism 1–338a; 4–34a
costume 3–618b
Easter edicts 4–366b
JEWS AND THE CATHOLIC CHURCH 7–0
Ashkenaz 1–586a
blood libel 2–276a
Ecclesia and Synagoga 4–371b
expulsions 4–564b
Western councils 3–641a
JEWS IN CHRISTIAN SPAIN 7–0
Aragon, Crown of 1–419b
converso 3–577b
Crescas 3–677b
expulsions 4–564b
massacres (1391) 3–137b
JEWS IN EGYPT 7–0
Alexandria 1–154b
JEWS IN EUROPE: BEFORE 900 7–0
pork prohibitions 1–300b
JEWS IN EUROPE: AFTER 900 7–0
Andrew of Saint Victor 1–244b
Ashkenaz 1–585b-586a
banking 2–76a, 80b
Benjamin of Tudela 2–181b
Black Death 3–439b, 481b
Clement VI 3–439b
Cologne 3–481b
crusades 3–481b; 4–34a
Exchequer 4–535a
expulsions 4–563b
merchants 4–555b
JEWS IN MUSLIM SPAIN 7–0
Córdoba 3–599b, 600a,b
JEWS IN NORTH AFRICA 7–0
JEWS IN RUSSIA 7–0
JEWS IN THE MIDDLE EAST 7–0
Arabia 1–370b, 375b
Babylonian captivity 2–33b
Baḥrayn 2–51a
Benjamin of Tudela 2–181b
Cairo Genizah 3–15a
exilarch 4–551b
JEWS IN THE PAPAL STATES 7–0
Jiawor 3–199a
JIHĀD 7–0
crusades 4–31a
diplomacy 4–197a, 198a, 201a
Islam 4–16a
JĪLĀNĪ, ʿABD AL-QĀDIR AL- 7–0
Jimémez de Cisneros, Cardinal
church reforms 3–368a
Jimena Díaz 3–73a, 74a
JINN 7–0
Jizya 3–594b
Joachim I of Brandenburg, King 2–362a
JOACHIM OF FIORE 7–0; 1–344a
Arnald of Villanova 1–537b
ecclesiology 4–375a
Franciscans 2–315a
Spirituals 3–369b
Western councils 3–640b
Joan, Perot 3–171b
Joan, Pope 2–287a
Joanica
See Kalojan
Joanna I
Avignon 2–15b
Joanna II
Angevins 1–253b
Joanna of Sicily, Queen 4–419b
Joanna the Mad of Spain 2–9a
Joannes de Nova Domo
See Jean de Maisonneuve
Joannes Fuldensis 1–422b
Joannot Martorell 1–420a
JOAN OF ARC, SAINT 7–0
Charles of Orléans 3–273a
Charles VII of France 3–271a
Chartier, Alain 3–275a
Ditié 3–317a
Orléans 3–150b
portrayal 4–265a
Joan of Navarre 4–593a
João de Santarem 4–561b
João Gonçalves Zarco
Madeiras 4–559a
Jobst of Moravia
Brandenburg 2–361b
Joca 1–404b, 405a, 407b
JOCELIN OF BRAKELOND 7–0
water clock 3–458b
Jochi 2–131a-b
Jocopo de' Barbari
bucentaur 2–395b
Jofre de Foixà 3–164b
Jogaila of Poland, King 2–67a
JOGLAR/JONGLEUR 7–0
chansonnier 3–255b
chansons de geste 3–259b
Cid legend 3–386b-389a
Johan, Pere 1–420a
Johanitsa
See John Asen II
JOHANNES ANDREAE 7–0
Durand 4–314b
Johannes Anglicus
See Langlois, Jean
JOHANNES CANAPARIUS 7–0
Johannes Ciconia
ars subtilior 1–558b
Johannes Dacus 1–218b
Johannes de Garlandia
consonance/dissonance 3–542a
JOHANNES DE GROCHEO 7–0
ars antiqua 1–545a
Johannes de Mirfeld
alphabetization 1–206a
Johannes de Muris
See Jehan des Murs
Johannes de Tinctoris 4–172a
Johannes de Tinemue 1–436a
Johannes Diaconus
See John the Deacon
JOHANNES HADLAUB 7–0
Johannes Henslini de Sitbor
See Johannes of Teplá
JOHANNES MONACHUS 7–0
Johannes Noviforensis
See Johannes of Středa
Johannes of Liège
See Jacques of Liège
Johannes of Neumarkt
See Johannes of Středa
JOHANNES OF SAINT ARNULF 7–0
JOHANNES OF SAINT PAUL IN ROME 7–0
JOHANNES OF SAINT VINCENT 7–0
Johannes of Středa 1–44b-45a
Johannes of Teplá 1–43b
Johannes Scholasticus
Apostolic Constitutions 1–350a
Johannes Scotus Erigena
See John Scottus Eriagena
Johannes Tauler
See Tauler, Johannes
JOHANNES TEUTONICUS 7–0; 1–127a,b; 4–245a
Azo 2–29a
conciliar theory 3–516a
decretum 4–127b
Johannes von Frankenstein
poetry 2–231a
Johann Geiler von Kaysersberg
Brant, Sebastian 2–364a
Johannitius of Baghdad
See Isḥāq al-ʿIbādī, Hunayn ibn
Johann Ulrich Surgant
ars praedicandi 1–556b
JOHANN VON WÜRZBURG 7–0
John XVI, Antipope 1–330b
John I, Pope 1–454b
John VIII, Pope
Byzantine church 2–463b, 465a
crusade propaganda 4–18b
Methodios, Saint 4–73b, 74a
John X, Pope
Croatia 4–4b
Tomislav 4–5a
John XI, Pope
Cluny order 3–470a
John XV, Pope 1–13a
John XIX, Pope
Cluny order 3–470a
John, Abbot 2–153b

John, Antipope 1–330a
JOHN, KING OF ENGLAND 7–0; 4–420a, 468a-469a,b, 471a-b
anti-Semitism 2–81a
archives 1–448b
Bordeaux 2–328a,b
Brittany, Duchy 2–380a
Burgh, de 2–421b
coronation 1–35b
Damietta 4–50b
deposition 4–160b
elections, church 4–423a
Fifth Crusade 4–49b
Langton 3–83b
Normandy 2–330b-331a
Philip II 1–367b
John IV, Pope
Easter 3–465b
JOHN XXI, POPE 7–0; 1–463b
conclave 3–524a
JOHN XXII, POPE 7–0; 1–13b; 2–1a; 4–103a
alchemy 1–137b
Angelus 1–252b
annate 1–304b
anointing of kings 1–308b
ars nova 1–548b
Avignonese papacy 3–362a-363b
Ayās rebuilding 2–19a
beguines 2–161b
Cambridge University 3–59a
Cilician-Roman church union 3–395a
college of cardinals 3–94a
Corpus Christi feast 3–608a
crusades 4–55b
curial staff 3–363b
Dominicans 4–253a
Donation of Constantine 4–259a
Durand, Guillaume 4–313b
ecclesiology 4–376b-377a
Edward II 4–475b
elections, royal 4–428b
Franciscans 2–163a
Italian policies 1–131a
Louis of Bavaria 3–515a
Marsilius of Padua 4–132a
Western councils 3–645a,b
John XXIII, Pope 1–330b; 2–8b
Bruni 2–391a
deposition 3–648b
Great Schism 3–366a
Western councils 3–647a-649b
John, Prester 1–32b
John, Saint, Basilica of 4–494b
John, Tzurillas
heresy 2–295b
John (Ivan) Alexander of Bulgaria 2–412b
art and architecture 2–417b
JOHN ASEN I (ASEN) **7–0**; 2–407b-408a
JOHN ASEN II 7–0; 2–408b-409b, 410a
Bogomils 2–295a
Byzantine Empire 2–498b
John Asen III 2–410b-411a
John Bekkos, Patriarch 2–465b
John Busch
Brethren of the Common Life 2–366b
John Cassian, Saint 2–13b
JOHN CHRYSOSTOM, SAINT 7–0; 1–653b
Antiochene homilies 1–327a
Armenian literature 1–507b
Armenian rite 1–516b
Ascension Feast 1–582a
bestiary 2–204a
Burgundio of Pisa 2–423b
Cassian 3–122a
Christian dogma 3–336a
Christmas 3–318a
Copts and Coptic church 3–595a
Cyril of Alexandria 4–74b
Divine Office 4–229b
doctor of the church 4–234a
eucharistic canon 2–468a
ornamented works 2–456b
patriarchy 2–461b
salvation theory 3–342a
veneration 2–459a
John Climacus of Sinai 2–442b
John Damascene, Saint 2–13a
John de Baliol 4–396a
John de Montfort 2–380a
John de Stratford, Archbishop
death 2–262a
John Duns Scotus
See Duns Scotus, John
John Geometres 2–506b, 524a
John Gerson
See Gerson, John
John Grammaticus
See Philoponus, John
JOHN GUALBERTI, SAINT 7–0
John Hemerken of Kempen
Brethren of the Common Life 2–367b
JOHN HUNYADI 7–0
JOHN ITALOS 7–0
John XIV Kalekas
Barlaam of Calabria 2–109b
John Kameniates 2–516a
John Kananos 2–517a
John Kantakouzenos
Byzantine throne 2–500b-501b
JOHN VI KANTAKOUZENOS 7–0; 4–135b
history 2–516b, 518a
holdings 2–479b
reign 2–501b
theological works 2–450b
JOHN KINNAMOS 7–0
history 2–515a
JOHN KLIMAKOS 7–0
JOHN II KOMNENOS 7–0; 4–93a
mausoleum 2–443b
patronage 2–522b-523a
reign 2–493b, 494a-b, 495a-b
John Kukuzelis 2–511b
John Kurkuas 2–490a
John Lackland, King
See John, King of England
John IV Laskaris
Arsenius Autorianus 1–560b
Byzantine throne 2–499a
John Lydus
See Ioannes Laurentii Lydus
John Major
Arthurian literature 1–565b
conciliar theory 3–519b, 520b
John Malalas of Antioch 2–512a-b
John Mauropous 2–507a, 511b, 524a
John of Acre, Saint 2–18a
JOHN OF AFFLIGHEM 7–0
Cistercian chant 3–402b
John of Antioch 2–512b
John of Antioch, Archbishop
Cyril of Alexandria, Saint 3–629a; 4–75a
John I of Aragon 1–417a; 3–168b, 170b
John II of Aragon 1–418b
John of Avis 3–137b
See John I of Portugal
John of Avranches
Divine Office 4–223a
John of Bavaria, Count 4–566a
John of Bohemia, King 2–8a, 300b
John I of Brandenburg 2–360b
John of Brienne, King of Jerusalem
Bulgaria 2–409b
Fifth Crusade 4–31b, 50a
John I of Brittany, Duke 2–380a
John II of Brittany, Duke 2–380a
John IV of Brittany, Duke 2–380a-b
Charles V 3–270a
John of Bromyard
florilegia 1–317b
John I of Brunswick, Duke 2–199a
John of Canterbury
Anglo-Norman chronicles 1–265b
JOHN OF CAPESTRANO 7–0
preaching missions 3–368a
John of Cappadocia
Corpus iuris civilis 3–608b
John I of Castile 3–137b
John II of Castile 3–138a
taxation 3–612a
John II of Cyprus 4–71a
JOHN OF DAMASCUS, SAINT 7–0; 1–458a; 2–524b
astrology 1–606a
Balavariani 2–54b
Burgundio of Pisa 2–423b
Christology 3–320b, 323a
church father 3–334b
Dialectica 4–170b
doctor of the church 4–234a-b
icons 2–463a
incarnation doctrine 3–631a
kanōn 2–511b
theology 2–466a,b; 3–336b
veneration 2–459a
John I of Denmark
Nordic union 4–156a
John of Dražice, Bishop 2–304a
JOHN OF EPHESUS 7–0
Nubian Christianity 3–314b
John of Epiphaneia 2–512b
John of Falkenberg 3–649b
John II of Flanders 2–30a
John Offord, Archbishop
death 2–262a
John of Fordun 4–392b-393a
John II of France 4–398a, 399a
capture 4–490b
Champagne 3–250a
Charles V 3–269a
John of Freiberg 1–129a, 206a
John of Fruttaria 2–174a
John of Gaddesden
contraception 3–572a
John of Gaèta
See Gelasius II, Pope
JOHN OF GARLAND 7–0; 1–183b
ars antiqua 1–543b, 544b-545b
ars poetica 1–554a
consonance/dissonance 3–542a
courtoisie 1–268b-269a
motet manuscripts 1–545a-b
musical teaching 1–309b
poetry 1–255a
JOHN OF GAUNT 7–0; 4–399a, 473a, 476a, 477b
Castilian throne 3–137b
Chaucer, Geoffrey 3–281a,b
Clanvowe, Sir John 3–408a
John of Gmunden
University of Vienna 1–613b
John of Holywood 3–539a
JOHN OF HOWDEN (HOVEDEN) **7–0**; 1–262b
poetry 1–255a
John of Jandun
See Jean de Jandun
John of Jenštejn, Archbishop 2–304b
John of Jerusalem 1–518b

John of Joinville
assassins 1–591a
chronicles 3–332b
John of La Rochelle 1–461b
Bonaventure, Saint 2–313a
John of Lichtenberg 1–129a-b
John of Lignères
Alfonsine Tables 1–159b, 160a, 612b
John of Lugio 3–184a,b
John of Luxemburg
See John of Bohemia
John of Monte Corvino 3–642a
Cilician-Roman church union 3–394b
John of Murs
See Jehan des Murs
John of Naples
Angevins 1–253b
John of Neumarkt
dictamen 4–176a
JOHN OF NIKIU 7–0
JOHN OF ŌJUN, SAINT 7–0; 1–480b, 481b, 482a
John of Palermo 1–438b
JOHN OF PARIS 7–0; 1–465a
Antichrist theology 1–322a
conciliar theory 3–517a, 518a, 521a
deposition, papal 4–483b
ecclesiology 4–376a,b
Engelbert of Admont 4–451b
John of Parma
Bonaventure, Saint 2–315a, 316b
JOHN OF PLANO CARPINI 7–0
Mongols 4–556b
John I of Portugal, King 3–137b
Aviz, Order of 2–17a
election 3–611b
John II of Portugal 1–21b
Columbus 4–559b-560a,b
Ethiopia 1–32b
exploration 4–562a-b
John of Ragusa
Basel council 3–651b
conciliar theory 3–512b
John of Ridewall 1–183b
John of Rila
Bulgaria 2–405b
John of Rupescissa
alchemy 1–138a
John of Sacrobosco 1–396a
astronomy manuals 1–612a
John of Saint Albans
Dominicans 4–245a
JOHN OF SALISBURY 7–0; 1–17b, 52a
Adrian IV 1–58b
antifeminism 1–323a, 324a
Arnold of Brescia 1–539b
astrology 1–607a
Bernard of Chartres 2–189b, 190a
Bernard of Clairvaux 2–191b
classical literary studies 3–434a,b
dialetic 4–170a
dualism 4–298a
Norman-Angevin England 4–471b
Policraticus 4–159b
John of Saxony
Alphonsine Tables 1–160a, 612b
John of Segovia
conciliar theory 3–515b
John of Seville 1–388a, 389a
astronomy 1–611a, 612a
John of Sicily
astronomy 1–612b
JOHN OF S. MARTÍN DE ALBARES 7–0
John II of Thessaly, Lord
Almogávares mercenaries 1–191a
John of Trani
eucharistic food 2–31b
John of Trevisa 3–325a, 329b
John of Turrecremata
conciliar theory 3–519b, 520b
John of Urtubia
Thebes 3–156b-157a
John of Vercelli 1–129a; 4–242a, 245a
John of Vicenza 4–250a
John of Viktring 3–405a
John of Wales 3–167b
JOHN V PALAIOLOGOS 7–0; 2–501a; 4–56a, 135b
Byzantine church 2–465b
ivory 2–457b
land holdings 2–481a
reign 2–501b-502b
John VII Palaiologos
Constantinople 2–502b, 503b
ivory 2–458a
JOHN VIII PALAIOLOGOS 7–0
church schism 2–465b-466a
reign 2–503b-504a
John Peckham
See Peckham, John
John Philophonos of Alexandria
astrolabe 1–603a
John Quidort
See John of Paris
John Rellach of Constance
Dominican theology 4–246a
JOHN SCOTTUS ERIUGENA 7–0; 1–228b
Alan of Lille 1–119b-120a
angel/angelology 1–250b
Biel, Gabriel 2–234a
Carolingians 3–103a
Christology 3–322a
dualism 4–297b
eucharist 2–188a
exegesis 2–213a, 224a; 4–542b
Periphyseon 4–169b
John Šišman 2–412b
John Stefan of Bulgaria 2–412a-b
John Studios, Saint, basilica 4–337b
John the Alchemist Hohenzollern 2–362a
John the Archpriest 1–136a
John the Baptist, Saint 2–86b
angel/angelology 1–249b
crucifixion image 4–12b
relics 1–518a
JOHN THE DEACON 7–0
Boethius 2–292a
John the Exarch
Bulgaria 2–404a
JOHN IV THE FASTER, PATRIARCH 7–0; 4–383a
Byzantine church 2–461a
charistikion 3–268a
clergy 3–447a
John the Fearless, Duke of Burgundy 2–427a
Cabochien riots 3–4a
Charles VII 3–270b
John the Grammarian
See Philoponus, John
John the Kat'ołikos
See John of Ōjun, Saint
John the Lydian 2–512b
John the Mild of Holstein 4–155a
John the Orphanotrophos
Byzantine throne 2–492a
John the Scribe
cartulary 2–73a
JOHN I TZIMISKES 7–0; 1–482b, 483b; 2–118b, 490a,b
Antioch 2–455a
Ašot III Ołormac 1–589b
Bardas Phokas 2–106b
Bardas Skleros 2–106b
Bulgaria 2–406a-b
Mount Athos monasteries 1–636b
sarcophagus 2–455b
John Tztezes 2–508a, 524b
JOHN III VATATZES 7–0
imports 2–457a
reign 2–498b
Tzamblakoi 2–479b
John Vladislav 2–407a
JOHN XIPHILINUS 7–0
Byzantine throne 2–492a
education 3–556b
JOINVILLE, JOHN OF 7–0
Champagne, County 3–245b
***JÓMSVIKINGA SAGA* 7–0**; 2–256a,b; 4–411a
Jonah Abū'l Walīd Merwān ibn Janāḥ
exegesis 4–539b
Jonas Fragment
See French language
JONAS OF ORLÉANS 7–0; 3–112a
Jongleur
See Joglar/Jongleur
Jón Halldórsson, Bishop 2–252a
Jón of Hólar, Saint 2–252B
JÓN ÖGMUNDARSON, SAINT 7–0
***JONS SAGA HELGA* 7–0**; 2–252a,b
Jónsson, Brand 1–151b
Jónsson of Hólar, Brandr, Bishop 1–152a
Joost de Hurtere
Azores 4–559b
JOOS VAN GHENT (VAN WASSENHOVE) 7–0
Ducal chamber 2–198a
JORDANES 7–0; 1–638a
Æsir 1–62b
JORDAN FANTOSME 7–0
JORDAN OF OSNABRÜCK 7–0
JORDAN OF QUEDLINBURG 7–0
Jordan of Saxony 1–127a
Dominican chant 4–240a
Dominican rite 4–241b
Dominicans' expansion 4–245a
mysticism 4–248a
Jordan River
baptism of Christ 2–86b
Jordanus de Nemore 1–436a, 438b
JORDI DE S. JORDI 7–0; 3–167a, 169b
Jordi Johan 1–420a
Jorge Inglés
See Inglés, Jorge
Josaphat
See Barlaam and Josaphat
Joscelin III of Edessa
Nūr al-Dīn 4–38b
Joscius of Tyre
Third Crusade 4–40a
JOSEPH II, PATRIARCH 7–0
church schism 2–465b-466a
Joseph Albo
biblical exegesis 2–212b
JOSEPH BEN ABRAHAM AL-BAṢIR 7–0
Joseph ben Isaac Bekhor Shor 2–212b; 4–541a
Joseph ben Isaac ibn Abitor 4–539b
Joseph ben Jacob ibn Ẓaddik 4–540a
JOSEPH BEN JUDAH BEN JACOB IBN 'AQNIN 7–0
Joseph della Reina
apocalyptic literature 1–346b
cabala 3–3a
JOSEPH IBN CASPI 7–0
JOSEPH IBN SADDIQ 7–0
Joseph Kara 2–212b

Joseph of Arimathea
deposition from the Cross 4–157a
Holy Grail tradition 1–134a
Seinte Resureccion 1–270a
Joseph of Exeter
See Josephus Iscanus
Joseph of Ḥamadan
cabala 3–2a,b
Joseph of Ireland 1–142b, 143a
Joseph of Pahn
Eznik of Kołb 4–571a
Joseph the Hymnographer 2–511b
Josephus, Flavius 1–152b
Josephus Iscanus
epic 4–496a
Josephus Scotus
acrostics 1–46a
JOSHUA ROLL 7–0; 2–454a
JOSHUA THE STYLITE 7–0
Josiane, Princess 1–267a
Jostice et Plet, Livre de
See Livres de Jostice et de Plet
JOURNAL 7–0
Jours of Troyes 3–249b, 250a
Jousting
See Games and Pastimes
Jouy, Guiard de 2–144a
Jovian, Emperor 1–476a
Aršak II 1–560a
Jovinus 1–121a
JOY, WILLIAM 7–0
Juana, Queen 1–418b
JUAN AND SIMON DE COLONIA 7–0
Juana of Castile 3–138b
JUAN DE BURGOS 7–0
JUAN DE FLANDES 7–0
Juan de Torquemada
Birgitta, Saint 2–247a
Dominican theology 4–248a
Juan Gil de Zamora
dictamen 4–175b
Juan-juan
See Abar/Apar
Juan Lobeira
Amadís de Gaula 1–227b
Juan Lorenzo de Astorga 1–152b
Juan I of Aragon
See John I of Aragon
Juan II of Aragon
See John II of Aragon
Juan of Trastámara 1–416b
Juan Rexach
See Rexach, Juan
Jubail (Gibelet) 4–22b
Jubail (Gibelet) Castle 4–22b
Jubayr, Ibn
fairs 4–588b-589a
Jubbā'ī, al-
Ash'arī, al- 1–582b
Jube
See Screen
JUBILEE 7–0
JUBILUS 7–0
Jubinal, Achille 1–271a
Júcar River 1–83b
Juchil, King 3–300b
Judah ben Elijah Hadassi 4–539b
JUDAH BEN SAMUEL HE-HASID 7–0
Judah ben Samuel ibn Bal'am 4–539b
JUDAH HALEVI 7–0
Judah ibn Tibbon 1–23a
Judah of Barcelona 1–387b
Judah the Pietist 4–420b
JUDAISM 7–0
Alexander romances 1–151a
astrology 1–605a-606b
Bible 2–210b, 212a
Iraqi 3–16a
Judāla tribe 1–198a,b
Judas of Jerusalem, Bishop
Helena, Saint 1–336b-337a
Judenhut 3–620b, 624a
JUDEO-ARABIC LANGUAGE 7–0
Cairo Genizah documents 3–16a
JUDEO-ARABIC LITERATURE 7–0
apocalyptic 1–344a
Baḥya ben Joseph 2–51a
JUDEO-FRENCH 7–0
Judeo-German
See Yiddish
JUDEO-GREEK 7–0
JUDEO-ITALIAN 7–0
JUDEO-LATIN 7–0
JUDEO-PERSIAN 7–0
JUDEO-PROVENÇAL 7–0
JUDEO-SPANISH 7–0
alphabet 1–208a
biblical exegesis 2–212a
Judeus, John, Bishop 3–185b
Judezmo
Hebrew alphabet 1–208a
Judgement Day II, The 1–277a
Judgment of Cambyses (Gerard David) 4–114b-115a
Judicael of Domnonia
Dagobert 2–378b
Judicia (al-Manṣur) 1–606b
Judiciary
decretum 4–129a
Judiciis astrorum, De (Aquinas) 1–607b
Judiciis nativitatum, De (Alī al-Khaiyāṭ) 1–606b
Judith 2–184a
English Bible 2–221b
Nowell Codex 1–280a
Jugement d'amour 1–268b
Juges-mages
assize 1–595b
dauphinal authority 4–109b
Juglares 4–63a
Juliana (Cynewulf) 1–278a, 279b
Juliana, Saint
Anglo-Norman life of 1–261b
Juliana of Liège, Saint
Corpus Christi feast 3–608a
Dominicans 4–248a
Julian calendar 3–18a-24b
Julianists sect 4–524b
Julian of Eclanum, Bishop
Augustine of Hippo 1–650a, 652b, 653b
Julian of Nobadia, Bishop
Nubian Christianity 3–314b
JULIAN OF NORWICH 7–0
Latin church 3–368b
Julian of Toledo, Saint 1–264a
JULIAN THE APOSTATE 7–0; 1–117a
Apollinarius 1–348a
Athanasius of Alexandria 1–633a
Frankish allies 2–94a
Persian campaign (363) 1–235b
reign 2–485a
JULIANUS OF TOLEDO 7–0
JULIANUS OF TOLEDO 7–19b
Julius I, Pope 1–454a
Apollinarius 1–348a
papal theory 3–341b
Julius II, Pope
conciliar theory 3–519a, 520a
coronation 3–605a
councils 3–655a
Jumièges Cathedral
architecture 1–255b
corbel table 3–597b
Jummal al-kabīr, al- 1–386b, 387a
Jummal aṣ-ṣaghīr, al- 1–386b, 387a
JUNAYD 7–0
Jund
revolts 1–70a-b, 71b, 72a
Jüngere Cambridger Liedersammlung, Die 1–319a
Jüngere Judith 2–227b
Jüngerer Titurel (Albrecht von Scharfenberg) 1–133b-134a
Junius, Franciscus 1–287a
Junius Bassus sarcophagus 4–350b, 357a,b
Junius manuscript 1–277a, 279b
Junqueres Convent 2–104a
Jurane Burgundy 2–428b
Jure electionis novorum prelatorum, De (William of Mandagout) 4–422b
Jureregni apud Scotos, De (George Buchanan) 3–522a
Jurés
See Échevins
JURY 7–0
assize 1–596b
Clarendon assize 3–409a
court leet 3–659b
Justianic Code
See Corpus iuris civilis
JUSTICES ITINERANT (IN EYRE) **7–0**
assize 1–594b, 595a, 598a
court of common pleas 3–491b
Normans 2–53a
JUSTICES OF COMMON PLEAS 7–0
court of common pleas 3–491b
JUSTICES OF THE KING'S BENCH 7–0
assize 1–595b, 598a
JUSTICES OF THE PEACE 7–0
assize 1–595b
constable, local 3–543a
JUSTICIAR 7–0
Justin I, Emperor 1–32a
Arians 1–454b
Justin II, Emperor 1–477a; 2–12b
consular title 3–18a
Great Palace of Constantinople 3–553a
Nicene-Constantinopolitan Creed 3–676b
Justina, Empress
Ambrose, Saint 1–231a
JUSTINIAN I 7–0; 1–32a, 422a, 454b
Africa 2–165a
Alani 1–121a
Anatolia 1–239b
Antioch rebuilding 1–325b, 326a
Armenia 1–473a, 477a-b, 515b
art 4–348a, 353a, 354a,b
astrology 1–606a
authority 3–343b
blasphemy 2–272a
bureaucracy 2–472b
Burgundio of Pisa 2–423b
caesaropapism 3–10b
calendar dating 3–18a
cataphracti 3–179b
celibacy laws 3–215b
church architecture 4–338a-339b
church-state relations 2–459a
classical literary studies 3–431a
Constantinople 3–551b
Corpus juris civilis 2–57a, 115a-b, 117b; 3–608b
dioceses 4–191b
dunatoi 4–307a
election of bishops 3–446a
empire restoration 2–95a

JUSTINIAN I (cont.)
Ephesus 4–494b
Great Palace of Constantinople 3–552b
Histories 1–67b
Italy 3–631b
Monophysitism 2–462a
Ostrogoths 2–94a
poetry 2–523b
public building projects 4–334a
Ravenna bishops 1–73a
reign 2–486a-b
Second Council of Constantinople (553) 3–630a
JUSTINIAN II 7–0; 1–479a
Armenian church 1–500a
Bulgaria 2–401a
Constantine IV 3–546a
Synod of Trullo (692) 3–630b
Justinianic Code
See Corpus iuris civilis
Justinian's Church of the Holy Apostles
architecture 3–379a
Justin Martyr
Christian theology 3–339a, 342a
defense of Christians 3–335a
Jutes
Canterbury 3–81a-b
family 4–599b
invasions 2–97a
Kent settlement 4–452b
literature 1–274a
origins and migration 1–289a
Juthungi tribe 1–117a
Jutland
Angles 2–96b
Danish exploration 4–554a
Germans 2–88a
Goths 2–90a
Juvenal of Jerusalem 2–461a; 3–629b
Juvencus 4–496a
Juwaynī, al-
Ashʿarī, al- 1–585a
Juzayy, ibn
Baṭṭūṭa, Ibn 2–130a
Jūzjānī 4–445b

K

KAABA 7–0; 1–16a
Arabia 1–373a
Ascension of the Prophet 1–581a
KABALA 7–0
Kaballarika themata
See Cavalry, Byzantine
Kaballarios
See Cavalry, Byzantine
KABA OF ZOROASTER 7–0
Kabbalah
See Cabala
Kabj, al-
See Caucasus Mountains
Kabk, al-
See Caucasus Mountains
Kabkh, al-
See Caucasus Mountains
Kabul 1–65b
Kabulistan 1–64a
Kadisiya, Battle of (635) 3–488a
Kāfkōh
See Caucasus Mountains
Kaftan
See Caftan
Kāfūr, Abū ʾl-Misk 4–405b
Kaherdin 1–266a
Kāhin 1–617a
K'aifeng
Jewish community 3–619b-620a
Kai-Khusraw I of Iconium
Cilicia 3–391b
K'ai-p'ing-fu
See Chandu
Kairouan
See Qayrawān
***KAISERCHRONIK* 7–0**
Annolied 1–306a
Kaǰberunids 1–423a
Kakheti
See Georgia: Geography
Kakhet Kingdom 2–49a
Kalām dialectic 4–116b
Kaleb, Emperor 1–32a
Kalend 3–20b
Kalenda maya 4–87b
Kalenderhane Camii church 4–344b
restoration 2–447a
Kalenić Monastery 2–450a; 4–347b
Kalgha 3–679b
Kali
See Rugs and Carpets
Kalīla wa-Dimna 1–106b, 379a; 3–31b
Kalliergis 2–450a
Kallikan, Ibn
See Khallikan, Ibn
Kallistos, Patriarch
death 2–502a
Kalmuck tribe 3–195a
Kalocsa 4–7a
Bosnian church 2–336a
KALOJAN 7–0
art and architecture 2–416a, 417a
Balkans 2–498a
reign 2–408a-b
KALONYMUS FAMILY 7–0
Kalwādhā 2–45a
Kamah
See Ani in Daranałik'
Kamariotissa Church 4–341b
Kamasarakan lords
Ani in Širak 1–290b
Kamaχ
See Ani in Daranałik'
Kamelaukion 3–615a
KAMENNAYA BABA 7–0
Kāmil, al-, Sultan 2–24a, 25a
Fourth Crusade 4–31b-32a
Kāmil fī al-Taʾrīkh (ʿIzz al-Dīn) 1–634b
KAMKHA 7–0
Kammerknechtschaft
See Servi camerae regis
KAMSARAKAN 7–0
Ayrarat principality 2–20a
church 1–493b
Kanobos
election 4–47a
***KANŌN* 7–0**
Byzantine 2–511a-b
canticle 3–84b
KANTAKOUZENOI 7–0
agricultural losses 1–78b
Byzantine Empire 2–500b-501b
holdings 2–479b
Kantakouzenos, John 1–246b
Kantara affair 4–72b-73a
Kantara fort 4–70b
Kanz al-Dawla 3–315a
Kapaḷak
See Qabala
Kapan Čoray
See Derbent
Kara, Joseph
exegesis 4–540b
Karabaş Kilise Church 3–92b
KARAGÖZ FIGURES 7–0
Karahisar plain
fair 4–589b
KARAITES 7–0
Cairo Genizah materials 3–16a
exegesis 2–212a; 4–539a-b
inheritance 4–607a
monogamy 4–606b
KARAJĪ, AL- 7–0
KARAKHANIDS 7–0
Bukhara 2–397a
Karakorum
Mongols 4–556b
Karamān
Bāyazīd I 2–136b
KARAMANIA 7–0; 1–352a
Basra 2–127a
Caesarea 3–9b
See Also Baḥrayn, Al-
KARA MUḤAMMAD 7–0
KARA QOYUNLU 7–0
Kara Su River 4–508b, 522a
KARA YUSUF 7–0
Karel de Grote
See Charlemagne
Karel ende Elegast 4–318b
KARGAH 7–0
KARIN (KARNOY K'AŁAK') 1–450b, 473a,b, 474a, 476a, 483b
Armenian Council 1–500a
Armenian Muslim emirates 1–512b, 513a
Erzincan 4–508b
Kariye Camii
See Kariye Djami
KARIYE DJAMI (CAMII), CONSTANTINOPLE **7–0**
Anastasis representation 1–239a
Annuciation 1–308a
Apocalypse illustration 1–344a
mosaics 2–449b-450a
paintings 2–449b, 451a, 457b
Theodore Metochites 2–449a-b, 450a
tomb sculptures 2–448b
Karkathiokerta 1–515a
Karkatʿiakert
See Karkathiokerta
Karkh 2–45b, 46a
***KARLAMAGNÚS SAGA* 7–0**; 3–258a
Karlmann of Bavaria, King 3–114a
KARLMEINET 7–0
KARLSKRÖNIKAN 7–0
Karmrawor, Saint, Church of 1–601b
***KĀRNAMAG I ARDEŠIR Ī PĀPAKĀN* 7–0**; 1–451b-452a
Karoussie church 4–359b
Karramiya
Afghanistan 1–65a-b
Karr wa ʾl-farr, al- 3–203b, 209b
KARS 7–0; 1–450b, 482b; 2–48b
sack (1064) 2–493a
KARTIR 7–0
Kartli
See Georgia: Geography
See Gurgeni of Iberia
K'ART'LIS C'XOVREBA 7–0
Karts
Herat 1–65a
K'asał
Aštarak 1–601a
KASHI 7–0

Kasia 2–511b
Kaspars von der Roen Heldenbuch
See Dresdener Heldenbuch
KASTORIA 7–0
Katarchai 1–619a
KATEPANO 7–0
Katharinenkirche
Brunsberg, H(e)inrich von 2–392b
KATHERINE GROUP 7–0
KATHOLIKON 7–0; 4–333b
Katholikon Church
architecture 3–379a
KATHOLIKOS 7–0; 4–552a
Albania 1–123b
Armenian church 1–501b, 502b-503a
Katʿołikos Anastas
calendar reform 1–238a
Katʿołikos Sahak the Parthian
See Sahak, Saint
Katranideh of Armenia, Queen
Ani Cathedral 1–291b
Katze, Die (Hartmann von Aue) 1–230a
Katzheimer, Lorenz 4–490a
Kaukasos
See Caucasus Mountains
Kauleas Church 4–343a
Kavkaz
See Caucasus Mountains
Kawkaz
See Caucasus Mountains
KAYKHOSRAW I 7–0
Kaysanid sect 1–174b
Kaysaniyya sect 1–173b
Kayseri
See Caesarea
Kazan
destruction 3–679b
fairs 4–587b
Kazbek, Mount 3–196a
Kecharitomene Convent
Anna Komnena 1–303b
KEDRENOS, GEORGIOS 7–0
Keep
See Dungeon
Kefe
See Caffa
KEKAUMENOS 7–0
akritai 1–116a
Kelheim 2–134b
Kelim
See Kilim
Kellia 1–637b; 4–333b
KELLS, BOOK OF 7–0; 3–221a, 223a,b
KEMPE, MARGERY (BURNHAM) **7–0**
businesses 4–603b
Kempis, Thomas á
Devotio Moderna 1–659b
religious communities 3–369a
KENNETH I MACALPIN 7–0; 4–78b
Kenneth of Aghaboe
See Cainnech of Aghaboe
Kenneth II of Scotland
Chester, Treaty of 3–299b-300a
KENNING 7–0
Kent
Anglo-Saxon 4–452b-453b, 455b
barbarian invasions 2–96b
Black Death 2–262b
Danelaw 1–164a
Old English texts 1–276a,b
KENTIGERN, SAINT 7–0
Kentish Psalm 1–280a
Kerak (Al-Karak) Castle 2–113a; 4–24b
Kerbogha of Mosul 2–309a
Kerkyra
Guiscard 1–158a
Roger II of Sicily 2–494a
Kermes 4–326b, 327b
Keroularios, Michael, Patriarch
Eastern-Western church schism 3–349a, 556a
Kęstutis of Lithuania, Grand Duke 2–67a
Ketilsobók 4–403b
***KETILS SAGA HÆNGS* 7–0**; 1–310b
Keyser, Konrad 1–318a
Keys to writings According to the Tradition of the Ancients 4–368a
Khabur River 2–43b
Khadīja 1–15a, 171b
Khaḍrāʾ, al-, Palace 3–37a
Damascus 4–83a
Khaghan Bayan 2–12b
Khaibar 1–4b
Khalaf al-Aḥmar 1–27b
KHALDŪN, IBN 7–0; 1–382a; 4–407b
alchemy 1–141b
astrology 1–618b
Baṭṭūṭa, Ibn 2–131a
Berbers 2–185b, 186a
commander of the faithful 3–488b
number systems 1–384b-385b
Khālid, Muḥammad ibn
Ašot I Mec 1–588a
KHALID IBN AL-WALĪD 7–0
Abū Bakr 1–373b
Khālid ibn Barmak 2–109b-110a
Khālid ibn Yazīd, Prince
alchemy 1–136a, 141a
Khalīfa
See Caliphate
Khalīl ibn Aḥmad, al- 4–443b-444a
astrology 1–617b
KHALLIKĀN, IBN 7–0
al-Athīr, ibn, family 1–634a-635a
biographies 2–238b
Khamekhia 1–123b
KHAN 7–0
KHANAGAH 7–0
Khanate of Crimea
See Crimea, Khanate of
Khandaq (moat) 3–678a
Khandaq, Al-, Battle of
See Trench, Battle of
Khandaq Tahir canal 2–45a
Khan Omortag 1–298a
Khānqāhs 4–407a, 408a
Khans of Crimea
See Crimea, Khanate of
Kharāj 1–194b
Copts and Coptic church 3–594b
Khārijites 1–16a
Abbasids 3–46a, 47a
ʿAlī 1–173a,b; 3–35a-b
Baḥrayn, al- 2–50b
Berbers 2–186a,b
caliphate 3–38a,b, 39a
commander of the faithful 3–488b
Ibadism 1–374b
poetry 1–400a
Sijilmass principality 1–641a
Umayyads 1–374a; 3–41a-b
***KHARJA* 7–0**
Kharjas
cantigas de amor 3–87a
Khātam an-nabiyyīn 1–178a
Khatchkʿars
See Xačʿkʿar
KHAṬĪB AL-BAGHDĀDĪ, AL- 7–0
biographies 2–237b, 238b
Khātima, Ibn
plague 2–264b
Khaṭṭ 3–51b
Khaṭṭ al-mansūb 2–135b-136a
Khaṭṭ al-raml 1–385a
Khawada Nameh
See Xwadāy Nāmag
Khawārij
See Kharijites
Khayl
See Cavalry, Islamic
Khazars
See Russian Nomads, Invasions of
KHAZARS, JEWISH 7–0
Cairo Genizah 3–16a
KHILʾA 7–0; 3–620b
Islamic costume 3–618a
Khilāfa
See Caliphate
Khilendar Monastery 1–79a, 637a
Khirokhitia, Battle of (1426) 4–71a
Khitān
See Islamic circumcision
Khludov Psalter 4–13a-b
Khorāsān 1–63b
Abbasids 1–7a-b, 8a, 9b, 10a-b; 3–41b, 49a
Alptigin 1–219b
Faḍl, al- 2–110b-111a
Khorezmian warriors
Latin Kingdom of Jerusalem 4–32a
Khosrau I of Persia
murder 1–66a
Khosrau II of Persia
Armenian church 1–499b
Khounni
See Huns
Khtachkʿar
See Xačʿkʿar
Khuff 3–616b
Khuld, al-, Palace 2–45b, 46a
KHURDADHBIH, IBN 7–0
merchants 4–555b
Khushdāshīya 3–399b
Khushqadam 3–400a
Khutsuri script 1–214b
Khuzāʿa
ʿAbd al-Muṭṭalib 1–15a
Khwārizmī, al- 1–383a
Zīj 1–611b
Khwārizmshāh Jalāl al-Dīn
Azerbaijan 2–27a
KHWARIZMSHAHS 7–0
Afghanistan 1–65a
KIBLA 7–0
Kiddush ha-Shem
See Martyrdom, Jewish
Kierzy Council (838) 1–75b
Kiestut
See Kęstutis
Kiev
Alexis of Moscow 1–159a
Byzantine church 2–464a
cathedrals 4–341a
fairs 4–587b-588a
Mongol invasions 1–100b; 2–131b
Varangians 4–555a
KIEVAN RUS 7–0
Kildare
See Cell-dara
Brigit, Saint 2–376a
Kilfenora, County Clare
stone monuments 3–223a
Kılıçlar Kilise 3–92a
Kilij Arslan, Sultan
First Crusade 4–30a, 34a-b, 35a
Kilij Arslan II
Byzantine Empire 2–495b
Danishmendids 4–93a
KILIM 7–0
Killarney
Eóganacht Locha Léin 3–121a
Killis, ibn 2–28a

KILWARDBY, ROBERT (CANTUAR) **7–0**; 1–461b, 463b
alphabetization 1–207a
ars antiqua 1–544a
Augustinism 1–660b
Bacon 2–35b
Canterbury 3–83b
Dominican theology 4–246b
indexes 1–206a
Kimḥi family
exegesis 4–541a-b
Kindah confederation 1–371b
Kindheit Jesu, Die (Konrad von Fusesbrunnen) 2–228b
KINDĪ, AL- 7–0; 1–458b
Arnald of Villanova 1–538a
Kingdom of Lesser Armenia
See Cilician Kingdom
King Horn 2–60b
King in Council 4–502b
King in Parliament 4–502b
***KINGIS QUAIR* 7–0**
King Mark and the Blond Iseut (Chrétien de Troyes) 3–308b
King Robert of Sicily 4–287b
King Saladin and Hugh of Tiberias (Hein van Aken) 4–319a
King's Bench, court of
creation 4–470a-b
equity 4–502a-b
King's Chapel at Clarendon
tiled pavements 3–237a
King's College, Cambridge 3–59b, 263b
KING'S EVIL (FRANCE AND ENGLAND) **7–0**
King's Hall, Royal College of 3–59b
Kingship
Anglo-Saxon laws 1–286a
Armenia 1–489a,b-490a
German 2–88b-89a
KINGSHIP (CORONATION), **RITUALS 7–0**
butler 2–434b
KINGSHIP, THEORIES OF: WESTERN EUROPE 7–0
anointing 1–308a
deposition 4–157b
Disputatio inter clericum et militem 4–218a
Egidius Colonna 4–400b
elective vs. hereditary principle 1–630a-b
English 4–473a-479b
equity 4–502a-b
King's Lynn
Black Death 2–261b
Kings' sagas 4–402b, 612b, 617b-618a
King's Summa, The 1–263a
Kingston upon Hull
charter (1440) 2–331b
Kinsai
Marco Polo 4–557a
Kinship
See articles under Family
KIOSK 7–0
KIOT 7–0
Kipchak 3–680a
Baybars al-Bunduqdārī 2–138a
Kirakos Arewelc'i
Synaxarion 1–521a
KIRAKOS OF GANJAK 7–0; 1–486a
KIRGIZ 7–0
Kirkburn
Anglo-Norman sculpture 1–256a
Kirmiz
See Qirmiz
Kirovabad
See Ganjak
Kisa' 1–172a
Kislev 3–26b
KISWA 7–0
Kitāb al-aḍdād (Ibn al-Sikkīt) 4–443b
Kitāb al-Aghānī 2–44a
Kitāb al-'ain (al-Khalīl ibn Aḥmad) 4–443b-444a
Kitāb al-alfāẓ (Ibn al-Sikkīt) 4–443a
Kitāb al-asṭurlāb (Kūshyār ibn Labbān) 1–385b
Kitab al-burhān (Eutychios) 4–525b
Kitāb al-filāḥa al nabaṭīya (Ibn Waḥshīya) 1–106a
Kitāb al-filāḥa al-rūmīya 1–106a
Kitāb al-imtā' wa'l-mu'ānasa (Abū Hayyān al-Tawḥīdī) 1–381a
Kitāb al-i'tibār (Usāma ibn Munqidh) 1–381a
Kitāb al-Jamhara (Ibn Durayd) 4–444a
Kitāb al-jīm (Abū 'Amr al-Shaybānī) 4–442b
Kitāb al-khalq al-insān (al-Aṣma'ī) 4–443a
Kitāb al-madkhal 'ilm'aḥkām al-nujūm (Abū Ma'shar) 1–618b
Kitāb al-mālidī ('Ali ibn al-'Abbas) 3–548b
Kitāb al-muṣannaf (Abū 'Ubayd) 4–443a
Kitāb al-Muwashshā 1–401a
Kitāb al-Shifā' (Ibn Sīnā) 1–136b
KITAB-KHANA 7–0
Kitāb segobiano (Içe de Gebir) 1–176a
Kitchens
European cookery 3–583a
Kivorii
See Darokhranitelnitsa
Kiwrakos Vardapet
Armenian Saints 1–520a
Kiwrikē I of Armenia 1–484b
Kiwrion of Georgia, Katholikos 1–499b
excommunication 1–499b
Kizil Arslan
Dwin 4–324b
***KJALNESINGA SAGA* 7–0**; 4–613b
Kjustendil
See Velbužd
Klage, Die (Hartmann van Aue) 1–230a
Klappvisier 1–526b, 527a
Klara Hätzlerin
See Hätzlerin, Klara
***KLÁRA SAGA* 7–0**; 4–289b
Kleidion, Battle of (1014) 2–119a
KLEIMO 7–0
Klešić, Pavle 2–338a
Kleterologion (Philotheos) 4–447a
KLIROS 7–0
Klokotnica, Battle of (1230) 2–409b
Klosterneuburg Monastery 1–448b
Knapdale family 3–407a
Knaresborough Forest
charcoal burning 3–267b
Kneecops 1–524b, 525b, 534a,b
Kneer, August
conciliar theory 3–514b
Knez Lazar
See Lazar Hrebel janović
Knight-banneret
See Banneret
Knight in the Panther Skin
See Shot'a Rustaveli
Knighton, Henry
Black Death 2–265a
KNIGHTS AND KNIGHT SERVICE 7–0; 1–523a
Ambraser Heldenbuch 1–229b
Ami et Amile 1–234a
Anglo-Norman *courtoisie* 1–268b
assize 1–595a, 598a
banneret 2–82a
baron 2–111b
cavalry 3–200a, 209a
chivalry 3–301b, 303b
Cilician kingdom 3–393b
class structure 3–412a-b, 413a, 414a-b, 419b, 420b, 421a
courtesy books 3–666b
Cyprus 4–72a
der von Kürenberg 4–161a
horse breeding 1–295a
See Also Azat
Knights Hospitalers
See Hospitalers, Knights
Knights of Alcántara 3–306b
Knights' sagas
See Riddarasögur
Knights Templar 2–1a; 3–244b
See Templars
KNIK'HAWADOY 7–0
Knin 4–4a
Knitting
See Textiles; Wool
Knollys, Sir Robert
expedition to France 3–408a
Know Thyself
See Ethica
KNUD LAVARD 7–0
***KNÝTLINGA SAGA* 7–0**
KOERBECKE, JOHANN 7–0
Kofman, Christofal
Cancionero General printing 3–63a
Kogovit 2–48a
Koh-i-nuh Mount
See Ararat, Mount
KOIMESIS 7–0
Koimesis Church 3–378a
Kokcha River 1–65a
KOKOSHNIK 7–0
Kolbítr 1–310b
KOLLEMA 7–0
KOLLESIS 7–0
Koloman I of Bulgaria 2–409b
Koloman II of Bulgaria 2–410a
Koloman of Hungary, King 4–7a-b, 8a
Kołt' 1–123b
Komitas 1–509a-b
Komnena, Anna 3–203a
Komnenian revolt (1081)
Alexiad 1–304a
KOMNENOI 7–0
agriculture and nutrition 1–79b
Alexios I of Trebizond 1–159a
Anatolia 1–241b
art 2–443b-446a, 447a, 457a
Byzantine Empire 2–493b-495a,b, 498a
Cyprus 4–70b
literature 2–509a, 521b-522a, 523b
KONÂK 7–0
KÖNIG LAURIN 7–0
***KÖNIG ROTHER* 7–0**; 4–304b-305a
Königsburg im Neumark 2–392b
Koninc Ermenrîkes Dôt
See Ermenrîkes Dôt
Konjic 2–339a
Konrad Fleck
See Fleck, Konrad
Konradins
Arnulf 3–114b
Konrad of Masovia 2–66b
Konrad von Heimesfurt
poetry 2–228b
KONRAD VON SOEST 7–0
KONRAD VON STOFFELN 7–0
KONRAD VON WÜRZBURG 7–0
Bussard, Der 2–434a

KONRÁÐS SAGA KEISARASONAR **7–0**
KONTAKION 7–0; 2–510b, 524b
Akathistos 1–114b
Asmatikon 1–586b
KONTSOVKA 7–0
Konunga sǫgur
See Kings' sagas
Konya
See Ikonion
KORAN 7–0
Aghlabid art 1–69b
Aghlabid doctrine 1–71a
ʿA'isha 1–113b
Allah 1–177a
alms tax 1–201b, 202a
Arabic alphabet 1–209a,b
Arabic language 1–377a
Ascension of the Prophet 1–581a
Ashʿarī, al- 1–583a-584a
Badr, Battle of 2–43a
Bible tales 2–214b-215a
blood money 2–276b
Bukhārī, al- 2–398b
calligraphy 3–52a-53a
concubinage 3–527a-b
contraception 3–573a, 575A
family 4–597a
Jewish dietary laws 4–178b
paradise 1–170b
Peter the Venerable 3–356b
Sacred Law 1–373b
umma concept 3–32b
ʿUthmān 3–35a
Korčēkʿ 1–472b
Korezmian Turks
Jerusalem 4–52b
KORIKOS 7–0
Korium 1–66b
KORIWN 7–0; 1–114a, 491b
Armenian church 1–498b
Armenian literature 1–508a
Armenian saints 1–518b
Bible translation 2–217a
Eznik of Kołb 4–570b, 571a
KORMAKS SAGA **7–0**; 2–255b; 4–612b-613a
Kosača family 2–337b
Köse Dağ, Battle of (1243) 1–241b
Kosmas of Maiuma 2–511b
Kosovo
See Serbia
Kossovo, Battle of (1389) 4–56a
Kossovo, Second Battle of (1448) 4–56a
Kotor 4–1b
Kotromanić, Stjepan 2–336b-337a
Bosnia 2–336b-337a
KOTZENMARE, DAS 7–0
Koumiss 2–209b
Koutloumousiou Monastery 1–638a
Kovrat 2–399a
KRAFFT, ADAM 7–0
Krajina 2–336b, 338b, 339b
KRAK DES CHEVALIERS 7–0
Baybars 2–138b
crusader art and architecture 4–24b, 25a,b
Knights of Saint John 3–304a
Krakow
fairs 4–587b
Krbava 4–4a
Kremikovci
art and architecture 2–417b
Kremlin
See Moscow Kremlin, art and architecture
Kreševo 2–334a
Kresimir II of Croatia 4–5a
Bosnia 2–334b
Kresimir IV of Croatia 4–8b, 61
Kreuziger, Der (Johannes von Frankenstein) 2–231a
KRISTNI SAGA **7–0**; 2–252a
KRITOVOULOS, MICHAEL 7–0
Krk, Isle of 4–6a
Kronidēs
Armenian saints 1–519b
Kronos, myth of
allegorical interpretation 1–181a
Kropotin, Peter
climatology 3–452b
Krstjani 2–342a,b
KRUM 7–0
Byzantine defeat 2–401a-b, 488b
Kruševac 4–347b
Kryptē
See Crypt
Kuban River basin 3–193b
Kublai Khan
Christian church in Persia 3–313a
Marco Polo 4–556b
Küchük-Kaynarji, Treaty of (1774) 3–679b
Kudanbes of Nubia, King 3–315a
KUDRUN **7–0**; 2–253a; 4–304b-305a
Ambraser Heldenbuch 1–230a
Kudugers
See Bogomilism
KUENE, KONRAD 7–0
KŪFA, AL- 7–0; 1–16a, 374a; 2–45a
ʿAlī ibn Abī Ṭālib 1–173b
Arab settlements 1–377a
caliphate headquarters 3–35b
Kufa, al-, Battle of (740) 1–174b
KŪFĪ **7–0**; 1–209b, 210a; 3–52a
calligraphy 3–54a
Kuirike Baneli, Bishop 2–70a
Kulan 2–336a
KULIN 7–0
trade 2–340b
Kunigunde, Saint
canonization 3–68b
Kupa River 4–4a
Kur 4–427a,b, 428a
Kura-Araks basin 3–195a
KURA RIVER 7–0; 1–123a-b, 125a, 421b; 2–26a; 3–195a
KURAYSH (QURAYSH)
See Quraysh
Kurdādbih, Ibn
See Khurdādhbih, Ibn
KURDS 7–0
Armenian Muslim Emirates 1–513b
Ayyubids 2–23a
Marwānids 1–423a
Kurkollegium 4–428a
Kurland
crusades 2–65a
Viking settlements 2–62b
Kürnberger, Der
See Der von Kürenberg
KURSI 7–0
Kusanacʿ Monastery 1–292a
Kushano-Kidarite dynasty
Afghanistan 1–64a
Kūshyār ibn Labbān 1–383a, 385b-387b
KUTAISI 7–0
Bagrat's cathedral 2–47b
Kutāma
Abū ʿAbd Allah 1–72a
Kuthayyir 1–115b
Kutlumus Monastery 1–637a
Kutná Hora 3–623b
silver mines 2–300a
Kutrigurs 2–12b
Kutubīya Mosque 1–191b
KUWAYT, AL- 7–0
Kviđa
Eddic poetry 4–390a-b, 391a
KVIÐUHÁTTR 7–0; 4–401a
Kydones, Prochoros 3–632b
Kykou Monastery 4–70b
Kyng Alisaunder 1–266b
KYRIALE 7–0
antiphonal 1–329b
KYRIE 7–0

L

LABARUM 7–0
La-Bastide-du-Levis 2–129a
Laboratores 3–358a
Laborers
class structure, Western 3–415b
corvée 3–613a
See Also Serfs, serfdom
Labourd
Basques 2–126a,b
Labrador
discovery 4–555a
LACERTINE 7–0
Lackland, John 4–420a
Lack of Steadfastness (Chaucer) 3–286a
Lacnunga 1–286a
Lacombe, Stephen
Dominican reform 4–253b
La Coruña 4–558a
Lactantius
Anglo-Saxon adaptations 1–280b
Lactantius Firmianus
Arnobius the Elder 1–539a
astrology 1–605b
LACTATIO 7–0
Lacy, Hugh de
Clonard 3–466a
Ladder of Monks, The (Guido II) 3–119a
Ladder of Paradise (John Climacus) 3–215a
LĀDHIQIYA, AL- 7–0
Ladino
See Judeo-Spanish
Ladislas of Naples 2–337a,b, 338a; 3–647b; 4–80a
Ladislaus Posthumus 2–8b, 9a
Ladoga, Lake
Aldeigjuborg 4–555a
Lady Chapel
See Chapel
"Lady Day" style calendar 3–20a
Lady-in-waiting
courtesy book 3–663b-664a
Lady of the Fountain, The 1–566b
Laetentur coeli decree (1439) 3–653b; 4–378a
La Ferté
Cistercian Order 3–403b
La Ferté-Gaucher
fairs 4–590b
Lag B'Omer 3–27a
Lagin
Brigit, Saint 2–376a
Lagny
fairs 4–590b, 591a-592b
Lagos
commerce 4–558a

LAGOS (cont.)
slaves 2–269a; 4–561a
Lagos, Gil Eanes de
Canaries 4–561a
Lagoudera Master 2–445b
Lahslit 4–91a
LAI, LAY 7–0
Anglo-Norman 1–268a-b
ars nova 1–552b
Arthurian literature 1–568a-b
descort 4–164a
fabliau 4–574a,b
Marie de France 1–271b; 3–277b
Lai de Lanval (Marie de France) 3–277b
***LAI DEL COR* 7–0**; 1–568a
***LAI DEL DÉSIRÉ* 7–0**; 1–268a
Lai de l'ombre 1–271b
Lai des dous amans 3–277b
Lai d'Haveloc 1–268a, 271a
Lai du cor (Robert Biket) 1–268a
Laikoi 3–338b
Laisren of Devenish
Clonard 3–465b
LAISSE 7–0; 3–72a-b
assonance 1–600b
chansonnier 3–255b
chansons de geste 3–261a
Laisso
See Āyās
Laity
Latin church 3–358a-360a, 368b
Lajassi
See Āyās
Lajazzo
See Āyās
LAJVARD 7–0
Lajvardina
ceramics 3–240a
LAKHMIDS 7–0
pre-Islamic Arabia 1–371b
La Lastra, Battle of (1304) 4–99b
Lamb
Islamic cookery 3–584a
Lambarde, William 1–287a
Lambert, Pierre
Bordeaux 2–328a
Lambertiners 3–107b
Lambert "le Bègue" ("the Stutterer") 2–158b
Lambert le Tort
Alexander romances 1–151a
Lambert of Auxerre
dialectic 4–170b
LAMBERT OF HERSFELD 7–0
Carmen de Bello Saxonico 3–97a
Lambertus
ars antiqua 1–542b, 545a
LAMBESPRINGE, BARTHOLOMEW 7–0
Lambeth Bible
Anglo-Norman art 1–258a
Lambeth Psalter 4–548b
Lamb of God
See Agnus Dei
Lambrequin 3–623b
LAMBRON 7–0; 3–391a
LAMENTATION 7–0
deposition from the Cross 4–157a
Lamentation (Petrus Christus) 3–324b
Lamentation on the Holy Cathedral of Vałaršapat (Step'anos Orbelean) 4–417b
Lamentations of Matheolus, The 1–323b
Lament for a Nightingale (Alcuin) 3–101a
Lamento di Tristano (dance) 4–88a
Lament of Oddrún
See Oddrúnargrátr
Laments
Anglo-Norman lyric poetry 1–269b
Byzantine literature 2–523a
Lamont family
Scottish clans 3–407a
Lamos
fairs 4–588a
LAMPRECHT 7–0
Book of Tobit 2–228a
Lamprecht of Trier
Alexander romances 1–150a
Lamps
See Lighting Devices
Lamtūna
See Almoravids
Lancastrian hereditary principle 4–477a-b
Lancastrian Order of Saints 3–307a
LANCE 7–0; 1–521b; 2–352b
history and development 1–522b, 526b
wielding 3–202b, 206a
Lancelot
See Arthurian literature
Lancelot (Chrétien de Troyes) 3–668a
Lancet arch
See Arch
LANCET WINDOW 7–0
Landesarchiv 1–448b
Landévennec
Celtic monasteries 3–227b
LANDINI, FRANCESCO 7–0
ars nova 1–553a
ballata 2–61a
Faenza Codex 4–580a
***LANDNÁMABÓK* 7–0**; 4–618a
Land ob der Enns 2–7b
Lando di Pietro
Agostino 1–76b
Land of Cockaigne 1–319b
***LANDOLFUS SAGA* 7–0**
Landshut
arms and armor 1–529a
founding 2–135a
Landshut, Mair von 4–490a
Land tenure, Byzantine 1–79a-b
LAND TENURE, ISLAMIC 7–0; 1–105b
agriculture 1–103a-b
LAND TENURE, SLAVIC 7–0
Bohemia-Moravia 2–302a
Bulgaria 2–406a, 408a
pomestie 1–101b-102a
serfdom 1–102a-b
LAND TENURE, WESTERN EUROPEAN 7–0
allod 1–190a
assize 1–596a-598a
banal monopolies 2–69b
Brittany, Celtic 2–382a
burgage tenure 2–420b-421a
Canterbury 3–82b
Castile 3–136a, 139b
colonus 3–482b
copyhold 3–596b
distress 4–220b
escheat system 4–508b
estate management 4–511a
LANFRANC OF BEC 7–0; 2–173b
Berengar 2–188a
church reform 4–466a,b
Dialectica 4–169b
exegesis 2–213a; 4–543a
Latin exegesis 4–543a
legal system 4–464a
LANFRANC OF MODENA 7–0
Lanfranc of Pavia 1–311b, 312a
LANGLAND, WILLIAM 7–0
allegory 1–186a
Black Death 2–265b
LANGLOIS, JEAN 7–0
Langobards 1–522a
Langres
Burgundians 2–423a
Langtoft, Peter
Anglo-Norman chronicles 1–265b
LANGTON, STEPHEN 7–0
Articles of the Barons 4–468b, 469a
biblical terms 2–213b
election 3–94b, 265b; 4–423a, 468b
Hebrew-Latin vocabulary 3–313b
Lambeth Council (1222) 3–578b
Lateran Council (1215) 3–640a-b
Latin exegesis 4–544a
Saint Augustine's Abbey 3–83b
Language of the Arabs (Ibn Manẓūr) 4–444a
Language of the Persians (Asadī al-Ṭūsī) 4–444b
Languages
document 3–253a
epigraphic studies 1–336a,b
See Also specific languages
LANGUEDOC 7–0
Black Death 2–261a
Cathars 3–189b
commune 3–497a
fairs 4–586a
seneschal 2–53a,b
Lanseloet van Denemarken 4–321a,b
Lanškroun
Waldensians 2–306b
LANTFRED 7–0
Lantfrid and Cobbo
Cambridge Song 3–58b
LANTPERT OF DEUTZ 7–0
Lanval (Marie de France) 1–268a
LANX 7–0
Lanzarote 3–61b, 62a-b; 4–558b
Laodicea
See Lādhiqiya, al-
Laodicea, Council of
cantor 3–87b
Laon
Adalbero 1–46b
commune 3–496a,b
Laon, School of 1–316a
Laon Cathedral
alternating supports 1–226a
basilica 2–125a
construction 3–564b, 565a
Laonikos Chalkokondyles 2–517b
Lapais Monastery 4–73a
LAPIDARIUM 7–0
Anglo-Norman literature 1–262a
Catalan 3–168b
Lapidarius 1–138b
Lapidary of Aristotle 1–136b, 137a
Lapini, Bernardo 3–169b
Lapis philosophicus 1–134b
Lapps 1–166b
LAQABI WARE 7–0
Laras family 3–130b
Lärbro 3–234b
Large, Robert 3–210a
Laribus, Battle of (909) 1–72a
Larissa
Bohemond I 2–308b
Norman siege (1082) 1–158a
Larnaca
See Les Salines
La Rochelle 2–328b
port 2–328b
La Rochelle, Battle of (1372) 3–137b
La Salle, Gadifer de
Canary Islands 3–62a-b
Lashkari Bāzār palace 4–569b

Las Huelgas Church 3–133a
Laskarid dynasty 4–345a
LASKARIDS 7–0; 4–345a
art patrons 2–446b
Byzantine Empire 2–498a, 499a,b
Ephesus 4–495a
Laskaris (Theodore or Constantine)
Fourth Crusade 4–48a
Las Navas de Tolosa, Battle of (1212)
1–195a, 641a; 3–131a
Calatrava Order 3–16b
Las Navas de Toloso 1–410b
Lassois 2–427a
LAST 7–0
Lastic, Jean de
Knights of Saint John 3–304a
Lastidianus 1–647b
Last Judgment
Apocalypse illustration 1–344a
Last Judgment (Pietro Cavallini) 3–198a
Last rites 4–119b-120a
LAST SUPPER 7–0
Last Things 1–262b
Lāt, al- 1–29a
Latakia
See Lādhiqiya, Al-
"Late Banns" 3–298b
LATEEN SAIL 7–0
La Tène art 3–218a
La Tène culture 3–232b
LATERAN 7–0; 4–102a, 332a-b
Adam of the Little Bridge 1–52a
breviary 2–372a, 373a
cardinal-bishop association with pope
3–93b
Donation of Constantine 4–258a
furnishings 4–361a
papal coronation 3–603a,b
Lateran Council, Second (1139) 3–637b
celibacy of clergy 3–443b
excommunication 3–445a
Lateran Council, Third (1179)
Basques 2–126b
Cathars 3–187a
church elections 4–422a
decretals 4–123b
papal election 3–94b
Lateran Councils
See Councils, Western
Fourth 3–540a
Later Cambridge Songs (869-1179) and
(1215-1274) 1–319a
Laterculus
See Polemius Silvius
Latgalians
See Lettgallians
Latimer, William 4–399a
impeachment 4–484b
Latin abacus
See Arabic numerals
Latin alphabet 1–207b, 209b, 212a-217b
Anglo-Saxon culture 1–274a
Celtic languages 3–233a
sequence of letters 1–204a-205a
Latin Anthology
See Anthologia Latina
Latin Averroism
See Rushd, Ibn (Averroës)
Latin Calvary Chapel 4–24a
Latin-Cornish glossary 3–234a
Latin Cross
See Cross, Forms of
LATIN EMPIRE OF CONSTANTINOPLE 7–0; 2–498a-499b
Baldwin I 2–58b
Bulgaria 2–409a-b
Conon de Béthune 3–538a
Constantinople 3–549a
decline 4–48b
founding 4–48a
Fourth Crusade 4–31b
Gregory IX 4–52a
Latin-French vocabularies 1–270a,b
Latin grammar
Celtic intellectual life 3–231b
LATINI, BRUNETTO 7–0; 3–168b,
196b; 4–96b, 449a
Latin Kingdom of Jerusalem
Byzantine Empire 4–25a
crusader art and architecture 4–21b
crusades 4–30b
decline 4–32a,b
Saladin 4–31a-b
LATIN LANGUAGE 7–0
administrative documents 1–260a
Anglo-Latin poetry 1–255a
Arabic texts 1–378b
Armenian language 1–507a
barbarian invasions 2–96a,b
Bible translations 2–211a-b
Castilian 3–141a
Cato's Distichs 3–193a
Cilician court 3–393a
dictamen 4–173b
Old English prose translations
1–284a-286b
LATIN LITERATURE 7–0
Ackerman 1–44b
acrostics 1–45b
Alexander romances 1–149b
Alfred the Great and translations
1–164b
Anglo-Latin poetry 1–254b
Anglo-Saxon literature 1–274b
anthologies 1–319a-320a
archpoet 1–449b
ars antiqua 1–544a, 546b
Arthurian literature 1–572b
Baudri of Bourgueil 2–132a
Calpurnius Siculus Titus 3–55b
Cambridge Songs 3–57a
Carmina Burana 3–97b
courtesy books 3–661a
courtly love 3–671b-672a
cuaderna vía 4–63a
cursus 4–66b
Endelechius 4–451a
Ennodius 4–491b
epic 4–495b
Eugenius Vulgarius 4–520b
LATIN METER 7–0
Auspicius of Toul 2–4a
Carolingian Latin poetry 3–100b
cursus 4–66b
epic 4–495b
LATIN PRINCIPALITIES AND FRANKISH STATES IN GREECE 7–0
Agobard 1–75b
Assizes of Romania 1–600a
Bulgaria 2–409a-b
Catalan Company 3–157a
crusader art and architecture 4–21b
Latin States 4–38b-39a
Latium
agriculture 1–86b-87a,b
La Tour family
butler 2–434b
La Tour-Landry, Geoffroy de 3–662b
Latreia 3–320b
La Trinité Abbey 3–8b
Latrocinium
See Robber Synod
Latvia
exploration 4–554a
Latvians 2–61b, 67b, 68a
LAUDA 7–0
Laudabiliter 1–58b
Laudabili vita coniugatorum, De (Denis
the Carthusian) 3–573b
LAUDES, ACCLAMATIONS 7–0
Celtic liturgy 3–230b
Divine Office 4–221b, 226-227, 229a
Office of the Dead 4–117b-118a
Laudes matutinales 3–67a
LAUDES MEDIOLANENSIS CIVITATIS 7–0
Laudibus divinae sapientiae, De (Alexander Neckham) 1–255a
Laudibus virginitatis, De (Aldhelm)
1–254b
Lauingen 1–127a
Laurac
Cathars 3–186a
Lauraton 4–354b
Laurence of Durham
Brigit, Saint 2–377a
Laurence of Somercote 4–422b
Laurent de Bois 3–167b
Laurent de Premierfait
Boccaccio 2–285b, 286b
Laurentian Chronicle 1–175b
Laurentian Library, Florence
chained books 3–240b
LAURENTIUS HISPANUS 7–0
LAURENTIUS OF MONTE CASSINO 7–0
***LAURENTIUS SAGA* 7–0**; 2–252a
Laurentiusson, Árni
Dunstanus saga 4–311b
Laurent of Saint Omer
florilegia 1–317a
Laurin 2–253a
LAUSAVÍSA 7–0
Lausavísur 4–401a
Lausiac History
See Palladios
Lausor de la Divinitat 3–167a
Lauzengiers 3–70b
La Vigne, André de 4–265a
LAVRA 7–0; 1–636b
Sabas, Saint 2–468a
Law
Champion in judicial combat 3–413a
LAW, ARMENIAN 7–0
Law, Breton 2–382a
LAW, BYZANTINE 7–0
Assizes of Romania 1–600a
basilics 2–125a
Basil I the Macedonian 2–117b
Bulgaria 2–402b
Codex Theodosianus 3–475a
Constantine VII Porphyrogenitos
3–547a
Corpus iuris civilis 3–608b
Eclogue 4–382b
Epanagoge 4–493a
Law, Canon
baptism 2–84b, 85b
casuistry 3–153b
confession 3–533b
corporation 3–606a-b, 607b, 608a-b
decretals 4–122b
decretists 4–127a
decretum 4–128a
degradation of clerics 4–133a
deposition of rulers, 4–159b
dispensation 4–216b
equity 4–503a
marriage annulment 1–306a
medicine, practice of 2–98a
suitability principle 4–427a,b
LAW, CANON: ARMENIAN 7–0

LAW, CANON: BYZANTINE 7–0; 2–466a-468a
Bulgaria 2–403a
clergy 3–447a
Eclogue 4–383a
Law, Carolingian 3–107a
Law, Cilician 3–393b
LAW, CIVIL 7–0
Bartolo da Sassoferrato 2–115a
Bracton, Henry de 2–357a
Bulgaria 2–401b
Burchard of Worms 2–420b
corporation 3–606a
Corpus iuris civilis 3–608b
equity 4–501a, 502a, 503a
lay curia 4–65b
Law, Cyprian 4–71b-72b
LAW, DANISH 7–0
LAW, EARLY GERMAN 7–0
Burgundians 2–423a
Law, English Common
bailiffs 2–52a
cartulary 3–120a
constable, local 3–542b
copyhold 3–596b
coroner 3–605a
corporation 3–606b, 607a-b
distress 4–220b
equity 4–501b-503b
Exchequer 4–533b, 534a-b
gage 2–81a
lay curia 4–65b
presentment of Englishry 4–487a
statutes 4–482b
LAW, ENGLISH COMMON: TO 1272 7–0; 4–480a-481a
Anglo-Norman 1–260a
Anglo-Saxon texts 1–286a
assize 1–594a, 598a-b
asylum, right of 1–631b
Bracton, Henry de 2–357a
Clarendon, Assize of 3–408b
common pleas, court of 3–491b
Norman-Angevin 4–464a-465a, 470a-b, 471b, 472a
Old English documents 1–275a, 286b
LAW, ENGLISH COMMON: AFTER 1272 7–0; 4–481b
assize 1–595a-b
Britton 2–382b
burgage tenure 2–420b-421a
common pleas, court of 3–492b
Edward I 4–396b
parliament 4–482a-483a
Law, French
capitulary 3–91a
LAW, FRENCH: IN NORTH 7–0
assize 1–594b-595a
bailli 2–52a
ban, *banalité* 2–69a
Beaumanoir, Philippe de 2–144a-145b
Châtelet 3–278a
Coutumes de Beauvaisis 3–674b
custumals of Normandy 4–68b
Établisssement de Saint Louis 4–515a
LAW, FRENCH: IN SOUTH 7–0
assize 1–595b-596a
ban, *banalité* 2–69a
LAW, GERMAN: AFTER THE CAROLINGIANS 7–0
Burchard of Worms 2–420b
Constitutio de feudis 3–557b
Eike von Repgowe 4–408b
LAW, IRISH 7–0
LAW, ISLAMIC 7–0
Abū Ḥanīfa 1–26a-b
Almohads 1–193b, 195a
Arabic prose literature 1–379a
blood money 2–276b
caliphate 3–32b-33a, 43b, 44a-b
commercial 2–79b
costume 3–616b, 619b, 620b
diet 4–178b
Egypt 4–407a
sources 3–41a
usury 2–79a-b
Law, Italian
Cino da Pistoia 3–397a
LAW, JEWISH 7–0
Eclogue 4–383a
Rabad 1–22b
Rhenish customary 4–420b
LAW, JEWRY 7–0
Law, maritime
Admiralty, Court of 1–56a
consulate of the sea 3–569b
LAW, PROCEDURES OF: 1000 TO 1500 7–0
False Decretals 4–126b
Law, Roman
annulment of marriage 1–306b
Beaumanoir, Philippe de 2–144b-145a
custumals of Normandy 4–68b
lawbooks 4–578a
LAW, RUSSIAN (MUSCOVITE) 7–0
agricultural 1–99a
sudebnik 1–101b
LAW, SCHOOLS OF 7–0
Bologna 2–312a
Bulgarus 2–417b
Corpus iuris civilis 3–608b-609a,b
decretists 4–127a
decretum 4–128a
LAW, SCOTTISH 7–0
LAW, SPANISH 7–0
Cantar de Mío Cid 3–74b, 79b
Castile 3–139a
Catalan literature 3–169a
Catalonia 3–175b-176a
cortes 3–611a,b
maritime 3–165a
LAW, SWEDISH 7–0
LAW, WELSH 7–0
agriculture 1–91b
Law of Hywel Dda 2–106a
LAW, CANON: TO GRATIAN 7–0; 3–348b-349a, 352b
Alger of Liège 1–167b
Anselm II of Lucca 1–311a
Carolingian age 4–373a-374a
Celtic church 3–229a,b
concubinage 3–530a-b
Deusdedit, Cardinal 4–165b
False Decretals 4–124a
Norman-Angevin England 4–464b, 466b, 471b
Western councils 3–635a-b, 637a-b, 638a-b
LAW, CANON: AFTER GRATIAN 7–0; 3–354a
Alexander III, Pope 1–146b
Antonius, Saint 1–342b
Beaumanoir, Philippe de 2–144b-145a
Bracton, Henry de 2–357a
Canterbury and York convocations 3–578b
Cistercians 3–405a
Clarendon, Constitutions of 3–409b
Clement V, Pope 3–438b
clericos laicos 3–447b
Corpus iuris civilis 3–609b-610a
deposition of rulers 4–159b
Durand 4–314b
Western councils 3–642a,b
LAW CODES: 1000 TO 1500 7–0
ban, *banalité* 2–69a
Burgundian 2–92b
corporation 3–606a
Lawrence, Antipope 1–330a
Lawrence of Milan, Bishop 1–422a
Laws (Henry I) 4–90b
Lawsuit of the Lady of Valor Against Bertran Tudela
See Procés de la Senyora de Valor contra En Bertran Tudela
Lawyers, status of 3–413a
***LAXDŒLA SAGA* 7–0;** 4–402b, 613b, 614a, 615a
Lay
See Lai, Lay
Layamon
See Brut, The
Layas, Layazzo
See Āyās
Lay de Paix (Alain Chartier) 3–275b
Laying on of hands
ordination rites 3–442b
Lay of Erik
See Eiríksmál and *Hákonarmál*
Lay of Hákon
See Eiríksmál and *Hákonarmál*
Lay of Sigrdrífa 4–386a, 387a
Lay of the Horn (Robert Biket) 1–268a
Lazarević, Stefan 2–338a
LAZAR HREBELJANOVIĆ 7–0
ŁAZAR P'ARPEC'I 7–0; 1–66b; 4–114a, 417b
Armenian literature 1–508b
Armenian saints 1–518b
Ełišē 4–433b
LAZARUS, RAISING OF 7–0
Lāzhuvard
See Azulejo
Lazica
See Georgia: Geography
Lāzuward
See Azulejo
LCz, Master
See Katzheimer, Lorenz
Leabar Gabálá Érenn 2–82b
Leabhar Breac
Irish apocrypha 1–347b
liturgical colors 3–484a
Lead mining
Bosnia 2–340a,b
LEAGUE 7–0
Lea River 4–456b
Danelaw border 4–91a
Leasing
English estate 4–512a-513b
LEATHER AND LEATHER WORKING 7–0
LEBANON 7–0
Beirut 2–163b
Damascus 4–80b
Le Bel, Jean
French chronicles 3–333a
Lebus 2–360b
Lechfeld, Battle of (955) 1–94a; 3–202b
Lech River 2–132b
LECTIONARY 7–0; 4–224a-b
Alcuin of York 1–143a
breviary 2–370b
evangeliary 4–525b
Lectionary of the Church of Jerusalem 1–518b, 520a-b
Lector 3–442a,b, 443a, 444a
Lector, Theodore 3–675b, 676a
Lectura in codicem (Cino da Pistoia) 3–397b
Lectura super Digesto veteri (Cino da Pistoia) 3–397b
Ledrede, Richard
Anglo-Latin poetry 1–255a

Leechbook
botany 2–345b
Leet jurisdiction 3–659b-660a
Le Fèvre, Jean
Cato's Distichs 3–193b
Lamentations of Matheolus, The 1–323b
LEFEVRE, RAOUL 7–0
LEGATE, PAPAL 7–0
church organization 3–373b, 375a, 376b
Western European diplomacy 4–203b
Legatus 4–205a
Legenda 4–224b
Legenda Aurea (Jacobus de Voragine)
See Golden Legend
Legendary Sagas
See Fornaldarsögur
Legend of Good Women (Chaucer) 3–281a, 289a,b
Legends of the Prophets 1–380b
Leges Henrici 4–487a
Legibus, De (Henry Bracton) 3–530b
Legname
See Madeira Islands
Legnano, Battle of (1176) 3–117b
Legumes 1–86b, 92b, 95a
Islamic cultivation 1–104b, 105a
Leich, Der (Walther von der Vogelweide) 2–228b
Leiden Papyrus 1–135b
Leiden Riddle 1–276a
Leidrad of Lyons, Bishop 1–75a
Leif Ericsson
Vinland 4–555a
LEINSTER 7–0
Leinster Tribute, The
See Bóraime Laigen
Leipzig
fair 4–583a
Leitha River 2–6a-b
LEIÐARVÍSAN 7–0
LEJRE CHRONICLE 7–0
Leken spieghel, Der 4–319b
Leliaerts 2–387a,b
LE LOUP, JEAN 7–0
Lemaire, William
conciliar theory 3–517b
Western councils 3–645b
Lembiotissa Monastery
cartulary 1–78b-79a
Lenburc, Princess 1–266b
Lendit
fair 4–585a
Leningrad Bede 1–275b
Leno, Antonius de 3–657b
LENSES AND EYEGLASSES 7–0
LENT 7–0
Advent 1–59a
carnival 3–99a
darokhranitelnitsa 4–105b
Easter 4–365a
ember days 4–435b
Lentienses 1–117a
LEO I, EMPEROR 7–0; 1–121b
LEO I, POPE 7–0; 1–499b, 500a
astrology 1–605b-606a
brandeum 2–362b
Byzantine Church 2–460b
Christmas 3–318a
Christology 3–321a
church unity 3–336b
clerical celibacy 3–443b
concubinage 3–530a
ecclesiology 4–372a,b
ecumenical councils 3–629b, 630a
elections, church 4–421a
ember days 4–436a
Eutyches 4–524a
Huns 2–93a
papal power 3–341b, 342a
LEO II, POPE 7–0
LEO III, POPE 7–0; 1–2b; 4–412a
Alcuin of York 1–143b
caesaropapism 3–11b
catacombs 3–154b
Charlemagne's coronation 3–110a-b
Christology 3–321b
Felix of Urgel 1–57b
Nicene-Constantinopolitan Creed 3–676a, 677a
Salzburg archbishopric 2–4b
Leo IV, Pope
Alfred the Great 1–163b
crusade propaganda 4–18b
Leo VII, Pope
Cluny order 3–470a
Leo VIII, Pope
papal coronation 3–604a
LEO IX, POPE 7–0; 1–47a, 58b; 4–427b
business volume 3–353b
Byzantine church 2–465a
clerical celibacy 3–217a
Desiderius of Monte Cassino 4–164b
elections, church 4–421b
monastic reform 4–374a
papal reform 3–93b, 348b, 350b, 351a
schisms: Eastern-Western church 3–349a
Western councils 3–633b, 634a
Leo X, Pope
church reform 3–367b
Leo XIII, Pope
Aquinas 1–365a
Leo, Archpresbyter 1–149b
Leo Africanus
Guzzūla fair 4–589a
Leo Choirosphaktes 2–507a
Leoffric 1–277a
Celtic church reforms 3–232a
Leofric Missal 1–273a
Leofric of Mercia, Earl 4–394b
León 1–409a, 410a; 3–131b
agriculture 1–82a, 83a-84b
Alfonso X 1–161a
Alfonso XI 1–162b
Asturias-León 1–625a
Cantar de Mío Cid 3–75a
cortes 3–611b-612a
dialects 3–141b
fairs 4–587b
Leonardo da Vinci 1–439b
astrarium 3–462a
Leonardo Dellaportas 2–523a
LEONARDO DI SER GIOVANNI 7–0
Leonard of Maurperg 1–138b
Leonardo Lomellini
slaves 2–270a
Leon Battista Alberti
artists' status 1–580a
Leonessa, Gentile da 3–531b
Léonin
Anonymous IV treatise 1–310a
ars antiqua 1–543a, 546a
LEONINUS 7–0
Leon of Thessalonica 1–434a
Leonora of Castile 1–415b
Leonor de Albuquerque 3–139b
Leonor de Guzmán 3–135a, 136b
Leontios Machairas 2–522b
Leontius of Balbissa 2–296a
Leontius of Byzantium
Christology 3–320b
Leonzio Pilato
Boccaccio 2–283a, 287a,b
LEO I/II OF ARMENIA 7–0
Ayās 2–19a
Cilician kingdom 3–391b
Leo II/III of Armenia 2–19a; 3–391b
Leo III/IV of Armenia
Cilician kingdom 3–391b
LEO V/VI OF ARMENIA 7–0
Cilician kingdom 3–393a, 395a
Leo of Chosroids 3–308a
Leo I/II of Cilicia 3–391b, 394a
Leo of Naples 1–152b
Leo of Ochrid, Archbishop 2–407a
eucharistic foods controversy 2–31b
Leo of Ohrid
See Leo of Ochrid
LEO OF OSTIA 7–0
Leo of Tripoli 2–489b
LEO OF VERCELLI 7–0
Leo Patrikios
Bible 2–440b
Leopold I, Margrave 2–6a, 33b
Leopold III, Margrave 2–6a,b
Leopold IV, Margrave 2–6b, 33B
Leopold III, Saint 2–33b
Leopold I of Austria, Duke 2–8a
Leopold II of Austria, Duke
Richard I the Lionhearted 4–70b, 467b
Leopold V of Austria, Duke 2–33b
Styria 2–6b-7a
Leopold VI of Austria, Duke 2–7a, 33b
Fifth Crusade 4–49b
Leo Sgouros
Byzantine Empire 2–496b
LEO V THE ARMENIAN, EMPEROR 7–0; 1–154a
Amorian dynasty 1–236a
Leo the Deacon 2–514b
LEO III THE ISAURIAN, EMPEROR 7–0
Anatolikon theme 1–236a
Bulgaria 2–402a
Byzantine church 2–462b
classical literary studies 3–431a
Eclogue 2–117b; 4–382b
heterodoxy 2–459a
iconoclastic movement 3–10b, 631a
reform measures 3–345a
reign 2–488a
LEO THE MATHEMATICIAN 7–0; 1–391b, 392a; 2–489a
Constantinople 3–556b
LEO VI THE WISE, EMPEROR 7–0; 3–203a
Basil I 2–117b, 118a
Basilics 2–125a
Book of the Eparch 4–494a
Book of the Prefect 2–478a
Bulgaria 2–404b
Byzantine councils 3–632a
canon law 2–467b
Constantine VII Porphyrogenitos 3–546b
crown 2–455a
Hagia Sophia 2–440a
marriage definition 4–594b
nobility 3–553a
reign 2–488b, 489b-490a
royal confessor 3–534b
Taktika 4–447a
Leo Tornikios
rebellion 2–492a
Leovigild 2–126a
Córdoba 3–597b
LEPROSY 7–0
Lérida 1–410b, 413b, 418b
bishopric 1–408a
Catalonian expansion 1–412b

LÉRIDA (cont.)
conquests 1–405b, 406a
fruit trees 1–82b
Muslim hamlets 1–408b
restoration of see 1–407b
university 3–415a
Valencia settlement 1–412a
Lerida Ferrer the Elder
See Ferrer the Elder, Jaime
Leroquais, Abbé
book of hours 2–326a
Le Roux de Lincy, Antoine Jean Victor 1–271a
Lesbos
Andronikos III Palaiologos 1–246b
Lescherius, Paul
dictamen 4–176b
Les Salines 4–72a
Lesser Armenia
See Armenia: Geography
Lesser Armenian Era 3–31a
Lesser Caucasus range 3–195a
Lesser Privilege 2–6b
Lesser Sophenē 1–515a
LETALD OF MICY 7–0
Leth Cam, Battle of (827) 3–397a
Letter from Valerius to Rufinus Against Taking a Wife (Walter Map) 1–323b
Letter of Cupid (Thomas Hoccleve) 1–324a
Letter of Tansar (Tansar) 1–452a
LETTER OF TANSAR 1–452a
Letters
See Alphabets
Letters, Book of
See Girk Tʿłtʿocʿ
Letters, diplomatic 4–208a-209a
Letters of exchange
fairs 4–584b, 585b
Letter to a lady containing admonitions concerning behavior to a lover 1–269a
Letter to Can Grande (Dante) 4–103a, 104b
Letter to the Brethren at Mont Dieu, A (William of Saint Thierry) 3–119a
Letter to the God of Love (Christine de Pisan) 1–324a
Letter to the Italian Cardinals (Dante) 4–103b
Letter writing, French
See Dictamen
Lettgallians 2–65a,b
"Let us bless the Lord"
See Benedicamus Domino
Levant 4–22a
Cid 3–73b
Columbus 4–560b
commerce 1–146a; 4–556a, 558a
Leven van Sinte Lutgart 4–320a
Leven van Sint Servaes 4–320a
LEVI BEN GERSON 7–0
Aristotelianism 1–460a
astronomy 1–613a
cross-staff 4–12a
exegesis 4–212b, 541b
Levon I
Armenian church 1–501a
Lewes, Battle of (1264) 2–112a; 4–395b
LEWES, SONG OF 7–0
ŁEWOND 7–0
Armenian saints 1–519a
Eznik of Kołb 4–571a
Lex Burgundionum 2–92b
Lexicography
Arabic 1–377a; 4–442b-444a
Latin 4–449b
Persian 4–444a-b
Lex innocentium 1–52b
Lex Romana Burgundionum 2–92b
Lex Romana Visigothorum 3–475b
Lex Salica
antrustiones 1–343a
LEYS D'AMORS 7–0; 4–87a
Liability, principle of unlimited 2–76b-77a
Libanius 2–120a
Libās
See Costume, Islamic
Libelli 4–225a
Libello of Dante 4–96b
Libellus ad Leonem X (Tommaso Giustiniani and Vincenzo Quirini) 3–520a
Libellus contra invasores et symoniacos (Cardinal Deusdedit) 4–165b
Libellus de adoranda cruce (Einhard) 4–412b
Libellus de Antichristo (Adso) 2–226b
Libellus de arte dictandi rethorice (Peter of Blois) 4–175a
Libellus de ecclesiastica et politica potestate (Edmond Richer) 3–521b
Libellus de malo senectutis et senii (Boncompagno of Signa) 2–320b
Libellus de modo vivendi hominum simul commorantium (Gerard Zerbolt) 4–166b
Libellus dictaminum et privilegiorum 4–175b
Libellus responsionum 1–645a,b
Liber abaci (Leonardo Fibonacci) 1–395b, 396a
Liberal arts
Fachschrifttum 4–577b-578b
Liber alghoarismi de practica arismetrice (John of Seville) 1–388a, 389a
Liber alter de consecratione ecclesiae sancti (Suger) 1–334a
Liber continens (al-Rāzī) 3–574a
Liber de amicitia (Boncompagno of Signa) 2–320b
Liber de arte contrapuncti (Johannes Tinctoris) 3–657b; 4–172a
Liber de bestiis et aliis rebus (Hugh of Saint Victor) 1–188b
Liber de causis 2–35b; 4–510b
Liber de corpore et sanguine Domini (Lanfranc of Bec) 4–169b
Liber decretorum (Burchard of Worms) 4–128b
Liber de moribus 1–317b
Liber de obsidione Ancone (Boncompagno of Signa) 2–320a-b
Liber de planctu naturae (Alan of Lille) 1–188b
Liber derivationum (Osbern of Gloucester) 4–449b
Liber de septuaginta (Jābir ibn Ḥayyān) 1–136a,b
Liber de vita Christiana (Bonizo of Sutri) 3–358b
Liber dictaminum (Baldwin) 4–175b
Liber dictaminum et salutatione (Alberic of Monte Cassino) 1–125b
Liber evangeliorum (Otfrid von Weissenburg) 2–225b
Liber extravagantium decretalium (Gregory IX) 3–353b, 638a
Liber Faceti 3–661a
Liber facetiarum (Poggio Bracciolini) 3–235a
Liber Flavus Fergusiorum (Bocht Ó Huiginn) 1–111b; 3–484a
Liber floridus (Lambert of Saint Omer) 4–448a-b
Liber floridus (Laurent) 1–317b
Apocalypse illustration 1–344a
Liber formularum (Georgius) 4–176a
Liber generationis
Christmas mass 3–319a
Liber gestarum (Petrus Marsilius) 3–165b
LIBERGIER, HUGUES 7–0
Liber glossarum (Aynard of St. Èrre) 2–19b; 4–449b
Liber hymnorum 3–231a
Liber illustrium virorum archisterii Casinensis (Peter the Deacon of Monte Cassino) 3–548b
Liber in gloria confessorum (Gregory of Tours) 3–540b
Liber introductorius (Michael Scot) 1–136b
Liber lucis (John of Rupescissa) 1–138a
Liber misericordiae (Jābir ibn Ḥayyān) 1–136a
Liber officialis (Amalarius of Metz) 1–228a
Liber ordinarius 4–225a
Liber particularis (Michael Scot) 1–136b
Liber poenitentialis (Alan of Lille) 1–120a
Liber pontificalis 1–331a, 645a
Agnus Dei chant 1–74a
Anastasius Bibliothecarius 1–239b
Celestine I 3–213b
ember days 4–436a
Pseudo-Isidore 4–125a
Telesphorus 3–317a
Liber regulae pastoralis (Saint Gregory) 1–274b
English translation 1–165a,b-166a
Liber secretorum (al-Rāzī) 1–136a-b
Liber sextus (Boniface VIII) 3–523b, 642a; 4–133b
Liber sufficientiae (Avicenna) 2–35b
Libertate arbitrii, De (Anselm of Canterbury) 1–312a, 314b
LIBERTY AND LIBERTIES 7–0
Liber Urbani (Daniel Churche) 3–661a
***LIBER USUALIS* 7–0**; 1–75a
Liber XXX differentiarum (John of Seville) 1–612a
LIBRARIES 7–0; 1–446b
catalog alphabetization 1–206a
chained books 3–240b
Libre Blanquerna (Ramon Lull) 3–157b
Libre d'Amic e Amat (Ramon Lull) 3–157b
Libre de concordances (Jaume March) 3–170b
Libre de consells (Jaume Roig) 3–173b
Libre de contemplació (Ramon Lull) 3–157b, 158a
Libre de cuina de sent Soví (Master Robert) 3–168b
Libre de Fortuna e Prudencia (Bernat Metge) 3–173b
Libre de Fra Bernat (Francesc de la Via) 3–173b
Libre de la saviesa o de doctrina (James I) 3–168a
Libre del Consolat del mar 1–413b; 3–165a, 169a
Libre de les dones (Francesc Eiximenis) 4–416b
Libre de les dones (Jaume Roig) 3–173b
Libre de les nobleses dels reys (Francesc) 3–166b
Libre del orde de cavayleria (Ramon Lull) 3–666a-b
Libre del rei En Pere d'Aragédels seus antecessors passats (Bernat Desclot) 3–165b

Libre dels angels (Francesc Eiximenis) 4–416b
Libre dels feyts (James II) 3–166a
Libre dels feyts del rey En Jacme (James I) 3–165b
Libre de meravelles (Ramon Lull) 3–157b
Libre de paraules de savis e de filòsofs (Jafuda Bonsenyor) 3–168a
Libri Carolini 1–143a; 3–110a, 321b
Libri dialogorum (Gregory the Great) 4–371a-b
Libri feudorum (Baldus)
 commentaries 2–57a
Libro de Alexandre (Gonzalo de Berceo) 2–187a
Libro de Apolonia 4–63b
Libro de buen amor
 See Ruiz, Juan
Libro de la montería 1–576b
Libro de las batallas 1–176a
Libro de Patronio 3–31b
Libros del saber de astronomia (Alfonso X of Castile) 1–613a; 3–458a
Libya
 alms tax 1–202b
 Berbers 2–185b
 Byzantine church 2–459b
Libyan Wars (Corippus) 3–601a
Licentius 1–647b
Licet de vitanda 3–94b
Licet in consuetudine (Clement VI) 3–524a
Lichfield Cathedral
 chapter house design 3–267a
Li congé (Adam de la Halle) 1–48b
Lidia 4–283a
Lido
 See St. Nicholas Island
LIÉDET, LOYSET 7–0
LIED VOM HÜRNEN SEYFRID, DAS 7–0
Liège
 Alger 1–167b
 Cathars 3–183a
 commune 3–497b
LIERNE 7–0
Lietard, Archbishop
 Church of the Annunciation at Nazareth 4–24b
Liet von Troya (Herbort von Fritzlar) 1–635b
LIEVIN VAN LATHEM 7–0
Life of Alfred (Asser) 1–165a,b
Life of Augustine (Possidius) 1–648b, 660a
Life of Constantine (Eusebius of Caesarea) 4–523b
Life of Edward the Confessor, The (Saint Ethelred) 4–517a
Life of Happiness, The (Augustine) 1–648a, 657a
LIFE OF MARY, MASTER OF THE 7–0
Life of Saint Anthony (Athanasius) 1–633b
Life of Saint Catherine, The 1–261b
Life of Saint Eigil (Candida of Fulda) 3–64a
Life of Saint Josaphat, The 1–260b
Life of Saint Ranieri (Antonio Veneziano) 1–342b
Life of the Seven Sleepers, The 1–260b, 261b; 3–267b
 See Vie des Set Dormanz
Life of the Virgin (Pietro Cavallini) 3–198a
Life of Willibrord (Alcuin) 3–100b, 101a
Li fet des Romains 3–331b
Liftina
 Boniface, Saint 2–322a
LIGATURE 7–0; 1–544b, 545a
Light cavalry 3–204a
Light for Lay People (Peter of Peckham) 1–263b
LIGHTING 7–0
LIGHTING DEVICES 7–0
Light of the Lord
 See Or Adonai
Lignum vitae (Saint Bonaventure) 2–316a
Liguria
 Ambrose, Saint 1–230b
 Lombards 2–95b
 Ravenna exarchate 4–529b
 Willem van Afflighem 4–320a
Liḥyān Kingdom 1–371a
Lika
 Croatia 4–4a
LÍKNARBRAUT 7–0
Lilith
 Jewish apocalyptic literature 1–346a
Lilja
 See Eysteinn Ásgrímsson
LILLE 7–0
 banking 2–74b
 fairs 4–585a-b
Limassol 4–70b, 72a
LIMBOURG BROTHERS 7–0
 book of hours 2–327a
Limburg life of Jesus 4–320a
Limburgse leven van Jezu 4–320a
Lime burning
 coal mining 3–472b
Limerick
 Norwegian 4–554b
Limes 2–88b; 3–143b
Limestone
 construction 3–566b-567a
LIMITANEI 7–0
Limoges, Battle of (1370) 4–399a
Limoges enamel
 See Enamel, Limoges
Limpieza de sangre, statutes of 3–139b
Lim River 2–337a
Linaje 3–76b
Lincoln
 commune 3–498a-499a
LINCOLN, RITE OF 7–0
Lincoln Cathedral 1–255b; 4–472a
Lincolnshire
 Black Death 2–262b
LINDISFARNE GOSPELS 7–0
 Anglo-Saxon conversion 4–458b
 glosses 2–221a; 4–548b
 Latin Campanian Gospel 2–180ba; 4–548b
 Northumbrian dialect 1–276a
 ornamentation 3–220a-b
 West Saxon version 1–285b
Lindisfarne Monastery
 Anglo-Latin poetry 1–254b
 Celtic church 3–226a
 sack (793) 4–456a
Line drawings 1–273a,b
LINEN 7–0
 Coptic textiles 3–589a
Linguistics
 Arabic language 1–377b
Lintel 1–424
Linz
 fairs 4–586a
Linzer Antichrist, Der 2–228a-b
Lion 2–206b, 243a
 beast epic 2–140b
Lion de Bourges
 German traslation 4–432b
Lionel of Clarence
 Burgh, de 2–422a
LIPARIT IV ORBELEAN 7–0
Liporita, Anthony
 dictamen 4–176b
LIPPO MEMMI 7–0
***LIPSANOTHECA* 7–0**
 classical form 4–352a
 container 4–361b
Liripipes 3–623b
Li Romanz d'Athis et Prophilias 1–635b
Lisān al-'Arab (Ibn Manẓūr) 4–444a
Lisbon
 sack (955) 1–627b
 siege (1147) 3–181a
 slaves 2–269a
Lists
 Old English texts 1–275a
LITANIES, GREATER AND LESSER 7–0
LITANY 7–0
 breviary 2–371b
LITERACY, BYZANTINE 7–0
LITERACY, ISLAMIC 7–0
LITERACY, WESTERN EUROPEAN 7–0
 clerk 3–448b
Literary texts
 Anglo-Saxon 1–274b
Literature
 See individual entries
Lithām
 See Almoravids
LITHUANIA 7–0
 Balt 2–61b
 Black Death 2–264a
 church 2–68a, 469b
 independence 2–67a-b
 Muscovy 4–232a
 Nowogródek 2–64b
 raiding 2–64a
 Swedes 4–554a
Litomyšl
 Bohemian Brethren 2–307a
Litterae calendarum 3–23b
Litteris colendis, De (Alcuin) 1–142b
Little Ararat Mountain 1–421b
Little Domesday
 See Domesday Book
Little Kabylia 1–641a
Liturgical Books
 See individual entries
Liturgical day 2–165b
Liturgical drama
 See Drama, Liturgical
Liturgical furnishings
 See Furniture, Liturgical
Liturgical poetry
 See Poetry, Liturgical
Liturgy
 bells 2–166a
 catacomb paintings 4–350a
 Evovae 4–529a
LITURGY, ARMENIAN CHURCH 7–0; 1–516a-517a
 Antiochene rite 1–326b
LITURGY, BYZANTINE CHURCH 7–0; 2–468a-469a
 Alexandrian rite 1–155a
 Ancient of Days 1–242b
 Antiochene rite 1–326b
 Aquileia rite 1–352b
 Basil the Great 2–120b-121a, 122a
 dedication of churches 4–130a
 elevation of the Holy Cross 4–430a
 Liber officialis 1–228a
LITURGY, CELTIC 7–0
 Celtic church 2–381b; 3–230a-231a

LITURGY, ISLAMIC 7–0
LITURGY, JEWISH 7–0
cantor 3–87b
circumcision 3–401b
LITURGY, STATIONAL 7–0; 4–333a
LITURGY, TREATISES ON 7–0
Anglo-Norman homilectic texts 1–263a
Apostolic Constitutions 1–349b
Divine Office 4–221b
liturgical colors 3–484a
Liturgy, Western European
See individual entries
Liudolfings family
Arnulf 3–114b
Liutbert of Mainz, Archbishop
biblical poetry 2–225b
LIUTHARD 7–0; 1–645a; 3–81b; 4–453b
Liutpoldings family
Arnulf 3–114b
Liutprand, Lombard King 2–96a
Charles Martel 3–272a
LIUTPRAND OF CREMONA 7–0
Livadia 3–156a-b
***LIVERE DE REIS DE BRITTANIE, LE, AND LE LIVERE DE REIS DE ENGLETERRE* 7–0**; 1–265a
Lives of the Abbots of Wearmouth and Jarrow (Bede) 2–155a
Lives of the Egyptian Fathers 1–518a
Livestock
See Animals
Living cross
See Cross, Forms of
Livingstone, Thomas
conciliar theory 3–520b
Livio, Tito
biographies 3–328b
Livländische Reimchronik 4–505b
Livno 4–4a
Livonia
crusader state 2–64b, 65a
serfdom 2–68a
Livonian War (1557-1583) 2–68a
LIVRE 7–0
Livre d'amours (Drouart La Vache) 1–189a
Livre de chevaleries (Geoffrey of Charni) 3–666a
Livre de divinacions (Nicole Oresme) 1–608b
Livre de la mutacion de fortune (Christine de Pizan) 3–316b
Livre de la prod'hommie de l'homme (Christine de Pizan) 3–316b
Livre de l'espérance, Le (Alain Chartier) 3–275b
Livre de Marco Polo, Le (Marco Polo) 3–332b
Livre de prudence (Christine de Pizan) 3–316b
Livre d'Eracles 3–331b
LIVRE DES ASSISES DE JÉRUSALEM 7–0
Livre des droiz 4–515b
Livre des estoires 3–331b
Livre de seyntz medicines (Henry, duke of Lancaster) 1–263b
Livre des faits d'armes et de chevalerie (Christine de Pizan) 3–302a
Livre de Sibylle (Philippe de Thaon) 1–262a
Livre des quatre dames, Le (Alain Chartier) 3–275b
Livre des saintes paroles et des bons faiz nostre roy saint Looys (John of Joinville) 3–332b
Livre des trois vertus (Christine de Pizan) 3–316b, 664b
Livre du chevalier de La Tour-Landry (Geoffroy de La Tour-Landry) 3–662b
Livre du corps de policie (Christine de Pizan) 3–316b
Livre du roy Modus et de la royne Ratio (Henri de Ferrières) 1–189b
Livre du voir dit (Guillaume de Machaut) 3–256a
Livre en forme de plaid (Philippe de Novare) 4–73a
LIVRES DE JOSTICE ET DE PLET, LI 7–0
Livres dou trésor, Li (Brunetto Latini) 3–168b; 4–449a
Līwān
See Eyvān
***LJÓSVETNINGA SAGA* 7–0**; 4–613b, 614a
Ljóđaháttr 4–384a,b, 388b, 390b-391a
Ljubostinja 4–347b
Ljudevit of Croatia, Prince 4–2a
Llancarfan
Celtic monasteries 3–7a, 227b
Llatai 4–69b
Lletres de batalla 3–169a
Llibre del coch (Master Robert) 3–168b
Llibre del Consolat del Mar 2–103b
Llibre del consolat de mar, 3–569b, 570a
Llobregat Valley, Catalonia 3–174b, 175a
Llonja 2–104b
Llull, Romeu 3–172a
Llwyd of Gogerddan, Ieuan 3–121b
Llwyd of Gwynedd, Gruffudd 3–121b
Llywarch of Dyfed, King 4–329b
LLYWELYN AP GRUFFUDD 7–0
Edward I 4–391a
Peace of Conway 3–579b, 580a
Llywelyn ap Iorwerth the Great 4–413a
Elidir Sais 4–431a
Loans
See Banking
Lob Salomonis, Das 2–227b
Locher, Jacob
Brant, Sebastian 2–363b
Loch Léin, kingdom 4–492b
LOCHNER, STEPHAN 7–0
Locis sanctis, De (Saint Adamnan) 1–53a
Locis sanctis, De (Bede) 2–154b
LOCK, ADAM 7–0
LO CODI 7–0
Lo conhort (Francesc Ferrer) 3–171b, 173b
Lo Crestià (Francesc Eiximenis) 3–157b; 4–416a-b
Loculi 3–155a
LOCULUS 7–0
Locus amoenus 1–184b
***LOCUS SANCTUS* 7–0**; 4–348b
Lofty among the equals 4–444b
Lof vanden Heilighen Sacramente (Anthonis de Roovere) 4–322b
Logic
See Dialectic
LOGIC, ISLAMIC 7–0
Logica Algazeli 4–170b
LOGOS, CHRIST 7–0
dogma 3–336a
LOGOTHETE 7–0
bureaucracy 2–473a,b
diplomacy 4–194b, 195a-b
evolution 2–487b
Logroño 3–131b
LOHENGRIN 7–0
Loher und Maller (Elisabeth of Nassau-Saarbrucken) 4–432b
Loire River 1–89a
***LOKASENNA* 7–0**; 4–386a, 391a,b
LOKI 7–0; 2–55b
Fáfnir 4–581a
LOLLARDS 7–0; 4–376b
Bible 2–222a
Bohemian Brethren 2–306a
Cambridge University 3–59a
Clanvowe, Sir John 3–408b
exegesis 4–547a,b, 548a
heretical dissent 3–370a-b
rise 4–484b
Lombard, Peter 1–52a, 109a, 127a; 4–381b
angel/angelology 1–250a
baptism 2–84a
Christology 3–322b, 323a
confirmation 3–536a
Peter of Candia 1–147a,b
Sentences 1–148a, 353b, 354b; 4–170a, 519a
Lombard arch
See Arch
LOMBARD ART 7–0
LOMBARD BANDS 7–0
LOMBARD LEAGUE 7–0
Byzantine support 2–494b
carroccio, use 3–117b
consuls, consulate 3–571a
Frederick Barbarossa 1–147a; 3–117b
LOMBARDS 7–0
agricultural tools 1–90b
Arianism 1–454b; 3–339b
Austria 2–4b
banking 2–76a
Byzantine Empire 2–486b
cavalry 3–201a
Charlemagne 3–107a, 268b
consolamentum 3–185a-b
Crusade of 1101 4–36a,b
Italy invasion 2–95a-96a
papacy 3–106a,b
Rome seige (756) 3–154b
LOMBARDS, KINGDOM OF 7–0
agriculture 1–86b, 87a
Albornoz 1–131a
Avars 2–12b
fairs 4–587a
feuds 4–60a
Frederick II 4–58b-59a,b
Peter of Candia 1–147b
Lombers
Cathar debate 3–183b
L'Ombrière, Castle 2–328a
LONDON 7–0
aldermen 1–144a
Alfred the Great 1–164a
Anglo-Norman chronicles 1–266a
Anglo-Saxon 4–457b
art trade 1–562a
barbers guild 2–99b
Black Death 2–262a-b
burgesses 4–465b
Chroniques de Londres 3–329b, 334a
commune 3–498a-499a, 502a
fairs 4–586b
money markets 2–78b
Norman-Angevin England 4–469b
Simon de Montfort the Younger 2–112a
Londres, Chroniques de
See Chroniques de Londres
Longbow
See Bow and Arrow/Crossbow
Longer Command, The (Augustine) 1–658a
Longer Letter, The (Augustine) 1–658a
Longest Letter, The (Augustine) 1–658a

Longinus
Anglo-Norman literature 1–270a
crucifixion 4–12a
Nubian Christianity 3–314b
Longobardorum leges 3–609b
Lonja 2–74a
Loores de Nuestra Señora (Gonzalo de Berceo) 2–187a-b
Lo pecador remut (Felip de Malla) 3–168a
Lope de Luna 1–416a
LOPES, FERNÃO 7–0
LÓPEZ DE AYALA, PERO 7–0
cuaderna vía 4–63a
Lop of Valencia, King 1–409a
Lopo Gonçalves
exploration 4–561b
Loptr 2–256a
Lorca
agriculture 1–82a
Lord's Prayer
baptismal sponsorship 2–86a
ceremonies of catechumen 2–83b
recitation by laity 3–359a
Lord Valley 3–174b
LORENZETTI, AMBROGIO 7–0; 1–343a
frescoes 1–73b
LORENZETTI, PIETRO 7–0; 2–113a
Assisi, San Francesco 1–593b-594a
Lorenz Helmschmied
arms and armor 1–533a
Lorenzo da Firenze
ballata 2–61a
Lorenzo della Volpaia 3–463b
LORENZO DI NICCOLÒ DI MARTINO 7–0
LORENZO MONACO 7–0
LORENZO VENEZIANO 7–0
Lore of Place Names
See Dinnshenchas
Lore of Places
See Dindshenchas
Lorica 3–231a
LORI/CORAGET 7–0
Lori-Joraget 2–48b
Loros 3–615a-b
Lorraine
See Lotharingia
Lorrenzetti, Ambroglio
Duccio 4–302b
Lorrenzetti, Pietro
Duccio 4–302b
Lorsch Monastery 1–306a
Los Toros de Guisando, pact of (1468) 3–138b
LOTE, STEPHEN 7–0
Lothair I, Emperor
Agobard 1–75a
Angelomus of Luxeuil 1–251b
Burgundy, County of 2–424a
Burgundy, Kingdom of 2–428b
Carolingians 3–112a,b
Clemens Scotus 3–438a
Einhard 4–412b
Lothair II/III, Emperor
Billungs 2–235b
Brandenburg 2–360b
election 2–424b; 4–427a
Lothair II of Lorraine, King 3–114a
Burgundy, Kingdom of 2–428b
Byzantine Empire 2–494a
Lothair of Segni
See Innocent III, Pope
Lothar
See Lothair
Lothar Cross 1–335a
Lotharingia 1–1b
Arnulf 1–541b
Black Death 2–262b
Burgundy, Duchy of 2–427a
champlevé enamels 4–438a,b
Charles the Simple 3–115a
Lothario di Segni
See Innocent III, Pope
Lothbrok, Ragnar 1–163b
Louis II, Emperor 3–114a
Albrecht von Scharfenberg 1–133b
Bari 2–108b
Burgundy, Kingdom of 2–428b
Louis IV, Emperor 2–8a, 135a
Andronikos II Palaiologos 1–246a
Avignonese papacy 3–363a
Brandenburg 2–361a
conciliar theory 3–515a
Defensor pacis 4–132a
Donation of Constantine 4–259a
election 4–428b
Mühldorf victory 2–7b
seal 1–333b
Louis, Saint
See Louis IX of France
Louis II de Male of Flanders, count 2–145a; 3–270a
Louis IV d'Outremer of France
Western Carolingian Empire 3–115a-b
Louis Ellies du Pin
conciliar theory 3–521b
Louis I of Anjou 3–270a
Apocalypse Tapestries 2–129b
Louis III of Anjou 1–417b
Louis I of Bavaria 2–134b-135a
Louis of Blois, Count
Crusades: Fourth 4–42a
Louis of Bourbon, Duke
biography 3–333a
Clanvowe, Sir John 3–408a
Louis III of France 3–114a
accession 4–426a
Louis V of France
death 3–115b
LOUIS VI OF FRANCE 7–0
Bernard of Clairvaux 2–191b
biography 2–236b, 239b
charters, town 3–494b
châtelet 3–278a
church reforms 3–347b
communes 3–496a,b
Eleanor of Aquitaine 4–419a
Hugh, lord of Le Puiset 3–145a
Normandy 4–462b
Louis VII of France
church reforms 3–347b
Eleanor of Aquitaine 1–367b; 3–245a
Henry II of England 4–467a
Second Crusade 4–30b, 37b-38b
Louis VIII of France
Albigensian crusade 3–189a,b
appanages 1–351b
Avignon siege 3–247b
Blanche of Castile 2–270b
LOUIS IX OF FRANCE 7–0
assassins 1–591a
banking, Jewish 2–81b
Baron's War 2–112a
Baybars al-Bunduqdārī 2–138a
Bible 2–215a; 4–25b
biography 2–236a, 240a
Blanch of Castile 2–270b
Boniface VIII 2–324a
Book of Judith 4–26a
Boucher, Guillaume 2–349b
Cathars 3–190a
chamberlain office 3–242b
chronicles 3–332b
courtesy books 3–661b
crusader art and architecture 4–25b
crusades 2–77b; 4–31b, 52b-54a, 59b, 396a
diplomacy 4–211a
dye industry 4–328b
Eudes of Montreuil 4–519a
Eudes Rigaud 4–519a
Henry III 1–148a
Leiden psalter 1–336a
Mansūra, Al- 4–32a
Mongolia 4–556b
Paris, Treaty of (1259) 1–367b
royal confessor 3–535a
Louis X of France
chronicles 3–332b
Jews expulsion 4–564a
LOUIS XI OF FRANCE 7–0
angelus bell 2–166a
Aragon, Crown of 1–418b
biography 2–237a
Bordeaux 2–328b
Bourdichon, Jean 2–349b
Brittany, Duchy 2–380b
Burgundy, County of 2–426a
Burgundy, Kingdom of 2–429b
Charles VII 3–271b
Comines' chronicles 3–333b, 487a,b
Dauphiné 4–109b
fairs 4–585b
Louis XII of France
Bourdichon, Jean 2–349b
Brittany, Duchy 2–380a
conciliar theory 3–520a
Louis I of Hungary 4–80a
Boccaccio 2–281a
Bosnia 2–337a
Byzantine Empire 2–502a
Christine de Pizan 3–316a
Cola di Rienzo 3–478b
Louis of Nevers
Bruges 2–387b
Louis I of Orléans
assassination 3–649b
Enguerrand VII of Coucy 4–490b, 491a
Louis of Orléans, Duke 3–272b
Louis the Blind
Burgundy, Kingdom of 2–428b
Louis III the Child of Germany 2–6a; 3–114b; 4–426a
Louis II the German 4–426a
Basil I 2–453b
Louis I the Pious 1–75a, 228a, 366b; 2–102b; 3–268b, 269a, 346b, 436b
All Saints' Day 1–176b
anointing 1–308b
Benedictine Rule 2–168a, 170b, 172a
biblical epics 2–225a-b
biography 2–236a-b
Brittany, Duchy 2–378b
caesaropapism 3–11b
canon laws 3–216b
capitularies 3–91b
Carolingian Empire 3–111a-112b
Celtic church 2–382a; 3–229a
church reforms 3–347b
deposition of rulers 4–159a
Einhard 4–412a-b
elections, royal 4–425b-426a
Ermoldus Nigellus 4–507b
Theodulf 3–100b
Louis the Roman
Brandenburg 2–361a-b
Louis II the Stammerer of France 3–114b
Aquitaine 1–367a
Louis Villiers de l'Isle-Adam
ceramics 3–238a

Louvain
Bouts, Dirk 2–350a
Flemish commune 3–497b
Louvre
renovation 4–295a
Love
allegory 1–183b-185a, 189a
Love, courtly
See Courtly love
Lovelich, Henry
Arthurian literature 1–573b, 574a
Lovers' Courtship
See Donnei des amanz
Lovers' Disasters (al-Sarrāj) 1–380b
Love sagas
See Family sagas, Icelandic
Love sleeve 3–625a
Lovocat
Celtic church 2–382a
Low Countries
coal mining 3–473a
communes 3–497a-498a, 500b, 502a, 503a
See Also Belgium
See Also Luxembourg
See Also Netherlands
Lower Armenia 2–20a
Lozano, Menachem ben Judah da 3–622a
LÜBECK 7–0
LUCA DI TOMMÈ 7–0
Lucan 1–162a; 2–236a
Córdoba 3–597b
Lucca
Alexander II 1–146a
banking 2–73b, 74a,b, 76b, 77b, 78b
codices 4–23a
commune 3–500a
dye industry 4–328a
Lucca Madonna (Jan van Eyck) 4–567a
Lucernarium 4–367a
Lucerne Passion 4–267b
Lucian of Samosata 3–334b
Lucić, Hanibal 4–80a
Lucidaire
See Elucidarium and Spanish *Lucidario*
Lucidarios
See Elucidarium and Spanish *Lucidario*
Lucidator astronomiae (Pietro d'Abano) 1–613a
Lucius III, Pope 3–186b
Cilician-Roman church union 3–394a
Lucius Cornelius Sulla
Athens, looting 1–334b
Lucy, Saint
Anglo-Norman life of 1–261b
Lucydary
See Elucidarium and Spanish *Lucidario*
Lüderitz
exploration 4–562b
Luder von Braunschweig 2–230b, 231b-232a
Ludger, Saint 1–226a
Ludolf of Saxony 3–167a
Ludolf of Sudheim
travel book 4–579a
Ludovici VIII
biography 2–236b
Ludus de adventu et interitu Antichristi 4–281b-282a
***LUDUS DE ANTICHRISTO* 7–0**; 3–98b; 4–281b-282a
Ludus super Anticlaudianum (Adam de la Bassée) 1–48a
Ludwig
See Louis
LUDWIGSLIED 7–0
Lughat-i Furs (Asadī al-Ṭūsī) 4–444b
Lugo 1–626a
Luis Dalmau
See Dalmau, Luis
Luitger the Frisian 1–142b
Luitpold, Margrave
Magyars 2–6a
Luitpoldingians 2–6a
Babenberg family 2–33b
Bavarian rule 2–134a
Luitprand of Cremona
See Liutprand of Cremona
LUKAS NOTARAS 7–0
Luke of Prague
Bohemian Brethren 2–307a-b
Luke of Sambucina 3–405b
Luke of Stiris, Saint
Hosios Lukas Monastery 2–442b
LULL, RAMON 7–0; 1–415b; 2–41a
alchemy 1–138a-b
Arnald of Villanova 1–538a
biblical exegesis 2–216b
Boniface, Saint 2–322b
Catalan language 3–157b, 158a, 160a,b, 161a,b, 163a-b
Catalan literature 3–165a, 170b
Christian Hebraists 3–314a
courtesy books 3–666a-b
exempla 4–551b
Vienne, Council of 3–644b
Lullus of Malmesbury 1–142b
Lully, Raymond
See Lull, Ramon
Luma' 1–583a, 584b, 585a
Lumen luminum (al-Rāzī) 1–136b
Lumere as lais (Peter of Peckham) 1–263b
"Luminous Doctrine"
Nestorianism 3–312b
Lunardo di Matteo Ducci
Brunelleschi, Filippo 2–388a
"Lunar jump" 3–22a-b
Lunar month 3–17b
Lunar year 3–17b
Lupi, Bonifazio 1–226b
LUPOLD OF BEDENBURG (BAMBERG) **7–0**
LUPUS OF FERRIÈRES 7–0; 3–112a
Chappes fair 4–590b
classical literary studies 3–433a
Lūqā, Qusṭa ibn 1–458a, 461a-b
Lusatia 2–300b
LUSIGNANS 7–0
crusades 4–54b-55b
Cyprus, Kingdom of 4–70b, 71a-b
Lusitania 1–121a
LUSTERWARE 7–0
Abbasid 1–5b
European 3–238a
Islamic 3–238b, 239a
Lustration
dedication of churches 4–130b
Luther, Martin 3–655a
Babylonian Captivity 2–34b
Biel 2–234a,b
Bohemian Brethren 2–307b
Brethren of the Common Life 2–369a-b
excommunication 4–538a
Reformation 1–660a
Luwāta
See Berbers
Luxorius
Anthologia latina 1–317a
Luzarches, Robert of
See Robert of Luzarches
Luzzi, Mondino dei
See Mondino dei Luzzi
Lycia 1–240a
LYDGATE, JOHN 7–0; 1–323b; 3–661a
Boccaccio 2–286b
dramas 4–279b
Lydus, John
See Ioannes Laurentii Lydus
Lyndsay, Sir David
allegory 4–287a
LYONESE RITE 7–0
Carthusian rite 3–118a
Lyonnais 2–428b
LYONS 7–0
Agobard 1–75a
Amalarius of Metz 1–228a
Burgundians 2–423a
Council (1245) 4–59a-b
duchy 2–428b
fairs 2–78b; 4–585b
Lyons, Councils of
See Councils, Western (869-1179) and (1215-1274
Lyons, Richard
impeachment 4–399a, 484b
Lyons, Second Council of (1274)
crusade propaganda 4–19b-20a
papal election constitution 3–94b-95a
Lyric
See entries under individual languages
Lytel John 3–661a-b

M

Ma'arrat al-Nu'mān
Raymond of Toulouse 4–35b
MA'ARRĪ, ABŪ 'L-'ALĀ' AḤMAD AL- 7–0; 1–381b, 401b
Mabādi' al-lugha (Muḥummad ibn 'Abd Allāh al-Iskāfī) 4–443a
Mabillon, Jean 3–252a, 318b
MABINOGI 7–0
Arthurian literature 1–566a
Dyfed 4–329b
Macaronic
Anglo-Norman lyric poetry 1–269a
MACBETH 8–0
Duncan I 4–308a
Mac Crimthainn, Feidlimid 3–121b
Maccus (Magnus), King
Chester, Treaty of 3–299b-300a
MacDonald clan 3–407a
MacDougall clan 3–407a
MACEDONIAN RENAISSANCE 8–0; 2–117b, 440b-441a, 442a, 453b-454b
Byzantine art 2–439a-443b, 453b
Byzantine poetry 1–523b
Cappadocia 3–92b
MACEDONIANS 8–0
Anatolia 1–241a
Andronikos II Palaiologos 1–246a
Basil II 2–119a
Bogomils 2–296a-b
Boris of Bulgaria 2–329a
Bulgaria 2–119a, 406b, 408b, 409a,b, 410a, 412a
Byzantine 2–479b; 4–595a
Catalan conquest 3–156a
Constantinople 3–552a
dunatoi 4–306b

Epiros despotate 4–499a
Turkish conquest 2–502a
villages 2–480b
MACHAUT, GUILLAUME DE 8–0; 1–185a, 189b
ars nova 1–548b, 552b
ars subtilior 1–558b
ballade 2–59a
chansonnier 3–256a
Faenza Codex 4–580a
poetized history 3–332b
Machecoul castle 3–146b
Machiavelli
condottieri 3–531b
MACHICOLATION 8–0; 3–146b, 147
Ayyubid 2–21a-b
Machicoulis
See Machicolation
Machoviensis
See Macsó
Maciot
Canary Islands settlement 3–62b, 63a
MacLachlan family 3–407a
MACLONAIN, FLANN 8–0
Mâconnais county 2–427a
Mac Regol of Birr
manuscript illumination 3–221b
Macrobiosis, theory of 1–134b
MACROBIUS 8–0
allegory 1–182a-b
astronomy 1–610b
Avianus 2–15b
fables 4–572a
Macrocosmos 1–604b
Macruaraidh lords 3–407a
Macsó 2–70a, 336a
MacSween family 3–407a
Mačva
See Macsó
Madā'in, al-
See Ctesiphon
Madara 2–399b, 401b
art and architecture 2–414b
Madder (*Rubia tinctorum*) 4–326b-327a
MADEIRA ISLANDS 8–0
exploration 4–559a
Madīnat al-Salām
See Round City
Madīnat al-Zahrā'
Córdoba 3–599a, 600a
Madog ab Einion
Peace of Conway 3–580a
Madog ap Maredudd 4–69b
Arthurian literature 1–578a
Madog Benfras 4–76b, 77a
Madog Fychan
Casnodyn 3–121b
Madonna and Child (Bernardo Daddi) 4–75b, 76a
Madonna and Child (Cimabue) 3–396b
Madonna and Child (Coppo di Marcovaldo) 3–585a
Madonna and Child Enthroned (Coppo di Marcovaldo) 3–585a
Madonna and Child Enthroned with Saints and Angels (Giovanni Baronzio) 2–113a
Madonna and Child (Pietro Cavallini) 3–198a
Madonna and Child with Donor (Barna da Siena) 2–111a
Madonna and Child with Saints (Bernardo Daddi) 4–76a
Madonna and Child with Saints (Giovanni Baronzio) 2–112b
Madonna at the Fountain (Jan van Eyck) 4–567a
Madonna in the Church (Jan van Eyck) 4–567a
Madonna of Mercy (Bartolo di Fredi) 2–116b
Madonna of the Chancellor Rodin (Jan van Eyck) 4–567a
Madonna of the Franciscans (Duccio di Buoninsegna) 4–302a
Madonna with Canon van der Paele (Jan van Eyck) 4–567a
Madonna with Saint Francis (Duccio di Buoninsegna) 4–302a
Madonna with Saints Francis and Jerome (Petrus Christus) 3–324b
MADRASA 8–0; 4–408a
Bukhara 2–397a
Madrasah 2–21b-22a
Damascus 4–83b
Madrid
fairs 4–587b
MADRIGAL 8–0
ars nova 1–552b-553a
caccia 3–4a,b
Máeldubh 1–144a
MAELGWN 8–0
Maerlant, Jacob van
didactic works 4–319b
romances 4–318b
MAESTÀ 8–0
Cimabue 3–396b
Duccio di Buoninsegna 4–302a-303a
Maffeo Polo 4–557a
MA FIN EST MON COMMENCEMENT 8–0
Magdeburg
Adalbert, Saint 1–47b
Mag Eo
Colman, Bishop of Lindisfarne 3–480a
Maghīla
See Berbers
Maghrebi 1–210a; 3–54b
Alexandrian Jews 1–153b, 154b
Maghrib
Almohads 1–194a,b, 195a
Almoravid art 1–196a
Almoravid invasion 1–200b
Berbers 1–198a; 2–186b
MAGHRIB, AL- 8–0; 1–622a
Maghribi art
Alhambra 1–171a
Magi, adoration of
art 4–497b
Epiphany 4–496b, 497a
MAGIC, BOOKISH 8–0
MAGIC AND FOLKLORE, ARMENIAN 8–0
MAGIC AND FOLKLORE, BYZANTINE 8–0
MAGIC AND FOLKLORE, ISLAMIC 8–0
Arabic numerals 1–384b
MAGIC AND FOLKLORE, JEWISH 8–0
MAGIC AND FOLKLORE, WESTERN EUROPEAN 8–0
Arthurian literature 1–564a
Bacon 2–38a-b
botany 2–348a
charms, old High German 3–273b
Egbert of Liège 4–399b
Fachschrifttum 4–579b
MAGISTER MILITUM 8–0; 1–491b
Alaric 1–122a
Magister militum per Orientum
Anatolikon theme 1–242a
MAGISTER OFFICIORUM 8–0
Magister scrinii
See Chancery
Magistri 3–111b
Magistri civium
communes 3–497b
Magistro fabro de Fontains
charcoal making 3–267b
MAGISTROS 8–0
MAGIUS 8–0
Mag Léna, Battle of (907) 3–602a
MAGNA CARTA 8–0
assize 1–598a
bailiff 2–51b
baronial claims 4–481b
common pleas court 3–492a
communes 3–499a
deposition of rulers 4–160b
distress 4–221a
French translation 1–260a
Henry I 4–462a
John, King 4–468b, 469a, 470b, 472a
Langton 3–83b
Magnae derivationes (Hugutio of Pisa) 4–449b, 450a
Magna glosatura (Peter Lombard) 2–221b
Magnaura Palace 3–553b
university 2–106a
Magnesia
Andronikos II Palaiologos 1–246a
Magnificat 3–84b
Magnificence 4–287a
Magnus, Albertus
See Albertus Magnus
Magnús Bareleg of Norway, King 4–414a
Magnus II Eriksson, King
Birgitta, Saint 2–247a
Black Death 2–261b
Erikskrönikan 4–505b
Magnus liber (Léonin) 1–310a
MAGNUS LIBER ORGANI 8–0
clausula 3–437a
Magnus of Denmark 4–152b, 153a
Magnus VII of Denmark, King 4–155a
Magnus I of Norway, King 4–395a
Magnus of Saxony 2–235a-b
See Billungs
Magnusson Erik 4–520a
Erikskrönikan 4–505b
Magret, Guillaume 4–110a
MÁGUS SAGA JARLS 8–0
Magyar Országos Levéltar 1–448b
MAGYARS 8–0
Austria 2–6a
Bohemia 2–299b
Bulgaria 2–404b, 405b
Burgundy, County of 2–424a
Byzantine Empire 2–489b
Carolingian Empire 3–114b
cavalry 3–203a
conversion 3–355b
Croatia 4–2b-4a
draft animals 1–296b
northern Europe raids 1–94a
MAHDĪ, AL- 8–0; 1–9a, 174b; 3–46b
Baghdad 2–46a
heresy suppression 3–43b, 48a
Mahdi, Ismaili 1–72a
Mahdia 1–194a
Mahdīyah, Al-, Tunisia 4–27b, 556a
Ma'hir Ibn Tibbon, Jacob ben 1–613a
Mahmūd 2–43b
Khwarizm 2–248b
Maḥmūd ibn Sebuktegin 1–65a
Mahoître shoulders 3–625b
Maide Kranz, Der (Von Mügeln) 1–138b
Mail 1–522a-b, 523a, 524a-b, 533b, 534a,b

Mailed cavalry 3–200a-b, 203a
MAIMONIDEAN CONTROVERSY 8–0
MAIMONIDES, ABRAHAM BEN MOSES 8–0
biblical exegesis 2–212a
MAIMONIDES, MOSES 8–0; 1–21b; 4–407b
Aristotelianism 1–460a
cookery, European 3–582b
Córdoba 3–600b
Crescas 3–677b
Eckhart 4–381b
exegesis 4–540a
Jewish apocalyptic literature 1–345b
Mishneh Torah 1–22b
MAINMORT 8–0
See Also Commune
Mainz
Adalbert, Saint 1–47b
commune 3–498a
Embricho 4–436b
Frankish invasions 2–94a
Jewish community 2–263b; 4–420b
Prague 2–304a
Maior domus 3–104b, 107b
***MAISTRE PIERRE PATHELIN* 8–0**
MAITANI, AMBROGIO 8–0
MAITANI, LORENZO 8–0; 1–251a
Maître Pierre Pathelin 4–265b
MAI UND BEAFLOR 8–0
Maius
See Magius
Majd al-Dīn Abū 'L-Sa'Ādāt Mubārak 1–634a, 635a
MAJESTAS DOMINI 8–0
Apocalypse illustration 1–344a
Majid, Ahmad ibn
exploration 4–563a
Majlis 3–33a
Majmū'a rasā'il fī aḥkām al-nujūm (Kūshyār ibn Labbān) 1–385b
MAJOLICA 8–0; 3–237b
commercial trade 1–561b
Majolus of Cluny 3–469a
Major, John
conciliar theory 3–519b, 520b
Majorca
agriculture 1–80a, 83b
Alfonso V 1–418a
archives 1–448b
commerce 1–561b; 4–559a
James II 1–414b
James the Conqueror 1–411b-412a,b, 413a
Jews, persecution of 1–419b
Martín I 1–417a
Pedro IV 1–415b-416a,b
slaves 2–268b, 270a
Majorian, Emperor 1–334a
Majūsī, al-
See Haly
Makarios I 4–525a
Makarios Melissenos 2–517a-b
Makarska 2–336b
Makeup
See Beauty aids, cosmetics
Makhairas, Leontios 4–73a
Makheras monastery 4–70b
Makhzūm 1–28b, 29b, 112b; 2–42b
Makīn, al- 4–525a
Makuria, Kingdom of
Nubian Christianity 3–314b
Malabranca, Francesco Frangipani 3–196b
Bernard of Clairvaux 2–191a
Celtic church reforms 3–232a
MALACHY, SAINT 8–0; 1–470a
Mālaga
fruit trees 1–82b
Málaháttr 4–384a, 388b-389a
Malā'ika 1–248b
MALALAS 8–0
Mälar, Lake 4–554a
Mälaren, Lake
Birka 2–247b
Malatesta, Pandolfo 3–531a
Malatya
Danishmendids 4–91b
Malazgert
See Manzikert
MALCOLM I OF ALBA 8–0
Malcolm I of Scotland
Chester, Treaty of 3–299b
MALCOLM II OF SCOTLAND 8–0
Duncan I 4–308a
MALCOLM III OF SCOTLAND 8–0
David I 4–110b
Donald III 4–256a
William the Conqueror 4–461b
MALCOLM IV OF SCOTLAND 8–0; 4–111a
Mal d'amor 3–87a
Maldon, Battle of (991) 4–90a, 457a
Mâle, Louis de, Counte of Flanders 2–145a
See Louis II de Male of Flanders
Male circumcision
See Circumcision
MALI 8–0
Maliasenoi family 2–479a
Malik, 'Abd al- 1–479a
Malik al-'Ādil Sayf al-Dīn, al-
Ayyubid art and architecture 2–21b
Malik al-Nāṣir, al- 3–398b
Malik al-Ṣāliḥ, al-
Saladin 4–39a
Malik al-Ṣāliḥ 'Ayyūb, al-
Baybars al-Bunduqdārī 2–138a
Malik al-Ṣāliḥ Najm al-Dīn Ayyūb, al-
Ayyubid art and architecture 2–21b-22a
blazon 2–272b
Malik al-Ẓāhir, al-
See Baybars al-Bunduqdārī
Malik-Ghāzi Gůmůshtigin 2–309a
MĀLIK IBN ANAS 8–0; 1–26b; 4–407a
Córdoba 3–598b
Maliki school of jurisprudence 1–71a
MALIKSHĀH 8–0; 1–118b, 485a; 4–82a
Alp Arslan 1–203b
Byzantine Empire 2–493a
Malimir of Bulgaria 2–402a, 406a
Mall, Eduard 1–271b
Malla, Felip de 3–168a
M'allaqa, Al- 4–361a
Malmédy
Pepin 3–104a-b
Malmesbury
Aldhelm 1–144a
Malocello, Lanzarotto 4–558b, 559a
Canary Islands exploration 3–61b
MALORY, SIR THOMAS 8–0
Arthurian literature 1–564a, 573b, 574a,b; 3–302b
courtly love 3–669b
MALOUEL, JEAN 8–0
Malqaf
See Bādgīr
***MÁLSHÁTTAKVÆÐI* 8–0**; 2–256a
MALTA 8–0
Malta, Knights of 3–303b-304a
Maltese cross 4–9b
"Maltese falcon" 3–304a
Maltese language 1–378b
MALTOLTE 8–0
MALWIYA 8–0
Maly Kavkaz
See Lesser Caucasus range
Mamai, Emir
Dmitri Ivanovich Donskoi 4–232b
Mambre
early Christian architecture 4–335a
Mambrē Vercanoł 1–509b
MAMIKONEAN 8–0; 4–112b
Armenia 1–478b, 479a
Bagratids 2–48a
social structure 1–489a
Mamistra 3–391a, 393a
MAMLŪK 8–0; 1–453a
Ayyubids 2–24a, 25a
Circassians 3–398a
military dress 3–618a-b
MAMLUK ART 8–0
MAMLUK DYNASTY 8–0
Acre 4–26a
Aleppo 1–145b
Alexandria 1–153b, 154a
Anatolia 1–241b
Antioch 1–326a
Āyās 2–19a; 3–393a
Ayyubid art 2–20b
Barqūq 2–113a
Baybars al-Bunduqdārī 2–138a
Beirut 2–164a
blazons 2–272b
cavalry 3–209b
Cilician kingdom 3–393a
Cilician-Roman church union 3–394b, 395a
Copts and Coptic church 3–594b
crusader art and architecture 4–22b, 25b
crusades 4–32a-33a, 54b, 55a-b, 56b
Damascus 4–82b, 83b, 84a-b, 85a
Egypt 1–12a; 3–51a; 4–406a, 408a
origins 2–138a
Ottoman war 2–137b
Sunnites 1–376a
Syria 3–14a
MAMMEN STYLE 8–0
MA'MŪN, AL- 8–0; 1–9b, 10a-b, 391b; 2–110b; 3–46b
Abū Nuwās 1–27b-28a
Baghdad 2–46b
caliphate 3–43a, 48a
Christian church in Persia 3–313a
exilarch 4–552a-b
Marrakech 1–195b
parentage 4–597b
Manarah
See Minaret
Manaw Gododdin 4–64b
MANAZKERT 8–0
Alp Arslan 1–203b, 302a; 4–33b
Arčēš 1–423a
Armenian Muslim emirates 1–512b, 513b
Romanos IV 2–493a
Turkish Islam 1–241a
Manazkert, Battle of (1071) 3–356a; 4–27b, 344a
MANAZKERT, COUNCIL OF 8–0; 1–501b
Mandamentum 2–69a
Mande, Hendrik
Devotio moderna 4–166b
Mandeville family
Tower of London 3–125a
***MANDEVILLE'S TRAVELS* 8–0**; 4–547a
MANDORLA 8–0
early Christian art 4–354b

MANDYLION 8–0
early Christian art 4–367b
Edessa 4–384a
Manē, Saint 1–519b
MANEGOLD OF LAUTENBACH 8–0
angelus 1–252a
Anselm of Laon 1–316a
dialectic 4–169b
Manekine, La (poem) 2–145a
Manfred, Bishop
Arnold of Brescia 1–539b
Manfredina, La 4–88a
Manfred of Athens, Duke 3–156b
MANFRED OF MAGDEBURG 8–0
Manfred of Sicily, King 1–412b; 4–60a-b, 95b, 330a
Angevins 1–253b
Epiros despotate 4–499b
Nicaea 2–498b, 499a
Manfred of Vercelli 4–250a
Mangonel 3–150b, 180a-b
castle location 3–143a-b
Mangujaqids 1–514a
Mangyt 3–680a
MANICHAEANS 8–0
Abbasid caliphate 3–43b
Augustine of Hippo 1–646b, 647a-b, 650b-661b
Docetism 4–233a-b
dualism 3–340a; 4–297b
MANIERA GRECA 8–0
MANIÈRE DE LANGAGE 8–0; 1–270b
Manifestation, Feast of
See Epiphany, Feast of
Manipulus florum (Thomas of Ireland) 1–207a
Manjacoria, Nicholas
Christian Hebraists 3–313b
Mankind 4–287b
Mankū Khān 2–43b
Mannered School
See Ars subtilior
Manners of the Drinking Companion 1–380a
MANNYNG, ROBERT, OF BRUNNE (BOURNE) 8–0; 1–263a; 3–662a
folk games 4–279b
Man of Sorrows
See Imago Pietatis
Manorial accounts 1–39a-40a
Manorialism
Norman-Angevin England 4–470a
MANRIQUE, JORGE 8–0; 3–104a
copla 3–584b
Manselli 4–512a
Mansi 4–512a
Mansionarius
hierarchy of clergy 3–444b
MANṢŪR, AL- 8–0; 1–8a, 9a, 392a
Abū Hanīfa 1–26a
Alid rebellion 1–174b
astronomy 1–619b-620a
Baghdad 2–44b
Barmakids 3–44a
caliphate 3–42a,b, 44a, 46b, 48a
diplomacy 4–200b
Rafiqah, al- 2–46b
Manṣūr, al-, Muḥammad ibn-abi-ʿĀmir
Alptigin 1–220a
Asturias-León 1–625b, 628a
Barcelona 2–102b
Catalonia 3–175b
Mansūra, Al-, Battle of (1250) 1–526a; 2–138a; 3–151b; 4–50b
Louis IX 4–32a, 53a
Manṣūr ʿAlī, al-
Barqūq 2–113a
Manṣūr ibn ʿAlī ibn ʿIrāq, Abū Naṣr 1–606b
Manṣūrīya, al-
See Qāhira, al-
Mantegna, Andrea 1–226b
engraving 4–487b, 489a, 490a
Mantel, Der (Heinrich von dem Türlîn) 1–229b
Mantel mautaillié 1–268a
Manticore 2–206a
Mantua
fairs 4–587a
Mantua, Council of (1064) 1–146b
Manual (Byrhtferth of Ramsey) 1–284a, 285b
Manual of Christian Iconography
See Hermeneia
MANUALS, ARTISTIC 8–0
ars praedicandi 1–555b-557b
Manuals, farming
Islamic 1–105b-106a
MANUEL, JUAN 8–0
Libro del Cavallero Zifar 3–197b
Manuel Angelos 2–479b
Manuel Butumites
Nicaea 4–35a
MANUEL CHRYSOLORAS 8–0
artists' status 1–580a
***MANUEL DES PECHÉS* 8–0**; 1–263a
Manuel Disypatos 2–457a
MANUEL EUGENIKOS 8–0
MANUEL I KOMNENOS 8–0; 1–159a, 614a
Andronikos I Komnenos 1–244a
Armenian church 1–500b
Bogomils 2–294b
Boniface of Montferrat 2–323a
Church of the Nativity 4–24b
crusades 4–37b, 38a-b
despot 4–165a
Hagia Sophia (Trebizond) 2–447a
Myriokephalon 1–241b
reign 2–493b, 494a-b, 495a-b
Manuel of Armenia the architect
Ałt'amar 1–220b
Manuel I of Portugal
Vasco da Gama 4–563a
MANUEL II PALAIOLOGOS 8–0
land holdings 2–481a
monasticism 2–478b
Pisa Council (1409) 1–147b
reign 2–502a-503b
MANUEL PANSELINOS 8–0; 2–448b
Manuel Philes 2–507b, 524a
epigrams 2–457b
Manumissions
Old English 1–286b
MANUSCRIPT AND BOOK BINDING 8–0
codicology 3–475b
MANUSCRIPT AND BOOK PRODUCTION 8–0
block book 2–274a
Caxton 3–210a
chained books 3–240b
classical literary studies 3–431a
codex 3–473b
codicology 3–475b
colophon 3–483b
Manuscript Illumination: Armenian 1–496b-497b
MANUSCRIPT ILLUMINATION: BYZANTINE AND ISLAMIC 8–0
Ahmad Mūsā 1–106b
Apocalypse illustrations 1–344a
Ayyubid 2–22b
Cilician 3–393b
Deesis 4–131b
early Christian art 4–350b-351a,b
Macedonian Dynasty 2–440b
Manuscript illumination: Coptic 3–590a-591b
MANUSCRIPT ILLUMINATION: HEBREW 8–0; 1–5b
MANUSCRIPT ILLUMINATION: WESTERN EUROPEAN 8–0
Ambraser Heldenbuch 1–229b
Apocalypse illustration 3–343b, 344a
Avila Bible, Master of 2–16b
bas-de-page 2–117a
Beatus manuscripts 2–143b
Boucicaut Master 2–349b
Brailes, William de 2–360a
Brittany, Duchy 2–379a
Bulgarian 2–417b
canon table 3–66a
carpet page 3–117a
Celtic 3–218a-219a,b, 220b, 221b, 223a,b
Cluny order 3–469a
codicology 3–475b
Colombe 3–482a
death and burial 4–121b
diaper pattern 4–171b
drollery 4–294a
Durrow, Books of 4–316b
early Christian art 4–348b, 352b-353a, 355b-357a
Ebgert of Trier 4–399b
Ebo of Rheims 4–368a
Emeterius of Tábara 4–436b
Ende 4–450b
Manuscripts and books
ars praedicandi 1–555b
Bosnian 2–342b
collections 1–335b-336a
dating 1–275b
Manuscripts and books: Anglo-Saxon 1–274a
MANUSCRIPTS AND BOOKS: CELTIC LITURGICAL 8–0
MANUSCRIPTS AND BOOKS: HEBREW 8–0
MANUSCRIPTS AND BOOKS: ISLAMIC 8–0
Bukhārī, al- 2–397b-399a
farming manuals 1–105b-106a
Man who blew into the little box, The
See Buskenblaser
Manx dialect 3–233a
Manzikert
See Manazkert
Manẓūr, ibn 4–444a
MAP (MAPES), WALTER 8–0
antifeminism 1–323a, 324a
Henry II's court 4–471b
MAPHORION 8–0
Maphrian 1–327b
Mappae clavicula 1–135b, 318a
MAPPA MUNDI 8–0
Maps 1–333a-b
Maqālāt al-Islāmiyyīn (al-Ashʿarī) 1–583a, 584b
MAQĀM 8–0
Maqāma genre
invention 1–381b
Maqāmāt (al-Harīrī) 2–22b
Maqdisī, al-
See Muqaddasī, Muḥammad al-
Maqqarī, al-
Córdoba 3–599a
Maqrīzī, al- 4–407b
Ethiopia 1–32b
Eutychios 4–525a
Nubian Christianity 3–315a

Mar Aba
  Christian Church in Persia 3–312b
Maragheh 1–621b, 622a
Marble
  cosmati work 3–614a
  excavations 1–337b
  reuse 1–333b-334b
MARBOD OF RENNES 8–0
  anthology of poems 1–318b, 319a
Marburg 1–93b
MARC 8–0
MARCABRU 8–0
  Cercamon 3–240b
  crusade poems 4–20b
  Fin'amor-Fals'amor opposition 3–669a
Marcadé, Eustache
  See Mercadé (Marcadé), Eustache
Marcellinus of Africa, Count 1–654a
Marcellus, General
  Córdoba 3–597b
Marcellus, Nonius
  classical literary studies 3–432a
Marcellus, Saint
  altar relic 1–337a
MARCH, AUSIÀS 8–0; 1–420a; 3–157b
  Catalan literature 3–171a
March, Jaume 3–170b, 171a, 173b
March, Pere 3–173b
Marche, Olivier de la
  chronicles 3–333b
Märchenhaft
  Eckenlied 4–380a
MARCHETTUS OF PADUA 8–0
  ars nova 1–550b
"March of Spain"
  Frankish protectorate 3–174b, 175a
March River 2–6a-b
Marcian, Emperor 2–93a; 3–629b
Marcion
  Gnosticism 3–335a
  revisionism 3–338a
MARCO POLO 8–0
  Arčēš 1–423a
  assassins 1–591b
  Baṭṭūṭa 2–130a
  Columbus 4–559b
  explorations 4–556b-557a, 558b
  French chronicles 3–332b
  travel account 1–332b
Marcus Agrippa 1–426a
Marcus Claudius Marcellus
  Syracuse 1–334b
Marcus Manilius 1–605a
Mardanīsh, ibn 1–194a
Mardi Gras 3–99b
Mardpetakan 1–451a
***MÄREN* 8–0**
  Bussard, Der 2–433b
  Die Bauernhochzeit 2–132a
Mareuil, Arnaut de 3–665a
Margaret, Maid of Norway 4–396a
Margaret, Queen of Scots
  church reforms 3–232a
  death 4–392b-393a
Margaret, Saint 1–285a
  Anglo-Norman life of 1–261b
Margaret of Denmark (Semiramis of the North) 4–155b
  Nordic Union 4–156a
Margaret of Flanders, Countess
  Burgundy, County of 2–426a
  diplomacy 4–209a
Margaret of France 2–151a
Margaret of Hungary, Saint 2–13b
  Boniface of Montferrat 2–323a
Margaret of Provence 2–271a
Margaret of Scotland, Saint
  son 4–110b
Margaret of Vaudémont and Joinville 4–432b
Margarita philosophica (Gregor Reisch) 4–449b
MARGRAVE, MARQUESS 8–0
  Brandenburg 2–360a-b
  power 3–659a
Marheshvan 3–26b
María de Molina of Castile, Queen 3–134b, 135a
María de Padilla 3–137a
Mariage des neuf filles du diable, La (Robert Grosseteste) 1–263b
Mariage des sept arts (Jean le Teinturier) 1–188b
Maria Gloriosa of Erfurt bell 2–166b
MARIA LEKAPENA 8–0
MARIAN FEASTS 8–0
Marian legends
  Dutch literature 4–320a-b
Marianos the monk
  See Morienus
Marianos the poet 2–506b
Maria Novella, Santa, Dominican Friary of
  frescoes 1–244a
MARIANUS SCOTUS 8–0
Maria of Alania 1–303a
Maria of Montpellier 1–410a
Maria Palaiologos
  Bulgaria 2–410b-411a
Marica, Battle of (1371) 2–413a
MARICA RIVER 8–0
Māridāniyya, al-, mausoleum 2–21b
Marie d'Angoulême 3–277b
Marie de Bar 4–491a
MARIE DE CHAMPAGNE 8–0; 3–247a; 4–419b
  Chevalier de la Charrette 3–308b
  Conon de Béthune 3–538a
  courtly love 3–89a, 669b, 673a
MARIE DE FRANCE 8–0; 1–268a
  Anglo-Norman literature 1–260b, 261b
  Espurgatoire Saint Patrice 4–509b
  fables 4–572b, 573a
  lais 1–568a-b; 2–370a; 3–277b; 4–574a,b, 613a
Marienburg Castle
  Teutonic Knights 3–306a
Marienkirche
  Brunsberg, H(e)inrich von 2–392b
Marie of Antioch
  Byzantine throne 2–496a
Marie of Brabant
  Cleomadés 1–55a
Marie of Clèves 3–272b
Marie of Lusignan 1–415a
MARIGNY, ENGUERRAN DE 8–0
MAR II 12–0
Mariken van Nieumeghen 4–322a
Marinē, Saint, Church of 1–601b
MARINIDS 8–0
  Almohad empire 1–195b, 196a
MARIOTTO DI NARDO 8–0
Marisco, Adae de
  See Marsh, Adam
Marius
  biology 2–241b
Marius, Gaius
  Teutones 2–88b
Maríu saga 4–402a
Marius Victorinus
  See Victorinus, C. Marius
Marj al-Sham
  Anatolikon theme 1–242a
MARJ DĀBIQ 8–0
MARJ RĀHIṬ 8–0
Mark, Saint 2–13a
Mark, Saint, Master of
  Destorrents, Ramón 4–165b
Marke, Collard de 2–75a
MARKETS, EUROPEAN 8–0
  Asturian 1–629b
  Barcelona 2–103b
  Brittany, Duchy 2–379b, 380b
  Bruges 2–386a, 387a
  Bulgaria 2–404b, 405b
  Burgage Tenure 2–421a
  Catalonia 3–175b
  See Also Commune
  See Also Fairs
MARKETS, ISLAMIC 8–0
  Alexandria 1–154a
  textiles 2–156a
MARK EUGENICUS 8–0
Markland
  See Newfoundland
Mark of Cornwall
  Tristan romance 1–266a
Mark of Ephesus
  church schism 2–466a
Mark of Montelfeltro 2–315b
MARKO KRALJEVIĆ 8–0
Mark the Gravedigger
  Cathar movement 3–183b-184a
  consolamentum 3–185a-b
Markward of Anweiler 4–58a-b
Marmara, Sea of 4–331b, 337b
  Dardanelles 4–105a
Marmaras
  Trnovo 2–479a-b
MARMION, SIMON 8–0
MARMOUSETS 8–0
Marmoutier, Abbey of 4–513a
Marmoutier, Sacramentary of
  altar cross 4–9a
MARNER, DER 8–0
MARONITE CHURCH 8–0; 1–326b
Marot, Clément
  chant royal 3–263b
Marqab Chapel 4–25b
Marquess
  See Margrave, Marquess
Marquet, Galceran 3–166a
MARQUETRY 8–0
MARRAKECH 8–0
  Almohads 1–193b, 194a, 195b, 200a,b
  Almoravid art 1–197b
  casbah 1–168a
  mosques 1–191b-193a
Marranos
  See New Christians
Marriage
  See Family
Marriage of Philology and Mercury (Martianus Capella) 1–182a
Marsan, Arnaut Guilhem de 3–665a
MARSEILLES 8–0
  agriculture 1–85a
  Aragon, Crown of 1–412a
  Black Death 2–260b
MARSH, ADAM 8–0; 1–461b; 2–40a
MARSHAL 8–0
  constable of the realm 3–543b
Marshal, William
  See William Marshal
Marsilius, Petrus 3–165b
MARSILIUS (MARSIGLIO) OF PADUA 8–0; 1–465a
  conciliar theory 3–512a, 515a-516a
  corporation 3–606a
  defensor pacis 4–132a,b, 133a
  ecclesiology 4–376b, 377b

John XXII 3–363b
Munich 2–135a
Marsilius von Inghen 1–464b
Biel 2–234a
Marston, Roger 1–461b; 3–59b
Martel, Charles
See Charles Martel
Martel, Geoffrey
Angevins 1–253a
Martha, Saint 1–261b
Martial, Marcus Valerius
codex 3–474a
Martial, Saint
cult 1–54b
Martial, Saint, Church
pilgrimage style 3–379b
MARTIANUS CAPELLA 8–0; 1–460b
allegory 1–182a-b, 188a-b
astronomy 1–610b
Aucassin et Nicolette genre 1–642a
encyclopedias and dictionaries 4–447b
Nuptiis Philologiae at Mercurii, De 4–168b
seven liberal arts 1–580a
Martígnes, Gerard de
Knights of Saint John of Jerusalem 3–303b
Martin V, Antipope 1–331b
concordats 3–526a
Constance council 1–108b, 109a; 3–650b-651a
Dominicans 4–253b
ecclesiology 4–378a
election 3–649a; 4–377b
Great Schism 2–465b-466a; 3–366a
papal conclave 3–524b
papal curia 4–66b
Pavia council 3–651b
reunion council 3–652b
Martin I, Pope
caesaropapism 3–10b
exile 1–76b; 2–462a; 3–344a, 544b
monothelitism 3–630b
Martin IV, Pope 1–414a
Andronikos II Palaiologos 1–245b
Boniface VIII 2–323a
Dominicans 4–251b
German Holy Roman Empire 1–149a
Peter III of Aragon 4–61a
Martin, Saint, Church
pilgrimage style 3–379b
Martín Cortés 4–12b
Martines, Fra Pero 3–168a
Martínez, Ferrán 3–197b
Libro del Cavallero Zifar 3–197b
Martini, Raymond
missionaries 4–252b
Martini, Simone
See Simone Martini
Martiniega tax 3–132a
Martin of Tours, Saint
Alcuin of York 1–143b
Audradus Modicus 1–644a
biography 2–236a
canon community 1–659a
monasticism 2–172a
relics 3–107b
Martin I the Humane of Aragon, King 4–416a
Catalan literature 3–166b, 169a, 170b
reign 1–416b, 417a
Marinus I, Pope 3–603b
MARTINUS BRAGA (BRACARA) **8–0**
contraception 3–573a
MARTINUS GOSIA 8–0; 2–417b
See Also Corpus iuris civilis
Martinus of Fano 2–29a
Martirio de San Lorenzo (Berceo) 2–188a
Martorana, Church of 4–346b
MARTORELL, BERNARDO 8–0
Martorell, Joanot 3–157b, 170a
MARTYRDOM, CHRISTIAN 8–0
Armenian saints 1–517b-521a
baptism 2–84b
Bruno of Querfurt, Saint 2–391b
canonization 3–67b
catacombs 3–154b
MARTYRDOM, ISLAMIC 8–0
MARTYRDOM, JEWISH 8–0
MARTYRIUM 8–0
Armenian saints 1–518a
basilican plan 2–124a
shrine 4–336b
MARTYROLOGY 8–0
Aelfric 1–285a
MARTYROLOGY, IRISH 8–0
Martyrology 1–176b, 276b, 284a
Martyropolis 1–473a
Marulić, Marko 4–80a
Mārūt 1–248b
Marvani
Moravia 2–297b
MARWĀN, ʿABD AL-MALIK IBN 8–0
ʿAbd Allāh ibn al-Zubayr 1–16a
Akhṭal, al- 1–115a,b
Arabic language and script 3–52a
Arabization 3–40a-b
Catalonia 3–175b
death 1–628a
diplomacy 4–200a,b
dīwān al-barīd 3–39b
Dome of the Rock 4–237a
succession authority 3–39a
MARWĀN I IBN AL-ḤAKAM 8–0; 1–16a; 3–39a
MARWĀN II IBN MUḤAMMAD 8–0; 1–479a
Abbasid uprising 3–41b
Marwānids
Arčēš 1–423a
Basil I 1–483b
caliphate 3–38b-40b
Daylamites 1–513b
Maryānos
See Morienus
Mary Magdalen, Saint 1–261b
Mary (Xena) of Antioch
Andronikos I Komnenos 1–245a
MARY OF BURGUNDY, MASTER OF 8–0
Mary of Egypt, Saint 1–261a
Aelfric 1–285a
Mary of Oignies 2–158b
Mary of Portugal, Queen 3–137a
Mary Plantagenet
Anglo-Norman chronicles 1–265b
Marzadga tax 3–132a
MARZAL DE SAX, ANDRÉS 8–0
MARZPANATE 8–0; 1–476b
Arsacids/Aršakuni 1–559b
Dwin 1–481a
MASACCIO, TOMMASO CASSAI 8–0
Brunelleschi, Filippo 2–390b
frescoes 1–226b
Masāʾil Nāfiʿ ibn al-Azraq (ʿAbd Allāh ibn al-ʿAbbās) 4–442b
Masdeu, Juan Francisco 3–386a
Masdovelles, Guillem de 3–171a
Masegne
See Dalle Masegne, Pierpaolo and Jacobello
Māshāʾallāh 1–385b, 606b
astrolabe 1–611a
MASHHAD 8–0
Mashhad al-Juyūshī 2–44b
MASHRABĪYA 8–0
Masis
See Ararat, Mount
Masjid al-Aqṣā 1–581a
Masjid Ḥaram 1–581a
Masjid-i Jumʿa mosque
eyvān 4–569b
Maslama
See Musaylima al-Kadhadhāb
Maṣmūda 2–186a
Tūmart, ibn 1–193b
MASO DI BANCO 8–0
MASOLINO 8–0
MASONS AND BUILDERS 8–0
engineering 3–564a
materials 3–561a-564a
MASORETES 8–0
Hebrew Old Testament 2–210b
MASS 8–0
Agnus Dei 1–74a
Alexandrian rite 1–155a
altar apparatus 1–221a
Amalric of Bène 1–228b
Anselm of Canterbury 1–314b
architecture, liturgical aspects 1–441b-442a,b, 445a
Armenian 3–394b
azymes 2–31b
Bangor rite 2–72a
Benedicamus Domino 2–167b
Berengar 2–188a
Celtic 3–230a,b
chalice 3–241b
Christmas 3–318a
confirmation 3–536a
Corpus Christi feast 3–405a
creeds 3–675a, 676b-677a
early church 3–338a
Easter 4–366a,b, 367b
Eastern-Western church schism 3–349a
Engelbert of Admont 4–451b
Ethiopian 1–155b
last rites 4–120a
New Testament symbols 2–84b
Nicene-Constantinopolitan Creed 3–676b
order of ceremonies 1–327a
Ordinary 1–74a
postbaptism 2–83b
MASS CYCLES, FOURTEENTH-CENTURY 8–0
MASS CYCLES, PLAINSONG 8–0
MASSES, VOTIVE 8–0
MASSINGHAM, JOHN 8–0
MASTARA 8–0
Master
See Doctor
Master Eckhart
See Eckhart, Meister
Master of Flémalle
See Campin, Robert
Master of Moulins
See Moulins, Master of
Master of the Soldiers
See Magister Militum
Maštocʿ
See Mesrob, Saint
MASʿŪDĪ, AL- 8–0; 1–381a
traveler accounts 1–332a
Masudic Canon (Bīrūnī) 2–248b, 249b, 250b
MATAKDAN I HAZAR DATASTAN 8–0
Matara Palace
Axumite art 2–17b
Materia medica, De (Dioscorides) 2–245a; 4–353a,b, 355b, 356a-b

Mathematical geography
Bīrūnī 2–249a-b
MATHEMATICS 8–0
Anania Širakac'i 1–238a
Arabic numerals 1–382b
Arabic science 1–377b
Archimedes 1–433b
astrolabe 1–602b
astronomy 1–612a
Bacon 2–38a-b
Boethius 2–291b
Bradwardine 2–358a
Brunelleschi 2–390b
study of 2–241a-b
Mathematicus (Bernard Silvester) 2–195a
Matheseos libri VIII (Firmicus Maternus) 1–605a
Mathgamain of Munster, King 4–77b
MATHIEU D'ARRAS 8–0
Matière de Bretagne
See Matter of Britain, Matter of France, Matter of Rome
Matière de Charlemagne
See Matter of Britain, Matter of France, Matter of Rome
Matière de France
See Matter of Britain, Matter of France, Matter of Rome
Matière de Rome
See Matter of Britain, Matter of France, Matter of Rome
Matilda (daughter of Henry I)
David I of Scotland 4–110b
Henry I 4–462b-463a
Henry II 4–475a
Stephen of Blois 1–253a; 4–463a-b
MATILDA OF TUSCANY 8–0
biography 4–261a-b
Canossa 3–69b
Marian office 2–274a
Matins
Bruges 2–387b
Divine Office 4–221b, 226, 228a-b
Office of the Dead 4–117b-118a
Matjar 1–154a
Matmonoc of Landévennec
tonsure 3–229a
Matrimony
See Family
Matroneum 1–442a, 443; 4–335b
Matteo of Perugia
ars subtilior 1–558b
Matteo Raverti
See Raverti, Matteo
Matt'ēos Uřhayec'i
See Matthew of Edessa
Matteo Villani
Black Death 2–266a
MATTER OF BRITAIN, MATTER OF FRANCE, MATTER OF ROME 8–0
Arthurian literature 1–572b
Matthaeus of Grabow
Devotio Moderna 4–166b
Matthew, Saint
Andreas 1–279a
Christian of Stablo 3–311b
Matthew Kantakouzenos
reign 2–501b
Matthew of Angers 1–52a
MATTHEW OF AQUASPARTA 8–0
MATTHEW OF EDESSA 8–0; 1–482b, 511b
Matthew of Paris
cameo drawing 1–335b
Chronica majora 1–333a
MATTHEW OF VENDÔME 8–0
ars poetica 1–553b
Bernard Silvester 2–195a
chronicles 2–236b
dictamen 4–175a
Milo 4–283a
MATTHEW PARIS 8–0; 2–174a
Albigensians 1–130b
assassins 1–591a
beguines 2–159b
Chronica majora 3–326b
Richard I 1–261b, 265a; 4–18b
Mattinata
See Aubade
Māturīdī, al-
Ash'arī, al- 1–585b
Mauclerc, Peter
Brittany, Duchy 2–380a
invasion of Champagne 3–247b
Mauger Worcester 4–423b
Maultasch, Margarete 2–8a
Maundy Thursday
See Holy Thursday
MAURICE, EMPEROR 8–0
Armenian church 1–499a
Armenian history 1–477b
Bahrām VI 2–50a
Byzantine economy and society 2–477b
Maurolico, Francesco 1–436b, 439a,b
Maurus, Hrabanus
Christian Hebraists 3–313b
confirmation 3–536a
Maurus, Rabanus 1–273a
See Also Maurus, Hrabanus
Mausoleum of Galla Placidia
architecture 3–379a
Mausoleum of Hadrian 1–335a
"Mausoleum of the Exodus" 3–592a
Mawālī 2–110a; 3–38a,b
Abbasid administration 3–44a
caliphate treatment 3–41b
Mawālīd 1–619a-b
Māwardī, al-
Buyids 2–436b
caliphate literature 3–50b
Mawlawīya order
dervish 4–163a
Maxentius
Constantine I 3–545a
Maximiam of Ravenna 4–361b
Maximianus Thracianus, Empress
death 1–117a
MAXIMILIAN I, EMPEROR 8–0
Ambraser Heldenbuch 1–229b
arms and armor 1–529a, 531a; 2–354b
Biterolf 2–253a
Brittany, Duchy 2–380b
Maximinus, Galerius Valerius 2–119b
Maximinus of Micy 2–16b
Maximos Kausokalybes 2–519a
MAXIMS, LEGAL 8–0
Maximus, Clemens, Emperor 1–231a
Maximus of Madauros
Augustine 1–650a,b
MAXIMUS THE CONFESSOR, SAINT 8–0
angel/angelology 1–250b
Byzantine theology 2–467a
Christology 3–320b, 322a
Constans II 3–544b
letters 2–520a
monothelitism 3–630b
veneration 2–459a
Maymūn, ibn
See Maimonides, Moses
MAYOR 8–0
aldermen 1–143b
Mayordomo mayor 3–139a
MAYOR OF THE PALACE 8–0
Charles Martel 3–272a
Mayyāfāriqīn
See Martyropolis
Mayyūn
See Perim
Maẓālim 3–43b
MAZDAKITES 8–0
Mazzoni, Francesco 4–103a
M'bin
See Nisibis
MC'XET'A 8–0
MEAD 8–0
brewing 2–374a
Islamic 2–208b
Measures
See Weights and measures
Mecatun 1–491a
MECCA 8–0
'Abbās, al- 1–4a,b
'Abd Allāh 1–15b-16a
'Abd al-Muṭṭalib 1–14b
Abū Sufyān 1–28b, 29a
'Ā'isha 1–113a-b
alms tax 1–201b
Badr, Battle of 2–42b
fairs 4–588b
Fatimid conquest 3–50b
locating 2–249b
Muḥammad 1–24b-25a
qibla 3–35b
settlement 1–372a,b
sharifs 1–175a
Mec Cop'k
See Sophanenē
See Greater Sophenē
Mechanical arts
Fachschrifttum 4–577a-578b
Mechanical clocks
See Clocks and reckoning of time
Mechanikos 4–335b
MECHTHILD OF MAGDEBURG 8–0; 2–160b
Medea 1–266b-267a
Media Atropatene 2–26b
Media Minor 2–26b
Median March 2–140a
Medicean chant 3–403a
MEDICI 8–0
art trade 1–561a
Florence bank 2–78b
mercantile banking 2–77a
Medici, Cosimo de'
Antoninus 1–342b
Medici Atlas
Madeiras 4–559a
Medicina apropriada a tot mal (Bernat Metge) 3–173b
Medicina de Quadrupedibus
Old English translation 1–286a
Medicine
Arnald of Villanova 1–537b
Black Death 2–264a-b
Constantine the African 3–548b
contraception, Islamic 3–574a
Fachschrifttum 4–578a,b
herbals 2–244b-246a
recipe anthologies 1–318a
texts 1–286a; 4–579b
treatises 1–275a
MEDICINE, BYZANTINE 8–0
MEDICINE, HISTORY OF 8–0
alchemy, Islamic 1–141a,b
astrology 1–604b, 618a
barber-surgery 2–97b
botany 2–347a
MEDICINE, SCHOOLS OF 8–0
Avicenna 1–458b

Bologna 2–312a
Medicine good for all diseases (Bernat Metge) 3–173b
Medikion Monastery
agriculture 1–78a
Medimnoi 1–78a
MEDINA 8–0
'Abbās, al- 1–4b
'Abd Allāh 1–15a,b-16a
Abū Bakr 1–24b-25a
'Ā'isha 1–112b-113b
alms tax 1–201b
Arabia 1–373a,b, 374a,b, 375a,b
caliphate 3–33a,b, 35a,b
Fatimids 3–50b
Muḥammad 1–171b, 373b; 2–43a
siege (656) 1–172b
Medinaceli 1–407a
Medina del Campo
fairs 4–587b
Medina de Pomar 3–125b
Medina de Rioseco
fairs 4–587b
Medinat al-Zahra0lordoba 1–168a
MEDITATIO 8–0
Meditation
Brethren of the Common Life 2–367b-368a
Meditationes vitae Christi (pseudo-Bonaventure) 1–347b
Meditation of the Sad Soul, The (Abraham bar Ḥiyya) 1–22a
Meditation on Human Redemption (Anselm of Canterbury) 1–313a, 314b
Meditatio redemptionis humanae (Anselm of Canterbury) 1–313a, 314b
Mediterranean
agriculture and nutrition 1–77b-88b
barrels use 2–114a
Mediterranean Sea
Anatolia 1–239b, 240
Atlas Mountains 1–639b
Crete 3–678a
MEDWALL, HENRY 8–0
Megas basileus 2–123a
Megas chartophylax 3–447a
Megas dux
Roger de Flor 3–156a
Megas oikonomos 3–447a
Megas sakkelarios 3–447a
Megas skeuophylax 3–447a
Megillat ha-Megalleh (Abraham bar Ḥiyya) 1–22a
MEGINHART OF FULDA 8–0
MEHMED (MUḤAMMAD) **I 8–0**; 1–70b
Abu Ja'far 1–71a
Byzantine Empire 2–503b
MEHMED (MUḤAMMAD) **II 8–0**; 1–70b; 4–56a
Alhambra 1–168b
Anatolia 1–242a
Bāyazīd II 2–137a
Bosporus 2–344a
Caffa 3–12b
Constantinople 2–504a-b; 3–552b
Ibrāhīm II 1–71b
Trebizond 1–159a
Meier Betz
See Bauernhochzeit, Die
Meilyr ap Gwalchmai 4–413a, 431a
MEILYR BRYDYDD 8–0
Meinhard of Bamberg
Carmen de Bello Saxonico authorship 3–97a
Meinhard II of Tyrol 2–8a
Meinhard of Uxküll, Bishop 2–64b
MEINLOH VON SEVELINGEN 8–0
Meinwerk of Paderborn, Bishop 1–332b
MEINZO OF CONSTANCE 8–0
Meir, Samuel ben
beekeeping 1–79a
Meir ben Baruch of Rothenburg
marital relations 4–606b
Meister Bertram
See Bertram, Meister
Meister Eckhart
See Eckhart, Meister
MEIT, CONRAD 8–0
MEKNES 8–0
Meknut'iwn i Verlucakann Aristoteli (David the Invincible) 4–114b
Meknut'iwn Storogut'eanc'n Aristoteli 4–114a
Melanchthon, Philipp
Biel 2–234a
Brethren of the Common Life 2–369a
Tetrabiblos 1–609a
Melchisedec 1–223b
MELCHITES 8–0
Alexandria 1–154b
Copts 3–594b
Eutychios 4–525a
Nubian Christianity 3–314b
Melcombe Regis
Black Death 2–261b
MELFI, CONSTITUTIONS OF 8–0
Melfi Synod (1089) 3–635a
Melilla 1–639b
Melintziani
households 2–480a
Melioramentum 3–181b, 185b
***MELIOR ET YDOINE* 8–0**
Anglo-Norman courtoisie 1–268b
Melisende, Queen
Anne's, Saint, Church 4–23b
coronation 4–22b
Jerusalem art and architecture 4–23a
Psalter 4–22a-23a, 24a, 25b
MELISMA 8–0
ars antiqua 1–546b
clausula 3–437a
Melissenos
Nicaea 2–493b
MELITENE 8–0
Armenia geography 1–472b, 473a
Bar Hebraeus 2–108a
Cilician kingdom 3–391a
pillage 2–493a
Melkites
See Melchites
Mellinus 1–251b
Melnik, Bulgaria 2–409a
MELODY 8–0
ars subtilior 1–559a
Melon dome 4–236a
Melor, Saint 1–261b
Melton, William
Corpus Christi play 4–286a
Memento mori 3–625a
MEMLING, HANS 8–0
David 4–114b
Memmo, Giambattista 1–439a
Mémoires sur les règnes de Louis XI et de Charles VIII (Philippe de Comines) 3–327b, 333b
Memoirs of the Right Honourable Marquis of Clanricarde 2–107a
Mémontois 2–427a
Memoranda rolls 4–534a
Memoria et reminiscentia commentarium, De (Aquinas) 3–197a
Memorial (Joan Francesc Boscà) 3–166b
Memorial de la fe cathólica (Francesc de Pertussa) 3–168a
Memoriale de prerogativa Romani imperii (Alexander of Roes) 1–148b
Memoriale sanctorum (Eulogius of Córdoba) 4–521b
Memorials of Saint Anselm 1–314a
MENA, JUAN DE 8–0
copla 3–584b
Tragicomedia de Calisto y Melibea 3–213a
Ménagier de Paris, Le 3–663b
Menahem ben Benjamin Recanati 4–541b
Menahem ben Ḥelbo 4–540b
Menahem ben Saruq 2–212a
Menahem ben Solomon Meiri 4–541b
Menaion (Book of Months) 2–468b
MENANDER PROTECTOR 8–0
Agathias 1–68a
Constantine VII Porphyrogenitos 3–547b
Mendacio, De (Saint Augustine) 3–153a
MENDICANT ORDERS 8–0
Augustinian friars 1–659b
beguines and beghards 2–157b
Caffa 3–12a
Carmelites 3–96a
Mendoza, Íñigo López de 3–140a
Menescalia (Manual Diez) 3–168b
Menger, Louis Emil 1–271b
Mennas, Saint 1–520a
MENOLOGIAN ART 8–0
Menologion
See Symeon Metaphrastes
Menologium
purpose 1–281a
MENORAH 8–0
Mensa 1–221b
Mensis exiens 3–21a
Mensis intrans 3–21a
Mensura astrolabii, De (Hermannus Contractus) 1–611a
Mensural Notation
ars nova 1–549a-550b
Mentel Bible 2–215b
Men Tenorio, Rodriquez 3–87a
Menyspreu del món, Del (Ramon Ros) 3–168a
Mequinenza 1–406a
fruit trees 1–82b
Merantune, Battle of (871) 1–163b
Mercadanzias 3–570a
MERCADÉ (MARCADÉ), **EUSTACHE 8–0**
Vengeance de Jésus-Christ, La 4–265a
Mercedarians
Barcelona 2–104a
Mercenaries
Catalan Company 3–156a
Mercers 3–210a
corporation 3–607a
Merchant Adventurers Company 3–210a-b
Merchants
See Trade
Mercia
Danelaw 1–164a
Danish invasion 4–456a
dominance 4–455a,b
emergence 2–96b
Mercian dialect
Old English texts 1–276a
Mercury clock 3–458a
Mercy and Justice, On (Alger of Liège) 1–167b
Mére, Huon de 1–188b
Meribanes, King of Chosroids 3–308a
Mérida
Alfonso IX 3–133b
MERIGARTO 8–0

Merinids
mosques 1–193a
Merino 3–132b
Merino mayor 3–139a
Merke, Thomas
dictamen 4–175b
Merkurios, King 3–315a
Merlijns boeck (Jacob von Maerlant) 4–318b
Merlin (Albrecht von Scharfenberg) 1–133a,b-134a
Merlin
See Arthurian literature
Merlin's book (Jacob von Maerlant) 4–318b
***MERLÍNÚSSPÁ* 8–0**; 2–365b-366a
Merlons 3–148a, 149
Mermedonian cannibals
Andreas 1–279a
MEROBAUDES 8–0
Mérode Altarpiece (Robert Campin) 3–61a-b
Annunciation painting 1–308a
Meroë 1–30b
Merovingian art
See Migration and Hiberno-Saxon art
MEROVINGIANS 8–0
Alamanni 1–117b
antrustiones 1–343a
Aquitaine 1–366b
Bavaria 2–134a
Bordeaux 2–327b
Bruges 2–386a
Cambridge Songs 3–57a
Carolingians 3–104a
ceramics 3–236a
chancery 3–252b-253b
Charles Martel 3–272a
church organization 3–373b
decline 3–345b
deposition of rulers 4–158a
duchies 4–303b
elections, royal 4–425b-426a
illiteracy 3–99b-100a
Salian Franks 2–94a
Merseburg Cathedral
charms, old High German 3–273b
Merseburger Zauberspruche
See Charms, Old High German
Merton College 1–436b
Aristotelianism 1–464a
MERURE DE SEINTE ÉGLISE 8–0; 1–263a
Anglo-Norman literature 1–261b
Meružan Arcruni 1–476a
Meseta 1–640a, 641a
Mesopotamia
alchemy 1–135a-136a
art and architecture 2–417a
Ayyubids 2–23a-b
Black Death 2–259a
Byzantines 2–410a,b, 411b, 412a,b
ceramics 2–101a; 3–238b
Diyarbakir 4–231b
Edessa 4–384a
Euphrates River 4–521b
Latin Kingdom of Jerusalem 4–30b
Marco Polo 4–556b
petty states 4–27b
Saladin 4–31a
Tamerlane 3–313a
Turks 2–493a
water buffalo use 1–298a
MESROB, SAINT 8–0; 1–518b, 520a-b
Albanian alphabet 1–123b
Armenian alphabet 1–66b, 214a-b, 491b, 507b
Armenian literature 1–510b
Arsacids/Aršakuni 1–559b
Bible translation 2–217a
David the Invincible 4–114a
Eznik of Kołb 4–570b
Theodore of Mopsuestia 1–498b
translations 1–507b
MESSEMBRIA 8–0
Messenger
See Angel; Angel/Angelology
Messiad (Eupolemius) 4–523a
Messiads 4–495b
Messianism, Jewish
See Apocalyptic literature and movement, Jewish
Messina
Aghlabid capture 1–70b
Black Death 2–259a
Richard I 4–40a
Messines
fairs 4–585a-b
MESTA 8–0
Castile 3–136a, 138b
***MESTER DE CLERECÍA* 8–0**; 3–140a
cuaderna vía 4–63a
decir 4–122b
MESTER DE JUGLARÍA 8–0
Mesura 3–78a
METALLURGY 8–0
alchemy 1–139b-140a
Bīrūnī 2–250b
bronze and brass 2–383a-385a
stone building 3–145b
Metalogicon (John of Salisbury) 1–52a; 3–434b; 4–170a
Metalogicus (John of Salisbury) 4–471b
METALSMITHS, GOLD AND SILVER 8–0
Boucher, Guillaume 2–349b
Conte Del Lello Orlandi 3–572a
Córdoba 3–599b
engraving 4–487b, 488a
Metalwork
Anglo-Saxon 1–273b, 274a
Ayyubid 2–22a
bells 2–165b
cannon 3–65a
Celtic art 3–218a
chip carving 3–301a
codex aureus 3–474b
engraving 4–488a
METALWORKERS 8–0
arms and armor 1–529a-b, 533b, 536a-b
émail brun 4–435b
Metamorphoses (Apuleius) 1–182a, 651b
Metamorphoses (Ovid) 1–131b, 162a, 180b
Metamorphosis
See Transfiguration
Metamorphosis of the Hoopoe, Swallow, and Nightingale, The (Chrétien de Troyes) 3–308b
Metaphor
allegory 1–179a
Old English poetry 1–277a
Metaphrastes, Symeon
See Symeon Metaphrastes
Metaphrastic Lives 2–519a
Metaphysics 1–361b-362a
Metaphysics (Aristotle) 2–36a
Aquinas 1–357a, 360b
Metatron
Jewish apocalyptic literature 1–344b
METEHI 8–0
METELLUS OF TEGERNSEE 8–0
METEORA 8–0
Meteora (Albertus Magnus) 1–137a
Meteorology (Aristotle) 1–136b
Meters (Boethius) 1–277b
METGE, BERNAT 8–0; 1–420a; 3–173b
Catalan language 3–157b, 158a, 161a, 163b
Methodios, Saint
See Cyril and Methodios, Saints
Methodios of Olympus 2–510a
Method of Calculation of the Hindus (al-Khwārizmī) 1–383a
Metochites, Theodore
Andronikos II Palaiologos 1–246a
education 3–556b
Metrophanes of Smyrna 2–511b
METROPOLITAN 8–0
church organization 3–373a,b, 374a-b, 375b
ecclesiology 4–373b
False decretals 4–126a
patriarch election 4–383b
Metropolitan Jonas 2–470a
Metz
bishops 1–203b
Franks 2–94a
siege 3–64a
METZ, USE OF 8–0
Metzen hochzit
See Bauernhochzeit, Die
Metz Psalter 2–218b
Meun, Jean de
alchemical poetry 1–138b
Meurig, Bishop 2–71b
Mexico-Tenochtitlán
siege (1521) 3–181a
Mexuar Hall 1–168b
Meyer, Paul 1–271b
Mher 4–112b, 113a
Miathi
Áedán 1–60a
MICHAEL III 8–0; 1–391b
Amorian dynasty 1–236a
Arabs 4–523a
Bardas Caesar 2–106a
Basil I the Macedonian 2–117a-b, 118a
Boris of Bulgaria 2–329a
church 2–464a
Cyril and Methodios, Saints 4–73b
minor arts 2–453b
reign 2–489a-b
Michael IV 1–484a
Michael I Angelos
See Michael I of Epiros
Michael II Angelos
See Michael II of Epiros
Michael (archangel) 1–433a
angelology 1–249a
Antichrist killing 1–322b
Jewish apocalyptic literature 1–344b
Mīkā'il 1–248b
Michael Asen 2–409b-410b
MICHAEL ASTRAPAS 8–0
MICHAEL ATTALEIATES 8–0
arts 2–455a
history 2–514b
Michael I Doukas
See Michael I of Epiros
Michael VII Doukas 4–263a
Budapest crown 4–437b
reign 2–491b, 492a, 493a
Michael Glykas 2–509a, 515b, 521b
Michael V Kalaphates ("the Calker")
Zoe 2–491b, 492a,b
MICHAEL KEROULARIOS 8–0
Byzantine throne 2–492b
church schism 2–465a
Michael Kritobulos of Mimbros 2–517b
MICHAEL OF CANTERBURY 8–0

Michael of Cesena
John XXII 3–363b
Michael of Ephesus
dialectic 4–170b
MICHAEL I OF EPIROS 8–0; 4–330a, 499a
Bulgaria 2–401b
Byzantine Empire 2–498a
MICHAEL II OF EPIROS 8–0
Bulgaria 2–401b
Byzantine Empire 2–498b, 499a
Pelagonia defeat 4–499a
Michael of Tver, Prince
Muscovy 4–232b
MICHAEL VIII PALAIOLOGOS 8–0
Andronikos II 1–245b
Arsenius Autorianus 1–560b
art 2–447b
autobiography 2–518a
Bulgaria 2–410a,b
Constantinople 3–552a
east-west church schism 2–465b
heterodoxy 2–459a
Nicaea 2–498b-499b
Western councils 3–632b, 641b, 642a-b
Michael IX Palaiologos
Almogávares 1–191a
Andronikos II 1–245b
reign 2–499b, 500a
Roger de Flor 3–156a
Michael Panaretos 2–517a
Michael Psellos 2–507b, 519b
Byzantine throne 2–492a
Chronography 2–514b
poetry 2–524b
MICHAEL SCOT 8–0; 1–461a
Michael Šišman, Czar
Bulgaria 2–411b-412a
Michael VI Stratiotikos
Byzantine throne 2–491b
Michael II the Amorian, Emperor 3–678a
dynasty 1–236a
Michael the artist
church decoration 2–448a
Michael IV the Paphlagonian
Zoe 2–491b, 492a
MICHAEL THE SYRIAN 8–0
Bar Hebraeus 2–108b
Michel, Francisque 1–271a
Michel, Jean
passion play 4–264b
MICHEL BEHEIM 8–0
Michel Colombe
See Colombe, Michel
MICHELOZZO DI BARTOLOMEO 8–0
Mich mac der tot von ir minnen wol scheiden (Albrecht von Johansdorf) 1–132b
MICON OF SAINT RIQUIER 8–0
Mico of Bulgaria 2–410a
Microcosmos 1–604b
Micrologus (Guido of Arezzo) 3–542a
Micy abbey 2–16b
MIDDLE AGES 8–0
Middle Angles 4–454a
Middle Armenian
See Armenian language
Middle Atlas Mountains 1–639b
Middle-class women
courtesy books 3–662b-663a, 664b
Middle English exegesis
See Exegesis, Middle English
MIDDLE ENGLISH LANGUAGE 8–0
MIDDLE ENGLISH LITERATURE 8–0
Aeneid translations 4–262b
Ancrene Riwle 1–243a
Anglo-Norman literature 1–266b, 267a
Arthurian literature 1–573a-575a
Bible 2–221b-222b; 4–545a
Capgrave 3–90a
Chaucer 3–279b
Clanvowe 3–408a
courtesy books 3–663a
Dunbar, William 4–307a
Everyman 4–526b
French Romances 1–573a-b
MIDDLE ENGLISH LITERATURE: ALLEGORY 8–0
MIDDLE ENGLISH LITERATURE: ALLITERATIVE VERSE 8–0
MIDDLE ENGLISH LITERATURE: LYRIC 8–0
Arthurian literature 1–568b, 571b
ballads 2–59b
Brut, The 2–393a-394a
MIDDLE ENGLISH LITERATURE: PROSODY AND VERSIFICATION 8–0; 1–320a
Middle French
See French Language
Middle High German literature 1–455a-b
Albrecht von Halberstadt 1–131b
Ambraser Heldenbuch 1–229b
Anegenge 1–246b
Anglo-Norman romances 1–266a
Annolied 1–306a
Arthurian literature 1–571b-572a
Athis und Prophilias 1–635b
Bauernhochzeit, Die 2–132a
biblical poetry 2–224b
Buch von Bern, Das 2–395b-396a
Bussard, Der 2–433b
Carmen de Bello Saxonico 3–97a
Carmina Burana 3–97b, 98a,b
courtly love 3–667b, 668b
der von Kürenberg 4–161a
Dietmar von Aist 4–184a
Dresdener Heldenbuch 4–292b
Dukus Horant 4–304b
Eckenlied 4–380a
Eckhart 4–380b
Middle Irish apocrypha 1–347a,b
Middle Saxons 4–454a
Middle Scots poetry 1–320a
Middlesex
Anglo-Saxons 4–454a
Middleton, Richard
contraception 3–573b
Middle Welsh period
See Celtic languages
MIDGARD SERPENT 8–0
Midi
agriculture and nutrition 1–80a, 85a-86a
Midons 3–668b, 670a
Midrash
See Exegesis, Jewish
Miélot, Jean
See Jean Miélot
Migetius
Adoptionism 1–57b
Migration, internal
See Reclamation
MIGRATION AND HIBERNO-SAXON ART 8–0
Breviary of Alaric 2–373b
Migration Period
See Barbarians, Invasions of
Mihna 3–48a
MIHRĀB 8–0
Aghlabid art 1–69b
Almohad art 1–193a
Almoravid art 1–197a
Mihranids
See Chosroids
Mihrnerseh 2–49b
Milagros de Nuestra Señora (Gonzalo de Berceo) 2–187b
MILAN 8–0
Alexander II 1–146a
Ambrose, Saint 1–230b
Ambrosian chant 1–232a
angelus 1–252b
Angilbert 1–254b
arms and armor 1–528b-529b
Arnulf of Milan 1–541b-542a
baptismal rites 2–83a,b
Black Death 2–260b
carroccio 3–117b
commune 3–499b, 500a
exchange banks 2–73b
fairs 4–587a
money markets 2–78b
Peter of Candia 1–147b
MILAN CATHEDRAL 8–0
Milanese Chant
See Ambrosian Chant
Milanese Mass Book 2–180b
MILANESE RITE 8–0
Ave Maria 2–13a
MILE 8–0
Miles
Boeve de Haumtone 1–267b
Mileševo Monastery
art 2–446b
Milet, Jacques
Destruction de Troye, La 4–265a
Milevis, Council of (416) 1–653a
Military architecture
See Castles and fortifications
Military dress
Byzantine 3–614b-615a
Islamic 3–618b
Military orders
Alfonso I 1–161a
Baltic countries 2–64b, 65b, 66b
Brittany, Duchy 2–379b
Castile 3–130b
crusader art and architecture 4–21b
crusades 4–55b, 56b-57a
Western councils 3–643b, 644a
See Also specific military orders
Milites (knights) 1–629b
Militia Christi 4–16a
Militia Saneti Petri 4–16a
Milk
cattle yield 1–301b
Islam 2–109b, 208b
Millau 1–410a
Millefiori
See Enamel, Millefiori
Millefleurs
See Tapestry, Millefleurs
MILLENIALISM 8–0
Airden Brátha 1–111a
MILLENIALISM, ISLAMIC 8–0
Miller, James
Chester plays 3–299a
Millet
See Grain Crops
MILLS 8–0
banal 2–69b
bread 2–364b-365a
Byzantine grain 1–77b
Russian 1–100b
Slavic 1–97a, 98a

Millstätter Exodus
See Altdeutsche Exodus
Milo 4–283a
Milon, Castellan of Chevreuse 3–145a
MILO OF SAINT AMAND 8–0
Miltiades, Pope
confirmation 3–536a
Milton Port, Somerset
Anglo-Norman sculpture 1–256a
Milutin, Stefan, of Serbia 4–330a, 347a
Bulgaria 2–411a
Milvian Bridge, Battle of (312)
Constantine I, the Great 3–545a,b
MÍMIR 8–0
Mimṭara 3–618a
Minā
fairs 4–588b
Mina, São Jorge da
slaves 2–269a
Minaeans
pre-Islamic Arabia 1–370a
MINAI WARE 8–0
ceramics 3–240a
MINARET 8–0
ajímez 1–114b
MINBAR 8–0
Aghlabid art 1–69b
Mindaugas 2–67a
Mindoug
See Mindaugas
Mineralibus, De (Albertus Magnus) 1–137a
Min erste liebe der ich ie began (Albrecht von Johansdorf) 1–132b-133a
Minerva Medica Palace 4–339a
Miniatures
Paris Psalter 2–441a-b
Minim
ars nova 1–549a-b
MINING 8–0
Bosnia 2–340a-b
Burgundy, County of 2–426b
coal 3–472b
costume 3–626a
Minio-Paluello, Lorenzo 1–52a
MINISTERIALS 8–0
Minneallegorie
See German literature: Allegory
MINNEBURG 8–0
Minnen loep, Der (Dirc Potter) 4–320a
MINNEREDEN 8–0
Minnesang
See Middle High German literature
MINNESINGERS 8–0
chivalry 3–302b
der von Kürenberg 4–161a
Dietmar von Aist 4–184b
Minoan civilization 3–678a
Minorca 1–412a
Catalan language 3–157b
slaves 2–268a
Minor Dialogue (Chardri) 1–264b; 3–267b
Minorites
Bernard Silvester 2–196a,b
MINORITIES 8–0
dayr 4–117a
MINSTRELS 8–0
Arthurian literature 1–573b
chansons de geste 3–257a
Colin Muset 3–479a
Middle English ballads 2–59b
Welsh bards 2–106a
Mintāsh of Melitene 2–113a
MINTS AND MONEY, ARMENIAN 8–0
Cilician kingdom 3–393a
MINTS AND MONEY, BYZANTINE 8–0
bracteates 2–355b
bronze and brass 2–384b
Bulgaria 2–407a, 412b
dinar 4–187a
nomisma 4–301a
MINTS AND MONEY, ISLAMIC 8–0
administration 3–34a-b
Arabization 3–40a-b
banking 2–80a
bronze and brass 2–384b
dinar 4–187a, 301b
dirham 4–215b
MINTS AND MONEY, RUSSIAN 8–0
MINTS AND MONEY, WESTERN EUROPEAN 8–0
Anglo-Saxon England 4–457a
banking 2–75a
bracteates 2–355b
Brittany, Duchy of 2–380a
bronze and brass 2–384b
Canterbury 3–82a
coin collections 1–335b
dinar 4–187a,b
dirham 4–215b
ducat 4–301a
Exchequer 4–531a
fairs 4–585a
Minucius Felix
early Christian movement 3–334b
Mi-parti 3–624b-625a
Miqṭorīn 3–618b
Mirabilia (Gregory the Englishman) 1–333a
Arthurian literature 1–564b-565a
Mirabilia urbis Romae 1–333a
Miracle de Théophile 4–264a
MIRACLE PLAYS 8–0
Dutch 4–322a
French 4–264b
German 4–268b
Miracles de Notre Dame 4–264a, 284b
Miracles of Saint Anthony (Donatello) 4–257b
Miracula sancti Benedicti (Adrevald de Fleury and Aimoin de Fleury) 1–110a, 244a
Miracula S. Dionysii
portable altars 1–225a
Mi ʿraj-nama 1–106b
MIR'ALI 8–0
Mīr ʿAlī al-Haravī 3–54b
Mirall dels divinals assots (Pero Martines) 3–168a
Mirall de trobar (Berenguer d'Anoya) 3–170a
Miralles, Melcior 3–166b
Miralomin 3–489a
Mirandola, Pico della
astrology 1–609a
Miravet 1–408b
Mirdāsid dynasty
Aleppo capture 1–145b
Mirepoix 2–129a
Mirian, King
Djvari 4–231b
Mirian III, King of Chosroids 3–308a
MÍRMANNS SAGA 8–0
Mirmumnus 3–489a
Miroir de mariage, Le (E. Deschamps) 4–163b
Miro II of Catalonia 3–175a
Miroslav 4–5a
Mirour de l'omme (John Gower) 1–263b
Mirozshki Monastery, Spaso Preobrazhenski 4–341a
Mirra (Boncompagno of Signa) 2–320b
Mirror, The (Jaume Roig) 3–171b-172a, 173b-174a
Mirror for Princes 1–220a
Mirror of Charity, The (Saint Ethelred) 4–517a
Mirror of Fools (Nigel Wireker (or Whiteacre)) 1–255a
Mirror of Holy Church (Saint Edmund) 1–263a
MIRROR OF JUSTICES 8–0
Mirror of love (Colijn van Rijssele) 4–322b
Mirror of Man (John Gower) 1–263b
Mirror of Marriage (Eustache Deschamps) 1–189b
antifeminism 1–324b
MIRROR OF PRINCES 8–0
Mirrors 2–148a
Miryam al-Qibṭiya 4–407b
MISA DE AMOR, LA 8–0
Miscellaneous Agama, The 4–528a
MISERICORD 8–0
Mishwar 1–168b
Misis (Mopsuestia) basilica 4–357a
Miṣr
See Fusṭāṭ, Al-
Missaglia 1–528b, 529b
MISSAL 8–0
Aquileia rite 1–353a
Bangor rite 2–72a
baptism 2–83a
books of hours 2–326a
Divine Office 4–225a
Stowe 3–676b
Missal VI 2–181a
Missale pro S. Aquileiensis ecclesiae ritu
Aquileia rite 1–353a
Missi 3–91a
***MISSI DOMINICI* 8–0**
capitulary 3–91b
Carolingians 3–108a
Charlemagne 3–268b
Charles the Bald 3–114b
Theodulf 3–102b
Missile weapons 3–205a-b
MISSION OF THE APOSTLES 8–0
MISSIONS AND MISSIONARIES, CHRISTIAN 8–0
Augustine of Canterbury 1–645b
Byzantine diplomacy 4–194b
Cilicia 3–394b
Columba, Saint 3–485a-b
confession 3–533a
Coptic monasticism 3–595a-b
Council of Vienne 3–644b
Cyril and Methodios, Saints 4–73a
Dominicans 4–252a-253a
See Also Church, Latin
***MISSORIUM* 8–0**
early Christian art 4–353b, 354b
Mistere du Viel Testament 4–264b
Misthotoi 4–494a
MISTRA 8–0
architecture 4–334b, 345a
planning 4–333b
Mitannians
Aleppo 1–145a
Miter 3–94a, 624a-b
Mithraism, cult of 1–605a
Mithridates 3–308a
Mitrovica
See Also Pannonia
Mittelfränkische Reimbibel 2–228a
Mīzān 1–141b
Mkhedruli script 1–214b
MOAT 8–0; 3–148a, 150a
MOBADAN MOBADH 8–0
Mobi Clarainech of Glasnevin 3–465b

***MOCEDADES DE RODRIGO* 8–0**
Cid legend 3–388a-389a
Modalism 3–625a-628b
MODAL NOTATION 8–0; 1–543b, 544a-b
ars nova 1–548b-550b
MODE 8–0
ars antiqua 1–543b
Model books
See Drawings and model books
Modena Cathedral
Arthur legend 1–567b
Moderno dictamine, De (Thomas Merke) 4–175b
Modes (melodic) 1–545b
ars nova 1–551b-552a
ars poetica 1–554b
Modestus of Fulda 3–438a
MODILLION 8–0
Modioi 1–78a
Modis uniendi et reformandi ecclesiae, De (Dietrich of Niem) 3–518b
MODOIN 8–0
Modoin of Autun
Theodulf 3–102b-103a
Mǫðruvallabók 4–294a, 401a, 403b
Modus
ars nova 1–549a
Modus liebinc (Heribert of Rothenburg) 3–58a
MODUS TENENDI PARLIAMENTUM 8–0
Modwenna, Saint 1–261a
Moego, Pero 3–87a
Moguer
trade 4–558a
Mohammed
See Muḥammad
Mohammed II 1–159a
See Mehmed (Muḥammad) II
Mohel 3–401a
MOISSAC, CHURCH OF SAINT PIERRE 8–0
Durandus 4–315b
Mojmír
Moravia 2–299a,b
Mokkʻ 1–472b, 473a,b; 2–48b
Molad adu 3–26b
Molad Beharad 3–25b
Molad betuthakpat 3–26b
Molad computations 3–25b-26b
Molad saken 3–25b
Molad tishri 3–25b-26b
Molad yaḥ 3–25b
Molad yaḥ-adu 3–26b
Molay, Jacques de
Knights Templars 3–304b
Moldavia
Bohemian Brethren 2–305b
Visigoths 2–90b
Moldboard plow 1–77a
MOLDING 8–0
Molesme abbey 3–403a-b, 406a
Molina 1–416b
Mollat, Georges
Avignonese papacy 3–362b
Molle Valley
agriculture 1–85b
Mollusks
dyes 4–327a
Mombaer, Jan
Brethren of the Common Life 2–368a
Devotio Moderna 4–167a
Monachus, Johannes
conciliar theory 3–517a
Monarchia (Dante) 4–102b-103a,b
Monarchy
See Kingship, Theories of
MONASTERY 8–0
anthologies 1–320a
Architectura, De 1–331b
Augustinism 1–661a
Bosnian church 2–342a-b
Brethren of the Common Life 2–366b, 367b
brewing 2–374b
Brittany, Duchy 2–379a
Burgundy, Duchy of 2–428a
Byzantine 1–636b, 637b
Celtic church 2–381b
chapter house design 3–266a
church reforms 3–347b
cloister 3–465a
Coptic 3–585a, 586a,b, 587a, 592b
dayr 4–117a
elections, church 4–424b-425a
time measurements 3–458b
Monastery of the Caves
See Pecherskaya Lavra
Monastic chant
See individual articles
Monastic exegesis 4–542b-543a
Monasticism
Alexandrian rite 1–155b
anchorites 1–242b
Ancrene Riwle 1–243a
Anglo-Saxon England 4–459a
Basil the Great 2–120a, 121b, 122a
Brethren of the Common Life 2–367b-368a
Carthusians 3–118a
celibacy 3–216b-217a
Celtic church 3–227b
Cistercian Order 3–403a
Cluny, Order of 3–468b
commendam 3–489b
Cyprus 4–72b-73a
Dauphiné 4–109b
dervish 4–163a
early church theology 3–342b, 343a
English reformers 1–61b
Ethelwold 4–518a
Latin church 3–368a
Old English prose 1–281b
MONASTICISM, BYZANTINE 8–0
architecture 4–333a-b, 343a, 344a
Armenian church 1–504b
Armenian Rite 1–516b-517a
Camaldolese Order 3–55b
Cappadocia 3–92a
Cassian 3–122a
charistikion 3–268a
economy and society 2–478b-479a
Mount Athos 1–636b, 637a
Monasticism, Celtic
See Celtic Church
MONASTICISM, ORIGINS 8–0
Ašot III Ołormac 1–589b
Benedictine Rule 2–171a,b
Benedictines 2–171b
Benedict of Nursia 2–168b
Bosnian Church 2–342a
Brigit, Saint 2–376a
Bulgaria 2–403b, 404a, 405b
Burgundy, County of 2–426b
Burgundy, Duchy of 2–427b-428a
Carmelites 3–96a
Celestines 3–214b
chapter 3–265a
Copts and Coptic church 3–595a
Monastir
fairs 4–589a
ribāṭ 1–69a-b
Monceau, Henri Duhamel de
charcoal burning 3–267a
MONDINO DEI LUZZI 8–0
MONEMVASIA 8–0
Moner of Rousillon, Squire
Catalan poetry 3–172a
Moneta di banco 2–75a
Moneta of Cremona
Dominican theology 4–247b
Money
See Banking, European
See Banking, Islamic
See Mints and Money
Money changing
banking, European 2–74a-b, 75b, 77b
banking, Islamic 2–80a
fairs 4–584b, 592b
Moneylending
European 2–73b
Islamic 2–79a-b
Money markets
European 2–78b
Islamic 2–80a
MÖngke, Great Khan
Cilician kingdom 3–391b
MONGOL EMPIRE: EUROPE AND WESTERN ASIA 8–0
agriculture 1–100b-101a
Argun 1–453a
Ayyubids to 2–23b
Azerbaijan 2–27a
Batu 2–131b
Caffa 3–12a
caliphate 3–50b-51a
Cilician kingdom 3–391b
Egypt 2–138b; 4–32a
exploration 4–556b, 558b
Muscovy 4–232a-b
MONGOL EMPIRE: FOUNDATIONS 8–0
Abbasids 1–12a
Afghanistan 1–65a,b
Aleppo 1–145b
alms tax 1–202b
Ani in Sirak 1–291a
Arčēš 1–423a
Armenia 1–485b-486a
Assassins 1–591a
Bukhara 2–397a
Caucasia 3–195a-b
crusades 4–31b
Seljuks 1–241b
Mongolian still 4–219b
Mongols
Abar/Apar 2–12a
agriculture 1–105a
bow and arrow/crossbow 2–350b, 352a
cavalry 3–209b
Moniage Guillaume 3–259a
Monica, Saint 1–646a, 647a, 650b
MONKEY HEAD 8–0
Monk of Montaudon
Arnaut Daniel 1–539a
Monks
divisions of society 3–358a, 359a
Monologion (Anselm of Canterbury) 1–311b, 314a
MONOPHONY 8–0
ars nova 1–552b
chansonnier 3–255b-256a
MONOPHYSITISM 8–0; 1–58a
Akhṭal, al- 1–115a
alphabet 1–212a
Antioch 2–460a
Antiochene rite 1–327a-b
Armenian church 1–499a
Axum kingdom 2–17b
Bar Hebraeus 2–108b
Bogomils 2–296a
Byzantine church 2–462a,b, 464b,

MONOPHYSITISM (cont.)
485b
caesaropapism 3–10b
Christology 3–320a
Constantinople 3–554b, 555b
Coptic church 3–594a-b
Council of Chalcedon 1–32a; 3–629a-b
Council of Constantinople 3–630a-b
Cyril of Alexandria 4–75a
Dominican mission 4–252b
early church 3–339b
Ekthesis 4–418b
Eutyches 4–523b
Eutychios the Melchite 4–525a
Latin Church 3–339b-340a
Nicene-Constantinopolitan Creed 3–676b
Nubian Christianity 3–314b
Monopolies
banal 2–69b
Monosticha (Saint Columbanus) 3–486b
Monotheism
pre-Islamic Arabia 1–370b, 372b
MONOTHELITISM 8–0; 3–344a
Antiochene rite 1–327b
Armenian church 1–499b-500a
Byzantine church 2–462a
Christology 3–320a
Constans II 3–544b
Council of Constantinople 3–630b
Ekthesis 4–418b
Monreal del Campo 1–406a
Monreale Cathedral
architecture 4–346b
doors 2–109a, 324b
mosaics 2–445b
Monreale monastery 1–87b
Mons Meg 4–393a
Monstrance 1–223b-224a
Monstrelet, Enguerrand de
chivalry 3–328a
chronicles 3–333b
Montagnac
fairs 4–584b, 586a
Montaillou
Catharism 3–360a
Montanism
Tertullian 3–335b
Montaperti
Ghibellines 3–196a
Montaperti, Battle of (1260) 3–117b; 4–96b
Montauban
bastide 2–128a, 129a,b
Montazgo 3–138b
Montdidier, Paien de
Knights Templars 3–304a
Montearagón 1–405b
Montebourg Psalter 1–262b; 2–218b
MONTE CASSINO 8–0
Alberic of 1–125b
atrium 1–641a
Benedict of Nursia 2–169a, 170b
Bertharius 2–199a
breviary 2–371a-b
Bruno of Segni, Saint 2–392a
Desiderius abbot 4–164b
Monte Cassino Passion 4–281b
Monte Cassino Vulgate 2–211b
Montecatini, Battle of (1315) 4–103b-104a
Monte Fumone, Castello di 2–323b
Monteg, Lunel de 3–665b
Montenegro 2–339a
Montereau, Pierre of
See Pierre of Montreuil
Montesa, Order of 1–415a
Montesión Church 1–20a
Montfort Castle
carving 4–25b
Montibus, silvis, fontibus, lacubus, fluminibus, stagnis seu paludibus et de dominibus..., De 2–286b
Montjuïc 2–103a
Montjuic, Jaume de 3–166b
Montpazier 2–129a
MONTPELLIER 8–0
Black Death 2–261a
Crown of Aragon 1–408b, 411b, 412b-413a, 416a
Inquisition 3–190a
money markets 2–78b
Montpellier, University of
Cistercian order 3–405a
Montpellier family
Cathar persecution 3–186b-187b
MONTPELLIER MS H 196 8–0
Montpensier, Battle of (892) 3–202b
Montréal
castellan 3–124b
Montreuil, Eudes of
See Eudes of Montreuil
Montreuil, Jean de
Christine de Pizan 3–316b
Montreuil, Pierre of
See Pierre of Montreuil
Monuments, stone
Celtic art 3–221b-223b
Moon age tables
Old English rules 1–285b
Moors
Alhambra 1–170a, 171a
Castile 3–135b
Santiago 4–561b
Second Crusade 4–37b
Visigoths 2–91a-b
Moosburg Ordinarium 1–582b
Moral allegory 1–179b-180a, 185b
Moral exempla
Canterbury Tales 3–294a-295b
Moralia in Job (Gregory the Great) 1–364a; 3–167a
codicology 3–476b
Moralité de l'alliance de foy et de loyalté 4–286b-287a
Moralité des sept pechés mortels et des sept vertus 4–286b
Moralité du pèlerinage de la vie humaine 4–286b
MORALITY PLAY 8–0
allegory 1–186a
Castle of Perserverance 3–142b
Dutch 4–322a
Everyman 4–526b
France 4–264b, 265a-b, 266a
Germany 4–269a-b, 271b
terminology 4–279a
Moral philosophy
Aquinas 1–364a-365a
Bacon 2–40a-b
Morals of the Catholic Church (Augustine) 1–648b, 650b, 656a
Morals of the Manichees (Augustine) 1–648b
Morant und Galie
See Karlmeinet
Morat, Battle of (1476) 3–205a
Morava phase of Serbian architecture 4–347b
Morava River
Macsó banat 2–70a
MORAVIA 8–0
agricultural tools 1–90b
Bohemian Brethren 2–305b
Bulgaria 2–402a-b
Byzantine church 2–463b-464a
Byzantine Empire 2–489a-b
Cyril and Methodios 4–73b-74a
Slavs 2–329a
See Also Bohemia-Moravia
Moravské Pole, Battle of (1278) 2–300a
Moray, Battle of (1130) 4–110b
More, Thomas 3–83b
MOREA 8–0
Byzantine Empire 2–499a, 503a,b, 504b
Kantakouzenoi 2–479b
***MOREA, CHRONICLE OF* 8–0**; 2–508a-b, 522b
MOREA, DESPOTATE OF 8–0
Morel, Eustache
See Deschamps, Eustache
MOREL, PIERRE 8–0
Morella 1–412a
Moreno, Joan 3–171b
Morgan clan 3–407a
Morgarten, Battle of (1315) 2–8a; 3–205a
Moriaen 4–318b-319a
Morienus
alchemy 1–136a,b, 141a
Morimond Abbey 3–403b
Morion 1–527b, 531a
MORITZ VON CRAUN 8–0
AMbraser Heldenbuch 1–229b
Morkinskinna 4–413b
Moroccan Rif
agricultural tools 1–80a
Morocco
Almoravids 1–198b-199a, 200b
Atlas Mountains 1–639b
rown of Aragon 1–414b
fairs 4–589b
Norwegians 4–554b
slaves 2–268a
Morosini, Thomas, Patriarch 3–552a
Morphosyntax
Catalan language 3–160a-163a
Morrer d'amor 3–87a
Morrone, Mount 3–214b
Mors (death)
crucifixion 4–13b
Mort Alixandre 1–151a
Mort d'ancestor 1–594b, 597b, 598a
Morte Darthur, Le
Caxton 3–211a
See Also Malory, Sir Thomas
Mortifications
Celtic spirituality 3–231a,b
Mortimer
deposition of Edward II 4–483a-b
Mortimer, Katherine 4–111b
Mortimer, Roger
death 4–398a
Isabella of France 4–397b
Mortimer family
Burgh, de 2–422a
MORTMAIN 8–0
Burgundy, Duchy of 2–427b
Edward I of England 4–396b
Morton, John, Archbishop
Canterbury 3–83b
Morum qualitate per exemplorum coaptationem, De 1–314a
Morvan
Brittany, Duchy of 2–378b
MOSAIC AND MOSAIC MAKING 8–0
Alhambra 1–171a
Annuciation 1–307b
Cavallini 3–198a
early Christian art 4–349b, 352a-b, 358a, 359a,b, 362a-b
Ephrem 4–495a

Hosios Lukas Monastery 2–442a-443a
MOSAN ART 8–0
bronze and brass 2–384a,b
champlevé enamels 4–438a,b
Moscow
Crimea, Khanate of 3–679b
fur trade 4–588a
patriarch of 2–10a
See Also Muscovy, Rise of
MOSCOW KREMLIN, ART AND ARCHITECTURE 8–0
MOSER, LUCAS 8–0
Moses Arragel of Guadalajara
Alba Bible 2–215b
Moses bar Kefa
Antiochene rite 1–327b
Moses ben Maimon
See Maimonides, Moses
Moses ben Naḥman
See Nahmanides, Moses
Moses ben Nakman
See Nahmanides, Moses
Moses ben Samuel ha-Kohen Gikatilla (Chiguatilla)
exegesis 4–539b
MOSES BEN SHEM TOV DE LEON 8–0
cabala 3–2a
Zohar 1–346a
Moses ben Simon of Burgos
cabala 3–2a
Moses ha-Darshan
exegesis 4–541a
Moses ibn Ḥanokh
Córdoba 3–600a
MOSQUE 8–0
Aghlabid architecture 1–69a
Almohad art 1–191b-193a
Almoravid 1–196b-197b
Islamic Egypt 4–408a
Mosque of Ibn Ṭūlūn 4–408a
Mosque of Manučʿē (Minūchihr) 1–292b
Mossel Bay
exploration 4–562b
MOSUL 8–0
Athīr, Ibn al-, family 1–634a
Ayyubids 2–23a
Badr al-Dīn 2–43b
exilarch 4–552b
ʿImād al-Dīn Zangī 4–37a-b
Saladin 4–31a
Mote, Jean de la 1–151b, 185b
Mote of Mark
ornamented molds 3–224a
MOTET 8–0
ars antiqua 1–542b
ars nova 1–550b-551b
ars subtilior 1–558b
Bamberg manuscript 2–68b
clausula 3–437a
duplum 4–313a
MOTET MANUSCRIPTS 8–0
ars antiqua 1–545a-b
ars nova 1–552a
Bamberg manuscript 2–68b
Mother Arax 1–421b
Motherhood
church fathers 1–323a
Mother-of-God, Church of the (Constantinople) 4–341b
Mother of God Eleousa, Church of the (Constantinople) 4–344a
Motibus celorum (Scot) 1–614b
Motte-and-bailey fortification 3–144a-145a
MÖTTULS SAGA 8–0
Motu octauae sphaerae, De (Thābit ibn Qurra) 1–612b
MOUCHETTE 8–0
Mouchroutas 2–443b
MOULINS, MASTER OF 8–0
"Mountain of Noah"
See Ararat, Mount
Mount Badon, Battle of (516)
Arthurian literature 1–564a,b
Mount of Olives
Antichrist 1–322b
Mourtzouphlos
Crusades 4–47a-48a
Mousket, Philippe
Chronique rimée 3–258a
Mouvance 3–260b
Movable feasts
Old English rules 1–285b
MOVSĒS DASXURANCʿI 8–0; 1–511a
Movsēs of Siwnikʿ, Bishop 1–510a
Movsēs of Tatʿew 1–520b
Movsēs the Grammarian 1–520a-b
MOVSĒS XORENACʿI 8–0; 1–510a, 519b
Aršak II 1–559b
Artašat 1–563a
Moxenē
See Mokkʿ
Moyses vir Dei 3–653b
MOZARABIC ART 8–0
MOZARABIC CHANT 8–0
Mozarabic dialects 3–141b
MOZARABIC KHARJAS 8–0
Mozarabic poetry
courtly love 3–672a
MOZARABIC RITE 8–0
Asturias-León 1–630b
conflict in Spain 3–129a
Mozarabs
Asturian raids 1–626a
Córdoba 3–598b, 599b, 600a
Eulogius 4–521b
MREN 8–0
Msr 4–113a
Msra Melikʿ 4–112b, 113a
Mtavari 2–29a
Mtkvari
See Kura River
MTSXETA 8–0
Djvari 4–231b
Muallaqa 4–361a
MUʿĀWIYA 8–0
ʿAbd Allāh 1–15b
Abode of Covenant 1–21a, 29a-b
ʿAlī ibn Abī Ṭālib 1–172b-173b
ʿAmr ibn al-ʿĀṣ 1–237a-b
Armenia 1–478a
caliphate 3–36a-38b
Damascus 4–81b, 83a, 85a
diplomacy 4–200a
MUʿĀWIYA ʿĀʾISHA 1–113b
Mu-ʿāwiya ibn Lope
Córdoba 3–600a
Mu'ayyad al-Dīn al-ʿUrḍī
astronomy 1–621a
Mu'ayyad Shaykh, al- 3–400a
Muʿayyid al-Dawla
Buyids 2–436a
Muḍāraba
See Commenda
Mudawwana (Saḥnūn) 1–71a
MUDÉJAR ART 8–0
ajímez 1–114b
Aragon 1–407a, 412a, 419b
Castile 3–134a, 135a
MUEZZIN 8–0
Mugello, Battle of (1303) 4–99a
Mughāwir, al-
See Almogávares
Mughīth al-Rūmī
Córdoba 3–598a
Muhallabī, al- 1–70a
MUḤAMMAD 8–0
ʿAbbās, al- 1–3b-4b
Abbasids 1–6b
ʿAbd Allāh 1–15a
ʿAbd al-Muṭṭalib 1–14a, 15a
Abode of Islam-Abode of War 1–20b
Abū Bakr 1–24a
Abū Sufyān 1–28b
Abū Ṭālib 1–29b-30a
ʿĀʾisha 1–112a
Alids 1–174b
ʿAlī ibn Abī Ṭālib 1–171b
Allah 1–177b-178b
alms tax 1–201b
ʿAmr ibn al-ʿĀṣ 1–236b
Ansāb al-Ashrāf 2–54a
Arabia, Islamic 1–373a-b
archangels 1–248b
Aristotle 1–458b
Ascension of the Prophet 1–581a
Badr, Battle of 2–42b
Bukhārī, al- 2–397b, 398b
Burāq 2–419b
calendar 3–27a,b
caliphate origins 3–32a-b
dietary laws 1–300b; 4–179b
diplomacy 4–200a
fairs 4–588b
marriage 4–597b, 598a
mi ʿrāj 1–106b
perfume 2–147a
wine 2–208b-a
Muḥammad I
See Mehmed (Muḥammad) I
Muḥammad II
See Mehmed (Muḥammad) II
Muḥammad V
Alhambra 1–168b
Muḥammad al-Amīn 1–9b, 10a
Muḥammad al-Bāqir 1–175a
Muḥammad al-Nāṣir 1–195a
Muḥammad Danishmendids 4–91b-93a
Muḥammad ibn ʿAbd al-Karīm 1–634a
Muḥammad ibn ʿAbd Allāh al-Iskāfī 4–443a
Muḥammad ibn ʿAbdullāh al-Nafs al-Zakiyya 1–174b
Muḥammad ibn al-Ḥanafiyya 1–173b, 174b
Muḥammad ibn ʿAlī ibn ʿAbd Allāh ibn al-ʿAbbās 1–7a
Muḥammad ibn Ḥasan al-Shaybānī 1–26b
Muḥammad ibn Ḥūd 1–195b
Muḥammad ibn Kathīr al-Farghānī
astronomy text 1–620b
Muḥammad ibn Maḥmūd al-Āmūlī 4–445b
Muḥammad ibn Mūsā al-Khwārizmī 1–53b
Sindhind 1–620a
Muḥammad ibn Mūsā ibn Shākir
astronomy text 1–620b
Muḥammad ibn Tāshfīn
Cid 3–384b, 385a, 387b
Muḥammad ibn Ṭughj 4–405b
Muḥammad ibn Tūmart
Almohads 1–191b, 193b
Muḥammad ibn Umail al-Tamimī
alchemy 1–136b
Mühldorf, Battle of (1322) 2–7b
***MUḤTASIB* 8–0**
caliphate 3–43a, 44b
Damascus 4–84a
divine right 3–46b

MUID 8–0
Mu'īn al-Dīn Unur
Second Crusade 4–38a
Muirchertach Ua Briain, King 4–77b
Muiredach at Monasterboice
Celtic art 3–221b, 222
Mχit'ar Gos
Cilician court 3–393b
MU'IZZ AL-DAWLA 8–0
Baghdad 1–11b
Buyids 2–435b
caliphate 3–50a
Mu'izz al-Dīn 2–23b
Mu'izz li-Dīn Allāh, al-
See Fatimids
Mukarrabūn, al- 1–248b
Mukharrim, al- 2–46a
Mukhaṣṣaṣ (Ibn Sīda) 4–443a
Mukhtār ibn Abī 'Ubayd, al- 1–16a
Mukkarnas
See Muqarnas
Muktafī, al- 1–11a
Mukūs 1–202a
Mulaththamūn
See Almoravids
MULDENFALTEN 8–0
Mule
draft animal 1–295b-296a
MULḤAM 8–0
Mulieribus claris, De (On Famous Women) (Boccaccio) 2–286b-287a, 288b
Müller, Johann (Regiomontanus)
Archimedes 1–436a, 439a,b
Müller, Johann
astrarium 3–462a
astronomy 1–613b
sundials 3–28b
Mulling, Book of
extreme unction 3–230b
MULLION 8–0
Multiplicatione, De 1–138a
Multiplicatione specierum, De (On the Multiplication of Species) (Bacon) 2–38a, 39a
Multivalencia 3–623b
MULTSCHER, HANS 8–0
Muluk aṭ-ṭawā'if
See Taifas
Mundi transitu, De (Saint Columbanus) 3–486b
Mundi universitate, De
See Cosmographia
Munich
founding 2–134b
Louis IV 2–135a
Munio of Zamora
Dominican sisters 4–254b
Munkar 1–248b
MUNNIUS 8–0
Beatus *Commentary* 4–255b
MUNSTER 8–0
Cashel 3–121a
Dál Cais kingship 4–77a-b
Eóganacht 4–492b
Münster (Ger.)
bishops 1–226a
Muntaner, Ramon 1–415b; 3–165b-166a
Catalan language 3–162a
Munyat al-Ruṣāfa
Córdoba 3–598a
Muqābasāt, al- (Abū Ḥayyān al-Tawḥīdī) 1–618a
MUQADDASĪ, MUḤAMMAD AL- 8–0; 2–33a
Armenia 1–485a
Armenian Muslim emirates 1–513b
Bukhara 2–397b
Muqaddima (Ibn Khaldūn) 1–384b-385b
MUQAFFA', 'ABD ALLĀH IBN AL- 8–0
Calīla e Digna 3–31b
prose literature 1–379a
***MUQARNAS* 8–0**
Alhambra 1–170a, 171a
Almoravid art 1–191b, 197b
Muqla, Ibn 2–135b
script styles 3–54b
MUQTADIR, AL- 8–0; 1–6a-b
ascension to throne 3–42b
Muqtadir of Sargossa, al- 1–405b
Cid 3–384a
Muqtafī, al-
caliphate 3–50b
Muqtanā, 'Alī Bahlā' al-Dīn al-
Druzes 4–296a
Mur, Raymond de
See Raymond de Mur
See Also Almoravids
Murābiṭūn, al- 1–71a
MURAD I 8–0; 2–136b
Anatolia 1–242a
Ankara occupation 1–302b
Bulgaria 2–413a
MURAD II 8–0; 2–137a
Byzantine Empire 2–503b, 504a
Muradiye
See Berkri
Murād Su River 4–522a
Murcia
agriculture 1–84b
Crown of Aragon 1–408b, 409b, 412b, 414b, 416b
Ferdinand III 3–134a
Murder
presentment of Englishry 4–487a
Muret 1–410b, 411a-b
Murji'a
Abū Ḥanīfa 1–26b
Umayyads 3–40a, 41a
Murtaḍā, al- 1–195b
Murtagh O'Loughlin
Clonard 3–466a
Murten, Battle of (1476)
bow and arrow/crossbow 2–352b
Murūj al-dhahab (Mas'ūdī) 1–381a
Mur Valley 2–7a
Mūsā al-Hādī 1–9a
Mūsā al-Kāẓim 1–175a
Mus'ab ibn al-Zubayr 1–16a
Muṣādara 3–39b
Musāfirids 2–27a
Mūsā ibn 'Abdullāh 1–175a
MUSALLA 8–0
Musaylima al-Kadhdhāb
caliphate 3–33b
MUSCOVY, RISE OF 8–0
boyar 2–355a
Dmitrii Ivanovich Donskoi 4–232a
duma 4–305b
pomestie estates 1–101b-102a
Mušeł 1–483a
Museł Mamikonean 1–290b, 479b
Mushtarak al-lafẓī, al- (al-Aṣma'ī) 4–443b
Music
Christmas mass 3–319a
Cluny Order 3–469a
MUSIC, ARABIC INFLUENCE IN 8–0
MUSIC, ARMENIAN 8–0
MUSIC, BYZANTINE 8–0
MUSIC, CELTIC 8–0
MUSIC, ISLAMIC 8–0
MUSIC, ISLAMIC INFLUENCE IN THE WEST 8–0
MUSIC, JEWISH IN THE MIDDLE EAST 8–0
cantor 3–87b
Music, Liturgical
ars subtilior 1–558b
Aurelian of Réôme 2–2b
Benedicamus Domino 2–167b
differentia 4–185a
MUSIC, MEDITERRANEAN 8–0
MUSIC, MIDDLE EASTERN 8–0
MUSIC, ORAL TRADITION IN 8–0
MUSIC, POPULAR 8–0
chansonnier 3–255b
Middle English ballads 2–59b
MUSIC, SLAVIC 8–0
MUSIC, SYRIAN 8–0
MUSIC, WESTERN EUROPEAN 8–0
antiphon 1–328b
ars antiqua 1–542b
ars subtilior 1–558a-559a
caccia 3–4a
cantiga 3–84b
chansonnier 3–255b
contrafactum 3–575b
contratenor 3–576b
counterpoint 3–658b
duplum 4–312b
song anthologies 1–319a,b
Musica, De (Alcuin) 1–142b
Musica, De (Grocheio) 4–87a
Musica disciplina (Aurelian of Réôme) 2–2b
Musica enchiriadis
clef 3–438a
diaphonia 4–172a,b
MUSICA FICTA 8–0
ars nova 1–552a
Musical instruments
bells 2–165b
MUSICAL INSTRUMENTS, EUROPEAN 8–0
dance 4–86b, 89b
MUSICAL INSTRUMENTS, MIDDLE EASTERN 8–0
MUSICAL NOTATION, ALPHABETIC 8–0
MUSICAL NOTATION, BILINGUAL 8–0
MUSICAL NOTATION, BYZANTINE 8–0
MUSICAL NOTATION, DASEIAN 8–0
MUSICAL NOTATION, EKPHONETIC 8–0
MUSICAL NOTATION, HUFNAGEL 8–0
MUSICAL NOTATION, MODAL 8–0; 1–543b
ars nova 1–548b-550b
counterpoint 3–657a-b
MUSICAL NOTATION, WESTERN 8–0; 1–542b
Agnus Dei 1–74b
ars antiqua 1–545b-547a
ars subtilior 1–558b
"Cambridge Songs" 1–319a
cantiga 3–85b
Carmina Burana 3–97b, 99a
chansonnier 3–255b
chansons de toile 3–263a
clef 3–438a
custos 4–68a
diaphonia 4–172a
diastemy 4–172b
MUSICAL ORNAMENTATION 8–0
MUSICAL PERFORMANCE 8–0
Ambrosian chant 1–232a
Bamberg manuscript and 13th century 2–68b

chansonnier 3–255b
MUSICAL TREATISES 8–0
Anonymous IV 1–309a, 310a
ars antiqua 1–544a-545a
ars nova 1–548b-550a
Aurelian of Réôme 2–2b
consonance/dissonance 3–541b
copula 3–595b
counterpoint 3–657b
MUSIC IN EDUCATION 8–0
MUSIC IN MEDIEVAL SOCIETY 8–0
ars subtilior 1–558a
centonization 3–235b
See Also Cistercian chant
Music theory
conductus 3–532a
copula 3–595b
diabolus in musica 4–167b
MUSICUS 8–0
Muslim, Qutayba ibn
Bukhara 2–397a
"Muslim Saint Augustine"
See Ghazālī, al-
***MUSPILLI* 8–0**; 2–225a
Mussato, Albertino (poet) 4–96a
Musta'īn, al- 3–400a
Cid 3–384a,b-385a
Mustakfī, al- 3–50a
MUSTANṢIR, AL- 8–0
Almohads 1–195b
Badr al-Jamālī 2–44a
Ismā'īliya 1–590a
Mustarshid, al- 4–91b
MUSTA'ṢIM, AL- 8–0
death 1–12a; 3–51a
Mustaṭraf, al- (al-Ibshīhī) 4–445a
Mu'taḍid, al- 1–11a
Baghdad 2–46b
Mu'tamid, al-
Armenia 1–480b
Mu'tamid ibn 'Abbād, al- 1–199b
Cid 3–384a,b
MUTANABBĪ, AL- 8–0; 1–401b
Buyids 2–437a
MU'TAṢIM, AL- 8–0; 1–10b-11a
Baghdad 2–46b
Turkish troops 3–49b
MUTAWAKKIL, AL- 8–0
Alexandria 1–153b-154a
Armenia 1–480a
Balādhurī 2–54a
costume edict 3–619b
medals 1–6b
murder 3–49b
Nestorians 3–312b
regulation of *ahl al-dhimma* 3–43b
science 1–391b
MU'TAZILA, AL- 8–0
Ash'arī, al- 1–583a-584a
Mu'tazilite kalam
influence 2–51a
Mu'tazilite school of theology 1–379b
Mu'tazz, Ibn al- 1–401b, 402b
Mutī', al-
Buyids 2–435b
Mutimir 4–2b
Muṭṭalib, al- 1–29b
'Abd al-Mu?t19ttalib 1–14b
Mutton
European cookery 3–581b
Muwaffaq, al- 1–11a
Muwalladūn
Córdoba 3–598b
Muwaqqit 1–623a-b
Muwashshaḥ 1–398a
Muwashshaḥāt 1–176a
Muwassin Mosque, al- 1–193a
Mxargrdzeli 1–235b
Mχargrdzeḷi, Ivanē
Ani in Širak 1–291a
Mχit'ar Anec'i 1–511b
Mχit'ar Ayrivaṇec'i 1–511b
MXIT'AR GOŠ 8–0; 1–511b, 512a
Mχit'ar Herac'i 1–512a
Mycenaeans
arch 1–423b
Mynyddog the Wealthy
Gododdin 1–247b
Mynyw (Menevia) Church 4–329b
Myrelaion Church 4–341a
MYRIOKEPHALON 8–0
Manuel I 1–241b
Myriokephalon, Battle of (1176) 4–93a
Myrrh
Arabia 1–370a
Mystère d'Adam
See Jeu d'Adam
Mystère du siège d'Orléans 4–265a
Mystère du Vieil Testamen 4–284b
MYSTERY PLAYS 8–0
barber guilds 2–99b
Dutch 4–321b-322a
terminology 4–279a
See Also Chester plays
MYSTERY RELIGIONS 9–0
Mystical Marriage of Saint Catherine (Barna da Siena) 2–111a
Mystical poetry, Arabic 1–402a
Mystical theology, Byzantine 2–467a
MYSTICAL WRITINGS, MIDDLE ENGLISH 9–0
MYSTICISM
beguines and beghards 2–160b-161a
Bonaventure, Saint 2–315b-316a
cathars 3–181a
Zosimus 1–135b-136a
MYSTICISM, BYZANTINE 9–0
Mount Athos 1–637b
mystical theology 2–467a
Mysticism, European
Birgitta, Saint 2–246b
Dominicans 4–248a-b
Dutch literature 4–319a-b, 320b
Eckhart 4–380b
See Also Church, Latin: 1305 to 1500
MYSTICISM, EUROPEAN: GERMANY 9–0
MYSTICISM, EUROPEAN: RUUSBROEC 9–0
MYSTICISM, EUROPEAN: WOMEN MYSTICS 9–0
MYSTICISM, ISLAMIC 9–0
Ascension of the Prophet 1–581b
Sufism 4–407a
Mysticism, Jewish
See Cabala
Myth of ten lost tribes
Jewish apocalyptic literature 1–346a,b
Mythography 1–183b
Mythologies (Fulgentius) 1–183b
Mythology
Alvíssmál 1–226b
interpretation 1–180b, 282a
MYTHOLOGY, CELTIC 9–0
Mžež Gnuni 1–477a

N

Nabataean Book of Agriculture (Ibn Wahshīya) 1–106a
Nabateans 1–371a
Iraq 1–106a
Nabuchodonosor 2–227b
NADĪM, IBN AL- 9–0; 1–389b, 390a
astrology/astronomy 1–616b
numerals 1–384a
Nafā'is al-funūn fī 'arā'is al-'uyūn 4–445b
Nafīs, Ibn al- 4–407b
Nafs al-Zakiyya, al- 1–374b
Nag Hammadi
angel/angelology 1–249b
NAGID 9–0
Nagy-Szent-Miklós
art and architecture 2–414b, 415a
Nahapet K'uč'ak 1–512a
Nahj al-balagha (al-Sharīf al-Raḍī) 1–173b
NAHMANIDES, MOSES 9–0
cabala 3–1b-2a
exegesis 2–212a
Nahrawān, Al-, Battle of (658) 1–173a; 3–36a
Nahray ben Nissim
Cairo Genizah 3–16a
Nahr Buq 2–45a
Naissance du chevalier au cygne 3–331a
Najac 2–129a
Nájera, Battle of (1367) 3–137a; 4–399a
Najralla, Jehoseph bar 1–168a
NAJRĀN 9–0; 1–375b
Nakīr 1–248b
Na'l 3–616b
Naloi
See Analoi
Nancy, Battle of (1477) 2–352b; 3–205a
Nanna 2–55b
NANNI DI BANCO 9–0
Nanni di Bartolo
See Giovanni (Nanni) di Bartolo
Nantcarfan
See Llancarfan
Nanteuil, Sanson de 1–262b
NAOS 9–0; 3–378a
NAPLES 9–0
banking 2–73b, 76a, 78b
Catalan language 3–157b
concordat (1451) 3–525b
Crown of Aragon 1–417b-418a, 420a
fruits and fruit trees 1–87a
Ravenna exarchate 4–530a
slaves 2–268b, 269b
trade 4–557b
Napoleon I
papal archives 1–448a
Naqīb al-ashrāf 1–175b
NAQSH 9–0
NAQSH HADIDA 9–0
NAQSH-I RUSTAM 9–0; 1–451b
Narbonnais, Les 2–201b
Narbonne 1–121a, 408b
Alani settlement 1–121a
Albigensian Crusade 3–188a-b, 189a
Black Death 2–260b
fairs 4–586a
inheritance 4–607a

Narbonne, Treaty of (1415) 3–649a
NARBONNE RITE 9–0
NARDO DI CIONE 9–0; 1–343a
Nardulus
  See Einhard
Narrenschiff, Das 2–363b-364a
Narses
  Ostrogoths 2–95b
NARTHEX 9–0
  basilicas 2–124a
  Coptic and Ethiopian churches 1–157a
Nashki
  See Naskhī
NASI 9–0
Nāṣir-i Khusraw
  Ismāʿīlism 1–65a
Nāṣir li-Din Allah, al- 1–12a
  art 1–6b
  caliphate 3–50b
Nāṣir Yūsuf, al- 2–23b-24a
***NASKHĪ* 9–0**; 3–54a
  Arabic alphabet 1–209b, 210a
Nass 1–175a
NASTʿALĪQ 9–0; 3–54a-b
Natalis, Hervaeus (Harvey Nedellec)
  Durand of Saint Pourçin 4–313b
Natalis solis invicti 3–317b
Natangians
  See Nattangians
Nathan ben Isaac ha-Bavli
  exilarchy 4–552a
Nativitatibus et interrogationibus, De (ʿUmar al-Ṭabarī) 1–606b
Nativities (horoscopes) 1–605b, 619a
NATIVITY 9–0
Nativity (Campin) 3–61a
Nativity, Church of the (Bethlehem) 4–359b, 495a
  crownings 4–22b
  crusader art and architecture 4–24b
Nattangians
  insurrection 2–67a
Natura boni, De (Albertus Magnus) 1–127a,b
Naturalis historia (Pliny) 1–605a, 610b; 4–442a, 447b
Natural science
  Aquinas 1–358b-359b
  Bradwardine 2–358a
Natura rerum, De
  See Natures of Things
Natureingang 3–98a
Naturen bloeme, Der (The best of Nature) 4–319b
Natures of Things (Bede) 2–154b; 4–448a
Natures of Things (Hrabanus Maurus) 4–448a
Natures of Things (Isidore of Seville) 4–448a
Natures of Things (Neckham) 1–607a; 2–205a; 4–448b
Naukratios 2–439a
Naum
  Bulgaria 3–403b
NAʿŪRA 9–0; 1–104a
Navarre, Collège de 1–108a
NAVARRE, KINGDOM OF 9–0
  Alfonso I of Aragon 1–160b
  Aragon 1–404a-b, 406b
  archives 1–448b
  Asturias-León 1–627b, 628b
  Basques 2–126a,b
  Castile 3–128b, 129a, 130b, 137b
  cortes 3–610b
  Crown of Aragon 1–409a, 410a, 416b
Navarrese-Aragonese dialects 3–141b
NAVE 9–0
  basilicas 2–124a
  crossing 4–12a
  See Also Church, types of
Navidad
  Columbus 4–561a
Navies, Byzantine
  See Warfare, Byzantine
NAVIES, ISLAMIC 9–0
NAVIES, WESTERN 9–0
  crusades of later middle ages 4–55b
NAVIGATION: INDIAN OCEAN, RED SEA 9–0
NAVIGATION: SOUTHERN MEDITERRANEAN 9–0
NAVIGATION: WESTERN EUROPEAN 9–0
  cross-staff 1–613a; 4–12a
  texts 4–579a
Navigatio Sancti Brendani
  See Voyage de Saint Brendan
Nawādir 4–442b
Nawfal ibn ʿAbd Manāf
  ʿAbd al-Muṭṭalib 1–14b
NAXARAR 9–0; 1–475a, 476b, 479a, 480a-b, 481b
  azat 2–25b
  cavalry 3–199a
  Cilician court 3–393b
  social structure 1–488a-b, 489a-b, 490a,b
NAXČAWAN 9–0; 1–473b
Naχekełecʿi 4–417a
NAXOS, DUCHY OF 9–0
Nazareth
  artistic activity 4–24b
  Church of the Annunciation 4–22b
  crusader art and architecture 4–21b
  Fourth Crusades 4–32a
  Frederick II 4–51b
Nazarius, Bishop
  Bogomils 2–294b, 295b, 297a,b
Naẓm al-jawhar (Eutychios) 4–525a
Nea (New church of Constantinople) 2–117b; 3–378b; 4–341b
Nea Moni (New Monastery) on Chios 3–378b; 4–341b, 345a
  art 2–443a
Near East
  agricultural style 1–89a-90a
  food animals 1–301b
  traveler accounts 1–332a-333b
  Vikings 4–554a
  water buffalo use 1–298a
Nebuchadnezzar
  Babylonian captivity 2–33b
  See Also Nabuchodonosor
NECHTAN, KING OF THE PICTS 9–0
  dating of Easter 3–228b
NECKHAM, ALEXANDER 9–0
  Adam of the Little Bridge 1–52a
  bestiary 2–205a
  castles and fortifications 3–145b-146a, 150b
  Christian Hebraists 3–313b
  coal mining 3–472b
  De laudibus divinae sapientiae 1–255a
  encyclopedias 4–448b
  fables 4–572b, 573b
  man as microcosm idea 1–607a
  on drawings 4–291b
Necrologies
  demography 4–138b
Nedroma
  Almoravid mosque 1–197a
Negroli 1–529b
Nehunyah ben Ha-Kanah
  cabala 3–1b
NEIDHART VON REUENTAL 9–0
  Die Bauernhochzeit 2–132b
Nelipić 2–336b
Nelli, Francesco
  Boccaccio 2–288b, 289a
Nemanjić dynasty 2–337a
NEMESIANUS 9–0
Nemesius of Emesa 1–458a, 506a
  Burgundio of Pisa 2–423b
Nemrut 1–470b
NENNIUS 9–0; 2–71b
  Arthurian literature 1–564b
  Aurelianus 2–2b
  Canterbury 3–81a
Neocaesarea, Pontus Polemoniacus 2–119b
Neopatras 1–415a; 3–156b
Neopatria
  See Neopatras
NEOPLATONISM 9–0; 1–458b
  Alfred's translation of Boethius 1–167a
  allegorical interpretation 1–181a
  Ambrose, Saint 1–231b
  Aristotelianism 1–457b-458a, 459b, 460a, 461b
  Augustine, Saint 1–647a
  Bacon, Roger 2–39a
  Baḥya ben Joseph 2–51b
  Boethius 2–291b, 292a
  cosmography 1–183a
  Dāwūd ibn Marwān al-Muqammiṣ 4–116b
  Eckhart 4–381b-382a
  Egidius 4–400a
  Pseudo-Dionysius the Areopagite 1–250b
  Zosimus 1–135b-136a
Nepotism
  Avignonese papacy 3–363a
Nequam, Alexander
  See Neckham, Alexander
Neretljani
  Croatia 4–2b, 4a
  pirates 4–2a-b
  Venice 4–5b
Nerezi, Master of
  paintings 2–444b-445a
NERI DI FIORAVANTI 9–0
Ne Romani (Clement V) 3–524a
Nerra, Count Fulk
  Angevins 1–253a
NERSES I THE GREAT, SAINT 9–0; 1–476a, 498a
  Aršak II 1–560a
NERSĒS II AŠTARAKACʿI (BAGREWANDACʿI) **9–0**
  Aštarak 1–601a
  literature 1–508b
NERSĒS III 9–0; 1–478b, 479a
NERSĒS LAMBRONACʿI 9–0
  Armenian Rite 1–516b
  Bible 2–217b
  Cilician-Roman church union 3–394b
  literature 1–512a
NERSĒS IV ŠNORHALI 9–0
  Armenian saints 1–520b
  literature 1–511b, 512a
Nerva
  accession (96) 1–236a
Neseb$$r
  See Mesembria
Neskhi
  See Naskhī
Nestorian alphabet 1–208a-209a
NESTORIANISM 9–0
  Antiochene rite 1–327a
  Armenia 1–499a; 2–49b

Cassian 3–122b
Celestine I 3–213b
Christian church in Persia 3–312a
church, early 3–339b
Constantinople 3–555b
Coptic church 3–594a
Cyril of Alexandria 4–74b-75a
Dominicans 4–252b
ecumenical councils 3–628b-629a, 630a
Edessa 4–384a
Eutyches 4–524a
influence 1–57b, 58a
See Also Christology
NESTORIUS 9–0
condemnation 2–459b, 460a, 485b
patriarchy 2–462a
Netherlands
altarpieces 1–225b
archives 1–448a
religious communities 3–368b
Nether Wroughton
See Ellandun Wroughton
Nettesheim, Cornelius Agrippa von
cabala 3–3b
Net Vault
See Vault
Neuberg
Boniface, Saint 2–322a
NEUMA 9–0
Neumark
Brandenburg 2–360b, 361b-362a
NEUME 9–0
"Cambridge Songs" 1–319a
diaphonia 4–172a
diastemy 4–172b
Neustria
Boniface, Saint 2–322a
Merovingian Francia 3–104a-106a
Nevelon, Jean de 1–151a
Neville, Anne
death 4–479a
Neville, William
See Clanvowe, Sir John
Neville's Cross, Battle of (1346) 4–111a
NEVSKY, ALEXANDER 9–0
Nevu'at ha-yeled (The prophecy of the child) 1–346b
Newark
Black Death 2–262b
New Book of Polite Accomplishments (al-Ibshīhī) 1–380b
Newcastle
charter 2–330b
Durham treaties 4–316a
Newcastle upon Tyne
commune 3–498a
New Catalonia
Crown of Aragon 1–408b
NEW CHRISTIANS 9–0
converso 3–578a
New Church of Constantinople
See Nea
Newfoundland
exploration 4–560a
Icelanders 4–555a
New Monastery at Cîteaux 3–403b
New Monastery on Chios
See Nea Moni (New Monastery) on Chios
New Order
See Aviz, Order of
New Phocaea
Andronikos III Palaiologos 1–246b
New Rome
See Constantinopole
New Testament
angel/angelology 1–248a, 249a
Antichrist doctrine 1–321b
anti-Semitism 1–339b
apostolic succession 1–350b
baptism 2–84b
canticle 3–84b
Easter 4–365b-366a
Old English translations 1–285b
See Also Church, early
Newton, Isaac 1–609a
Newton in Cleveland
Anglo-Norman sculpture 1–256a
New World
agriculture 1–94b, 95a
Christianization 4–21a
Neyshābūr
Bukhārī, al- 2–398b
Nhutscelle abbey
See Nursling abbey
Niall of the Nine Hostages 3–407b
Nibelungen family 3–107b
***NIBELUNGENLIED* 9–0**; 1–229b; 2–7a, 253a
Atlamál and tradition of 1–639a
Bible 2–216b
Brynhild 2–394b, 395a
Buch von Bern, Das 2–396a
Burgundians 2–422b
Nicaea (Iznik)
Andronikos III Palaiologos 1–246b
Crusader-Byzantine siege 1–158a-b
crusades 2–308b; 4–30a, 35a
Seljukid sultanate 4–27b
NICAEA, COUNCILS OF 9–0
Nicaea, First Council of (325) 1–633a; 3–312a, 627b-628a; 4–365a
Arianism 1–650a
Byzantine clergy 3–446b
caesaropapism 3–10b
Christian dogma 3–336a
church organization 3–372b
Constantine I 2–484b; 3–341a
episcopal synods 2–459b
Eusebius of Caesarea 4–523b
Nicaea, Second Council of 1–143a, 579a; 3–631a; 4–365a, 373b
Charlemagne 2–465a
Christology 3–320b, 321b
iconoclasm 2–488b; 3–110a, 346b
NICAEA, EMPIRE OF 9–0
Arsenius Avtorianus 1–560a
Bulgaria 2–409b-410a
Byzantines 2–498a,b-499a
Turks 2–493b, 495a
NICCOLA DA VERONA 9–0; 1–579a
Niccolò, Lorenzo di
See Lorenzo di Niccolò di Martino
Niccolo Crescentius
marble 1–334b
NICCOLÒ DA BOLOGNA 9–0
Niccolo da Martoni
travel accounts 1–333a
Niccolò da Montefalcone
Boccaccio 2–289a
Niccolò da Perugia 2–61a
Niccolò da Prato 4–99b
Niccolò da Verona
See Niccola da Verona
Niccolò di Bartolo Del Buono
Boccaccio 2–287b
NICCOLÒ DI BUONACCORSO 9–0
Niccolò di Giacomo
See Niccolò da Bologna
NICCOLÒ DI PIETRO GERINI 9–0
Niccolò Niccoli
art trade 1–561a
Niccolo Polo 4–557a
Nice
agriculture 1–85a
Nicene-Constantinopolitan Creed
See Nicene Creed
Nicene Creed 1–453b, 454a; 3–627b-628b, 632a, 675b-677a
Apollinarius 1–348a
Athanasius of Alexandria 1–632b, 633a
conciliar theory 3–510b
Latin version 4–74a
Nicephorus I
See Nikephoros I
Nicephorus Phokas
See Nikephoros II Phokas
Nicetas Chionates
See Niketas Choniates
NICHE 9–0
Nicholas V, Antipope 1–330a
NICHOLAS I, POPE 9–0; 2–58a; 3–346b
Anastasius 1–239a
anti-Semitism 3–620b
Bulgaria 2–402b, 403a
Byzantine arts 2–453b
Byzantine church 2–465a
council development 3–633b
Cyril and Methodios, Saints 4–73b
Nicholas II, Pope 1–330b
Alexander II as papal legate under 1–146a
coronation 3–604a
Desiderius of Monte Cassino 4–164b
elections, church 4–421a
electoral decree 3–93b
Lateran synod (1059) 3–634b
papal conclave 3–523b
papal reform 3–351a,b
Nicholas III, Pope
breviary 2–372b
curial staff 3–363b
Dante's *Comedy* 4–98b
Franciscans 3–645a; 4–376b, 377a
Nicholas IV, Pope 1–453a
Bacon, Roger 2–35a-b
Boniface VIII 2–323a
cardinals' income 3–94a
crusades 4–54b-55a
Nicholas V, Pope 1–439a
Alberti 1–126a
concordats 3–526a
election 3–654a
Great Schism 3–366b
slaves 2–268b
University of Bologna 2–312b
Nicholas Dybinus of Dresden
dictamen 4–176a
Nicholas Maliasenos
See Nikolaos Maliasenos
Nicholas Manjacoria
Bible text 2–213b
Nicholas Mystikos
See Nikolaos I Mystikos
NICHOLAS OF AUTRECOURT 9–0; 1–464b
Nicholas of Clairvaux 3–246a
NICHOLAS OF CLAMANGES 9–0; 4–424a
Collège de Navarre 1–108a
NICHOLAS OF CUSA 9–0; 1–437b
Albertus Magnus 1–129b
alphabets 1–218a
astronomy 1–615b
bleeding hosts 3–371a
conciliar movement 3–365b, 511a,b, 515b, 520a
Council of Basel 3–23b
Devotio Moderna 4–167a
Donation of Constantine 4–257b
ecclesiology 4–378a

NICHOLAS OF CUSA (cont.)
Western councils 3–652b, 653a
NICHOLAS OF ELY 9–0
Nicholas of Leiden
See Gerhaerts, Nicholas
NICHOLAS OF LYRA 9–0
biblical exegesis 2–214a, 224b
Christian Hebraists 3–314a
commentaries 3–167a
exegesis 4–545b, 546a, 548a
Latin exegesis 4–544a
Rashi 4–540b
Nicholas of Myra, Saint
barrel symbol 2–114a
NICHOLAS OF VERDUN 9–0
Klosterneuburg altar 4–439a
Nicholas Trevet
See Trevet, Nicholas
Nichomachean Ethics (Aristotle) 4–501a
Albert the Great 1–353b, 357a
Nicodemus, Apocryphal Gospel of
Anastasis 1–239a
NICOLAITANS 9–0
NICOLA PISANO 9–0
Nicolas de Bray
Gesta Ludovici VIII 2–236b
Nicolaus Hermanni, Blessed 2–247a
NICOLE BOZON 9–0
Nicoloso da Recco
Canary Islands 4–558b
Nicomachus
Boethius 2–291b
Nicomedia (İZMIT)
Anatolia 1–239b, 240
Andronikos III Palaiologos 1–246b
Peasants' Crusade 4–34a
surrender to Ottomans 2–500b
NICOPOLIS 9–0
Bāyazīd I 2–136b
Bulgaria 2–413a
crusades of later Middle Ages 4–56a
Enguerrand VII of Coucy 4–490b, 491a
Nicostratus
fables 4–572a
NIELLO 9–0
Niels, King 4–152b
Niğde
monuments 1–241b
NIGEL OF LONGCHAMP (WIREKER) **9–0**
Nigg stone 3–222b, 223b
"Nightingale"
See Rossignos
Night Office
Cistercian rite 3–406a
See Also Matins
Nigri, Peter
See Schwartz, Peter
Nika Revolt (532) 2–486a
demes 4–135a
Nike (Victory)
angel 1–248a
Nikephoritzes
Byzantine throne 2–492a
NIKEPHOROS I 9–0
allelengyon 1–189b
Bulgaria 2–401a
reign 2–488b
NIKEPHOROS, PATRIARCH 9–0; 2–461b-462a, 513b
icons 2–463a
Incarnation doctrine 3–631a
Nikephoros Basilakios
rebellion 2–492a
Nikephoros Blemmydes 2–518a
Nikephoros III Botaneiates 1–303a
Byzantine throne 2–491b, 492a,b
Doukas 4–263a
rebellion 2–492a
NIKEPHOROS BRYENNIOS 9–0; 1–158b
Byzantine throne 2–495b
Material for History 2–514b
rebellion 2–492a
Nikephoros Chrysoberges 2–507b
NIKEPHOROS GREGORAS 9–0
Nikephoros Kallistos Xanthopoulos 2–517a
Nikephoros Melissenos
rebellion 2–492a
Nikephoros Ouranos 2–119a
Taktika 4–447a
Nikephoros Phokas 2–118a
NIKEPHOROS II PHOKAS 9–0; 2–118b; 4–447a, 494a
Aleppo 1–145a
Bulgaria 2–406a
Cyprus 4–70b
dux 4–323a
monasticism 2–478b
Mount Athos monastery 1–636b
murder 2–106b
reign 2–490a-b
Nikephoros the Hesychast 1–637b
Nikephoros Uranos
See Nikephoros Ouranos
Niketas
Cathar movement 2–297a; 3–183b-184a, 185a-b
Niketas, Bible of 2–454b
NIKETAS CHONIATES 9–0
Constantinople 1–334b
history 2–515a-b
Niketas Eugenianos 2–508a, 522a
Niketas of Constantinople
Bogomils 2–296a
Niketas Stethatos
eucharistic foods 2–31b
NIKITIN, AFANASII 9–0
Nikiu
ʿAmr ibn al-ʿĀṣ 1–237a
Nikolaos Kallikles 2–507a
NIKOLAOS KAVASILAS 9–0
Nikolaos Maliasenos
holdings 2–479a
NIKOLAOS MESARITES 9–0
NIKOLAOS I MYSTIKOS 9–0
Bulgaria 2–404b-405a
Byzantine theology 2–467b
missionaries 2–464a
Nikolaos of Methone 2–519a
Nikon Metanoietes, Saint 2–454b
NIKORCMINDA 9–0
Niksar
See Neocaesarea
Nikšić 2–339a
Nilant, Freédéric
fables 4–573a
NILE 9–0
ʿAmr ibn al-ʿĀṣ 1–237b
Axum 2–17a
NIL SORSKY, SAINT 9–0
NIMBUS 9–0
early Christian art 4–354b
NIMBUS, CRUCIFORM 9–0
Nîmes
fairs 4–586a
Nimrod 1–262a
Nin 4–2a, 4a
Nine Books on the Romans' Famous Deeds and Sayings (Valerius Maximus) 3–166b
Nine Herbs Charm 1–281a
Nineveh
traveler accounts 1–332a
Ninfale fiesolano (Boccaccio) 2–282b-283a
NINIAN, SAINT 9–0
Celtic church 3–225b, 229a
Ninnid of Inishmacsaint 3–465b
NINO, SAINT 9–0
Nino of the Georgians, Saint
See Nunē, Saint
Ninoslav
Hungary 2–336a
trade 2–340a
Niphon
Bogomilism 2–296a
Niš 2–407b, 408b
Hungarians 2–493a
Niṣāb
alms tax 1–201b
Nisābūrī, al-
"Clever Madmen" 1–380b
NISART, PEDRO 9–0
NISHAPUR 9–0
art 1–5b
Nishwār al-muḥāḍara 1–380b
NISIBIS 9–0
Nisibis, School of
See Syrian Christianity
NISI PRIUS 9–0
assize 1–595a
NITHARD 9–0; 3–202b
Niđarós 4–411b
Nitra (Nyitra)
Peasants' Crusade 4–34a
NIVARDUS OF FLEURY 9–0
Nivardus of Ghent 4–496a
beast epic 2–141a
Latin epic 4–496a
Nivernais 2–427a
NIẒĀM AL-MULK 9–0; 1–203a, 220a
Ashʿarī, al- 1–585a
Nizār
assassins 1–590a
Nizārī branch of Ismailis 1–118b, 590a
Nizhni Novgorod
fairs 4–587b
***NJÁLS SAGA* 9–0**; 4–613b, 614a, 615a, 617a,b
Darrađarljóđ 4–105b
NJǪRĐR 9–0
Æsir 1–63a
Noah's Ark 1–422a
Nobadia
Nubian Christianity 3–314b
NOBILITY AND NOBLES 9–0
Armenia 1–488b
baron 2–111b
Bosnian church 2–342b
Bulgaria 2–402b, 408a
castellan 3–124b
county 3–658a
courtesy books 3–664a
courtly love 3–668b-669a
training schools 3–660b
See Also Class structure, Western
Nocera, Battle of (1132) 3–203b
Noctes Atticae (Aulus Gellius) 1–52a
Nocturns 3–67a
See Also Matins
NOEANNOE 9–0
Noëfort convent 1–18a
Nogajs
Bulgaria 2–410b, 411a
NOGARET, GUILLAUME DE 9–0; 3–644a
Ausculta fili 2–4a
Boniface VIII 2–324a
NOLI ME TANGERE 9–0
Nomenoë
Brittany 2–378b, 379a

NOMEN SACRUM **9–0**
Bible 4–355b
Nominale sive verbale in Gallicis cum expositione eiusdem in Anglicis 1–270b
NOMINALISM 9–0
Biel, Gabriel 2–234a
Brethren of the Common Life 2–369a
Burley, Walter 2–433a
conceptualism 3–510a
Latin church: 1305 to 1500 3–361b
Nominibus utensilium, De (Nequam) 1–52a
NOMISMA 9–0; 4–301a
NOMOCANON 9–0
Nomos Rodion nautikos 3–569b
Nona 4–4a
None 3–20b; 4–221b, 227, 229a
Nonnos of Panopolis
Dionysiaca 2–506a, 524a
Nonnosos 2–512b
NORAVANK' AT AMAŁU 9–0
NORBERT OF IBERG 9–0
Norbert of Xanten
Premonstratensians 3–354b
Nordic Union 4–156a
Nördlingen
fairs 4–586a
Nordmark
Brandenburg 2–360b
Noria 1–104a
Noricum 2–4b
Roman rule 2–133a-b
Norman Anonymous
celibacy of clergy 3–217a; 4–374b-375a
Norman Conquest 4–394b, 459a
Bangor (Wales) reorganization 2–71b
NORMANS AND NORMANDY 9–0
agriculture 1–105a
Almohads 1–194a
Angevins 1–253a
bailli 2–53a-b
Bari of 2–108b
Bayeux Tapestry 2–139a
Bordeaux 2–327b
Brittany, duchy 2–379b
Brut, The 3–393b-394a
Burgundy, duchy of 2–427a
butler 2–434b
Byzantine Empire 1–157b-158a; 2–494a-b, 496b-497a
Caen 3–8b
castellans 3–124b-125a
cavalry 3–203b
chronicles 4–304a
church, Latin 3–351a-b, 353a, 356a
custumals 4–68b
duchies 4–304a
fairs 4–585b, 586a
First Crusade 4–34a
hearth lists 4–138a
Ireland 1–347b
Norman-Angevin England 4–459b
North Africa 4–27b
political crusades 4–58a
power of earls 3–659a
Sicily 4–33b, 346b
NORNA-GESTS ÞÁTTR 9–0; 4–391b
NORNS 9–0
Darraðarljóð 4–106b
NORSE FLYTING 9–0
Norse-Icelandic romances
Alexanders Saga 1–152a
chansons de geste 3–258a
darraðarljóð 4–106a
See Also Riddarasöogur
NORSE KINGS' SAGAS 9–0
Áns Saga Bogsveigis 1–310b
arms and armor 1–523a
Norsemen
Latin church: 1054-1305 3–355b
northern Europe raids 1–94a
See Also Vikings
Nor Širakan
See Adiabene
North Africa
Alani settlement 1–121a
Atlas Mountains 1–639b
casbahs 3–121a
Children's Crusade 4–14a
Islamic cavalry 3–209a,b
Northallerton, Battle of (1138) 3–203b
Northampton
commune 3–499a
fairs 4–586b
Northampton, Statute of (1332) 3–543a
North Britain, Synod of
penitential documents 3–229b
North Caucasia 3–193b, 195a-b
Northern Ireland
archives 1–448b
North Rhine-Westphalia
Aachen 1–1a
North Semitic alphabet 1–208a, 209b
Northumbria 2–96b; 4–454b-455a
Aidan of Lindisfarne 1–107a
Celtic art 3–218b, 219b, 220a, 221a, 223b
church 2–153b
cultural revival 4–458b
Danish invasion 4–456a
monastic scriptoria 1–331b
treaties of Durham 4–316a-b
Northumbrian dialect 1–276a
Norton, Thomas 1–139a
NORWAY 9–0
Anglo-Saxon settlements 1–289b
bracteates 2–356a-b
Cistercian order 3–404a
explorations 4–554a-555a
stave churches 3–382
Norwegian runic alphabet 1–215b
Norwich
art trade 1–562a
Norwich Cathedral
architecture 1–255b
Benedictines 3–265b
clock automata 3–459b
horologia 3–460b
planetary clockwork 3–464b
Notabilia
decretists 4–127b
Notarial contract 2–78a
Notaries 1–446a
Notary public
cartularies 3–120a
Notation, musical
Anonymous IV 1–309b
Notes on the World (Alexander of Roes) 1–148b, 149a
NOTGER OF LIÈGE 9–0
Nothelm of London 1–645a
Noticari (Toralles) 3–166a-b
Notices et extraits des manuscrits (Paul Meyer) 1–271b
Noticia seculi (Alexander of Roes) 1–148b, 149a
NOTITIA DIGNITATUM **9–0**; 3–201a
Notitia ecclesiarum urbis Romae 1–333a
NOTKE, BERNT 9–0; 4–93a
NOTKER BALBULUS 9–0
Notker Labeo
See Notker Teutonicus
Notker of Saint Gall
See Notker Teutonicus
NOTKER TEUTONICUS 9–0; 2–174a
Bible translation 2–215a
Fachschrifttum 4–578b
Notre Dame at Tartūs
crusader art and architecture 4–25b
NOTRE DAME DE PARIS, CATHEDRAL OF 9–0; 1–431a
architecture 1–255b; 3–565a
ars antiqua 1–543a, 546a
excavation 1–336b
NOTRE DAME SCHOOL 9–0
Anonymous IV 1–309a
ars antiqua 1–543a,b, 545a
conductus 3–532a
copula 3–596a
discantor 4–216b
duplum 4–312b
Notstal 3–180a
Nótt 1–116b
Nottingham
Borough-English 2–332a
Nottinghamshire
Black Death 2–262b
Notula
See Chansonnier
Notule auree (Boncompagno) 2–320a
NOUVELLE 9–0
Novara 1–147b
Novare, Philippe de
See Philippe de Novare
Nova Scotia
Leif Ericsson 4–555a
Novatian, Antipope 1–330a
Novatian schism 4–70a
Novel disseisin
See Assize
See Petty Assizes, English
Novella 6 (Justinian) 3–446a
Novella 120 (Justinian)
Byzantine clergy 3–447a
Novellae
See Corpus iuris civilis
Novelle (Matteo Bandello) 3–277b
Novello da Polenta, Guido 4–104a
Noves rimades
Catalan narrative 3–173a
NOVGOROD 9–0; 1–101a
Bogoliubskii 2–203b, 293b
boyar 2–354b
Byzantine church 2–464a
cathedrals 4–341a
fairs 4–587b, 588a
See Also Holmgard
Novgorodok
Byzantine church 2–469b
Novi (Hercegnovi) 2–339a
Novissimis et Antichristo, De (Damian) 1–111b
Novo ordem
See Aviz, Order of
Nowell, Laurence 1–286b
Nowell Codex 1–277a
Noyon
commune 3–496a
Noyon Cathedral
alternating supports 1–226a
Np'kert
See Martyropolis
N-TOWN PLAYS 9–0
Nubia
Christianity 3–314a
slaves 2–268a
Nude statuary
medieval collections 1–335a
Nuestra Señora del Monte Carmelo Church (Barcelona) 1–20a
Nuestra Señora del Pino Church (Barcelona) 1–20a

Nūḥ ibn Naṣr
Alptigin 1–220a
Nujūm
See Astrology/astronomy, Islamic
Numbers, numerals
See Arabic numerals
Num Christus corporeis oculis Deum videre pocuerit 3–64a
Numerology
Arabic numerals 1–384b
Numidia Cirtensis 1–646a
Numidjkath
Bukhara 2–397a
Numismatics
See Mints and money
Numudar
Arabic numerals 1–386a
Nunc Dimittis 3–84b
NUNCIO, PAPAL 9–0
Nuncius
diplomacy 4–201b-203a, 204a, 205a-b
Nunē, Saint 1–519a
Núñes, Airas 3–87a
Núñez, Count Nuño
Brañosera charter 3–127b
Nunnaminster, Book of
Celtic spirituality 3–231a
Nunnius
See Munnius
Nuno Alvares Pereira
Arthurian literature 1–576b
NUNS 9–0
Dominicans 4–254a-b
Nuptiis Philologiae et Mercurii, De (Martianus Capella) 1–188a-b, 610b, 642b; 3–432a; 4–168b, 447b
Nūr al-Dīn 1–145b; 2–23a
Damascus 4–83b, 84a,b-85a
Danishmendids 4–93a
Edessa capture 4–384a
First Crusade 4–30b-31a
Latin states 4–38b-39a
mausoleums 2–21b
Saladin 4–39a
Unur, Mu'īn al-Dīn 4–38a
Nūr al-Dīn Arslān Shāh 1–635a
Nūr al-Dīn Maḥmūd
Damascus 4–82a-b
Nureddin 3–679b
NUREMBERG 9–0
arms and armor 1–529a
Black Death 2–262b
city walls 3–151b
Nuremberg chronicle (Hartmann Schedel) 3–329a
Nuremberg hours 3–24b
Nuremberg Passion, Master of the 4–488b, 489b
Nur Mountains
See Amanus Mountains
Nursling abbey 2–321a
Nutrition
See Agriculture and nutrition
Nuwayrī, al-
contraception 3–574b
Nuzhat al-albāb (al-Tīfāshī) 1–380b
Nyköping Castle 4–505b
NYMPHAEUM 9–0
NYMPHAION 9–0; 4–334b
Nymphs of Fiesole (Boccaccio) 2–282b-283a

O

Oasis populations 1–371a
OATH 9–0
barber guilds 2–99b
basileus 2–123a
champion in judicial combat 3–257a
OATH MORE JUDAICO 9–0
Oats
See Grain Crops
OBECO 9–0
Obiurgatio (Augustine) 1–658a
Obra de agricultura (Herrera) 1–81b
O'Brien, Donal, King 2–421b
Ó BROLCHAN, MAEL ISU 9–0
Obsequium
See Opsikion
Observatories 1–622a-b
Oca
Castilian settlement 3–128a
Occitan
See Provençal language
Occitania
Aragon, Crown of 1–408a,b, 410a,b, 412b
Cathars 3–181b, 186a
mercenary troops 3–186b, 187a
See Also Languedoc
Occitan ritual 3–184a
Oceanus
Crucifixion 4–13b
OCHRID 9–0; 2–329b, 403b
Bulgaria 2–406b, 407a, 409a
Byzantine church 2–464a
Ociosa, Petrus Frater Dictus Palma 3–657b
OCKHAM, WILLIAM OF 9–0
Albert of Saxony 1–125b
Aristotelianism 1–464a-b, 465a, 467a-b
Bradwardine, Thomas 2–358b
Buridan, Jean 2–430a
Burley, Walter 2–433a
conceptualism 3–510a
conciliar theory 3–512a, 515a, 516a
dialectic 4–170b
ecclesiology 4–376b-377a,b
John XXII, Pope 3–363b
Munich 2–135a
nominalist theology 3–371a
O'Connor, Tairdelbach
Connacht 3–538a
OCTATEUCH 9–0
Octavian
See Augustus
Octavius (Minucius Felix) 3–334b
OCTOECHOS 9–0
Octo vitiis principalibus, De (Saint Columbanus) 3–486b
Ó DALAIGH, DONNCHADH MOR 9–0
Ó DALAIGH, GOFRAIDH FIONN 9–0
Ó DALAIGH, MUIREDACH ALBANACH 9–0
O'Daly, Donogh Mór
See Donnchadh Mó ó Dálaigh
ODA OF CANTERBURY 9–0
Oddaverja þáttr 2–252b
ODDR SNORRASON 9–0
ODDRÚNARGRÁTR 9–0; 4–386b
Odeljan, Peter 2–407b
Oderic de Pordenone
See Odoric of Pordenone
Odericus
See Oderisi, Pietro
Oderigi da Gubbio 1–579a
ODERISI, PIETRO 9–0
ODILO OF CLUNY, SAINT 9–0; 3–469a
All Souls' Day 1–177a
monastic reform 3–348a
ODIN 9–0; 1–62b
Alvíssmál 1–227a
Baldr 2–55a
Baldrs Draumar 2–56a
divine function 1–63a
Fáfnir 4–581a
ODINGTON, WALTER 9–0; 1–138a
Odo, King
Arnulf 1–541b
Carolingians 3–115a
ODOACER 9–0
Burgundians 2–422b
Ostrogoth invasions 2–93a-b
Odo Colonna
See Martin V, Pope
Odo de Saint Amand
Knights Templar 3–304b
ODOFREDUS 9–0
Odo of Bayeux
Bayeux Tapestry 2–139a
Odo II of Blois-Chartres-Tours
Burgundy, Kingdom of 2–429a
Champagne 3–244a
Odo of Burgundy
Cistercians 3–403b
Crusade of 1101 4–36a
Odo of Châteaudun
Robert IV 3–89b
ODO OF CLUNY, SAINT 9–0; 3–469a
Odo of Corbie 2–173b
Odo of Deuil
Second Crusade 3–356b
ODO OF METZ 9–0
ODO OF MEUN (MEUNG) **9–0**
Odo of Sully 2–13b
Odoric of Pordenone
Assassins 1–591b
travel account 1–332b
Odo Rigaldus
See Eudes Rigaud
Odyssey 4–401b
Oeconomica (Conrad of Megenberg) 3–539a
Oecumenical patriarch
See Ecumenical patriarch
Óengus mac Fergusa, King 4–78b
Óengus mac Nad Froích
Eóganacht 4–492b
Ofen
See Buda
Offa of Mercia, King 2–184b; 4–455a
witenagemot (764) 3–82a
Offa's Dyke 4–452b, 455a
OFFERTORY 9–0; 1–442a-b
antiphon 1–328b
Offertory rite
basilica plan 4–335b
Office chants
Cistercian chant 3–402a
Officium Gazarie (Khazariae)
Caffa 3–12a
Of the training of women (Tertullian) 1–322b, 323a
Ögedey, Great Khan 2–131b
Ogee arch 1–423b, 424
building materials 3–563b

OGHAM **9–0**; 1–207a, 215a-216a, 217b; 2–2a
Celtic languages 3–233a
Oghuz Turkic tribes
Alp Arslan 1–203a
Ogier de Saint Donat 4–110a
Ogive arch
See Ogee arch
Ó HEOGHUSA, EOCHAIDH **9–0**
Ohrmizd IV, King 3–308a
Ó Huiginn, Philip Bocht 1–111b
Ó HUIGINN, TADHG DALL **9–0**
Ó HUIGINN, TADHG ÓG **9–0**
Oil of exorcism 2–177a-b
Oil of thanksgiving 2–177a
OIL PAINTING **9–0**
Oils, holy 2–177a-b
Oisín 1–33b, 34a
OJUN **9–0**
Okaz
fairs 4–588b
Okol'Nichie
See Duma
Olaf, King 4–155b-156a
Olaf Haraldsson, King
saga 2–255a
Óláfr, Saint 4–411b
Óláfsdrápa
See Geisli
ÓLÁFS SAGA HELGA **9–0**; 2–254a, 255b
ÓLÁFS SAGA TRYGGVASONAR **9–0**
Bjarni Kolbeinsson 2–256a
Olaf Tryggvason, King 4–554b-555a
Olbia
camel use 1–296b
water buffalo 1–298a
Old Abyssinian alphabet
See Ethiopic alphabet
Old Brethren
See Bohemian Brethren
Old Breton dialect
Celtic languages 3–234a
Old Bulgarian 1–216a
Old Cairo
See Fusṭāṭ, Al-
Old Catalonia 1–417a,b
Crown of Aragon 1–408b, 410b-411a
Old Church Slavic 1–216a
Old English
Anglo-Saxon art 1–273b
Ethelwold and the Benedictine Rule 4–518a-b
Old English dialects
Anglo-Saxon literature 1–274b
Old English literature
See Anglo-Saxon literature
Old English poetry
dialect mixture 1–276b
Old English scholarship 1–286b-287b
Old French
chanson de geste 3–257a
See Also French language
Old French Bible 4–25b
Old French dialects
Anglo-Norman 1–259a
Old French texts
Anglo-Norman scholarship 1–271a
OLD HALL MS **9–0**
Old Irish period
See Celtic languages
Old Norse 4–389a
eddic meters 4–388b-389a
eddic poetry 4–385a
Erex Saga 4–504b
Old Provençal
chanson de geste 3–258a
OLD ROMAN CHANT **9–0**
Old Roman Creed 3–676a
Old Sacristy of San Lorenzo (Florence) 2–388a
OLD SAINT PETER'S, ROME
architecture 4–338a
art 4–352a, 354a, 358b, 361a
basilica 2–124a
campanile 3–60a
crypt 1–442b
See Also Coronation, papal
OLD SARUM **9–0**
Anglo-Norman features 1–255b
Old Testament
allegory 1–180b, 181b-182a
angel/angelology 1–247b, 249a
baptism 2–84b
Book of Proverbs (florilegia) 1–317a
canticle 3–84b
centonization 3–235b
dedication of churches 4–131a
Junius manuscript 1–279b
Old English paraphrase 1–273b
Old English translations 1–285a,b
Old Testament Trinity
See Trinity, Old Testament
Old Welsh period
See Celtic languages
OLEG **9–0**
OLGA/HELEN **9–0**
Byzantine church 2–464a
Constantine VII Porphyrogenitos 3–547a
Olgierd
See Algirdas
OLIBA **9–0**; 3–175b
OLIPHANT **9–0**
Oliva (Boncompagno) 2–320a
Oliver, Bernat 3–168a
Oliver of Paderborn
Fifth Crusade 4–49b
Olivi, Peter John
See Peter John Olivi
Olivier de Clisson
Brittany, Duchy 2–380b
Oliviero Forza (Forzetta)
manuscript collections 1–336a
Olleguer of Barcelona, Bishop 3–178a
Oller, Berenguer 2–104a
Olmen, Ferdinand van
See Dulmo, Fernão
Olomouc
bishopric 2–304a
Olybrius
Burgundians 2–422b
Olympias
Aršak II 1–560a
Olympiodorus
alchemy 1–136a
Oman
ʿAmr ibn al-ʿĀṣ 1–236b
Kharijites 1–374b
Omar I
See ʿUmar I ibn al-Khaṭṭāb
Omar II
See ʿUmar II ibn ʿAbd al-Azīz
Omar Khayyam
See ʿUmar Khayyām
Omiš 2–338b
Omnem
corpus iuris civilis 3–609a
Omnis utriusque sexus fidelis 1–263a
OMOFOR **9–0**; 3–616a
Omophorion
See Omofor
Omurtag 2–401a,b-402a
art and architecture 2–414b
Onager 2–243a; 3–180a
On Being and Essence (Aquinas) 1–358a
On Christian Doctrine (Augustine) 3–342b; 4–447b
One Hundred Twelve (Jābir ibn Ḥayyān) 1–136a
O'Neill kings 3–407a
See Also Uí Néill
On Elegance and Elegant People (al-Washshāʾ) 3–618a
On emptiness (Meister Eckhart) 4–381b
On Grace and Free Choice (Bernard of Clairvaux) 2–191a
Onguyon, Jacques de 1–151a
On Heaven and Earth (Aristotle)
Aquinas 1–356a, 357a
On Interpretation (Aristotle)
Aquinas 1–356a, 357a
Onion dome 4–235b, 236a
Onkelos
See Aquila (Onkelos)
On Loving God (Bernard of Clairvaux) 2–191a
On Lying (Augustine) 1–649a
On Mountains, Forests, Springs, Lakes, Rivers, Marshes, or Swamps . . . (Boccaccio) 2–286b
On noble men (Meister Eckhart) 4–381a
On Precept and Dispensation (Bernard of Clairvaux) 2–191a
On Singing Girls (al-Jāḥiẓ) 1–379b
On Spiritual Friendship (Ethelred of Rievaulx) 3–405a
On the Administration of the Empire (Constantine VII) 3–547b
On the Book of Causes (Thomas Aquinas) 1–356b
On the Ceremonies (Constantine VII) 3–547b
On the Coming of Antichrist (Arnald of Villanova) 1–537b
On the Divine Names (Pseudo-Dionysius)
Aquinas 1–357b, 358a
On the Doings of Pelagius (Augustine) 1–652b, 653b
On the Erection of the Walls of New Ross 1–265b
On the Eternity of the World (Aquinas) 1–356b, 357a
On the Faith and the Creed (Augustine) 1–649a
On the Fifteen Signs Preceding Judgment Day 1–111b
On the Gospel of John (Augustine) 1–657a
On the Identical and the Diverse (Adelard of Bath) 1–53b-54a
On the Incarnation of the Word (Athanasius) 1–633a
On the Multiplication of Species (Bacon) 2–38a, 39a
On the Multiplication of Species
See *De multiplicatione specierum*
On the Perfection of Human Justice (Augustine) 1–652b
On the Power of God (Aquinas) 1–363b
On the Principles of Nature
Aquinas 1–358b
On the seven ways of holy love (Beatrijs van Nazareth) 4–319a
On the Soul (Ethelred of Rievaulx) 3–405a
On the Soul (Aristotle)
Aquinas 1–357a
On the sparkling stone (Jan van Ruusbroec) 4–320b
On the Spirit and the Letter (Augustine) 1–653a
On the Themes (Constantine VII) 3–547b

On the Trinity (Eugenius II of Toledo) 4–520b
On the Trinity (Boethius)
Aquinas 1–355a, 357b
On the Unicity of Intellect Against the Averroists (Thomas Aquinas) 1–356b, 357a
On the Virgin Conception and on Original Sin (Anselm of Canterbury) 1–313a, 314b
On Truth (Anselm of Canterbury) 1–312a, 314b
ONULF OF SPEYER 9–0
Open-field agriculture 1–80b, 91b
Opitz, Martin 1–306a
Oporto 1–627a
Opsikion 1–241a
OPSIKION, THEME OF 9–0
Optatianus Porfyrius, Publilius 1–45b-46a
Optatus of Meleve
Christmas celebration 3–318a
OPTICS, ARABIC 9–0
OPTICS, WESTERN EUROPEAN 9–0
Bacon, Roger 2–38b-39b
OPUS ALEXANDRINUM 9–0
OPUS ANGLICANUM 9–0
art trade 1–561a
Opuscula sacra (Boethius) 2–292a
Opusculum de passione Domini 3–64a
OPUS FRANCIGENUM 9–0
Opus lemovicense 4–438b
Opus maius (Bacon) 2–36a, 37a,b-40b, 41a
Opus minus (Bacon) 2–40b
OPUS MIXTUM 9–0
OPUS RETICULATUM 9–0
Opus sancti Eligii 4–437b
OPUS SECTILE 9–0
Opus tertium (Bacon) 1–137a-b; 2–39a, 40b
Opus tripartitum (Eckhart) 4–381b
Oració (Roís de Corella) 3–171b
Or Adonai (Crescas) 3–677b
"Oralist" theory 3–78b-79b
Oral story-telling
Anglo-Saxon 1–274b
Orange, First Council of (441)
confirmation 3–535b
Orange, House of
archives 1–448a
Orange, Second Council of (529) 3–122b
ORANT 9–0
ORAR 9–0
Orarion
See Orar
Orator
diplomacy 4–205a,b
Oratores
social divisions 3–358a
Oratorio of San Giorgio
frescoes 1–226b
ORATORY 9–0
chasovnya 3–277a
Orbais, Jean d'
See Jean d'Orbais
ORBAN II, POPE 12–0
ORBĚLEAN, STEPʻANNOS 9–0
Armenian history 1–486a
Cilician-Roman church union 3–394b
Orbeli family
Amirspasalar 1–235b
ORCAGNA (**ANDREA DI CIONE**) **9–0**
ORCHARD, WILLIAM 9–0
ORDEALS 9–0
Ordelaffi, Scarpetta degli 4–99a
Ordelaffi of Forlì 1–131a
Ordenacions (Peter III) 4–416b
Ordenamiento de Alcalá (Alfonso XI of Castile) 3–135a, 611b
Ordene de chevalerie 1–189a; 3–666a
Order (Augustine) 1–648a
ORDERICUS VITALIS 9–0; 2–3a, 174a
"Order of a Monastery" (Augustine) 1–658a
"Order of a Monastery Given to Women" (Augustine) 1–658a
Order of Friars Preachers
See Dominicans
Order of Preachers
See Dominicans
Order of the Temple
chamberlain office 3–242a
Order of the Teutonic Knights
See Teutonic Knights
Ordinacions de la reial casa d'Aragó sobre lo regiment de tots los oficials de la sua cort 3–169a
ORDINALE 9–0
Ordinal of Alchemy (Norton) 1–139a
Ordinals
baptismal rites 2–83a
Sibert of Beka 3–96a
Ordinamenta et consuetudo maris edita per consules civitatis Tranis 3–570a
ORDINANCE (FRENCH AND ENGLISH) **9–0**
Ordinances
chancery practices 3–252b, 253a
Ordinances of 1311 4–397b
ORDINARIUS LIBER 9–0
Ordinary of a diocese
recognition of saints 3–68a,b
Ordinary of the Mass
Agnus Dei music 1–74a
Ethiopian 1–155b
ORDINATION 9–0
Byzantine clergy 3–446a
celibacy 3–216a
Celtic church 2–381b-382a
clergy 3–441b, 442a,b
Ordines 4–225a, 230b
Celtic liturgy 3–230b
customary 4–68a
ORDINES ROMANI 9–0
liturgical colors 3–484a
Ordini del cavalcare (Grisone) 3–206b
Ordo (Angilbert of Saint Riquier) 4–117a-b
Ordo baptismi 2–83a-b
Celtic church 3–229a, 230b
Ordo breviarii secundum consuetudinem Aquilegensis et Tergestinae ecclesiae per anni circulum
rite of Aquileia 1–353a
Ordo monasterii (Augustine) 1–658a
Divine Office 4–222a
Ordo monasterii feminis data (Augustine) 1–658a
Ordóñez, García
Cid 3–74b, 75a, 76a
Ordoño I 1–626b-627a
Ordoño II 1–627a,b
Ordoño III 1–627b
Ordoño IV the Bad 1–627b
Ordo prophetarum 1–270a
Ordo representacionis Adae
See Jeu d'Adam
Ordo romanus I
cantatorium 3–80b
Ordo romanus VII 3–676a
Ordo stellae 2–9b
Ordo virtutum 4–286b
Ordre de bel ayse 1–269b
Ordulf of Saxony 2–235a
See Billungs
ORENDEL 9–0
Oren-Kala 2–139a
ORESME, NICOLE 9–0
Albert of Saxony 1–125b
Arabic numerals 1–396b
astrology 1–608a-b
Bradwardine, Thomas 2–358a
Buridan, Jean 1–464b
Burley, Walter 2–433a
universe concept 1–615b
William of Moerbeke 1–438a
ORFEO, SIR 9–0
ORGAN 9–0
ars nova 1–553a
ORGANUM 9–0
Anonymous IV treatise 1–310a
ars antiqua 1–543a,b, 544b, 545b, 546a
clausula 3–437a,b
consonance/dissonance 3–541b
copula 3–596a
diaphonia 4–172a
ORIEL WINDOW 9–0
Oriental languages
Bible translations 2–211a
biblical exegesis 2–214b
ORIENTIUS 9–0
ORIGEN 9–0
angel/angelology 1–249b
Bible translations 2–211a
biblical exegesis 2–223b-224a
Byzantine theology 2–467a
Christian doctrine 3–342a
Christmas celebration 3–317b
church father 3–335b
Origenes (Isidore of Seville) 1–152b
Origenistic Hexapla 4–223b
Original Sin
Annuciation 1–308a
early church 3–340b
Origine actibusque Getarum, De (Jordanes) 3–123a
Origine potestatum et jurisdictionum, De (Durand of Saint Pourçain) 4–313b
"Origin of Sin" (Prudentius) 1–181a-b
Orkahn 2–500b
Anatolia 1–242a
ORKNEYINGA SAGA 9–0
Orkney Islands
Áedán's expedition 1–60a
exploration 4–554a
mythology 4–106b
Orlando furioso (Ariosto) 3–258a
Orléanais 1–121a
Orléans 3–150b
Cathars 3–183a
Orléans, Charles of
See Charles of Orléans
Orléron, laws of 1–56a-b
ORMULUM 9–0
exegesis, Middle English 4–546a
Ormuz
exploration 4–563a
Marco Polo 4–556b, 557a
Orne fragment of psalter 1–262b
ORNEMENT DES DAMES 9–0
Western European costume 3–623b-625a
O ROMA NOBILIS 9–0
Orontid dynasty 2–20a, 48a
Bagratids 2–48b
OROSIUS, PAULUS 9–0
Alfred the Great 1–164b, 165a-166b
mission for Augustine of Hippo 1–653a
ORPHANOTROPHOS 9–0
ORPHERY 9–0

Orse
See Erzincan
Orseille (*Rocella tinctoria*) 4–326b
Orsini, Cardinal Gaetano
Bonaventure, Saint 2–316b, 317a
Orsini, Matteo
papal conclave 3–523b
Orsini, Niccolò
Boccaccio 2–289b
Orsini, Nicholas 4–499b
Orthodox Baptistery, Ravenna 2–88a
Orthodox Eastern church
See Byzantine church
***ORTHOGRAPHIA GALLICA* 9–0**; 1–270b
Orthographia, De (Alcuin of York) 1–142b
Orthographia, De (Bede) 2–154b
Orthographia, De (Cassiodorus) 3–124a
Orthography
French instruction 1–270b
Old English manuscripts 1–275b-276b
ORTNIT 9–0
Ambraser Heldenbuch 1–230a
ORTOKID ART 9–0
Ortokids
See Artuqids
Ortolf of Bayerland 4–579b
Ortu . . . et fine romani imperii, De (Engelbert) 4–451b
***ÖRVAR-ODDS SAGA* 9–0**; 1–310b
Orvieto
Black Death 2–260a-b, 264a-b
Osberht, King
chronicles 1–264b
Osbern of Exeter 1–258a
Aelfric Bata 1–62b
Osbern of Gloucester
encyclopedia 4–449b
Osburh (mother of Alfred the Great) 1–163b
O'Scanlain, Patrick 1–470a
Oscheret 2–427a
Osculatorium 1–224b
OSEBERG 9–0
OSEBERG STYLE 9–0
Ó SINAICH, CELLACH 9–0
Armagh 1–470a
OŠKI 9–0; 1–519a
OSMAN I 9–0
Osmanlis
See Ottomans
Osona 3–175a
Osona, Rodrigo de
See Rodrigo de Osona
Ospedale degli Innocenti
Brunelleschi, Filippo 2–388b
Ostan 1–489a
Ostan Hayoc' 2–20a
Ostanik' 1–489a
Ostarrichi 2–6b
Ostasio da Polenta
Boccaccio 2–287b
Österreich
See Ostarrichi
Ostia
Augustine of Hippo in 1–648a-b
castrum 3–152b
OSTIKAN 9–0
Armenia 1–479a, 481a
Ostoja, King
Bosnian church 2–342b
reign 2–337b-338b
Ostojić, Stefan 2–338b
OSTROGOTHS 9–0; 1–422a
Arian Christians 3–339b
Austria 2–4b
Byzantines 2–95a, 486b
coalescence 2–90a
Crete 3–678a
Hunnish domination 2–90a,b
invasions 2–92b-94a
Justinian 3–343b
OSWALD, SAINT: EPICS 9–0
Oswald of Northumbia, King 1–107a,b
OSWALD OF RAMSEY 9–0
Oswald of Worcester, Bishop 4–457a
Aelfric 1–61b
reforms 4–518a
Oswald of York, Archbishop 1–12b-13a
OSWALD VON WOLKENSTEIN 9–0
Oswy of Northumbria, King 4–454b
Roman Christianity 3–344b
Osyth, Saint 1–261a
Otakar IV, Duke of Styria 2–6b
Otakars 2–7a
OTAQ 9–0
Otenē
See Utik'
OTFRID VON WEISSENBURG 9–0; 3–325a
biblical poetry 2–225b-226a
Other Armenia
Pentarchy 1–515b
Othman
See Osman I
OTLOH OF SAINT EMMERAM 9–0; 3–98b
Otranto Cathedral
Arthurian literature 1–567b
Ottar 4–555a
Ottaviani, Cardinal 4–60a
Otto (brother of Louis the Bavarian) 2–361a-b
OTTO I THE GREAT, EMPEROR 9–0
Aachen 1–1b
Billungs 2–235a
Brandenburg 2–360a
Burgundy, Kingdom of 2–429a
church reforms 3–347b
coronation 1–35b
elections, royal 4–426b
Magyars 2–6A
Prague 2–304a
Otto II, Emperor 2–33b
Alpert of Metz 1–203b
OTTO III, EMPEROR 9–0
Aachen 1–1b
Bernward 2–197b
Bruno of Querfurt, Saint 2–391b
Burchard of Worms 2–420a
church reforms 3–347b
election 4–426b
papal coronation 3–604a
Otto IV, Emperor
anointing of kings 1–308b
election 4–425a,b, 427b
John of England 4–468b-469a
Otto-Guillaume
Burgundy, county of 2–424b
Ottokar II of Bohemia, King
Austria 2–7b
Prussians 2–66b
Ottoman-Mamluk war (1485-1491) 2–137b
OTTOMANS 9–0
Adrianople 1–59a
agriculture 1–105a
Aleppo 1–145b-146a
Anatolia 1–242a
Ankara 1–302b
Arčēš 1–423a
Armenia 1–474a
Armenian church 1–504a
Ayrarat 2–20b
Balkans 4–32b
banats 2–70a
Bāyazīd I 2–136a
Bāyazīd II 2–137a
Beirut 2–164a
Bosnia 2–338a-339b
Bosporus 2–344a
bow and arrow/crossbow 2–350b
Brusa 2–392b
Buda 2–396b
Bulgaria 2–413a-b
Bulgarian art and architecture 2–417b
Byzantine Empire 2–500a,b, 501a,b-504b; 4–32b
Caesarea 3–9b
Catalan expansion 3–157a
crusade propaganda 4–21a
crusades of later middle ages 4–54b
Damascus 4–84a
Dardanelles 4–105a
despotate of Epiros 4–500a
Dubrovnik 4–300b
Dyrrachium 4–330a
Egypt 1–12a
Ephesus 4–495a
Erzincan 4–508b
Khanate of Crimea 3–678b-679a
Latin church: 1054 to 1305 3–355b
Palaiologans 1–246a,b
textiles 2–156a
Ottoman-Venetian War (1497-1502) 2–137b
Ottonian architecture
alternating supports 1–226a
See Also Pre-Romanesque Architecture
Ottonian art 4–399b
See Also Pre-Romanesque art
Ottonian dynasty
Bavarian rule 2–134a
Otto of Ballenstedt
Saxony 2–235b
OTTO OF BAMBERG, SAINT 9–0
Otto I of Bavaria 2–134b
Otto III of Brandenburg 2–360b
Otto of Brunswick 1–367b
Otto I of Burgundy, Count 2–424b
OTTO OF FREISING 9–0; 2–6a
Arnold of Brescia 1–539b
Babenberg family 2–33a
Bernard of Clairvaux 2–192a
Cistercian historical writing 3–405a
Frederick II 2–239b-240a
Otto II of Meran, Count of Burgundy 2–424b
Otto IV of Meran, Count of Burgundy 2–424b, 429b
Otto of Nordheim
Billungs 2–235a
Otto of Saxony 4–426a
OTTO VON BOTENLAUBEN 9–0
Ouar
See Avars
Oubliette
See Châtelet
OUNCE 9–0
Ouroboros 1–139b
Ouse River 4–456b
Danelaw border 4–91a
Ousia
Basil the Great 2–121b
Outer crypt
See Crypt
OUTLAWRY 9–0
OUWATER, ALBERT VAN 9–0
Ouzes
Byzantine Empire 2–492b, 493a
See Also Oghuz Turkic tribes

OVENS 9–0
alchemy 1–139a
bread 2–364b
Ovide moralisé
See Ovid moralisé
OVID IN THE MIDDLE AGES 9–0
Albrecht von Halberstadt 1–131b
Alcuin of York 3–101a-b
Alfonsine literary court 1–162a
allegorical interpretation tradition 1–180b, 181b, 182a, 183b-184a
Catalan translations 3–169a
courtly love 3–667b, 671a
French allegory 1–189a,b
OVID MORALISÉ 9–0
French allegory 1–183b, 189b
Ovid's Surfaces Interpreted (John of Garland) 1–183b
Ovidus moralizatus (Bersuire) 1–183b
Oviedo
Asturian court 1–626b
Owain ap Guffydd ap Gwenwynwyn
Peace of Conway 3–580a
Owain Bleddyn
Peace of Conway 3–580a
Owain Brogyntyn
Peace of Conway 3–580a
OWAIN GWYNEDD 9–0; 2–71b
Owein 1–578a
OWL AND THE NIGHTINGALE, THE 9–0; 1–264b
antifeminism 1–324b
débat 4–122a
Øxarflokkr (Einarr Skúlason) 4–411b
Oxen
draft animals 1–293b-294a
European cookery 3–581b
Oxford
Black Death 2–262a
Council of (1222) 1–263a
Gui de Warewic 1–267b
OXFORD PSALTER 9–0
Anglo-Norman text 1–262a
OXFORD UNIVERSITY 9–0
Aristotelianism 1–461a,b, 463b
Bacon, Roger 2–35a, 39a, 41a
Bradwardine, Thomas 2–358a
brewing 2–375a
"Calculators" 1–396b
Cambridge University 3–59a-60a
Cistercian order 3–405a
medical training 2–98b
Vacarius 4–501b
Oxides, metallic
See Ceramics, European
Oxygen dating
climatology 3–453b
Oxyrhynchos
Coptic art 3–588a
OYER AND TERMINER, TRAILBASTON 9–0
piracy issues 1–56b
Oyster
food animal 1–301a

P

Pacheco, John 3–138a
PACHER, MICHAEL 9–0
Pachomius, Saint
Copts and Coptic church 3–595a
monasticism 3–342b
Pachoras (Faras)
Nubian Christianity 3–315a
Pacianus, Bishop 2–102b
Pacifico of Verona
collectarium 3–479b
PACINO DI BONAGUIDA 9–0
Pacioli, Luca 1–41a-b
Padua
Angelus 1–252b
fairs 4–587a
Padua, University of
Arabic numerals 1–396a
founding 2–312b
Paestum
architectural plans 3–152b
Paganism
Augustine of Hippo 1–650a
Page
courtesy book 3–660b, 661b
Pagès, William
Cathars 3–190a
PAGUS 9–0
Burgundy, County of 2–424a
Burgundy, Duchy of 2–427a
Pahak Honacʿ
See Derbent
Pahlavi alphabet
See Persian alphabet
PAHLAVI LITERATURE 9–0
PAHLAWUNI 9–0
Pahlawuni, Grigor 1–292a
Paideia
classical literary studies 3–430b, 431a
PAIKULI 9–0
"Painful Mountain"
See Ararat, Mount
Painting
Anglo-Norman 1–256b
Anglo-Saxon art 1–273a
antependium 1–316b
Armenian 1–496a-497b
art trade 1–561b
catacomb walls 3–155b
Coptic 3–591b-593a
Nubian Christianity 3–315a
Pakistan
alms tax 1–202b
PAKUDA, IBN 9–0
Palace Academy, Aachen 1–1b
Palace architecture
early Christian and Byzantine 4–334b, 343a-b
Palace Church of the Citadel 1–291b
Palace of the Blachernae 3–553a
Palacio de Pinohermoso 1–197b
PALA D'ORO 9–0; 4–438a
Palaeo-Caucasian languages
Caucasia 3–195a
Palaeologan dynasty
See Palaiologoi
Palaiologan-Renaissance learning
Bessarion 2–203a
PALAIOLOGOI 9–0
Andronikos II 1–245b
architecture 4–344b-345b
art 2–447b-451a, 457a-b
autocrator 2–10b
Bulgaria 2–413b
Bulgarian art and architecture 2–417b
Byzantine rules 2–498b-504b
coronation of basileus 2–123a
earthenware 3–237b
East-West church schism 2–465b
Maliasenoi 2–479a
poetry 2–523b, 524a
Tzamblakoi 2–479b
Palaiologos, George
Alexiad 1–304a
Palamas, Gregory 3–632b; 4–135b
angel/angelology 1–250b
PALATINATES 9–0
Treaty of Pavia (1329) 2–135a
Palatine Anthologies 2–524a
Palatine Court
See Charlemagne
Palatium
Carolingians 3–107b
Palazzo dei Consoli 1–251a
Palazzo dei Priori 1–251a
Palazzo del Capitano
astronomical clock 3–29b
Palazzo Pretorio and Gubbio 1–251a
Palazzo Rucellai 1–126b
Paleae
decretum 4–129b
Palencia
fairs 4–587b
Paleo-Christian art 4–349a-350b
Paleodemography 4–136b
PALEOGRAPHY, ARABIC AND PERSIAN 9–0
Bawwāb, Ibn al- 2–135a
PALEOGRAPHY, WESTERN EUROPEAN 9–0
chancery 3–251b
Codiology 3–475b
Old English manuscripts 1–275b
See Also Alphabets
PALERMO 9–0
Aghlabids 1–70b
agriculture 1–87b
art 1–5b
exchange banks 2–73b
money markets 2–78b
public banks 2–76a
PALESTINE 9–0
ʿAmr ibn al-ʿĀṣ 1–237a
Ayyubid art 2–20b
Black Death 2–259a
Byzantine Empire 2–495a
church of Jerusalem 2–461a
early Christian and Byzantine architecture 4–337a-b
Fourth Crusade 4–43b
Frederick II 4–32a
Latin Kingdom of Jerusalem 4–30b
Louis IX 4–53b
pilgrimages 4–27b
See Also Church, Early
Palestinian system of vowel indicators 1–208a
Palestrina 2–324a
PALIA 9–0
Palice of Honour (Gavin Douglas) 4–262b
PALIMPSEST 9–0
PALIOTTO 9–0
Angilbert of Milan 1–254b
Pall 1–224a
Palladinus, Jacobus 1–44a
PALLADIUS 9–0; 3–214a, 595a
Coptic church 3–595a
Divine Office 4–229b
Pallars 1–409b, 413b
PALLIUM 9–0
Anselm of Canterbury 1–312a,b
Brandeum 2–362a
papal coronation 3–604a,b
Palm
blessing of 2–177b-178a
Palma (Boncompagno of Signa) 2–320a
Palma Cathedral 3–568b-569a

Palma de Mallorca
money markets 2–78b
Palmesel 4–492a
PALMETTE 9–0
Palmette, Sasanian
See Palmette
Palmette, Wing
See Palmette
"Palmgroves" 1–371a
Palm Sunday
entry into Jerusalem 4–491b
PALMYRA 9–0
Palol, Berenguer de 3–164b
Palos
Columbus 4–560b
trade 4–558a
***PÁLS SAGA BISKUPS* 9–0**; 2–252a,b
Paltasar 4–112b, 113a
PALUDAMENTUM 9–0
Paludanus, Peter
Christology 3–324a
Pamir plateau
Marco Polo 4–556b
Pammakaristos Church 4–345b, 346
Pamphlet on the Case of Formosus (Eugenius Vulgarius) 4–520b
Pamplona 3–131b
Aragon 1–404a, 405a-b
Charlemagne 2–126a
Panagia, Church of (Chios) 4–345a
Panagia tou Arakou, Church of the
paintings 2–445b
Panchatantra 1–455b; 3–31b
Pancorbo, Gap of
Castilian settlement 3–128a
Panegyricon Berengarii
See Berengarii Imperatoris Gesta
Panegyrics
Arabic poetry 1–400b, 402a
PANEL PAINTING 9–0
antependium 1–316b
Paneutychestatos 4–165a
Pannonia 2–4b
Avars 1–90b; 2–12b
Lombard settlement 2–95a
Magyars 4–4a
map 2–298
Ostrogoth settlement 2–93a
Pannonian Croatia 4–1b, 2a, 8a
Sirmium 2–299b
Vandals settlement 2–91b
Panodoros 3–18b
Panormia (Ivo of Chartres) 1–607a
PANORMITANUS 9–0
conciliar movement 3–365b
conciliar theory 3–511b, 572b
Panphilus 4–283a
Pantaenus
Catechetical School of Alexandria 3–593b
Pantaléon, Jacques
feast of Corpus Christi 3–608a
Pantanassa, Church of the 2–451a; 4–345a
Pantegni (Constantine the African) 3–548b
PANTEIRON 9–0
Pantheon 1–426a,b
Panther, The 1–280b
Panticapaeum
camel use 1–296b
PANTOKRATOR 9–0
Christology 3–320b
Emmanuel 4–437a
Pantokrator Monastery 1–637a; 2–456b; 4–344a
Pantoleon 2–438b
Paolina da Venezi
Boccaccio 2–286a
Paolino Piero
Arthurian literature 1–572b-573a
Paolo da Castro
Baldus 2–57a
Paolo da Perugia
royal library 2–278a
Paolo del Pozzo Toscannelli
Columbus 4–559b
PAOLO DI GIOVANNI FEI 9–0
art trade 1–562b
PAOLO VENEZIANO 9–0
PAPACY, ORIGINS AND DEVELOPMENT
Alexios I Komnenos 4–30a
antipopes 1–330a
archives 1–446a
Augustinus Triumphus 2–1a-b
Avignon 1–108a; 2–15b; 4–376a-377a
banking 2–77b, 81a
Carolingians 3–109a
Cluny 4–33b
Council of Vienne 3–643a
crusade concept 4–15b-16b, 17a,b-18a
crusade of later middle ages 4–54b-55a,b, 57a
crusade propaganda 4–18b
Defensor pacis 4–132a
ecclesiology 4–372a
election to 3–638a-b
Frederick II 4–51a
German Holy Roman Empire 1–148b-149a
Hohenstaufens 4–17b
Louis IX 4–53b
Photian Council 2–117b
See Also Church, Latin
PAPACY, ORIGINS AND DEVELOPMENT OF 9–0
abbreviator 1–13b
accounting system 1–37a-b, 39a,b
Auxilius 2–11b
Babylonian captivity 2–33b
Boniface VIII 2–324b
bulls 2–418a
canonization 3–68a-b
Carolingians 3–106a,b
College of Cardinals 3–93b
conclaves 3–523b
consistorium 3–541b
coronations 3–602b
cross 4–9b
decretals 4–122b
Desiderius of Monte Cassino 4–164b
dictatus papae 4–177a
documents and records 1–206b; 3–19b-20a
Ennodius 4–491b
Eugenius Vulgarius 4–520b
False Decretals 4–124a
money markets 2–78b
papal curia 4–65b
See Also Church, Early
See Also Church, Latin: to 1054
Pāpak 1–451b
PAPAL CURIA, LITURGY OF 9–0
Breviary 2–371b-372a
Papal Jubilee 3–360a
PAPAL STATES 9–0
Albornoz 1–130b
political crusades 4–57b
PAPER, INTRODUCTION OF 9–0
chancery 3–253b
codicology, Western European 3–475b
Islamic calligraphy 3–54a
PAPERT 9–0
Paphnutius, Saint 1–261b
Paphos 4–72a
PAPIAS 9–0
dictionary 1–204b-205a; 4–449b
PAPYRUS 9–0
charters 3–274b
codex 3–474a
codicology, Western European 3–475b
Merovingian documents 3–253b
Parable
allegory form 1–188a
Paracelsus
alcohol 4–219b
Paraclet, Le, Convent 1–17a,b
PARADISE, ISLAMIC 9–0
PARADISE, WESTERN CONCEPT OF 9–0
Paradise of the Fathers (Palladius) 3–595a
Paradiso (Dante) 3–258a; 4–94a
Paradisus cloisters 1–128a
Paralipomenon 1–110b
P'aranjem
Aršak II 1–560a
PARAPHONISTA 9–0
Parastatic clock 3–28a
PARCHMENT 9–0
codicology, Western European 3–475b
Paréage 2–128a,b, 129a
PAREKKLESION 9–0; 4–345b, 346
Byzantine art 2–448b-449a
Parement de Narbonne 2–310a
PARES (PARRYS), JOHN 9–0
Parfait du paon (Jean de la Mote) 1–151b
Parias (tributes) 3–128b, 132a, 136a
Parigoritissa church 4–345a-b
PARIS 9–0
archeological excavations 1–336b
arms and armor 1–529a
art trade 1–562a
astronomy school 1–612b
châtelet 3–278a
Dante 4–101a-b
medicine 2–98b
money markets 2–78b
physicians and barbers 2–100b
Vikings 3–103b
Paris, Council of (1210)
Amalric of Bène 1–228b
Paris, Gaston 1–271b
Paris, Matthew
See Matthew Paris
Paris, Synod of (849) 1–644a
Paris, Treaty of (1259) 4–519a
PARIS, UNIVERSITY OF 9–0; 2–311b
Albert of Saxony 1–125b
Albertus Magnus 1–127a
Alexander of Hales 1–148a
Arabic numerals 1–396b
Aristotelianism 1–461a-b, 463a,b
ars antiqua 1–543a-b
ars praedicandi 1–555b-556a
Augustinianism 4–309a
Bacon 2–35a, 41a
Bonaventure, Saint 2–313a-b, 317b
Buridan, Jean 2–430a
celibacy laws 3–217b
classical literary studies 3–434b
Courson 3–659a
d'Ailly 1–108a
Dominicans 4–251b
ecclesiology 4–377b
Eckhart 4–381a
Egidius Colonna 4–400a
Paris and Vienne 3–210b
PARISH, ORIGIN AND DEVELOPMENT OF 9–0
Carolingian system 3–109a

PARISH, ORIGIN AND DEVELOPMENT OF (cont.)
church, Latin 3–372b
dioceses 4–191a
Parisiensis secunda 4–123b
P'arisos 2–48b
PARIS PSALTER 9–0; 2–221a, 441a-b, 451b
alliterative patterns 1–277a
Old English poetry 1–280a
Old English translations 1–285a,b
Paris, Treaty of (1229) 3–189a-b
Paris, Treaty of (1259) 1–367b
Paris, Treaty of (1303) 1–367b
Parker, Henry
Boccaccio 2–287a,b, 288a
Parker, Matthew, Archbishop of Canterbury 1–286b
Parker Chronicle 1–284a-b
Parlement, French 4–65b
Brittany, Duchy 2–380a
PARLEMENT OF PARIS 9–0
Eudes Rigaud 4–519a
PARLER, JOHANNES 9–0; 2–392b
PARLER, PETER 9–0; 2–392b
PARLIAMENT 9–0
Parliament, English 4–478a, 479a,b-486a
Edward I 4–395b, 396b
Edward III 4–398a,b
PARLIAMENT, IRISH 9–0
PARLIAMENT, SCOTTISH 9–0
Parliament of Fowls (Chaucer) 3–286b-287b
Parloir aux Bourgeois
châtelet 3–279b
P'arnavaz, King 4–506a
PARODY, LATIN 9–0
PAROIKOI 9–0
Paronymy
Anselm of Canterbury 1–314a
PAROUSIA 9–0; 3–337b, 340b
Saint George Church 4–359a
Parrot, Friedrich 1–422a
Parrys, John
See Pares, John
Pārs 1–451b, 452a
Parskahayk' 1–472b, 473b-474a
***PARTALOPA SAGA* 9–0**
Partav
See Perozapat
Partaw
See Bardha'a
Parthenius 1–117b, 422a
PARTHIANS 9–0
PARTIMEN 9–0
Partnerships
accounting 1–40b
mercantile banking 2–76a-77a
Partridge, The 1–280b
Parts of Animals (Aristotle) 1–356a
Paruchia
Celtic church 3–226a, 227b
Parva naturalia (Albertus Magnus) 1–128a
Parvipontanus, Adamus
See Adam of the Little Bridge
Parvo Ponte, Adam de
See Adam of the Little Bridge
Parvus, Joannes
See Petit, Jean
Parzival 2–228b
Pascal, Blaise
casuistry 3–153b
Pascentius, Count 1–654a
Paschal, Antipope 1–330a
Paschal III, Antipope 1–330a
Paschal I, Pope
arts 2–453b, 455a
catacombs 3–154b
PASCHAL II, POPE 9–0; 1–313a
Alfonso I 1–160b
Bruno of Segni, Saint 2–392a
Camaldolese Order 3–56a
First Crusade 4–36a
Knights of Saint John of Jerusalem 3–303b
Western councils 3–635b-636a
Paschal candle 4–367a,b
***PASCHALE CHRONICON* 9–0**
Paschalis rhythmus ad procedendrum
See Easter Song
Paschal Proclamation
exultet roll 4–565b
PASCHASIUS RADBERT OF CORBIE 9–0; 3–112a
Agius of Corvey 1–72b
biblical exegesis 2–224a
dialectic 4–169b
Latin exegesis 4–542b
PASHA 9–0
Pasqual, Joan 3–169b
Pasqual, Pere, Bishop 3–167b
Passaggerii, Rolandino
dictamen 4–174b
University of Bologna 2–312b
Passau
bishoprics 2–134a
Boniface, Saint 2–322a
"Passauer Anonymous" 1–322a
Passeggieri, Rolandino
See Passaggerii, Rolandino
Passió de Jesucrist (Francesc Alegre) 3–169b
Passio martyrum Marcellini et Petri (Einhard) 4–412b
Passional 4–224b
PASSION CYCLE 9–0
Passion du Palatinus 4–264a
PASSION PLAYS, FRENCH 9–0; 4–264a-265a
Passion plays, German 4–267a-268a
Passio sanctae Eulaliae Barcinonensis 3–164a
Passiun (anon.) 1–261a
***PASSIUN SEINT EDMUND, LA* 9–0**
Passover 3–27a; 4–365a
azymes 2–31b
dating of Easter 3–228a,b
Paston, Sir John 1–320a
PASTON LETTERS 9–0
Pastophorium (sacristy) 4–335b
PASTOPHORY 9–0
Pastor aeternus 3–518b-519a, 655a
Pastoral Care (Saint Gregory) 1–165a-b, 167a, 281a, 284b
Alfred the Great translations 1–274b, 276a
West Saxon dialect 1–276b
Pastorale (Francesc Eiximensis) 4–416b
Pastoralism, Islamic 1–103a-b
Pastoral letters 1–285a
PASTOUREAUX 9–0
Blanche of Castile 2–271a
Children's Crusade 4–15a
Eudes Rigaud 4–519b
***PASTOURELLE* 9–0**; 1–269a; 4–122a
Aucassin et Nicolette 1–643b
Bodel 2–290b
Cercamon 3–240a
PASTURE, RIGHTS OF 9–0
Byzantine agriculture 1–78b-79a
Islamic 1–103b
Patarines
Alexander II 1–146a
Italian communes 3–499b
Patarins
dualism 2–296b
See Also Bosnia
PATEN 9–0; 1–223a
ordination rites 3–442b
Patengoli family
Angela Merici 1–250b
PATERIKON 9–0
Paterna faience 3–238a
Paternoster
Cathar liturgy 3–181b
Path of Eloquence
See Nahj al-balagha
Patmos
agriculture and nutrition 1–77a
PATMUT'IWN (YERKRIN), **TARONOY 9–0**
Patracius
consolamentum 3–185a-b
PATRIARCH 9–0
Byzantine clergy 3–447a
Cathar attitudes 3–184b
of Constantinople 2–10a,b
of Moscow 2–10a
of Rome 2–10a
Patriarch Paulinus
rite of Aquileia 1–353a
PATRICIAN, ROMAN 9–0
PATRICIAN, URBAN 9–0
Bruges 2–386b
PATRICK, SAINT 9–0; 2–220a; 1–261a
Celtic church 3–225b, 229a
espurgatoire Saint Patrice 4–509b
Finn and Fiana 1–33b, 34a
monasticism 3–344b
Patrington, Stephen 3–535a
Patristic heritage
death and burial 4–118b-119b
ecclesiology 4–372a-b
Patrocinio
See Commendatio
Patrologia latina (Saint Columbanus) 3–486b
PATRONAGE 9–0
Arthurian literature 1–574a
art trade 1–560b
Badr al-Dīn 2–43b
Buyids 2–437a
commendation 3–490a
PATRONQMOBA 9–0
Pattern books 4–291b
Patzinaks
See Pechenegs
See Russian Nomads, Invasions of
PAUCAPALEA 9–0
decretist 4–127b
Paul, Patriarch
heresy 2–462a
Paul I, Pope
relics 3–154b
Paul II, Pope
cardinal's purple 4–327b
carnival promotion 3–99b
Paul III, Pope
breviary 2–373a
Paul V, Pope
archives 1–448a
Paul, Saint
bulls 2–418b
theology 3–338b
Ankaran address 1–302a
Ephesus 4–494a
See Also individual epistles
Paul Aurelian, Saint
Brittany, Duchy 2–377b
Pauldrons 1–525b, 530b, 534a
PAULICIANS 9–0
Armenian church 1–501b

Basil II the Macedonian 2–118b
Bogomils 2–294b, 296a
Byzantine Empire 4–523a
Docetism 4–233a
Pauline Epistles
Celtic language 3–233a
PAULINUS OF AQUILEIA 9–0; 1–142b
Carolingian latin poetry 3–101b
Charlemagne's reform of clergy 3–109b
Nicene-Constantinopolitan Creed 3–677a
pseudonym 3–100a
PAULINUS OF BÉZIERS 9–0
PAULINUS OF NOLA 9–0; 4–358a
bells 2–165b
Cassian 3–122b
liturgical books 2–180a,b
PAULINUS OF PELLA 9–0
PAULINUS OF PÉRIGUEUX 9–0
Paulinus the Minorite 1–333b
Paul of Burgos, Bishop
Christian Hebraists 3–314a
Paul of Hungary
Dominicans 4–244a
Paul of Venice 1–465a
PAUL THE DEACON 9–0
beast epic 2–141a
Calpurnius Siculus Titus, influence 3–55b
Carolingian latin poetry 3–100b, 101b-102a
Charlemagne, court 3–268b
Charlemagne's reform of clergy 3–109b
Cistercian rite 3–406b
Erchenbert of Monte Cassino 4–504a
exegesis 4–543a, 550a
homilies 1–284b
Paul the Hermit, Saint 1–261b
Paul the Silentiary
Hagia Sophia 2–506a
Paulus Diaconus
See Paul the Deacon
Paulus of Heredia
cabala 3–3a
Pau of Bellviure 3–171a
Paupertate honesta, De 1–317a
Pausanias
Periegesis 1–333a
Pauses and rests, musical
Anonymous IV 1–309b
Pavely, John
Admiralty Court 1–57a
Pavese
agriculture 1–87b
Pavia
commune 3–500a
fairs 4–587a
Lombard invasion 2–95b
Pavia, Treaty of (1329) 2–135a
Pavia, Council of (1160) 1–146b
Pavia, Council of (1423-1424) 3–651b
Pavise 1–528a,b
Pavlović, Ivaniš 2–339a
Pavlović, Peter 2–338b
Pavlović, Radoslav 2–338a-b, 339a
Pavlovići 2–337b, 340a
Pavlov-Obnorsky Monastery
art 4–192a
Pavo (Alexander of Roes) 1–148b, 149a
Pawnbroking
European 2–76a
Jewish banking in Europe 2–80b
P'AWSTOS BUZAND 9–0; 2–48a; 4–417a
Aršak II 1–559b
church 1–498a
literature 1–508a
saints 1–517a, 518a, 519a
Pax brede 1–224b
Pax Islamica
See Abode of Islam--Abode of War
Payens, Hugh de
Knights Templars 3–304a
Payne and Sorow of Evyll Maryage, The (John Lydgate) 1–323b
P'aytakaran
Albania 1–123b, 124b-125a
Armenia 1–472b, 473b
See Also Baylakān
Pazzi Chapel of the Church of Santa Croce
Brunelleschi 2–388a, 389b, 390a
Peace movement
crusade concept 4–15a
Peace of Constance (1183) 3–627a; 4–203b
PEACE OF GOD, TRUCE OF GOD 9–0; 3–177a
chivalry 3–302a
Latin church: 1054 to 1305 3–356a-b
Peace of Lodi (1454)
conciliar movement 3–367b
Peace of the Church 3–337a
dedication of churches 4–130b
Peace of Venice (1177) 1–147a
Peacock
food animal 1–301a
***PEARL, THE* 9–0**
allegory 1–186a
Peasants
northern European 1–94a-b
See Also Class Structure, Western (1000-1300)
See Also Class Structure, Western (1300-1500)
Peasants' Crusade (1096) 4–34a
PEASANTS' REBELLION (1381) **9–0**; 4–424b, 484b
Anonimalle chronicle 1–265b
Chaucer, Geoffrey 3–290a
copyhold 3–596b
Enguerrand VII of Coucy 4–491a
Simon of Sudbury 3–83b
Peasants' Wedding, The
See Bauernhochzeit, Die
Peat bogs
climatology 3–454b
pollen studies 3–453b
Pechenegs
Alexiad 1–303b
Bulgaria 2–489b
Byzantine Empire 2–492b, 493b, 494a,b
See Also Russian Nomads, Invasions of
PECHERSKAYA LAVRA 9–0; 1–636b
Alimpi 1–175b
PECIA 9–0
PECK 9–0
PECKHAM (PECHAM), **JOHN 9–0**; 1–264a
Anglo-Latin poetry 1–255a
Aristotle 1–461b
Augustinism 1–660b
Bacon, Roger 2–38b, 39b, 41a
Canterbury 3–83b
Thomistic theses 4–247a
Peć Monastery
art 2–446b
PECOCK, REGINALD 9–0
Pedilavium
See Feet, Washing of
Pedralbes convent 2–128a
Pedro da Evora
Africa 4–562a
PEDRO DE CÓRDOBA 9–0
PEDRO EL CEREMENIOSO, LITERARY COURT OF
Eiximenis 4–416a
Pedro el Ceremonioso 1–415b-417a,b
Barcelona government 2–104b
Christian calendar 3–18b
PEDRO EL CEREMONIOSO, LITERARY COURT OF 9–0
Catalan literature 3–166a,b, 169a, 170b
Pedro I of Aragon 1–160a-b, 405b-406a
Pedro II of Aragon 1–410a-411a
Albigensians 3–188b
court 3–164b
heretics 3–187a-b
Pedro III of Aragon 1–412b-414a
Arnald of Villanova 1–537b
cortes 3–611a,b
poets 4–189b
Sicilian Kingdom 4–61a
Pedro of Barcelos, Count 3–86b; 4–190a,b
Pedro Serra
See Serra, Pedro and Jaime
Pedro IV the Ceremonius of Aragon
See Pedro el Ceremonioso
Pedro I the Cruel of Castile 3–136b-137a
Albornoz 1–130b
Aragon 1–416b
Chaucer 3–280b, 284b
Pegasides pleyn ende den lust-hof der maeghden (Jan Baptist Houwaert) 4–322b
Pegged dial
clocks 3–459b
Pegolotti, Francesco Balducci
Asian trade 4–557a-b
Cyprus 4–72a
PEIRE CARDENAL 9–0
PEIRE D'ALVERNHA 9–0
courtly love 3–668a
Peire D'Auvergne
Arnaut Daniel 1–539a
PEIRE VIDAL 9–0
Peitrel 1–529a
Peking
See Also Cambaluc
Peláez, Bishop Diego 2–194b
Pelagians
Bradwardine, Thomas 2–358a
Celestine I combat vs. 3–214a
PELAGIUS 9–0
alchemy 1–136a
Augustine of Hippo 1–652a-654a
Cassian 3–122b
Irish Bible 2–220a
origin of Celtic church 3–225b
Pelagius I, Pope
ordination 3–441b
Pelagius II, Pope
exarch 4–529b
Pelagius, Cardinal
Fifth Crusade 4–50a-51a
PELAGONIA 9–0
Byzantine Empire 2–498b
Pelayo 1–625b-626a
Pelecanum
Andronikos III Palaiologos 1–246b
PELENA 9–0
Pèlerin, Richart le
chronicles 3–331a
Pèlerinage de Charlemagne 3–258b
Pélerinage de la vie humaine (Guillaume de Guilleville) 1–189b; 3–281a

Pelican
  crucifixion 4–13b
Pellegrino of Padua 2–99a
Pellet bow 2–353a
Peltas
  Celtic art 3–218b
Pembroke 4–329a
PENANCE AND PENITENTIALS 9–0
  Burchard of Worms 2–420b
  casuistry 3–153b
  Celtic church 3–229b-230a,b
  confession 3–533a
  confessor, royal 3–534b
  contraception 3–573a
  ember days 4–435b
  excommunication 4–538a
  funeral rights 3–231a
Pencerdd 2–106a; 4–69b, 76b
Pendant vault
  See Vault
PENDENTIVE 9–0
  dome 4–234b-235b, 236a
  domed churches 3–378a,b
Pendilia 3–615a
***PENETES* 9–0**
  dunatoi 4–307a
Pénicaud dynasty
  Limoges enamel 4–439b, 441b
Peñíscola 1–411b, 412a
Penitentia, De
  decretum 4–129a,b
Penitential (Pseudo-Egbert) 1–286a
Penna, Lucas de 4–502a
"Penniless Prodromos"
  See Theodore Prodromos
PENNY 9–0
Pentapolis
  ʿAmr ibn al-ʿĀṣ 1–237a; 4–403b
  Byzantine church 2–459b
  Ravenna exarchate 4–529b
PENTARCHY 9–0
  Armenian 1–514b-516a
PENTATEUCH 9–0
  Jewish exegesis 4–539a
PENTECOST 9–0
  Ascension, Feast of the 1–582a
  baptism 2–85b
  confirmation 3–536a
  Easter 4–365b
  ember days 4–435b
PENTECOST (ART) 9–0
PEOPLE OF THE BOOK 9–0; 1–20b
PEPIN (AND DONATION OF PE-PIN) 9–0; 3–106a-b, 346a
  Alamanni 1–118a
  Alanni 1–118a
  anointing 1–308b
  brewing 2–374b
  Byzantine church 2–463a
  Capetians 3–89b
  deposition of rulers 4–158b, 159a
  diplomacy, Islamic 4–200b
  Divine Office 4–230a
  ecclesiastical reform 3–108b-109a
  election as king 3–345b
  Saxon tribute 3–202a
Pepin III
  See Pepin (and Donation of Pepin)
Pepin I of Aquitaine
  Carolingian Empire rule 3–112a
  Ermoldus Nigellus 4–507b
Pepin II of Héristal 3–104b-106b
  Alamanni 1–118a
  Boniface, Saint 2–321a
  Frankish kingdom 3–345b
Pepin the Elder 3–104a-b
Pepin the Hunchback
  Frankfurt capitulary 3–91b
Pepin the Short
  See Pepin (and Donation of Pepin)
Pepin the Younger
  See Pepin (and Donation of Pepin)
Pepo
  corpus iuris civilis 3–609b
Per Abbat
  Cantar de Mío Cid, authorship 3–79b
PERA-GALATA 9–0
Peraldus (Perault), William
  Dominican theology 4–247b
***PERCEVAL, ROMAN DE* 9–0**; 1–567a, 571a
***PERCEVALS SAGA* 9–0**
PERCH 9–0
Peredur
  See Mabinogion
Peredur Son of Efrawg 1–567a, 578a
Perego, Camillo
  La regola del canto fermo ambrosiano 1–233a
Peregrinatio 3–344b
Peregrinatio ad loca sancta Silviae (Aetheria of Gaul) 1–332a
Peregrinatio Aetheriae
  See Itinerarium Egeriae
Peregrinatio pro amore Christi 3–231b
Pereiaslav
  Mongol invasions 2–131b
Perejaslavec 2–406a
Père Lachaise Cemetery 1–18b
Perellós, Ramon de 3–170a
Pere I of Catalonia
  See Pedro II of Aragon
Pere II of Catalonia
  See Pedro II of Aragon
Pere III of Catalonia
  See Pedro el Ceremonioso
PÈRES, LA VIE DES ANCIENS 9–0
Pérez, Miquel 3–168a
Perez de Guzman, Ferna
  See Spanish Literature: Biographical
Perez de Martel of Seville, Gonzalo
  Canary Islands expedition 3–61b
***PERFECTIO* 9–0**
Perfectione vitae ad sorores, De (Bonaventure) 2–316a
Perfecto magisterio, De (Aristotle) 1–136b
Perfume 2–146a,b-147b
Pergri
  See Berkri
Pericles
  classical literary studies 3–430b
PERICOPES 9–0
Periculis novissimorum temporum, De (William of Saint Amour) 1–128a
Periegesis (Pausanias) 1–333a
Perigrini
  Celtic spirituality 3–231b
Peri hermeneias (Apuleius of Madaura) 4–168b
Perim 2–32a
Peripatetics
  Boethius 2–292a
  eternity doctrine 1–45a
Periphyseon (John Scottus Eriugena) 4–169b
Periplus maris Erythraei 1–32a
Peristrema Valley 3–92a
Perizoma 4–13a,b
Perkri
  See Berkri
***PERLESVAUS* 9–0**; 1–567a, 571a, 578a
Permin
  Carolingian Empire 3–106a
Pero da Covilhão
  exploration 4–562b-563a
Pero de Escobar
  exploration 4–561b
PERO TAFUR 9–0
PEROTINUS 9–0
  Anonymous IV 1–310a
  ars antiqua 1–543a, 546a
  clausula 3–437b
  conductus 3–532a
Pērōzāpāt 1–123b, 124b-125a; 2–26a
Pērōz-Kawādh
  See Pērōzāpāt
PERPETUAL SYNOD 9–0
Perpetuus, Bishop
  Christmas celebration 3–318a
Perpignan
  Black Death 2–260b
  Crown of Aragon 1–413b, 414a, 415b, 417a, 419a,b, 420a
Perpignan, Council of (1408) 3–646a
Perriers 3–150b
Persarmenia 2–48a
  See Parskahaykʿ
Persepolis
  traveler accounts 1–332b
Pershore Cathedral
  architecture 1–256a
Persia
  See Iran; Sasanians
  Abbasid caliphate 3–49a
  Alamūt 1–118a
  Antioch 1–325b
  Antiochene rite 1–327a
  Armenian saints 1–518b-519a
  astrology 1–604a
  ʿAzīz, al- 2–28a
  Byzantine church 2–460a
  Byzantine Empire 2–486b-487a
  ceramics 3–238a
  Chosroids 3–307b
  Christian church 3–312a
  Marco Polo 4–556b
  water buffalo 1–298a
Persian Gulf
  Euphrates River 4–521b
  Marco Polo 4–556b
Persian language
  alphabets 1–209b, 214b
  literature 1–378a-b
Persona mixta
  anointing of kings 1–308b
Personification
  See Allegory
Perspectiva
  See Optics
Perturbator 1–331a
Pertussa, Francesc de 3–168a
Perugia
  Baldus 2–57a
  fountain 1–251a
  Ravenna exarchate 4–530a
Perugia, University of
  Bartolo da Sassoferrato 2–115a
Per Uno da Siena
  fables 4–572b
Perutilis logica (Albert of Saxony) 4–170b
Peruzzi banking company 2–77a,b, 287a
Pervasor 1–331a
Pervigilium Veneris 1–317a
Pessagno, Bartolomeo 4–558b
Pessagno, Carlo 4–558b
Pessagno, Lanzarote 2–29b; 4–558b, 559a
Pessagno, Manuel 4–558b
Pessagnos of Portugal
  Castile 4–558a
Pesto-Capaccio
  Amatus 1–229a
Petaḥia of Regensburg 2–181b

Petchenegs 1–157b, 158a
  Constantinople 3–552a
  See Also Pechenegs
Peter, Archbishop 1–453b
PETER, MASTER 9–0
Peter, Saint
  altar relic 1–337a
  papal bulls 2–418b
PETER ALFONSI 9–0
PETER AUREOLI 9–0
Peter Bartholomew
  First Crusade 4–35b
Peterborough
  chronicles 1–284b
Peterborough Abbey
  estates 4–512b
PETER COMESTOR 9–0
  biblical exegesis 2–219a-b, 231b
  Latin exegesis 4–543b
  Middle English exegesis 4–545a,b, 546b, 547a,b
Peter cross 4–9b
PETER DAMIAN, SAINT 9–0
  Camaldolese Order 3–56a
  canonical reform 3–355a
  Celestine V 3–214b
  dialectic 4–169b
  dictatus papae 4–177b
  Divine Office 4–223a
  ecclesiology 4–375a
  excommunication 4–536b
  Marian office 2–274a
  monasteries 3–354b
  papal reform 3–348a, 351a
Peter de Coninck
  Bruges 2–387a
Peter de Honestis
  Marian offices 2–274a
Peter della Vigna
  See Peter of Vinea
Peter I Getadarj 1–484a
PETER GETADARZ 9–0
Peterhausen sacramentary
  Anno 1–306a
Peterhof
  fairs 4–588a
Peter John Olivi
  beguins 2–162a
  Bernardino of Siena 2–196b
Peter Kresimir IV of Croatia, King 4–79b
PETER LANGTOFT 9–0
PETER LOMBARD 9–0
  Biel 2–233b
  Burgundio of Pisa 2–423b
  Duns Scotus, commentary 4–308b
  exegesis 2–213b, 218b, 221b; 4–543b, 546a, 547a,b
  Sentences 2–313a, 314a
Peter Martyr, Saint
  murder 3–190b
Peter of Abernon
  See Peter of Peckham
Peter of Alexandria
  Armenian saints 1–518b
  bestiary 2–204a
  Sefer tekunah 4–12a
Peter II of Aragon
  See Pedro II of Aragon
Peter III the Great of Aragon
  See Pedro III of Aragon
Peter IV of Aragon
  See Pedro el Ceremonioso
Peter of Aragon, Friar 4–416a
Peter of Benevento 3–189a
PETER OF BLOIS 9–0
  brewing 2–375a
  church elections 4–423a
  dictamen 4–175a
Peter of Bruys
  anticlericalism 3–358b
  Bernard of Clairvaux 2–192a
  ecclesiology 4–374b
PETER OF BULGARIA 9–0; 2–405a-b
  Bogomils 2–294a
  boyar 2–403a
Peter of Byzantium, Patriarch
  heresy 2–462a
Peter of Candia
  See Alexander V, Pope
Peter of Castelnau
  heretics 3–187b, 188a
Peter I of Castile
  See Pedro I the Cruel of Castile
Peter of Celle
  Carthusian influence 3–119a
  Henry I 3–246a
Peter of Cornwall
  biblical dictionary 1–205b
Peter of Croatia, King 4–7a
Peter I of Cyprus 4–71a,b, 72a
  Āyās captured 2–19a
  Cilician kingdom 3–393a
Peter II of Cyprus, King 4–71a
Peter of Dreux
  See Mauclerc, Peter
Peter of Dusburg
  Baltic religion 2–64a
Peter of Fetcham
  See Peter of Peckham
Peter of Ickham
  Le livere de reis de Britannie et le livere de reis de Engleterre 1–265a
Peter of Isernia
  See Celestine V, Pope
Peter of La Ferté, Archbishop
  Cistercian Order 3–405b
Peter of Lusignan, King 4–55a-b
  Alexandria 1–153b
Peter of Maricourt
  See Peter Peregrinus of Maricourt
Peter of Medina 4–12b
Peter of Morrone
  See Celestine V, Pope
PETER OF MOSCOW 9–0
Peter of Pavia
  heretics 3–187a
PETER OF PECKHAM 9–0
  Light for Lay People 1–263a
  Secret des Secretes 1–264b
  Wyche, Richard 1–261b
PETER OF PISA 9–0
  Aachen, Palace School 1–142b
  Carolingian Latin poetry 3–100b, 101b
  Charlemagne 3–109b
  classical literary studies 3–433a
PETER OF SPAIN 9–0
  dialectic 4–170b
Peter of Tarentaise
  Albertus Magnus 1–128a
  Bonaventure, Saint 2–319a
  church reform 3–641b
  See Also Innocent V, Pope
Peter of Ulm
  surgical text 4–579b
Peter of Verona
  preaching 4–250b
Peter of Vinea
  dictamen 4–174b, 175a, 176b
  diplomacy 4–204b
PETER PEREGRINUS OF MARICOURT 9–0
PETER RIGA 9–0
Peters, Gerlach
  Devotio moderna 4–166b
PETER THE CHANTER 9–0
  contraception 3–572a
  Courson 3–659a
  Latin exegesis 4–544a
  medicine 2–100b-101a
PETER THE DEACON OF MONTE CASSINO 9–0
  See Also Constantine the African
Peter the Fuller, Bishop 3–676b
PETER THE HERMIT 9–0
  Chanson d'Antioche 3–254a
  Council of Clermont 3–449a
  crusades 1–158a; 4–30a, 33b, 34a-b
PETER THE VENERABLE 9–0
  Abelard and Heloise 1–18a, 19b
  Carthusian influence 3–119a
  Cluniac rite 3–467b
  Cluny Abbey 3–468a, 469a, 471a
  Koran translation 3–356b
  Marian offices 2–274a
PETER URSEOLUS 9–0
PETER VON PRACHTATITZ 9–0
Petit, Jean 3–649b
  Council of Constance 1–109a
Petit Brut 1–265b
***PETITE PHILOSOPHIE, LA* 9–0**; 1–263b
Petit Plet (Chardri) 1–264b; 3–267b
Petit traitise 3–661a
Petrajolo dei Negroni da Ello 1–528b
Petra monastery 1–637a
PETRARCH (FRANCESCO) **9–0**
  Ackermann 1–45a
  Babylonian captivity 2–34a
  biographical writing 2–239b
  Black Death 2–257b
  Boccaccio 2–289a,b
  Brant, Sebastian 2–363b
  Bruni, Leonardo 2–391a
  Catalan translations 3–169b
  Chaucer 3–283a, 284b
  Cino da Pistoia 3–397b
  classical literary studies 3–435a,b
  coin collection 1–335b
  See Also Cola di Rienzo
Petrarch, Giovanni
  Boccaccio 2–285b
***PETRI EXCEPTIONES* 9–0**
Petro d'Ancarano
  Baldus disciple 2–57a
Petroni, Pietro
  Boccaccio 2–288a
Petros of Siwnik', Bishop
  literature 1–509a
Petros Philargos
  See Alexander V
Petrucci, Federico
  Baldus 2–57a
Petruce de Cruce
  ars antiqua 1–545b
PETRUS 9–0
Petrus Alfonsi
  Disciplina clericals 4–216b
  exempla 4–551b
Petrus Bonus 1–138a
Petrus de Alliaco
  See Ailly, Pierre d'
Petrus de Crescentiis 4–513a
PETRUS DE CRUSE 9–0
  ars antiqua 1–542b, 543b, 547a
Petrus Helie
  classical literary studies 3–434b
Petrus Hispanus
  See John XXI, Pope
  See Peter of Spain
***PETRUSLIED* 9–0**
Petrus of Picardy 1–544b

Petrus Ramus
dialectic 4–171a
PETTY ASSIZES, ENGLISH 9–0; 1–596b
Petty baillis 2–52b
Peuerbach, Georg 1–614b
astronomy 1–613b
Pézenas
fairs 4–584b, 586a
Pfaffe Amis
See Stricker, Der
Pfaffe Konrad
See Rolandslied
Pfaffe Lamprecht
See Lamprecht
Pflug
See Plows
Phaedrus
fables 2–15b; 4–572a,b
Phaletolum
See Utensilibus, De
Phanagoria
camel use 1–296b
Phantom's Frenzy, The 1–567a-b
PHARMACOPIAE 9–0
Bīrūnī 2–250b-251a
Pharos 1–154a
Pharsalia (Lucan) 1–162a
Phasis River
See Rioni River
Phelonion 3–615b
Phenology
climatology 3–451a
Phiale 4–333b
Philadelphia
Byzantine independence 1–241b
Philae
Egyptian frontier 4–404a
Philanthropoteron 4–383a
Philaretos Vakhramios
See P'ilartos Varažnuni
Philip, Antipope 1–330a
Philip, Provincial of the Holy Land
Dominicans 4–252b
PHILIP II AUGUSTUS 9–0
Angevins 1–253a
appanages 1–351b
assize 1–594a
bailli 2–53a-b
biographies 2–236b, 240a
Boniface of Montferrat 2–323a
Burgundy, Duchy of 2–428a
castles 3–148b
Cathars 3–187b-188a, 189a
Children's Crusade 4–15a
Easter style calendar 3–20a
Eleanor of Aquitaine 4–420a
expulsion of Jews 4–563b-564a
Fifth Crusade 4–49b
John of England 1–367b
Norman-Angevin England 4–467a,b, 468a-469a
nutrition 1–96a
perfumers guild 2–147a
Richard I 4–18b
royal seal 3–254a
Summa de legibus 4–69a
Third Crusade 4–31b, 40a-b
Philip de Rouvre
Burgundy, County of 2–426a
PHILIP VI DE VALOIS 9–0
Aquitaine 1–368a
Brittany, Duchy 2–380a
Burgundy, Kingdom of 2–429b
Clement VI 3–439a
dauphin 4–108a
Dauphiné 4–109a
Durand 4–313b
Philipoctus of Caserta
ars subtilior 1–558b
Philip of Flanders, Count
Conte du Graal (Chrétien de Troyes) 3–308b
Philip I of France
Council of Clermont 3–449a
William the Conqueror 4–461b
Philip of Heinsberg, Archbishop 3–481a
Philip of Swabia
Boniface of Montferrat 4–43a
Cilicia 3–391a
election of 4–425a,b, 427b
Fourth Crusade 2–497a
Philippa of Hainault, Queen 4–398b
Jehan Froissart 3–333a
Philippe de Beaumanoir
See Beaumanoir, Philippe de
Philippe de Comines
See Comines (Commynes), Philippe de
PHILIPPE DE GREVE 9–0
PHILIPPE DE HARVENGT 9–0
Philippe de Mézières
astrology 1–608b
PHILIPPE DE NOVARE 9–0; 4–73a
Assizes of Jerusalem 1–598b-599a
chronicles 3–332b
PHILIPPE DE THAON 9–0
PHILIPPE DE VITRY 9–0; 1–542b, 545b
ars nova 1–548a,b, 549a
PHILIPPE MOUSKET 9–0
Philippines
Christianization 4–21a
PHILIPPOPOLIS 9–0; 2–119b, 409a, 410a, 411b, 412b
Philipp von Seldeneck
firearms 4–579a
Philip III the Bold
Adenet le Roi 1–55a
Broederlam, Melchior 2–383a
Burgundy, County of 2–426a
Burgundy, Duchy 2–428a
Burgundy, Duchy of 2–427a
chamberlain office 3–242b
Champagne, rule 3–249b
chronicles 3–165b, 331b
Crown of Aragon 1–414a
Egidius 4–400a
invasion of Aragon 1–190b
mausoleum 4–186a
political crusades 4–61a-b
Philip the Bold of Burgundy
Bible illumination 3–478a
Philip the Chancellor of Paris
conductus 3–532a
Philip I the Fair of Spain
marriage 2–9a
Philip the Good
arts 4–566a
Aubert 1–642b
Burgundy, Duchy of 2–427a
Cent nouvelles nouvelles 3–235a
Treaty of Troyes 3–271a
Philip V the Tall
Ethiopia 1–32b
PHILLIP IV THE FAIR 9–0
archives 1–447a
Argun 1–453a
Augustinus Triumphus 2–1b
Ausculta fili 2–3b
Beaumanoir 2–144a
Boniface VIII 2–324a; 3–515a
Bruges 2–387a-b
Burgundy, County of 2–426a
Burgundy, Kingdom of 2–429b
Celestine foundations 3–214b
Champagne, rule 3–249b
châtelet 3–279a
Clement V 3–438b
clericis laicos 3–447b, 448a
dauphin 4–108a
degradation of clerics 4–133b
Disputatio inter clericum et militem 4–218a
Donation of 4–259a
Duns Scotus 4–308b
ecclesiology 4–376a,b
expulsion of Jews 4–564a
Knights Templars 3–304b
marriage 4–593a
political crusades 4–61b
portable clock 3–462a
royal confessor 3–535a
tutor 4–400a
vidame of Amiens 1–59b
Western councils 3–643b-644b
Philobiblon
See Bury, Richard de
Philocalian Calendar (354)
Christmas 3–317b
Philo Judaeus
angel/angelology 1–250b
Armenian Hellenizing School 1–505b
biblical exegesis 2–223b
church father 3–334b
Philokalia (Basil the Great) 2–120b
Philology
Arabic literature 1–379a
Philomelion
Alexios I 1–158b
Philomena (John Peckham) 1–255a
Philomena, Peter
astronomical calendar 1–612a
Philoponus, John 1–457b-458a
education 3–556b
iconoclasm 2–488b, 489a
Philosopher's stone (*lapis philosophicus*) 1–134b, 140a, 141b
Philosophia (Philip Elephant) 1–138a
"Philosophical School" (Constantinople) 1–392a
Philosophy
alchemy 1–139b-140a
PHILOSOPHY AND THEOLOGY, BYZANTINE 9–0; 2–466a-468a
Apollinarius 1–348a
Armenian Hellenizing School 1–505a
Christology 3–319b
Greek 3–335b
PHILOSOPHY AND THEOLOGY, ISLAMIC 9–0
angel/angelology 1–250b
Arabic prose literature 1–379b
Arabic translations 1–377b
Aristotelianism 1–458a-459b
Ash'arī, al- 1–582b-585b
PHILOSOPHY AND THEOLOGY, JEWISH: ISLAMIC WORLD 9–0
Aristotelianism 1–459b-460a
Dāwūd ibn Marwān al-Muqammiṣ 4–116a
PHILOSOPHY AND THEOLOGY, JEWISH: NORTHERN EUROPE 9–0
Apocalyptic literature and movement 1–344b
PHILOSOPHY AND THEOLOGY, WESTERN EUROPEAN: TO EARLY TWELFTH CENTURY 9–0
Anselm of Canterbury 1–314b, 316a
Anselm of Laon 1–315b, 316a
Augustine 1–646b
Bernard of Clairvaux 2–190b
Boethius 2–292a-b
Bruno of Segni 2–392a

Christology 3–319b-322a
PHILOSOPHY AND THEOLOGY, WESTERN EUROPEAN: TWELFTH CENTURY TO AQUINAS 9–0
Alan of Lille 1–119a
Albertus Magnus 1–127a-b
Alexander of Hales 1–148a
Anegenge 1–246b
Anselm of Canterbury 1–314b, 315a
Anthony of Padua 1–321a
Aquinas 1–353b, 362a-363a
Aristotelianism 1–460b-465b
Bacon 2–35a
Bernard of Clairvaux 2–190b
Bernard Silvester 2–194b
Cavalcanti 3–196a
Christology 3–322b-324a
Duns Scotus 4–308b
essence and exitence 4–510a
PHILOSOPHY AND THEOLOGY, WESTERN EUROPEAN: LATE MEDIEVAL 9–0
Antoninus, Saint 1–342b
Biel 2–233b
Bradwardine, Thomas 2–358a-b
Buridan, Jean 2–430a
Burley, Walter 2–432b
Christology 3–324a
PHILOSOPHY AND THEOLOGY, WESTERN EUROPEAN: TERMINOLOGY 9–0
angel 1–247b
disciplines 2–241a-242a
PHILOSTORGIOS 9–0
PHILOTHEOS 9–0
Kletorologion 2–456a; 4–447a
PHILOTHEOS KOKKINOS, PATRIARCH 9–0
Council of 1368 3–632b
patriarchate 2–462a
Philoxenos cistern
See Binbirdirek
Phlebotomy 1–604b; 2–99a
Phoenician alphabet 1–204a
Phoenix 2–206b
Phoenix, The 1–280b
rhyme patterns 1–277a
PHOKAS 9–0
exarchos 4–529b
Phokas, Nikephoros
Crete expedition 3–678b
Phonetics
Catalan language 3–159b-160a
Phonology
See Celtic languages
PHOTIAN COUNCIL (870) **9–0**
Amorians 1–236a
Basil I the Macedonian 2–117b
Photian schism
See Schism, Photian
PHOTIOS 9–0
Arabic numerals 1–391b, 392a
Armenian church 1–500a
Ašot I Mec 1–588a
Basil I the Macedonian 2–117b
Bulgaria 2–402a
canon law 2–468a
Constantinople 3–556a
councils 3–631b-632a, 633a
Cyril and Methodios, Saints 2–299a; 4–73b, 74a
education 3–556b
encyclopedias and dictionaries 4–446b
Epanagoge 4–493a
Filioque 2–214b, 465a
letters 2–520a
Magnaura Palace university 2–106a
patriarchate 2–462a
Slavs 2–489a
Phrygia
Anatolikon theme 1–242a
Turkish invasion 2–493a
Phrygian cap 3–623b
Phrygium
papal coronation 3–603b
Phundagiagitae 2–295b
Physicians
barbers, barber-surgeons 2–97a
university-trained 2–100a-b
PHYSICS 9–0
Albert of Saxony 1–125b
Buridan, Jean 2–430b-431b
Burley, Walter 2–433a
study of 2–241b
Physics (Aristotle)
Aquinas commentaries 1–356a, 357a
Physika kai mystika (Democritus) 1–135b
Physiologus
See Ebo of Rheims
Physiologus (bestiary) 2–203b-204a, 205a,b-206a, 243a,b; 4–369a-b
Physiologus (Josephus) 1–152b
Piacenza
Alexander V 1–147b
merchants 4–557b
Piacenza, Councils 3–635a, 636b
PIAST DYNASTY 9–0
land tenure 1–102a
PICARD LANGUAGE 9–0
Amadas et Ydoine 1–227a
PICARD LITERATURE 9–0
Arthurian literature 1–569a
Picards
Bohemian Brethren 2–306a
Picardy
Black Death 2–261a
Enguerrand VII of Coucy 4–490b
Piccinino 1–529b
Pico
Flemings 4–559b
Henry the Navigator 2–30a
Pico della Mirandola
cabala 3–3b
Christian Hebraists 3–314a
PICTISH ART 9–0
Pictor, Hugh
book illumination 1–258a
Pictor, Petrus
poems 1–318b
PICTS 9–0
Áedán 1–60a
Anglo-Saxon origins and migration 1–288b, 289b
Dál Riata 4–78a,b
Latin alphabet 1–212b
threat to Britain 2–96a
Vortigern fighting against 2–2b
See Also Celtic church
Pidal, Ramon Menendez 3–386a
Piedmont
grain crops 1–86a,b
Pier Innocenzo da Faerno of Milan 1–529b
PIERO DELLA VINEA 9–0
PIERO DI GIOVANNI TEDESCO 9–0
Pierre III, Archbishop
Bordeaux 2–328b
PIERRE CARDENA 9–0
Pierre de Bauffremont
Burgundy, Duchy of 2–428a
Pierre de Belleperche 3–397b
Pierre de Chalon
benefices 2–179b
PIERRE DE FONTAINES, CONSEIL 9–0
PIERRE DE LA CROIX 9–0
PIERRE DE MONTREUIL 9–0
Pierre de Saint Cloud 2–140b
See Roman de Renart
PIERRE DESCHAMPS 9–0
PIERRE DUBOIS 9–0
Pierrefonds, Château de 3–151b
entrance 3–148a
Pierre II Legros 4–371b
Pierre Olivi
See Peter John Olivi
Piers
See Also Construction: Engineering
Piers Plowman (William Langland) 1–186a, 319b
See Also Langland, William
PIETÀ 9–0
deposition from the Cross 4–157a
Pietro, Maestro 2–99a
PIETRO DA RIMINI 9–0
Pietro d'Assisi 2–115a
Pietro Oderisi
See Oderisi, Pietro
Pietro Piccolo da Monteforte
Boccaccio 2–278a
Pietro Spagnuolo
See Berruguete, Pedro
Pieusse
Cathar council 3–189b
Pig
Anglo-Saxon England 1–302a
food animal 1–299a
Pignon, Laurens
Durand 4–313b
Pike 3–204b
See Also Lance
P'ilartos Varažnuni 1–484b
Cilicia 2–493b
PILASTER 9–0
Bulgarian art and architecture 2–417a
PILASTER STRIPS 9–0
Pilate
Seinte Resureccion 1–270a
Pileus cornutus 3–620b, 621b
PILGRAM, ANTON 9–0
PILGRIMAGE, CELTIC 9–0
spirituality 3–231b
PILGRIMAGE, ISLAMIC 9–0
Ba?t19tūṭa, Ibn 2–130a
PILGRIMAGE, JEWISH 9–0
Pilgrimage church 2–124b; 3–379b, 382
Pilgrimage of Human Life (Guillaume de Deguileville) 1–185b
Pilgrimage of Jesus Christ (Guillaume de Deguileville) 1–185b
Pilgrimage of the Soul (Deguileville) 1–185b
PILGRIMAGES, RUSSIAN 9–0
PILGRIMAGES, WESTERN EUROPE 9–0; 3–356a
Burgundy, County of 2–426b
Canterbury 3–83a, 84a
Canterbury Tales 3–290b-296a
catacombs 3–154b
exploration 4–553a,b
Santiago de Compostela 1–630b
Pilgrim of Bordeaux
Itinerarium Burdigalense 1–332a
Pilgrim's Castle
crusader art and architecture 4–25b
PILGRIM'S GUIDE 9–0
Pilgrim's Progress (John Bunyan) 1–185b
P'ilon Tirakac'i 1–506a
Piloti, Emmanuel 1–154b
Pimalniya 3–619a
Pinakes (Callimachus) 1–204b
Pinzón, Martin Alonso
Colulbes 4–560b

PIPE ROLLS 9–0
archives 1–446a
Exchequer 4–530b, 531b, 532a, 533b
Pipino, Giovanni
See Also Cola di Rienzo
Piracy
Admiralty, Court of 1–56a,b-57a
Crete 3–678b
Piramus, Denis
literature 1–261a
PIRMIN, SAINT 9–0
PISA 9–0
Andrea da Firenze 1–244a
angelus 1–252b
Black Death 2–259a
Byzantine Empire 2–494b, 496a
campanile 3–60b
commune 3–500a
Crown of Aragon 1–412a
exchange banks 2–73b
Genoa 4–59a
maritime law 3–569b
money markets 2–78b
slaves 2–269b
trade 4–557b
PISA, CATHEDRAL 9–0
Buscheto of Pisa 2–433b
Cimabue mosaic 3–396a
Leaning Tower 2–324b
Pisa, *conciliabulum* of (1511-1512) 3–367a
Pisa, University of
Bartolo da Sassoferrato 2–115a
surgery chair 2–100b
Pisa Camposanto
Antonio Veneziano 1–342b, 343a
Pisa, Council of (1135) 3–636b, 637a
Pisa, Council of (1409) 1–147b; 3–646a-647a; 4–377a
PISANELLO, ANTONIO 9–0
sketchbook 4–292a
PISANO, ANDREA 9–0
Pisano, Giovanni 2–325a; 4–498a-b
Pisano, Nicola 2–325b
Arnolfo di Cambio 1–541a
Pisan style calendar 3–20a
PISHTAQ 9–0
Pisidia
Anatolikon theme 1–242a
civil government 1–240a
Pistoia
Guelphs factionalism 4–97b, 98a-99b
Pistoia, Cino da 4–96b
Pistoia Cathedral
Brunelleschi, Filippo 2–388a
Pitres, Edict of (864) 4–512a
Pit saws 3–145b
Pitsunda
See Bitshvinta
Pius II, Pope
abbreviators 1–14a
Carthusians 3–119b
church reform 3–367b
conciliar movement 3–366b
conciliar theory 3–518b, 519a
councils 3–654b, 655a
crusade propaganda 4–21a
crusades of later middle ages 4–56b
Pius V, Pope
abbreviators 2–14a
Breviary 2–373a
doctors of the church 4–234a
Roman missal (1570) 1–353a
Pius XI, Pope
Albertus Magnus 1–129a
Carthusians 3–119b
Pius XII, Pope
Ad Deum 1–129a
Piyyut
See Hebrew Poetry
Placebo 4–117b
PLACENTINUS 9–0
corpus iuris civilis 3–609b
Place value
See Arabic numerals
Placitum Generale 3–111b
PLACITUS 9–0
Plagiarism
Arabic poetry 1–403a
PLAGUES, EUROPEAN 9–0
Anonimalle chronicle 1–265b
Black Death 2–257a
Circassians 3–400a
PLAGUES IN THE ISLAMIC WORLD 9–0
Alexandria 1–154b
Plainchant/Plainsong
Anonymous IV treatise 1–309b
centonization 3–235b
contrafactum 3–575b
Dominicans 4–240a
Gregorian Chant 5–661a
Plain of Vic 1–419b
PLAINSONG, EASTERN EUROPEAN 9–0
PLAINSONG, SOURCES OF 9–0
Plainte
Anglo-Norman lyric poetry 1–269a
Plaint of Nature (Alan of Lille) 1–183a
Planctu naturae, De (Alan of Lille) 1–119a
***PLANCTUS* 9–0**; 3–100a,b
¿Ay, Iherusalem! 2–18a
Planetary Hypotheses (Ptolemy) 1–261a, 612b, 620b
Planetary theory
See Astrology/Astronomy
Planh
Cercamon 3–240b
Planisphaerium (Ptolemy) 1–611b
PLANO CARPINI, JOHN OF 9–0
PLANTAGENETS 9–0
Angevins 1–253a
Aquitaine 1–368a-369a
Crown of Aragon 1–408b-409b
Henry II 4–462b
Plantis, De (Albertus Magnus) 1–128a
Plants
climatology 3–451a
study of 2–241a, 244b-246a
Plantus de obitu Karoli 2–18b
Planudean Anthologies 2–524a
Planudes, Maximus 1–391b, 392a
classical literary studies 3–431b
Planus
accentual pattern 4–67a
Planys del cavaller Mataró 3–173b
PLASHCHANITSA 9–0
PLATERSEQUE STYLE 9–0
PLATO IN THE MIDDLE AGES 9–0
Adelard of Bath 1–54a
allegorical interpretation tradition 1–180b-181b, 183a, 185b
Aquinas 1–357b-358b
Arabic translations 1–377b
Armenian Hellenizing School 1–505b
astrology 1–604b
Bernard of Chartres 2–190a
Bernard Silvester 2–195a
biology studies 2–241b, 242a
Byzantine theology 2–467b
church father 3–334b
dialectic 4–168a
dualism 4–298a
"two cities" image 1–654b
Platonic Academy of Athens 1–606a
Plato of Tivoli
Abraham bar Ḥiyya 1–22a
Archimedes 1–435a
Tetrabiblos 1–606b
PLATYTERA 9–0
PLAYING CARDS, MASTER OF THE 9–0
engraving 4–488b, 489b
***PLAY OF DANIEL* 9–0**; 3–532a
PLAY OF HEROD 9–0
Plea rolls
court of common pleas 3–492a
Plegmund, Archbishop 1–165a,b
***PLEIER, DER* 9–0**
***PLENA POTESTAS* 9–0**; 4–208b
Plenipotentiary
See Procurator
***PLENITUDO POTESTATIS* 9–0**
Pope Leo I 3–342a
Plethon, Gemisthos
classical literary studies 3–432a
PLEURANT 9–0
PLEYDENWORFF, HANS 9–0
PLICA 9–0
Pliny
alphabet 1–218a
astrology 1–605a
astronomy 1–610b
botany 2–345a
Natural History 1–335b; 4–447b
plant studies 2–245a
plow design 1–90a
Pliska 2–399b, 401a,b
art and architecture 2–414b
basilica 2–329a
Pliva 4–4a
Plotinus
Aristotle 1–457b
church father 3–334b
Plough
See Plow
Plovdiv
art and architecture 2–417b
See Also Philippopolis
Plovum
See Plow
Plow 1–90a-91b
ard 1–104a
heavy 1–90a-91b, 97a,b-98a, 100b
light 1–97b, 98b, 100b
Roman 1–80a
sole-ard type 1–77a
Plowman
See Class Structure, Western (1000-1300)
Plowman from Bohemia, The
See Ackermann aus Böhmen, der
Plug
See Plow
Plurality of forms 2–36b-37a
Augustinism 1–660b
Pneumatomachians 2–121a,b
Pneumonia
demography 4–142b
Pneumonic plague
demography 4–142b
Poblet monastery 1–408b, 420a; 3–165b
POCKETBOOKS 9–0
Pocquet, Antoine 3–215a
PODESTÀ 9–0
Podrina 2–335a
Podsechnoe zemledelie
See Slash and burn tillage systems
Podseka
See Slash and burn tillage systems
Poema de Alfonso XI 1–162b
Poema de Fernán González 1–162b; 4–63b

Poema del Salado (Afonso Giraldes) 1–163a
Poema de Yūsuf 1–176a
Poème moral 1–264a
Poetic Edda 1–226b; 4–385a-b, 388a
Poetria nova (Geoffrey of Vinsauf) 1–255a, 452b
Poetry
  alchemical 1–138b-139a
  Alvíssmál 1–226b
  Angilbert, Saint 1–254a
  Anglo-Saxon 1–276b-281a
  Anthologia latina 1–317a, 318b
  antifeminism 1–324b
  Arabic language 1–377a
  Armenian 1–511b-512a
  Byzantine 2–523a,b-525a
  Carolingian 3–99b
  Catalan 3–170a-172a
  centonization 3–235b
  chanson 3–254b
  Charles of Orléans 3–273a
  Chrétien de Troyes 3–308b
  Cid 3–386b-389a
  Cino da Pistoia 3–397b
  florilegia 1–318a
  Libro de Apolonio 1–348b
Poetry, Arabic 1–398a-403b
POETRY, LITURGICAL 9–0
  Anglo-Latin 1–254b
  Byzantine 2–505b, 510a-511b, 524a-b
Poetry, lyric
  Anglo-Norman literature 1–269a,b
Poetry, pre-Islamic 1–398b-400a
Poetry, secular
  Byzantine 2–506a-510a
Poets of Princes 4–430b
Pogesania
  Poles and Pomeranians 2–65a, 66a
Poggeto, Bertrando del, Cardinal 4–103a
POGOST 9–0
Poillevillain, Nicholas
  See Nicholas of Clamanges
Pointed arch 1–423b-425a
Poitevins
  Canary Island 3–62a-b
Poitiers
  Eleanor of Aquitaine 4–419b
Poitiers, Council of (1100) 4–36a
POITIERS, BATTLE OF (732) **9–0**
  cavalry 3–201a
Poitiers, Battle of (1356)
  bow and arrow/crossbow 2–353b
  cavalry 3–205b
  Edward III 4–398a
  Edward the Black Prince 4–399a
  Estates General 4–109b
P'ok'r Cop'k'
  See Lesser Sophenē
P'ok'r Mher 4–112b, 113a
POKROV 9–0
POLAND 9–0
  agriculture 1–98a
  Balts, border warfare 2–64a
  Black Death 2–264a
  Bohemian Brethren 2–305b
  Byzantine church 2–469b
  Cisiojanus 3–21b
  Cistercian Order 3–404a
  Culm 2–66a,b
  dictamen 4–176a
  dwarf cattle 1–293b
  fairs 4–588a
  food animals 1–299b
  German migrants 1–97b-98a
  Innocent III, Pope 3–353b
  Jews 1–586a; 2–263b
  monasteries 2–172a
  Mongol invasions 2–131b
  Polish-Lithuanian state 2–67a
  serfdom 1–102a
  Teutonic Knights 3–306a
Poland-Lithuania
  Angevin interests 1–253b
Pole, Michael de la 3–426b
Polemics
  Bacon 2–40b
POLEMICS, CHRISTIAN-JEWISH 10–0
  Cathars 3–182a, 184b
POLEMICS, ISLAMIC-JEWISH 10–0
POLEMIUS SILVIUS 10–0
Policraticus (John of Salisbury) 1–324a, 607a; 4–159b, 471b
***POLISTORIE* 10–0**; 1–265b
Political songs
  Anglo-Norman 1–269b, 271a
POLITICAL THEORY, BYZANTINE 10–0
  Epanagoge 4–493a
POLITICAL THEORY, ISLAMIC 10–0
POLITICAL THEORY, WESTERN EUROPEAN: TO 1100 10–0
  deposition of rulers 4–157b-159b
  Disputatio inter clericum et militem 4–218a
POLITICAL THEORY, WESTERN EUROPEAN: 1100-1485 10–0
  defensor pacis 4–132a
  deposition of rulers 4–159b-160b
  Engelbert of Admont 4–451b
Political verse
  Byzantine 2–521a-b, 524b
Politics (Aristotle)
  Aquinas 1–357a
Poliziano, Angelo
  planetarium 3–463b
Polizze 2–75a
Pollaiuolo, Antonio
  engraving 4–489a
Pollen studies 3–451b, 453b, 454a
POLL-TAX, ENGLISH 10–0
POLL-TAX, ISLAMIC 10–0
Połos Tarawnec'i
  Armenian literature 1–512a
Polotsk
  Varangians 4–555a
Polovetsians
  See Cumans
  See Russian Nomads, Invasions of
Polovtzi
  transhumance 1–79a
Polvoraria, Battle of (878) 1–627a
POLYCANDELON 10–0
Polycarp
  postapostolic writing 3–334b
Polychrome ceramics 3–237b, 238a
Polychronicon (Higden) 2–222a
  historical translation 3–325a
Polyculture
  Byzantium 1–77b
  Italy 1–86b-87b
  Mediterranean region 1–81a
  Portugal 1–85a
Polydore Vergil
  Arthurian literature 1–565b
Polygamy
  Islamic family 4–598b
Polyglot Bible 2–215b
Polygyny
  Jewish family 4–606b
  Western European 4–609a
Polyphonic songs
  chansonnier 3–256a-b
Polyphony
  Anonymous IV treatise 1–309b
  conductus 3–531b
  contrafactum 3–575b
  copula 3–596a
  diaphonia 4–172a
Polypticum (Atto of Vercelli) 1–641b
POLYPTYCH 10–0
  demography 4–137b
  ecclesiastical estates 4–511b
Polystaurion 3–615b, 616a
Polytheism
  pre-Islamic Arabia 1–370b
Pomander 3–625a
Pomerania
  Balts, border warfare 2–64a
  Brandenburg 2–360b
Pomeranians
  Pogesania settlement 2–66a
Pomeshchiki 1–101b-102a
Pomestie 1–101b-102a
Pommeraie, La, abbey 1–18a
Ponet, John, Bishop of Winchester
  conciliar theory 3–521b
Pons of Cluny 3–469a
Pons of Provence
  dictamen 4–175a
Ponthus et la belle Sidoyne (Geoffrey de la Tour Landry) 4–429a
  See Also Pontus und Sidonia
Pontic Mountains 1–470b
PONTIFICALS 10–0
  Bangor rite 2–72a
  baptismal rites 2–83a
  consecration of cemeteries 3–540b
  dedication of churches 4–131a
  Durand, Guillaume 4–314b-315a
Pontigny
  Cistercian abbey 3–403b
PONTUS 10–0
  Andronikos I Komnenos 1–244a
  Antiochene rite 1–326b
  Byzantine church 2–460b
  Byzantine Empire 2–493a,b
  civil government 1–240a
  Crusade of 1101 4–36b
Pontus und Sidonia 4–429a-b
Poor Clares
  Barcelona 2–104a
Poor Knights of Christ
  chivalry 3–304a-b
Poor Ladies of Saint Clare 2–317a
POPE 10–0
  antipopes 1–330a
  apostolic succession 1–350a
  beatification 2–142b
  chancery 3–252b
  See Also Clergy
POPPEHOWE, THOMAS 10–0
Poppo, Archbishop
  Cambridge Songs 3–57b
Poppo of Stavelot, Saint 1–47b
Population
  Ani in Širak 1–291a
  demography 4–136a
  Denmark 4–149b
  northern European agriculture 1–94a,b
Porcelain, Chinese 3–240a
Porcelos, Diego Rodríguez
  Castile 3–128a
Porcupine, French Order of 3–307a
Porete, Marguerite 2–160b
Pork
  European cookery 3–581b
Pork prohibitions 1–300b
Porphyrogenitos, Constantine
  Croatia 4–4a,b, 5a
PORPHYROGENITUS 10–0

Porphyry
Apollinarius 1–348a
Aquinas 1–357b, 358a
Aristotle 1–457b
Armenian Hellenizing School 1–505b
Boethius 2–292a
Porphyry rock
Coptic art 3–587b
Porpoise
European cookery 3–581b
Porrée, Gilbert de la 1–52a
Portable clocks 3–462a, 463b
Porta della Carta of the Doge's Palace 2–419b
PORTCULLIS 10–0; 3–148a, 149b
Porte-Dieu 1–223b
Porter 3–441a, 442a
Portinari, Beatrice
See Beatrice
Portois 2–424a
Porto Santo
exploration 4–559a
Portrait, donor
See Donor portrait
Portrait of a Man in a Red Turban (Jan van Eyck) 4–567b
PORTUGAL 10–0
agricultural tools 1–80a
agriculture and nutrition 1–84b-85a
Anthony of Padua, Saint 1–320b
archives 1–448b
Azores 2–29b
Black Death 2–263b-264a
Canary Islands and Béthencourt 3–61b; 4–559a
commerce 4–557b-558a,b
concordat (1289) 3–525b
cortes 3–610b, 611b-612a
Crown of Aragon 1–410a
dictamen 4–175b
expulsion of Jews 4–564b
independence 3–130a
Innocent III, Pope 3–353b
Order of Aviz 2–17b
orders of chivalry 3–306b
slaves 2–268b, 269b-270a
PORTUGUESE LANGUAGE 10–0
Catalan 3–160a-b
PORTUGUESE LITERATURE 10–0
Arthurian literature 1–573a, 575b-576b
assonance 1–600b
cantigas de amor, amigo, and escarnio 3–86b
poetry 4–189b-190a
PORTULAN CHART 10–0
Posidonius
astrological determinism 1–604b, 605a
Posidonius of Apamea
bards 2–105b
Possessory assizes
See Petty Assizes, English
Possidius, Bishop
Augustine of Hippo 1–648b, 649b, 660b
Augustinian friars 1–659b
POSTAL AND INTELLIGENCE SERVICES, BYZANTINE 10–0
POSTAL AND INTELLIGENCE SERVICES, ISLAMIC 10–0
Postbaptism ceremonies 2–83b, 84a
Postburial rites 4–121a
Posterior Analytics (Aristotle)
Aquinas 1–357a
POSTGLOSSATORS 10–0
Potentes
See Dunatoi
Potentiae
allegory 1–186a
Potentiores
See Dunatoi
Potestas 2–69a
Potestate regia et papali, De (John of Paris) 4–376a
Potter, Dirc 4–320a
POTTERY 10–0
art trade 1–561b
ceramics, European 3–236a
ceramics, Islamic 3–238a
Pou, Pere 3–171a
Poulaines (shoes) 3–623a, 625b
POUND, MONEY 10–0
POUND, WEIGHT 10–0
Pourpoint 3–623a, 625b
Po Valley
agriculture 1–90a
Lombard invasion 2–95b
Poverty
apostolic 3–363b
Power
See Class structure, Western
Power of Women, Master of the 4–488a
Powys 4–69b
Prachatitz, Peter von
See Peter von Prachtatitz
Practica seu arte tripudii vulgare opusculum, De (Guglielmo Ebreo) 4–89a
Praecepta dictaminum (Adalbert of Samaria) 4–174a
Praeceptum (Augustine) 1–658a
Praeceptum longius (Augustine) 1–658a
Praeconium paschale 4–367a
PRAEMUNIRE 10–0
Praetextatus 1–460b
Praetoria 3–152b
PRAETORIAN PREFECT 10–0
Byzantine bureaucracy 2–472a-b, 484b, 487b
Praevalitana 4–79b
PRAGMATIC SANCTION OF BOURGES (1438) **10–0**; 3–526a
annate payments 1–305a
Charles VII of France 3–271b
conciliar movement 3–367a
ecclesiology 4–378a
Western council 3–654a
Prague
bishopric 2–304a
Cosmas 3–164a
development 2–300b, 302b-303b
fairs 4–587b
Hus 3–649b-650a
midday angelus 1–252b
university 2–312b
Praises of the Lord (Dracontius) 4–520b
Prayers
Alexandrian rite 1–156a
benedictions 2–177a
canonical hours 3–66a
Celtic spirituality 3–231a
charms, old High German 3–274a
creeds, liturgical use 3–675a
obligations of clergy 3–444b
Old English poetry 1–281a
Prayers, Jewish
apostolic constitutions 1–350a
Preachers
education of laity 3–359a
Preachers, Order of
See Dominicans
PREACHING AND SERMONS, ISLAMIC 10–0
PREACHING AND SERMONS, JEWISH 10–0
PREACHING AND SERMONS, WESTERN EUROPEAN 10–0
ars praedicandi 1–555b
Bernard of Clairvaux 2–190b
Berthold von Regensburg 2–199b
crusade propaganda 4–20b
Dominicans 4–239b, 248b-252a
drama 4–285b-287a
exempla 4–551a
Prebaptism ceremonies 2–83b
Prebendaries
hierarchy of clergy 3–444b
Precedent, law of 4–480a-b
PRECENTOR 10–0; 3–444b
cantor 3–87b
Precession
calendars 3–22b-23a
theory 1–614b-615a
Precipitation data 3–452b
***PREDELLA* 10–0**; 1–222b
Predestination
Augustine 1–653b
Predicatione sanctae crucis, De (Romans) 4–20b
Preemption rights
Byzantine family 4–595a
Preface of Gildas on Penance
Celtic church 3–229b
Preljubovič, Thomas 4–500a
PREMONSTRATENSIAN RITE 10–0
PREMONSTRATENSIANS 10–0
bastides 2–128b
beguines 2–158a
Marian office 2–274a
Norbert of Xanten 3–354b
PŘEMYSLID DYNASTY 10–0
Bohemia 2–299b-300b
land tenure 1–102a
wealth 2–7a
Přemysl I of Bohemia
church 2–304a
Přemysl Ottokar I
reign 2–300a
Přemysl Ottokar II
reign 2–300a
PRENTYS, THOMAS 10–0
PREPENDULIA 10–0
PREROGATIVE 10–0
PRE-ROMANESQUE ARCHITECTURE 10–0
Aachen palace chapel 1–2b-3b
PRE-ROMANESQUE ART 10–0
bronze and brass 2–384a
Bulgarian art and architecture 2–417a
Demetrios Presbyter 4–136a
Ebo of Rheims 4–368b
Egbert of Trier 4–399b
Presbytera
celibacy laws 3–216a
***PRESBYTERIUM* 10–0**
Presbyteroi
early church 3–338b
Presbyters 3–372b, 441a
Presbytery 1–443a
PRESENTATION, RIGHT OF 10–0
PRESENTATION IN THE TEMPLE 10–0
Presentment
Henry II 4–470b
Presiam
Boris 2–329a, 402a
Preslav
art and architecture 2–414b
Boris 2–329b, 403b, 406a
Omurtag 2–401b
Peter and Asen 2–407b, 408a
Symeon 2–404a,b
Preslav, Council of (893) 2–329b, 404a

Presles, Raoul de 3–167a
Prespa
Samuil 2–406b
Pressura
Asturias-León 1–629b
Pressuris ecclesiasticis, De (Atto of Vercelli) 1–641a
PRESTER JOHN 10–0
commerce 4–558b
Portugal 4–562a,b
Prestige
See Class structure, Western
Pretiosa margarita novella (Petrus Bonus) 1–138a
Prévôt
See Provost
Pribina
Croatia 4–5a
Moravia 2–299a
PRICKINGS 10–0
Pride of Life 4–287a
PRIE-DIEU 10–0
Priest 3–440a-445b
chaplain 3–264a
early Church 3–338b
"Priester Johannes"
Ambraser Heldenbuch 1–230a
See Also Clergy
Prijezda
Bosnia 2–336a
PRIMARY CHRONICLE RUSSIAN 10–0
Primary History of Armenia 2–47b
Primas
See Hugh (Primas) of Orléans
Primasius 2–11a
Primat 2–236b
clerical chronicles 3–327b
French chronicles 3–331b
Primate, office of 4–126a,b
Prime
Divine Office 4–221b, 227, 229a
Primera crónica general 3–71b
Primicerius
hierarchy of clergy 3–444b
Primicerius notariorum
chancery 3–257a
Primissaries 3–444b
Primitiua ecclesia et synodo Nicena, De
False Decretals 4–124b-125a
PRIMITIVE CHURCH, CONCEPT OF 10–0
Primitive Norse language
Eddic poetry 4–389a
Primogeniture 2–332a; 4–475b
appanages 1–351a
Armenia 1–488b
Basque rule 2–126b
Primorje 4–4a
PRINCE 10–0
boyar 2–354b
Prince of Princes
See Archon ton Archonton
Prince of Wales 4–108a
Princess
courtesy books 3–664b
Principe
exploration 4–561b
Principia (Peter of Candia) 1–147b
Principles of philology (Muḥammad ibn ʿAbd Allāh al-Iskāfī) 4–443a
Principles of philology
See Mabādi' al-lugha
PRINTING, ORIGINS OF 10–0
alphabetical works 1–207a
astrology texts 1–608b-609a
block book 2–274a
Bois Protat 2–309b
Carthusian centers 3–119a-b
Caxton 3–210a
engraving 4–487b
PRINTS AND PRINTMAKING 10–0
block book 2–274a
Bois Protat 2–309b
burin 2–432a
Prior and Prioress
See Clergy
Pripet Marshes
West Slav boundary 1–96b
PRISCIAN 10–0
Auraicept na nÉces 2–2a
classical literary studies 3–432a
grammar 2–107b
Priscilla catacombs
angel 1–248a
PRISCILLIAN 10–0
Airdena Brátha 1–111a
astrological beliefs 1–606a
dualism 4–297b
Prise de Defur 1–151a
Prise d'Orange 3–257a
Prison
Châtelet 3–278a
Private devotions
Celtic spirituality 3–231a
Privilegio de los Votos 2–187a
Privilegium maius (Rudolf IV Habsburg) 2–8a
Privilegium minus 2–134b
Prizren 4–347a
Problemata (Abelard) 1–17b
Problems of Nāfiʿ ibn al Azraq (ʿAbd Allāh ibn al-ʿAbbās) 4–442b
Proboslav, Prince
Brandenburg 2–360b
Probst
See Provost
Probus, Emperor 1–117a
Procés de la Senyora de Valor contra En Bertran Tudela (Francesc de la Via) 3–173b
Procés de les olives (Mossèn Bernat Fenollar) 3–171b
Procession of the Holy Spirit, The (Anselm of Canterbury) 1–313b, 314b
PROCESSIONS 10–0
Ascension, Feast of the 1–582a
conductus 3–531b
funerals 4–120b
Processus Belial (Jacobus Palladinus) 1–44a
***PROCHEIROS NOMOS* 10–0**
Basilics 2–125b
Epanagoge 4–493a
Prochoros
Aquinas 4–135b
Proclus
Aristotle 1–457b-458a
Armenian literature 1–507b
astrological beliefs 1–606a
Proconessus 4–331b
PROCOPIUS 10–0
Agathias 1–67b
architecture 4–338b
Bulgaria 2–399a
Procurator
ratification of acts 4–213b-214a
Western European diplomacy 4–203a-205b, 207b
Prodheiron
Basil I the Macedonian 2–117b
Profit calculation 1–40a,b
Profuturus of Braga
dedication of churches 4–130b
Prognosticum futuri saeculi (Saint Julian of Toledo) 1–264a
Programmatic Capitulary (802) 3–91b, 108b
Prohemio (Marques of Santillana) 3–171a
PROKHOR OF GORODETS 10–0
PROLATIO 10–0
Prolation
ars nova 1–549a, 550a
Prolegomena tēs philosophias 4–114a
Promotio per saltum
interstices of clergy 3–442b
PRONOIA 10–0
Bulgaria 2–407b
Proof of the Incarnation of God According to the Image of Man (Apollinarius) 1–348a
PROPAGANDA, WESTERN EUROPEAN 10–0
crusades 4–18b, 54b-55a, 56b
Propagation of force, theory of 2–38a
Property law
See Class structure, Western
Prophatius Judaeus
See Maʿhir Ibn Tibbon, Jacob ben
Prophecies of Merlin 1–265b
Prophecy
rabbinic concept 1–21b
PROPHECY, POLITICAL: MIDDLE ENGLISH 10–0
Prophecy of the Child, The 1–346b
Prophet, the
See Muḥammad
Prophets
Allah 1–178a
Prophilias
See Athis und Prophilias
Propositiones ad acuendos juvenes (Alcuin) 1–142b
***PROPRIETAS* 10–0**
Proprietatibus rerum, De (Anglicus) 2–205a; 3–168b; 4–448b
Prosa
See Sequence
Prosdocimus de Beldemandis 3–657b
Prose
Old English 1–281b-286b
Prose anthologies 1–318a
Prose Edda (Snorri Sturluson) 2–254a,b; 4–385b, 387a-b, 415a
PROSE LANCELOT 10–0
Prose Romance of Alexander 1–151a
Prosimetrum 1–642b
Proskunēsis
Christology 3–320b
***PROSKYNESIS* 10–0**
Charlemagne 3–110a
PROSKYNETARION 10–0
Proslogion (Anselm of Canterbury) 1–311b, 314a, 649b
PROSPER OF AQUITAINE 10–0; 3–214a
Cassian 1–653b; 3–122a
Prostitutes
cosmetics 2–147b
Protase, Saint
tomb 1–254b
Protat family
Bois Protat 2–309b
Protaton, Church of the 2–448a
Protestantism
Brethren of the Common Life 2–369a-b
Protestant Reformation
celibacy laws 3–217b
Protevangelium of James
Annuciation 1–307b
Protheselaus (Hue de Rotelande) 1–266b
PROTHESIS 10–0
apse 1–352a

Protocol
chancery documents 3–253a
Protocuropalates 4–66b
Protodeutera 3–631b
Protonotarius
See Chancery
PROTOSPATHARIOS 10–0
PROVENÇAL LANGUAGE 10–0
albas 1–123a
Castilian 3–142a
Catalan language 3–157b, 158a-159a
Catalan narrative in verse 3–173a
PROVENÇAL LITERATURE: TO 1200 10–0
Arnaut Daniel 1–539a
Basques, depiction of 2–126b
Canso 3–69b-70a
Catalan literature 3–164a-b, 170b
Cercamon 3–240a
chansons de femme 3–257a
chansons de malmariée 3–262b
courtly love 3–667b, 668a-b, 670a
débat 4–122a
Ermengaud 4–506b
lyric poetry 1–184a, 185a
PROVENÇAL LITERATURE: AFTER 1200 10–0
assonance 1–600b
PROVENCE 10–0
bastide 2–128a, 129b
Burgundy, Kingdom of 2–428b
canonical reform 3–355a
commune 3–497a
courtesy books 3–660b
Crown of Aragon 1–408b, 409b-410a, 412b
Dauphiné 4–108a
establishment 3–114a
field systems 1–85a-b
hearth lists 4–138a
Jewish exegesis 4–541a
mercenary troops 3–186b, 187a
Merovingians 3–104a
Proverbia trifaria 1–269b
PROVERBS AND SENTENTIAE 10–0
Old English poetry 1–281a
Proverbs of Seneca
alphabetization 1–204b
Proverbs of Solomon (Sanson de Nanteuil) 1–262b
PROVINCE, ECCLESIASTICAL 10–0
Byzantine Clergy 3–446a
Dominicans 4–244a-b
Latin church 3–372b
Provins
fairs 4–585b, 590b, 591a-592
PROVISIONS, ECCLESIASTICAL 10–0
Babylonian Captivity 2–33b
PROVISIONS OF OXFORD (1258) **10–0**
Baron's War 2–112a
Edward I 4–395b
French translation 1–260a
parliament 4–481a,b
Provisions of Westminster (1259)
Baron's War 2–112a
PROVOST 10–0
assize 1–595a
bailli 2–52b-53a
Burgundy, Duchy of 2–427b
castellan 3–124b
châtelet 3–278a
hierarchy of clergy 3–444b
Provveditori alla Sanità 2–100b
Próxita, Gilabert de 3–171a
PRUDDE, JOHN 10–0
PRUDENTIUS 10–0; 1–273b
allegory 1–180a, 181a-182a
church art 4–358b
church fathers 3–336a
Eulalia, Saint, hymn 4–521a
Latin epic 4–495b
pagan art 4–351a
Prusa
See Brusa
Prussia
Bohemian Brethren 2–305b
Christian conversion 2–66a-b
Cisiojanus 3–21b
Treaty of Christburg (1249) 2–66b
Prussians 2–61b, 67b
Prutenic Tables 1–160a
Psalm Against the Party of Donatus (Augustine) 1–649a
Psalmody
Celtic divine office 3–230b
Psalms
antiphon 1–328b
antiphonal 1–329b
Armenian rite 1–516b-517a
Psalms-collects
rite of Aquileia 1–352b
PSALM TONES 10–0
differentia 4–185a
Evovae 4–529a
PSALTER 10–0
Airbertach 1–110b
Anglo-Norman literature 1–262b
Arundel 1–580b
bas-de-page 2–117a
breviary 2–370b, 371a,b
collecting 1–336a
Divine Office 4–223b-224a
Old English 1–275a-277b
Old English exegesis 4–548b
Psalteri (Roìs de Corella) 3–167a
Psalter of Basil II 2–442a
Psalter of Cashel (Cormac) 3–602a
Psalter of Queen Melisende 2–447a
Psalter of Theodore 2–443a
Psalter of the Quatrains, The 1–347b
See Also Saltair na Rann
***PSALTIKON* 10–0**
Akathistos 1–114b
Asmatikon 1–586b
PSELLOS, MICHAEL 10–0
agriculture 1–78a
Anna Komnena 1–303b
Attaleiates 1–641b
biographical writing 2–240a
classical literary studies 3–431a
dialectic 4–170b
education in Constantinople 3–556b
Pset 4–4a
Pseudo-Alcuin
Christmas celebration 3–318a
Divine Office 4–223a
Pseudo-Apuleius
herbal 2–245a,b
Old English translation 1–286a
Pseudo-Bonaventure
ars praedicandi 1–557a
Pseudo-Callisthenes
Alexander romances 1–149b
Armenian literature 1–508b
Pseudo-Clement
apostolic constitutions 1–349b
Pseudo-Clementines 4–125a
Pseudo-Council of Pisa (1409) 1–342a
PSEUDO-DIONYSIUS THE AREOPAGITE 10–0
Albertus Magnus 1–127a,b
angel/angelology 1–249b, 250a
Aquinas 1–357b, 358a
Aristotle 1–458a
Armenian Hellenizing School 1–506a
Celestial Hierarchy 1–248a, 249b
Christology 3–321b, 322a
liturgy 2–468b
Pseudo-Egbert
penitential texts 1–286a
Pseudo-Germanus
Divine Office 4–222b
Pseudo-Ignatius
apostolic constitutions 1–349b
Pseudo-Isidore
False Decretals 3–374b
Pseudo-Jerome
Christian Hebraists 3–313b
PSEUDO KODINOS 10–0
Byzantine clergy 3–447a
Byzantine handbook 4–447a
Pseudo-Methodius
Antichrist doctrine 1–321b
PSEUDO-NICCOLÒ 10–0
Pseudo-Odo
Cistercian chant 3–402b
Pseudo-Remedius of Chur collection 4–125b
PSEUDO-TURPIN 10–0
Pseudo-Turpin Chronicle 1–260b
French translations 3–331b
Pskov
Boyar 2–354b
trade 1–101a
Psychomachia (Prudentius) 1–188a, 273b; 2–11a; 4–495b
allegory 1–180a, 181a-182a
See Also Virtues and Vices
PSYCHOPOMP 10–0
PTŁNI 10–0
Ptochoptodromos
See Theodore Prodromos
Ptolemaeus, Claudius
astrology manual 1–604b
PTOLEMAIC ASTRONOMY 10–0
acceptance of 1–614a
Alfonsine Tables 1–160a
Almagest 1–610a, 612a
astrolabe description 1–602b-603a
astrology 1–604b
Boethius 2–291b
Byzantine commentaries 1–613b
Canterbury 3–81a
Islamic astrology 1–617a
Islamic astronomy 1–620a-623a
mathematics condemnation 2–38b
objections to 1–614b
precession phenomenon 3–22b
PTOLEMY OF LUCCA 10–0
Public health
barbers, barber-surgeons 2–100b
Publilius Optatianus Porphyrius 1–218a
PUCELLE, JEAN 10–0
breviary 2–371a,b
Puebla de Montalbán 3–213b
Puerto de Santa Maria
commerce 4–558a
Puig de Cebolla 1–412a
Puits de Moïse 2–428b
Pulgar, Hernando del
See Spanish biographical literature
Pulpit
ambo 1–229a
Pulse 1–95a
Pumpkin dome 4–236a
PUNCTUATION 10–0
Punctuation poems
antifeminism 1–324b, 325a
Punic War, Second 2–126a
Puppet plays
chansons de geste 3–258a

Purgatorio (Dante) 3–417a; 4–94b, 95b, 97a, 98a, 99b, 102a-b, 103b
PURGATORY, ISLAMIC 10–0
PURGATORY, WESTERN CONCEPT OF 10–0
 Espurgatoire Saint Patrice 4–509b
Purim 3–27a
Purple
 dyes 4–327a-b
 liturgical color 3–484a
Purpura
 dyes 4–327a
Purvey, John
 Middle English exegesis 4–547b, 548a
Push to the East
 See Drang nach dem Osten
PÜTERICH VON REICHERTSHAUSEN, JAKOB III 10–0
Putul 1–142b, 143a
PUY 10–0; 1–48a
Puy, Raymond du
 Knights of Saint John of Jerusalem 3–303b
Pygmalion myth 1–185a
PYNSON, RICHARD 10–0
 Everyman 4–527b
Pyrame et Thisbé 3–277b
Pyramus River
 See Ceyhan River
Pyrenees
 Basques 2–126a
 Catalonia 3–174a
Pyrgi
 castrum 3–152b
Pyrrhus, Patriarch
 heresy 2–462a
Pythagoreans
 astrology 1–604a-b
Pyx 1–223b; 4–361b
Pyxides
 Coptic art 3–587a
PYXIS 10–0

Q

QA'A 10–0
Qabā' 3–616b, 618b, 619b, 620b
 See Kaaba
Qaba, Al-
 See Caucasus Mountains
Qabala 1–123b
Qābūs ibn Washmgīr
 Bīrūnī 2–248b
Qadarīya
 Umayyad caliphate 3–41a,b
QADI 10–0
Qadi (office)
 Damascus 4–84a
Qāḍī al-Quḍāt 3–44b, 48a
Qadi'l qudāt
 Alexandria 1–153b
Qādir, al-, King
 Cid 3–385a
Qāhira, Al- 3–13b
QAHIR BI'LLAH, AL- 10–0
Qahulga
 See Derbent
QA'IM, AL- 10–0
 medallion 1–6b
Qairawān, Great Mosque of 1–191b, 196b
Qaisariya
 See Caesarea
QA'ITBAY, AL-ASHRAF 10–0
Qalāmdan
 See Dawat
Qalandarī
 dervish 4–163a
***QALANSUWA* 10–0**; 3–619b, 620a
Qalansuwa ṭawīla 3–618a
Qal'at al-hamra 1–168a
Qal'at Banī Ḥammād 1–197b
Qal'at Sim'an
 monastery 4–333a-b
QALA'UN, AL-MANṢUR 10–0
 Circassians 3–398b
Qalā'ūn College
 construction 3–14b
Qalonimide dynasty 4–420b
Qalqashandī, al-
 Mamluk history 3–398a
 secretaries handbook 1–382a, 445b
Qamīṣ 3–616b
Qāmūs al-muḥīṭ, al- (al-Fīrūzābādī) 4–444a
Qanāt 1–104a
QĀNṢŪH AL GHAWRĪ 10–0
Qānūn, al- (Ibn Sīn13a) 3–574a
Qānūn al-Mas'ūdī, al-
 See Masudic Canon
Qaraja of Haran
 Crusade of 1101 4–36b
Qarakhanids
 Ghaznevids 1–65a
Qara Qoyunlu 1–423a; 2–27a
Qarāqūsh 1–194b, 195a
Qarawīyīn Mosque 1–197a-b
Qara Yülüg Osman
 Aq Qoyunlu 1–352a
Qarmaṭians
 Al-Baḥrayn 2–50b
 Basra 2–127b
 Ismailis 1–375a
 See Also Carmatiens
Qaṣaba
 See Casbah
Qaṣā'id fī-al-gharīb 4–442b
Qasba
 See Casbah
Qaṣīda 1–398b, 400a
QASR 10–0
Qasr Ibrim 3–315a
Qastamonu 2–136b
Qāsyūn, Mount 4–83b, 85a
Qatabān
 pre-Islamic Arabia 1–370a,b
Qaṭā'ia, Al- 3–13b
Qaṭrabbul 2–45a
Qayrawān
 Aghlabids 1–70a,b, 71b
 exegesis 2–212b
 Great Mosque 1–5b, 69a-b, 70b
QAYRAWĀN, AL- 10–0
Qays
 Taghlib war 1–115a
QAYSARĪYA 10–0
Qays Ibn Nushbah 1–617a
Qaysites
 Arčeš 1–513a
 Armenia 1–481a, 482a
Qayyim al-Jawzīyyah, Ibn
 attack on astrology 1–617b, 618b
Qazvīn 1–118a
QBOU 10–0
Qibla 1–191b, 196b
 See Kibla
Qiblas 1–602b
Qifṭī, Ibn al- 4–408a
QILIJ ARSLAN II 10–0
Qipčaq Turks
 Circassians 3–398b
Qirāḍ
 See Commenda
QIRMIZ (KIRMIZ) **10–0**
 Artašat 1–564a
Qiṭ'a 1–398b
QMA 10–0
Qolobūs 3–618b
Quadi 1–117a
Quadrans novus 1–163a
Quadrant (measuring device) 1–662b; 3–28b
Quadrant arch 1–424, 425a
QUADRANTS 10–0
Quadrilogue invectif, Le (Alain Chartier) 3–275b
Quadripartite vault
 See Vault
QUADRIVIUM 10–0
 seven liberal arts 1–580a
Quaestio
 glosses by decretists 4–127b
***QUAESTIO IN UTRAMQUE PARTEM* 10–0**
QUAESTIONES 10–0
Quaestiones (Cino da Pistoia) 3–397b
Quaestiones Disputatae (Thomas Aquinas) 1–363b
Quaestiones grammaticalae (Abbo of Fleury) 1–13a
Quaestiones morales (Martin Le Maistre) 3–573b
Quaestiones naturales (Adelard of Bath) 1–53b
Quaestiones Nicolai Peripatetici 1–137a
Quaestiones Quodlibetales (Thomas Aquinas) 1–363b
Quaestiones tam essentiales quam accidentales (Arnald of Villanova) 1–138a
Quantity of the Soul, The (Augustine) 1–648b, 656a
Quantum Praedecessores 4–19b
Quarrels
 missiles 2–353b
QUARTER 10–0
Quartodecimans 3–628a
Quarton, Enguerrand
 See Charonton (Quarton), Enguerrand
QUATREFOIL 10–0
 cusp 4–68a
***QUATRE LIVRE DES REIS, LI* 10–0**; 1–262b
Quatre souhaits Saint Martin, Les 1–269b
Quatro Ribeiras 2–30a
Quattuor temporum 4–435b, 436a
Qubasar
 amirspasalar 1–235b
QUBBA 10–0
Qubba of 'Alī ibn Yūsuf 1–197b
Quḍā'a tribes
 'Amr ibn al-'Āṣ 1–237a
Queen Margaret Psalter 2–215b-216a
Queens' College, Cambridge 3–59b
Quem quaeritis 4–272b-277b, 280b, 281a
Queralt, Pere de 3–171a
Quercia, Jacopo della 4–79a
QUEROLUS 10–0
Quesnes
 See Conon de Béthune
Questio de situ aque et terre (Dante) 4–104a
Questiones naturales (Seneca) 1–605a
Questiones super librum Topicorum (Boethius) 4–170a
Questions of John 3–182a, 184a,b
Quévaise
 Brittany, Celtic 2–382a

Quicksilver-sulfur theory 1–141b
Quiercy, Council of (853)
Christology 3–321b
Quierzy, Capitulary of (877) 3–114b
Quimperlé
fairs 4–586a
Quincunx church 3–378b; 4–341a-b
Quinisext Synod (692) 1–66a; 3–630b
apostolic constitutions 1–350a
Byzantine bishops 3–446a
canon of Scripture 2–466b
celibacy laws 3–215b
charistikion 3–268a
Quinquagenta curialitatibus ad mensam, De (Riva) 3–66ba
Quinque compilationes antiquae 3–638a; 4–422b
Quintessence of profane traditions, The 4–444b
Quintilian
allegory 1–179a-b
Quintus Curtius Rufus
Alexander romances 1–149b, 151b
Quintus of Smyrna 2–524a
Quintus Symmachus 1–231a
***QUINZE JOIES DE MARIAGE, LES* 10–0**
QUIRE 10–0
codex 3–474a
Quiriace of Provins, Saint
canon of Champagne 3–246a
Quiricus, Bishop 2–102b
Quirini, Vincenzo
conciliar theory 3–520b, 655a
Qui sint rebelles (Bartolo da Sassoferrato) 2–115a
Quivers
bow and arrow/crossbow 2–352a, 354a-b
Qul 2–136a
QUODLIBET 10–0
Quodvultdeus
Christmas mass 3–319a
Quomodo substantiae (Boethius) 4–510b
Quoniam homines (Alan of Lille) 1–119b
Qur'ān
See Koran
Qurashī, Muḥammad ibn al-Wahb al-
Druzes 4–296a
QURAYSH 10–0; 1–112b
ʿAbbās, Al- 1–3b-4b
ʿAbd Allāh 1–15a
ʿAbd al-Muṭṭalib 1–14a
Abū Bakr 1–24a-25b
Abū Sufyān 1–28b
Abū Ṭālib 1–29b-30a
ʿAmr ibn al-ʿĀṣ 1–236b
Ansāb al-Ashrāf 2–54a
Badr, Battle of 2–42b
pre-Islamic Arabia 1–372a,b
Quriltay 2–131b
Qurna, al- 4–522a
Quṣayy
Mecca 1–372a
Qusṭūs 1–106a
Qutayba, Ibn
contraception 3–574b
encyclopedia 1–379b; 4–444b
Quṭb al-Dīn al-Shīrāzī 1–621b
Quṭun
See Cotton
Quṭuz 2–138a
Quzmān, Ibn 1–401a

R

Rabad
See Abraham Ben David of Posquiéres
Rabad I
See Abraham ibn Daud
Rabanus Maurus
See Hrabanus Maurus
Raba River 2–4b
RABAT 10–0
ʿAbd al-Mu'min 1–194a
Almohad art 1–191b, 193a
Rabbanites
biblical exegesis 2–212a
Rabban Sauma 1–453a
Rabban Ṣāwmā
Mongol-Christian alliance 3–313a
Rabbenu Tam
See Jacob ben Meir (Rabbenu Tam)
RABBINATE 10–0
Rabbinic script
See Rashi (rabbinic) script
Rabbit
food animal 1–301a
Rabenschlacht
See Buch von Bern, Das
RABER, VIRGIL 10–0
comedies 4–271b
Rabīʿa ibn al-Ḥārith
ʿAbbās, al- 1–4a
Rabiʿ ibn Zaid
Córdoba 3–600a
Rābiṭṭ
dervish 4–163a
Rabula Gospels
chairete 3–241a
colobium 3–480b
crucifixion 4–13a
decorations 4–356a, 357a
Rachimburgi 4–379a
RADBOD OF UTRECHT 10–0
Boniface, Saint 2–321a
Radegonde, Saint
exploration 4–553b
Radegunda, Queen
consecration of cemeteries 3–540b
Radenović, Pavle 2–337b, 338a
Radewijns, Florens
Brethren of the Common Life 2–367a
Devotio moderna 4–166a
religious communities 3–368b
Radhanites
See Economic Life, Jewish
RĀḌĪ, AL- 10–0
caliphate decline 3–50a
Radical Aristotelianism
See Rushd, Ibn
Radič Sandović 2–337b
Radimlja
cemetery 2–341a
Radin
Bosnian church 2–339b
RADOLF OF LIÈGE 10–0
astrolabe 1–611a
Radulfus Glaber
See Raoul Glaber
RADULFUS TORTARIUS 10–0
Ami et Amile 1–234a
Radulphus of Laon 1–315b
Latin exegesis 4–543b
Raffael da Noli 4–561b
Rāfiqah, al- 1–9b; 2–46b
Ragallach mac Uatach
See Connacht
Raghib al-Iṣfahānī, al-
contraception 3–574b
RAGIMBOLD OF COLOGNE 10–0
Eiríksmál and Hákonarmál 4–414b
RAGNARǪK 10–0
***RAGNARS SAGA LOÐBRÓKAR* 10–0**
Raguel
angel/angelology 1–249b
Ragusa
Arab siege (867) 2–117b
Ragusans
Bosnia 2–336a,b-337a, 340a-341a
Ragusium
See Dubrovnik
Rahere 4–586b
RAHEWIN 10–0
Raḥim 4–596b
RAHLE 10–0
Raḥmān the Merciful One 1–370b
RAIMBAUT D'AURENGA 10–0
RAIMBAUT DE VAQUEIRAS 10–0
RAIMON DE CORNET 10–0
RAIMON DE MIRAVAL 10–0
Raimondo de' Liuzzi
See Mondino dei Luzzi
Raimond V of Toulouse 1–410a
Raimond VI of Toulouse 1–410a
Raimond VII of Toulouse 1–410b
RAIMON VIDAL DE BESALÙ 10–0
RAINALD OF DASSEL 10–0
archpoet 1–449b-450a
RAINALDUS 10–0
Rain data 3–452b, 453a, 454b
RAINER OF HUY 10–0
Rainier of Ponza
heretics 3–187b
Rā'iq, Ibn 3–50a
Ra'īs al-balad 4–84a,b
Raising of Lazarus
See Lazarus, Raising of
Raithliu 4–492b
Rajaz 1–398a
Rakkada 1–71b, 72a
Ralbag
See Levi ben Gershom
Raleigh, William
Bracton, Henry de 2–356b, 357b
Ralo
See Plows
Ralph, Abbot of Battle
Anselm of Canterbury 1–315a
Ralph of Fontfroide
heretics 3–187b
Ralph of Longchamp 1–120a
Ralph of Shrewsbury
Black Death 2–261b-262a
Ralph of Tiberias
Assizes of Jerusalem 1–599a
RAMADAN 10–0; 3–27b
alms tax 1–202b
Ramanazanids
Cicilia 1–241b
Ramat-el-khalil
See Mambre
Ramban
See Maimonides, Moses
RAMIK 10–0; 1–488b, 489b
Ramiro II of Aragon 1–406b
election 1–161a
Ramiro I of Asturias-León 1–626b
Ramiro II of Asturias-León 1–627b

Ramiro I of Navarre 1–404a, 405a
marriage 3–76a
Ramla
Church of Saint John 4–24b
Ramnoux II
Aquitaine 1–367a
Ramon, Abbot
Knights of Calatrava 3–306b
Ramon Berenguer I
Aragon 1–408b
Catalonia 3–176b-177a
Ramon Berenguer II
Catalonia 3–177a-b
Ramon Berenguer III
Aragon 1–409b-410a
Catalonia 3–177b, 178a
RAMON BERENGUER IV 10–0
Aragon and Barcelona union 3–130a
Catalonia 3–178b
Crown of Aragon 1–406b, 408a-b
Ramon de Caldes 1–411a
Ramon de Montcada 1–412a
Ramon de Muntaner 1–191a
Ramon Destorrents
See Destorrents, Ramón
RAMSEY, JOHN 10–0
RAMSEY, WILLIAM 10–0
Ramsey Abbey
estates 4–512b
RÁN 10–0
See Also Albania (Caucasian)
RANGERIUS OF LUCCA 10–0
Rani
See Albania (Caucasian)
Ranieri da Perugia
University of Bologna 2–312b
Rank List
Armenia 1–489a
Raonament d'Avinyó (Arnald of Villanova) 3–157b
Raonament entre Francesc Alegre i Esperonça (Francesc Alegre) 3–169b
Raonament fet entre Scipió e Aníbal (Antoni Canals) 3–169b
Raoul de Cambrai 3–258b, 259b, 330b
RAOUL DE HOUDENC 10–0
Arthurian literature 1–570a
Raoul de Presles
Bible 2–218b, 219b
RAOUL GLABER 10–0
Raoul le Tourtier
See Radulfus Tortarius
Raoul of Bath
angelus 1–252b
Rape of Proserpine (Claudian) 1–182a
Raphael (archangel) 1–249b, 433a
RAPULARIUS 10–0
RAQQA 10–0; 2–22a
Rashbam
See Samuel ben Meïr
RASHI (RABBI SOLOMON BEN ISAAC) 10–0
biblical exegesis 2–212a-b, 213b
exegesis 4–540b
marital relations 4–606b
Rashīd, al- 1–195b
Rashīd al-Dīn
language 1–378a,b
Rāshidūn caliphs 3–33a,b, 35b
Rashi (rabbinic) script 1–208a,b
Rasica
Serbs 2–494a
Raška
Bulgaria 2–406b
Rasós de trobar (Ramon Vidal de Besalú) 3–164b
Raspe, Henry 4–428a
Rass, al-
See Araks River
Rastislav of Moravia 4–73b
Cyril and Methodios, Saints 4–73b
Rastko
See Sava, Saint
Rasulids
Sunnite dynasty 1–375b, 376a
Rathbreasail, Synod of (1111)
Clonard 3–466a
RATHER OF LIÈGE 10–0
RATHER OF VERONA 10–0
Rationale divinorum officiorum (Guillaume Durand) 3–541a; 4–315b
Ratione fidei, De (Agnellus of Ravenna, Saint) 1–73a
Rationes seminales 1–649b, 656a
Rationibus fidei, De (Aquinas) 1–354a,b
Ratislav
Byzantine Church 2–463b
Moravia 2–299a
RATPERT OF SAINT GALL 10–0
Ekkehard IV of Saint Gall 4–418b
RATRAMNUS OF CORBIE 10–0
dialectic 4–169b
eucharist 2–188a
RAUḌA 10–0
Alhambra 1–170b
Ravello
cathedral 2–109a
RAVENNA 10–0
Agnellus, Saint 1–73a
architecture 1–423b
campanile 3–60b
Dante's stay 4–103b, 104a-b
early Christian art 4–352a, 353a, 358a,b, 361b
exarchate 3–106b; 4–529b
maps 4–553b
spolia of marble and mosaics 1–333b
Ravenna sacramentary
rite of Aquileia 1–353a
RAVERTI, MATTEO 10–0
Rāwīs
Arabic poetry 1–398b
Rawwādids 2–27a
Dwin 4–324a
Rayḥāna
Bīrūnī 2–250a
Rayhanī 3–54a
Raymond de Béziers 3–31b
RAYMOND DE MUR 10–0
Raymond de Saint Gilles
Antioch 2–309a
Raymond du Temple
Louvre 4–295a
Raymond Gayrard of Toulouse
See Gayrard, Raymond
Raymond Lully
See Lull, Ramon
Raymond of Antioch 4–419b
Raymond of Burgundy 3–130a
Raymond of Cahors 3–288b
Raymond of Capua
Dominican reform 4–253b-254a
Raymond of Fietero
Calatrava, Order of 3–16b
Raymond of Marseilles
astronomical tables 1–611b
RAYMOND OF PEÑAFORT 10–0
casuistry 3–153b
decretals 4–124a
Dominican theology 4–247a-b
language schools 4–252a
master general 4–245a
Raymond IV of Toulouse 4–36a
Albara 4–35b
Council of Clermnot 3–449b
Crusade of 1101 4–36b
First Crusade 4–30a, 33b, 34a,b-35a
Ma'arrat al-Nu'mān 4–35b
Tripoli 4–37a
Raymond V of Toulouse
Bernart de Ventadorn 2–197a
heresy 3–187a
Raymond VI of Toulouse
Albigensian Crusade 3–188a-b, 189a
heresy 3–187a-188a, 640a-b
Raymond VII of Toulouse
Blanche of Castile 2–271a
Cathars 3–190a
consuls, consulate 3–571b
Raymond III of Tripoli
Nūr al-Dīn 4–38b
Rayner Sacconi
Bogomils 2–295a, 297a
Rayy
Buyids 2–436a
Razès 1–410a
Ramon Berenguer III 3–178a
RĀZĪ, ABŪ BAKR MUḤAMMAD IBN ZAKARĪYYA, AL- 10–0; 1–136a,b, 137b
alchemy 1–141a,b, 142a
astrology/astronomy 1–618b
contraception 3–574a,b
encyclopedias 4–445b
RAZON DE AMOR 10–0
Razors 2–148a,b
Reading, Battle of (871) 1–163b
Re aedificatoria, De (Alberti) 1–126b
Realgestech 1–533a
REALISM 10–0
Burley, Walter 2–433a
conceptualism 3–510a
Reason (Guillaume de Lorris) 1–185b
Rebais
fairs 4–590b, 591a
"Rebuke, The" (Augustine) 1–658a
Rebus in administratione sua gestis, Re (Suger of Saint Denis) 1–335b
Recanati, Menahem
cabala 3–2b, 3a
Recared, King 3–344a
Arianism 3–676b
Reccared
See Recared
Recco, Nicoloso da
Canary Islands 3–61b
"Received Rule, The" (Augustine) 1–658a
Rechtfertigungsschrift (Meister Eckhart) 4–381a
Reciting Tone
See Psalm Tones
Récits d'un ménestrel de Reims 3–332b
RECLAMATION
Brittany, Duchy of 2–377b-378a
RECLAMATION OF LAND 10–0
Recort (Gabriel Turell) 3–166b
Rectangulus 1–613a-b
Rectitudo (Anselm of Canterbury) 1–314b
Recueil des histoires de Troye, Les 3–210b
Red
liturgical color 3–484b
Red Church of Perushtica 2–414b
Re diplomatica, De (Jean Mabillon) 3–252a
Redditio symboli 3–675b
Reden der Unterscheidung (Meister Eckhart) 4–381a
Redon, Concordat of (1441) 3–526a
Red Sea
Bab al-Mandab 2–32a

RED SEA (cont.)
exploration 4–562b
trade 1–30b
Red Sea canal
ʿAmr ibn al-ʿĀṣ 1–237b
Reductione artium ad theologiam, De (Bonaventure) 2–314b
Reductorium morale de proprietatibus rerum (Pierre Bersuire) 4–449a
REEVE 10–0
estate management 4–514a
REFECTORY 10–0
Referendarius
See Chancery
Reform
calendar 3–22b-23b
REFORM, IDEA OF 10–0
Carthusians 3–118a
conciliar theory 3–510b
Western councils 3–645a-b, 650a-651a,b, 652a-b, 653a
Reformatio in melius 3–347a
Reformation
altarpiece destruction 1–225b
Augustinian friars 1–660a
Carthusians 3–119a
Reformatione virium animae, De (Zerbolt) 4–166b
Refrigeria 4–336a
Regaim 3–24b
Regensburg
Albertus Magnus 1–128b-129a
bishoprices 2–134a
Boniface, Saint 2–322a
See Also Castra Regina
Regensburg, Council of (792)
Christology 3–321b
Reges 1–117b
Reggimento e costumi di donna (Francesco da Barberino) 3–664a
REGIMEN SANITATIS SALERNITANUM 10–0
Regiment de la cosa pública, El (Eiximenis) 4–416b
Regimiento 3–136b
Regimine animae, De (Bonaventure) 2–317b
Regimine civitatis, De
See "Government of the City-State, On the"
Regimine principum, De (Egidius) 4–400a,b
Regina caeli laetare 1–329a
Reginald
Xerigordon 4–34a-b
Reginald, Abbot of Abingdon
book illumination 1–258a
REGINALD OF CANTERBURY 10–0
Anglo-Latin poetry 1–254b
Reginald of Châtillon
crusades 1–375b; 4–39b
REGINO OF PRÜM 10–0
Cistercian chant 3–402b
contraception 3–572b
Reginsmál 4–386a, 390b
REGINSMÁL AND FÁFNISMÁL 10–0; 4–386a, 390b
Fáfnir 4–581b
Regiomontanus
See Müller, Johann
Registers
chancery practices 3–252b
Regles de trobar (Jofre de Foixà) 3–164b
REGNAULT DE CORMONT 10–0
Regnitz River
Bavaria border 2–132b
Regnum
papal coronation 3–603b
Regola del canto fermo ambrosiano, La (Camillo Perego) 1–233a
Regulae morales (Basil the Great) 2–120b
Regula magistri (RM)
Benedictine Rule 2–169a-b
Regula recepta (Augustine) 1–658a
Regularis concordia (Dunstan) 3–82b
church elections 4–421b
Ethelwold 4–518b
liturgical drama 4–274a, 276b, 280b
monastic reform 3–348a
Old English texts 1–286b
Regularis concordia Sancti Ethelwoldi
angelus 1–252a
Regularis informatio (Augustine) 1–658a
Regula sancti Benedicti 4–518b
Rehinlik 3–679a
Řehoř of Prague
See Gregory of Prague
Reichersberg, Gerhoh von
papal curia 4–66a
Reichstag
See Representative Assemblies
Reification allegory 1–179a-b, 180b, 181a, 183a, 184a, 186a
Reigenlied 3–116a
Reims
Utrecht Psalter 1–273b
Reinaert I 2–141b, 142a
Reinaert II 2–142a
Reine Sebile 4–432b
REINFRID VON BRAUNSCHWEIG 10–0
Reinhold, Erasmus
Prutenic Tables 1–160a
Reinke Vos 2–142a
REINMAR VON HAGENAU 10–0
REINMAR VON ZWETER 10–0
Reisch, Gregor 4–449b
Reis glorios (Giraut de Bornelh) 1–123a
Reis van Sinte Brandean 4–318b
RELICS, WESTERN EUROPEAN 10–0
altar apparatus 1–221a
ampulla 1–236b
archeological excavations 1–336b-337b
Armenian saints 1–518a
Brandeum 2–362a-363a
canonical legislation 3–229a
canonization 3–68a
chapels 3–263b
crypt 4–62a
magi 4–498b
Relieving arch 1–425a
Religious allegory 1–185b
RELIGIOUS INSTRUCTION 10–0
RELIQUARY 10–0
early Christian art 4–348b, 352a, 361b
enameled 4–438a, 439a
Remaniement 1–270a
chansons de geste 3–260b
Remedes d'amour (Jacques d'Amiens) 1–189a
Remedies of Love (Ovid) 1–184a; 3–671a,b
Remediis fortuitorum, De 1–264b
Remediis utriusque fortunae, De (Petrarch) 3–213a
Remi, Gilles de 2–144a
Remi, Jean de 2–144a
Remi, Philippe de
See Remin, Philippe de
Remi, Raoul de 2–144a
Rémi, Saint 3–634a
Champagne county 3–243b
Remigius
See Rémi, Saint
REMIGIUS OF AUXERRE 10–0
biblical exegesis 2–213a
classical literary studies 3–433a
Latin exegesis 4–542b
Re militari, De (Vegetius) 3–200b, 302a
Remin, Philippe de 2–144a
***REMUNDAR SAGA KEISARASONAR* 10–0**
RENAISSANCES AND REVIVALS IN MEDIEVAL ART 10–0
RENARD THE FOX 10–0; 2–141b
beast epic 2–140b, 141b-142a
Dutch literature 4–319a
fables 4–572b
Renart
See Renard the Fox
Renaud II
Burgundy, County of 2–424b
Renaud III
Burgundy, County of 2–424b
Renaud, Count of Boulogne
Pseudo-Turpin Chronicle translations 3–331b
Renaud de Montauban 2–128a
RENAUT DE BEUJEU 10–0
Arthurian literature 1–570a, 574b
René I
Angevins 1–253b
book of hours 2–326b
chronicles 3–333b
Naples 1–417b
Rennen 1–533a
Rennes
fairs 4–586a
Rennhut 1–533a
Renntartsche 1–533a
Renouard, Yves
Avignonese papacy 3–362b
Renout van Montalbaen 4–318b
Renovatio concept 4–521a
Rents
demography 4–139a
Réole, La, monastery 1–109b; 2–327b
Abbo of Fleury 1–13a
Reply to Gaunilo (Anselm of Canterbury) 1–311b
REPOUSSÉ 10–0
REPRESENTATIVE ASSEMBLIES 10–0
parliament 4–484a-485b
REPRESENTATIVE ASSEMBLIES, FRENCH 10–0
Reprobatione Monarchiae, De (Vernani) 4–103a
Republicanism
defensor pacis 4–132b
Republic (Cicero) 1–181a
Republic (Plato) 1–180b-181a, 654b
moral allegory 1–181a
Requesens, Lluís de 3–171b
Requests, Court of 4–503a
Rerebrace 1–525b, 534a
REREDOS 10–0; 1–222a
Resafa
conch church 3–378a
RESCRIPTS 10–0
Rescuer from Error (Al-Ghazālī) 1–381a
Resende, Garcia de 3–63b
RESERVATION OF THE SACRAMENT 10–0
Res gestae (Ammianus Marcellinus) 1–235b
Res gestae Alexandri Macedonis (Valerius) 1–149b
RESPONSORY 10–0; 4–224b-225a
antiphonal 1–329b
Responsum literature, Islamic
See Fatwā

RESPONSUM LITERATURE, JEWISH 10–0
Restor du paon (Jean Brisebarre) 1–151b
Resurrection
early Christian movement 3–335a
See Also Easter
Resurrection, Church of the (Jerusalem)
See Anastatis
RESURRECTION, ISLAMIC 10–0
"Resurrection, The" 3–299a
RESURRECTION CYCLE 10–0
RETABLE 10–0
Rete of astrolabe 1–602a; 3–29a
Reticules 3–625a
Retractions (Augustine) 1–653a
Reuchlin, Johann 4–450a
Christian Hebraists 3–314a
Reuda
Dál Riata 4–78a
Reuenthal, Neidhart von
crusading song 3–97b
Reval 2–65b
Revedun, Bishop 2–71b
Reveillé
See Aubade
Revelationes (Saint Brigid of Sweden) 3–61a
Revelations (Peter of Aragon) 4–416a
Revelations of Divine Love (Julian of Norwich) 3–368b
REVERDIE 10–0
Reversarias
Anglo-Norman lyric poetry 1–269a
Reverter 1–200a
Révigny, Jacques de
Cino da Pistoia 3–397b
Revue des langues romanes 1–271a
REXACH, JUAN 10–0
REYKDŒLA SAGA **10–0**; 4–613b, 618a
Reynes, Henry of
See Henry of Reynes
Reynes, Robert
commonplace books 3–493a
Reynolds, Walter
parliament 4–483b
Rhain ap Cadwgan, King 4–329b
Rheged
ornamented molds 3–224a
Rheims
Ebo of 4–368a
fairs 4–590b
False Decretals 4–125b-126a
Rheims, Councils of 3–186b, 634a, 636a-b
RHEIMS CATHEDRAL 10–0; 3–276a
archaelogical study 1–431a
architect 2–194b
bar tracery 2–116b
buttress 2–435a
engineering 3–564b-565a, 568a
Rhenish cults
charms 3–273b
Rhens, Declaration of (1338) 4–428b
RHETICIUS OF AUTUN 10–0
Rheticus
astrology 1–609a
Rhetorica antiqua sive Boncompagnus (Boncampagno of Signa) 2–320a
Rhetoricale wercken (Anthonis de Roovere of Bruges) 4–322b
Rhetorica novissima (Boncompagno of Signa) 2–320b; 4–174b
Rhetorica et virtutibus, De (Alcuin of York) 1–142b
RHETORIC: ARABIC, HEBREW, AND PERSIAN 10–0
RHETORIC: BYZANTINE 10–0
RHETORIC: WESTERN EUROPEAN 10–0
allegory 1–179a-b, 180a-b
ars poetica 1–554a
ars praedicandi 1–556b
Boncompagno 2–320a
Capellanus 3–89a
dictamen 4–173b
Ennodius 4–491b
Rhetorimachia (Anselm of Besate) 1–311b
RHÉTORIQUEURS 10–0
Rhieingerdd 3–121b
Rhineland
Burgundian settlement 2–92a,b
canonical reform 3–355a
Cathars 3–181b
Cistercian Order 3–404a
fairs 4–585b
Oliver of Paderborn 4–49b
religious communities 3–368b
Rhine-Main region
Capetians 3–89b
Rhine-Meuse region
Capetians 3–89b
Rhine River
Alamanni raids 1–117a
boundary 2–88b
Burgundians 2–422b
RHODES 10–0
crusader art and architecture 4–26b
Rhodes, Knights of 3–303b-304a
Rhodian Law
consulate of the sea 3–569b
Rhodri ab Owain Gwynedd, Prince 4–430b
RHODRI MAWR 10–0
Rhön, Kaspar von der
Heldenbuch 4–292b
Rhône River
Avignon 2–15b
Dauphiné 4–108a
Rhône Valley 4–110a
agriculture 1–85b
Burgundian kingdom 2–92a
Rhyme
Arabic poetry 1–398a
assonance 1–600a-b
canso 3–70a
chansons de geste 3–261b
RHYMED OFFICES 10–0
Rhys ap Gruffudd 4–415b
Peace of Conway 3–580a
Rhys Fychan ap Rhys ap Maelgwn
Peace of Conway 3–580a
RHYS OF DEHEUBARTH 10–0
RHYTHM 10–0
Anonymous IV 1–309b
Arabic poetry 1–398a
ars antiqua 1–544a-b, 545b
ars nova 1–550a
ars subtilior 1–558b-559a
RIB 10–0
RIB, RIDGE 10–0
Ribā 2–79a-b
Ribagorza 1–404a, 405a,b, 407b
RIBAṬ 10–0; 1–69a-b
Almoravids 1–198a,b
murābiṭūn 1–71a
Ribāt al-Fatḥ
See Rabat
Ribatego
agriculture 1–85a
Ribeira dos Flamengos 2–30a
Ribera district 2–104a
Ribes Valley 1–84a
Rib vault
See Vault
Riccardiano
fables 4–572b
Ricciardi company of Lucca 2–76b, 77b
wine 2–328b
Riccomanni, Leonardo 4–79a
Rice
See Grain crops
Islamic cookery 3–584a
Ricemarch Psalter 3–224a
Rich, Edmund
Canterbury 3–83b
Richard (son of Eleanor of Aquitaine) 1–367b
RICHARD I THE LIONHEARTED 10–0; 4–467b-468a, 471a
Aquitaine 1–367b
Ayyubids 2–23b
Bertran de Born 2–201b
Burgundy, Duchy of 2–428a
Cistercians 3–405a
communes 3–499a
court of common pleas 3–491b, 492a
crusades 4–31b, 40a-b
Cyprus 2–497a; 4–70b
Eleanor of Aquitaine 4–420a
French chronicles 3–331a
kidnapping 2–7a, 330b-331a
See Also Crusade and Death of Richard I
RICHARD II 10–0; 1–253a
Admiralty, Court of 1–57a
annate payments 1–305a
anointing of kings 1–308b
Champion of England 3–251a
Chaucer, Geoffrey 3–283b
Clanvowe, Sir John 3–408a
deposition 4–485a
deposition of rulers 4–160b
right to kingship 4–476a-b
RICHARD III 10–0
right to kingship 4–478b-479b
succession 4–485b
Richard, Duke of Gloucester
See Richard III
Richard de Beauchamp 4–510b
RICHARD DE BURY 10–0
Bradwardine, Thomas 2–358a
Burley, Walter 2–432b
Philobiblon 1–324a
Richard de Fishacre 1–461b
Richard de Fournival
Bestiaire d'amour 2–203b, 205b
Richard le Barber 2–99b
Richard le Justicier 2–427a
Richard of Chichester, Saint 1–261a
Richard of Cornwall
Barons' War 2–112a
crusade 4–51b-52b
election 4–428a
Ṣāliḥ Ayyūb, al- 4–32a
Richard of Devizes 4–420a
Richard of Hampole
See Rolle, Richard
Richard of Middleton
See Richardus de Mediavilla
RICHARD OF SAINT VICTOR 10–0
encyclopedias 4–448b
exegesis 2–213b
Richard of Thetford
ars praedicandi 1–556a
RICHARD OF WALLINGFORD 12–0
astronomical clock 3–459b, 461a, 464b
astronomy 1–613a-b; 3–29b
Richard of Ware
Roman marbles 1–334a
Richard of Wendover
See Richard the Englishman

Richard of York
claim to throne 4–477b-478a
See Also Richard III
Richard the Bishop 2–190a
Richard the Good of Normandy, Duke 4–394b
Richard the Pilgrim
Chanson d'Antioche 3–254b
RICHARDUS DE MEDIAVILLA 10–0
Richarius, Saint
Alcuin of York 1–143b
Richemont, Arthur de
See Arthur de Richemont
RICHER OF SAINT REMI 10–0
Richerzeche 3–481b, 482a
Richeza 1–311b
Richfort, Simon 3–466a
Ricoldo da Montecroce 4–253a
Ridā 3–616b
Ridda 1–25a; 3–32a, 33b
ʿAmr ibn al-ʿĀṣ 1–237a
***RIDDARASÖGUR* 10–0**; 4–612b
Bevers saga 2–209b
Elis saga ok Rosamundu 4–431b
RIDDLES 10–0
Old English poetry 1–281a
Ridevall, John 4–544b
Ridiculum 3–57b
Riḍwān, Ibn 1–617a
RIED, BENEDICT 10–0
Ried, Hans
Ambraser Heldenbuch 1–229b
Biterolf 2–253a
RIEMENSCHNEIDER, TILMAN 10–0
Rienzi, Cola di 2–34a
Rieti
vineyards 1–87a
Rievaulx
Ethelred, Saint 4–516b
Rifāda 1–4a, 14b
Rif Mountains 1–639b
Riga 2–65b
Riga, Petrus 1–319a
Rigbod 1–143a
Rights of the Bourgeoisie
Bruges 2–386a
Rigmel 1–266b
RIGORD 10–0
Philip II Augustus 2–236b, 240a
RÍGSÞULA 10–0; 4–387a, 391a,b
Riḥla (Ibn Baṭṭūṭa) 2–130a-131a
Rijeka 4–2a, 4a
Rijkel, Denys
See Denys the Carthusian
Rijmkroniek van Holland 4–319b
Rijssele, Colijn van 4–322b
Rila
art and architecture 2–417b
Rimas derivatas 1–269a
RIMBERT 10–0
Baltic descriptions 2–62b
Riming Poem, The 1–277a
Rimini, Council of (359)
See Ariminum (Rimini) Council
***RÍMUR* 10–0**
Ála flekks saga 1–116b
Bósa saga 2–333b
Rindr 2–56a
Ring, Der (Wittenwiler) 2–132b
RINGERIKE STYLE 10–0
Celtic art 3–223a
Ring of the Dove (Ibn Ḥazm) 1–381b
Rinn Seimne 1–60a
Rio de Oro
trade 4–561a
Rio do Padrao
See Congo River
Rio dos Escravos
slaves 2–269a,b, 270a
Rioni River 3–195a
Río Tinto
trade 4–558a
Ripley, George 1–139a
Ripoll 3–76b, 164a
ecclesiastical culture 3–175a,b
wood-carving 3–120b
Ripuarians 2–94a
Riquier, Guiraut
See Guiraut Riquier
Ritterfahrt des Johann von Michelsberg (Heinrich von Freiberg) 1–636a
Ritter vom Turn, Der (Stein) 3–662b
RITUALE 10–0
Ritual murder
anti-Semitism 1–340a-341a
Rituals
Baldr myth 2–55b
baptism 2–83a
botany 2–348a
churching of women 3–382b
circumcision, Islamic 3–400b
circumcision, Jewish 3–401a
Riurik
See Rurik
Riva San Vitale
baptistery 2–88a
Rivers, Anthony Earl 3–211a
RIWAQ 10–0
ROADS AND BRIDGES, WESTERN EUROPEAN 10–0
ROADS AND COMMUNICATIONS, BYZANTINE 10–0
ROADS IN THE ISLAMIC WORLD 10–0
Robber Synod (449) 3–629B; 4–524a
Robbia
See Della Robbia
Robert, Abbot
Elis saga ok Rosamundu 4–431b
ROBERT D'ARBRISSEL 10–0; 4–374b
ROBERT DE BORON 10–0
Arthurian literature 1–570b, 571a
ROBERT DE CLARI 10–0
Constantinople 1–334b
Robert de Ho 1–264a
Robert de Ketene 1–136b
ROBERT DE LUZARCHES 10–0
Robert de Torote
feast of Corpus Christi 3–608a
Robert de Veneys 2–173b
Robert Grosseteste
See Grosseteste, Robert
ROBERT GUISCARD 10–0; 2–308b
Alexios I Komnenos 1–157b-158a
Byzantine Empire 2–492b, 493b, 494a
First Crusade 4–34a
Robertinians
See Capetian family origins
Robert Kilwardby
See Kilwardby, Robert (Cantuar)
ROBERT LE DIABLE 10–0
Robert I of Artois 2–270b
crusade 4–53a
Robert II of Artois
Adam de la Halle 1–48b
Robert of Basevorn
ars praedicandi 1–556a, 557a,b
Robert of Blois 3–664a, 665b
Robert II of Burgundy, Duke 2–426a; 4–109a
Robert of Champagne 3–243b
Robert of Chester
astronomical tables 1–611b
Robert of Courson
See Courson (Courçon), Robert of
Robert of Epernon 3–183b
Robert II of France
Abbo of Fleury 1–13a
Adalbero of Laon 1–46b
Burgundy, Duchy of 2–427a
ROBERT OF GREATHAM 10–0; 1–262b, 263b
Robert of Holcot 3–59b
Bradwardine, Thomas 2–358b
Robert II of Jerusalem, Count of Flanders
First Crusade 4–34a,b
Robert of Jerusalem, Patriarch
¿Ay, Iherusalem! 2–18b
ROBERT OF JUMIÈGES 10–0
Robert of London, bISHOP 1–256B
Robert of Luzarches
Amiens Cathedral 1–234b
ROBERT OF MELUN 10–0
Christology 3–322b
Robert of Molesme 3–355a
Robert of Naples, King
Augustinus Triumphus 2–1a
Henry VII 4–102a
Robert I of Neustria
Carolingian Empire 3–115a
Robert II of Normandy, Duke
First Crusade 4–20a, 34a,b
Robert of Sabilone 1–544b
ROBERT I OF SCOTLAND 10–0; 2–102a
Bannockburn 3–204b
Burgh, de 2–421b
David II 4–111a
Dublin 4–299b
Edward I of England 4–396b
ROBERT II OF SCOTLAND 10–0
Robert of Sicily, King 4–109a
Roberto of Sahagún 3–129a
Robertsbridge Codex
ars nova 1–553a
Robert the Englishman
See Robertus Anglicus
Robert IV the Strong, Count of Anjou
Rhineland holdings 3–89b
Robertus Anglicus
clocks 3–29a-b, 459a
ROBIN HOOD 10–0
Fouke III 1–268a
Rocabertí, Bernat Hug de 3–169b, 172a
Roch, Saint
plague 2–265a
Rochester Cathedral
Anglo-Norman features 1–255b
Benedictine monastery 3–265b
Rockingham Council of (1095) 1–312a
Roda
See Ribagorza
Rodrigo, Mocedades De
See Mocedades de Rodrigo
RODRIGO DE OSONA 10–0
Rodrigo Díaz de Bivar
See Cid
RODRÍGUEZ DEL PADRÓN, JUAN 10–0
Rodríguez de Montalvo, Garcí 1–227b
Rodynton, John 2–358b
ROFFREDUS DE EPIPHANIIS OF BENEVENTO 10–0; 2–29a
Roffud of Benevento
See Roffredus de Epiphaniis of Benevento
Rogationtide 1–281b
Roger, Pierre
See Clement VI, Pope
Roger Bernard de Foix 1–413b
ROGER DE FLOR 10–0; 3–165b
Andronikos II Palaiologos 1–190b-191a, 246a

Catalan Company 2–500a; 3–156a
Roger de Wendover
See Roger of Wendover
Roger Hauteville 2–492b
ROGERIUS 10–0
Roger II of Béziers 1–410a
ROGER OF HELMARSHAUSEN 10–0
Roger of Hereford
astronomical tables 1–611b
Roger of Howden (Hoveden) 4–18b
Roger of Loira 1–414a
Roger of Salerno
surgery 2–98b
ROGER OF SALISBURY 10–0
ROGER I OF SICILY 10–0; 4–33a
Carthusians 3–118b
duana 1–37b
ROGER II OF SICILY 10–0; 1–378b
Byzantine Empire 2–494a; 4–38a
Roger of Stoke
planetary clockwork 3–464b
Roger of Wendover 1–265a; 4–18b
Roger of York 2–152a-b
Rogers, Robert 3–298b
ROHAN MASTER 10–0
Roi de Sicile, Le (Adam de la Halle) 1–48b
Roig, Jaume 3–171b-172a, 173b-174a
Roís de Corella, Joan 3–167a, 168a, 169b, 171b
Rojas, Fernando de
La Celestina 3–212a
Rokycana, Jan 2–306b
Roland
Brittany 2–378b
***ROLAND, SONG OF* 10–0**; 1–271a, 643a; 3–257b-258a, 259b, 260b-261a, 330b
chivalry 3–301b, 302b
historical writing 3–325b
versions 1–260b; 3–257a
Rolandinus de Padua 2–320a
Roland of Cremona 1–462a; 4–246a
***ROLANDSLIED* 10–0**
ROLANDUS 10–0
ROLFE, THOMAS 10–0
Rolin, Nicolas
Burgundy, duchy of 2–427b
Rollant
Knights Templars 3–304a
ROLLE, RICHARD 10–0
Anglo-Latin poetry 1–255a
exegesis 4–547a
mysticism 3–368b
psalter 2–221b
Rollo
Charles the Bald 3–115a
Roman alphabet
See Latin alphabet
Roman art
influence on early Christian art 4–348a
Roman calendar 3–18a-b, 20b
divisions of months 3–20b-21a
names of days 3–21b
Roman de Brut (Wace) 1–264b, 565a-b
Romanç del setge de Rodas (Francesc Ferrer) 3–171b
***ROMANCE OF HORN* (MASTER THOMAS) 10–0**; 1–266b
***ROMANCE OF THE ROSE* 10–0**; 1–138b; 2–237a; 3–311a
alchemy 1–138b
antifeminism 1–324a
botany 2–348b
Chaucer 3–281a
Christine de Pizan 3–316b
courtly love 3–670b, 671a
Dante 4–101b
encyclopedias 4–449a
French allegory 1–183b, 184a-186a, 189a-b
Middle English exegesis 4–547a
Romancero 3–258a
Romances
Anglo-Norman literature 1–266a-268a
Byzantine 2–508a-b
Old English prose 1–285a
Roman d'Alexandre 1–150a, 151a
Anglo-Norman literature 1–260b
Libro de Alexandre 1–152b
Roman d'Auberon 3–259a
Roman d'aventures et d'amour 1–267a
Roman de Brut (Wace) 3–255b, 331a; 4–419b
Roman de Fauvel
See Fauvel, Roman de
Roman de Flamenca 3–256a
Roman de la Rose
See Romance of the Rose
Roman de la Violette 3–263a
Roman de philosophie (Simund de Freine) 1–264a
Roman de Renart
See Renard the Fox
Roman de Rou (Wace) 3–331a
Roman des eles (Raoul de Houdenc) 1–188b-189a
***ROMAN DE TOUTE CHEVALERIE* (THOMAS OF KENT) 10–0**; 1–151b, 266a
Roman de Troie (Benoît de Sainte-Maure) 2–182a; 4–419b
Roman du châtelain de Coucy et la dame de Fayel (Jakemes) 3–277b
ROMAN EGYPT, LATE 10–0
Byzantine church 2–459b
Coptic art 3–585b
ROMAN EMPIRE, LATE 10–0
agriculture and nutrition 1–76b-79b
Alamanni 1–117a
Alani 1–120b
Alaric 1–122a
Anglo-Saxon colonization 1–288b
animal breeding 1–293b-295b
Antichrist 1–322a
anti-Semitism 1–339a
architecture 4–331b
Armenia 1–476a
arms and armor 1–522a
art 4–348b, 350b-353b
barbarian invasions 2–89a-b, 97a-b
basileus 2–123a
brick 2–375b
bronze and brass 2–384a
Burgundians 2–422b-423b, 427b
camels 1–296b
castrum 3–152b
cavalry 3–200a-201a
Champagne 3–243a
consistorium 3–541b
Constantine I 3–545a
Constantinople 3–549a-551b
cultural decline 1–182a,b
dioceses 4–191b
duchies 4–303b
estate management 4–511a-b
fairs 4–583b
fortifications 3–143b-144a
See Also Byzantine Empire: History (330-1025)
Roman Empire of the German Nation
See Holy Roman Empire
ROMANESQUE ARCHITECTURE 10–0
arch 1–423b, 425a
archivolt 1–449a
basilica 2–124b, 125a
bay system 2–139b
Benedictine plan 2–175a
brick 2–375b
Burgundy, Duchy of 2–428a
Buscheto of Pisa 2–433b
buttress 2–435a
capital 3–90b
Castile 3–133a
Cistercian churches 3–404b
Cluny, Abbey Church 3–468b
corbel 3–597a,b
Durham Cathedral 4–315b
See Also Church, types of
ROMANESQUE ART 10–0
Anglo-Norman art 1–255b
bronze and brass 2–384b
Roman History (Livy) 3–166b
ROMANIA 10–0
asses 1–295b
camels 1–296b
ROMANIAN LANGUAGE AND LITERATURE 10–0
ROMAN NUMERALS 10–0
See Also Arabic numerals
Romanos III Argyros
allelengyon 1–190a
Hagia Sophia 2–443a
Zoe 2–491b
ROMANOS IV DIOGENES 10–0
Byzantine throne 2–491b, 492b, 493a
Doukas family 4–263a
ivories 2–454b
Manazkert 1–203b
ROMANOS II 10–0
Anna 1–303a
Basil II 2–118a
ROMANOS I LEKAPENOS 10–0
Byzantine law 2–477b
Constantine VII Porphyrogenitos 3–546b
dunatoi 4–306b-307a
Myrelaion Church 4–341a
preemption rights 4–595a
reign 2–490a
ROMANOS MELODOS 10–0
Armenian saints 1–520a
hymns 2–469a
Kontakia 2–510b-511a
poetic forms 2–524b
Romanos of Bulgaria 2–406b
Roman Pontifical 4–314b-315a
Roman rite
baptism 2–83a-84a
dedication of churches 4–130b
Romanus
Benedict of Nursia 2–168b
Roman Vergil 4–356a
Romaunz de temptacioun de secle (Guischart de Beaulieu) 1–262b
ROME 10–0
Adrian IV, Pope 1–58b
Alaric 1–122a, 654a; 2–90b-91a
architecture 4–332a-b
archives 1–445b, 446a
Arnold of Brescia 1–540a
art 4–348b, 351a-352b
barbarian invasions 2–88a
Byzantine church 2–459b, 461a
Byzantine Empire 2–481b
classical literary studies 3–430a,b
cola di Rienzo 3–478a
dating of Easter 3–228a
Lombard domination 2–95b
patriarch of 2–10a
Ravenna exarchate 4–530a
siege (756) 3–154b

ROME (cont.)
spolia 1–333b
topographic views 1–333b
traveler accounts 1–332a-333b
Vandals 2–91b
Rome, Council of (1412-1413) 3–647a-b
Rome, Synod of (1059)
canonical reform 3–355a
papal elector rights 3–93b
Romsey Cathedral 1–256a
ROMUALD OF RAVENNA, SAINT 10–0
Bruno of Querfurt 2–391ab
Camaldolese Order 3–55b
eremitic movement 3–354b
monastic reform 3–348a
ROMULUS 10–0
Romulus (fable) '4–572a-b, 573a,b
Romulus Augustulus, Emperor 2–93a
***RÓMVERJA SAGA* 10–0**
Roncaglia, Diet of (1158) 1–58b
Bulgarus 2–418a
RONCESVALLES 10–0
Rondache 1–528a
RONDEAU 10–0; 4–86b, 87a
Anglo-Norman lyric poetry 1–269a
ars nova 1–552a-b
ars subtilior 1–558b
ballette 2–61a
chansonnier 3–255b
Charles of Orléans 3–273a
Chartier, Alain 3–275b
RONDELLUS 10–0; 1–547a
Rood screen 1–442b, 443
Roovere, Anthonis de 4–322b
RORICZER, CONRAD 10–0
RORICZER, MATHES 10–0
Rory O Connor, King
Cinéal Eóghain 3–397a
Ros, Ramon 3–168a
Rosa anglica (John of Gaddesden) 3–572a
Ros Ailithir 1–110a
Rosamunda
See *Elis saga ok Rosamundu*
Rosarius (Arnald of Villanova) 1–138a
ROSARY 10–0
Ave Maria 2–13a
Islamic 1–178a
lay devotion 3–359a
Roscelin of Compiègne
Abelard 1–16a, 17a, 18b
ROSCELINUS 10–0
Rose, Die (Van Aken) 4–319a
ROSELLO DI JACOPO FRANCHI 10–0
***ROSENGARTEN* 10–0**; 2–253a
ROSENPLÜT, HANS 10–0
drama 4–271b
Roses, Wars of the
See Wars of the Roses
Rosetti, Gioanventura 4–329a
Rosetum exercitiorum spiritualium et sacrarum mediatationum (Jan Mombaer) 4–167a
Rosewater 2–147a
ROSE WINDOW 10–0
Rosh Hashanah 3–26b, 27a
Rosh Ḥodesh 3–25a
***ROSKILDE CHRONICLE* 10–0**
Rossano Gospels 4–357a
Rosselli, Francesco 4–489a
Rossignos (John of Hovden) 1–262b
Rossikon (Mt. Athos) 1–637a
Rosso
See Giovanni (Nanni) de Bartolo
Rostislav Mihajlović 2–410a
Rostock
Dominican priory 1–128a
Rostov 4–555a
***ROTA* 10–0**
Rota (badge) 3–620b, 621a
Rota Romana 4–66a
Rota Veneris (Boncompagno of Signa) 2–320b
Ṙotěstak
See Hrak'ot-Perož
ROTH, RICHARD 10–0
Rothad of Soissons
Engelmodus 4–452a
False Decretals 4–373a
Rothar, King 1–90b
Rother, Martin
Bible translation 2–215b
Rothwell, William 1–272a
***ROTROUENGE* 10–0**
Anglo-Norman lyric poetry 1–269a
chansonnier 3–255b
Rotte 4–88a
Rotundellus 4–87a
Rouelle 3–621b
ROUEN 10–0
Black Death 2–261a
commune 3–497a
Eudes Rigaud 4–519a
Exchequer 3–8b
ROUEN, RITE OF 10–0
Rouen Cathedral
architecture 1–255b
Round arch 1–424, 425a
Round Church (Preslav) 2–414b, 415a-b
Round City (Baghdad) 1–8b; 2–45a,b
Round Table, knights 3–307a
See Also Arthurian Literature
Roupenids
See Rubenids
ROUSSEL DE BAILLEUL 10–0
rebellion 2–492a, 493b
Roussillon 1–409b, 416a, 418b-419a
agriculture 1–85b, 86a
Catalan language 3–159a-b
Crown of Aragon 1–413a
Routiers
See Great Companies
Royal Library Prayer Book 3–231a
Royal Psalter 4–548b
Royal unction 1–308a
Rrekontamiento de Rrey Ališandere 1–176a
Ruadan of Lorrha 3–465b
RUBEN I 10–0
RUBENIDS 10–0
Byzantine Empire 2–495a
Cilician Kingdom 3–391a
Cilician-Roman church union 3–394a
Rubens, Peter Paul
Gemma Tiberiana 1–335a-b
RUBLEV, ANDREI 10–0
Rubrics
antiphonal 1–330a
Rucellai Madonna (Duccio) 4–301b
Rūdbār 1–118a
Rudel, Jaufré
See Jaufré Rudel
Rudimenta astronomica (John of Seville) 1–612a
Rudolf I of Burgundy 2–429a
Rudolf II of Burgundy 2–424a, 429a
Rudolf III of Burgundy 2–429a
RUDOLF OF FULDA 10–0
Rudolf of Rheinfelden
election 3–69b; 4–427a
RUDOLF OF SAINT TROND 10–0
Rudolf of Swabia
See Rudolf of Rheinfelden
Rudolf IV the Founder of Austria 2–8a
RUDOLF VON EMS 10–0
Bligger von Steinach 2–274b
Bussard, Der 2–434a
poetry 2–229a
Rudolph of Bruges 1–393b
Ruḍwān of Aleppo
Crusade of 1101 4–36b
Ruffus, Jordanus 3–206b
RUFINUS (CANON LAWYER) 10–0
archbishop of Sorrento 4–422a
bishop of Assisi 3–638a
deposition of rulers 4–159b
irregularities of clergy 3–444a
summary of *Decretum* 4–127b
Rufinus (church father)
bestiary 2–204a
biblical exegesis 2–224a
Catechetical School of Alexandria 3–594a
Copts and Coptic church 3–595a
rite of Aquileia 1–352b
theology of Western church 3–336a
Rufinus (Greek calligrapher)
Armenian alphabet 1–492a
Rufus, Richard 2–36a
Rufus, William
See William II of England
Rugians 2–95a
RUGS AND CARPETS 10–0
rūh al-amīn, al- 1–248b
RUIZ, JUAN 10–0; 3–140a
fables 4–572b
Libro del Cavallero Zifar 3–197b
verse form 4–63b
Ruiz de Avendaño, Martin
Canary Islands 3–61b; 4–559a
Ruiz de Ulibarri, Juan
Cantar de Mío Cid 3–70b
Rukn al-Dawla 2–435b
Rukn al-Dīn Khūrshāh 1–118b
Rudolf I Habsburg 2–7b; 4–60a, 428b
election 1–133b, 161b; 2–300a
Rule of Chrodegang 1–286b
Rule of Columbanus 2–170a; 3–230a,b
Rule of Life for a Recluse, A (Saint Ethelred) 4–517a
Rule of Saint Augustine 1–657b-658b; 4–243a,b
Augustinian canons 1–659a
Augustinism 1–660b
Devotio Moderna 4–166b
Rule of Saint Benedict
See Benedictine Rule
"Rule of the Master" 3–343a
Rule of the Third Order of Saint Francis
Devotio Moderna 4–166b
RULING 10–0
RUM 10–0
Rümeli Ḥiṣār 2–504a
RŪMĪ (JALĀL AL-DĪN 10–0; 1–402a
Rune Poem, The 1–281a
RUNES 10–0; 1–207b, 212a-215b
Anglo-Saxon culture 1–274a
Old English texts 1–275a
***RUODLIEB* 10–0**; 1–94a; 4–496a
Ruodpreht Group 4–399b
RUOTGER OF COLOGNE 10–0
Rupert, Saint 2–4b, 134a
RUPERT OF DEUTZ 10–0; 2–174a
Alger of Liège 1–167b
Divine Office 4–223a
RURIK 10–0
Holmgard 4–555a
Rurik dynasty 1–100a, 102a
Rus
pirates 2–107a
Ruṣāfah, al- 2–46a

RUSHD, IBN (AVERROËS) **10–0**
Abū Yūsuf 1–194b, 195a
Albertus Magnus 1–127a
angel/angelology 1–250b
Aquinas, Thomas 1–356a,b-357a
Aristotelianism 1–459a-b, 463a, 465a, 467b-468a; 2–243b
Arnald of Villanova 1–538a
astronomy 1–614b, 621a
Burley, Walter 2–433a
Cavalcanti, Guido 3–197a
Córdoba 3–600b
dialectic 4–170b
Rushworth Gospels 2–221a
Mercian dialect 1–276a
Northumbrian dialect 1–276a
West Saxon version 1–285b
Russell, John 3–661b
Russia
agriculture 1–99b-102a
Baltic countries 2–64a
Black Death 4–142a
Byzantine church 2–464a, 469b-470a
Byzantine Empire 2–118b, 490b
camels 1–296b
cattles 1–293b, 294a
Christianity conversion 1–303a
Crimean khanate 3–679a-b
fairs 4–587b-588a
food animals 1–299b
Islamic currency 4–215b
Jews 2–263b
Lithuania 2–67a
Mongols 1–96b, 100b-101a
patrimonial principalities 1–101a
traveler accounts 1–332b
Varangians 4–555a
Vikings 4–554a
water buffalo 1–298a
See Also Kievan Rus
See Also Muscovy
See Also Novgorod
RUSSIAN AND SLAVIC ART 10–0
Dionysios the Greek 4–192a
Dubrovnik 4–300b
icons 1–238a
Theophanes 2–450b-451a
RUSSIAN ARCHITECTURE 10–0
bochka 2–290b
dome 4–236a
RUSSIAN NOMADS, INVASIONS OF 10–0
Albania 1–124a-b
Armenia 1–478b, 479a
Bulgaria 2–404b, 406a, 407b, 408a-b
Byzantine Empire 2–492b-493a
Caucasia 3–195a
Cyril and Methodios, Saints 2–463b
Derbent 4–162a
North Caucasia 3–195a
See Also Cumans
See Also Pechenegs
RUSSIAN ORTHODOX CHURCH 10–0
agriculture 1–100a-b
Byzantine church 2–461b
caesaropapism 3–11b
Constantinople 2–469b-470a
Russkaya pravda
See Law, Russian
Rustamids 3–49a
Taher 1–641a
Rusticiano da Pisa 1–572b; 2–522b
Rusticus 1–647b
Rustumids
See Rustamids
RUTEBEUF 10–0; 2–237a
crusade poems 4–20b
fabliaux 4–574a, 576b
Miracle de Théophile 4–264a
Ruthwell Cross 1–276a
Rutilius Taurus Aemilianus Palladius 4–511a
RUTILUS NAMATIANUS 10–0; 4–511a
RUUSBROEC, JAN VAN 10–0; 4–320b
RUUSBROEC AND HIS ASSOCIATES 10–0
Ruy de Sequeira 4–561b
Ruyelle, Guillaume 2–74b
Ryazan 2–131b
Rye
See Grain crops, Western European
Ryman, James
carols 3–116a

S

Saadiah ben Joseph al-Fayyumi
exegesis 4–538b
SAADIAH GAON 10–0
exegesis 2–212a
Jewish apocalyptic literature 1–345b
Saba
See Sabaeans
SABAEANS 10–0; 1–370a,b
Sabatons 1–534a
Sabbas
See Sava, Saint
Sabbath 3–25b
Sabīka
Alhambra 1–168a
SABĪL 10–0
Sabinianus, Pope
bells 2–165b; 3–28b
Sābiqa 3–34b
Ṣabruguera, Romeu 3–167a
ŠĀBUHR (SHAHPUHR) **I 10–0**; 1–452a
Šābuhr I 2–25b
Avesta collection 2–14b
Bishapur 2–251b
ŠĀBUHR (SHAHPUHR) **II 10–0**
Šābuhr II
Armenia 1–476a
Diyarbakir 4–231b
Šābulhr I
See Šābuhr (Shahpuhr) I
Sabur
See Bishapur
Sac
See Soc, sac, and sec
Saccelli 1–223b
Sacchetti, Franco 1–562a
Sacconi, Rainier 3–182a, 186a
***SACHSENSPIEGEL* 10–0**
Conrad IV 4–428a
Eike von Repgowe 4–408b
Sächsische Weltchronik 4–409a
SACK 10–0
SACK, FRIARS OF THE 10–0
Sacra coena, De (Berengar) 2–188a
Sacralias
See Zallaqa
Sacramentarium patriarchale secundum morem S. Comensis ecclesiae 1–353a
SACRAMENTARY (ART) **10–0**
SACRAMENTARY (LITURGY) **10–0**
Agnus Dei music 1–74b
Alcuin of York 1–143a
baptismal rites 2–83a
collectarium 3–479b
Divine Office 4–223a-b
rite of Aquileia 1–353a
Sacramentary, Gelasian 4–120b
Sacramentary, Gregorian
Christmas Mass 3–318b
Sacramentary of Angoulême
dedication of churches 4–131a
Sacrament of the Lord's Body and Blood, On the (Alger of Liège) 1–167b
Sacraments
Armenian church 1–502a
Augustine 1–660b
Celtic liturgy 3–230b, 231a
Decretum 4–129b
early church 3–338a
extreme unction 4–565a
patristic heritage of ecclesiology 4–372b
See Also individual listings
Sacraments of the Church, The (Anselm of Canterbury) 1–313b, 315a
Sacred Law
Koran 1–373b
Sacrifice of Isaac 2–388a,b
Sacrifice of Unleavened and Leavened Bread, The (Anselm of Canterbury) 1–313b, 314b
Sacrificio de la Misa (Berceo) 2–187a
Sacristan
hierarchy of clergy 3–444b
SACRISTY 10–0; 1–442b
Sacro Eremo di Camaldoli monastery 3–56a
Sacrosancta 3–511a; 4–483b
SAʿD 10–0
Saddles
high-backed 3–202b
SAʿDI 10–0
Saʿdites
mosque types 1–193a
Sādjids
See Sājids
Saeborg 2–62b
Sælden Hort, Der 2–230b
Sæmundr Edda 4–385b
Sæmundr Sigfússon the Learned 4–385b
Safad
Baybars' recapture 2–138b
Ṣafadī, al-
biographies 2–237b
Safawids
Aq Qoyunlu 1–352b
Ayrarat 2–20b
Azerbaijan 2–27a
Bāyazīd 2–137b
SAFFĀH, ABŪ 'L-ʿABBĀS AL- 10–0
SAFFARIDS 10–0
rise to power 1–64b
Safflower (*Carthamus tinctorius*) 4–326a
Saffron (*Crocus sativus*) 4–326a, 328a
Ṣafiyya 1–15a
Safont, Jaume 3–166b
SAGA 10–0
Alexanders saga 1–152a
Áns saga bogsveigis 1–310b
Ásmundar saga Kappabana 1–586b-587b
Atlamál 1–638b
Bandamanna saga 2–70b
Bósa saga 2–333b
See Also Family Sagas, Icelandic
SAGA HREDU 11–0

Saga of Droplaug's Sons
See Droplaugarsona saga
"Saga of the Confederate Chieftains"
See Bandamanna Saga
Sagrajas, Battle of (1086) 3–129b, 384a
Sagreres 2–103a
Sagristà i la burgesa, El (Verger and the bourgeoise) 3–173b
Sahagún 3–131b-132a
Sahak (ninth-century martyr) 1–519b
SAHAK, SAINT 10–0; 1–498b, 518a,b
Armenian literature 1–508a
Armenian rite 1–516b
Arsacids/Aršakuni 1–559b
Bible 2–217a
Eznik of Kołb 4–571a
Sahak Arcruni, Prince 1–479b, 519a
Sahak Bagratuni 2–48a
Sahakduxt 1–510a
Sahak III Kat'ołikos 1–500a
Sahak of Jorap'or 1–509b
Sahak the Parthian, Kat'ołikos
Ējmiaçin 4–417a
ŠAHAN-ŠAH 10–0; 1–485b
Šahapivan, Council of 1–498b, 508a, 518a
Sahara Desert
Atlas Mountains 1–639b
Berbers 2–186a,b
Saharan tribes
Islamization 1–199a
Sahē
See Sophenē
Šah-i Armen dynasty 1–485a
Şah Ismā'il 2–137b
Sahm al-sa'ādah 1–619b
Sahmank' Imastasirut'ean
See Prolegomena tēs philosophias
Sahm clan
Kuraysh 1–236b
SAHN 10–0
Saḥnūn
Aghlabids 1–71a
Şaho 1–31b
Šāhphur II, King
See Shapur II
Sa'īd, Ibn
Córdoba 3–599a
Sa'īd al-Mu'taḍid, al- 1–195b
Sa'īd ibn al-'Āṣ 1–15b
Saif al-Dīn Ghaāzī I
Unur 4–38a
Sail vault
See Pendentive
Saint Albans
clerical chronicles 3–327a
Saint Albans Cathedral
architecture 1–255b
Saint Albans Psalter
art 1–258a
Saint Amand monastery
Ebarcius 4–368a
Saint André Cathedral 2–328a
Saint Andrew on the Clivus Scauri, Monastery 1–644b
SAINT ANDREWS 10–0
Saint Andrews Manuscript
See Wolfenbüttel, Helmstedt MS 628
Saint Anne's Church 4–22b
Saint Anthony, Order of 3–307a
Saint Augustine, Monastery of 1–265b
Saint Augustine Abbey 3–81b, 82b
Cambridge Songs 3–57a
Clonard 3–466a
Saint Augustine Cathedral
architecture 1–255b
Saint Ayoul fair 4–585b, 591a, 592a
Saint Barbara Church 3–92b
SAINT BARTHOLOMEW, MASTER OF 10–0
Saint Bartholomew fair 4–586b
Saint Bernard, College of 3–405a
Saint Catharine's College, Cambridge 3–59b
Saint Catherine, Monastery of (Sinai)
art 3–446a; 4–354b, 355a, 356, 357b, 358b, 359a, 361a
icons 2–439a, 445b
SAINT CECILIA MASTER 10–0
Assisi 1–593b
SAINT CHAD, BOOK OF 10–0; 1–285a
Saint Chrysostomos, Church of 2–444b
Saint Clair-sur-Epte, Treaty of (911) 3–115a
Saint Claude Church 2–426b
Saint Cuthbert Church (Edinburgh) 4–392b
SAINT DAVID'S 10–0
SAINT DENIS, ABBEY CHURCH 10–0; 3–192a
Abelard 1–17a,b
architecture 4–346a
chronicles 1–109b
fair 4–585a
Historia regum Francorum 3–332a
Pepin the Younger 3–108b-109a
tiled pavements 3–237a
Saint Donation Church (Bruges) 2–386a-b
Sainte ampoule
French coronation rites 1–308b
Saint Ebbe's Church (Oxford)
sculpture 1–256a
SAINTE CHAPELLE, PARIS 10–0; 3–263b
Sainte Croix Abbey 2–327b
Sainte Geneviève Church (Paris) 3–467a
Sainte Madeleine de Traînel Convent 1–18a
Sainte Maria Donnaregina Church (Anjou) 3–198a
Saint Emmeram Monastery 2–134a
Saint Erasmus, Master of 4–489a
Saint Étienne Cathedral (Caen)
alternating supports 1–226a
groin vaulting 2–125a
Saint Étienne of Troyes 3–246a
Saint Eustace Church
sculpture 1–256a
Saint Èvre Monastery
Aynard 2–19b
Saint Felix-de-Caraman
Cathars 3–183b
Saint Flavit Convent 1–18a
Saint Gall, Church of 3–378b
Saint Gall Monastery 2–139b
"Saint-Gatien" Anthology 1–319a
Saint George (Donatello) 4–257a
Saint George Church (Brinsop)
sculpture 1–256b
Saint George Church (Kurbinovo) 2–445b
Saint Georg of the Mangana (Constantinople)
art 2–443a
Saint Gereon Church (Cologne) 3–378a
Saint Germain-des-Prés Church
portal 1–427b
Saint Germain l'Auxerrois
Black Death 2–261a
Saint German, Christopher 4–503a
Saint Germigny-des-Prés Church 4–347a
Saint Gilles 1–408b
Saint Guildas of Rhuys Abbey 1–17b
Saint Jacques Convent (Paris) 1–127a
Saint Jaume Church (Barcelona) 2–103a
Saint John Lateran Church (Rome)
See Lateran
Saint John of Jerusalem, Knights of 3–303b-304a
Saint John's fair 4–585b, 592a
Saint John the Baptist Monastery (Dawid-Garedja) 4–116a
Saint John the Evangelist Church (Ephesus) 4–339a
Saint-Julien-du-Petit-Quevilly Chapel
Anglo-Norman art 1–258a
Saint Lazarus Convent 4–23b
Saint Louis of Toulouse (Donatello) 4–257a
Saint Malo
city walls 3–151b
Saint Maria Church (Cosmedin) 1–333b
Saint Mark's (Venice)
See San Marco, Venice
SAINT MARTIAL SCHOOL 10–0
Saint Martin Church (Canterbury) 4–453b
Saint Martin de Boran Convent 1–18a
Saint Martin's fair 4–592a
Saint Mary Abbey
Anonimalle Chronicle 1–309a
Saint Mary-le-Bow Church (London) 1–433b
Saint Mary Magdalene Convent 1–147a
Saint Mary Magdalene Hospital
Stourbridge fair 4–587a
Saint Mary of Bethlehem, Priory of Bedlam 2–157a
SAINT MARY'S ABBEY, DUBLIN 10–0
Saint Mary's at Clonard 3–466a
Saint Mary's at Warwick 4–510b
Saint Mary's of the Germans
Teutonic Knights 3–306a
Saint Maur, Congregation of 1–427b
Saint Memmie Abbey
fair 4–591a
Saint Michael Monastery (Hildesheim) 2–198a
Saint Michael's Church (Hildesheim)
alternating supports 1–226a
double-ended basilica 2–124b
Saint Nicholas Church (Curtea-de-Arges) 2–450a
Saint Nicholas Island 4–43a
Saint Nicholas Orphanou Church (Thessaloniki) 2–450a
Saint Niklas Church (Cheb) 1–44a
Saint Omer
commune 3–497b
Saint Panteleimon Monastery (Mount Athos) 1–638a
Saint Panteleiomon Church (Nerezi)
paintings 2–444b-445a
SAINT PATRICK'S PURGATORY 10–0; 1–185b, 261b
Saint Paul's Cathedral (London)
Bradwardine, Thomas 2–358a
clocks 3–29b, 460a
estates 4–512b
Saint Paul's Descent into Hell 1–261b
Saint Paul's Outside the Walls
See San Paolo fuori le Mura
SAINT PETER, LITURGY OF 10–0
Saint Peter's Abbey
Clonard 3–466a
Saint Peter's Church (Rome)
See Old Saint Peter's, Rome
Saint Peter's fair 4–592a
Saint Peter's Gloucester
estate management 4–513b
Saint Pierre sur Dives Church
tiled pavements 3–237a

Saint-Pol family
butler 2–434b
Saint Quentin
commune 3–496a
Saint Quentin, collegial church 3–192a
Saint Quiriace fair 4–592a
Saint Rémi fair 4–592a
Saint Rémi Monastery 3–634a
Saint Riquier Monastery
Angilbert, Saint 1–254a
Saint Saviour Monastery 3–122b
Saints Cosmas and Damian Church (Rome) 4–352a, 358b, 359a,b
Saints' days
calendar dating 3–21b
Saints Sergios and Bakchos, church of (Constantinople) 4–338b
Saint Sergius Church (Gaza)
dome 3–378a
SAINT SERNIN, TOULOUSE 10–0
pilgrimage church style 3–379b, 382
triforium 2–125a
Saint Seurin Church (Bordeaux) 2–328a
Saint Sever Abbey 2–327b
Saints' lives
Aelfric homilies 1–285a
Anglo-Norman literature 1–261a-262b
Anglo-Saxon literature 1–275a, 279a
Cistercian order 3–405a
French chronicles 3–332b
historical chronicles 3–325b
See Also Hagiography
Saint Sophia Church
decoration 2–453b
Saints Peter and Paul, Abbey of
See Saint Augustine Abbey
Saints Peter and Paul Church (Canterbury)
Augustine of Canterbury 1–645b
Saints Peter and Victor Monastery 3–122a
Saints' sagas 4–612b
"Saint Sulpice" 1–562b
Saint-Théodard Abbey 2–128a
Saint Theodore Church 4–358b
Saint Therapont Monastery
art 4–192a
Saint Titus Church (Gortyna) 4–339a
Saint Vaast Church (Arras) 4–105b
SAINT VERONICA, MASTER OF 10–0
Saint Victor, School of 1–51a
SAINT VICTOR MANUSCRIPT 10–0
Saint Vitus Cathedral (Prague) 3–614a
Saint Yves
fairs 4–586b
Saisset, Bernard, Bishop of Pamiers
Boniface VIII 2–324a
Sājids 1–513b; 2–27a
Ašot II Erkatʿ 1–589a
Sajjada
See Rugs and carpets
Sakarya River
See Sangarius River
Šakašēn 1–123b
Ṣakhr ibn Ḥarb
See Abū Sufyān ibn Ḥarb ibn Umayya
Sakkos 3–615a,b
SALADIN 10–0
Aleppo 1–145b
Alexandria 1–153b, 154b
Athīr, Ibn al- 1–634a,b
Ayyubid dynastic establishment 2–23a-b, 24a
Ayyubid fortification architecture 2–21a, 25a
Cairo 3–14a
crusader art and architecture 4–25a
crusades 4–31a-b, 38b, 39a-40b
Damascus 4–82b
dirham 4–215b
Fatimid dynasty 2–28a
Islamic Egypt 4–406a, 407a
reign 1–375b
Salado, Battle of (1340) 3–135a
Ṣalāḥ al-Dīn
See Saladin
Ṣalāḥ al-Dīn of Yemen 2–23b
Salala 1–472b
Salamanca, University of 3–212a
Cistercian order 3–405a
Salamis
See Constantia
Salces
fortress 3–152a
Sale, Antoine de la
Cent nouvelles nouvelles 3–235a
Salef River 4–40a
Salerno, University of
medicine 1–219a; 4–579b
Salian dynasty
Babenberg family 2–6b, 33b
Bavarian rule 2–134a
royal election 2–94a; 4–427a
Salian Law
agriculture 1–90b
Clovis 3–467a
Salic Law
See Salian Law
Ṣāliḥ Ayyūb, al-
Richard of Cornwall 4–32a
Ṣāliḥ Ḥājjī, al-
Barqūq's control 2–113a
Ṣāliḥ ibn Ayyūb, al- 2–24a
SALIMBENE 10–0
Boncompagno 2–320a
Salisbury, rite of
See Sarum rite
SALISBURY CATHEDRAL 10–0
chapter house design 3–267a
Sallarids
Dwin 4–324a
Sallet 1–527a, 530a
Sallus 2–236a
Sallust 3–77a
Sallustius 1–181a
***SALMAN UND MOROLF* 10–0**
Salmon ben Jeroḥam
exegesis 4–539b
Salomon, Duke of Brittany 2–379a
Salomon family (Swabia)
Arnulf 3–114b
SALOMO OF CONSTANCE 10–0
Salona 4–79b
Ṣalt, Ibn al- 1–617a
***SALTAIR NA RANN: THE PSALTER OF QUATRAINS* 10–0**; 1–347b
Airbertach 1–110b
Airdena Brátha 1–111b, 112a
Saltarello 4–88a
SALT TRADE 10–0
Burgundy, County of 2–424b, 426b
Cistercians 3–404a
Saltuqids 1–514a
Saltu lunae, De (Columbanus, Saint) 3–486b
Saltus lunae 3–22a-b
Salutati, Coluccio
Boccaccio 2–287b, 289a
Bruni, Leonardo 2–390b
classical literary studies 3–435b
Salut d'Amor 3–173a
Salvatge, Pere 3–164b
Salvation
early church theory 3–342a
rabbinic concept 1–21b
SALVATORIS HODIE 10–0
Salvatoris, Sancti, Basilica
papal coronation 3–602b
Salve regina 1–329a
SALVIAN OF MARSEILLES 10–0
Salvo
Ermenrich of Ellwangen 4–507a
Salzburg
archbishopric 2–4b-6a
bishoprics 2–134a
Boniface, Saint 2–322a
Samael
Jewish apocalyptic literature 1–344b, 346a,b
Samālū, Battle of 2–110a
Samandağ
See Seleucia-Pieria
SAMANID ART AND ARCHITECTURE 10–0
SAMANIDS 10–0
Alptigin 1–219a
Bukhara 2–397a
Buyids 2–435b
emirs 4–437a
Samaritani, Adalberto
University of Bologna 2–312b
SAMARITANS 10–0
SAMARKAND 10–0
Bukhara 2–397a
SAMARKAND WARE 10–0
SAMARRA 10–0
Abbasid capital 1–11a; 2–46b; 3–49b
architecture 1–5a-b
Sambatyon River
Jewish apocalyptic literature 1–346b
Sambians 2–66b
Samḥ, Ibn al- 1–385b
Sāmī fī-al-asāmī, al- (Nīshāpūrī) 4–444b
Samlanders
See Sambians
Samogitia
Semgallians 2–65b
Samogitians
Battle of Durben (1260) 2–66b-67a
Samosata 4–522a, 523a
Byzantine capture (873) 2–118a
SAMPIRUS OF ASTERGA 10–0
Sampson, William
excommunication 4–537b-538a
Samson, Saint
Brittany 2–377b
Samson of Bury Saint Edmund's 2–173b, 175b; 4–424b
***SAMSONS SAGA FAGRA* 10–0**
Samtíða sǫgur 4–612b
Samuel
tekufot 3–26b-27a
Samuel ben Hophni
Pentateuch 4–539a
Samuel ben Meïr
exegesis 2–212b; 4–540b
Samuēl Kamrǰajorecʿ
literature 1–510b, 511b
Samuēl of Ani 1–511b
SAMUIL OF BULGARIA 10–0;
2–118b, 406b
Bosnia 2–334b
Byzantine church 2–464a
Byzantine Empire 2–490b; 4–5b
Samur River 2–26a
SANA 10–0
Islamic center 1–375a,b
San Agostino Church (San Gimignanao) 2–116b
SANAHIN 10–0; 1–589b
San Ambrogio Church (Milan) 4–361a
San Antonio
Anthony of Padua, Saint 1–320b

San Antonio Church (Padua)
frescoes 1–226b
San Apollinare in Classe Church (Ravenna) 4–358b
San Apollinare Nuovo Church (Ravenna) 4–358b, 361b
San Aquilino Church (Milan) 4–358b
San Aṙak'eloc' Church 1–292a
Sanasar 4–112b, 113a
Sanas Cormaic (Cormac) 3–602a
Sanatruk Aršakuni 2–139a
Sanç 1–415a
San Cassiano a Settimo
doors 2–233b
Sancha of Castile 1–409a
Sanche-Guillaume 1–367a
Bordeaux 2–327b
Sanchez, Ferdinand 1–413a
Sancho García of Castile 3–128b
Sancho I of Asturias-León 1–627b
Sancho II of Castile 3–129a
Cid 3–383b
Sancho III of Castile
See Sancho III of Navarre
Sancho IV of Castile
reign 3–134b
Sancho III of Navarre 3–130b
Basques 2–126b
Calatrava, Order of 3–16b
Castile 1–404a; 3–128b
conquest of León 1–628b
Sancho IV of Navarre 1–405b
Sancho II of Portugal
right to rule 4–160a
Sancho Ramírez of Aragon 1–404a-b
son 1–160a
Sancho the Great of Castile
See Sancho III of Navarre
Sancho VI of Navarre
Castile 3–130b
Sanctity
canonization 3–67b
SANCTIUS 10–0
Sanctuary 1–442b, 443, 444a
liturgical action 4–343b-344a
Sanctuary, right of 1–631a
SANCTUS 10–0
Alexandrian Anaphora of Mark 1–156a-b
SANDALJ HRANIĆ KOSAČA 10–0
territories 2–337b, 338a-339a, 340a
Sandals
Western European 3–625b
Sandek
Jewish circumcision 3–401b
San Domenico Church (Bologna)
Dalle Masegne 4–79a
San Domenico Church (Pesaro)
Dalle Masegne 4–79a
San Domingo de Silos Church 3–133a
Sanduxt, Saint 1–519a
San Fosca Church (Torcello) 4–346a
San Francisco Church (Bologna)
Dalle Masegne 4–79a
Islamization 1–198a-b
Sangarius bridge 1–240a
Sangarius River 4–334a
San Germano, Treaty of (1230) 4–58b
San Gimignano, Collegiata of 2–116b
San Giorgio Church (Velabro) 3–198a
San Giovanni in Fonte Church (Naples) 4–358a
San Grigor Church 1–292a
San Grigor Lusaworic' Church 1–292a
Ṣanhāja
Berbers 2–185b, 186a
Sanjar, Sultan 4–91b
San Joan de les Abadesses Monastery 3–175a
San Juan de la Peña 1–404a
San Juan de los Caballeros Church 1–114b
San Julián de los Prados Church (Oviedo) 1–624b
Sankovići family 2–337b
Sankt Jakob Church (Straubing)
Burghausen, Hanns von 2–422a
Sankt Martin Church (Landshut)
Burghausen, Hanns von 2–422a
San Lorenzo Church 3–378a
San Lorenzo Church (Florence) 2–390a
San Lorenzo Church (Milan) 3–378a; 4–352a
San Lorenzo fuori le Mura (Rome)
ambulatory 1–234a
San Lorenzo Outside the Walls 4–352a, 359a
SAN MARCO, VENICE 10–0
bronze horses 1–335a
doors 2–202a-b
enamels 2–443b
iconostasis 4–79a
San Marco Convent 1–342b
San Maria Maggiore Church of Rome 4–337b-338a, 357a, 358b-359a
San Miguel de Lillo Church 1–630b
San Miquel of Cuixà Monastery 3–175a
San Paolo fuori le Mura 3–198a; 4–352a, 359a
architecture 4–338a
bronze doors 2–456a
SAN PEDRO, DIEGO DE 10–0
San Pedro de Cardeña Monastery 3–73a
Cid 3–76a
Estoria del Cid 3–71b
San Pere Convent 2–104a
San Petronio Church (Milan)
Dalle Masegne 4–79a
San P'rkič' Church 1–292a
San Sabina Church (Rome) 4–360, 361a
San Salvador (Watling's Island)
Columbus 4–560b
San Salvatore Church (Lucca)
portal 2–233b
San Satiro Church 4–346a
San Sebastian
trade 4–558a
San Sebastiano Church (Mantua) 1–126b
San Sepolcro, Church of 4–193b
SANSON DE NANTEUIL 10–0
San Stefano Church (Venice)
Dalle Masegne 4–79a
Santa Agnese 4–352a
Santa Cecilia Church 3–198a
Santa Cecilia Church (Rome) 3–198a,b
Santa Clara Convent (Vivar) 3–70b
Santa Coloma de Queralt
slaves 2–268b
Santa Costanza Church (Rome) 4–358a,b
mausoleum 4–350b
Santa Creu Hospital 2–104b
Santa Cristina de Lena Church 1–630b
Santa Croce Church (Florence)
Pazzi Chapel 2–388a, 389b, 390a
Santa Maria Antiqua Church (Rome) 4–353b, 358b
Santa Maria Church (Trastevere) 3–198a; 4–355a
Santa Maria Church 4–353b
Santa Maria Degli Angeli Church (Florence)
Brunelleschi, Filippo 2–390a
Santa Maria de la Torre
Bruno the Carthusian 2–392b
Santa Maria del Carmine Church (Milan) 2–196b
Santa Maria del Fiore Church (Florence) 1–431a
Santa Maria della Carità Church (Venice)
Buon, Giovanni and Bartolomeo 2–419b
Santa Maria dell'Orto Church (Venice)
Buon, Giovanni and Bartolomeo 2–419b
Santa Maria del Mar Church (Barcelona) 2–103a
Santa María de Naranco Church 1–630b
Santa Maria Maggiore Church of Jerusalem
Christmas mass 3–318b
Santa Maria Maggiore Church of Rome 4–332b, 337b-338a
angels 1–248a
Annuciation 1–248a, 307b
mosaics 4–357a, 358b
Santa Maria Novella Church (Florence) 1–126b
Brunelleschi, Filippo 2–388a
Santa Maria Novella Church 4–101a
Santa Miguel Church (Barcelona) 2–103a
Santander
Asturias-León 1–625a
Castile 3–125b
trade 4–558a
Sant'Andrea Church (Mantua) 1–126b
Sant'Apollinare in Classe Church
altar apparatus 1–221b
Santa Pudenziana Church 4–351b, 352a, 358b, 526a
angels 1–248a
Santarém 1–194b
Santa Sabina 4–352a
Santa Sabina Church (Rome)
doors 4–360, 361a
Santa Salvatore 4–353b
Santa Tecla Church (Milan) 4–336a
Santes Creus Monastery 1–408b
Santiago
exploration 4–561b
Santiago, Knights of
Marian office 2–274a
SANTIAGO DE COMPOSTELA 10–0; 2–194b
Asturias-León 1–626b, 627a, 629b, 630b
cantigas de amigo 3–86b
Castilian development 3–131b-132a
cathedral 1–224b, 625b
fairs 4–587b
Latin church: 1054 to 1305 3–356a
Muslim attack on (997) 1–628a
pilgrimage church style 3–379b
pilgrimmage to 4–16a
Romanesque architecture 3–133a
trade 1–404b
SANTIAGO DE COMPOSTELA, SCHOOL OF 10–0
Santiago de Compostella, Order of 3–306b
Santi Giovanne e Paolo Church (Venice)
Dalle Masegne 4–79a
SANTILLANA, MARQUÉS DE 10–0
Catalan literature 3–169b, 171a
Santillana del Mar Church 3–133a
Santissima Trinità di Delia Church 4–346b
Santos Just i Pastor Church (Barcelona) 2–102b
Santo Spirito Church (Florence)
Brunelleschi 2–389a, 390a
Santo Stefano dei Mori (Rome) 1–32b

Santo Tomaso in Formis church (Rome)
cosmati work 3–614a
Santritter, Joannes Lucilius
Alfonsine Tables canons 1–160a
San Victorián
See Sobrarbe
San Vitale Church (Ravenna) 1–3a; 4–336, 339a, 347a, 353a, 354a,b, 359a,b, 361b, 526a
São Jorge
settlement 2–29b
São Jorge da Mina
slaves 2–268b, 269a
trade 4–562a
São Miguel
colonization 2–29b; 4–559b
Saone (Sahyun)
castle site 4–24b
São Thome 4–561b
Saplana, Dalmau 3–168b
Saplana, Pere 3–168b
Sapor
See Šābulhr I
Ṣaps 3–144b, 146a
Šapuh, Prince
Armenian literature 1–510b
Ṣaqāliba 1–70a
Córdoba 3–600a
Sāqiṭ 1–386b, 387a
Saracen besants 2–203a
See Also Besant
Saracens
Aucassin et Nicolette 1–642b
Crown of Aragon 1–408a-b, 413a
Pope Leo IV 4–18b
Saragossa
agriculture 1–82a
Alfonso I 1–160b
Alfonso VII 1–408a
Almoravid conquest 1–200a
Aragon 1–403b, 404b, 405b, 406a,b, 407a,b
Braulio, Saint 2–364b
Crown of Aragon 1–409a, 411b, 413b, 414a, 415b, 417a, 419a
Sarajevo
See Vrhbosna
Sarakhsi
banking 2–79b
Ṣarāt Canal
Baghdad 2–44b, 45a
SARAY 10–0
Sarcophagus 4–121a,b
Apocalypse illustration 1–343b
Celtic art 3–223a,b
SARDICA 10–0
Krum 2–401a
Sardica, Council of (343)
canons (343) 3–632a
interstices of clergy 3–442b
origin of Celtic church 3–225b
Sardinia
agricultural tools 1–80a
agriculture and nutrition 1–88a
Catalan language 3–157b
Crown of Aragon 1–414b, 415a, 416a,b, 417a,b, 419a
Genoans 4–556a
Sardis
Anatolia 1–239b
Sargis (Armenian *vestes*) 1–484a
SARGIS PICAK 10–0
Sargis the General, Saint 1–519a
Sariel
angel/angelology 1–249b
Sarigürzel sarcophagus 4–351b
angel 1–248a
Sarjīs ibn Ḥilya 1–106a
Sarkland 4–555b
SARMATIANS 10–0
arms and armor 1–522a, 534b
north Caucasia 3–195a
Sarōsh 1–249a
SARRACINUS 10–0
Sarrāj, al-
Lovers' Disasters 1–380b
SARUM CHANT 10–0
Sarum Manual 4–565b
SARUM RITE 10–0
Bangor, Rite of 2–72a
SASANIAN ART AND ARCHITECTURE 10–0
Bulgarian art and architecture 2–414b, 417a
Ctesiphon 4–62b
eyvān 4–569b
SASANIANS 10–0
Abbasid caliphate 3–42a
Abū Bakr 1–25b
Afghanistan 1–64a,b
Ankara occupation 1–302a
Ardešīr I 1–451b
Armenia 1–475b, 476b-478a
Arsacids/Aršakuni 1–559a,b
Avarayr 2–12a
Azerbaijan 2–26b-27a
Bahrām V Gōr 2–49b
Bahrām VI Čōbēn 2–50a
Bishapur 2–251b
Buyids 2–436b-437a
Byzantine Empire 2–486b, 487a
caliphate 3–38a
Chosroids 3–308a
See Also Christian church in Persia
Sasanids
See Sasanians
Sasi
mining 2–340a
Sasna Cṙer
David of Sasun 4–112b
SASSETTA 10–0
Sassoferrato, Bartolo da
See Bartolo da Sassoferrato
Sasun, David of
See David of Sasun
Sasuncʿi dawitʿ
See David of Sasun
Satan
angel/angelology 1–249b
Satire
Anglo-Norman lyric poetry 1–269b
anthologies 1–319a,b
antifeminism 1–323b
Arabic poetry 1–402a
Deschamps 4–164a
fabliau 3–293a,b; 4–575b
Sermones (Amarcius) 1–228b
Satisfaction (Dracontius) 4–520b
Satisfaction theory of atonement
Anselm of Canterbury 1–314b
Satyre of the Thrie Estaitis 4–287a
Saucer dome 4–236a
Saule, Battle of (1236) 2–65b
SAVA, SAINT 10–0; 2–339a
Mount Athos 1–637a
Serbian church 2–469a
Savage, Sir John
Chester plays 3–298b
Sava River 2–334a-b
banats 2–70a
Slavonia border 4–4a
SAVIGNY 10–0
Cistercian order 3–404a
Savior, Church of the (Nereditsa) 4–341a
Savonarola, Girolamo
burning 2–307b
church reforms 3–368a
Dominican studies 4–246a-b
ecclesiology 4–378a
preaching 4–250a
SAVOY, COUNTY OF 10–0
Dauphiné 4–108a
Savrīqīn 3–618b
Sawāda, Djaḥḥāf ibn
Ašot I Mec 1–588a
Sawīrus ibn al-Muqaffaʿ
Eutychios 4–525a
Saxnot
renunciation in baptismal vows 2–87a
SAXO, POETA 10–0
SAXO GRAMMATICUS 10–0
Ásmundar saga Kappabana 1–586b-587b
Baldr 2–55a
Bjarkamál 2–254b
Browulf 2–184b
Gesta Danorum 1–310b; 3–327a; 4–152a
Hryggjarstykki 4–414a
SAXON ARCHITECTURE 10–0
SAXON DYNASTY 10–0; 4–421a-b
Saxons
Anglo-Saxon literature 1–274a
Anglo-Saxon origins and migration 1–289a
arms and armor 1–522a
Canterbury settlement 3–81a
invasions 2–96b-97a
kinship group 4–599b
sundial 3–457a
Vortigern 2–2b
See Also England: Anglo-Saxon
SAXONY 10–0
arms and armor 1–529b
barbarians 2–96b
Billungs 2–235a
Carmen de bello saxonico 3–97a
Charlemagne's conquests 3–107a
Henry the Lion 2–134b
Prague 2–303a
Say, Lord
Cade's Rebellion 3–5a
Sayf al-Dawla 4–523a
Aleppo 1–145a
Constantine VII Porphyrogenitos 3–547a
Sayf ibn Dhī Yazan
Arabia 1–371b
Sayol, Ferrer 3–168b
Sayyid 1–175b; 3–33b
Muʿāwiya 3–36b-37a
Sayyids
Islamic Arabia 1–375a
Scabies parasites 1–377b
Scabini 3–658b
Cologne 3–482a
Scabinus
See Échevin
Scacs d'amor (Fenollar) 3–171b
Scala, Alboino della 4–99a
SCALACRONICA 10–0; 1–265b
Scala de contemplació (Canals) 3–167b
Scala Dei (Eiximensis) 4–416b
Scale of Perfection, The (Hilton) 3–368b
Scalloped capital 3–90b
Scandinavia
Adam of Bremen 1–50a-b
Adrian IV 1–58a
animal style 1–293b
archives 1–449a
banking 2–74a
Black Death 2–261a-b
climatology 3–451a, 454a, 455a
dwarf cattle 1–293b

SCANDINAVIA (cont.)
fairs 4–587b
Goths 2–90a
Islamic currency 4–215b
stave churches 3–379b, 382
trade with Baltic countries 2–62b-63a
SCANDINAVIA, ARABIC SOURCES IN 10–0
SCANDINAVIA: BEFORE 800 10–0
bracteates 2–355b
SCANDINAVIAN LANGUAGES 10–0
alphabets 1–212b, 215a,b
SCANDINAVIAN LITERATURE: BALLADS 10–0
Draumkvæde 4–290a
SCANDINAVIAN LITERATURE: GRAMMATICAL 10–0
SCANDINAVIAN LITERATURE: RELIGIOUS 10–0
SCANDINAVIAN LITERATURE: RHYMED CHORNICLES
Erikskrönikan 4–505b
SCANDINAVIAN MYTHOLOGY 10–0
Æsir 1–62b
Baldr 2–55a
Baldrs Draumar 2–56a
berserks 2–198a
Bragi Boddason the Old 2–359a
Darrađarljóđ 4–106b
Fáfnir 4–581a
Scandinavians
exploration 4–553b-555b
SCANDINAVIAN TEMPLES 10–0
SCANDINAVIA: POLITICAL AND LEGAL ORGANIZATION 10–0
Scaramangion 3–615a
Scéla Laí Brátha 1–347b
Scéla na h-Esérgi 1–347b
Schaffhausen
John XXIII 3–648a
SCHAMPIFLOR, DER 10–0
Schedel, Hartmann
Nuremberg chronicle 3–329a
Weltkronik 4–578b
Schematibus et tropis, De 2–154b
Schiltrons 3–205a
SCHISM, ARMENIAN-BYZANTINE 11–0
Albanian church 1–123b
SCHISM, ARMENIAN-GEORGIAN 11–0
SCHISM, GREAT 11–0; 3–365a-366b
Ailly 1–108a
Alexander V 1–147a
antipope 1–331a
Antoninus, Saint 1–342a
Avignon 2–16a
Babylonian Captivity 2–34b
Carthusians 3–119a
celibacy laws 3–217b
Charles V of France 3–270a
church organizaton 3–377a
Cistercians 3–405b
conciliar movement 4–484b
conciliar theory 3–510b
conclave, papal 3–524a-b
crusades 4–56a
deposition of rulers 4–160a
ecclesiology 4–377a-378a
papal coronation 3–604b
theology 4–416a
Western councils 3–642a, 645b-649a, 651a
SCHISM, PHOTIAN 11–0
Schismatics
crusade against 4–17a
Schisms
Acacian 4–491b
Antioch 3–122a
Frangipani and Pierleoni factions 3–94a
Innocentian-Anacletian 3–637a
Novatian 4–70a
SCHISMS, EASTERN-WESTERN CHURCH 11–0; 2–464b-466a, 485b-486a
Alexander III 1–147a
azymes 2–31b
Constantine IX Monomachos 3–548a
Council of Chalcedon 3–630a
Latin church: to 1054 3–349a-b
See Also Church, Latin: 1054 to 1305
Schleswig
Vikings 4–554a
Schloss Ambras (Alto Adige)
Ambraser Heldenbuch 1–229b
Schmelzen
See Enamel
Schnabelschuhe
See Poulaines
Schnapps 4–220a
***SCHOLAE* 11–0**
Byzantine bureaucracy 2–472a
See Also Schools, palace
Scholar's Guide
See Disciplina clericalis
Scholarship
Anglo-Norman literature 1–271a-272a
Cistercian order 3–404b
Old English 1–286b-287b
SCHOLARSHIP, BYZANTINE CLASSICAL 11–0
Scholars Primer
See Auricept na nÉces
Scholastica, Saint 1–125b
SCHOLASTICISM, SCHOLASTIC METHOD 11–0
Abrabanel 1–22a
Adelard of Bath 1–53b
alchemy 1–137b, 140a
alphabet 1–218a,b
angel/angelology 1–250b
Arabic numerals 1–396b
Aristotelianism 1–458a, 460a, 464a, 465a, 468a
ars antiqua 1–543a-b
astrology 1–607b
Bacon 2–35a, 36b-37a
Bernard of Chartres 2–189b
Biel 2–233b
blasphemy 2–271b
botany 2–345a
Bradwardine 2–357b
Crescas 3–677b
dialectic 4–578a
ecclesiology 4–375b
Eckhart 4–381b
encyclopedia development 4–448b
Engelbert of Admont 4–451b
eternity doctrine 1–45a
exegesis 2–213a,b; 4–543a-544b
Latin church 3–357a-358a
universals 1–18b
Scholasticus
chancery 3–252a
hierarchy of clergy 3–444b
Scholia tēs Porphyriou eisogogēs 4–114a
Schönebeck, Brun von
poetry 2–229a-b
Schöner, Johannes
astronomical observations 1–613b
SCHONGAUER, MARTIN 11–0
engraving 4–487b, 488b, 489a, 490a
Schools
Charlemagne 3–268b
Latin church 3–357a-358a
Schools, Byzantine
See Universities, Byzantine
SCHOOLS, CATHEDRAL 11–0
English 4–471b-472a
SCHOOLS, GRAMMAR 11–0
Cato's Distichs 3–193a
SCHOOLS, ISLAMIC 11–0
Azhar, al- 2–27b
SCHOOLS, JEWISH 11–0
exegesis 4–538b
SCHOOLS, MONASTIC 11–0
SCHOOLS, PALACE 11–0
SCHOOLS, URBAN 11–0
***SCHRÄTEL UND WASSERBÄR* 11–0**
SCHÜCHLEIN, HANS 11–0
***SCHULER VON PARIS, DER* 11–0**
***SCHWABENSPIEGEL* 11–0**
Schwartz, Peter
Dominican theology 4–246a
Schwartzenberg family 1–448b
Schwyz 2–7b
Science
alchemy 1–142a
Bacon 2–39b-40a
Old English treatises 1–285b
SCIENCE, ISLAMIC 11–0; 1–377b
Adelard of Bath 1–53b
influx into Europe 1–183a
SCIENCE, JEWISH 11–0
Scientia stellarum, De (Plato of Tivoli) 1–611b
SCIENTIFIC INSTRUMENTS 11–0
Scimitar 3–209a
Scipió e Aníbal (Canals) 3–167b
"Scipio vision" literature 1–185b
Scodra 4–79b
Scop 2–106a
Scorpion
See Mangonel
Scot, Michael 1–614b
alchemy 1–136b-137a
Scotism
See Duns Scotus, John
SCOTLAND: HISTORY 11–0
Anglo-Saxons 1–288b, 289b
archives 1–448b
Barbour 2–102a
Black Death 2–262b
Burgh, de 2–421b
Celtic art 3–218a
Celtic church 3–225a, 344a-b
chalder 3–241a
Cistercians 3–404a
clans 3–407a
Columban church 1–52b
conciliar theory 3–520b
coroner 3–605b
Dál Riata 1–60a; 4–78a-b
David I 4–110b
David II 4–111a
Donald III 4–256a
Duncan I 4–308a
Edward III of England 2–202b
Edward I of England 4–396a-b
Falkirk, Battle of 3–205a
Henry II of England 4–467a
hunting laws 1–300b
Latin church 3–344a,b
measures 2–310b
southern border 4–459b
treaties of Durham 4–316a
Treaty of Chester 3–299b
Vikings 4–554a
Vortigern 2–2b
Scott, John
Everyman 4–527b
Scott, Sir Walter 2–60a
Eyrbyggja saga 4–568a

Scottish language
See Celtic languages
SCOTTISH LITERATURE, GAELIC 11–0
bardic grammar 2–107a
bards 2–105b
See Also Celtic languages
Scotus, John Duns
See Duns Scotus, John
Scratch plow 1–90a,b
SCREEN 11–0
altar apparatus 1–222a
Atherington 4–263a-b
Daw 4–115a
SCREEN, CHANCEL 11–0
Scribes
Islamic 3–53b-54a
SCRINIUM 11–0
Byzantine diplomacy 4–194b-195a
Script
Arabic language 1–376b
chanceries 3–253b
Islamic calligraphy 3–51b
Old English manuscripts 1–275b-276b
SCRIPTORIUM 11–0
Alcuin Bibles 1–143a
Carolingian 3–109b-110a
Cassiodorus 3–123b-124a
Celtic intellectual life 3–231b
Scriptorum de musica medii aevi nova series (de Coussemaker) 1–309a
Scriptuaries
See People of the Book
"Scriptum super cantilenam Guidonis de Cavalcantibus" (Dino del Garbo) 3–196b
Scripturarum claves iuxta traditionem seniorum 4–368a
SCROLL, INHABITED 11–0
Scroll of the Revealer, The
See Megillat ha-Megallah
Scrolls
Celtic art 3–218b
exultet roll 4–565b
Scrope, Stephen 3–666a
Scrovegni, Enrico 1–453a
Sculpture
Amiens Cathedral 1–235a
Anglo-Norman 1–256a
animal style 1–293a
Armenian 1–494a-496a
art trade 1–561b
Broun, Robert 2–385a
Celtic art 3–221b-222b
Chartres Cathedral 3–276a
Ciuffagni, Bernardo 3–407a
Cluniac order 3–469a
Colombe, Michel 3–482b, 483a
Coptic 3–587a-588b
Donatello 4–256b
early Christian and Byzantine Architecture 4–339b
images of death 4–121b
See Also individual topics
Scuolo della Misericordia
Buon, Giovanni and Bartolomeo 2–419b
SCUTAGE 11–0; 4–469b
Scutari
Fourth Crusades 4–45a
Scylacium
Vivarium monastery 3–123a
Scylitzes, Joannes 1–303b
Scyphus 1–222b
Scythe 1–92a, 98a
Scythia Minor 2–12b
Scythians
north Caucasia 3–195a
Scythian-Sarmatian horses 1–294b
Seafarer, The 1–281a
Ezra Pound translation 1–287b
Seafaring
See Ships and ship building
Seal of faith
See Knik' Hawaddy
Seals
See Sigillography
Sea merchants
crusades 4–32b-33a
See Also Trade, European
Sea of Darkness
See Baḥr al-Muḥīt
Seasons for Fasting, The 1–281a
SEBASTE (SIVAS) 11–0; 1–472b, 473a
Arcrunis 1–451a-b
Armenian saints 1–518b
Danishmendids 4–91b
pillage 2–493a
Seljuk control of Anatolia 1–241b
Sebastian, King 2–102a
Sebastian, Saint
altar relic 1–337a
plague 2–265a
SEBASTOKRATOR 11–0
caesar 3–9a
SEBEOS 11–0
Armenian cavalry 3–199a
Armenian church 1–500a
Armenian literature 1–509b
Arsacids 2–50a
Heraklios 2–513a
SEBÜKTIGIN 11–0
Alptigin 1–220a,b
Second Coming
See Parousia
Second rose 4–319a
***SECOND SHEPHERD'S PLAY, THE* 11–0**
Secret des secrets (Pierre d'Abernun of Peckham) 1–264b
Secret Supper 3–182a
Secretum 4–493b
Secretum secretorum 2–38a, 39b, 40b
SECTS, ISLAMIC 11–0
Sects, Jewish
See Karaites
Sedacer, Guillem
alchemy 1–138a
"Sederunt" (Pérotin) 1–310a
SEDILLA 11–0
SEDULIUS SCOTTUS 11–0
Carmen paschale 4–496a
Carolingian court 3–103a
Ecclesia and Synagoga 4–371a
Latin exegesis 4–542b
meter 3–100b
Seed-natures, cosmic theory of 1–649b, 656a, 660b
Seehausen Priory 1–128a
Sefer ha-roqeaḥ (Eleazar Ben Judah of Worms) 4–420b
Sefer massao't (Benjamin of Tudela) 1–613a
Sefer tekunah (Levi ben Gerson) 1–613a
cross-staff 4–12a-b
Sefer yezirah (Abū Sahl ibn Tamīm) 1–387b
Sefirot 3–1a-b
Segene, Abbot of Iona 1–107a
dating of Easter 3–228b
Segius, Saint
See Anu Sarga
Segmental arch 1–424, 425a
SEGNA DI BONAVENTURA 11–0
Duccio 4–302b
Segovia
Asturian raids 1–626a
fuero privileges 3–131b
Segovian Book (Içe de Gebir) 1–176a
Segre Valley 1–84a
Seifrid de Ardemont (Albrecht von Scharfenberg) 1–133a
SEIFRIED HELBLING 11–0
Seignorial system
communes 3–493b, 494a
***SEINTE RESURRECION* 11–0**; 1–270a
SEISIN, DISSEISIN 11–0; 3–413b
assize 1–596b-597a
Claendon, Assize of 3–408b
escheat 4–509a
Seisyll 4–329b
Seisyll Bryffwrch 4–69b
Sejeut 3–680a
Sekretikon 4–71b
SELAMLIK 11–0
Selden, John 4–525a-b
Seleucia, Anatolia 1–239b
See Also Ctesiphon
Seleucia Mesopotamia
Christian church 3–312a
katholikos 1–327a
See Also Ctesiphon
Seleucia-Pieria
conch church 3–378a
Seleucids
south Caucasia 3–25a, 195b
Seleucus Nicator
Aleppo 1–145a
Self bow 2–350b-351a, 352a,b
Seligenstadt Monastery 4–412b
SELIM I 11–0
Anatolia 1–242a
Bāyazīd II 2–137a
Crimea Khanate 3–679a
Egypt 4–407a
Selinus
architectural plans 3–152b
SELJUK ART AND ARCHITECTURE 11–0
Great Palace, Constantinople 2–443b
SELJUKS 11–0
Abbassids 1–11b
agriculture 1–105a
Aleppo annexed (1085) 1–145b
Alp Arslan 1–203a
Anatolia 4–344a
Ani in Širak 1–290b
Ankara occupation 1–302a,b
Antioch domination 1–326a
Arabia 1–375b
Arčēš 1–423a
Arcn 1–450b
Armenia 1–474a, 484a-485a
Armenian Muslim emirates 1–514a
atabeg position 1–632a
Ayrarat 2–20b
Azerbaijan 2–27a
Badr al-Jamālī 2–44a
Baghdad 2–47a; 3–50b
Bosporus 2–344a
bow and arrow 2–350b, 352a
Buyids 2–436a
Byzantine Empire 2–493a,b, 494b-495b, 496b
Cappadocia 4–27b-30a
cavalry 3–209a
Christian church relations 3–313a, 355b-356a
Cilician kingdom 3–391b
Constantinople 3–552a
crusades 4–30a, 33b, 37b
Damascus 4–81b, 82a, 83b, 84b
Danishmendids rivalry 4–91b

SELJUKS (cont.)
Derbent 4–162b
Gandzha 1–125a
Georgians 4–112a
military dress 3–618a-b
Syria 4–27b
ʿUyūnids 2–51a
SELJUKS OF RŪM 11–0; 1–514a
Anatolia 1–241b
Armenia 1–485a
Caesarea 3–9a-b
Ephesus 4–495a
Erzincan 4–508b
Selkirk 4–110b
Selschoss 3–180a
Semgallians
crusader alliance 2–65b
Semi-Arians
See Homoeans
Semibreve
ars nova 1–549a
Semidome 4–236a
Semigallians
See Semgallians
Semita recta (Albertus Magnus) 1–137a
SEMITECHOLO, NICOLET 11–0
Semitic alphabet 1–208a, 209b
Semitic languages
Arabic 1–376b
Sempach, Battle of (1386) 2–8b; 3–205a
Şempringham Chronicles 1–265a
ŠEM ṬOB 11–0
cabala 3–3a
Senatorium 4–335b, 442a, 443a
Senchas Fer nAlban 4–78a
Seneca
Alani 1–120b
astrology 1–605a
Bacon 2–40a
Catalan translations 3–169b
Senegal
slaves 2–269a
Senekʿerim-Yovhannēs Arcruni 1–451a, 483a, 484a,b
SENESCHAL 11–0
assize 1–594b, 595b
bailli 1–53a,b
Gascony 1–368b, 369a
Seneschaucy 4–513b, 514a
Senhal 3–668b
Sennacherib 1–451a
Byzantine Empire 2–493a
Sens, Council of (1140-1141) 1–18a; 3–322b
Sens, Council of (1252)
Champagne property 3–249b
Sentence of Guadalupe (1486) 1–420a
Sentences
See Proverbs and *sententiae*
Sentences (Peter Lombard) 1–109a, 127a,b, 147a, 148a; 4–381b, 519a
Aquinas 1–353b, 354b
Bonaventure, Saint 2–313a, 314a
Christology 3–322b, 323a
Duns Scotus 4–308b
SEPHARDIM 11–0
alphabet 1–208a
biblical exegesis 2–212a
Sephirot 1–346a
Septiformi spiritu, De (Aelfric) 1–284b
Septimania
Visigoth settlement 2–91a
Septimius Severus
See Severus, Septimius
Sept psaumes allégorisés (Christine de Pizan) 3–316b
Septuagint 2–210b-211a,b
Armenian Bible 2–217b
texts 2–214a,b
Septuagint Psalter 4–223b
***SEPUH* 11–0**
Armenian social structure 1–488b-489a, 490a
Sepúlveda
fuero privileges 3–131b
SEQUENCE (PROSA) 11–0
SEQUENCE, LATE 11–0
Adam of Saint Victor 1–51a
Cambridge Songs 3–57a
Séquence de Sainte Eulalie 4–521a
See Also Eulalie
Sequin
See Ducat
SERAPH 11–0
Seraphic Doctor
See Bonaventure, Saint
Serapion of Thmuis, Bishop 1–155a
SERBIA 11–0
Andronikos I Komnenos 1–245a
autocephalos 2–10a
Bogomils 2–296b
Bosnia 2–334a,b, 335b-336a,b, 337a, 338a
Bulgaria 2–402a, 405a, 409a, 411a,b-413b
Byzantine church 2–469a
Byzantine civil war 1–246b
Byzantine Empire 2–118b, 492a, 500a,b-501a, 502a,b
conversion 2–117b
Croatia 4–5a
crusades 4–56a
despotate of Epiros 4–500a
metal trade 4–300a
serfdom 1–102a
SERBIAN ART AND ARCHITECTURE 11–0
early Christian architecture 4–347a-b
monasteries 2–446b-447a
SERDICA 11–0
agriculture and nutrition 1–78a,b
Basil II 2–118b
ŞEREFE 11–0
SERF, SERFDOM: RUSSIA 11–0
rise of 1–102a-b
SERF, SERFDOM: WESTERN EUROPEAN 11–0
Baltic countries 2–67b-68a
class structure 3–415a,b-416a, 424a
colonus 3–482b
commendation 3–490a
copyhold 3–596b
corvée 3–613a
Dauphiné 4–110a
decline 1–102a-b
estate management 4–512b
Sergas de Esplandián (Amadís de Gaula) 1–227b
SERGEANT 11–0
estate management 4–514a
SERGIOS I 11–0; 2–461b
Monotheletism 2–462a; 3–630b; 4–418b
Sergius I, Pope
Agnus Dei chant 1–73b
Agnus Dei music 1–74a
Sergius III, Pope 1–330b
imprisonment of Eugenius Vulgarius 4–520b
reenactment of decrees against Formosus 2–11b
Sergius, Saint 1–520a
Sergius of Radonezh, Saint
Alexis of Moscow 1–159b
Sericulture
south Italy 1–78a
Serie 3–72a-b
Series romana
rite of Aquileia 1–352b
Serments de Strasbroug
See French language
See Strasbourg Oaths
Sermo ad Anglos (Wulfstan) 1–285a
Sermó (Metge) 3–173b
Sermó (Muntaner) 3–165b
Sermones
Amarcius 1–228b
Sermones dominicales per annum (Anthony of Padua) 1–321a
Sermones in laudem et honorem beatae Mariae Virginis (Anthony of Padua) 1–321a
Sermones in solemnitatibus sanctorum (Anthony of Padua) 1–321a
Sermon on Antichrist 1–262b
Sermons
Aelfric of Eynsham 1–284b
Anglo-Saxon 1–274b, 284a
Chaucer's Parson's Tale 3–295b
Cistercian order 3–405a
See Also Preaching
Sermons (Saint Vincent Ferrer) 3–159b, 161b-162a
SERRA, PEDRO AND JAIME 11–0
Serradell de Vic, Bernat 3–170a, 173b
Serrai
Tzamblakoi 2–479b
Servatus
See Lupus of Ferrières
SERVI CAMERAE NOSTRAE 11–0
Servicio 3–138b
Serviens
See Sergeant
Servites
Augustinism 1–661a
Servius
accessus 1–34b
agriculture 1–90a
classical literary studies 3–432a
Sescas, En Amanieu de 3–663b, 665b, 672b
Seselles, Blai 3–171a
SETIER 11–0
Sétif, Battle of (1152) 1–194a
Seusenhofer
arms and armor 1–529b, 536b
Sevan, Lake
See Sewan, Lake
Seven Books of History Against the Pagans (Orosius) 1–653a
Seven Cities, Island of the 4–559b-560a
SEVEN DEADLY SINS 11–0
Brant, Sebastian 2–364a
Cassian 3–122b
Chaucer's Parson's Tale 3–295b-296a
Seveners
See Ismailis
Seven liberal arts
See Arts, seven liberal
SEVEN SLEEPERS OF EPHESUS 11–0; 3–267b; 4–494b
Aelfric 1–285a
Seventeen Towns 4–592a
Seven Thrones
Ascension of the Prophet 1–581b
Seven Tribes
Bulgaria 2–399b
76 Questions on Nature
See Quaestiones naturales
Severan dynasty 4–350a
Severian of Gabala, Bishop 1–507b
Severin 2–70a
Severinus, Saint
Bavaria 2–134a

Eugippius 4–521a
Severus, Septimius
Cilician Gates 3–390b
Constantinople 3–549b
Severus of Antioch, Patriarch 2–13a
Monophysitism 4–524b
Severus of Ashmunein
See Sawīrus ibn al-Muqaffa'
Severus Sanctus qui et Enedelechius
See Endelechius
SEVILLE 11–0
agriculture 1–84b
Almoravids 1–199b
Castile 3–134a, 135a, 136a
Norwegians 4–554b
slaves 2–268b
trade 4–557b
Seville, Great Mosque of 1–191b
SEWAN, LAKE 11–0; 1–470b, 589a
Sewing songs
Chansons de toile 3–263a
Sew Learn
Armenian Council 1–501b
SEX AETATES MUNDI 11–0
Sexpartite vault
See Vault
Sext
Divine Office 4–221b, 227, 229a
Sextus Amarcius Gallus Piosistratus
See Amarcius
Sexual abstinence
See Celibacy
Sézanne
fairs 4–590b, 591a
Sfax
Great Mosque 1–70b
Sffin, Battle of (657) 1–172b-173a
SFORZA 11–0
Sforza, Francesco
condottieri 3–531a
Sforza, Ludovico il Moro
diplomacy 4–212b
Sforza, Muzio Attendolo
condottieri 3–531b
Sforza, Tristano
diplomacy 4–204b
Sgraffito decoration
ceramics 3–237a,b
SHÂH-ARMAN 11–0; 1–514a
Sha'aṭnez 3–619b
Sha'ban, Sultan
execution 2–113a
SHADDADIDS 11–0; 2–27a
Ani in Širak 1–290b, 514a
Armenia 1–482b, 483a, 484a,b, 485a
Dwin 1–513b; 4–324a
Ghandzha 1–125a
SHADIRVAN 11–0
Shadows
time reckoning 2–250a; 3–23b
Shadows (Bīrūnī) 2–250a
Shadow theater, Egyptian 4–407b
SHĀFI'Ī, AL- 11–0; 1–374b
Abū Ḥanīfa 1–26b
Damascus 4–84b
tomb 3–14b
Shahāda 1–178a
Islamic calligraphy 3–52b
Shahanshah
See Šāhan-šāh
Shāh Maḥmūd Nīshāpūrī 3–54b
***SHĀHNĀMA* 11–0**; 2–50b
Aḥmad Mūsā 1–106b
Shahristān
Bukhara 2–397a
SHAH RUKH I 11–0
Shāhrukh ibn Tīmūr 1–65b
Shajar al-Durr
concubinage 3–529a
Shakki 2–26a, 27a
Shamakha 2–26a, 27a
Shams al-Dīn Muḥammad
See Ḥāfiẓ
Shams al-Dīn Muḥammad ibn 'Abd Allah Ibn Baṭṭūṭa
See Baṭṭūṭa, Ibn
Shams-i-Munshī 4–444b
Shanfarā 1–400a
Shannon
Norwegians 4–554b
Shansabanids
See Ghurids
Shapur, Grotto of 2–252a
Shapur, Iran
See Bishapur
Shapur I
See Šābuhr
Sharaf, al-
fruit trees 1–82b
Sharaf al-Dīn 1–634b
Sharbūsh (cap) 3–618b
Sharī'a 1–178a, 373b; 2–79a; 4–84b, 445a
Sharifs
Mecca 1–175a,b, 375a
Shāṭir, Ibn al- 1–621b, 622b
Shatt al-Arab River 4–522a
Shaubak
Krak de Montreal 4–22b
Shaving 2–148a-b
Shavuoth 3–27a; 4–365b
Shaw, Ralph 4–478b
Shayba ibn Hāshim ibn 'Abd Manāf ibn Quṣayy
See 'Abd al-Muṭṭalib
Shaybānids 1–513a
She'azana 1–32a
Sheep
food animal 1–299a, 301b
Sheep farming
Cistercians 3–404a
Sheki 1–125a
Shell keep 3–144a-b
Shemakha
See Khamekhia
Shemariah ben Elijah ben Jacob
exegesis 4–541b
Shem Tov ibn Shem Tov
See Šem Ṭob
Shenute (theol.)
Coptic architecture 3–586b
Shepherd of Hermas 1–182b
Shepherds
costume 3–626a
Shepherd's Chapel (Ani) 1–494a
Sherborne
Aldhelm 1–144a
SHERIFF 11–0
accounting 4–530b, 533b
assize 1–596b-597a
bailiff 2–52a
constable 3–542b
court leet 3–659b
escheat 4–509a
Norman-Angevin England 4–464b-465a, 469b
Shetland Islands
exploration 4–554a
SHĪ'A 11–0
'Abbās, al- 1–4a
Abbasid caliphate 3–46a
'Alī's party 1–174b
Assassins 1–589b
caliphate 3–35b, 38a,b, 47a
Egypt 4–406a
Ismaili movement 3–50a
sects 1–174b-175b
Umayyad caliphate 3–41a-b
Shield 1–521b, 522b, 524b, 525b, 528a, 534a
Byzantines 1–523b
cavalry 3–200b, 201b, 202b
Goths 1–523b
Lithuanians 1–523b
Normans 1–523a-524a
orders of chivalry 3–303b, 304b, 306a
Saxons 1–523a
Vikings 1–523b
Shifā', al- (Sīna, Ibn) 1–458b
Shihāb al-Dīn Toghril 1–634a
Shihāb al-Zuhrī, Ibn 4–84b
Shiḥna
Damascus 4–84a
Shiism
Ash'arī, al- 1–585b
Buyids 2–435b, 436a,b
commander of the faithful 3–488b
Copts and Coptic church 3–594b
See Also Shī'a
Shiites
'Alī ibn Abī Ṭālib 1–171b
imams' origins 1–173b
Shikasta 3–54b
SHILLING 11–0
shimāsah, al- 1–114a
Ship of Fools, The 2–363b-364a
SHIPS AND SHIPBUILDING, MEDITERRANEAN 11–0
SHIPS AND SHIPBUILDING, NORTHERN EUROPEAN 11–0
SHIPS AND SHIPBUILDING, RED SEA AND PERSIAN GULF 11–0
SHĪRĀZ 11–0
Buyids 2–435b
SHIRE 11–0
Anglo-Saxon England 4–457b
Norman-Angevin England 4–464b
Shirin clan 3–680a
Shīrkūh, Asad al-Dīn
Ayyubids 2–23a
Nūr al-Dīn 4–39a
Shirley, John 1–320a
SHIRVAN 11–0; 1–125a
Azerbaijan 2–26a, 27a
Derbent 4–162b
Shishman, King 2–136b
Shock cavalry
See Cavalry, European
SHOES AND SHOEMAKERS 11–0
Western European 3–625b-626a
Shohet 4–182a
Shorte Treatise of Politicke Power (Ponet) 3–521b
SHOT'A RUSTAVELI 11–0
Shoulder Bite, The (Chrétien de Troyes) 3–308b
Shrewsbury
commune 3–499a
Shrine of Saint Anno
brattishing 2–364a
Shrines
early Christian and Byzantine architecture 4–336a-337a
See Also Celtic art
Shrove Tuesday
carnival 3–99b
Shu'ayb 4–296b
Shuhayd, Ibn
Treatise of Familiar Spirits and Demons 1–381b
Shūrā 3–35a, 37a
Shushtarī, al- 1–402a
Shu'ūbīya 1–380a

Si aliquis
contraception 3–573a
Sibert of Beka
Ordinal 3–96a
Sibille (Elisabeth of Nassau-Saarbrücken) 4–432b
SIBYLLINE ORACLES 11–0
Sicard of Cremona
Divine Office 4–223a
Sic et non (Abelard) 1–17b, 18b; 4–170a
SICILIAN POETRY 11–0
SICILIAN VESPERS 11–0; 2–499b; 4–95b
Andronikos II Palaiologos 1–245b
political crusades 4–60b-61a
Sicily
Aghlabids 1–70b, 71a
agricultural tools 1–80a
agriculture and nutrition 1–87b-88a
Angevins 1–253a
architecture 1–256a; 4–346b
Black Death 4–142a
Byzantine church 2–463a
Catalan language 3–157b
ceramics 3–237b
Crown of Aragon 1–413b-415b, 416b, 417a,b, 418a,b
crusades 4–40a
Frederick II 4–51b
fruits and fruit trees 1–87a-b
Islamic currency 4–215b
medicine 2–98b
Norman kingdom of 4–58a
SICILY, ISLAMIC 11–0
SICILY, KINGDOM OF 11–0
Black Death 2–259a
Byzantine empire 2–499b
Catalan Company 3–157a
despotate of Epiros 4–499a
financial system 4–532a
political crusades 4–57b
slaves 2–269a,b
Swedes 4–555b
Sickle 1–92a, 98a
Byzantine 1–77b
Siculus, Diodorus
Historical Library 3–325a
Sid, Isaac ben 1–159b
Sīda, Ibn 4–443a-b
Siddhānta
See *Sindhind*
Ṣiddī, al-
See Abū Bakr
Side 1–239b
Sidereal year 3–18a
Siderocastron 3–156b
Sidon
Fourth Crusade 4–32a
Louis IX 4–25b
SIDONIUS APOLLINARIS 11–0
Sidraga 4–4a
Siege trains 3–65a-b
Siege warfare 3–145a
Siege weapons 3–150a-b
Siegfried
See Sigurd
Siegmund of Tyrol, Duke 4–429a
SIENA 11–0
Barna da 2–111a
Black Death 2–260a
Bonsignori company 2–76b, 77b
commune 3–500a
exchange banks 2–73b
merchants 4–592b
money markets 2–78b
painting 4–301b
Siena Cathedral
Antonio Veneziano 1–342a
Sierra Nevada
Alhambra 1–168a
***SIETE PARTIDAS* 11–0**
Almogávares 1–190b; 3–169a
Castile 3–135a
Siferth
See Chester, Treaty of
ṢIFFĪN 11–0
ʿAmr ibn al-ʿĀṣ 1–237b
caliphate 3–36a
S'i' fosse fuoco, arderei 'l mondo (Cecco Angiolieri) 3–212a
Sigebert I, King
Avars 2–12b
Sigebert III, King
Carolingians 3–104b
SIGEBERT OF GEMBLOUX 11–0
biographical writing 2–239a-b
SIGEHARD OF SAINT MAXIMIN 11–0
Sigena
Anglo-Norman art 1–258a
Sigeric, Archbishop 4–90a
SIGER OF BRABANT 11–0
Albertus Magnus 1–129a
Aristotelianism 1–463a
Bonaventure, Saint 2–317b
Siger of Lille
Dominican nuns 4–248a
SIGILLOGRAPHY
papal bull 2–418a,b
SIGILLOGRAPHY, BYZANTINE 11–0
SIGILLOGRAPHY, EUROPEAN 11–0
SIGILLOGRAPHY, ISLAMIC 11–0
SIGILLOGRAPHY, SASANIAN 11–0
Sigismund, King of Burgundy 2–423a
Sigismund, King of Hungary and Bohemia
Byzantine Empire 2–503a
Council of Constance 3–647b, 648a, 650a,b
Lating church 3–366a
Order of the Dragon 3–306b
Bohemian throne 2–300b
Sigismund King of Tyrol 2–9a
Sigismund of Brandenburg 2–361b-362a
Sigismund of Luxembourg
Hungarian throne 2–337a-338a
Sigla 4–127b
SIGNATURES 11–0
Significatione planetarum in nativitatibus, De (Māshā'allāh) 1–606b
Signos del Juicio Final (Berceo Gonzalo de) 2–187a
***SIGRDRÍFUMÁL* 11–0**; 4–386a, 387a
SIGDRIFUMAL 11–0
Sigulf 1–142b, 143a
SIGURD 11–0
Brynhild 2–394b
***SIGURÐARKVIÐA IN FORNA* 11–0**
Brynhild 2–394b
***SIGURÐARKVIÐA IN MEIRI* 11–0**; 4–387a, 390b
Brynhild 2–394b, 395a
***SIGURÐARKVIÐA IN SKAMM* 11–0**; 4–386a, 390a,b
Brynhild 2–394b
Sigurðar saga 4–385b
SIGURÐAR SAGA FÓTS 11–0
SIGURÐAR SAGA THÖGLA 11–0
Sigurðr I Jerusalem Farer 4–411a
Sigurðr Slembidjákn 4–414a
Ṣiḥāḥ al-Furs (Shams-i-Munshī) 4–444b
Sijilmāsa
Zanāta revolt (1055) 1–198b
SIKAND GUMANIG WIZAR 11–0
Sikidites
See Michael Glykas
Sikkīt, Ibn al- 4–443a,b
Silesia 2–300b
Cisiojanus dating method 3–21b
cultivation 1–97a
Silian, Saint
Thuringia 2–321b
Silistria 2–407a
SILK 11–0
Byzantium 2–452b-453a
Coptic textiles 3–589a
Córdoba 3–599b
Dībāj 4–173a
dyeing 4–328a
Sil Muiredaig
See Connacht
Sil nÁeda Sláne
Uí Néill power 1–60b
Silver
Bosnia 2–340a,b, 341b
Celtic art 3–221a
Córdoba 3–599b
Silver mining
Cistercians 3–404a
Silversmiths
See Metalsmiths, gold and silver
Silvester IV, Antipope 1–330a
Silvester I, Pope
Donation of 4–258a
Donation of Constantine 3–346a
SILVESTER II POPE 11–0; 1–436a; 3–175b, 346b
Adalbold of Utrecht 1–47b
All Souls' Day 1–177a
Armillary sphere 1–521b
astronomy 1–611a
Bohemian Brethren 2–306a
church reforms 3–347b
clerical prestige 3–417b
dialectic 4–169b
dualism 4–298a
ghubār numerals 1–395b
Silvester, Bernard
classical literary studies 3–434a
man as microcosm idea 1–607a
Simancas, Battle of (939) 1–627b
Simeon ben Yoḥai
cabala 3–2a
Simeon Manscript 1–319b
Simeon Stylites, Saint 4–333a
Simeon the Young
biblical exegesis 2–214b
Simḥat Torah 3–27a
Simnel, Lambert
Dublin 4–299b
Simon, Earl of Leicester
Anglo-Latin poetry 1–255a
Simon de Colonia
See Juan and Simon Colonia
Simon de Covina
plague 2–264b
SIMON DE MONTFORT 11–0
Bracton, Henry de 2–356b
Cathars 3–188b, 189a
Crown of Aragon 1–410b, 411a
distress 4–221a
Dominicans 4–239b
Gascony 1–368b
Lateran Council (1215) 3–640a-b
SIMON DE MONTFORT THE YOUNGER 11–0
Baron's War 2–112a
Edward I 4–395b
parliament 4–481a
SIMONE DA BOLOGNA (CROCEFISSI) 11–0
SIMONE MARTINI 11–0; 2–16a, 111a
Assisi, San Francesco 1–594a
Destorrents, Ramón 4–165b
Duccio 4–302b

Simon le Coustellier
Cabochien riots 3–3b
Simon Magnus
tonsure 3–229a
Simon of Bisignano
summary of *Decretum* 4–127b
Simon of Cramaud
Council of Pisa (1409) 3–646b
Simon of Reading 2–173b
Simon of Saint Albans
Anglo-Norman art 1–258a
Simon of Sudbury
beheading 3–83b
Simon Stock, Saint
Carmelite rule 3–96b
Simon Ushakov
See Ushakov, Simon
SIMONY 11–0
papal reform 1–146a,b
Western councils 3–634a,b, 635a, 636b, 637a
Simplicianus 1–230b
Simplicius 1–457b, 458a
SIMUND DE FREINE 11–0; 1–261a, 264a
SINĀ, IBN 11–0; 1–377b; 2–35b
actualism 1–46b
alchemy 1–136b, 137a,b, 141b
angel/angelology 1–250b
Aristotelianism 1–458b-459a
Arnald of Villanova 1–538a
astrology 1–618a
Bar Hebraeus 2–108a
Bīrūnī 2–251a
Buyids 2–437a
contraception 3–572a,b, 574a-b
cosmetics 2–147a,b
dialectic 4–170b
encyclopedias 4–445b
essence and existence 4–510b
mathematics 2–38b
philosophy 2–241b
Sinai
archbishops 2–10a
Sinai Christ icon 4–363a
ŠINAKAN 11–0; 1–488b, 489b, 491a
Sindhind 1–620a
Sind ibn ʿAlī 1–391b
Sinecure
castellan 3–124b
Sinell of Cleenish
Clonard 3–465b
ṢINF 11–0
SINFJǪTLI 11–0
Sinibaldi, Cino de'
tomb 1–73b, 76b
Sinibuldi, Guittoncino
See Cino da Pistoia
Sinjār 2–43b
Sinope 1–239b
SINOPIA 11–0; 4–291a
Sipʿan Mountain 1–470b
Sippe 4–599b
Siqāya 1–4a, 14b
Ṣira, Simeon ben Jesus ben 3–15b
ŠIRAK 11–0; 1–473b
Širakawan, Council of 1–500a
Sīrat Baybars 2–138b
Sir Beues of Hamtown
See Bevers saga
SIRDAB 11–0
Siresa, Benedictine House of 1–403b, 404a,b
Sir Gawain and the Green Knight
See Gawain and the Green Knight, Sir
Siricius, Pope
Christmas celebration 3–318a
Epiphany 4–497a
interstices of clergy 3–442b
papal theory 3–341b
requirements of clergy 3–443a
SIRMIUM 11–0
Basil II 2–407a
Methodios 2–299b; 4–73b, 74a
Ormurtag 2–401b
Siroccos 3–452a
Sir Orfeo
See Orfeo, Sir
SIRVENTES 11–0
Sirwāl 3–616b
SIS 11–0; 3–391, 391b, 393b
Sis, Council of (1307) 1–501a-b
Cilician-Roman church union 3–394b
Sisakan
See Siwnikʿ
SISEBUT 11–0
Sisebuto, Abbot 3–76a
Sisinnios
goblet 2–454b
Sisinnios II, Patriarch
matrimony 4–594b
Ṣīṣit 3–619a
Šišman
Vidir 2–411a
Šišman, Tamara 2–413a
Sistan 1–63b, 64b
Sisteron, Albert de 4–110a
Sisters of the Common Life 2–366a-b
Devotio moderna 4–166a
Sitta 3–54b
Situ orbis, De (Pomponius Mela) 1–110b
SITULA 11–0
Siurana 1–408b
Sivas
See Sebaste
Siward of Northumbria 4–394b
SIWNIKʿ 11–0; 1–472b, 473a,b
Six Ages of the World
See Sex Aetates Mundi
Six Days of Creation (Eugenius II of Toledo) 4–520b
Sixtus III, Pope 4–332b
Christmas mass 3–318b
Sixtus IV, Pope 1–13b, 14a
Bonaventure, Saint 2–319a
conciliar theory 3–519a
councils 3–655a
Dominicans 4–254a
papal revenues 3–367b
Sixtus V, Pope
Bonaventure, Saint 2–319a
carnivals restraint 3–99b
Siyāsat-nāma 1–220a
Sizjī, Abu Saʿīd al-
astrolabe 2–250a
SKAÐI 11–0
Skálaholt
bishop's seat 4–618a
sagas 2–252a-b
SKÁLDATAL 11–0
SKALDIC POETRY 11–0
Bjarnar saga 2–255b
Bjarni 2–255b
Bragi Boddason the Old 2–359a-b
Breta Sǫgur 2–366a
dróttkvætt 4–294b
eddic poetry 4–385a, 389a,b, 391a,b
Egill Skallagrímsson 4–400b
Eilífr Goðrúnarson 4–409b
Einarr Helgason Skálaglamm 4–410b
Einarr Skúlason 4–412a
Eiríksmál and Hákonarmál 4–414b
Eyrbyggja saga 4–568a
Eysteinn Ásgrímsson 4–568b
Eyvindr 4–570a
Iceland 4–613b, 618a
***SKÁLDSKAPARMÁL* 11–0**; 4–409b, 411a
SKANDERBEG 11–0
Skanör
fairs 4–587b
Skelton, John
chronicles 3–325a
Magnificence 4–287a
Sketchbooks 4–292a
Skeuophylakion 4–335b
SKEWRA 11–0
***SKÍRNISMÁL* 11–0**; 4–386b, 389b, 390a,b, 391a,b
***SKJǪLDUNGA SAGA* 11–0**
Bjarkamál 2–254a
Skop 2–106a
Skopje
Basil II 2–407a,b
Byzantine capture 2–119a
Isak-Beg 2–338a
SKRÆLINGS 11–0
Skullcap 1–526b
SKYLITZES 11–0
Skylitzes, John 2–514b
Slash and burn tillage system 1–77a, 96b, 97a-b, 98b, 99b
SLAVERY, ISLAMIC WORLD 11–0; 2–268a,b
Aghlabids 1–70a
Almohads 1–194b
Circassians 3–398a, 399b
concubinage 3–527a
SLAVERY, SLAVE TRADE 11–0; 2–268a-270a
Armenia 1–488b, 489b
Asturias-León 1–630a
Byzantine church 2–461b
concubines 3–216a
Portugal 4–561a, 562a
Russia 1–100a
Slavic art
See Russian and Slavic art
Slavic church
Croatia 4–6a
SLAVIC LANGUAGES AND LITERATURE 11–0
alphabet 2–299a
Bible translations 2–215b
Bulgaria 2–329a,b, 403b, 404a, 407a, 414a
Dubrovnik 4–300b
Slavonia
banus 2–82b
Croatia 4–4a, 5a
Hungary 4–5b-6a
Zvonimir 4–6a-b
Slavonic alphabets 1–207b, 212b, 216a-217b
SLAVS 11–0
agricultural tools 1–90b
agriculture and nutrition 1–96b-103a
Austria 2–4b
Avars 2–12b
Bosnia 2–334b
Bulgaria 2–329b, 399a-b, 401a, 403b
Byzantine church 2–463b-464b, 469a
Byzantine Empire 2–477a, 486b, 489a-b
Crete 3–678a
Cyril and Methodios 4–73a-b
Dalmatia 4–79b
fairs 4–587b
First Crusade 4–34b
serfdom 1–102a-b
Sledges
draft animals 1–293a
Sleeves 3–625a

Slide cars
draft animals 1–293a
Slip painting
Islamic ceramics 3–239a
Sluis, Battle of (1340) 1–56b; 4–398a
SLUTER, CLAUS 11–0
Burgundy, Duchy of 2–428a
Chartreuse de Champmol 4–186a
Smalt
See Enamel
Smaltjan
See Enamel
Smaltum
See Enamel
SMARAGDUS OF SAINT MIHIEL 11–0
exarch 4–529b
Latin exegesis 4–542b
Smbat 1–478b
Smbat II, King 1–483a
Cathedral of Ani 1–291b
Smbat Bagratuni 1–477a
Smbat Bagratuni the Confessor 2–48a
SMBAT SPARAPET 11–0; 1–479b, 480a, 489a; 3–199a
Armenian literature 1–511b, 512a
SMBAT I THE MARTYR 11–0; 1–449a, 481b, 519b
Dwin 4–324a
Smbat II Tiezerakal 1–482a
Smerdy 1–100a
Smilec, Czar
Bulgaria 2–411a
Smithfield
fair 4–586b
Smiths
See Metalsmiths, gold and silver
Smyrna 1–242a
agriculture and nutrition 1–78a
Anatolia 1–239b
Bogomils 2–295b
Christian capture (1342-45) 4–55b
Smyrna Codex 2–206a
Snaffle bit 3–203a
***SNORRA EDDA* 11–0**; 1–226b; 2–256a; 4–385b, 401a
America discovery 4–554b
Baldr 2–55a
Baldrs Draumar 2–57a
Bragi Boddason the Old 2–359a
Eilífr Gođrúnarson 4–409b
Einarr Helgason Skálaglamm 4–410b
Snorri godi
saga 4–568a
SNORRI STURLUSON 11–0; 1–310b
Æsir 1–63a
Eddic poetry 4–385a-b
Egill Saga Skallagrímssonar 4–403a
Einarr Skúlason 4–411a
Eiríker Oddsson 4–414a
explorations 4–554b
Olaf sagas 2–254a
Snow Child (Heribert of Rogthenburg) 3–58a
So, Bernat de 3–173b
Soares de Paiva, João 3–86b
Sobrarbe 1–404a,b, 405b, 407a
Soc
See Sac and Soc
Social mobility
See Class structure, Western
Società dei Piovuti
Cimabue 3–396a
Societas
See Commenda
Societas Ricciardorum 2–76b
Socrates
Aquinas, Thomas 1–357b, 359b
SOCRATES SCHOLASTICUS 11–0
Armenian Hellenizing School 1–506a
Constantinople 3–551a
ecclesiastical history 2–512b-513a
Soeiro da Costa
exploration 4–561b
Soest, Konrad von
See Konrad von Soest
Sofala
exploration 4–563a
Sofia
See Saerdica
Soğanli Valley 3–92a
Soiscél Molaise 3–221b
Soissons
commune 3–496b
Soissons, Battle of (486 or 487) 3–104a
Soissons, Council of (1121) 1–17a
Soissons Cathedral 3–276a
spolia 1–334a
Sokha
See Plows
Sokkason, Bergr
Saint Dunstan 4–311b
Solage
ars subtilior 1–558b
Solar cycle 3–23b
***SÓLARLJÐ* 11–0**; *4–389a*
Solar year
length 3–17b
***SOLDIERS' PORTION* 11–0**
***SOLEA* 11–0**; 1–442a, 443
ambo 1–229a
Sole-ard plow 1–77a
Soler, Guillermus
Azores 4–559a
SOLESMES 11–0
Soli 2–334a, 335a, 336b, 338a
Solidus 4–187a, 301a
Soliloquies, The (Augustine)
translations 1–167a, 284a, 648a
Soliloquium (Saint Bonaventure) 2–316a
Sol invictus
Christmas 3–317b
Solitary Life (Petrarch) 3–215a
Sol iustitiae
Christmas 3–317b
Sollemnitatibus et sabbatis et neomeniis, De (Saint Columbanus) 3–486b
SOLMIZATION 11–0
SOLOMON AND MARCOLE 11–0
Solomon and Saturn 1–280b
Solomon ben Aret
cabala 3–1b
Solomon ben Isaac of Troyes
See Rashi (Rabbi Solomon ben Isaac)
SOLOMON BEN JUDAH IBN GABIROL 11–0; 2–35b
Aristotelianism 1–459b-460a
exegesis 4–540a
palace of Najralla 1–168a
Solomonid dynasty 1–32b
Solomon of Aarhus
Dominicans 4–244a
Solutiones contrariorum 4–127b
Somateia 4–494a
Somerled 3–407a
Somerset
Black Death 2–262a
Sommaire philosophique 1–138b
Somme le roi 1–263a
Somme le Roy (Laurent de Bois) 3–167b
Somme rurale (Boutillier) 4–515b
Somner, William 1–287a
Somni (Francesc Alegre) 3–169b
Somni, Lo (Metge) 3–157b
Somni de Joan Joan, Lo (Gasull) 3–171b
Somnium Scipionis (Cicero) 1–610b
***SOMNIUM VIRIDARII* 11–0**
Somχet'i
See Gugark'
Sonatorrek (Lament for my sons)
Egils Saga Skallagrímssonar 4–400b, 401a, 403a
SONDERGOTIK 11–0
Songbooks
Cambridge Songs 1–318b, 319a
polyphonic music 3–256b
Songe d'enfer (Houdenc) 1–185b
Songe du castel 1–189a
Song of Azarias
Daniel 1–280a
Song of Dermot and the Earl 1–265b
SONG OF ROLAND 1–643a
Song of Saint Faith 2–126b
Song of Songs (Bernard of Clairvaux) 2–191a
exegesis 2–213a; 4–543a
Song of the Three Children
Daniel 1–280a
Songs of Beuren
See Carmina Burana
Sophanenē 1–472b
Sophenē 1–472b
Pentarchy 1–514b
Sophenē/Cop'K' 2–140b
Sophistici elenchi 1–52a
Sophronius of Jerusalem, Patriarch
condemnation of monothelitism 2–510b; 3–630b; 4–418b
Sopočani Church 4–347a
Sopočani monastery
art 2–446b
Sopra corpo 2–77a
Sorbonne
library 1–206a,b
Sorcery
See Magic; Witchcraft
Sordello 3–665a, 672b
Sorghum
See Grain crops
Soria 1–406a, 407a
***SÖRLA SAGA STERKA* 11–0**
Sors, Lleonard de 3–171b
Sorted rarities (Abū 'Ubayd) 4–443a
Sort feta en laor de les monges de Valldonzella (Antoni de Vallmanya) 3–169b
Sortibus, De (Aquinas) 1–607b
Soslani, David 2–207a
Soterichos Panteugenos 3–632a
Soteriology
early church 3–342a
See Also Christology
Sottie des copieurs et lardeurs 4–265b
Souakin
exploration 4–562b
SOUFFLET 11–0
Soul
Augustine of Hippo 1–656a-b
Soul, On the (Saint Ethelred) 4–517a
Soule
Basques 2–126a,b
Soul-friend
Celtic liturgy 3–230b
Sousse
fairs 4–589a
ribāṭ 1–69a-b
Southampton
Black Death 2–261b
South Caucasia 3–193b-195a,b
South Saxons 4–454a
South Semitic script 1–209b
South Slavs 1–96b
agriculture 1–98b-99a

Soviet Union
Araks River 1–421b
Caucasus Mountains 3–195b
SOZOMEN 11–0
ecclesiastical history 2–512b-513a
Sozopetra
Byzantine capture 2–118a
Spade bit 3–203a
SPAHBAD 11–0
Spain
admiral, use of title 1–55b
Adoptionism 1–57b
agricultural tools 1–80a
agriculture 1–83a-84b, 96a, 105a
Alani kingdoms 1–121a
Almohads 1–194a-195b,b
alodial tenure 1–190b
Arabic philosophy and science 1–378b
archives 1–448b
arms and armor 1–528a
art 1–5b
banking 2–74a, 75b
Baptism 2–83a,b
Barcelona 2–102a
Black Death 4–142a
Canaries 4–559a
Canary Island rights 3–63a
canonical reform 3–355a
casbahs 3–121a
cavalry 3–203a
ceramics 3–236b, 237b, 238a,b
Christmas celebration 3–318a
Christology 3–321b
Cid, history and legend of 3–383b
Cistercian Order 3–404a
colonus 3–482b
Columbus 4–560a,b
commerce 4–557b-558a
converso 3–577b
Córdoba 3–597b, 678a
cotton production 3–626b
Crown of Aragon 1–408a
crusades 4–17b, 21a
dervish 4–163a
dictamen 4–175b
expulsion of Jews 2–81b; 4–564b
fairs 4–587b
illustration of Apocalypse 1–344a
inheritance 4–607a
Islamic cavalry 3–209a,b
Jewish family 4–605b
Latin church 3–344a
maritime law 3–570a
Moors 2–91a,b
Muslim scientific influence 1–606b
noble class 3–414b
Norwegians 4–554b
orders of chivalry 3–306b
reconquest 1–161a,b; 3–356b, 357a; 4–33b, 36a
slaves 2–268a-b, 269b
Umayyads 3–49a, 50b
Vandals invasion 2–91b
Visigoth settlement 2–91a
Spain, Bank of 2–75b
SPAIN, CHRISTIAN-MUSLIM RELATIONS 11–0
Almoravids 1–199a-200b
Aragon 1–403b
Castile 3–133b-134a
Catalonia 3–174a
dinar 4–187a,b
dirham 4–215b
SPAIN, MUSLIM KINGDOMS OF 11–0
Almoravids 1–199a-200b
Arab Green Revolution 1–81b-82b
Aragon 1–403b-404a
SPANDREL 11–0
Spangenhelm 1–522a, 527a
Spangröls 1–530b
Spanheims 2–7b
SPANISH ERA 11–0; 3–18b
Spanish knights 4–33b
SPANISH LANGUAGE 11–0
Alfonsine court 1–161b
Bible translations 2–215b
Castilian 3–141a
Catalan 3–157a
chansons de geste 3–258a
SPANISH LITERATURE 11–0
Alfonso X's literary court 1–161b-162a
Aljamiado literature 1–176a
Amadís de Gaula 1–227b
Arthurian literature 1–575b-576b
Calila e Digna 3–31b
Cancionero General 3–63b
exempla 4–551b
La Celestina 3–212a
Libro de Apolonio 1–348b
Libro del Cavallero Zifar 3–197b
SPANISH LITERATURE: BALLADS 11–0
SPANISH LITERATURE: BIBLE, TRANSLATIONS 11–0
Jewish exegesis 4–539b-540b
SPANISH LITERATURE: BIOGRAPHY 11–0
SPANISH LITERATURE: CHRONICLES 11–0
SPANISH LITERATURE: DAWN AND SPRING SONGS 11–0
SPANISH LITERATURE: DRAMA 11–0
Auto de los Reyes Magos 2–9a
La Celestina 3–212a
SPANISH LITERATURE: EPIC POETRY 11–0
Cantar de Mío Cid 3–70b, 386b-388b
Poema de Alfonso XI 1–162b
SPANISH LITERATURE: HAGIOGRAPHY 11–0
SPANISH LITERATURE: INSTRUCTIONAL 11–0
SPANISH LITERATURE: LATIN 11–0
Eugenius II of Toledo 4–520b
SPANISH LITERATURE: LOST WORKS 11–0
Eugenius II of Toledo 4–520b
SPANISH LITERATURE: LYRIC POETRY 11–0
decir 4–122b
SPANISH LITERATURE: NON-BIBLICAL TRANSLATIONS 11–0
SPANISH LITERATURE: POPULAR POETRY 11–0
assonance 1–600b
courtly love 3–671b-672a
SPANISH LITERATURE: ROMANCES 11–0
Arthurian literature 1–573a
Libro de Alexandre 1–152b
Libro de Apolonio 1–348b
Libro del Cavallero Zifar 3–197b
SPANISH LITERATURE: SATIRE 11–0
Dança general de la Muerte 4–85b
La Celestina 3–212a
SPANISH LITERATURE: SENTIMENTAL ROMANCES 11–0
SPANISH LITERATURE: SERMONS 11–0
SPANISH LITERATURE: TROY STORY 11–0
SPANISH LITERATURE: VERSIFICATION AND PROSODY 11–0
Cantar de Mío Cid 3–70b
copla 3–584b
cuaderna vía 4–63a
Spanish March (778) 1–412b; 3–107a
Spanish painting
Beatus manuscripts 2–143b
Span piece
See Collar beam
SPARAPET 11–0; 1–490a-b
Speaking Is Better Than Silence (Al-Jāḥiẓ) 1–379b
Spear
See Lance
Specchio della croce (Domenico Cavalca) 3–168a
Speculis comburentis, De (Bacon) 2–39a
Speculum Artis Bene Moriendi 1–547b
Speculum astronomiae 1–607b-608a
Speculum duorum (Giraldus Cambrensis)
Anglo-Norman languages 1–260a
Speculum historiale (Jaume Domenec) 3–166b
Speculum historiale (Vincent of Beauvais) 4–311b
SPECULUM HUMANAE SALVATIONIS 11–0
Speculum iudiciale (Guillaume Durand) 4–314b
Speculum maius (Vincent of Beauvais) 4–449a
Speculum secretorum 1–137b
Speculum stultorum (Nigel Wireker) 1–255a
SPECULUM VIRGINUM 11–0
Speier
commune 3–498a
Speilmann 2–106a
Sper 2–48a,b
Speraindeo, Abbot 4–521b
SPERBER, DER 11–0
SPERVOGEL AND HERGER 11–0
Sphaera mundi (John of Holywood)
translation 3–539a
Spherical astrolabe 1–602b
Spices
European cookery 3–581b
Spiegel der minnen (Colijn van Rijssele) 4–322b
Spielmannsdichtung 2–227b
Spielmannsepik 4–390b
Spiel von Frau Jutten 4–268b
SPIERINC, NICOLAS 11–0
Spill (Jaume Roig) 3–173b-174a
Spill de la vida religiosa 3–168a
SPINELLO ARETINO 11–0
Spirals
Celtic art 3–218b, 220a
Spiritual discoveries (al-Ibshīhī) 4–445a
Spiritual Friendship, On (Saint Ethelred) 4–517a
Spiritualibus ascensionibus, De (Gerard Zerbolt) 4–166b
Spiritual Ladder
See John Climachus
Spirituals
Boniface VIII 2–323b
Franciscan Order 2–163a, 315a; 3–369b
Spiritus et animae, De (Bacon) 2–36b
Spitakavor, Church of 1–601b
Spitalkirche hall church 3–379a
Split 2–337a; 4–1b, 79b, 80a
Spoleto
foundations 2–95b
SPOLIA 11–0; 1–333b-334b
Sponsorship, baptismal 2–86a

Springald 3–180a
Springolf 3–180a
Spruchdichtung 2–228b
Spurihalz
charms, old High German 3–274a
Spytihněv 2–299b
SQUARCIALUPI MANUSCRIPT 11–0
Squillace
Vivarium monastery 3–123a,b-124a
SQUINCH 11–0; 4–234b-235b, 341b-343a
Karmrawor, Church of Saint 1–601b
SQUIRE, ESQUIRE 11–0
courtesy book 3–665b
Srebrnica 2–338a
silver 2–340a
Srednogora
Bulgaria 2–411a-b
St.
See Saint
Stabili, Francesco
See Ascoli, Cecco d'
Stadtvogt
Cologne 3–481a
Stafford, Sir Humphrey
Cade's Rebellion 3–5a
Staging and theatre
See Drama
STAINED GLASS 11–0
Chartres Cathedral 3–276a
Stalactite vault
See Vault
Stallion 2–243a
Stamford Bridge, Battle of (1066) 4–395a
Standard, Battle of (1138) 4–110b
Standing army 3–206b
Standonck, Jean
church reforms 3–368a
Stans puer ad mensam (John Lydgate) 3–661a
Stantipes 4–87a-88b
See Also Dance
Stanzaic Life of Christ 2–222a
Chester plays 3–299a
Staraya Ladoga
cattle castration 1–294a
Stargard
Brunsberg, H(e)inrich von 2–392b
STARKAÐR 11–0
Staro Nagoričino 4–347a
"Starr" (contract) 2–81a
Star vault
See Vault
Stational liturgy 4–333a
STATIONS OF THE CROSS 11–0
Statues
medieval collections 1–335a
Statuta antiqua 3–118a
Statuta ecclesiae antiqua (Gennadius of Marseilles) 3–441a
Statuta et consuetudines
See Très ancien coutumier
Statuta nova 3–118a
STATUTE 11–0
"Statute, equity of" 4–502a
Statute of Gruffudd ap Cynan 4–415b
Statute of Marlborough (1267) 2–112b
Statute rolls (1278)
French translation 1–260a
Staupitz, Johann
Biel 2–234a
Staurakios 2–401a
STAUROGRAM 11–0
early Christian art 4–355b
See Also Cross, forms of
STAVE 11–0
Stave church 3–379b, 382b
Stavrakios 2–456a
Steatite
Byzantine art 2–456a,b
STEELMAKING 11–0
Stefan Dragutin 2–336a
STEFAN LAZAREVIĆ 11–0
STEFAN NEMANJA 11–0; 4–347a
Bogomils 2–296b
STEFAN PRVOVENČANI 11–0
STEFAN TOMAŠ 11–0; 2–339a
STEFAN TOMAŠEVIĆ 11–0; 2–339b-340a
Bogomils 2–296b
STEFAN UROŠ IV DUŠAN
Bulgaria 2–412b
Byzantine Empire 2–501a
STEFEN UROŠ II MILUTIN 11–0
STEFAN VUKČIĆ KOSAČA 11–0
Stein, Marquard vom 3–662b
STEINMAR 11–0
STEP'ANOS ASOŁIK TARONEC'I 11–0; 1–482a
Step'anos of Siwnik', Bishop
Armenian literature 1–510a
Step'anos Orbelean, Archbishop 4–417b
Armenian literature 1–511b
Step'anos Siwnec'i 1–506a
Step'anos Tarawnec'i Asołik 1–510b
Stephanos, King
Djvari 4–231b
Stephanos Sachlikis 2–523a
Stephanus of Alexandria 1–614a
Stephaton
crucifixion 4–12a-b
Stephen II, Bishop
Clermont-Ferrand abbey 1–144b
Stephen I, Pope 4–70a
STEPHEN II, POPE 11–0
anointing 1–308b
Byzantine church 2–463a
papal policies 3–345b
Pepin III 3–106b, 346a
Stephen IX, Pope
Ambrosian chant 2–181a
papal reform 3–348b
STEPHEN, CROWN OF SAINT 11–0
Stephen Harding
See Harding, Stephen
Stephen-Henry of Blois-Chartres-Meaux 3–244b
Stephen of Alexandria
alchemy 1–136a
Stephen of Alvastra, Archbishop
Cistercian Order 3–405b
Stephen of Blois, King 4–424b, 463a-b
Angevins 1–253a
crusades 4–20a, 34a,b, 35b, 36a,b
death 4–37a
Treaties of Durham 4–316a
Stephen of Bourbon
preaching 4–250a
Stephen of Burgundy, Count
Crusade of 1101 4–36a
Stephen of Chloyes
Children's Crusade 4–14a-b
Stephen of Grandmont
Marian offices 2–274a
STEPHEN I OF HUNGARY, SAINT 11–0
Stephen of Lexington
Cistercian Order 3–405a
Stephen of Meaux-Troyes
Champagne 3–243b
Stephen of Muret
eremitic movement 3–354b
Stephen of Orléans
See Stephen of Tournai
Stephen of Tarōn
See Step'anos Asołik Tarōnec'i
STEPHEN OF TOURNAI 11–0
Decretum 4–127b
Stephen of Ulnia
Armenian saints 1–519b
STEPHEN THE FIRST CROWNED 11–0
Stephen the Great of Wallachia
Bāyazīd II 2–137b
Stepped cross 4–9b
Steps of Humility and Pride, The (Bernard of Clairvaux) 2–191a
Stereographic projection, theory of 1–622b
Stethaimer, Hans
See Burghausen, Hans von
Steward
estate management 4–514a,b
Stewardship accounting 1–36b-40a
STIACCIATO 11–0
Sticharion 3–615b
STICHERON 11–0
STICHOMETRY 11–0
Stigand, Archbishop 4–459a
excommunication 3–82b
STIKARION 11–0
Stilicho, Flavius 1–652a
Alaric 1–122a
Stilted arch 1–424, 425a
Stilted dome 4–236a
Stimulus amoris (Saint Bonaventure) 3–168a
Stipes 1–221b
Stirrup
Arab adoption 3–208b
cavalry development 1–294b
Romans 3–200b
westward diffusion 3–201b, 202a
Stirrup, symbolic 3–346a
Stjepan I
Croatia 4–6a
STJEPAN KOTROMANIC 11–0; 2–336a-b
economy 2–340a,b
Stjepan Tomaš
Bosnian church 2–343a
Stockholm Bloodbath 4–156a
Stockholm Papyrus 1–135b
STOCKTON, THOMAS 11–0
Stoeffler, John
planetary clocks 3–465a
Stoicism
allegorical interpretation 1–181a
Aristotelianism 1–458b
astrological determinism 1–604b, 605a
Boethius 2–292a
Stojkovic of Ragusa, John
Dominican theology 4–248a
Stokton, Dame Elizabeth
businesses 4–603b
STONE 11–0
Stone castles 3–144a-152a
Stonehenge
topographic views 1–333b
Stoneland
See Helluland
Stones
See Masonry
Stone sculpture
Celtic art 3–221b, 222, 223a-b
Stoneware
Chinese 3–238b
European ceramics 3–238a
Storia de l'amat Frondino e de Brisona 3–173a
Story of My Misfortunes, The (Peter Abelard) 1–323b
Story of the loved Frondoin and Brisona 3–173a

Story of the people of Oddi
  See Oddaverja páttr
Story of the Ten Martyrs 1–344b
STOSS, VEIT 11–0
Stourbridge
  fairs 4–586b, 587a
Stour River
  Canterbury 3–81a
Stow
  Black Death 2–262b
STOWELL, JOHN 11–0
Stowe Missal 2–83b; 3–676b
  Celtic church 3–229a, 230b
  Celtic liturgy 3–230a
  extreme unction directions 3–230b
  funeral rites 3–231a
Strabo 2–29a
Strabo, Walafrid
  See Walafrid Strabo
Stracimir, John
  Bulgaria 2–412b, 413a
Strait of Gibraltar
  trade 4–557b
Strambotto
  See Estrabot
STRASBOURG 11–0
  commune 3–498a
STRASBOURG CATHEDRAL 11–0; 1–428a,b
  Anastasis representation 1–239a
  construction 2–182a
  Master Erwin 4–508a
Strassburg
  exchange banks 2–74a,b
Stratagem of Urard mac Coisse 1–114a
Strategikon (Kekaumenos) 1–116a
Strategikon (Maurice) 3–199b, 202a; 4–447a
Strategikon (Nikephoros Phokas) 4–447a
Strategopouloi family 2–479a
STRATEGOS 11–0; 1–491b
  Anatolikon theme 1–236a, 242a
Stratford, John, Archbishop
  convocations of Canterbury and York 3–578b
STRATHCLYDE, KINGDOM OF 11–0
  ornamented molds 3–224a
STRATIOTAI 11–0
Stratiotika
  See Soldiers' portion
Stratiotika ktemata 3–199b
Stratophilos, Bishop
  cathedral 2–253b
Straubing 2–134b, 135a
Strausberg Priory 1–128a
***STRENGLEIKAR* 11–0**; 4–432a
Strez
  Bulgaria 2–409a
***STRICKER, DER* 11–0**; 1–229b
  Ambraser Heldenbuch 1–230a
STRINGCOURSE 11–0
Stroma magistri Rolandi 4–127b
Struk 1–488b, 489b
Studenica Monastery 4–347a
  art 2–446b
Studentis, T. H. Parisii 1–270b
STUDIOS, MONASTERY 11–0
  liturgy 2–468a
Studium generale 3–59a
Stuñiga 3–140a
STURLA ÞHORÐARSON 11–0
***STURLAUGS SAGA STARFSAMA* 11–0**
***STURLUNGA SAGA* 11–0**; 4–612b
Sturluson, Snorri
  See Snorri Sturluson
Sturmi, Abbot 4–408b
Sturry, Sir Richard
  See Clanvowe, Sir John
Stuteville, William de
  charcoal burning 3–267a
"Style of the Châtelet" 3–279b
STYLUS 11–0
Styria 2–4b, 8b, 9a
  Babenberg family 2–33b
  Bohemia 2–300a
Subdeacon 3–442a-b
Ṣubḥ al-a'shā' (Qalqashandī) 3–54a; 4–445b
Šubić, Pavao
  Bosnia 2–336a
Šubići
  Bosnia 2–336a,b
Subkī, al- 1–634a
Subpoena
  English common law 4–502b
Subsistence theory
  Christology 3–322b, 323a
"Subtle Doctor" (*Doctor Subtilis*)
  See Duns Scotus, John
Süb?üdey 2–131b
Succession, dynastic principle of 3–42b-43a
Succession, rights of
  See Kingship, Theories of
Suckenie 3–624b
***SUDA* 11–0**; 4–447a
  classical literary studies 3–431a
  See Also Vozdukh
SUDAN 11–0
Sudanis
  Almoravids 1–199a
Sudavians
  See Sudovians
Sudbury
  Black Death 2–262b
Sudebnik 1–101b
Sudovians 2–64b, 67a
Suel, Adam de
  Cato's Ditichs 3–193b
Suero de Quiñones
  Arthurian literature 1–576b
Suetonius 2–236a, 239b
Suevi 2–94a
  agriculture 1–84b
  Alamanni 1–117a
  Arianism 1–454b
  invasions 2–91b, 92a
Suez
  exploration 4–562b
SUFFA 11–0
Sufism
  Allah 1–178b
  cabala 3–2b
  Cairo 3–14b
  dervish 4–163a
  Islamic Egypt 4–107a
  See Also Mysticism, Islamic
Suftaja 2–79b
Sufyānī
  caliphate 3–36b-38b, 46a
SUGER, ABBOT OF SAINT DENIS 11–0; 1–17a,b, 426a, 427b; 2–173b; 4–346a, 419b
  architecture 2–175a
  castles and fortifications reports 3–145a
  chevet 3–300b
  church rebuilding 1–334a
  church reforms 3–347b
  De rebus in administratione sua gestis 1–335b
  Louis VI 2–236b, 239b
  Louis VII 1–367b; 4–38a
  memoirs 2–237a
Suhrawardī al-Maktūl, al-
  angels 1–249a
Suibne
  Áed Sláne 1–60b
SUIDAS/SUDA 11–0
Suidger of Bamberg (Clement II) 1–47a
Suitability, principle of 4–427a,b
Suk'ias 1–519b
Sukkot 3–27a
Sul
  See Derbent
Sulayhid dynasty
  Yemen 1–375a,b
Sulaymān ibn 'Abd al-Malik
  'ahd 3–39a
  costume 3–616b
Suleiman I 2–137a
  Knights of Malta 3–304a
Sulien 3–224a,b
Sulien, Bishop 2–71b
Sulpicius Severus of Tours
  Helena, Saint 1–336b
  Martin, Saint 2–236a
SULTAN 11–0
  Ayyubids 2–24b
Suma de filosofia 3–169a
SUMER IS ICUMEN IN 11–0; 1–319b
Summa artis notariae (Rolandino Passaggerii) 4–174b
Summa Britonis (William Brito) 4–450a
Summa collationum (John of Wales) 3–167b
Summa contra gentiles (Thomas Aquinas) 1–354a,b, 607b; 4–381b, 510a
  Demetrios Kydones 4–135b
Summa (Robert of Courson) 3–659a
Summa de casibus (Raymond of Peñafort) 3–153b
Summa decretorum (Rufinus) 4–422a-b
Summa de ecclesia (Juan de Torquemada) 3–519b, 520b; 4–378a
Summa de ecclesiastica potestate (Augustinus Triumphus) 2–1a
Summa de electione (Bernard of Pavia) 4–123b
Summa de l'altra vida (Joan Pasqual) 3–169b
Summa de legibus 4–68b-69a
Summa de ligibus Normannie
  See Custumals of Normandy
Summa de sacramentis (Peter the Chanter) 3–572b
Summa dictaminis (Bernard of Meun) 4–175a
Summa dictaminis (Dominicus Dominici Visentinus) 4–175b
Summa dictaminis (Pons of Provence) 4–175a
Summa Fratris Alexandri (Alexander of Hales) 1–148a-b
Summa gramatica (Johannes Dacus)
  alphabets 1–218b
Summa (Lambert of Auxerre) 4–170b
Summa logicae (William of Ockham) 4–170b
Summa moralis (Antoninus) 1–342b
Summa on the Cathars and the Poor of Lyons (Rainier Sacconi) 3–182a
Summa Parisiensis (Albertus Magnus) 1–127a
Summa perfectionis magisterii (Jābir ibn Ḥayyān) 1–137b-138a
Summa philosophiae 2–41a
Summa predicantium (John of Bromyard)
  florilegia 1–317b
Summa recreatorum
  Bohemian anthology 1–320a

Summa theologiae (Thomas Aquinas) 1–323b, 354a-b, 356a; 4–501b
alphabets 1–218b
angel/angelology 1–250b
Demetrios Kydones 4–135b
Summa theologica (Antoninus) 1–342b
Summer Church
Ambrosian liturgy 1–233a,b
Summulae logicales (Petrus Hispanus) 4–170b
Summule dialectices (Roger Bacon) 4–170b
SUMPTUARY LAWS 11–0
Alfonso X 3–136a-b
European cookery 3–583a
Jewish costume 3–619b, 620b-621a
Western costume 3–622a
SUMPTUARY LAWS, ISLAMIC 11–0
costume 3–616b
"Sunday Gospels"
See Evangiles des domnees
SUNDIALS 11–0; 1–622b; 3–27b, 28a-b, 457b
Sunifred II 3–175a
Sunifred of Carcassonne 3–174b
Sunitai
See Siwnik'
***SUNNA* 11–0**; 3–32b, 33a
blood money 2–276b
concubinage 3–527b
SUNNI 11–0
Abū Ḥanīfa 1–26b
Alamūt 1–118b
Allah 1–178b
Ash'arī, al- 1–585a
Assassins 1–590b
Ayyubids 2–23b
Azhar, al- 2–27b
Bukhara 2–397a
Bukhārī, al- 2–397b
Buyids 2–435b, 436a,b
commander of the faithful 3–488b
Damascus 4–84b-85a
Islamic Arabia 1–374a, 375b-376a
Nūr al-Dīn 4–82a
Seljuks 1–11b
Sunyer 3–175a
Sup'an
See Sophanenē
Superpositio
Celtic mortifications 3–231b
Suppedaneum cross 4–9b
Supplicationes
Decretum 4–128a
Supputatio romana
dating of Easter 3–228a
SUQ 11–0
Sūq al-khayl 4–83b
Surcoat 3–625a
Surgery
barbers 2–97b
Old English text 1–286a
Surhan-David
relics 1–519a
Sur les états du monde 1–269b
Surnames
concept of family 3–413a
SURTR 11–0
Survey of the sciences 4–445a
Surveys, manorial, fiscal
demography 4–137b
Susa
barbotine technique 2–101a
ceramics 3–23a
Šušanik 1–518b
Susannah (The Pistel of Swete Susan) 2–221b
SUSO (SEUSE), **HEINRICH 11–0**
Albertus Magnus 1–129b
Clock of Wisdom 3–462b
Dominican mysticism 4–248b
German mysticism 3–368b
Ruusbroec 4–320b
Sussex
Anglo-Saxon 4–454a
borough-English 2–332a
emergence of kingdom 2–96b
SUTRI, SYNOD OF (1046) **11–0**; 1–47a
papal reform 3–348b
SUTTON, ROBERT 11–0
SUTTON HOO 11–0
Celtic art 3–219b
disk brooch 1–281a
royal treasure 2–184b
ship burial 1–274a
Ṣuwar al-kawākib ('Abd al-Raḥmān al-Ṣūfī) 1–623a
SUYŪṬI, AL 11–0
Suzay
ars subtilior 1–558b
Suzdal
city walls 3–151b
SVARFDÆLA SAGA 11–0; 4–613b
Svatopluk, Prince 2–299b; 4–73b
SVEN AGGESEN 11–0
SVERRIS SAGA 11–0
Sveta Sofia 2–414b
SVETT CXOVELI 11–0
Sveti Ivan Aliturgitos, Church of 2–416a, 417a
Svetoslav 4–5a-b
SVFER, HANS 11–0
***SVIPDAGSMAL* 11–0**; 4–387b
Svjatoslav, Prince 2–404a, 406a
SWABIA 11–0
Swabian-Rhenish League
class conflicts 3–428b
Swabian Welfs
Bavarian rule 2–134a
Swan 2–206b
Swan, Brandenburg Order of 3–307a
SWEDEN 11–0
Anglo-Saxon origins and migration 1–289a,b
Birka 2–247b
bracteates 2–356a
exploration 4–553b-554a, 555a-b
national peasantry 3–424b
Swedish language
chansons de geste 3–258a
runic alphabet 1–215b
Sweyn II Estridsen, King 1–47a
Sweyn Estridsen, King 1–47a; 4–152b
independent archbishop 4–154a
Sweyn Forkbeard, King 3–82a, 471b; 4–394b, 457a
Viking period 4–151b
Swine, wild
hunting laws 1–301a
SWINESHEAD, RICHARD 11–0; 1–396b, 464b
Bradwardine, Thomas 2–358a
Swiss Confederation 2–8a
Swithulf, Bishop 1–165b
SWITZERLAND 11–0
Alamanni settlement 1–117b
camel use 1–296b
cattle breeding 1–293b
consuls, consulate 3–570b
drama 4–269a
fairs 4–585b
infantry 3–204b-205a
Latin church: to 1054 3–344b
Sword, Knights of (Cyprus) 3–306b
SWORDS AND DAGGERS 11–0; 1–521b, 522b
falchion 4–593b
Swynford, Katherine
Chaucer 3–281a
Syagrius
Clovis 3–466a
Frankish invasions 2–94a-b
SYFER, HANS 11–0
Sylvester
See Silvester
Symbols of numbers
See Arabic numerals
Symeon 2–507b
SYMEON METAPHRASTES 11–0; 2–519a
SYMEON OF BULGARIA 11–0; 2–404a-406a
art and architecture 2–414b
Byzantine church 2–464a
Byzantine Empire 2–489b-490a; 4–4b
Constantinople 3–552a
Croatia 4–4b
Vladimir 2–329b
Symeon of Thessaloniki, Archbishop
Bogomils 2–296b
Symeon Seth 1–78a
Symeon Stylites, Saint 2–455a
SYMEON THE LOGOTHETE 11–0
chronicle 2–514b
SYMEON THE NEW THEOLOGIAN 11–0
Byzantine theology 2–467a
hymns 2–524b
Symmachus 1–647a
pagan party 1–650a-b
Symmachus, Quintus Aurelius Memmius
Boethius 2–291a
Symphoniae
See Consonance/dissonance
Symphosius riddles
Anthologia Latina 1–317a
Symposium (Methodius) 1–182b
Synadenoi
holdings 2–479b
Synagoga
See Ecclesia and Synogoga
SYNAGOGUE 11–0; 1–442a
bema 2–167a
SYNAXARION 11–0
saints 1–521a
SYNAXARY 11–0
SYNDIC 11–0
Synekdemos
See Hierokles
Synesios of Cyrene 2–510b, 524b
alchemy 1–136a
Synkellos
Byzantine clergy 3–447a
SYNKELLUS 11–0
Synodia . . . de conciliis (Matthias Ugonius) 3–520b
***SYNODIKON OF ORTHODOXY* 11–0**
Byzantine councils 3–631b
Synod in Trullo
See Quinisext Synod
Synod of Alexandria (378)
condemnation of Apollinarius 1–348a
Synod of Antioch (379)
condemnation of Apollinarius 1–348a
Synod of 843
Amorian dynasty 1–236a
Synod of Paris (1074)
celibacy of clergy 3–217a
Synod of Quierzy (838) 1–228a
Synod of Rheims (1148)
clash of cardinals adn bishops 3–94b

T

Synod of Rome (377)
Apollinarius 1–348a
Synod of Sens (1346)
angelus 1–252b
Synod of Whitby (664)
calendrical dispute 3–81b
Synodoi
See Councils (Ecumenical)
Synopsis major of Basilics 2–125b
Syntax
Anglo-Norman 1–272a
chansons de geste 3–261a,b
Old English texts 1–276a
***SYNTHRONON* 11–0**; 1–442a, 443; 4–335b
Syracuse
Aghlabids 1–70b
Romans 1–334b
SYRIA 11–0
Abbasids 1–7a, 11a,b
Abū Bakr 1–25b
Aleppo 1–145a
ʿAmr ibn al-ʿĀṣ 1–237a
architecture 4–337a-b, 343b
Armenians 2–492a
Assassins 1–590b, 591a
Axum kingdom 2–17a-b
Ayyubid art 2–20b, 21b
Ayyubid rule 2–23a-b, 24a, 25a
Bādiya 2–42b
baptism 4–497a-b
Barqūq 2–113a
Black Death 2–259a
Byzantine church 2–462a, 468a
Byzantine defeat 2–487a
caliphate reestablishiment 3–36b
ceramics 3–238b
Cilician Gates 3–390b
Circassians 3–398a
conch church 3–378a
conquest 1–4b
crusades 2–138b; 4–32a
Cyprus 4–72a
Damascus 4–80b
Druzes 4–295b
Fatimids 3–50b; 4–27b
hereditary governorship 3–49a
Louis IX 4–53b
Mamluks 3–14a-b
Muʿāwiya 1–172b; 3–36a
petty states 4–27b
Saladin 4–31a
Seljukid 4–27b
Swedes 4–555b
Umayyads 1–16a
verse 2–510b
Syriac alphabet 1–207b-209a, 218a
Syriac Bible 4–356b, 357a
Syriac language
Bar Hebraeus' revival 2–108a
Syriac-Peshitta biblical text 2–211a, 217b
SYRIAN CHRISTIANITY 11–0; 3–339a, 340a, 344a
Syrian Franks
Latin states 4–38b
Syrian Gates
See Cilician Gates
Syrian March 1–514b-515a; 2–140b
SYRIAN RITES 11–0; 1–326b
Syria-Palestine
crusader art and architecture 4–22a
Syro-Malabar alphabet 1–208b
Syro-Palestinian littoral 4–30b
Systemata 4–494a
System of Iamblichus, The 1–135b
SZÉKESFHERVÁR 11–0

TAAIAN 11–0
TÂamar, Queen
Dwin 4–324b
Tábara
Emeterius 4–436b
ṬABARĪ, AL- 11–0; 2–50a
Armenia 1–478a
Athīr, Ibn al- 1–634b
Burāq 2–419b
encyclopedias and dictionaries 4–442a
Koran 2–215a
Tabernacles
altar apparatus 1–223b
TABLION 11–0
TABRĪZ 11–0; 2–26b
Tabrobane
See Ceylon
Tabūk 1–24b
***TABULA ANSATA* 11–0**
Tabulae resolutae
Alfonsine Tables 1–159b
***TABULA PEUTINGERIANA* 11–0**; 1–333a
Tabula smaragdina 1–136a, 141b
Tacitus
Baltic countries/Balts 2–61b-62a
barbarian invasions 2–89a
deposition of rulers 4–157b
early Christian movement 3–334b
Tactica (Leo VI) 3–199b, 203a
TADDEO DI BARTOLO 11–0
Tafur, Pero
See Pero Tafur
Tʿagadir 1–489a
Tagaste 1–646a
Augustine's community 1–648b
Tagelied
aubade 1–642a
Taghlib 1–115a
Taghrībirdī, Ibn 3–399a; 4–407b
Circassians 3–400a
Tagliacozzo, Battle of (1268) 4–60b, 95b
TAGMATA 11–0
Tagrit
Antiochene rite 1–326b
Tagus River basin
Asturias-León boundary 1–625a
Tāhert, King
Aghlabids 1–70b-71a
ṬĀHIR IBN AL-ḤUSAYN 11–0
TAHIRIDS 11–0
Taḥrīr al-Majisṭī (Naṣīr al-Dīn al-Ṭūsī) 1–620b
Ṭāʾif, al- 1–16a
conquest 1–29a
Taifa 3–177a
Taifas 1–196b, 198a
Almoravids 1–199b-200a; 3–129b
Castile 3–128b
emergence 1–628b
parias 3–132a
TAILLE, TALLAGE 11–0; 4–469b
Charles VII 3–271b
Taillefer 1–265a
TAÍN BÓ CÚAILGNE 11–0
Tairdelbach Ua Briain, King 4–77b
Taisabun
See Ctesiphon
Tāj al-lugha wa ṣiḥāḥ al-ʿarabiya (al-Jawharī) 4–444a
Takkanot 3–621a
Taktika (Nikephoros Uranos) 4–447a
Taktika (Leo VI) 4–447a
Taktikon (Pseudo-Kodinos) 4–447a
Taktikon Uspenski 4–447a
Talbot, Robert
codicology 3–477a
TALENTI, FRANCESCO 11–0; 1–540b
Tales of women 2–82b
Ṭalḥa ibn ʿUbayd Allāh 3–35b
ʿĀʾisha 1–113b
ʿAlī 1–172b
TALIESIN 11–0
Arthurian literature 1–577b
Celtic language 3–234a
Gododdin 1–247b
TʿALIN 11–0; 1–493b
Talinn
See Reval
Taʿlīq al-ʾarṣād (Ibn al-Shāṭir) 1–622b
Talisman Gate 1–6b
Tallies
Exchequer 4–530b
Tallith 3–619a
Ṭallīt qāṭān 3–619a
Talmud
Babylonian 3–618b
contraception 3–573a
costume 3–618b, 619b
Jerusalem 3–618b
TALMUD, EXEGESIS AND STUDY OF 11–0; 2–212a-b; 4–538a
Rabad 1–22b
Tʿamar 2–207a
amirspasalar 1–235b
Ani in Širak 1–291a
Bagratids, Georgian 2–49a
Dwin 1–485b
TAMARA 11–0
Tamarón, Battle of (1037) 1–628b; 3–128b
TAMERLANE 11–0
Anatolia 1–242a
Ankara 1–302b
Aq Qoyunlu confederation 1–352a
Armenia 1–486a
Azerbaijan 2–27a
Barqūq 2–113b
Bāyazīd I 2–136b
Brusa 2–393a
Byzantine Empire 2–503a
Damascus 4–82b, 83b-84a
Erzincan 4–508b
Mesopotamia 3–313a
Western Asia 3–398b
Tamīmī, Ismāʿīl ibn MuḤammad al-
Druzes 4–296a
Tʿamtʿa
Xlatʿ 1–486a
Tana
Black Death 2–258b
trade 4–557a,b
TANCRED (CANONIST) 11–0
TANCRED (CRUSADER) 11–0
Bohemond I 2–309a
crusades 4–34a,b, 35a, 40a
Tangermünde
Brunsberg, H(e)inrich von 2–392b
TANGIER 11–0
Almoravids 1–199a
Tanjīm
See Astrology/Astronomy, Islamic
Tannenberg, Battle of (1410) 2–67a
TANNHÄUSER, DER 11–0

Tansar, Letter of
See Letter of Tansar
Tanta
fairs 4–589b
Tanta (Justinian)
Corpus iuris civilis 3–609a
Tanūkhī, al-
Deliverance After Distress 1–380b
TANUTĒR 11–0
Tanutēr (lord) 1–480b, 488b, 489a, 490a
Tao
See Tayk'
Taormina
Aghlabids 1–70b, 71b
Byzantine conquest 2–118a
TAPESTRY, ART OF 11–0
Bataille 2–129b
Bayeux 2–139a
trade 1–561a-b
TAPESTRY, MILLEFLEURS 11–0
botany 2–348b
TAPESTRY: WEAVING 11–0
Coptic textiles 3–589b, 590a
Tapissier 3–256b
Taq-e Khusro 4–62b
TAQ-I BOSTAN 11–0
Ṭāq-i Kisrā
See Taq-e Khusro
Taqlīb al-ḥurūf 4–444a
TARA 11–0
Cormac Mac Airt 3–601a
kings 1–60b
Tara brooch 3–220a-222
TARASIOS, PATRIARCH 11–0; 2–461b
iconoclasm 2–488b
letters 2–520a
Tarazona 1–160a, 406a, 407b, 416b
Tarchaneoites, John
Andronikos II Palaiologos 1–245b
Tardif, Guillaume
fables 4–572b
Tardus 4–67a
Targe
See Shield
Tarifa
Alfonso VI conquest 1–199b
Sancho's conquest 3–134b
Ta'rīkh al-Bāhir ('Izz al-Dīn) 1–634b
Ṭarīqa
dervish 4–163a
Tarlati, Guido, Bishop
tomb 1–73b, 76b
Tarn-et-Garonne
See Montauban
TARŌN 11–0; 1–474a; 2–48b
Tarragona 1–408a, 410b, 412b
archbishopric 3–178a
restoration (1118) 3–178a
Tarshish
See Córdoba
TARSUS 11–0
Anatolia 1–239b
Armenian council 1–501a
Cilician kingdom 3–391a, 393a
Tartaglia, Niccolò 1–438a, 439b
Tāshfīn ibn 'Alī Yūsuf 1–200a-b
Tashkent
Swedes 4–555b
Tassets 1–529a, 531b, 534a
Tassilo III, Duke 2–4b
Bavarian independence 2–94b-95a
deposition 2–134a
Tasyīr 1–619b
Tatars
Bāyazīd II alliance 2–137a
Boucher, Guillaume 2–349b
Bulgaria 2–409b, 410a,b-411a
Crimea Khanate 3–678a
Lithuania 2–67a
Polos 4–557a
See Also Mongol Empire
"Tatar yoke," era of 1–100b-101a
Tategan 3–393a
TAT'EW 11–0
TATIAN 11–0
Tatian the Assyrian
defense of Christians 3–335a
Tatikios
First Crusade 4–35a
Tats 3–195a
T'at'ul 1–484b, 519b
TATWINE OF CANTERBURY 11–0
Tau cross 4–9b
Tauern 2–4b
Taula de Canvi de Barcelona 2–75b
TAULER, JOHANNES 11–0
Albertus Magnus 1–129b
Dominican mysticism 4–248b
German mysticism 3–368b
Ruusbroec 4–320b
Taurus Mountains, 4–522a
Cilician Gates 3–390b
Cilician kingdom 3–391a
Tavadi 2–29a
Taverner, Peter 2–157b
Tavşanlı Kilise 3–92a
Tawḥīdī, al-
alchemy 1–141b
Tawq al-hamāma (Ibn Ḥazm) 3–672a
Taxation
alnage 1–203a
Bulgaria 2–407a
Castile 3–132a-b, 136a-b, 138b
communal government 3–501b
Copts and Coptic church 3–594b
cortes 3–611b-612a
TAXATION, BYZANTINE 11–0
agriculture 1–79b
bureaucracy 2–472a, 473a
Constantine VII Porphyrogenitos 3–547a
economy and society 2–476a,b, 477a, 480a
epibolé 4–495b
Komnenoi 2–496a
TAXATION, CHURCH 11–0
annate 1–304b
clericis laicos 3–447b
concordat 3–525b, 526b
convocations of Canterbury and York 3–578b-579b
crusades 4–51a,b, 53b
Innocent III 3–353b
political crusades 4–61b-62a
TAXATION, ENGLISH 11–0
danegeld 4–90a
England (1216-1485) 4–484a
Exchequer 4–530b
Norman-Angevin England 4–469a
TAXATION, FRENCH
Burgundians 2–423a
Burgundy, Duchy of 2–427b
Crown of Aragon 1–411b
TAXATION, FRENCH: HISTORY OF 11–0
Brittany, Duchy 2–380b
Charles V 3–269b
TAXATION, ISLAMIC 11–0
Abode of Islam--Abode of War 1–20b
agriculture 1–103a-b
alms tax 1–201b
Buyids 2–437b
Muḥammad 1–25a
Taxation, Mongol
Ani in Širak 1–291b
Taxation, Slavic 1–102b
TAXT-I SULEIMAN 11–0
Ṭayālisa (mantle) 3–619b
TAYK' 11–0; 1–472b, 473a,b; 2–48b
Bana 2–70a
See Also David of Tao
ṬAYLASĀN 11–0
Taymâ
crusader attack 1–375b
Taym-Allāh 1–26a
Taym clan 1–24a, 112b
TAYMĪYA, IBN 11–0; 3–51a
Tazarfatti, Rabbi Reuben
cabala 3–3a
TBILISI 11–0; 1–124b, 473b
Teacher, The (Augustine) 1–648b
Teaching centers
See Schools; Universities
TECHNOLOGY, BYZANTINE 11–0
TECHNOLOGY, ISLAMIC 11–0
TECHNOLOGY, TREATISES ON 11–0
TECHNOLOGY, WESTERN 11–0
barrels 2–114a
cannon 3–64a
charcoal burning 3–267a
gunpowder 3–205a, 206b
Tederic 3–168b
TE DEUM 11–0
Tegernsee, Monastery 2–134a
TEGLIACCI, NICOLÒ DI SER SOZZO 11–0
Teifi River 4–329b
TEKOR 11–0
Tekufot 3–26b-27a
Telanissus 4–333b
Telesphorus, Pope
Christmas celebration 3–317a
Tell Atlas Mountains 1–639b
Telles, Fernão
Seven Cities 4–559b
Tellurium
clocks 3–460b
Tëmny
See Basil II, Muscovite Grand Prince
TEMPERA PAINTING 11–0
Temperatures
climatology 3–452b, 453a
Tempier, Étienne, Bishop
Aristotelianism 1–463a-b
censure of astrology 1–608a
courtly love 3–671a
Tempier, Stephen
Thomistic theses 4–247a
Tempio Malatestiano (Rimini) 1–126b
Templars 2–1a; 3–244b, 304a-b
bastides 2–128b
Bernard of Chartres 2–191a,b
Bernard of Clairvaux, Saint 4–17a-b
Clement V 3–362a
Crown of Aragon 1–408a,b, 410b, 411a-b, 415a
crusader art and architecture 4–21b
crusades 4–32a
Hospitalers 4–52a,b
Jem Sultan 2–137a
papal funds 2–77b
Vienne Council 3–643b, 644a
See Also Chivalry, orders of
Temple of Ahura Mazda (Ani in Daranalik') 1–290a
Temple of Ceres (Rome) 1–333b
Temple of Concord (Rome) 1–333b
Temple of Solomon (Jerusalem)
angel 1–248a
Temples, Greek and Roman 1–442a
Templon screen
See Screen

Templum Domini
  Dome of the Rock 4–24a
Temporale
  antiphonal 1–330a
Temporibus, De (Bede) 2–154b
Temporibus anni, De (Aelfric) 1–285b
Temporum ratione, De (Bede) 1–606a, 610b
"Temptations of the World, The"
  See Romaunz de temtacioun de secle
Tempus
  ars nova 1–549a
Tendürük 1–470b
TENOR 11–0
  ars antiqua 1–545b
  ars nova 1–551a,b
  contratenor 3–576b
  counterpoint 3–657a
Tenorio, Peter, Archbishop 3–645b
***TENSO* 11–0**
  Cercamon 3–240b
Tenths
  See Tithes
T'ēodoros K'rt'enawor 1–509b
Tēr 1–488b
Terce
  Divine Office 4–221b, 227, 229a
Terceira 2–29b
  Flemings 4–559b
Terek River 3–193b
TEREM 11–0
Tēr Israyēl
  Synaxarion 1–521a
TERMINISM 11–0
  See Also Ockham, William of
TERRA SIGILLATA 11–0
Terreni, Guido 4–377a
Terres de Beauvais 3–238a
Territorial law
  See Class structure, Western
Terter River
  Bardha'a 2–107a
Tertry, Battle of (687) 1–118a; 3–106a
Tertullian
  antifeminism 1–322b
  apostolic succession 1–350b, 351a
  Christmas 3–317b
  Christology 3–320b
  Montanism 3–335b
  religious pictures 4–349a
  theology 3–334b, 342a
Teruel 1–409a
Tervel 2–401a
  art and architecture 2–414b
Tesaur (Pierre de Corbiac) 3–657a
Tesdik 3–679a
Teseida delle nozze d'Emilia 2–280a-b
  Chaucer 3–282b
TESSERA 11–0
Testament (Serradell) 3–170a, 173b
Testament of Abraham
  angel/angelology 1–249b
Testamentum 1–138b
Tester 1–222a
Tetarteron 4–494a
Tetrabiblos (Ptolemy) 1–604b, 606a,b, 608a, 609a, 617a, 619a
TETRACONCH 11–0
  Bana 2–70a
  church types 1–378a, 380
TETRAMORPH 11–0
Teutones
  invasions 2–88b
Teutonia
  Albertus Magnus 1–127b-128b
Teutonic Knights 3–306a
  accounting system 1–38a
  Baltic countries 2–66b-67a; 4–17b
  Estonia 2–65b
  Montfort 4–25b
  poems 2–231a
  Prussia 2–67b
  Severin 2–70a
  water buffalo 1–298b
  See Also Chivalry, orders of
Tévar
  Cid's victory 3–73b
Tevdos (Theodosios) III, King 4–113b
Tewkesbury Cathedral
  architecture 1–256a
Texier, Jean (Jean de Beauce)
  Chartres Cathedral 3–276a
TEXTBOOKS 11–0
  ars praedicandi 1–555b
  medicine 1–458b, 459a
TEXTILES 11–0
  Alexandria 1–154a-b
  Byzantine costume 3–615b
  canvas 3–88a
  Coptic 3–588b-590a
  Córdoba 3–600b
  cotton 3–626b
  dyes and dyeing 4–325a
  Western European costumes 3–622b-623a,b, 624b
TEXTILES, ISLAMIC 11–0
  bedestan 2–156a
  costume 3–616b-618a
  Dībāj 4–173a
  pastoralism 1–103b
TEXTILE TECHNOLOGY 11–0
TEXTILE WORKERS 11–0
Textus Roffensis 1–286a,b
  manuscript dating 1–275b
Tha'ālibī, al-
  poet biographies 2–238b
Thābit ibn Qurra
  Almagest 1–620a
  Archimedes 1–434b, 438a
  astronomy 1–612b, 622a
  sundials 3–28b
  trepidation theory 1–614b
THADDEUS, SAINT 11–0; 1–519a
Thaddeus of Suëssa
  Council of Lyons (1245) 3–641a
Thadeus of Parma
  astronomy 1–613a
ÞÆTTIR 11–0
Thagr 1–153b
Thaïs, Saint 1–261b
Thaleia (Arius) 1–453b
Thames River
  Anglo-Saxon kingdoms 4–452b-454a
  Black Death 2–261b, 262a
  Danelaw border 4–91a
THANGMAR OF HILDESHEIM 11–0
Thaon, Philippe de 1–271a,b
  moralizing literature 1–262a
Thatched roofing 3–559b
That Monasteries Should Not Be Given Over to Laymen (John IV of Antioch) 3–268a
ÞÁTTR AF RAGNARS SONUM 11–0
Thawb 3–616b
Thaz entphangana 3–274a
Theaetetus (Plato) 1–654b
Theater
  See Drama
Thebanus 1–152b
Thebes (Greece)
  Alexander romances 1–150b
  Byzantine Empire 2–494a
  Catalan Company 3–156a-b
Theca 1–223b
THEGANUS 11–0
THEGN 11–0
The Ill-cut Coat 1–268a
The King's Summa 1–263a
Themata
  See Themes
Thematibus, De 4–446b
THEMES 11–0
  Anatolia 1–241a
  Armenia 1–474a
  Armeniakon 1–491b
  Byzantine bureaucracy 2–473b, 474b
  Byzantine Empire 2–487b
  Constans II 3–544b
  divisions 3–199b
  Ephesus 4–494b
Themistius
  dialectic 4–168b
Themo the Jew 1–396b
Theobald of Blois, Count
  anti-Semitism 1–340b
Theobald of Canterbury, Archbishop 3–83a
  Becket 2–151a
  John of Salisbury 3–83a
Theobaldus-Physiologus 2–205b
Theodibert II
  Aquitaine 1–366b
Theodicy
  early church 3–340a
THEODOFRID OF CORBIE 11–0
THEODORA I, EMPRESS 11–0; 2–165a
  cosmetics 2–147b
  Nubian Christianity 3–314b
THEODORA II, EMPRESS 11–0
  Amorian dynasty 1–236a
  Bardas Caesar 2–106a
  reign 2–489a
Theodora of Bulgaria, wife of John Alexander 2–412b
Theodora of Bulgaria, wife of Michael Šišman 2–412a
THEODORA THE MACEDONIAN, EMPRESS 11–0
  reign 2–491b, 492a
THEODORE 11–0
Theodore, Antipope 1–330a
Theodore, Saint
  Bulgarian art and architecture 2–415b, 417a
Theodore Anagnostes 2–517a
Theodore Angelos Komnenos Doukas 2–498b
  Epiros 2–409a
Theodore Apseudes 2–445b
THEODORE BALSAMON 11–0; 2–507a
THEODORE I LASKARIS 11–0
  Brusa 2–392b
  reign 2–498a,b
THEODORE II LASKARIS 11–0
Theodore Mankaphas
  Byzantine Empire 2–496b
Theodore Meliteniotes 2–510a
THEODORE METOCHITES 11–0; 2–507b, 518a, 519a
  art patron 2–449a-450a, 451b
  donor portrait 4–261b
  icons 2–457b
Theodore of Candia
  University of Bologna 2–312b
THEODORE OF CANTERBURY, SAINT 11–0; 2–153b; 4–458b
  Canterbury 3–82a
  Celtic penitentials 3–229b
  classical literary studies 3–432b
  expulsion of Wilfrid 1–144a
  mass books 2–180b
  parental authority 4–599b

THEODORE OF CANTERBURY, SAINT (cont.)
horsemeat prohibition 1–300a
THEODORE OF FREIBERG 11–0
Theodore of Mopsuestia
Antiochene school 3–336a
Armenian church 1–498b
catechetical homilies 1–327a
Christology 3–320a
Irish Bible 2–220a
Nestorius 4–75a
Old English exegesis 4–549a
Second Council of Constantinople 3–630a
THEODORE OF STUDIOS 11–0; 1–78a; 2–506b, 511a,b
epigrams 2–524a
iconoclasm 2–488b
icons 2–463a
Incarnation doctrine 3–631a
letters 2–520a
veneration 2–459a
Theodore of Tarsus
See Theodore of Canterbury, Saint
Theodore Palaiologos
Manuel II 2–503a
THEODORE PRODROMOS 11–0; 2–506b, 507a, 508a,b, 521b
poetic forms 2–524a,b
Theodore Rštuni 1–478a,b
Theodore Skutariotes 2–517a
Theodore Svetoslav 2–411a-b
Theodore the Stratelates
Armenian saints 1–518b
THEODORET OF CYR 11–0; 2–512b-513a
Christian dogma 3–336a
ecumenical councils 3–630a
Theodoric, Antipope 1–330a
THEODORIC, MASTER 11–0
Theodoric, son of Thiudmir 2–93a
Theodoric, son of Triarius 2–93a
Theodoric of Cervia, Bishop
surgical practice 2–98a
Theodoric I of Metz, Bishop 1–203b
Theodoric II of Metz, Bishop
Alpert of Metz 1–203b
Theodoric IV the Merovingian
Charles Martel 3–272b
THEODORIC THE OSTROGOTH, EMPEROR 11–0; 1–219a, 422a
Alamanni 1–117b
Arians 1–454b
barbarian invasions 2–93a-b
Boethius 1–166b; 2–291b
Burgundians 2–422b
Cassiodorus 3–123a-b
chancery 3–252a
Ennodius 4–491b
vandalism 1–334a
Theodoric I the Visigoth
Catalaunian Fields 2–92b
Theodoric II the Visigoth
Aquitaine 1–366b
Theodosia
Caffa 3–12a
Theodosian code
See Codex Theodosianus
"Theodosian renaissance" 4–352a,b
Theodosiopolis
See Karin (Karnoy K'ałak')
Theodosios, Saint
See Theodosius of the Caves, Saint
Theodosios of Trnovo
Bulgaria 2–413b
Theodosius I, Emperor
Ambrose 1–231b
Arianism 1–454a
Armenia 1–472b, 518b
Christianity 2–459b; 3–337b; 4–337a
Constantinople 3–551a
Nicene orthodoxy 3–628b
reign 2–485a-b
Visigoths 2–90b
THEODOSIUS OF THE CAVES, SAINT 11–0
Mount Athos 1–636b
THEODOSIUS II THE CALLIGRAPHER 11–0
Codex Theodosianus 3–475a
Constantinople 2–485b; 3–556b
Constantinople fortifications 2–485b
Council of Ephesus, First (431) 3–629a
Council of Ephesus, Second (449) 3–629b
Eutyches 4–524a
Theodosius the Deacon 2–506b
THEODULF OF ORLÉANS 11–0; 1–286b
Carolingian court 3–109b, 268b
Carolingian Latin poetry 3–102a-103a
contraception 3–573a
pseudonym 3–100a
royal communications 1–143a
Vulgate 2–211b
Theofan Grek
See Theophanes the Greek
Theoktistos 3–678a
Theologia Christiana (Abelard) 1–17b
Theologia "Scholarium" (Abelard) 1–18a
Theologia "Summi Boni" (Abelard) 1–17a
Theologicae regulae (Alan of Lille) 1–119b, 120a
Theological hierarchies
Christian art 4–354b-355b
Theologos
See Ephesus
Theology
See Philosophy and theology
THEOLOGY, SCHOOLS OF 11–0
Bosnian Church 2–342a
Theology of Aristotle 1–606a
Theon of Alexandria
Byzantine commentaries 1–613b-614a
THEOPHANES CONFESSOR 11–0
world chronicle 2–513a-b, 514a
***THEOPHANES CONTINUATUS* 11–0**; 3–546b-547a
Theophanes Graptos 2–511b
Theophanes Nonnos 4–446b
THEOPHANES THE GREEK 11–0
painting 2–450b-451a
THEOPHANO, EMPRESS 11–0
Anna 1–303a
Basil 2–118b
Theophilitzes 2–117a
Theophilos, Emperor
Amorian dynasty 1–236a
Great Palace of Constantinople 3–553a
Leo the Mathematician 1–391b
monogram 2–453b
reign 2–488b-489a
THEOPHILUS 11–0
bells 2–166a
bronze and brass 2–384a,b
enamels 4–438b
metalworking 4–435b
Theophilus, Patriarch
Coptic architecture 3–586a
Theophilus 4–320b
Theophilus Miracle (play) 4–268b
Theophilus of Antioch
defense of Christians 3–335a
Theophrastus
botany 2–244b-245a, 345a
coal mining 3–472b
Golden Book on Marriage 1–323a
Theophylact of Constantinople, Archbishop
Bogomils 2–294a
Bulgarian church 2–407a
THEOPHYLAKTOS SIMOKATTES 11–0
Avars 2–12a
Byzantine Empire 2–50a, 512a, 513a
Theoricae novae planetarum (Peuerbach) 1–613b, 614b
Theorica planetarum (Andalò di Nigro) 1–613a
Theorica planetarum (anon.) 1–612a-b
Theorica planetarum (Campanus of Novara) 1–612b; 3–461b; 4–500b
THEOTOKOS 11–0
Christology 3–320a
Cyril of Alexandria, Saint 4–75a
Theotokos Church at Hosios Lukas (Phocis) 3–378b
Theotokos Church of Constantine Lips (Constantinople) 1–445a
Thesaurus (Hickes) 1–278a,b, 286b, 287a
Thesaurus linguae latine (Estienne) 4–450a
Thesaurus pauperum (Petrus Hispanus) 3–168b
Theseid of the Marriage of Emilia, The (Boccaccio) 2–280a-b
Thesprotia
despotate of Epiros 4–499a
THESSALONIKI 11–0
Andronikos I Komnenos 1–245a
Boniface of Montferrat 2–323a
Bulgaria 2–404b, 407b, 408b
Byzantine church 2–463b
Byzantine Empire 2–498b, 502b, 503b
church art 2–450a
despotate of Epiros 4–499a
fairs 4–588b
magnates 2–479b
sacking 2–489b
Theodosius I 1–231b
Zealots 2–501a,b
Thessaly
Basil II 2–119a
Bulgaria 2–406b
Byzantine Empire 2–500a, 501a
Catalan conquest 3–156a
despotate of Epiros 4–499a
magnates 2–479a-b
Palaiologoi 1–246a,b
Theuderich II the Merovingian
Alamanni 1–117b
Columbanus, Saint 3–486a
Theuderich III the Merovingian
Pepin 3–104b-106a
Thewis of Gud Women, The 3–663a
Thibaut de Chepoy
Catalan Company 3–156a
Thibaut I of Champagne 3–244a
Thibaut II of Champagne 3–244b, 245a
THIBAUT IV OF CHAMPAGNE 11–0
Blanche of Castile 2–270b
Boniface of Montferrat 2–323a
crusade of 4–51b-52b
Fourth Crusade 3–247a; 4–42a
Jerusalem 4–32a
Thibaut V of Champagne 3–249b
Thielt, Battle of (1128) 3–203b
Thiemo of Salzburg, Archbishop
crusade of 1101 4–36a-b
Thierry of Alsace
communes 3–497a

THIERRY OF CHARTRES 11–0
Adam of the Little Bridge 1–52a
arts, seven liberal 1–580a
Neoplatonic cosmography 1–183a
Thietmar of Saxony
See Billungs
THIETMAR VON MERSEBURG 11–0
Ðingeyrar monastery 4–618a
THIOFRID OF ECHTERNACH 11–0
Thionville, Capitulary of (805) 3–91b, 108b, 110a
Thionville, Council of (835) 1–75b
Third Order of Penance of Saint Dominic 4–243a, 254b
Third Order of Saint Francis
beguines 2–161b, 162a
THIRSK, JOHN 11–0
Thirst Market 2–46a
Thirteen Year War (1454-1466)
Prussians 2–67b
***ÞIÐREKS SAGA* 11–0**; 2–253a; 4–380a
Atlamál and tradition of 1–639a
Brynhild 2–394b, 395a
***ÞJÓÐÓLFR ÓR HVÍNI* 11–0**
Thodosak 1–632b
Thomas à Becket
See Becket, Thomas, Saint
THOMAS À KEMPIS 11–0
biblical exegesis 2–214a
Brethren of the Common Life 2–368a-b
Devotio Moderna 4–166b
Thomas Aquinas
See Aquinas , Saint Thomas
THOMAS DE CORMONT 11–0
Thomas de Pisan
astrology 1–608a
THOMASIN VON ZERKLAERE 11–0
courtesy books 3–665a
Thomas of Armenia, Saint 1–519b
Anglo-Norman literature 1–266a,b
Thomas of Bologna
alchemy 1–138a
Thomas of Britain 4–419b
Arthurian literature 1–569a-b, 570a
See Also Tristan, legend of
See Also Tristan, Roman de
THOMAS OF CANTIMPRÉ 11–0
alchemy 1–137a
bestiary 2–205a
encyclopedia 4–448b-449a, 577b
plant study 2–245b
Thomas of Celano
Dies irae 4–121b
Francis, Saint 2–316b
Thomas of Cobham 3–59b
Thomas of Erceldoune 2–60a
THOMAS OF HALES 11–0
sermon 1–262b
Thomas of Ireland
Manipulus florum 1–206a
Thomas of Kent 1–151b, 261b, 266a
Thomas of Lancaster 4–397b
THOMAS OF MEDZOP 11–0
Thomas of Melsanby 4–423b
Thomas of Monmouth
chronicle of Saint William 1–340a
Thomas of Savoy
diplomacy 4–209a
Thomas of York 1–461b; 2–71b; 3–59b
***THÓMAS SAGA ERKIBYSKUPS* 11–0**
THOMAS THE SLAV 11–0
Amorians 1–236a
Bulgaria 2–401b
revolt 2–489a
THOMISM AND ITS OPPONENTS 11–0
Barlaam of Calabria 2–109b
Durand of Saint Pourçain 4–313b
Egidius Colonna 4–400a
See Also Aquinas, Saint Thomas
THOR 11–0
Alvíssm?al 1–226b
Anglo-Saxon worship 1–289a
divine function 1–63a
Eilífr Goðrúnarson 4–409b
Þórbjǫrbn hornklofi 1–638b
Thorfinn Karlsefni
exploration 4–555a
Þorgilsson, Ari
Eyrbyggja saga 4–568a
Thorkelin, Grímr Jónsson 1–287a
Þorlákr, Saint
sagas 2–252a-b
Þormóðr Kolbrúnarskáld 2–254a
Thornbjórg 1–116b
THORNTON, JOHN 11–0
Thoros
See T'oros
Thoros II the Roupenid
See T'oros II the Roupenid
Thorpe, Chief Justice 4–482b-483a
Þórsdrápa (Eilífr Goðrúnarson) 4–409a
Þórsnes clan
saga 4–568a
***ÞORSTEINS SAGA VÍKINGSSONAR* 11–0**
***ÞORSTEINS ÞÁTTR BAEJARMAGNS BÆJARMAGNS* 11–0**
Ðorsteins Ðáttr stangarhǫggs 4–615a-b
***ÞÓRÐAR SAGA HREÐU* 11–0**
Þórðr Kilbeinsson 2–255a
Þórðr Sturluson 4–568a
Thorvald Ericsson
exploration 4–555a
Þorvaldr Ingjaldson
Droplaugarsona saga 4–294b, 612b
***THOUSAND AND ONE NIGHTS* 11–0**; 1–382a
Bussard, Der 2–434a
Thrace
Bogomils 2–295b, 296a-b, 297a
Bulgaria 2–404b, 405a, 406a, 408b, 409b, 410a,b, 411b
Byzantine church 2–460b
Byzantine families 2–479b
Catalan Company 2–500a
Catalan conquest 3–156a
Palaiologoi 1–246a,b
villages 2–480b
"Three Chapters" heresy
Columbanus, Saint 3–486a
Three-field rotation system 1–92a-93a, 101a
Slavs 1–97a,b
"Three hypostases, doctrine of" 3–628b
Three Marys at the Tomb (Eyck) 4–566b, 567
Threnos
See Lamentation
Threshing
Byzantine tools 1–77b
Thrush and the Nightingale, The
antifeminism 1–324b
***ÞRYMSKVIÐA* 11–0**; 4–386b, 410a
Baldrs Draumar, similarities 2–56b
Eddic poetry 4–390a,b, 391a,b
THULUTH 11–0
Islamic calligraphy 3–54a
Thunaer
baptismal vows 2–87a
Thurible 1–224b
Thuringia
Boniface, Saint 2–321b
Thuringians
Merovingians 3–104a
Tiara
papal coronation 3–603b
Tibbon family
exegesis 4–541a
Tiberian system (Hebrew orthography) 1–208a
Tiberius, Emperor 2–88b
Lombards 2–95a
Tide tables
Old English rules 1–285b
Tidings of Doomsday 1–111b, 347b
Tidings of the Resurrection 1–111b, 347b
Tien Shan Mountains
exploration 4–556b
TIERCERON 11–0
Tierra de Campos
Asturian raids 1–626a
Tierstimmendichtung
Cambridge Songs 3–58a
Tīfāshī, al-
Nuzhat al-albāb 1–380b
Tiflis
See Tbilisi
Ṭighnarī, al- 1–106a
Tignonville, Guillaume de 3–316b
Tigranes the Great 2–140a
TIGRAN HONENC' 11–0
Tigrini, Francesco
Baldus 2–57a
Tigris River 1–470b
Baghdad 2–44b
Euphrates 4–522a,b
Tihomir 2–407b
Tiles
building materials 3–563b
ceramics 3–237a
Tillage
Slavic 1–96b, 97a-98a
Tilo von Kulm 2–230b
Timaeus (Plato) 1–604b, 610b
allegory 1–183a
Aquinas 1–358b
TIMBUKTU 11–0
exploration 4–562a
Time, reckoning of
See Calendars and reckoning of time
Time deposits 2–74b
Timothius Aelurus 1–505b
Timothy of Constantinople, Patriarch
Nicene-Constantinopolitan Creed 3–676b
Timurbughā 3–400a
TIMURIDS 11–0
Afghanistan 1–65a,b
Uzun Ḥasan 1–352a
Timur Leng
See Tamerlane
Tin
Bordeaux 2–327b
Tinchebray, Battle of (1106) 3–203b; 4–462b
Tinctoris, Johannes 3–657b-658a
Tin glazing
ceramics 3–238b
Tinmel 1–191b, 193b, 641a
TINO DI CAMAINO 11–0; 1–76b
TINTAGEL 11–0
TINTERN 11–0
Tipoukeitos 2–125b
Tirada 3–72a-b
Tirant lo Blanch (Martorell) 3–157b, 158a, 161a,b, 166a, 170a
Arthurian literature 1–576b
***ṬIRĀZ* 11–0**
garments 3–616b-618a
Tirechán
See Connacht
Tirel, Walter 4–462a

Tiridates
    See Trdat
Tirkash Abuletisdze
    amirspasalar 1–235b
Tiro prosper
    See prosper of aquitaine
TITHES 11–0
Titian
    frescoes 1–226b
Titianus
    fables 4–572a
Tituli
    cardinal-priests 3–93b
Titurel (Wolfram von Eschenbach)
    Ambraser Heldenbuch 1–230a
Tkadleček 1–44a-b
Tlemcen
    Almohads 1–194a, 195b
Tlemcen, Great Mosque of 1–197a,b
TMUTARAKAN, KHANATE OF 11–0
Tobias 1–249b
    See Also Tobit
Tobias ben Moses ha-Avel
    exegesis 4–539b
Tobit 1–249b
    See Also Tobias
Tocco, Carlo 4–500a
To eparchikon biblion
    See Eparch, Book of the
TOGHRIL-BEG 11–0
    Alp Arslan 1–203a
"To His Purse" (Chaucer) 3–290b
Toiseach 3–407a
Tokalı Kilise, New Church 3–92b, 93a
Tokalı Kilise, Old Church 3–92a
Tokhta, Khan
    Caffa 3–12a
Tokhtamısh, Khan
    Muscovy 4–232b
Tolbac, Battle of (506)
    Clovis 3–467a
Toledan numerals
    See Ghubār numerals
TOLEDAN TABLES 11–0
TOLEDO 11–0
    agriculture 1–82a
    Alfonso VI 1–199b
    Braulio of Saragossa, Saint 2–364b
    Castile 1–84a; 3–129a,b, 131b, 178a
    Eugenius II 4–520b
    fairs 4–587b
    inheritance 4–607a
    school of translators 1–161b, 162a, 613a
Toledo, Martínez de
    See Martínez de Toledo, Alfonso
Toledo, First Council of (400)
    concubinage 3–530a
Toledo, Third Council of (589) 3–676b
Toledo, Fifth Council of (636)
    deposition of rulers 4–158b, 159a
Toledo, Seventeenth Council of (694) 4–366a
Toledo, Twelfth Council of (681) 4–421a-b
To Leucippus Book V 1–135b
Tomas
    Arthurian literature 1–573b
Tombs
    crypt 4–62a
Tome of Leo 3–321a, 342a, 629b; 4–524a
    See Also Leo I, Pope
Tome of the Holy Mountain 1–637b
"Tome of Union" 3–632a
"Tome to Flavian" (Leo I)
    See Tome of Leo
Tomich, Pere 3–166b
TOMISLAV 11–0
    Bulgaria 2–405a
    Croatia 4–2b
Tommaso da Missaglia 1–528b
Tomos hagioreitikos 1–637b
TONARY 12–0
    differentia 4–185a
TONES, MUSICAL 12–0
TONES, READING AND DIALOGUE 12–0
Tonsure 3–442a
    Celtic church 2–381b; 3–228b-229a
TOOLS, AGRICULTURAL 12–0
    Byzantine 1–77a-b
    horse harness 1–93a
    horseshoe 1–93b
    Mediterranean region 1–80a
    northern Europe 1–89b-91b
    Russian 1–100b
    Slavic 1–97b-98b, 99b
TOOLS, AGRICULTURAL: ISLAMIC 12–0
TOOLS, ARTISINAL: ISLAMIC 12–0
Top beam
    See Collar beam
Topia, Karl 4–330a
Topics (Aristotle) 1–52a
Topkapi Palace 1–168b
Tor
    exploration 4–562b
Toralles of Vic, Joan 3–166a-b
Torches
    See Lighting devices
Torcimany (Lluís d'Averçó) 3–170b
TOREL, WILLIAM 12–0
Torf-Einarr, Earl 2–256a
Torhout
    fairs 4–585a-b
TORNADA 12–0
Tornadas 3–70a
Torna-fuye 3–203a-b
T'ornik 1–484b
Toron
    Crusades: Fourth 4–32a
T'oros 1–484b
    Edessa 4–35a
"To Rosamond" (Chaucer) 3–290b
T'OROS ROSLIN 12–0; 1–497a
    Cilician kingdom 3–393b
T'OROS TARÔNEC'I 12–0
T'oros II the Roupenid 2–495a
Torquemada, Juan de 4–378a
Torre
    Carthusian foundation 3–118b
Torre degli Agli (Florence)
    frescoes 1–343a
Torriano, Gianello 3–463b
TORRIGIANO, PIETRO 12–0
TORRITI, JACOPO 12–0
    Assisi, San Francesco 1–593b
Torroella, Guillem de 3–173a
Torroella, Pere 3–171b
Tors, Lambert li 1–152b
Tortosa 1–406a, 408a,b, 415b
    Crusade of 1101 4–36b
Tosaphists
    Bible research 4–540b
"Tota celestis philosophia" (Courson) 3–659a
"To the Young on How to Derive Profit from Reading of Pagan Literature" (Basil the Great) 2–121a, 122a
Totila
    Benedict of Nursia 2–168b
Toul
    Frankish invasions 2–94a
TOULOUSE 12–0
    agriculture 1–85b-86a
    Alani settlement 1–121a
    Black Death 2–260b
    Cathars 3–183b, 188b-189b
    county 3–658b
    Crown of Aragon 1–409b-410b, 412b
    hearth lists 4–138a
    Inquisition 3–190a
    literature 3–170b-171a
    Montauban 2–128a
Toulouse, Council of (1119) 3–186b, 636a
Toulouse-Saint Gilles
    counts of 3–186b-187a
Touraine
    fairs 4–586a
Tourma 3–199b
Tournament of Antichrist, The (Huon de Méri) 1–185b, 188b
Tournament 3–202b-203a
    cavalry 3–204a
    See Also Games and pastimes
Tournoiement de l'Antéchrist (Huon de Méri) 1–185b, 188b
Tours
    Alcuin of York 1–143a-b
    arms and armor 1–529a
    fairs 4–586a
    translatio studii 1–142a
Tours, Battle of (732)
    Charles Martel 3–345b
Tours, Council of (1163) 1–130b; 3–186b, 637b-638a
T'OVMA ARCRUNI 12–0; 1–510b
    Armenian literature 1–510b
T'ovma Continuatus 1–510b
T'OVMA MECOP'EC'I 12–0; 1–511b
TOWER 12–0
    Bulgarian art and architecture 2–417a
Tower of Comares 1–170a
Tower of London
    building materials 3–562a
    keeper 3–125a
Tower of the Women 1–168b
Town charters
    See Communes
TOWNELEY PLAYS 12–0; 4–284b
Towns
    demography 4–141a,b
    fairs 4–584b
    Western European families 4–602b
    See Also Urbanism
TRACERY 12–0
Tract
    cantatorium 3–80b
Tractat de cavalleria de Sant Jordi 3–169a
Tractat de confessió (Canals) 3–167b
Tractat de les penes particulars d'Infern (Pasqual) 3–169b
Tractates of York
    anointing 1–308a
Tractatus artis bene moriendi 1–547b
Tractatus astrarii (Giovanni de' Dondi) 3–464b
Tractatus astrolabii (Māshā'allāh) 1–611a
Tractatus de apocalypsis (Beatus of Liébana) 1–630b
Tractatus de auctoritate ecclesiae et conciliorum generalium (Almain) 3–521a
Tractatus de computo (John of Sacrobosco) 1–612a
Tractatus de corpore domini (Engelbert) 4–451b
Tractatus de crudelitate mortis 1–44a
Tractatus de legibus
    canon law 4–129a
Tractatus de materia concilii generalis (Pierre d'Ailly) 3–518b, 650a

Tractatus de modo concilio celebrandi (Guillaume Durand) 3–645b
Tractatus de musica 1–544b
Tractatus de potestate regia et papali (John of Paris) 3–517a, 518a
Tractatus de purgatorio sancti Patricii (Hugh of Saltrey) 4–509b
Tractatus de schismate (Zabarella) 3–511b
Tractatus de sphaera (John of Sacrobosco) 1–612a
Tractatus horologii astronomici (Richard of Wallingford) 3–464b
Tractatus orthographiae 1–270b
Tractatus parabolicus (Arnald of Villanova) 1–138b
Tractatus seu summa de electionibus episcoporum (Laurence of Somercote) 4–422b
Tractatus super concilium generale (Quirini) 3–520b
Tractatus virtutum (Boncompagno) 2–320a
Traction plow
  draft animals 1–293a
TRADE
  Cologne 3–481a
  commune 3–493b
  economic separation 3–416b
  merchant class 2–103b; 4–416b, 419b, 422b
TRADE, ARMENIAN 12–0
  Artašat 1–563b
  Baylakān 2–139a
  Dwin 4–324b-325a
TRADE, BYZANTINE 12–0
  Alexandria 1–154a,b
  Book of the Eparch 4–493b
  Constantinople 3–554b-555a
  economy and society 2–475b-476a
  shipping 2–477b
  See Also Guilds, Byzantine
TRADE, EUROPEAN 12–0
  art trade 1–560b-562b
  Assizes of Jerusalem 1–598b
  Ayās 2–19a
  Baltic countries 2–62b-63a, 64a
  banking 2–72b-73a, 74b, 75b, 76a-77b
  Bavaria 2–134b
  Bosporus 2–344a
  botany 2–347b
  Burgundy, County of 2–424b, 426a
  Caffa 3–12a
  Castile 3–135b
  commenda 3–489a
  commercial credit 2–74b
  crusades 4–54b
  Cyprus, Kingdom of 4–70b, 72a
  decline of Roman civilization and 2–72a
  Denmark 4–149a,b
  Edinburgh 4–393b
  European expansion 2–72b-73a
  fairs 4–582b, 590b
  Norman-Angevin England 4–465a-b, 470a
  Russian 1–99a, 101a
TRADE, ISLAMIC 12–0
  Afghanistan 1–65b
  Aghlabids 1–70b, 71b
  Aleppo 1–145b-146a
  Basra 2–127b
  Buyids 2–437a
  Damascus 4–81a-b, 83b
  fairs 4–588b-589b
  Islamic banking 2–79a
TRADE, REGULATION OF 12–0
Trade routes
  Bagratid Armenia 1–291a,b
  Khanate of Crimea 3–679b
  North Africa 1–640b
  pre-Islamic Arabia 1–370a, 372a
TRADITIO CLAVIUM 12–0
TRADITIO LEGIS 12–0; 4–351a, 361b
Tradition literature
  Arabic language 1–377a, 378a
  See Also Ḥadīth
Traditio symboli 3–675b
Tragèdia de Caldesa (Roís de Corella) 3–171b
Tragicomedia de Calisto y Melibea
  See Celestina, La
Trailbaston
  See Oyer and Terminer, Trailbaston
  assize 1–595b
TRAINI, FRANCESCO 12–0
"Training in Lawfulness" (Augustine) 1–658a
Traité de la maladie de l'amour ou mélancholie erotique (Ferrand) 3–196b
Traité pour apprendre la langue (Walter of Bibbesworth) 1–270b
Traitié selonc les auctours pour essampler les amantz marietz (Gower) 1–263a
Trajan, Emperor 1–123b
Trajan's Column 3–200a
Trajan's Gate 2–118b
Trani
  Barisanus 2–109a
Transcaucasia
  Azerbaijan 2–26a, 27a
  Seljuks 1–203a
  See Also Caucasia
TRANSENNA 12–0
TRANSEPT 12–0
  crossing 4–12a
TRANSFIGURATION 12–0; 4–358b
  early Christian art 4–354b-355a, 356, 358b
Transfiguration, Church of the (Novgorod)
  painting 2–450b
Transhumance 1–78b, 79a, 83a, 84a
Transitus Mariae 1–347b
Transjordan
  Ayyubid principality of 2–24a
  Jerusalem 4–32a
Transjurane Burgundy 4–108b
  Burgundy, County of 2–424a
Translatio et miracula sanctorum Marcelli et Petri (Einhard) 1–337a; 4–412b
Translation and translators, Armenian
  Hellenizing School 1–505a-506a
  literature 1–507b-508a,b
TRANSLATION AND TRANSLATORS, ISLAMIC 12–0
  Arabic astrological treatises 1–606b-607a
  Arabic language 1–377b
TRANSLATION AND TRANSLATORS, JEWISH 12–0
TRANSLATION AND TRANSLATORS, WESTERN EUROPEAN 12–0
  Burgundio of Pisa 2–423b
  Caxton 3–210b-211a
  historical chronicles 3–325a
TRANSLATION OF BISHOPS 12–0
TRANSLATION OF EMPIRE 12–0
TRANSLATION OF SAINTS 12–0
  Brandeum 2–363a
  catacombs 3–154a
  dedication of churches 4–130a
TRANSLATIONS AND TRANSLATORS, BYZANTINE 12–0
  classical literary studies 3–431b
TRANSLATIONS AND TRANSLATORS, WESTERN EUROPEAN
  Alfred the Great 1–164b
  Bessarion 2–203a
  Catalan literature 3–164b-165a, 166b-170a
  Dionysius Exiguus 4–192b
  Douglas, Gavin 4–262a
  Eleonore of Austria 4–429a
  Elucidarium 4–434a
  Ethelwold 4–518a
  Eufemiavisor 4–519b
Translatio studii 1–142a,b
Transmutation
  See Alchemy
TRANSOXIANA 12–0
  Alptigin 1–219a
  Bukhara 2–396b
Transport
  draft animals 1–293a
Transubstantiation
  accident 1–35b
Transverse arch
  See Arch, forms of
Transylvania
  cultivation 1–97a
  water buffalo use 1–298b
Trapani 1–413b
Trapeza 4–333b
Trappists
  Cistercian chant 3–403a
  See Also Cistercians of the Strict Observance
Trás-os-Montes
  agriculture 1–85a
Trastámaras family 3–135a, 136b, 137a, 138a, 139a
Trattatello in laude de Dante (Boccaccio) 2–288a
Trattato dell'oreficeria (Cellini) 4–438b
Trauma, treatment of 2–99a
Traumlied 4–387a
Traun 2–4b
Traungau 2–4b, 7a-b
TRAVEL AND TRANSPORT, ISLAMIC 12–0
  antiquarianism 1–332a-333b
TRAVEL AND TRANSPORT, WESTERN EUROPEAN 12–0
  antiquarianism 1–332a-333b
  draft animals 1–293a
Traveler guidebooks 1–333a
Travels (Ibn Baṭṭūṭa) 1–382a
  See Also Riḥla
TRAVERSARI, AMBROGIO 12–0
  Camaldolese order 3–56a
  councils 3–653a
TRDAT 12–0
  cathedral of Ani 1–291b, 494a
  Hagia Sophia (Constantinople) 1–483a
Trdat II
  Ayrarat 2–20a
TRDAT III/IV THE GREAT
  Armenian saints 1–517b-518a
TRDAT III/IV THE GREAT, SAINT 12–0; 1–475b
  Arsacids/Aršakuni 1–559a
  conversion 1–66a
  Ejmiacin 4–417a
TREASON 12–0
Treasurer
  chamberlain 3–242a
  hierarchy of clergy 3–444b
Treasures of the Sciences in the Brides of the Springs 4–445b
Treasury, English
  See Exchequer

Treaties
  Byzantine diplomacy 4–195b-196a
  ratification 4–213b-214a
  Western European diplomacy 4–202b
Treatise of Familiar Spirits and Demons (Ibn Shuhayd) 1–381b
Treatise on Asthma (Maimonides) 3–582b
Treatise on the Astrolabe (Chaucer) 3–290b
Treatise on the Emanations on the Left (Isaac ben Jacob ha-Kohen) 1–346a
Treatise on the Laws and Customs of England (Glanville) 4–470a
Treatise on the Prerogatives of the Roman Empire (Alexander of Roes) 1–148b, 149a
Treatise to Give Examples from Writers to Married Lovers (Gower) 1–263b
Trebinje
  Samuil 2–406b
TREBIZOND 12–0
  Alexios I 1–159a
  Anatolia 1–239b
  Aq Qoyunlu 1–352a
  Byzantine Empire 2–498a
  caravan route 1–450b
  fairs 4–588a-b
Trebizond Palace 4–334b
Trebor
  ars subtilior 1–558b
Trebuchet 3–148a, 150b, 180b-181a
  castle location 3–143a-b
TRECENTO ART 12–0
  Agnolo di Ventura 1–73b
TRECENTO MUSIC 12–0
  ars nova 1–548b
  cacce 3–4b
TREE OF JESSE 12–0
  iconography 2–348b
TREE OF LIFE 12–0
  living cross 4–9b
Tree rings
  climatology 3–450b, 451a
TREFOIL 12–0; 4–68a
Trefologion
  See Paterikon
Tréguier
  fairs 4–586a
Trelleborgs
  Vikings 4–151b
Trémoille, Georges de La
  Charles VII 3–271a
"Tremulous hand"
  manuscripts 1–276a
Trencavel, Raymond-Roger
  Albigensian Crusade 3–187a, 188a,b, 189a
  Cathars 3–190a
Trencavel, Roger 3–187a
Trencavel family
  attack on heresy 3–186b-188a
Trencavel of Béziers 1–408b
Trench, Battle of the (627)
  al-ʿAbbās 1–4a
Trenchers
  cookery 3–581b
Trent, Council of
  astrology 1–609a
  concubinage 3–530b
  dedication of churches 4–131a
  dispensation 4–218a
  excommunication 4–538a
  Latin church organization 3–376a
  patriarchate rite 1–353a
TRENT CODICES 12–0
Trent River 4–509a,b
Trepidation, theory of 1–614b
Très ancien coutumier (Normandy) 4–68b
Très ancienne coutume de Bretagne 4–515b
Tres libri Codicis
  Corpus iuris civilis 3–609b
Trésor de la cité des dames (Christine de Pizan) 3–316b
TRESPASS 12–0
***TRÈS RICHES HEURES* 12–0**
  Colombe, Jean 3–482a
Tressours 3–624a
Tresvents, Bartomeu 3–168b
Tretiz pur aprise de langwage (Walter of Bibbesworth) 1–270b
"Treue Gattin, Die" 1–230a
TREVET, NICHOLAS 12–0
  chronicles 1–265b
TREVISA, JOHN 12–0
  Caxton 3–211a
  Disputatio inter clericum et militem 4–218a
  Wycliffe Bible 2–222a
Trevisan, Domenico 1–154b
Trewhiddle style
  Celtic art 3–221a
Treytz family 1–529b
"Trial and Flagellation of Christ" 3–299a
TRIBELON 12–0
Tribes
  Islamic family 4–596b
  See Also Barbarians, invasions of
Tribonian
  Corpus iuris civilis 3–608b
Tribunal de corte 3–139a
Tribunals
  cardinals 3–95a
TRIBUNE 12–0
  Aachen Palace Chapel 1–2b-3a
Tribur
  Henry IV 3–69a
TRICLINIUM 12–0
Triduum 4–365a, 366b
Trier
  Ebgert 4–399b
  Frankish invasions 2–94a
  Himmerod 1–43a
  monastery 1–47b
TRIFORIUM 12–0
  basilica 2–125a
Trigetus 1–647b
Trigonometry
  astrolabe 1–602b
Triklinios, Demetrios
  classical literary studies 3–431b
Trilogium astrologiae theologizatae (Charlier) 1–608b
Trination 1–177a
TRINITARIAN DOCTRINE 12–0
Trinité, La, Abbey
  Anglo-Norman features 1–255b
Trinity
  Abelard 1–18b-19a
  adoptionism 1–57b
  Agnus Dei music 1–74b
  Cathar beliefs 3–184b
  debates 3–628a
  early Church 3–338b-339b
  three hypostases of 1–178b
TRINITY, OLD TESTAMENT 12–0
Trinity (Augustine) 1–656a,b, 657a,b
Trinity Sergius Monastery 1–101b
Triodion 2–468b
Trioedd Ynys Prydein 1–577b
Trionfo, Agostino 4–377a
Tripartita
  Ivo of Chartres 4–128b
Triple church basilica
  See Church, types of
Triplici via, De (Bonaventure) 2–316a
Triplum
  ars nova 1–551a
  motet 1–546b-547a
TRIPOLI 12–0
  ʿAmr ibn al-ʿĀṣ 1–237a
  Ayyubids 2–23a
  crusader art and architecture 4–21b
  crusades 4–30b, 37a, 38a,b
  exploration 4–556b
  Islamic march on (880) 3–209a
  Saladin 4–25a
  slaves 2–269a
Tripolitania
  Knights of Malta 3–304a
TRIPTYCH 12–0
Triptych of the Madonna (Eyck) 4–567a
Triskeles
  Celtic art 3–218b
Trispondaicus 4–67a
TRISTAN, LEGEND OF 12–0
  Arthurian literature 1–569a-570a, 578a
  Chrétien de Troyes 3–308b
  Donnei des amants 4–261b
TRISTAN, ROMAN DE 12–0; 1–260b
  Anglo-Norman literature 1–260b, 266a,b
  Aristotle and Phyllis 1–455b
  Breton Literature 2–370a
Tristan rossignol, 4–261b
Tristan und Isolt (Gottfried von Strassburg) 1–266a; 5–634a-637b
Tristão Vaz Teixeira
  Madeiras 4–559a
***TRISTRAMS SAGA OK ÍSÖNDAR* 12–0**; 4–431b
TRIUMPHAL ARCH 12–0
TRIVIUM 12–0
  arts, seven liberal 1–580a
  Fachschrifttum 4–577a-579a
Trnovo 2–408a, 409a, 410b, 412b, 413a
  Bāyazīd 2–136b
  Byzantine church 2–464a
***TROBAIRITZ* 12–0**; 3–670a-b
Trogir 4–1b
Troilus and Criseyde (Chaucer) 3–287b-289a
Troilus and Criseyde legend
  Benoît 2–182a
  See Also Troy story
Trois dames qui trouverent un vit, Les 1–269b
Trois savoirs, Les 1–269b
Trojan Chronicle 3–212a
Trojan story
  See Troy story
***TRÓJUMANNA SAGA* 12–0**
  Breta Sǫgur 2–365b
Trondheim
  See Niđarós
TROPAR 12–0
TROPARION 12–0; 2–510b
Tropes
  ars poetica 1–554b
  Benedicamus Domino 2–167b
TROPES TO THE ORDINARY OF THE MASS 12–0
  Agnus Dei music 1–74b-75a
TROPES TO THE PROPER OF THE MASS 12–0
Tropological allegory 1–179b-180a
TROTA AND TROTULA 12–0
Trotto 4–88a

TROUBADOUR, TROUVÈRE, TROVADORES 12–0
alba 1–123a
Alfonso X 1–162a
Arnaut Daniel 1–539a
ballade form 2–59a
bard 2–106a
Bernart de Ventadorn 2–197a
Blondel de Nesle 2–276a
Bodel 2–290b
Breviari d'amor 4–506b
Canso 3–69b
cantiga melodies 3–85b-86a
cantigas de amor 3–87a
Catalan 3–157b, 164b, 173a-b
Cercamon 3–240a
chanson 3–254b
Chansonnier 3–255b-256a
Charles of Orléans 3–273a
chivalry 3–302b
Conon de Béthune 3–538a
contrafactum 3–576a-b
courtly love 3–667b, 668b-669b,b, 671b-672a, 673a
Cuaderna vía 4–63a
Dauphiné 4–110a
descort 4–164a
Portugal 4–190a
trobairitz 3–670a-b
Trouvère
See Troubadours, Trouvère, Trovadores
Trovadores
See Troubadours, Trouvère, Trovadores
Troyes
fairs 4–585b, 590b, 591a-592
TROYES, RITE OF 12–0
Troyes, Treaty of (1420)
Charles VI 3–271a
Troyes Cathedral 1–426a
TROY STORY 12–0
Breta Sǫgur 2–365b
Byzantine literature 2–522b
Byzantine poetry 2–508a, 509b
Chaucer 3–287b
Latin epic 4–495b
Trpimir I 4–2b
Trpimirović dynasty 4–2b
Truce of God 3–176a, 356a
chivalry 3–302a
True Cross
archaeological excavations 1–337a
Church of S. P'rkič' 1–292a
crusades 4–33a
Limburg an der Lahn 2–455a,b
True Cross cult
Elene 1–279a
True Religion (Augustine) 1–648b, 649a, 655a
TRULLA 12–0
Trullanum
See Synod in Trullo
Trullo, Synod in
See Quinisext Synod
Trullon Palace
Third Council of Constantinople 3–630b
See Also Quinisext Synod
TRUMEAU 12–0
Trunnion 3–65a
"Truth" (Chaucer) 3–286a
Tskarost'avi Gospels 2–164b
TSROMI (C'ROMI) **12–0**
Tuam 1–470a
Tuath
See Irish society
Tuatha Dé Danann 1–33b
Tubba' dynasty
pre-Islamic Arabia 1–370b
Tu B'Shevat 3–27a
Tudela 1–160b
Aragon 1–404b, 405b, 406a, 407a
Tudellén, Treaty of (1151) 3–130a-b
Tudeschis, Nicholaus de
conciliar theory 3–511a, 512b, 514a
Tudor, Henry
See Henry VII of England
TUDOR, OWEN 12–0
Tudor arch
See Arch, types of
Tuesday Market 2–45b, 46a
Ṭufayl, Ibn 1–194b, 459a
Tughra
Islamic calligraphy 3–52b
Ṭughrā'ī, al-
alchemy 1–141b
Ṭughrıl Bak
See Tughril Beg
TUGHRIL BEG 12–0; 1–11b; 2–493a
Ṭūlūn, Aḥmad ibn 1–153b; 4–405b, 406a
Ibrāhīm II 1–71b
mosque 1–196b
TULUNIDS 12–0
Antioch 1–326a
Copts and Coptic church 3–594b
Damascus 4–81b, 82a
Egypt 1–72a; 4–405b-406a
Tūmārt, Ibn 1–191b
Tun 1–488b-490a
Tunbudhī, al-
jund revolt 1–70b, 71b
Tunic
Byzantine 3–614a-b, 615a,b
Jewish 3–618b
Western European 3–624b
TUNIS 12–0
Ayyubids 2–23a
Crown of Aragon 1–413b
Great Mosque 1–70b
slaves 2–268b
Tunisia
agricultural labor 1–105b
agricultural tools 1–80a
Atlas Mountains 1–639b
Crown of Aragon 1–414b
Knights of Malta 3–304a
Louis IX 4–53b-54a
Tuns
See Barrels
TUOTILO 12–0
Tūrān Shāh
assassination 2–138a
concubinage 3–529a
Turba philosophorum 1–141a
Turbe
See *Gumbat*
TURCOMANS 12–0
Alp Arslan 1–203a
Anatolia 1–241b
Aq Qoyunlu 1–352a
Armenia 1–485a, 486a
cavalry 3–209a
migration 1–145b
Turell, Gabriel 3–166b
Turin-Milan Hours 4–566a
Turkestan
Ephthalites 2–12a
Turkey
Ani in Daranalik' 1–290a
Arabic language 1–378b
Araks River 1–421b
Arčēš 1–423a
ceramics 3–240a
crusader art and architecture 4–26b
food animals 1–301a
Turkic language family
Caucasia 3–195a
Turkil 1–262a
Turkish language
Arabic alphabet 1–209b
Hebrew alphabet 1–208a
Turkomans
See Turcomans
Turks
Abbasid army 1–10b-11a
Andronikos II Palaiologos 1–246a
Ankara 1–302a,b
Avars 2–12b
'Azīz, al- 2–28a
crusade propaganda 4–19a
fairs 4–589b
First Crusade 4–16a
Jerusalem 4–25b
Peasants' crusades 4–34b
Urban II, Pope 4–19a
Turks, Ottoman
See Ottomans
Turks, Seljuk
See Seljuks
TURMEDA, ANSELM 12–0; 3–168a
Turmeric
dyes 4–326a
Turner, William
botany 2–246a
TUROLDUS 12–0
Turpin
See Pseudo-Turpin
Turrecremata, Johannes de
conciliar theory 3–515a
Turri
siege (1281) 3–211b
Turris 1–223b
Turuberan 1–472b, 473a,b
Tuscans
pawnbroking 2–76a
TUSCANY 12–0
Cathar decline 3–190b
fruits and fruit trees 1–87a
Lombard invasion 2–95b
Tusfun
See Ctesiphon
Ṭūsī, Naṣīr al-Dīn, al- 1–261b, 434b, 620b, 621b
TUTILO 12–0
Tutush
Damascus 4–83b
Túy 1–626b
TVRTKO I 12–0
mining 2–340a
reign 2–337a-b
TVRTKO II 12–0; 2–338a,b
Tweede rose 4–319a
Twelve Apostles of Ireland 3–465b
TWELVE GREAT FEASTS 12–0
Twelver Shiite sect 1–175a, 374b
Two-field tillage system 1–99b
"Two natures" doctrine 4–524a
Two Souls: Against the Manichees (Augustine) 1–648b
TWO SWORDS, DOCTRINE OF 12–0
Two Ways, The (Clanvowe) 3–408b
Tychikos 1–238a
Tycho Brahe
See Brahe, Tycho
Tyler, Wat
Anonimalle Chronicle 1–309a
TYMPANUM 12–0
Anglo-Norman sculpture 1–256a
archivolt 1–449a
Armenian sculpture 1–495b-496a
Typikon
Mount Athos 1–637a-b

Typological allegory 1–179b-180b, 185b, 186a-b
Psychomachia 1–181b-182a
Typos (Constans II) 3–630b
caesaropapism 3–10b
Týr 1–63a
Tyrannia, De (Bartolo da Sassoferrato) 2–115a
Tyrannicide 3–649b
Tyrannius Rufinus of Aquileia
excavations 1–336b, 337a
Tyre
Alexander's siege 1–150b
Crusader art and architecture 4–24b
Saladin 4–25a, 40a
Third Crusade 4–31b
Tyrol 2–8a, 9b
Tywy River 4–329b
Tzachas 1–158a
Byzantine Empire 2–494b
Tzamblakoi
holdings 2–479b

U

Ua Conchobuir
See Uí Néill
Ua Mael Sechnaill
See Uí Néill
Ubaldo of Florence
public clocks 3–463a
'Ubayd Allāh
Aghlabids 1–72a
Ubeda
grape production 1–82b
Uberti, Farinata degli 4–95b
Ubi periculum (Gregory X) 3–94b-95a, 523b, 524a,b, 641b-642a
UCCELLO, PAOLO 12–0
Brunelleschi, Filippo 2–390b
Uchelwyr 4–76a
Uckermark
Brandenburg 2–360b
Udo of Toul
Marian offices 2–274a
Ufilias, Bishop 1–650a
Ugnus, Bishop 2–102b
Ugo da Campione 2–324b
Ugo da San Severino
Boccaccio 2–289b
UGOLINO DA SIENA 12–0
Duccio 4–302b
Ugolino di Nerio
See Ubolino da Siena
UGOLINO DI VIERI 12–0; 4–439a
Ugonius, Matthias
conciliar theory 3–520b
Uguccione della Faggiuola 4–103b-104a
Uḥud, Battle of (625) 2–43a
Abū Sufyān 1–29a
Uí Ailella 3–537a
Uí Briain 4–77b
Uí Briúin 3–537a
Uí Fiachrach 3–537a-b, 538a
Uí Fiachrach Aidni 3–537b; 4–77a
Uí Fiachrach Muaide 3–537b
UÍ NÉILL 12–0; 4–493a
Áed mac Ainmuirech 1–60a
Áed Sláne 1–60b
Cashel 3–121b
Cinéal Eóghain 3–396b
Connacht 3–537a
Cormac Mac Airt 3–601a
Cormac Mac Cuilennáin 3–601b
Uisnech, Synod of (1111)
Clonard 3–466a
Uí Thairdelbaig 4–77a
'Ukaylids
Aleppo capture (1079) 1–145b
Ukhaidir palace
eyvān 4–569b
Ukhaydirid dynasty 1–175a
Ukraine
agriculture 1–99a
camel use 1–296b
Crimean Tatars 3–679b
food animals 1–299b
Ulaid, King
Báetán mac Cairill 1–60a
***'ULAMĀ'* 12–0**; 3–40a
caliphate 3–41a, 47b-48b
Damascus 4–83a, 84a
Ulema
See 'Ulamā'
Ulfilas, Bishop 1–212a
Arianism 1–454a
Bible translation 2–211b
ÚLFR UGGASON (HUSDRAPA) 12–0
ULJAYTU 12–0
ULLR 12–0
Ulmannus 1–138b
Ulric, Bishop of Imola
celibacy of clergy 3–217a
ULRICH FÜETRER 12–0
Ulrich Funk the Elder 1–229b
Ulrich of Augsburg, Bishop
Marian office 2–273b
Ulrich of Celje, Count 2–8b
ULRICH OF ENSINGEN 12–0
Ulrich of Strassburg
Albertus Magnus 1–129a
ULRICH VON ESCHENBACH 12–0
ULRICH VON LIECHTENSTEIN 12–0
Ambraser Heldenbuch 1–230a
ULRICH VON SINGENBERG 12–0
ULRICH VON TÜRHEIM 12–0
Arthurian literature 1–572a
ULRICH VON WINTERSTETTEN 12–0
ULRICH VON ZAZIKHOVEN 12–0
ULSTER 12–0
Burgh, de 2–421b
Ultán, Bishop
Brigit, Saint 2–376b
Ultimogeniture 2–332a
ULUGH BEG 12–0
Ulugh Beg Observatory 1–622b
'UMAR II IBN 'ABD AL-AZĪZ 12–0
alms tax 1–201b
caliphate 3–41b
Nestorians 3–312b
'Umar, Pact of 3–619b
Umarā'
See Emir
'Umar al-Ṭabarī 1–606b
'Umar ibn abī Rabī'a (Islamic poet) 1–400a
'UMAR I IBN AL-KHAṬṬĀB 12–0; 1–112b-113a, 373b
'Abbās, al- 1–4b
Abū Bakr 1–24b, 25b
'Alī ibn Abī Ṭālib 1–172a
'Amr ibn al-'Āṣ 1–237a
caliphate 3–33b-34a
commander of the faithful 3–488a
'UMAR KHAYYĀM 12–0
UMAYYAD ART 12–0
Abbasid art and architecture 1–5a-b
arabesque pattern 1–369b
ceramics 3–238b
UMAYYADS 12–0; 1–29b, 112b
Abbasids 1–6b-7b, 8a; 3–45b-46a
Abū Sufyān 1–28b
Afganistan 1–64b
Aghlabids 1–70a
Akhṭal, al- 1–115a
Alexandria, rule of 1–153b
alms tax 1–202a
Antioch domination 1–326a
Arabia, Islamic 1–374a
bāb usage 2–32a
bādiya 2–42b
Basra 2–127b
Beirut 2–164a
caliphate 1–15a-16a, 198a; 3–35a, 36b-41b
Constans II 3–544b
costume 3–616b-618a
Damascus 4–81b, 82a, 83a, 84b
dinar 4–187b
diplomacy 4–200a
Marwanids 3–38b-40b
poetry 1–400a,b
slaves 2–268a
Taghlib 1–115a
UMAYYADS OF CÓRDOBA 12–0; 3–598a, 600a
Umbo 1–522b
Umbraculum 1–222a
Umbrella dome 4–236a
Umma 4–596b
caliphate 3–32b-34a, 36a, 40a, 47a,b-48b
Umm al-walad
Islamic concubinage 3–528b
Umm Ḥabība
'Ā'isha 1–112b
Umm Rūmān
'Ā'isha 1–112b
Umm Salama
'Ā'isha 1–112b
Umru' al-Qays, King 1–371b
Unam sanctam (1302) 4–376a
Una persona et duabus naturis Christi, De (Boethius) 3–321a
Una ventura (Vincenç Comes) 3–173b
Uncompleted Book on the Text of Genesis (Augustine) 1–649a
Uncompleted Work Against Julian (Augustine) 1–652b
Unction
evolution of kingship 4–475b
UNCTION OF THE SICK 12–0
death and burial in Europe 4–119b-120a
Extreme Unction 4–565a
Unequal hours
time reckoning 3–23b
water clock 3–28a
UNIBOS 12–0
UNICORN 12–0; 2–243a
Unifiers of Saint Gregory the Illuminator 4–253a
Union of the Churches (1274)
Bulgaria 2–410b
Unique Necklace (Ibn 'Abd Rabbih) 1–380b
Unitas Fratrum 2–305b
Uintate intellectus contra verroistas, De (Albertus Magnus) 1–128a
Unity of Brethren
See Bohemian Brethren
Universal astrolabe 1–602b
Universal History (Seven Books of History against the Pagans) (Orosius) 1–165a, 166a-b

Universal hylomorphism
Augustinism 1–660b
Bacon 2–35b-36b
UNIVERSALS 12–0; 1–467a
Abelard 1–18b
Adelard of Bath 1–54a
Bacon 2–39b
Burley, Walter 2–432b-433a
conceptualism 3–510a
Universitate temporum, De (Alpert of Metz) 1–203b
UNIVERSITIES 12–0
Aristotelianism 1–461a-463a,b, 464b, 465a
Bacon 2–37a
Bologna 2–311b
Cambridge 3–58b
Clement V, Pope 3–439a
doctor 4–233b
medical training 2–98a-b
physicians 2–100a
See Also Classical literary studies
UNIVERSITIES, BYZANTINE 12–0
Constantinople 3–556b
Universities, Islamic
See Schools, Islamic
Universo libri XXII, De (Hrabanus Maurus) 1–606b
Unodl
Gododdin 1–247a
Ūnqelay 3–618b
Unrochs family 3–107b
Unterwalden 2–7b
Un traitié selonc les auctours pour essampler les amantz marietz (John Gower) 1–263b
Upper Armenia
See Armenia: Geography
Upper Burgundy 2–428b
Upper Lusatia
Brandenburg 2–360b
Upper Palatinate
Bavaria border 2–132b
Treaty of Pavia (1329) 2–135a
Uppington
Anglo-Norman sculpture 1–256a
Uppsala
temple 1–50b
Uqlīdīsī, al- 1–383a, 384b
Urartu
See Ayrarat
URBAIN LE COURTOIS **12–0**; 1–264b; 3–661a
Urban VI, Antipope 1–331b
Urban I, Pope
confirmation 3–536a
URBAN II, POPE 12–0; 1–426b; 3–178a
Alexios I Komnenos 4–30a
Anselm of Canterbury 1–312a-313a
bells 2–166a
Bruno of Segni, Saint 2–392a
Bruno the Carthusian, Saint 2–392a
Byzantines 3–356a
Cluny order 3–470b
Council of Clermont 3–449a
crusade concept 4–15b
crusade propaganda 4–20a
crusades 1–93b, 158a; 2–308b; 3–356b
Crusade sermons 2–216a
crusades to 1192 4–33b, 34a, 36a
Decretum of Ivo of Chartres 4–128b
Marian office 2–274a
papal curia 4–66a
papal reform 3–351b, 352a
Western councils 3–635a-b
Urban IV, Pope
Ave Maria 2–13b
Bonaventure, Saint 2–316b, 317a
Celestines 3–214b
election 1–128b
feast of Corpus Christi 3–608a
political crusades 4–60b
Urban V, Pope
Avignonese papacy 3–362a
Byzantine Empire 2–502a
Urban VI, Pope
Birgitta, Saint 2–247a
cardinals deposition 3–95b
election 2–16a; 3–514b
Great Schism 3–365a,b, 645b
Urban VIII, Pope
beatification 2–143a
Urban chronicles 3–328b-329b
URBANISI 12–0
URBANISM, BYZANTINE 12–0
architecture 4–331b-333b
Ephesus 4–494b
URBANISM, ISLAMIC WORLD 12–0
agriculture 1–103a,b
Bukhara 2–397a-b
casbahs 3–121a
Damascus 4–82b-84a
Urbanism, Russian 1–102b
URBANISM, WESTERN EUROPEAN: TO 1000 12–0
Anglo-Saxon England 4–457b-458a
Barcelona 2–102a-103a
Brittany, Duchy 2–379b
Bulgaria 2–399b, 401b
Cologne 3–481a
URBANISM, WESTERN EUROPEAN: 1000-1300 12–0
Barcelona 2–103a-104a
bastide 2–128a
Bruges 2–386a-b
Castile 3–132a
consuls, consulate 3–570b-571a
échevins 4–379a
Norman-Angevin England 4–465a-b, 469b-470a
See Also Demography
URBANISM, WESTERN EUROPEAN: 1300-1500 12–0
Armenia 1–490b-491a
Barcelona 2–104a-105a
castles and fortifications 3–151a
Denmark 4–149a-B
See Also Class structure, Western
Urbanitatis (courtesy book) 3–661a
URBNISI 12–0
Urfa
See Edessa
Urgell 1–411b, 412a, 413b, 415a; 3–174b
Urhayecʻi, Mattʻeos 1–291a
Uri 2–7b
Uriel
angel/angelology 1–249b
URIEN RHEGED 12–0
URMIA, LAKE 12–0; 1–470b
URNES STYLE 12–0
Celtic art 3–223a
Uroš, Symeon 4–500a
Urraca
marriage 3–129b-130a
Ursicinus
Asian campaign 1–235b
Ursinus, Antipope 1–330a
Ursulines
Angela Merici 1–250b
Uruššа
See Erzincan
Urusu
See Erzincan
Usāma ibn Munqidh 1–381a
Usāma ibn Zayd 1–25a
Usatges of Barcelona 1–191a, 408b, 412a; 3–156b, 157b
Usefulness of Believing, The (Augustine) 1–648b
USHAKOV, SIMON 12–0
USK, THOMAS 12–0
Usora 2–334a, 335a, 336a,b, 337a, 338a
Ustādh
Circassians 3–399b
USUARD 12–0
Uṣūl ḥisāb al-hind (Kūshyar ibn Labbān) 1–385b
USURY 12–0
European banking and prohibition 2–73b
Islamic banking 2–79a-b
Jewish banking in Europe 2–80b
pawnbroking 2–76a
USURY, ISLAMIC LAW 12–0
USURY, JEWISH LAW 12–0
Utensilibus, De (Adam of the Little Bridge) 1–52a
ʿUthmān 1–373b
ʿAbd Allāh 1–15b
ʿĀʾisha 1–113a-b
ʿAlī ibn Abī Ṭālib 1–172a-b
ʿAmr ibn al-ʿĀṣ 1–237a
assassination 1–172a-b
caliphate 3–35a-b
ʿUthmān al-Battī 1–26b
ʿUthmānids 1–513a
Utikʻ 1–123b, 472b, 473b
Bardhaʿa 2–107a
Utilitatibus astrolabii, De (Hermannus Contractus) 1–611a
Utopia (Thomas More) 3–83b
Utraquists 2–306a, 307b
Utrecht
Adalbold 1–47b
fairs 4–586b
Flemish commune 3–497b
UTRECHT PSALTER 12–0; 1–273b; 4–292b
Ebo of Rheims 4–368b
medieval copies 1–336a
Utrum
See Petty Assizes, English
Uwāl
See Baḥrayn, al-
Uxküll 2–64b
ʿUyūn al-akhbār 4–444b
ʿUyūnids
Baḥrayn, al- 2–51a
UZUN ḤASAN 12–0
Aq Qoyunlu 1–352a
Caffa 3–12b
Uzur 3–619b

V

VACARIUS 12–0; 4–466b
equity 4–501b-502a
Vačʻē II 2–107a
Vache, Sir Philip de La
See Clanvowe, Sir John
Vadstena Abbey 2–247a
VAFÞRÚÐNISMÁL **12–0**; 2–56b; 4–385b, 386b, 388a, 390a, 391a
Vahan Mamikonean 1–476b, 477a
Ējmiacin 4–417b

Vahan of Gołt'n, Prince 1–519a
VAHKA CASTLE 12–0
Vahrām Čobēn 1–477a
Vahrām Pahlawuni 1–484a
Vahrām Rabuni 1–511b, 512a
Vaillant
  ars subtilior 1–558b
Vakhtang Gurgasali
  See Wakhtang Gurgaslani
Valabsapat
  See Ējmiacin
Valamir, King 2–93a
Vałaršapat
  Armenian council 1–502a
  See Also Ējmiacin
Valaxš V 1–451b
Valdambrino, Francesco di
  See Francesco di Valdambrino
Val d'Aran 1–415a
Valdejunquera, Battle of (920) 1–627b
Valdemora, Battle of (878) 1–627a
Valdo, Peter 4–374b
Valence
  Inquisition 3–190a
VALENCIA 12–0; 1–406a, 407a
  agriculture 1–83b, 84b
  Almoravid conquest 1–199b
  archives 1–448b
  Baçó, Jaime 2–34b
  Catalan language 3–157b
  Cid, The 3–383b
  Cid's victory 3–73b, 75a
  Crown of Aragon 1–408b, 409a-b, 412a-b, 413a-b, 415a, 416a, 417a,b, 418a, 419a-b, 420a
  exchange banks 2–74a,b
  hearth lists 4–138a
  literary festivals 3–171b
  money markets 2–78b
  slaves 2–268b, 270a
  trade 2–104b; 4–557b
Valens, Emperor 2–120b
  Constantinople building 3–551a
  death 1–236a
  reign 2–485a
  Visigoths 2–90b
Valens, Vettius 1–605a
Valentinian I, Emperor
  Ambrose, Saint 1–230b
  reign 2–485a
Valentinian II 1–231a
Valentinums of Hadrumentum 1–653b
Valentinus
  Gnosticism 3–335a
Valerius, Bishop 1–648b
Valerius, Julius 1–152b
  Alexander romances 1–149b
Valerius Maximus 3–166b
Vale Royal Abbey 3–562a
Valettus
  Chaucer 3–281a, 282b
VALHALLA 12–0
  Eiríksmál and Hákonarmál 4–414b
Valkenburg
  fairs 4–586b
VALKYRIE 12–0
  charms, old High German 3–273b
  darraðarljóð 4–106a-b
Valla, Lorenzo
  dialectic 4–171a
  Donation of Constantine 4–257b
Valladolid
  cortes meeting 3–137a
***VALLA-LJÓTS SAGA* 12–0**; 4–612b
Valle, Laurent
  fables 4–572b
***VALLE CRUCIS* 12–0**
Vallmanya, Antoni de (writ.) 3–169b, 172a
VALOIS, DYNASTY 12–0
  Burgundy, County of 2–426a
  Burgundy, Duchy of 2–427a,b, 428a
Valpuesta
  Castilian settlement 3–128a
Valvassores
  Constitutio de feudis 3–557b, 558a
VALVERS ÞÁTTR 12–0
Vambrace 1–525b, 534a
Van
  See Vaspurakan
VAN, LAKE 12–0; 1–423a, 470b, 473b, 479b, 483b
VANAND 12–0
Vandalism
  legislation 1–334a
VANDALS 12–0; 2–94a
  Alani 1–121a
  Arian Christians 3–339b
  Arianism 1–654a
  Augustinian friars 1–659b
  Bordeaux 2–327b
  Byzantines 2–486b
  invasions 2–91b-92a
  Justinian 3–343b
  taxation 2–423a
Vanden blinckenden steen (Jan van Ruusbroec) 4–320b
Van den Coninc Saladijn ende van Hughen van Tabaryen (Hein van Aken) 4–319a
Vanden levene ons Heren 4–320a
Van den Velde, Heymerich
  Albertist school 1–129b
Van den Vos Reinaerde (Willem) 4–319a
Vanden winter en vanden somer 4–321a,b
Vander Mollenfeeste (Anthonis de Roovere) 4–322b
Van Diest
  Elckerlijc 4–419a
Van Eyck, Jan
  Annunciation painting 1–308a
  Christus, Petrus 3–324b
  Dalmaú 4–80b
Van Heer Halewijn 4–321a
VANIR 12–0
  Æsir 1–63a
Van Leyden, Lucas
  etching 4–516b
Vannes
  Celtic language 3–233b, 234a
VANNI, ANDREA 12–0
  Bartolo di Fredi 2–116b
VANNI, LIPPO 12–0
Van't kind van twalef jaren 4–321a
Van zeven manieren van heiliger minnen (Beatrijs van Nazareth) 4–319a
***VÁPNFIRÐINGA SAGA* 12–0**; 4–613b, 614a
Vaqueiras, Raimbaut de 4–87b
Varais 2–424a
VARANGIAN GUARD 12–0
  Constantinople 4–45b
Varangians
  Caspian Sea 4–556b
  explorations 4–555a-b
  See Also Vikings
Varaz-Bakur 3–308a
Varaz-Tiridates II
  death 1–125a
Varaztiroc' 1–477a
Varazvałan Siwni 1–476b
VARDAN AREWELC' I 12–0; 1–511b, 512a
Vardan Aygekc'i 1–512a
VARDAN MAMIKONEAN 12–0; 1–476b
  Armenian saints 1–518b
  Avarayr battle 2–12a
  Ełišē 4–433a
Vardan II Mamikonean 1–477a
VARDAPET 12–0
  Armenian church 1–504b
Vardapet, Vardan 2–20b
Vard Patrik 1–477a
Vardulia
  See Castile
Vardzia
  See Wardzia
Varela de Salamanca, Juan 4–86a
Variae (Cassiodorus) 3–123a-b, 252b
VARIATIO 12–0
VARNA 12–0
Varna, Battle of (1444) 4–56a
Varos 1–519b
Varro 1–656a
  classical literary studies 3–430b
  history of encyclopedias 4–447b
Vasak 1–476b
Vasco da Gama
  Islamic Arabia 1–376a
Vasconia 2–127a
Vase collections 1–335b
Vasilii II
  boyars 4–306a
VASPURAKAN 12–0; 1–472b, 473a,b, 474a, 481b
  Arcrunis 1–451a-b
  Berkri 2–189a
  Byzantine Empire 2–493a
Vassalage
  Bulgaria 2–413a
  commendation 3–490a
  Constitutio de Feudis 3–557b
VASSALLETUS 12–0
Vassi dominici
  Carolingian administration 3–107b-108a
Vatican
  archives 1–448a
Vaticana (song book) 3–86b
Vatican Archives 1–446b
Vatican Bible manuscript 2–214a
Vatican Council (1099)
  ecclesiastical investiture 1–313a
VATNSDÆLA SAGA 12–0; 4–613b, 614a
Vatopedi monastery 1–636b
VAULT 12–0
  alternating supports 1–226a
  Amiens Cathedral 1–234b
  Armenian architecture 1–493b
  barrel 2–125a
  boss 2–344a
  buttress 2–435a
  centering 3–234b, 235a
  construction 3–562b-563b, 564b-565a
  groin 2–125a
  See Also Church, typesof
Vaulted arch 4–338a-339b
Vazir 1–632a
Vedast, Saint
  Alcuin of York 1–143b
Vega, Lope de
  La Celestina 3–212b
Vegetables
  climatology 3–452b
  European cookery 3–581b
  Islamic cookery 3–584a
VEGETIUS RENATUS, FLAVIUS 12–0
  De re militari 3–302a
  military theories 4–578b

Veguer 3–156b
VEHICLES 12–0
draft animals 1–293a
VEHICLES, ISLAMIC 12–0
Veit Fiedler
Ambraser Heldenbuch 1–229b
Velásquez, Diego
Knights of Calatrava 3–306b
Velbužd 2–412a
Veldeke, Hendrik van 4–318a
poetry 4–320a
Veldener, John 3–210b
Vellekla (Einarr Helgason Skálaglamm) 4–410b
Vellert, Dirk
etching 4–516b
VELLUM 12–0
Velox (accentual pattern) 4–67a
VENANTIUS FORTUNATUS 12–0; 3–57b
acrostics 1–46a
Merovingians 3–100a
Vendīdād
See Vīdēvdād
Venerabilem (Innocent III) 4–427b
Venerable Bede
See Bede
Venetia
Ravenna exarchate 4–529b
Venetians
Bosporus 2–344a
Catalans 3–156b
Crete 3–678b
VENETS 12–0
Vengeance de Jésus-Christ, La (Eustache Merradé) 4–265a
Vengement Alixandre (Gui de Cambrai) 1–151a
Veni, Sancte Spiritus (Stephen Langton) 3–83b
VENICE 12–0
Andronikos II Palaiologos 1–245b
angelus bells 1–252a
banking 2–76a
banking location 2–74a, 75b
Black Death 2–259a, 260b
Bosnia 2–338a, 339b
Bucentaur 2–395b
Byzantine Empire 2–494b, 496a, 499a, 502a
commerce 4–556a
commune 3–499b
Croatia 4–2a-b, 5b, 8a
Crown of Aragon 1–416a,b
crusades of later middle ages 4–55b
currency 4–301a
Dalmatia 4–79b
Dante 4–104a
diplomacy 4–202a, 203a, 204a-b, 205b-206a, 207a-208a, 209a-b, 210a-211b, 212b, 213a,b
Dubrovnik 4–300a,b
dyes 4–328a
Dyrrachium 4–330a
exchange banks 2–73b-74a
fairs 4–587a
Fourth Crusades 4–42a, 43a-b
fruits and fruit trees 1–87a
Marco Polo 4–557a,b
maritime law 3–570a
money markets 2–78b
Ottoman war 2–137a
physicians and surgeons 2–99a, 100b
slaves 2–269b
Thessaloniki 2–503b
Venice, Treaty of (1201) 4–42a-b
VENI CREATOR SPIRITUS 12–0
Venison
hunting laws 1–301a
Venjance Alixandre (Jean de Nevelon) 1–151a
Ventadorn, Bernart de
courtly love 3–669a
Ventadorn Castle 2–197a
Vento, Ugo
Castile 4–557b
Venturino of Bergamo
preaching 4–250a,b
Venturós pelegrí, Lo (Perellós) 3–169b
Verborum significatu, De (Varrius Flaccus) 4–449b
Verbum abbreviatum (John Dastin) 1–137b, 138a
Vercellae
Cimbri 2–88b
Vercelli
See Vercellae
Vercelli Book 1–277a, 278a-281a,b, 284b
Verdun, Treaty of (843) 3–112b
Burgundy, County of 2–424a
Burgundy, Duchy of 2–427a
VERECUNDUS OF JUNCA 12–0
Verfasserfragment 1–133b
Vergeboard
See Bargeboard
Verge dels Consellers (Luis Dalmaú) 4–80b
Vergerio, Pier Paolo 3–654b
Vergier lez une fontenele, En un 3–263a
VERGIL IN THE MIDDLE AGES 12–0; 3–55b
Aenead translations 4–262b
Agius of Corvey 1–72b
allegorical interpretation tradition 1–180b-181a
Augustine 1–656b
Dante 4–94b, 102b
Enéas, Roman d' 4–451a
Latin epic 4–495b
plow design 1–90a
Vergilius Maro Grammaticus
Irish Bible 2–220a
Verhkehrte Wirt, Der 1–230a
Veritate, De (Anselm of Canterbury) 1–312a, 314b
Verlucut'iwn neracut'eann Porp'iwri 4–114a
See Scholia tēs Porphyriou eisogogēs
Vermandois, Count
Champagne history 3–243b
Vermiculé enamel
See Enamel, vermiculé
Vermudo III, King 3–128b
Vernacular
Dante 4–95a, 100a-b
legal writing 4–409a
Vernani, Guido 4–103a
VERNICLE 12–0
Vernon Manuscripts 1–319b
Veroli Casket 2–454b
Verona
Cathar decline 3–190b
Dante 4–99a, 103a-b
fairs 4–587a
Verrius Flaccus 4–449b
VERS 12–0
Vers de la mort (Hélinandus de Froidmont) 1–264a
Verse anthologies 1–318a-320b
Verse translations
Old English poetry 1–281a
Versicles
angelus 1–252a
VERTUE, ROBERT AND WILLIAM 12–0
Vesió (Bernat de So) 3–173b
Vespasian Psalter 2–221a; 4–548b
Mercian dialect 1–276a
Vespers 3–67a
Alexandrian rite 1–157a
Angevins 1–253b
Divine Office 4–221b, 227-228, 229a
Office of the Dead 4–117b-118a
VESTMENTS 12–0
dalmatic 4–80a
epitrakhil 4–500a
liturgical colors 3–484a
ordination rites 3–442b
Western European costume 3–624a-b
Veterinary science
text 4–579b
Vettius Valens 1–617a
Vetus Latina Psalter 4–223b
Vexin burials
ceramics 3–236a
VÉZELAY, CHURCH OF LA MADELEINE 12–0
Via, Francesc de la 3–173b
Via Appia
Ad Catacumbas 3–154a
Via cessionis 1–108b; 3–646a
Via concilii 1–108b
Via Egnatia
Dyrrachium 4–329b
Via Latina catacomb 3–155b; 4–350b, 351a, 363a
***VIA MODERNA* 12–0**
Durand 4–313b
Viatge al purgatori de Sant Patrici (Ramon de Perellós) 3–169b-170a
Viaticum 4–119b, 120a, 565a
Vic
ecclesiastical culture 3–175b
Vic, plain of 3–174b
VICAR 12–0
Vicar-general
hierarchy of clergy 3–444b
Vicarius Christi 4–374a,b, 375b
Vicarius Petri 4–373b
Vice-dominus
See Vidame
Vicentino 3–658a
Vicenza 1–147b
Victor IV, Antipope 1–330a; 3–637b-638a; 4–517a
Danish church 4–153b
Victor I, Pope
papal theory 3–341b
Victor III, Pope
See Desiderius of Monte Cassino
Victorines
biblical exegesis 2–212b, 213b
VICTORINUS, G. MARIUS 12–0; 1–460b
dialectic 4–169a
Victorius of Aquitaine
dating of Easter 3–228a
Vida de Jesucrist (Francesc Eiximenis) 4–416b
Vida de San Mill?Olan de la Cogolla (Gonzalo de Berceo) 2–187a
Vida de Santa Oria (Gonzalo de Berceo) 2–187b-188a
Vida de Santo Domingo de Silos (Gonzalo de Berceo) 2–187a
Vidal, Ramon, of Besalú 3–164b, 173b
Vidame 1–59b
VIDAS 12–0
Videndo Deo, De (Augustine) 1–167a
VIDERUNT OMNES 12–0; 1–310a
***VĪDĒVDĀD* 12–0**; 2–14b, 15a
Vidin 2–409b, 410b, 411a, 412b, 413a

***VIE D'EDOUARD LE CONFESSEUR* 12–0**
Vie de Guillaume le Mareschal 3–332b
***VIE DE SAINT ALEXIS* 12–0**
***VIE DE SAINT AUBAN* 12–0**; 1–271b
VIE DE SAINT CATHERINE 12–0; 1–261b
***VIE DE SAINTE CATHERINE D'ALEXANDRIE* 12–0**
VIE DE SAINT EDMUND LE REI 12–0; 1–261a
***VIE DE SAINTE MARGUERITE* 12–0**
VIE DE SAINTE MARGUERITE 12–0
***VIE DE SAINTE MODWENNE* 12–0**
***VIE DE SAINT GILLES* 12–0**
VIE DE SAINT GILLES 12–0; 1–261b
Vie de Saint Grégoire (Angier) 1–254a
***VIE DE SAINT LAURENT* 12–0**
Vie de Saint Louis, La 3–332b
VIE DE SAINT MODWENNA 12–0
VIE DE SAINT THOMAS A BECKET 12–0; 1–261a
***VIE DE SAINT THOMAS BECKET* 12–0**; 1–260b
***VIE DES ANCIENS PÈRES, LA* 12–0**; 1–261b
Vie de Seint Josaphaz (Chardri) 1–260b, 261b; 3–267b
Vie de Seint Martin (play) 4–265a
Vie des Set Dormanz (Chardri) 1–260b, 261b; 3–267b
Vie du prince noir 1–266a
Vielle
  chansonnier 3–256a
Vienna 2–7a
  archives 1–448b
Vienna, Concordat of (1448) 3–525b, 526a
Vienna, University of
  Albert of Saxony 1–125b
  astronomers 1–613b
Vienne, Council of (1311-1312) 3–643a-645b; 4–400a
  Avignonese papacy 3–364b
  beguines 2–161a
  Christian Hebraists 3–314a
  Clement V, Pope 3–438b
  Knights Templar 3–362a
Vienne, counts of
  dauphin title 4–107b
Vienne, Kingdom of 2–428b
  See Also Burgundy, Kingdom of
Viennois 2–428b
***VIE SEINT EDMUND LE REI, LA* 12–0**
***VÍGA-GLÚMS SAGA* 12–0**; 4–612b
Vigila 1–390a,b
Vigilia crucis
  Celtic mortifications 3–231b
Vigiliae mortuorum 4–117b
VIGILIUS, POPE 12–0; 2–422a
  caesaropapism 3–10b
  dedication of churches 4–130b
  Second Council of Constantinople (553) 3–630a-b
VIGIL RABER 12–0
Vigils 3–67a
  Armenian rite 1–517a
  Celtic divine office 3–230a-b
***VÍGLUNDAR SAGA* 12–0**
Vigna Massima catacombs
  angel 1–248a
Viguiers
  castellans 3–124b
Vihāra
  Bukhara 2–397a
VIKING ART 12–0
  Anglo-Saxon 1–273b
  Borre style 2–332b
VIKING NAVIGATION 12–0
VIKINGS 12–0
  acclamations 1–35b
  Anglo-Saxon art 1–272a
  Anglo-Saxon England 4–455b-459a
  arms and armor 1–522b-523a
  Arnulf 1–541b
  Baltic tribes 2–62b
  bow and arrow/crossbow 2–352b
  Brittany, Duchy 2–379a
  Bruges 2–386a
  Canterbury 3–82a
  Carolingian Empire 3–114b-115a
  Celtic art 3–218a
  Cologne 3–481a
  danegeld 4–90a,b
  Danelaw 4–91a
  Denmark 4–148b, 151b, 152a
  Dublin 4–298b-299a
  exploration 4–554a
  fabrics 4–328a
  Flanders 2–58a
  raids 1–163b-164a
  The Battle of Maldon 1–279a
Vilain and the Bird
  courtoisie 1–268b
Vilain and the Serpent
  courtoisie 1–268b
Vilaragut, Antoni 3–169b
Vilarrasa, Lluís de 3–171b
VILLAGE LIFE 12–0
VILLAGES 12–0
  Byzantine 1–79a-b
Villaleon
  fairs 4–587b
***VILLANCICOS* 12–0**
  chansons de femme 3–257a
Villani, Filippo
  artist's status 1–579b
  biographies 2–240a
Villani, Giovanni
  assassins 1–590b
  carroccio 3–117a,b
  demography 4–137a
  food animals 1–300a
  plague 2–265a
Villani, Matteo
  food animals 1–300a
Villani family
  Boccaccio 2–287b
  chronicles of Florence 3–329b
Villanova
  Barcelona 2–103a, 104a
Villarcayo
  Castile 3–125b
VILLARD DE HONNECOURT 12–0; 3–145a
  clock automata 3–460a
  drawings 1–335a
  sketchbook 4–292a
  wood 3–561a
Villaret, Fulque de
  Knights of Saint John 3–304a
Villefranche-de-Rouergue 2–128b
VILLEHARDOUIN, GEOFFROI DE 12–0
  Châtelain de Coucy 3–277b
  Conon de Béthune 3–538a
  Conquête de Constantinople 3–328a
  Constantinople 1–334b
  crusades 3–247a; 4–42a,b, 43b, 46a,b
  diplomacy 4–203b, 210a
  French chronicles 3–332a
Villeinage
  copyhold 3–596b
VILLENA, ENRIQUE DE 12–0
  Catalan literature 3–170b
Villiers, Philippe
  Knights of Malta 3–304a
Villis, De (capitulary) 4–511b
VILLON, FRANÇOIS 12–0; 2–237a
  ballade 2–59a
  fabliau 4–577a
***VILMUNDAR SAGA VIÐUTAN* 12–0**
VIMARA 12–0
Vincent Ferrer, Saint 3–167b
  Eiximenis, 4–416a
  preaching 4–250a,b
  preaching missions 3–368a
  Western councils 3–646a
VINCENTIUS HISPANUS 12–0
VINCENT OF BEAUVAIS 12–0; 1–137a
  bestiary 2–205a
  Bible 2–216b
  Dominican studies 4–247b
  encyclopedias 4–449a
  Ermengaud 4–506b
  fables 4–572a
  plant study 2–245b
Vindiciae contra tyrannos
  conciliar theory 3–522a
Vindicta salvatoris 1–285b
Vineam domini Sabaoth (bull) 3–639b
Vineyards
  See Fruits and fruit trees
Vinland
  Leif Ericsson 4–555a
VINLAND SAGAS 12–0; 4–613b
  Eyrbyggja saga 4–568a
Vintners Guild
  corporation 3–607a
Violant of Hungary
  See Ioland of Hungary
Viollet-le-Duc, Eugene Emmanuel
  Amiens Cathedral 1–235a
Viratarrak
  See Derbent
VIRELAI 12–0; 1–558b
  ars nova 1–552a-b
  ballata 2–60b
  ballette 2–61a
  cantiga 3–85b
  chansonnier 3–255a
  dance 4–87a
VIRGATE 12–0
  peasant land 3–415a, 423b
Virgil
  See Vergil in the Middle Ages
Virgilio, Giovanni del 1–183b
Virgilius Bishop of Salzburg
  Carolingian church 3–109a
VIRGIL THE GRAMMARIAN 12–0
VIRGINAL 12–0
Virgin at Trikomo, Church of the 2–444b
Virginity
  church fathers 1–323a
Virgin Mary
  Annuciation 1–307b
  crucifixion 4–12b
  Marian offices 2–273b
Virgin of Mercy (Enguerrand Charonton) 3–274b
Virgin of the Pharos, Church of
  decoration 2–439b
Virgin of Vladimir 4–429b, 430a
Virgin Pammakaristos, Monastery of the 2–448b
Virgin Peribleptos, Church of the (Och-rid) 2–448a; 4–524b
Virgin Phorviotissa at Asinou, Church of the 2–444b
Virgin Stanimaka, Church of the (Bul-garia) 2–417a

Virgo inter virgines (Gerard David) 4–115a
VIRTUES AND VICES 12–0
allegory 1–181a-b, 183a-b, 184a-b, 185b, 186a
Anticlaudianus 1–119b
female personification 1–181b
Virtutibus et vitiis et de donis Spiritus sancti, De (Alan of Lille) 1–120a
Visby, Battle of (1361)
arms and armor 1–525a
VISCHER THE ELDER, PETER 12–0
VISCONTI 12–0
Albornoz 1–131a
monuments 2–324b
Visconti, Bernabò
Chaucer 3–283b, 286a
monument 2–324b
revolt against popes 3–439b
Visconti, Gian Galeazzo 2–79a, 390b
astrarium 3–462a
de' Dondi patronage 4–260b, 261a
Milan cathedral 2–196b
Peter of Candia 1–147b
Visconti, Giovanni
Petrarch 2–288a
Visconti, Stefano
monument 2–324b
Visconti, Valentina 3–272b
monument 2–324b
Višeslav, Prince 4–2a
Viseu
Ferdinand I 3–128b
VISIGOTHIC ART 12–0
See Also Early Christian art
Visigothic script
Arabic numerals 1–392b-394b
VISIGOTHS 12–0; 1–454b; 2–90a-91b
Alani 1–121a
Alaric 1–122a
Aquitaine 1–366b
Aragon 1–403b, 404a,b
Arian Christians 3–339b
Arianism 3–676b
Asturias-León 1–625b, 626b, 629a, 630a-b, 631a
Barcelona 2–102a-b
Basque independence 2–126a
blasphemy 2–272a
Bordeaux 2–327b
Byzantine Empire 2–485a,b
Castilian language 3–141b
Clovis 3–466b
deposition of rulers 4–158b
Franks 2–94b
invasions 2–90a-91b
Justinian 3–343b
language 1–212a
Roman cavalry 3–201a
Spanish settlement 2–95a
Vising, Johan 1–271b
Visio (Walafrid Strabo) 3–103a
Visió de Tundal (Ramon de Perellós) 1–185b; 3–169b
Visio Filiberti 4–63a
Vision
See Optics
Vision (Bernat de So) 3–173b
Vision de Tondale, La 1–261b
Vision of Adamnán, The 1–347b
Vision of Isaiah 3–182a, 184b
Vision of Mac Con-Glinne, The
See Aislinge meic Con-Glinne
Vision of Saint Paul 1–285b
VISIONS, LITERARY FORM 12–0
allegory 1–182a-b, 183a, 184a-186b
Dante 4–97a
Draumkvæde 4–290a
Visio Pauli
Irish apocrypha 1–347b
VISITATION 12–0
VISITATIO SEPULCHRI 12–0
Visoko 2–334a
Visor 1–526b, 530a, 534a
arms and armor 1–524a
Vistula River 2–66b
VĪS U RĀMĪN 12–0
Vita
crucifixion 4–13b
Vita Abbonis (Aimoin de Fleury) 1–109b-110a
Vita Beati Aemiliani (Braulio) 2–187a
Vita Beati Dominici (Grimaldus) 2–187a
Vita Caroli Magni (Einhard) 4–412b
Vita Christi (Ludolf of Saxony) 3–167a
Vita Columbae (Saint Adamnan) 1–52b-53a; 4–78a
Vita Constantini
See Eusebius of Caesarea
Vita curiali, De (Chartier) 3–275b
Vita Dunstani (Adelard of Ghent) 4–311b
Vitae Caesarum I (Suetonius) 3–331b
***VITAE PATRUM* (RUFIN) 12–0**; 3–167a
***VITAE SANCTORUM WALLENSIUM* 12–0**
Vita gauzlini abbatis floriacensis monasterii (André de Fleury) 1–244a
Vita Geraldi (Odo of Cluny) 3–469a
VITAL DE BLOIS 12–0
plays 4–283a
Vital du Four
Augustinism 1–660b
Vitalis, Ordericus 3–636b
Anglo-Norman languages 1–260a
Vita Mahumeti (Embricho of Mainz) 4–436b
Vita nuova (Dante) 3–196b; 4–94b, 96a,b-97a, 98a, 100a, 104b, 506b
VITA OF KOTOR 12–0
Vita Paldonis, Tatonis, et Tasonis (Ambrosius Autpertus) 2–11a
Vita Richerii (Angelram of Saint Riquier) 1–252a
Vita sancti Anscharii 2–62b
Vita sancti Eadmundi (Abbo of Fleury) 1–13a
Vita sancti Magni 4–414a
Vita sanctorum Amici et Amelii 1–234a
Vita Waltharii manufortis (Ekkehard I of Saint Gall) 4–418a,b
Viterbo fair
Muslim ceramics 3–237b
Viticulture
Burgundy, Duchy of 2–428a
Vitoria
founding 2–126a
Vitruvius 1–435a
De architectura 1–331b
sundials 3–457b
water clock 3–28a
Vitry, Jacques de
See Jacques de Vitry
Vitry, Philippe de
See Philippe de Vitry
Vitulo, Abbot 3–127a
Vitus 2–67a
Vivaldi, Ugolino 4–558b
Vivaldi, Vadino 4–558b
Vivarium monastery 3–123a,b-124a
Vivolo, Bishop
Passau 2–322a
Vizcaya
Basques 2–126a
VIZIER 12–0
Badr al-Jamālī 2–44a
caliphate 3–44a
divine right 3–46b
VLACHS 12–0; 2–340a, 341a
Bulgaria 2–399a, 407b
transhumance practice 1–79a
Vladimir (city)
captur by Mongols 2–131b
cathedrals 4–341a
Vladimir, King of Bulgaria 2–404a
overthrow 2–329b
VLADIMIR, SAINT 12–0
Anna 1–303a
baptism 2–490b
Basil II alliance 2–118b
Byzantine church 2–464a
VLADIMIR MONOMAKH 12–0
VLADIMIR-SUZDAL 12–0
Bogoliubskii 2–293b
Dmitrii Ivanovich Donskoi 4–232a
Vladimir Uspensky Cathedral and Golden Gate 2–293b
VLADIMIR VIRGIN 12–0
Vladislav I
Bohemia 2–299b-300a
Vladislav II
Bohemia 2–300a
Vladislav of Bulgaria 2–412a
***VOCABULARIUS SANCTI GALLI* 12–0**
Vocabulary
Anglo-Norman 1–259b
Catalan 3–163a-b
Hebrew-Latin 3–313b
Latin-French 1–270a,b
Old English texts 1–276a
Vodka 4–220a
Voeux du paon (Jacques de Longuyon) 1–151a-b
Vogt
See Advocate
Voice movement
Anonymous IV 1–310a
Voie d'enfer et de paradis (Jehan de le Mote) 1–185b
Voie de paradis (Rutebeuf) 1–185b
Vojsalić, Djuraj 2–338b
Vojteh, George
Bulgaria 2–407b
VOLGA BULGARS 12–0
Sübüdey 2–131b
Volga River
camels 1–296a,b
Danes 4–554a
exploration 4–556b
Volkbücher
development 4–432b-433a
Eleonore of Austria 4–429b
Völkerwanderung
See Barbarians, Invasions of
Volkhov River
Aldeigjuborg 2–555a
Danes 4–554a
Volkmar
Peasants' Crusade 4–34a
Vologases
See Valaxš
Vologases (Parthian)
Avesta collection 2–14b
***VǪLSUNGA SAGA* 12–0**; 4–387a
Brynhild 2–394b, 395a
VOLTO SANTO 12–0
Volucracy
Anglo-Norman literature 1–262a
VOLUMEN 12–0
VǪLUNDARKVITHA 12–0;
4–3865-3387a, 388b, 390a

VQLUSPÁ **12–0**; 1–63a; 2–224b; 4–386b, 387a, 390a, 391a,b
Baldrs Draumar 2–56b
Vǫluspá in skamma 4–387b, 391a,b
Volvellae 4–500b
Vom edlen Menschen (Meister Eckhart) 4–381a
Von Abegescheidenheit (Meister Eckhart) 4–381b
Von Bern, Dietrich
Ermenrîkes Dôt 4–507a
Von Bern, Ermanaric
Ermenrîkes Dôt 4–507a
Von der Vogelweide, Walther 2–7a
Von Gierke, Otto
conciliar theory 3–521b
VON KÜRENBERG, DER 12–0
Von Mügeln, Heinrich 1–138b
Von Ruysbroeck, Jan
mysticism 3–368b
Von siben Ingesigeln (Tilo von Kulm) 2–230b
Von Steinbach
See Erwin, Master
Von Ürslingen, Werner
condottieri 3–531a
Voragine, Jacobus de
Golden Legend 3–286a
Vorauer Bücher Mosis, Die 2–227a-228a
Vorkauf 4–494a
Vorsänger 3–116a
Vortigern, King 2–2b-3a
Votādinī
Gododdin 1–247a
Votchina 1–101b, 102a
Votive antiphons 1–329a
VOTIVE CROWN 12–0
Votive portraits 4–262a
VOUSSOIR 12–0; 1–423b
archivolt 1–449a
Vowels
Anglo-Norman 1–259b
Arabic language 1–376b
Vows of the peacock (Jacques de Longuyon) 1–151a-b
Vox in excelso 3–644b
Voyage de Charlemagne à Jérusalem et à Constantinople 3–258b
VOYAGE DE SAINT BRENDAN, LE **12–0**; 1–185b, 261a, 262a
Voyage of Trivaile of Sire Jehan de Manderville, Knight (Jean à la Barbe) 1–332b
Vratislav II
Henry IV 2–299b
Vrbanja 2–334a
Vrbas River
Croatian boundary 4–2a
VRELANT, WILLEM 12–0
Vrhbosna 2–334a, 339a
Vrtʿanēs Kʿertʿoł 1–509b
V tabulae salutationum (Boncompagno) 2–320a
Vukčić, Hrvoje
Bosnia 2–337b-338b
Vukčić, Stefan 2–337b, 339a-b
Vuk of Bosnia 2–337a
Vuković, Vlatko 2–337b
VULGAR LATIN 12–0
Vulgari eloquentia, De (Dante) 4–99b-100b, 101b, 102b
VULGATE 12–0; 2–211a-b, 212b
Arthurian literature 1–571a, 572a, 574a, 575b
Brethren of the Common Life 2–367b
Catalan translation 3–167a
Cistercian Bible 2–218a
exegesis 2–213a
French Bible 2–219a-b
Hugh of Saint Cher 4–246a
Ireland 2–220a
Latin exegesis 4–542a
Middle English exegesis 4–545b
Spain 2–215b
Vulpis, Nicholas
dictamen 4–176b
VUZURG-FRAMADAR 12–0
Vytautas 2–67a

W

WACE 12–0
Arthurian literature 1–565a, 576a
Brut, The 2–393a-b
French chronicles 3–331a
writing 2–236b
Wadi Natrun monasteries
Coptic architecture 3–587a
Wærferth, Bishop 1–165a,b, 167a
Old English translations 1–284a
Wafayāt al-aʿyān waanbāʾ al-zamān (Ibn Khallikān) 1–634a
Wāfid, Ibn (Abenguefith) 1–106a
Wagon fortress 3–206b
Wahhāb, Salāma ibn ʿAbd al-
Druzes 4–296a
Waḥshīya, Ibn 1–106a
Wajjāj ibn Zalwah al-Lamṭī 1–198a
Wakefield Plays
See Towneley plays
WAKHTANG GURGASLANI 12–0; 3–308a
WAKHUSHT 12–0
Wala 3–112a
Charlemagne 3–111a
exile 3–111b
WALAFRID STRABO 12–0; 3–112a
biology 2–242b-243a
Carolingian Latin poetry 3–103a
Divine Office 4–223a
Einhard 4–412a, 413a
exegesis 2–213a; 4–542b, 543b
Nicene-Constantinople creed 3–677a
Walcher of Malvern
astrolabe 1–611b
WALDEF, L'ESTOIRE DE **12–0**
Waldemar I of Denmark
monarchy 4–153a,b, 154a
Waldemar II of Denmark 2–65b
hereditary succession 4–154b
territory 4–154a
Waldemar's Land Book 4–149b
Waldensian bestiary 2–205b
WALDENSIANS 12–0; 3–369b-370a
Alan of Lille 1–119a
Albigensians 1–130b
Bible 2–215a,b, 218b
Bohemian Brethren 2–306a
Cathar decline 3–190b
condemnation 3–640b
Dauphiné establishments 4–109b
ecclesiological developments 4–374b
See Also Bohemian Brethren
Waldere (Walter of Aquitaine) 1–278b
WALDES 12–0; 3–359a, 369b
Waldo, Peter
See Waldes
WALDRAMMUS 12–0
Wales
archers 3–205a
borough 2–329b
Celtic art 3–219a, 224a-b
chalder measure 3–241a
coroner 3–605b
Wales, Statute of (1284) 4–396a
WALES: HISTORY 12–0
Bangor bishopric 2–70a
Celtic church 3–225a, 344a
Celtic population 1–290a
Chester, Treaty of 3–299b
Cistercian order 3–404a
Conway, Peace of 3–579b
Cunedda Wledig 4–64b
Dyfed 4–329a
Edward I of England 4–396a
Exchequer 4–534a
Henry II of England 4–467a
WALES: MARCHER LORDS 12–0
Walewein (Penninc and Vostaert) 4–318b
Waleys, Thomas
ars praedicandi 1–556a, 557a,b
exegesis 4–544b
Wālī al-madīna
Damascus 4–84a
Wāliba ibn al-Ḥubāb 1–27a-b
WALĪD I IBN ʿABD AL-MALIK AL- 12–0
Beirut 2–164a
Damascus 4–83a
Umayyad caliphate 3–40b
Walīd II ibn Yazīd, al
costume 3–616b
Wallace, Sir William 4–396b
Wallingford, Richard
See Richard of Wallingford
WALO OF AUTUN 12–0
Walpott, Hermann
Teutonic Knights 3–306a
Wälsche Gast, Der (Zerklaere) 3–665a
Walshe, Gerald 3–466a
Walsingham, Alan of
See Alan of Walsingham
Walsingham, Thomas
clerical chronicles 3–327a,b
WALTER, HUBERT 12–0; 4–468b, 471a-b
acclamations 1–35b
accounting 4–534a
court of common pleas 3–492a
Walter Map
See Map (Mapes), Walter
Walter of Albano 1–312b
Walter of Aquitaine 1–278b
WALTER OF BIBBESWORTH 12–0
vocabulary 1–270b
Walter of Brienne
Almogávares merrcenaries 1–191a
Catalan Company 3–156a
WALTER OF CHÂTILLON 12–0
Alexander romances 1–150a
Alexanders Saga 1–152a
anthology of poems 1–318b, 319a
conductus 3–532a
Latin epic 4–496a
Libro de Alexandre 1–152b
WALTER OF COLCHESTER 12–0
Walter of England
Romulus 4–572a-b
Walter of Evesham
See Odington, Walter
WALTER OF HENLEY 12–0
estate management 4–513b, 514a
Walter of Lille
See Walter of Châtillon
WALTER OF MAURETANIA 12–0

Walter of Odington
See Odington, Walter
Walter of Saint Victor
Contra quattor labyrinthos Franciae 4–170a
Walter of Strasbourg 4–248a
Walter of Wimborne 1–255a
Walter the Penniless
Peasants' Crusade 4–34a
Waltham Abbey 1–256a, 257
WALTHARIUS **12–0**; 2–253a; 4–496a
Ekkehard I of Saint Gall 4–418a
Walther, Bernard
astronomical observations 1–613b
WALTHER VON DER VOGELWEIDE 12–0
biblical poetry 2–228b
crusade poems 4–20b
WALTHER VON SPEIER 12–0
Wamba, King
anointing 1–308b
Wanderer, The 1–281a, 282, 283a-b
alliterative patterns 1–277a
WANDERING JEW LEGEND 12–0
Wangara
gold trade 4–561b
Wanley, Humfrey 1–286b
codicology 1–278a; 3–477a
WAQF 12–0
WĀQIDĪ, ABŪ 'ABD ALLĀH MUḤAMMAD IBN 'UMAR, AL- 12–0
WAQ-WAQ ISLANDS 12–0
Wardrobe of the royal household
finances 4–532b
WARDZIA 12–0
WARFARE, BYZANTINE 12–0
Armenian cavalry 3–198b
Byzantine cavalry 3–199b
encyclopedias 4–447a
WARFARE, ISLAMIC 12–0
cavalry 3–208a
WARFARE, WESTERN EUROPEAN 12–0
arms and armor 1–521b
canon 3–64a
castles and fortifications 3–143a-b, 145a, 146a-150b
catapults 3–179b
cavalry 1–294a,b; 3–200a
condottieri 3–531a
Fachschrifttum 4–578a,b
food animals 1–300a
standing army 3–206b
Warhorse 3–204b, 206a,b
costs 3–412a
Warin fitz-Gerold
Pseudo-Turpin Chronicle 3–331b
Wark Castle
David I of Scotland 4–316b
Warmians
insurrection (1260) 2–67a
WARNERIUS OF BASEL 12–0
War of Saint Sardos 1–367b; 2–128b, 129a
Wars (Procopius) 1–67b
Wars of the Lord (Abner of Burgos) 3–577b
Wars of the Lord, The (Levi ben Gerson) 4–12a
WARS OF THE ROSES 12–0; 4–477b-479b, 484b
chronicles 3–329b
WARTBURGKRIEG 12–0
Warwick
Gui de Warewic 1–267b
Wash, The 4–454a
map 4–453a-b
Washī 3–616b
Washshā, al- 3–618a
WĀSIṬ 12–0
WĀSIṬĪ, YAḤYĀ IBN MAḤMŪD, AL- 12–0
WASTELL, JOHN 12–0
Water buffalo
draft animal 1–296b-298b
food animal 1–299a
Water clocks 3–27b-28a, 457b, 458b-460a
Waterford
Vikings 4–554b
WATERMARKS 12–0
Water mill
See Mills
Waterrecht 3–570a
WATERWORKS 12–0
Watha's rebellion (1044)
horsemeat 1–300a
Wāthiq, al- 1–195b; 3–46b
Watling's Island
See San Salvador
WAUQUELIN, JEAN 12–0
WAX TABLETS 12–0
Way to Salvation, The 4–86b
Wazīr 1–634a; 2–110a,b
See Also Vizier
Weapons
arms and armor 1–521b
bow and arrow 2–350b
cannon 3–64a
Wearmouth 4–458b
Wearmouth and Jarrow, Monastery of 1–275b
Weavers
Córdoba 3–599b
Weavers Guild 3–607a
Wedricus of Liessie 1–258a
Weight-driven clocks 3–29a-b
WEIGHTS AND MEASURES, BYZANTINE 12–0
agriculture 1–77b-78a
WEIGHTS AND MEASURES, ISLAMIC 12–0
WEIGHTS AND MEASURES, WESTERN EUROPEAN 12–0
acre 1–45b
alnage 1–202b
arpent 1–542a
barrel 2–113b
boisseau 2–310a
boll 2–310b
bushel 2–433b
chalder measure 3–241a
fairs 4–586b
plowland units 1–93b
Weingartner Liederhandschrift 2–274b
WEINSCHWELG, DER **12–0**
Weland
Deor 1–278b
Welf IV of Bavaria
Crusade of 1101 4–36a,b
Second Crusade 4–38a
Welfs
Angevin alliance 4–467a
Bavaria 2–33b, 134b
Burgundy, County of 2–424a
Hohenstaufen feud 2–6b
See Also Guelphs and Ghibellines
Well poisoning
anti-Semitism 1–341a,b
Wells
Black Death 2–261b-262a
Wells Cathedral
chapter house design 3–267a
Wellustige mensch, De (Jan van den Berge) 4–322b
Welsh language
Bible translation 2–216a
chansons de geste 3–258a
See Also Celtic Languages
WELSH LITERATURE 12–0
Arthurian literature 1–565b-567a, 571b, 576b-578a
bards 2–106a
Brut, The 2–393b
eisteddfod 4–415a
Elidir Sais 4–430b
WELSH LITERATURE: POETRY 12–0
Arthurian literature 1–564b
bardic grammars 2–107a
Casnodyn 3–121b
Cynddelw Brydydd Mawr 4–69b
Dafydd ap Gwilym 4–76a
Einon ap Gwalchmai 4–413a
WELSH LITERATURE: PROSE 12–0
Areithian prose 1–452a
WELSH LITERATURE: RELIGIOUS 12–0
Weltchronik, Die (Rudolf von Ems) 2–229a
Wenceslas, Saint
crown of 2–300b
Wenceslas of Luxembourg 3–333a
Wenceslas IV
Bohemia 2–300b, 301a-b, 304b
Brandenburg 2–361b
WENDS 12–0
Second Crusade 4–37b
Wenzel Bible 2–215b
Werden casket 1–308a
WERGILD 12–0
Werl Altarpiece (Robert Campin) 3–61b
Werner, Johann 1–439a
Werner of Magdeburg 2–391b
WERNHER DER GARTENAER 12–0
Ambraser Heldenbuch 1–230a
WERNHER VON ELMENDORF 12–0
WERVE, CLAUS DE 12–0
Burgundy, Duchy of 2–428a
Chartreuse de Champmol 4–186a
Wessel Gansfort
Brethren of the Common Life 2–368b
Wessex
Alfred the Great 1–163b
Anglo-Saxons 2–96b; 4–454a
emergence of Kingdom 2–96b
See Also West Saxons
WESSOBRUNNER GEBET 12–0
West Antiochene rites 1–326b
Western Schism
See Schism, Great
Westminster
Court of Exchequer 4–533b
Westminster, Agreement of (1107)
See Compromise of Bec
Westminster, Council of (1163)
benefit of clergy 2–151b
WESTMINSTER, STATUTES OF 12–0
estate management 4–514b
Statute of 1285 4–514b
WESTMINSTER ABBEY 12–0
Anglo-Norman features 1–255b
building materials 3–562a
chapter house design 3–266b
Edward the Confessor 4–394a, 395b
Old English documents 1–286b
tiled pavements 3–237a
Westminster accounting 4–514a
West Saxon dialect
Old English texts 1–276b
West Saxon Gospels 1–275b, 285b
West Saxons 4–454a
supremacy 4–455a-457a

West Slavs
agriculture and nutrition 1–96b-99a
WESTWORK 12–0
Carolingian 2–124b
Wetti 3–103a
Wexford
Vikings 4–554b
WEYDEN, ROGIER VAN DER 12–0
Bouts, Dirk 2–350a
Campin, Robert 3–61b
Christus, Petrus 3–324b
Whale
cookery 3–581b
Whale, The 1–280b
Wheat
Islamic cookery 3–584a
See Also Grain crops, Western European
WHEEL OF FORTUNE 12–0
WHEEL WINDOW 12–0
Whitacre, Nigel
See Wireker (Whitacre), Nigel
Whitby 1–107b, 277b
WHITBY, SYNOD OF (664) 12–0; 1–107b; 4–454b, 458b
Celtic church 2–382a; 3–226a, 228b
Colman of Lindisfarne 3–480a
Latin church 3–344b, 373b
White
liturgical color 3–484a
White besants 2–203a
White Elephant, Order of the 3–307a
White Monastery
See Deir el-Abiad (Sohag)
White Monks
See Cistercian Order
White Sea
discovery 4–555a
White ware 3–238b, 239b
Whitsun Plays
See Also Chester Plays
Why God Became a Man (Anselm of Canterbury) 1–312b, 314b
WIBALD OF STAVELOT 12–0
WIBERT OF CANTERBURY 12–0
WIBERT OF TOUL 12–0
Wichmann I Billung 2–235a
WICHRAM OF SAINT GALL 12–0
Wiclif
See Wyclif, John
Widsith 1–278b
WIDUKIND OF CORVEI 12–0
royal election 4–426a
Wiener Genesis
See Altdeutsche Genesis
Wienerwald 2–4b
"Wie sich minne hebt" (Albrecht von Johansdorf) 1–132b
Wife's Lament, The 1–281a
WIGBODUS 12–0
***WIGMORE ABBEY, CHRONICLE OF* 12–0**
Andrew of Saint Victor 1–244b
Wigod of Wallingford 1–267b
Wikfried of Cologne, Archbishop 4–426b
Wild, Hans
See Hemmel, Peter
Wilde, John 1–319b
***WILDE ALEXANDER, DER* 12–0**
Wilfrid of Northumbria
Aeddi 1–61a
Benedictine Rule 2–170a
expulsion from England 1–144a
Wilfrid of York, Saint
missionary to Frisia 3–344b
Wilhelmus
See William
WILIGELMUS OF MODENA 12–0
Willame
See Adgar
Willehalm (Wolfram von Eschenbach) 2–228b
Willem
beast epic 4–319a
Willem of Hulsterlo 2–141b
Wille the priest 4–571b
William Bona Anima of Rouen 4–375a
William Carver
See Carver, William (Bromflet)
William Clito of Normandy
communes 3–497a
William de Brailes
See Brailes, William de
William II of England 4–461b, 462a
Angevins 1–253a
Anselm of Canterbury 1–312a-313a
Estoire des Engleis (Geffrei Gaimar) 1–264b
William-Jordan of Toulouse
Tripoli 4–37a
WILLIAM MARSHAL 12–0
biography 2–236b
knightly standard 3–303a
WILLIAM OF APULIA 12–0
William I of Aquitaine
Cluny monastery 3–468b
WILLIAM IX OF AQUITAINE 12–0; 3–668b
Crusade of 1101 4–36a,b
troubadour lyrics 3–669b; 4–576a
William X of Aquitaine 3–240b
WILLIAM OF AUVERGNE 12–0
Aristotle 1–462a
William of Blois
Alda 4–283a
WILLIAM OF BRIANE 12–0
William of Canterbury
See William the Englishman
WILLIAM OF CHAMPEAUX 12–0
Abelard 1–16b, 18b
scientific theology 1–316a
WILLIAM OF CHAMPLITTE 12–0
Fourth Crusade 3–247a
WILLIAM OF CONCHES 12–0; 3–168b
allegory 1–183a
astrology 1–607a
fables 4–572b
WILLIAM I OF ENGLAND 12–0; 4–33a
Angevins 1–253a
Anglo-Norman chronicles 1–265a
Bayeux Tapestry 2–139a
Brittany 2–379b; 3–8b
Canterbury 3–82b
coronation 1–35b
court of common pleas 3–491b
demography 4–137b
Domesday Book 2–330a-b; 4–237b
Edward the Confessor 4–395a
financial system 4–530b
presentment of Englishry 4–487a
reign 4–461a-462a, 463b, 464b, 465b-466a
wooden castles 3–145a
William II of England 2–71b
Clarendon Constitutions 3–409b
reign 4–461b-462a, 466a
Scotland 4–256a
William of Grosseto
beatification 2–143a
WILLIAM OF HIRSAU 12–0
Marian offices 2–274a
time measurements 3–458b
William of Holland
Aachen 4–59b
election 4–428a
WILLIAM OF JUMIÈGES 12–0
chronicles 3–331a
WILLIAM OF MALMESBURY 12–0
Aldhelm 1–144a, 278a
Alfred the Great 1–165a
Arthurian literature 1–565a
De gestis regum Anglorum 2–3a
oral tradition 1–274b
William of Mandagout 4–422b
William of Mara
Christian Hebraists 3–314a
William of Meliton
Alexander of Hales 1–148b
Bonaventure, Saint 2–313a
William of Militona
See William of Meliton
William of Modena 2–65b
WILLIAM OF MOERBEKE 12–0
Archimedes 1–434a, 437a-439b
Aristotle 1–461a
Dominican theology 4–247b
William of Montpellier 3–187a
William II of Nevers, Count
Crusade of 1101 4–36a,b
William of Newburgh
Arthurian literature 1–565b
William of Normandy, Duke
See William I of England
William of Ockham
See Ockham, William of
William of Orange
chanson de geste 3–258b-261a
William of Paris
royal confessor 3–535a
William of Pembroke
French chronicles 3–332b
WILLIAM OF POITIERS 12–0
Cambridge Songs 3–57b
William of Rheims 3–247a
William of Rubruck
Assassins 1–591b
exploration 4–556b, 557a
William of Rubruquis
See William of Rubruck
William of Saint Amour
allegory 1–189a
beguines and beghards 2–159b
Bonaventure, Saint 2–315a5b
Dominicans 1–128a; 4–251b
Franciscans 4–375b
William of Saint Carilef
illuminated manuscripts 1–256b
William of Saint Cloud
astronomy 1–612b
WILLIAM OF SAINT THIERRY 12–0; 1–607a
Abelard 1–18a
astrology 2–174a
Bernard of Clairvaux 2–191a, 192a
Bernard Silvester 2–195a
Carthusians 3–119a
exegesis 4–543a
WILLIAM OF SENS 12–0
William of Sherwood
dialectic 4–170b
William I of Sicily
Adrian IV, Pope 1–58b
Bari 2–108b
William II of Sicily
Byzantine Empire 1–245a; 2–496b
donor portrait 4–261b
William of Soissons 1–52a
William of Toulouse
Frankish protectorate 3–174b
William of Tripoli
missions 3–357a; 4–252b, 253a

WILLIAM OF TYRE 12–0
Alexandria 1–154a54a
Assassins 1–590b
Bogomils 2–294b
chronicles 3–331b
Eutyches 4–525a
fairs 4–589a
William of Valence 4–423b
WILLIAM OF VOLPIANO 12–0; 2–173b
William of Warelwast 1–313a
WILLIAM OF WINCHESTER 12–0
William of Ypres
communes 3–497a
William Rufus
See William II of England
William the Conqueror
See William I of England
WILLIAM THE ENGLISHMAN 12–0
William the Lion
chronicles 1–265a
Henry II of England 4–467a
William Torel
See Torel, William
Willibald 2–321a
Willibald, Saint
water buffalo use 1–298a
Willibrord (Clement) of Utrecht, Saint 2–172a
Alcuin of York 1–143b
Boniface, Saint 2–321a
Carolingian Empire 3–106a
Denmark 4–151a
Willigis of Mainz
Bernward 2–197b
WILLIRAM VON EBERSBERG 12–0
Wills
Old English documents 1–286b
Wilthair of Nomentana 3–109a
Wilton, Battle of (871) 1–163b
Wilton Diptych 4–476a-b, 477a
Wimple 3–624a
WINCHCOMBE, RICHARD 12–0
Winchester
Black Death 2–262a
elections, church 4–423b
Ethelwold 4–518a-b
fairs 4–586b
Old English chronicles 1–284b
treasury 4–530b
Winchester, Statute of (1285) 3–543a
Winchester, Treaty of (1153) 4–463b
Winchester accounting 4–514a
Winchester Bible
drawings 4–291a
Winchester Cathedral
Anglo-Norman architecture 1–255b
Anglo-Norman sculpture 1–256b
Anglo-Saxon art 1–272b, 273a
Benedictine monastery 3–265b
Winchester scriptoria 1–276b
***WINCHESTER TROPER* 12–0**; 4–518b
Wind beam
See Collar beam
Windesheim Congregation 3–368b, 369a
Devotio Moderna 4–166b, 167a
Windmill 1–98a
Byzantium 1–77b
Cistercians 3–404a
See Also Mills
Windsor Castle
building materials 3–145b
Royal Chapel 2–188b
WINE 12–0
banal monopolies 2–69b
butler 2–434b
Cistercians 3–404a
distilled liquors 4–219a-b
Islam 2–208b-209a
Jewish dietary laws 4–183a
Spain 1–82b
See Also Cookery, European
WINE TRADE 12–0
Aquitaine 1–368a,b
Bordeaux 2–327b, 328b
Winfrid
See Boniface, Saint
Winfrith, Saint
Frisia 3–344b
Winileodae 3–257a
Wino of Helmarshausen
travel accounts 1–332b
WINSBECKE 12–0
Winsbeke, Der 3–662a-b
Winsbekin, Die 3–663a
Winter Church (Milan)
Ambrosian chant 1–233a,b
Winwaed, Battle of (654) 4–454b
WIPO OF BURGUNDY 12–0
Cambridge Songs 3–58a
royal elections 4–426b-427a
Wireker (Whitacre), Nigel
Speculum stultorum 1–255a
WIRNT VON GRAFENBERG 12–0
***WIRT, DER* 12–0**
Wisby, Laws of 3–570a
Wisdom poetry
Anglo-Saxon literature 1–280b, 281a
See Also Gnomic Literature
Wise, Council of
Italian communes 3–499b
Wissembourg
Adelbert, Saint 1–47b
fables 4–572a
WITAN, WITENAGEMOT 12–0
Canterbury 3–82a
Harold III 4–395a
WITCHCRAFT, EUROPEAN 12–0
WITCHCRAFT, ISLAMIC 12–0
Witelo 2–38b, 39b, 41a
Archimedes 1–438b
Witham 3–118b
Witiza
See Benedict of Aniane
WITTELSBACHS 12–0
Bavaria 2–134b-135b
Brandenburg 2–361a-b
WITTENGAU, MASTER OF 12–0
WITTENWILER, HEINRICH 12–0
Bauernhochzeit, Die 2–132b
Wittenwiller, Hugo
Lehre von den Zeichen des Hirsches 4–579b
WITZ, KONRAD 12–0
danse macabre 4–93a
WIZLAW III VON RÜGEN 12–0
Woad 4–325b
Wodan
baptismal vows 2–87a
charms, Old High German 3–273b
See Also Woden
Woden
Anglo-Saxon worship 1–289a
Woldemar of Brandenburg 2–360b-361a
Wolf
beast epic 2–140b; 4–369a
***WOLFDIETRICH* 12–0**
Ambraser Heldenbuch 1–230a
WOLFENBÜTTEL, HELMSTEDT MS 628 12–0
Wolfenbüttelbók 4–403b
Wolfenbüttel model book 4–292a
Wolf-fox antagonism
Ecbasis Captivi 4–369a
WOLFHERE OF HILDESHEIM 12–0
WOLFRAM VON ESCHENBACH 12–0; 1–133a,b
Ambraser Heldenbuch 1–230a
Arthurian literature 1–572a, 574a
crusade poems 4–20b
Willehalm 2–228b
WOLGEMUT, MICHAEL 12–0
Wolin
draft animals 1–295a
food animals 1–301a
WOLVINUS OF MILAN 12–0
paliotto 1–254b
Woman Washing Her Feet, A (Urs Graf) 4–516a,b
Women, status of
Bansenchas 2–82b
Jewish banking 2–81a,b
See Also Class structure, Western
See Also Family
Wonders of the East, The 1–286a
Wood
building material 3–558b-561a
castles 3–145a-b
charcoal 3–267a
WOODCUT 12–0
block book 2–274a
Woodham, Adam 2–358b
Woodland
See Newfoundland
Woodstock
Black Death 2–262a
Woodville, Elizabeth
marriage 4–478b, 479a
WOOL 12–0
Bruges 2–386a
Castilian economy 3–139b
Chaucer 3–283a,b
Cistercians 3–404a
Coptic textiles 3–589a
Córdoba 3–599b
Worcester
Old English chronicles 1–284b
Old English scriptoria 1–276a
WORCESTER, SCHOOL OF 12–0
Worcester Cathedral
Anglo-Norman architecture 1–255b
Benedictine monastery 3–265b
Wordplay
See Acrostics-Wordplay
Work of the Four Elements 1–135b
World era 3–24b-25a
Worms
Alani 1–121a
charms 3–274a
commune 3–498a
Eleazar Ben Judah 4–420b
Gregory VII 3–69a
WORMS, CONCORDAT OF (1122) **12–0**; 3–525a
church elections 4–422a
papal reform 3–352a
Western Councils 3–636a,b
Wrake van Ragisel, Die (Vengeance for Ragisel) 4–319a
WRITING MATERIALS, ISLAMIC 12–0
calligraphy 3–53b, 54a
dawāt 4–115b
WRITING MATERIALS, WESTERN EUROPEAN 12–0
codex 3–473b
diptych 4–214b
Writ of naifty 3–415b
Writ of right
inheritance laws 3–414a
Wrought-iron guns 3–65a
Wroxham chronicles 1–265a
Wulfad, Abbot 1–12b

Wulf and Eadwacer 1–281a
Wulfsige of Sherborne 1–61b
WULFSTAN 12–0; 4–459a
Aelfric 1–61b
clerical texts 1–286a
Cnut the Great 3–472a
sermons 1–275b, 281b, 284b, 285a
***WUNDERER, DER* 12–0**
Würzburg
Boniface, Saint 2–322a
Wuwashshah 3–257a
WUZURG GRAMADĀR 12–0
Wyche, Richard 1–261b
WYCLIF, JOHN 12–0
Avignon 2–34a
Bible translation 2–215a, 222a-b
ecclesiology 4–376b, 377a,b
exegesis 4–544b, 547b-548a
heretical dissent 3–59a, 370a-371a
Western councils 3–647b, 649b-650a
Wycombe
Black Death 2–262a
Wynbercht, Abbot 2–321a
WYNFORD, WILLIAM 12–0
WYNKYN DE WORDE 12–0
Caxton, William 3–211a
courtesy books 3–661b
Middle English ballads 2–60a
treatise on death 4–527b-528a
WYSBECK, JOHN 12–0

X

Xač'atur Keč'areč'i 1–511b
Xač'ik-Gagik
See Gagik/Xač'ik-Gagik
Xač'ik I
See Gagik I
***XAČ'K'AR* 12–0**; 1–495a,b
Aštarak 1–601a
Xanadu
See Chandu
XAXULI 12–0
Xenophontos Monastery 1–636b
Xerigordon Castle 4–34a-b
Xeropotamou Monastery 1–638a
Ximénez de Cisneros 3–644b
Ximenis
See Eiximenis, Francesc
Xiphilinus, John
See John Xiphilinus
XLAT' 12–0; 1–473b
Armenian Muslim Emirates 1–513a,b
Xosrau
See Xusrō
Xosrov Anjewac'i 1–511a
Xosrovanoyš, Queen 1–589b
Xosroviduxt, Saint 1–519b
Xosrovik 1–509b
Xosrov II the Arsacid
Dwin 4–323b
Xosrov III/IV the Arsacid 1–476a
Xostakdars 1–489b
Xoyt' 4–112b
X tabulae salutationum (Boncompagno) 2–320a
XUSRŌ II ABARWĒZ 12–0
Bahrām VI Čōbēn 1–477a,b; 2–50a
Christian church 3–312b
Ctesiphon 4–62b
XUSRŌ I ANŌŠARWĀN 12–0; 1–477a
Christian church 3–312b
Ctesiphon 2–49b; 4–62b
Derbent 4–162a
***XWADĀY NĀMAG* 12–0**; 2–50a

Y

Yabhalaha III, Katholikos
Persian church 3–313a
Yačaxapatum Čaṙk' 1–508b-509a
Yáenz, Rodrigo
Poema de Alfonso XI 1–162b
Yaghıbasan 4–93a
Yāghısıyān 4–35a
Yaghmurāsin 1–195b
Yaḥhaf, Ibn 3–385b
Yaḥyā ibn ʿAbdullāh
Alids 1–174b-175a
Yaḥyā ibn Ghāniya
Almohads 1–194b-195a
Yaḥyā ibn Ibrāhīm al-Judālī
Almoravids 1–198a,b
Yaḥyā ibn Khalīd
Barmakids 2–110a,b
Yaḥyā ibn Maḥmūd al-Wāsiṭī
See Wāsiṭī, Yaḥyā ibn Maḥmūd, al-
Yaḥyā ibn Saʿīd
See Yahya of Antioch
Yaḥyā ibn ʿUmar 1–198b
YAHYA OF ANTIOCH 12–0; 4–525a
YAM 12–0
Yamāma, Al-
Ukhaydirid dynasty 1–175a
Yantar 3–132b
YAʿQŪBĪ, AL- 12–0
Yaʿqūb ibn Dawūd 1–174b
YAʿQŪB IBN LAYTH 12–0
Yāqūt al-Mustaʿṣimī
script styles 3–54b
Yāqūt al-Rūmī 2–33a, 47a
Yardland
peasant land 3–415a, 423b
Yared, Saint 1–155b
Yarmūk, Battle of (ca. 636)
ʿAbd Allāh 1–15b
Abū Sufyān 1–29b
YARMŪK RIVER 12–0
YAROSLAVL 12–0
Yaroslav of Kiev
See Yaroslav the Wise
YAROSLAV THE WISE 12–0
Nowogródek founding 2–64b
YASTS 12–0
Yathrib
See Medina
Yazdagird I 2–49b
Yazdagird II 1–476b; 3–308a
Armenian church 1–498b
Bahrām V 2–49b
Yazdgard
See Yazdagird
Yazīd (son of Abū Sufyān) 1–29a-b
Yazīd II ibn ʿAbd al-Malik
caliphate 3–41b
YAZĪD I IBN MUʿĀWIYA 12–0
iconoclasm 3–345a
reign 1–15b-16a
Year Books 2–357a
Yellow
liturgical color 3–484b
Yellow Book of Lecan 1–347b
YEMEN 12–0
Ayyubid rule 2–23a-b
Jewish exilarch 4–552b
Zaydite imamate 1–175a
See Also Arabia
Yerebatan cistern 4–334b
Yeshiva
See Schools, Jewish
YEVELE, HENRY 12–0
Canterbury Cathedral 3–83b
Yggdrasil 2–348a
YIDDISH 12–0
Hebrew alphabet 1–208a
Ylbughā
murder 2–113a
Ylbughā al-Nāṣirī
Barqūq 2–113a
Ymage du monde, L' 4–449a
Ymbrenfæstenum
See Ember days
Ynglingasaga (Snorri Sturluson) 1–63a, 116b
Ynglingatal 4–570a,b
***YNGVARS SAGA VÍÐFÖRLA* 12–0**
Yolanda/Irene of Montferrat 1–245b
Yolande of Anjou 3–275a
Yolande of Saint Pol 3–331b
Yom Ashoora 3–27b
Yom Kippur 3–26b, 27a
York
Alcuin 1–142a
barber-surgeon guild 2–99b
commune 3–498a
convocations 3–578a
ecclesiastical courts 1–433b
York, Statute of (1322) 4–397b, 481b
YORK, TREATY OF 12–0
York Cathedral
chapter house design 3–267a
YORK PLAYS 12–0; 4–284b, 285a, 286a
YORK RITE 12–0
Yorkshire
Danelaw 4–91a-b
YORK TRACTATES 12–0
anointing of kings 1–308b
Yovhannēs Awjnec'i 1–509b, 520b
Yovhannēs Drasxanakertec'i
literature 1–510b
saints 1–518b, 519a
Yovhannēs Kozeṙn 1–511a
Yovhannēs Mandakuni 1–508b
Armenian Rite 1–516b
Yovhannēs Mayragomec'i 1–509b
Yovhannēs of Erzincan 1–511b
Yovhannēs of Ōjnec'i
See Yovhannēs of Awjnec'i
Yovhannēs Orotnec'i 1–512a, 520b
Yovhannēs Sarkawag 1–512a
Armenian calendar 3–31a
Yovhannēs-Smbat Bagratuni 1–483a, 484a
Yovhannēs T'lkranc'i 1–512a
Yovhan of Ekełik' 2–217a
Yovsēp' of Constantinople 1–511a
Yovsēp' of Karin 1–519b
Yovsēp' of Pałnatun 2–217a
YPRES 12–0
fairs 4–585a-b
***YSENGRIMUS* 12–0**; 2–141a-b; 4–496a
Ysopets
See Isopets
Ystorya Bown de Hamtwn 2–210a
Yúçef of Marruecos 3–73b
See Also Yūsuf ibn Tāshfīn

Yugoslavia
Bosnia 2–334a
Yugoslavian architecture
arches 1–423b
Yumurtalik
See Ayās
Yunaban dproc'
See Armenian Hellenizing School
Yunnan
Black Death 2–258a
Yūsuf I (Nasrid)
Alhambra 1–168b
Yūsuf al-Fihrī
Córdoba 3–598a
Yūsuf ibn Abū'l Sāj 1–481b, 482a
Arcrunis 1–451a
Ašot II Erkat' 1–588b, 589a
Dwin 4–324a
Yūsuf ibn Taghrībirdī
concubinage 3–529a
Yūsuf ibn Tāshfīn 1–199a-200a
Cid 3–73b, 384a-385a, 386b, 387b
Yūsuf of Himyarite dynasty 1–371b
Yvori de Monbrant 1–267b

Z

Zāb
Aghlabids 1–70a
Zabānīya, al- 1–248b
ZABARELLA, FRANCESCO 12–0; 2–57a
conciliar movement 3–365b
Western councils 3–647a, 650a
Zabel (Isabel) (daughter of Leo I/II)
Cilician-Roman church union 3–395a
Zabel (Isabel) (daughter of Leo II/III)
Cilician kingdom 3–393a
Zabulistan 1–64a
Zaccaria, Benedetto 4–557b
Zacharias, Pope
Boniface, Saint 2–322a
clergy requirements 3–443a
papal policies 3–345b
Pepin 3–106b
ZACHARIAS OF MYTILENE 12–0
ecclesiastical history 2–512b-513a
Zacharias Scholasticus
See Zacharias of Mytilene
Zacharids
See Zak'arids
Zacher Epitome 1–266b
Zacuto, Abraham 1–613a
Zadar
See Zara
Ẓafar, Ibn 1–381b
Zagora 2–402b
Zagreb
bishopric 4–7a
Zagwe dynasty 1–32b
Zaharije 2–405a; 4–4b
Ẓāhir 1–202a
Ẓāhir Barqūq, al-
Christians 3–398a
***ZAHN, DER* 12–0**
Zahrāwī, al- 1–385b
Zahumlje 2–406b
See Also Hercegovina
Zainab 1–198b-199a
Zā'iraja 1–385a
Zajal 1–398b
cantigas 3–85a-b
Zak'areans
See Zak'arids
Zak'arē Mχargrzeli
See Zak'arids
Zak'aria of Gnunik' 1–511b
Zak'aria of Jag 1–511a
ZAK'ARIDS 12–0; 1–235b
Ani in Širak 1–291a,b
Armenia 1–474a, 485b
art 1–495b
churches 1–292a
Dwin 4–324b, 325a
social structure 1–490b
Zakāt 1–201b-202b
Zallaqa, Battle of (1086) 1–199b
Zamakhsharī, al- 4–443b, 444b
Zamatun
See Gawit'
Zamora 1–627a
siege (1072) 3–129a
Zamrak, Ibn 1–170a
ZAMZAM 12–0
'Abbās, al- 1–4a
'Abd al-Muṭṭalib 1–14b
Zanaga (Azànegue) Berbers 4–561a
Zanāta Berbers 2–185b
Islamization 1–198a-b
Zand Āgāhīh
See Bundahishn
Zangī 2–23a
Aleppo 1–145b
Edessa 4–30b
Saladin 4–39b
Zangid dynasty
Athīr, Ibn al- 1–634a,b
Ayyubid culture 2–22a
Badr al-Dīn 2–43b
ZANJ 12–0; 2–127b, 268b; 3–49a
Abbasids 1–374b
Zankid dynasty
See Zangid dynasty
Zannekin, Nicolas
Bruges 2–387b
Zanobi da Strada 2–277b, 288b
Zaporog Cossacks
Khanate of Crimea 3–679a
Zara 4–1b
conquest 4–44a-b
Zara, Treaty of 4–44b-45a, 46a
Zaragoza
See Saragossa
Zarathustra
teachings 2–14a-15a
Zar'a Ya'qob, Emperor 1–32b
Zarlino 3–658a
Zarqālī, al- 1–611b
Završje 2–336b, 337a, 339b
ZĀWIYA 12–0
Zayd ibn 'Alī 1–174b
ZAYDIS 12–0; 1–174b-175a, 374b-375a
Barmakids 2–110b-111a
Zaydites
See Zaydis
Zaydūn, Ibn
biographies 2–238b
poetry 1–401a
Zaynab
'Ā'isha 1–113a
Zayton
trade 4–557a,b
Zdeslav, Prince 4–2b
ZEALOTS 12–0
iconoclasm 2–488b, 489a
Thessaloniki 2–501a,b
Zechin
See Ducat
Zemen
art and architecture 2–417b
Zemljanik 2–334a
Zengi
See Zangi
Zenica 2–334a
Zenobius of Amida
Armenian Literature 1–508a
ZENO THE ISAURIAN 12–0
Armenian Hellenizing School 1–505b
caesaropapism 3–10b
Christian church in Persia 3–312a
Coptic architecture 3–586a
Ostrogoths 2–93a-b
reign 2–468a
Zerahyah ha-Levi 1–22b, 23a
Zerbolt, Gerard 2–368a
Devotio Moderna 4–166b
Zero
Arabic numerals 1–383b, 388b-389a, 394a,b, 395b
Zerubbabel 1–344b-345b
Zeta 2–494a
Zeugologia 1–79a
Zeyrek Camii
See Christ Pantokrator, Monastery of
Zgorzelec
armaments 2–303a
Ziani, Pietro 3–570a
Zibaldone laurenziano (Boccaccio) 2–287a
Zibaldone magliabechiano (Boccaccio) 2–286a, 287a
Žiča Monastery
art 2–446b
Zigabenos, Euthymios 1–303b
Zīj 1–611b
Zimām 1–383b-384a, 385a
Zindīq
See Manichaeans
Zinzendorf, Nikolaus
Bohemian Brethren 2–305b
"Zion"
See Darokhranitelnitsa
Zion, Basilica of
See Bolnisi Sioni
ZIRIDS 12–0
Ziryāb 3–598b
Zischägge 1–532a
ZIYADA 12–0
Ziyādat Allāh I 1–70b
Great Mosque of Qayrawān 1–69a
Ziyādat Allāh II 1–70b
Ziyādat Allāh III 1–72a
Ziyanid dynasty
Almohad empire 1–195b, 196a
Ziyarids
Ghaznavids 1–65a
Žižka, Jan 3–206b
ZOË THE MACEDONIAN 12–0
Hagia Sophia 2–443a
reign 2–491b, 492a
Zographou Monastery 1–636b
Zohar (Moses ben Shem Tov de Leon) 1–346a; 3–2a-b
ZONARAS, JOHN 12–0; 1–303b
canon law 2–468a
chronicle 2–515b
Zoology
See Animals
See Biology
Zōrnamak 3–199a
ZOROASTRIANISM 12–0
Ardešīr 1–451b-452a
Armenia 1–476b; 2–12a
Avesta 2–14a
Bundahishn 2–419a
Dēnkard 4–148a

ZOROASTRIANISM (cont.)
Persia 3–312a
Zorro, João 3–87a
ZOSIMUS 12–0
alchemy 1–135b-136a,b
Pelagius 1–653b
Zu'ar
Damascus 4–82b
Zuart'noc'
See Zwart'noc'
Zubayda 1–374a,b
pilgrimage route to Mecca 1–374a,b
Zubayr ibn al-'Awwām, al- 1–4a, 15a
'Ā'isha 1–113b, 172b; 3–35b
Zuccho, Accio
fables 4–572b
Zuccone (Donatello) 4–257a
Zug 2–8a
Zuhra 1–248b
Zuhr Abū Marwān, Ibn
See Avenzoar
Zunnār 3–616b
Županijaş
See Župas
Župans 4–1b
Župas 4–1a, 4a
Zurārids 1–513a
Zurich 2–8a
ZURVANISM 12–0
Zurzach
fairs 4–586a
Zutphen
fairs 4–586b
Zvartnots
See Zwart'noc'
Zvonimir 4–6a-b, 7b
ZWART'NOC' 12–0; 1–292a, 493b; 2–70a
Zwingli, Huldreich
Bohemian Brethren 2–307b
Zwolle
Brethren of the Common Life 2–367a